Bootleggers and
Beer Barons of
the Prohibition Era

Bootleggers and Beer Barons of the Prohibition Era

J. ANNE FUNDERBURG

McFarland & Company, Inc., Publishers
Jefferson, North Carolina

LIBRARY OF CONGRESS CATALOGUING-IN-PUBLICATION DATA

Funderburg, J. Anne, 1946–
Bootleggers and beer barons of the Prohibition era / J. Anne Funderburg.
p.   cm.
Includes bibliographical references and index.

ISBN 978-0-7864-7961-0 (softcover : acid free paper) ∞

ISBN 978-1-4766-1619-3 (ebook)

1. Prohibition—United States—History—20th century.   2. Distilling, Illicit—
United States—History—20th century.   3. Liquor industry—United States—
History—20th century.   4. Liquor laws—United States—History—20th century.
5. Crime—United States—History—20th century.   6. Outlaws—United States—
Biography.   7. United States—Social conditions—1918–1932.   I. Title.
HV5089.F88 2014   363.4'1097309042—dc23   2014007937

BRITISH LIBRARY CATALOGUING DATA ARE AVAILABLE

On the cover: police confiscating alcohol during Prohibition 1920-1933 (Photofest)

Printed in the United States of America

*McFarland & Company, Inc., Publishers
Box 611, Jefferson, North Carolina 28640
www.mcfarlandpub.com*

To Murry, my sounding board,
touchstone, and soul mate

Contents

Part III.
Choice versus Prohibition: The Cycle of History

Preface

The enactment of Prohibition unleashed a massive crime wave from coast to coast. Millions of Americans broke the Volstead law and felt no remorse about it. The central player in this criminal plague was the bootlegger who delivered booze to the marketplace. He or she worked in an industry ruled by guns rather than government regulations. Brutal, ruthless men rose to the top of the illegal liquor traffic. Through the media, the public came to know these men who called the shots in the underworld. Pop culture turned them into famous antiheroes admired by drinkers and hated by Prohibitionists.

Early in the Volstead Era a stereotype emerged of the bootlegger as an urban mobster who packed heat and reveled in shootouts with lawmen and rival gangsters. The media's stereotypical beer baron had a strong ethnic identity and was an immigrant or first-generation American. In reality, many bootleggers fit this mold, but many did not. In some areas the typical bootlegger belonged to an old-stock family with deep roots in American soil. He or she valued individualism, liked small-town life, and had no desire to belong to an urban-style gang. Yet the public image of the Volstead lawbreaker has been rather narrowly defined, with the urban mob boss dominating in pop culture.

To provide a balanced view of Volstead crime, *Bootleggers and Beer Barons of the Prohibition Era* looks at the business of bootlegging in multiple locations, spanning the country from New York City to Seattle, Washington. The book tells the stories of rural and small-town hooch haulers as well as urban liquor lords. The nationwide survey reveals that the members of the bootlegging fraternity shared commonalities, but some aspects of the business were unique to certain areas. Each gin jogger was an individual with a distinctive personality, although a few basic goals and traits may be attributed to the vast majority of bootleggers. The liquor runners lived dangerous lives outside the mainstream, supplying an illegal commodity to average Americans. They were criminals aided and abetted by corrupt lawmen, malfeasant officials, straw men, mob lawyers, moonshiners, alky cookers, forgers, counterfeiters, and — most of all — consumers who thirsted for something stronger than lemonade.

A NOTE ON SPELLING: *"Whisky" and "whiskey" are variant spellings of the same word. Traditionally, "whisky" was the preferred spelling in British and Canadian English while American English had no firm rule. In some publications, "whisky" refers to the Scotch and Canadian varieties while "whiskey" is used for American and Irish products. For consistency, this book uses "whiskey" in all contexts.*

PART I.
THE VOLSTEAD LAW:
KING ALCOHOL DETHRONED

1. Satan's Best Friend, God's Worst Enemy

The American republic has solemnly placed itself on record as prohibiting the greatest enemy of life, liberty, and the pursuit of happiness. There are not enough society creampuffs, political grafters, underworld gunmen, or social morons in the land to prevent the fulfillment of that prohibition.—Wayne Wheeler, General Counsel, Anti-Saloon League of America[1]

January 17, 1920, was Al Capone's twenty-first birthday, but he didn't celebrate with a legal drink at the corner saloon. The Volstead Act took effect at 12:01 a.m., knocking King Alcohol off his throne and sending him into exile. The activists behind Prohibition knew with absolute certainty that the new dry law would improve society in every way. The law would turn the habitual drunkard into a sober, hardworking, devoted family man. Instead of wasting his paycheck on booze, the reformed sot would spend his wages wisely. He would pay his debts and open a savings account. His children would have shoes and warm winter coats. He would enjoy wholesome fun with his family, and America would become a land of innocent pleasures. Clean, sober Christian fellowship would provide all the social life anybody could possibly want.

Al Capone's instincts told him the drys were all wet. Despite his youth, he already had a fondness for what he called the "light pleasures"—drinking, gambling, and visiting brothels. He didn't plan to give up his fun, and he didn't expect other drinkers to become teetotalers just because a bunch of meddling do-gooders passed a law. Growing up poor in a crime-ridden tenement district, Capone had learned to grab what he could take and fight for what he wanted. He had street smarts, greedy ambition, gangland connections, and few scruples to slow him down. For him, and his ilk, Prohibition would open the door to riches, power, and infamy.

The dry forces had fought a long, arduous war against Demon Rum. For decades, the liquor issue had divided the United States into two camps: the drys who demanded alcohol abstinence, enforced by law if necessary, and the wets who believed that drinking should be a personal choice. The middle class, church folk, nativists, farmers, and small-town residents formed the backbone of the dry faction. Urbanites, ethnic minorities, immigrants, and blue-collar workers generally favored little or no regulation of the liquor traffic. Protestants tended to support strict liquor control laws, while a majority of Catholics and Jews viewed drinking as a personal decision.

3

Efforts to restrict the liquor traffic dated back to Colonial America, but the dry movement didn't become a political juggernaut until the late nineteenth century. Before the Civil War, most dry leaders were temperance advocates who preached moderation, not total abstinence. After the war, the dry movement evolved in a more militant direction. Turning all Americans into teetotalers became the goal of the postwar cold water coalition. Social conservatives, religious crusaders, and progressive reformers banded together because they all believed that banishing King Alcohol would greatly benefit the nation.

The nativist social conservatives wanted to preserve what they believed to be true American values and the American way of life. Religious crusaders wanted to save the drunkard's soul and foster Christian family life. Progressive reformers wanted to improve society by eradicating vice, crime, and corruption. They formed countless investigative committees, issued tons of reports, and sought to pass legislation that would further their vision of a better tomorrow. Of course, many dry activists had overlapping goals; a religious crusader could also be a progressive reformer, for example.

The dry movement was tinged with xenophobia and racism, especially in the nativist faction. Bigots told lurid stories about drunken Negroes who ran amok and committed heinous acts, like cannibalism or "the nameless crime" (AKA rape). An editorial in a Nashville, Tennessee, newspaper singled out "the Negro problem" as the most urgent reason for closing the saloons. "The Negro, fairly docile and industrious, becomes, when filled with liquor, turbulent and dangerous and a menace to life, property, and the repose of the community," warned the paper. An Illinois dry leader called the grogshop "the Negro's center of power." She declared, "Better whiskey and more of it is the rallying cry of great dark-faced mobs."[2]

Xenophobes feared that the country's minorities would overwhelm the old-stock Americans. They demanded strict immigration quotas, and they supported programs of Americanization to mold newcomers into their rigid vision of the true American. The nativists favored Prohibition because they believed certain ethnic groups were predisposed to chronic drunkenness and the ills that came with it. Moreover, they viewed the liquor industry as an un–American business. In their narrow world of stereotypes, brewers were German, distillers Jewish, and vintners Italian, and all belonged to the undesirable "foreign element." Congressman John Tillman (D-AR) melded racism with xenophobia in a speech to the House of Representatives; he read aloud a list of distillers whose names sounded foreign and accused them of inciting black violence. "I am not attacking an American institution," he said. "I am attacking mainly a foreign enterprise."[3] Nativist groups, including the Ku Klux Klan, endorsed Prohibition as a means of keeping liquor away from racial and ethnic minorities.

The drys believed that alcohol caused virtually every societal ill, so removing liquor from American life would create utopia — or a very close facsimile. At first, the dry activists chose moral suasion and temperance education as the pathway to their ideal society. But they grew impatient because those tactics didn't work fast enough. They decided that a law mandating total alcohol abstinence would quickly dry up America. They saw enforced sobriety as the noblest of causes because it would save families, reduce crime, and elevate mankind in every way. With the focused zeal of true believers, the dry activists preached and proselytized. They organized, petitioned, marched, lobbied, and voted for their noble cause.

The wets, in stark contrast to their dry foes, lacked strong leadership and unity of purpose. Since the wet movement threatened the liquor trade, drinkers expected the industry to fight it. America's vintners, brewers, and distillers had a vested interest in stopping Prohibition, but they failed to unite because they viewed the threat differently. Vintners and brewers felt their products were beneficial to society, unlike the distilled spirits that were closely associated with drunkenness, crime, poverty, and broken homes. The makers of beer and wine worried that their products might be subjected to more regulation, but they believed only ardent spirits would be banned if a national dry law were enacted. Since the industry leaders didn't feel the same level of threat, they didn't form a solid front to battle the dry forces.

Outside the liquor industry, a few civil liberties groups opposed Prohibition but didn't make the issue their top priority. The Association against the Prohibition Amendment (AAPA), formed in 1918, tried to stop the implementation of the Eighteenth Amendment. But the AAPA entered the fray at a late date and was a wet Lilliputian fighting a dry giant. While the Prohibition forces mounted a nationwide offensive, the wet faction barely mustered enough troops for guerrilla warfare. In the crucial battles, the drys overwhelmed the wets.

For Rent: Hell

On the eve of the Great Drought, both wets and drys commemorated the occasion — but with very different attitudes. Jubilant dry Americans welcomed Prohibition with victory parades, rousing speeches, and church services. Across the USA, they marched through the streets, burned King Alcohol in effigy, and held funeral services for John Barleycorn. The celebrations ranged from noisy and circus-like in Atlanta, Georgia, to sedate and dignified in Washington, D.C.

Atlanta's dry forces held a victory celebration for the city's white residents. The KKK joined the Anti-Saloon League (ASL) in a parade down Peachtree Street, the city's major roadway. A squad of mounted policemen led the parade, which included revenue agents carrying a moonshine still. The Klansmen, wearing white robes and holding lit torches, were "a sight that chilled the marrow in the bones of the more imaginative and called forth memories or ideas of days long ago," wrote a reporter. The parade ended at Five Points, the city's hub, where people "jammed into every inch of space." Confiscated liquor fueled a roaring bonfire, and the flames threw light on "the picturesque figures" of the KKK. The revenue agents smashed the still and tossed the battered parts on the fire. An effigy of John Barleycorn burned "to a crackling crisp" on the hot flames.[4]

Optimism prevailed in Boston, where a cheering crowd paraded through the streets on the South End. A truck carried John Barleycorn's coffin and a demijohn while Uncle Sam rode on a city water wagon. The parade stopped for a jubilee service at Morgan Memorial Methodist Church, where social workers and clergymen lauded Prohibition. Reformed drunkards gave testimonials praising the Volstead law. The speakers forecast a rosy future because the saloons had closed and a spirit of renewal was taking hold in Bean Town.[5]

In Chicago churches and temperance groups held prayer meetings to thank God for Prohibition. The Chicago Sunday School Association hosted a party at a popular café, where the guests toasted Volstead with grape juice. The restaurant manager, setting a high standard in customer service, went beyond his usual duties and lay in a casket, posing as Demon

These brewery workers, photographed in San Francisco in 1919, would lose their jobs when the Volstead law took effect in January 1920 (San Francisco History Center, San Francisco Public Library).

Rum. Funeral dirges played while the pallbearers carried the casket to the bier. A minister held funeral rites for the deceased.[6]

On the West Coast, dry activists celebrated at sedate, churchy affairs. In San Francisco, the Woman's Christian Temperance Union (WCTU) joined other dry crusaders in an all-day prayer and thanksgiving service at the First Congregational Church. A spokeswoman for the WCTU said Prohibition was "God's present to the nation." She proclaimed that Americans had reached "the never-never country," where sobriety would create paradise on earth. Other dry celebrants, including a youth group, gathered at San Francisco's First Baptist Church. The event featured a "play hour," when the young people enjoyed wholesome games while their elders watched, to prevent any impropriety.[7]

Dry activists in Los Angeles held multiple celebrations. Southern California's WCTU leaders convened for a day-long event at the Temperance Temple, where they enjoyed a praise service, prayer, singing, and a basket luncheon. Other dry observances were held at the Trinity Auditorium and the Los Angeles City Club, where the dignitaries included pro–Volstead politicos and the head of the Good Templars temperance society. At the City Club, the guests raised "their glasses of aqueduct water in a toast of gladness and thanksgiving."[8]

In Washington, D.C., government officials joined the cold water coalition for a celebratory parade. Later that evening eminent dry leaders gathered for a dignified watch-night service at the First Congregational Church. The notables included Prohibition Commissioner John Kramer, Secretary of the Navy Josephus Daniels, elder statesman William Jennings Bryan, Bishop James Cannon Jr., and ASL attorney Wayne Wheeler plus a generous sprinkling of U.S. senators and representatives.

Wheeler, wielding the ASL's considerable clout, had personally chosen Kramer for the new job of Prohibition commissioner, Volstead's top cop. Kramer, a frail man who looked more like a librarian than a lawman, addressed the congregation. He assured his listeners that he would mop up every drop of illegal alcohol. "This law will be obeyed in cities large and small ... and where it is not obeyed, it will be enforced." Liquor will not be "manufactured nor sold nor given away nor hauled in anything on the surface of the earth, or under the earth, or in the air." At midnight, "after five hours of speeches, joyful demonstrations, and rejoicings," the wet leaders, their hearts bursting with joy, observed the dawn of the Golden Age of Sobriety.[9]

The Reverend Billy Sunday, super-star evangelist, preached the mother of all funerals for John Barleycorn in Norfolk, Virginia. A pro baseball player turned Bible thumper, Sunday was a natural showman who liked to weave sports metaphors into his theatrical sermons. He used his storytelling skills, his powerful voice, and his acting talents to stage worship services as entertaining as vaudeville.

At the Norfolk train station, John Barleycorn's coffin arrived on a railcar that purportedly came from beer-soaked Milwaukee. Pallbearers were waiting to move it to Sunday's revival tabernacle. A man dressed as Satan, complete with horns and a tail, sobbed while the coffin was loaded onto a wagon. A crowd of thousands watched as the wagon rolled slowly down the street, accompanied by the pallbearers and a band playing funeral dirges. The pallbearers carried the coffin into the tabernacle and sang "John Barleycorn's Body Lies A-moulding in the Clay."

Standing over the coffin, Sunday roared, "Good-bye, John! You were God's worst enemy. You were hell's best friend." He berated the deceased for egregious sins: "You corrupted our courts. You defied our laws. You destroyed both soul and body. You darkened our homes. You broke our hearts.... You led men to commit every conceivable crime." But the righteous had banded together, fought "the blood sucker of the universe," and defeated King Alcohol. "The reign of tears is over!" Sunday declared. "The slums will soon be a memory. We will turn our prisons into factories and our jails into storehouses and corncribs. Man will walk upright now, women will smile, and the children will laugh."

With showmanship befitting a master magician, Sunday nailed the wood coffin shut. The crowd watched his every move, cheering wildly.

"Hell will be forever for rent!" he bellowed.

For his grand closing, he grabbed a giant American flag and waved it as the delirious congregation sang the Doxology.

"Praise Father, Son, and Holy Ghost!"[10]

Where's the Orgy?

The press predicted January 16 would bring "orgies of drink," but reporters looking for bacchanalia found little to write about. Under state or local law, much of the country was already dry, so Volstead brought no major change in those jurisdictions. A widespread influenza outbreak put a damper on celebrations in the big cities because public health officials advised people to avoid crowds. In the Northeast and Midwest, winter storms kept people at home as freezing weather disabled motorcars, leaving only horse traffic on the roads.

Even in America's wettest cities, the farewell events didn't turn into boozy riots. "There were parties galore, but the wild night that had been predicted was almost dismal" in New York City. As the Big Apple bid adieu to liquor, funereal themes were the favorite motif and King Alcohol's coffin took center stage. The caskets ranged from expensive silver-and-ebony models to humble, homemade boxes cobbled together out of wood crates or soap-boxes.[11]

On Broadway, drinkers formed funeral processions and carried coffins through the bright light district. "Weeping Bacchante" led the mourning at a wake at the Park Avenue Hotel. The guests wore black, they ate black caviar at tables covered with black cloth, and King Alcohol's casket was filled with black bottles. The Café de Paris held a Cinderella Ball: at midnight the liquor vanished. Patrons at a popular Broadway nightspot danced around a coffin and received miniature caskets to take home. At a lavish party in the Della Robbia Room at the Hotel Vanderbilt, drinkers sipped champagne while the orchestra played "Good-by, Forever." The revelers polished off one hundred cases of the hotel's finest bub-bly.[12]

Boston officials told drinkers to celebrate on January 15 because the hotels and cafés would close early on the sixteenth. Hotels gave their farewell events special names, such as the Very Last Time Party, the Passing of the King Party, and the Grand Testimonial Cele-bration to King Barleycorn. Dutiful Bostonians who wanted a final fling went pub crawling on the fifteenth. On January 16 "there was no attempt at revelry in any of the hotels or cafés, all the devotees of King Alcohol appearing to feel that they had done the thing up so thoroughly the night before that anything more would be an anticlimax."[13]

At the National Press Club in Washington, D.C., newsmen met to observe the dawn of the Arid Era. As a group, reporters had a reputation as heavy drinkers, so many of them were glum about the long drought that lay on the horizon. The highlight of the evening was a humorous skit, "Crowning Prohibition," written and performed by members of the press corps. The skit parodied Washington insiders, including Senator John Morris Sheppard (D-TX), known as "the father of the Eighteenth Amendment."

The Chicago Automobile Club held a wake "with penitential simplicity." White cloths with black borders covered the tables, and the guests sipped the last of the club's best liquor from tin cups. Elsewhere in Chicago tipplers took their own liquor to nightspots that had already sold all or most of their booze. "All hips were oversize. All traveling bags gurgled," reported a newspaper. "Those who had liquor drank, and laughed, and shouted until they were tired." However, the revels were "attended by no larger than the usual Friday night crowd."[14]

San Francisco's party animals took two nights to say good-bye to their favorite indoor sport. The city's nightspots promoted January 15 as the time to celebrate "with a touch of the carnival spirit." On that night fun-loving residents partied into the wee hours at popular watering holes. On January 16, the saloons were open and diehard drinkers showed up, but officials ordered barkeepers to shut their doors at 11:30 p.m. to avoid any conflict with the new dry law.[15]

In Los Angeles, drinkers flocked to popular nightspots to mourn King Alcohol's demise. Streamers of black and blue crepe paper set the dark mood at Al Levy's Café. At midnight an effigy of John Barleycorn was stuffed into a garbage can for a satiric funeral service. At McKee's Cabaret "pretty girls" acted as pallbearers, waving farewell banners and carrying a demijohn on a stretcher as they paraded around the club in King Alcohol's funeral procession.

Confetti and streamers flew through the air as drinkers gulped down their last legal cocktails during a dinner dance at another trendy nightspot, the Marcell Café.[16]

Instant Extinction

January 16, 1920, was the last day on the job for countless Americans who worked in the legal liquor industry. The Volstead law threatened the livelihood of everybody in the liquor trade from the big bosses down to the guys who swept the barroom floor. Some lucky workers already had new jobs lined up. The others faced an uncertain future. According to the Bureau of Internal Revenue, Prohibition was closing 236 distilleries, one thousand breweries, and 177,790 retail liquor outlets.[17]

To reduce monetary losses, firms with liquor inventories rushed to dispose of them in the final weeks before Volstead began. Some manufacturers and wholesalers avoided financial disaster by selling their stock abroad. Liquor worth millions of dollars sailed out of ports along the Atlantic Seaboard and the Gulf of Mexico headed for Europe, Central America, or the Caribbean. On the West Coast, exporters shipped liquor to the Asian mainland and islands in the Pacific. One western syndicate bought vast quantities of California wine for shipment to Japan. Canny speculators, who foresaw a U.S. market for liquor despite the dry law, sent cargos of whiskey to offshore warehouses. They planned to bring it back later and sell it to parched Americans willing to pay top dollar for decent booze.

Prohibition would inflict serious economic damage in the states where breweries, wineries, and/or distilleries were major employers. Kentucky's bourbon distillers expected to be the hardest hit because they had fewer options than the wine and beer companies. Vintners could continue to cultivate their vineyards and sell grapes and/or unfermented grape juice. They also had the option of chopping down their grapevines in order to grow other crops.

Brewers could apply for a government license to make near beer, a cereal beverage with an alcohol content of less than one-half of one percent. In addition to producing legal near beer, breweries could be revamped to make a wide variety of items. They had industrial refrigeration systems that allowed them to produce and warehouse foodstuffs. Mega-brewer Anheuser-Busch was among the companies that would diversify to stay in business. Its new product mix would include ice cream, ginger ale, root beer, grape drinks, syrups, yeast, tonics, starch, glucose, malt extract, and livestock feed as well as near beer. Busch plants would also fabricate ice cream cabinets, coolers for drugstores, and refrigerated trucks.[18]

Kentucky's distilleries were uniquely designed for making bourbon and couldn't be easily converted to another product. As Volstead neared, distillers in the Blue Grass State rushed to sell as much inventory as possible. Exporters shipped millions of gallons of Kentucky bourbon to England and Ireland. Germany was also a popular destination, due to the availability of cheap warehouse space in Hamburg. Small quantities of bourbon went to wine-loving France, where whiskey drinkers were somewhat rare.[19] Although the bourbon exporters claimed they would sell the whiskey overseas, skeptics predicted liquor traffickers would bring much of it back to the United States.

Real estate investors had little interest in the bourbon distilleries because they were situated on isolated sites chosen for their access to pure limestone water. A few enterprising distillers dismantled their Kentucky plants and moved them abroad, mostly to Canada. Other distilleries were sealed shut, with the whiskey still aging in the barrels. The owners hoped to secure government permits to sell their stock legally under the exemptions to the Volstead law. The most pessimistic distillers planned to shutter their plants and sell their machinery as junk. One owner said he would plant ivy around his distillery and "there let it stand in ruins, a monument to the folly of this generation, for other generations to gaze on."[20]

Taking Stock

In the final pre–Volstead days, foresighted drinkers stockpiled their favorite alcoholic beverages so they wouldn't have to go cold turkey. Most liquor stores had already gone out of business, and customers besieged those that remained open. Buyers hauled their booze home in cars, trucks, horse-drawn wagons, pony carts, wheelbarrows, and even baby buggies. As the legal stock dwindled, consumers paid premium prices. In New York City a bottle of scotch or rye cost up to $20—at a time when the average apartment rented for $15 per month. French champagne brought $30 or more per bottle; domestic bubbly was a bargain at $10.[21]

On the West Coast, Californians rushed to fill their cupboards with potent potables. In San Francisco buyers from all walks of life bought as much liquor as they could afford. "Bankers and brokers, shipping men, mining men, real estate men, butchers and bakers, and candlestick makers — men of every rank and every degree who could raise the price of the liquor — were hurrying to their homes or other people's homes in vehicles piled high with liquor," wrote an observer. "Fair ladies sat in limousines behind alluring barricades of cases; businessmen in runabouts had cases on their knees."

In Wine Country "a host of vintage seekers" besieged Sonoma County's wineries to buy bottles and barrels of vino. "Whence they came from, where they were going, or whence returning, no one seemed to know," wrote a reporter. Nevertheless, "a marvelous procession of motor vehicles passed through town loaded to the gunwales with [the] wine which has made Sonoma Valley famous."[22]

While the typical consumer could afford only a modest stockpile, the wealthy spared no expense. Senator Boies Penrose (R-PA) stashed $125,000 worth of liquor in his Philadelphia townhouse. Senator John Sharp Williams (D-MS) publicly boasted that he had a "splendid" supply of liquor, enough for the rest of his life. Banker J.P. Morgan bought one thousand cases of fine French champagne to enhance his wine cellar. In Maryland, banker Wallace Lanahan filled his cellar with rare wines, brandies, and other alcoholic beverages. The mother of America's Sweetheart, actress Mary Pickford, bought the entire inventory of a liquor store in Los Angeles. A well-known judge stored $100,000 worth of potent potables at his summer home in Stockbridge, Massachusetts. Financier Joseph Leiter spent more than $350,000 on liquor to ensure adequate supplies at his country house in Virginia and his estate in Massachusetts.[23]

When the Great Drought began, a humorist said Prohibition divided drinkers into two classes: those who still had a little and those who had a little still. Clearly there was a third class — wealthy Americans who had stockpiled more than a little and owned enough liquor to ignore the dry law for years. They wouldn't go thirsty, but the future looked bleak for the average drinker. Would he guzzle homemade booze, pay high prices for bootleg whiskey, or join the brotherhood of teetotalers?

2. Volstead 101: Prohibition Basics

Safeguarding and facilitating the lawful use of alcohol is as much a part of Prohibition enforcement as preventing and suppressing its unlawful use. — Roy A. Haynes, Assistant Secretary, U.S. Treasury Department[1]

Like most legislation, the Volstead Act was the product of compromise. The dry forces demanded a tough law while the wets wanted to minimize the impact of Prohibition. After lengthy debate, the factions agreed on a ban with exemptions for using alcohol in medicine, industry, and religious rites. Pragmatic dry leaders persuaded their fanatical colleagues to accept these sensible, necessary exceptions to the ban. Wet leaders wanted more exemptions but had to settle for what they could get. Dry lawmakers expected to plug the loopholes after Prohibition went into effect and everybody saw the wondrous, transforming benefits of life without liquor. Wets, on the other hand, hoped to modify Volstead to weaken the ban.

One thing wets and drys agreed on: Volstead was an imperfect law.

Thou Shall Not

The Eighteenth Amendment to the U.S. Constitution set up a general, nonspecific framework for Prohibition. The three short paragraphs outlawed intoxicating liquors in the United States and its territories but did not define "intoxicating liquors." One clause empowered the federal and state governments to enforce Prohibition but set up no mechanism for doing so. To fill in these significant gaps, Congress passed the Volstead Act, which specified exactly what Prohibition entailed and how it would be enforced.

The Volstead Act outlawed the manufacture, sale, barter, transportation, importation, exportation, delivery, provision, or possession of intoxicating beverages with an alcohol content above one-half of one percent, except for specified legal exemptions. Although a sale implies a buyer, Congress did not make buying alcohol a crime, thereby placing the onus on the seller, rather than the purchaser. A drinker was not breaking the law when he imbibed socially as a bona fide guest at someone else's home. If he drank at a speakeasy or other illicit establishment, he was guilty of patronizing an illegal business; but buying and consuming alcohol were not crimes per se. (Dry fanatics wanted to make both buying and drinking illegal, but the moderates in Congress refused to vote for such a draconian law.)

11

The Volstead Act specified rules for using alcohol for medicinal, sacramental, or industrial purposes. A doctor, dentist, or veterinarian could obtain a permit from the federal government to buy alcohol for use in treating patients. A licensed doctor could write prescriptions for liquor, with one pint every ten days as the per-patient limit. Hospitals and sanitariums could secure a government license to buy and use liquor to treat diseases, including alcoholism.

After obtaining a government permit, an individual or business could make, sell, and/or transport liquor for religious use. Authorized religious leaders could buy and resell wine to be used in the Eucharist or other sacred rituals.

A citizen or business could acquire a government permit to make, sell, and/or transport liquor for non-beverage purposes, including industrial use. Volstead also had provisions for trade in flavoring extracts, syrups, vinegar, preserved sweet cider, and alcoholic liquids unfit for beverage purposes, including antiseptics, toiletries, and denatured distilled spirits.

Some businesses, especially distilleries, had sizable inventories of alcoholic beverages stored in warehouses. Under the dry law a business could obtain government approval to sell its pre–Volstead inventory for legal purposes, such as medical use. To keep this alcohol off the black market, strict regulations set forth the requirements for storing, selling, and shipping it.[2]

A citizen could have his own private liquor supply if he complied with a few simple rules. He could keep all the hooch he had purchased legally before midnight January 16, 1920, if he stored it at his private residence and served it only to his family or bona fide guests. If an individual owned or rented more than one residence, he could keep a supply at each of them. If he moved, he must obtain a government permit to take his liquor with him. A temporary abode, such as a room in a hotel or boardinghouse, did not qualify as a residence. Law enforcement could confiscate any private liquor kept in public storage, such as a warehouse or a clubhouse locker.[3]

Volstead outlawed the sale and purchase of recipes or formulas for making alcoholic beverages. Authorities made few attempts to enforce this ban, and it had little impact. Only the most delusional drys thought they could control the flow of information despite the constitutional guarantee of a free press. Wet activists defied the embargo by handing out copies of George Washington's beer recipe, which he had written in his notebook while serving in the Virginia militia.[4]

In a rare instance of enforcement, lawmen in Richmond, Virginia, arrested an African American newspaper editor for printing pamphlets with formulas for making liquor. Due to the South's general hysteria over the danger of inebriated Negroes, his race may have been the reason for targeting him. Ironically, the federal government issued publications that violated the ban on printing recipes for making potable alcohol. Nine years after Volstead began, the U.S. Department of Agriculture was still circulating Bulletin #1075, which gave directions for making alcoholic beverages at home.[5]

The ban on recipes and formulas presented a quandary for public libraries. Cookbooks were especially suspect because many contained recipes for making wine, cordials, ratafias, cider, and the like. Librarians were divided on the issue of banning books with liquor recipes; some removed offending tomes from their shelves; others refused to do so. The librarian at the San Francisco Public Library said, "It would be far-fetched to eliminate volumes dealing with alcohol." He noted that strict enforcement would ban books on chemistry, cookery, viticulture, distilling, and industrial processes.[6]

Under the Volstead law, anyone could make beverages containing not more than one-half of one percent alcohol. Although fermentation might occur in homemade cider or other fruit juices, they were presumed to be legal, non-intoxicating beverages unless a judge or jury found them to be intoxicating. This created a loophole for the individual who wanted to make a personal supply of wine or cider at home. If he made fruit juice that fermented, he might have an intoxicating beverage, but it was highly unlikely that he would be arrested and taken to court to verify its alcohol content.[7]

Volstead forbade the manufacture, advertising, sale, or possession with intent to sell of any utensil, contrivance, machine, compound, tablet, preparation, or substance designed for or intended for use in the unlawful production of intoxicating beverages. Although Volstead banned the sale of these items, stores stocked them due to the brisk demand. Drinkers could buy a wide range of do-it-yourself (DIY) supplies at specialty shops and mass merchandisers. An estimated twenty-five thousand retailers, including Woolworth's and Kresge's dime-store chains, sold items needed to make and bottle alcoholic beverages. In *Danovitz v. U.S.* the Supreme Court ruled that the government could seize a merchant's inventory if making illegal liquor was its sole or primary use.[8] Items like wort or malt extract had legal usages as well as illegal uses, so proving a case against a merchant was very difficult. Although law enforcement raided a few DIY stores, the trade went on with barely a hiccup after the Supreme Court ruling. Prohibition policy makers put a higher priority on fighting other types of Volstead crime.

The dry law prohibited liquor advertising aimed at general consumers, but it allowed specialized advertising for a targeted audience. Thus, trade journals could print alcohol ads for legal markets, such as the medical and pharmaceutical sectors. Magazines and newspapers defied the law by printing ads for products used in making liquor. At least one newspaper in Texas went even further and carried display ads for an illegal liquor store. The publisher, who apparently had no fear of Prohibition agents, even printed the brand names and the liquor prices![9]

Poison!

Economic factors precluded a ban on using alcohol in industry because it was a basic ingredient in many necessary, everyday products. "Few, if any, more important articles of legitimate commerce are manufactured or sold in the United States than alcohol. Without it, the industry of the nation could neither progress nor maintain itself," explained a Treasury Department official.[10]

Alcohol was used in making numerous products, including dyes, hair tonics, lotions, perfumes, patent medicines, liniment, mouthwash, synthetic silk, explosives, varnish, lacquer, shellac, celluloid, fungicides, insecticides, disinfectants, antifreeze, and embalming fluids. Common industrial processes utilized the nonpoisonous intoxicant ethyl alcohol (AKA grain alcohol) and/or methyl alcohol (AKA wood alcohol), a poison made from sawdust or wood cellulose. In Volstead's latter years, American industry greatly expanded its use of synthetic methyl alcohol (AKA methanol).

When federal lawmakers wrote the Volstead act, they grappled with a tricky task — crafting rules that guaranteed a steady supply of alcohol for industry while preventing people from drinking it. To ensure that drinkers didn't guzzle alcohol intended for industrial use,

Volstead required distillers to render it unpotable by adding at least one noxious substance — a process called "denaturing." Denatured alcohol contained "poisons, astringents, or corrosives, strong enough to cause intense suffering and lingering physical decay." Only ethyl alcohol designated for use in foods, pharmaceuticals, or scientific research was exempt from denaturing.[11]

The Volstead law specified two types of denatured alcohol: completely denatured and specially denatured. Both were unfit for human consumption, and some denaturing formulas could cause death. Completely denatured alcohol was used in antifreeze, radiator fluid, paints, varnishes, household fuel, and similar products. The general public could buy products containing completely denatured alcohol, but the packaging carried a forceful warning: a skull-and-crossbones plus the word "POISON." The text of the warning label read: "Completely denatured alcohol is a violent poison. It cannot be applied externally to human or animal tissues without serious injurious results. It cannot be taken internally without inducing blindness and general physical decay, ultimately resulting in death."

Specially denatured alcohol was a common ingredient in cosmetics, toiletries, personal care products, and pharmaceuticals. Very strict, detailed regulations governed the packaging and branding of specially denatured alcohol. It was always produced, sold, and transported under bond to prevent bootleggers from obtaining it. "No effort is spared to prevent diversion and manipulation of specially denatured alcohol," said a top Prohibition official.[12]

In the early 1920s the government issued six formulas for completely denatured alcohol and seventy for specially denatured alcohol. Each completely denatured formula contained at least two of the following: wood alcohol, benzine, pyridine, kerosene, ether, gasoline, nitrobenzene, or ortho-nitrotoluene. The additives imparted an unpleasant odor and/or taste so the consumer would know the alcohol was contaminated, even if he somehow failed to see the bold warning label.[13]

Each formula for specially denatured alcohol used a combination of ingredients from a long list that included sulfuric acid, iodine, camphor, oil of peppermint, carbolic acid, menthol crystals, tobacco, formaldehyde, tannic acid, mercury bi-chloride, and hydrochloric acid. Specially denatured formulas didn't use wood alcohol because it had a strong, repugnant odor that made it unfit for such products as perfume.[14]

Completely denatured alcohol could not be detoxified by any method known during Prohibition. However, a skilled chemist with a fractionating still could remove the adulterants from specially denatured alcohol. The result was drinkable ethyl alcohol that could be flavored and/or colored to imitate aged whiskey or brandy. Regrettably, bootleggers weren't always willing to pay for a chemist and the equipment to do the job right. Greedy gangsters did their own redistillation, and their "cleaned" alcohol was still adulterated to some degree. If the cleaning removed most of the poison, the drinker suffered only nausea or a hellacious hangover. In the worst case scenario, he became seriously ill and died.

Denatured alcohol added a scientific element to the battle between the bootleggers and the Volstead enforcers. Whenever the liquor traffickers figured out how to clean one type of denatured alcohol, the government would retire that formula or beef it up with more additives. "From adventure on the high seas and hide-and-seek along the borders, the chief interest in the Prohibition battle is now centered in chemical warfare. The laboratory has become the frontline, with government chemists pitted against the chemists of bootleggers," wrote a reporter in 1927.[15]

Due to a dramatic spike in alcohol-related deaths in the mid-Twenties, wet politicians accused the government of trying to kill drinkers with denatured alcohol. A high-ranking Prohibition official replied, "Our chemists are not seeking more deadly poisons ... but merely something that the bootlegger can't take out of alcohol. They are seeking something which the ultimate consumer ... will readily recognize from its odor and taste, so that he will know instantly that he is in possession of denatured alcohol."[16]

A furor swirled around the release of a new denatured alcohol formula in 1927. Compared to previous formulas, this one doubled the amount of wood alcohol. Due to the relative boiling points of the two types of alcohol, it was impossible to boil off all the poisonous methyl before the nontoxic ethyl also began evaporating. In theory, the double dose of wood alcohol made the product "not twice as poisonous, but half as likely" to be consumed. To intensify the repugnant odor, the new

A government chemist analyzes samples of bootleg whiskey in this 1920 photograph (Library of Congress).

formula also called for aldehol, an oxidation product of kerosene. The addition of benzine and pyridine bases completed the recipe. Reportedly, three drinks of this new formula caused blindness. Death might also result.[17]

Predictably, bootleggers tried to clean the new formula denatured alcohol, with mixed success. Even when they failed to remove all the contaminants, they sold it to gullible consumers. Senator Edward Edwards (D-NJ) called the new denaturing formula "legalized murder." Wet leaders accused Washington of trying to terrorize drinkers into abstinence. Secretary of the Treasury Andrew Mellon said he didn't like using poison but the government had no option until chemists could find a nonlethal denaturant that bootleggers couldn't remove.

Speaking for the dry faction, ASL attorney Wayne Wheeler said, "The government is under no obligation to furnish the people with alcohol that is drinkable when the Constitution prohibits it." He argued that the real killer was not denatured alcohol but the bootlegger who sold it. Drinkers who consumed the new formula were committing "deliberate suicide." Furthermore, Wheeler said, "It tastes like the seepage of a garbage can flavored with overheated oil."[18] (He didn't explain how he knew what it tasted like. Had he sampled it?)

In 1930 Prohibition officials finally found the stinky, sickening, but nonfatal ingredient they needed. Prohibition Commissioner James Doran announced plans to use alcotate — a noxious, nonlethal substance marketed by Standard Oil of California. A byproduct of petroleum cracking, alcotate induced nausea but did not blind or kill the drinker. Doran likened its putrid odor to "spoiled eggs and garlic." Although he wouldn't reveal alcotate's composition, he said chemists were confident it could not be "precipitated from or distilled out of grain alcohol."[19]

Industrious Bootleggers

As the U.S. economy expanded during the Roaring Twenties, industry's demand for alcohol nearly doubled. To satisfy this growing need, the federal government licensed plants to convert distilled spirits into denatured industrial alcohol, using the formulas issued by the Prohibition Unit. Businesses with a legitimate need for industrial alcohol could obtain a government permit to buy it from a licensed plant. To prevent the diversion of industrial alcohol into illegal channels, the Prohibition Unit controlled the production, storage, sales, and transportation of all industrial alcohol. The feds' strict oversight kept bootleggers from obtaining it — in theory, at least.

Enterprising mobsters set up sham companies to secure government permits to legally buy industrial alcohol. Starting a company to manufacture toiletries was a popular choice. In New Jersey, Prohibition officials discovered that the Percheron Products Company, which claimed to make toiletries, had never made so much as a bottle of shaving lotion. An upstart perfume maker in New York bought twenty-five times more industrial alcohol than a legitimate brand, Coty Perfumes. Chicago gangster Vincent "Schemer" Drucci set up the Cosmo Hair Tonic Company, which made a small amount of hair tonic and paid celebrities to endorse it. Drucci's real moneymaker was bootlegging the industrial alcohol he bought for Cosmo. Crooks too lazy to start a sham company could buy industrial alcohol from a dishonest plant manager, who would falsify his records to hide the transaction from the Prohibition Unit.[20]

Bootleggers with permits for sham companies had little to fear because an acute shortage of manpower kept the Prohibition Unit from closely monitoring sales of industrial alcohol. For example, in Wisconsin the Prohibition squad had only two inspectors to watch more than four thousand permit holders. Prohibition officials in Philadelphia licensed roughly five hundred firms that claimed to have a legitimate need for alcohol. The Philly police department estimated that only eight percent of the permit holders ran bona fide businesses, but the Prohibition Unit didn't have the resources for thorough investigations.[21]

Despite Washington's efforts to control every aspect of the industrial alcohol business, much of the licensed plants' output ended up in the hands of bootleggers. In fact, Assistant U.S. Attorney General Mabel Willebrandt stated that the licensed plants were "the greatest single source of liquor" for the illegal traffic. She said oversight was so lax that it was "well-nigh impossible" to stop the licensees from selling to bootleggers.[22]

Many Washington officials agreed with Willebrandt's assessment of the situation, but Prohibition Commissioner James Doran found no reason to be alarmed. He claimed that little industrial alcohol leaked into bootleg channels. In 1930 he ordered cutbacks in the production of industrial alcohol and boasted that improved Volstead enforcement had removed it from the illegal marketplace. However, there was another plausible reason for the ample supply of industrial alky. The Great Depression was shrinking the U.S. economy, and manufacturers needed less of almost everything. Realists said the bad economy, not better Volstead enforcement, explained the oversupply of industrial alcohol.[23]

Baby Volstead

The Eighteenth Amendment gave the federal and state governments "concurrent power" to enforce Prohibition "by appropriate legislation." To supplement the national law, most state legislatures enacted a "baby Volstead" statute to stipulate exactly how Prohibition would be enforced at the state and local levels. Bone-dry state legislators seized this opportunity to pass measures even more restrictive than the federal law. Some baby Volsteads made buying liquor a crime. Others limited alcohol content to even less than one-half of one percent and defined "intoxicant" to include flavoring extracts, toilet waters, canned heat, and similar items. The federal dry law allowed doctors to prescribe alcohol for medicinal use, but twenty-one states prohibited such prescriptions. Several states that allowed doctors to prescribe medical alcohol limited the quantity to one-half or even one-fourth of what federal regulations permitted.[24]

Georgia and Indiana criminalized the possession of liquor even if the owner had acquired it for personal use before Prohibition began. Under Indiana's baby Volstead, an empty container that smelled of liquor was sufficient evidence to arrest someone for possession. The Indiana statute also banned medical alcohol and prohibited merchants from exhibiting cocktail shakers or whiskey flasks in their display windows. For a time, Indiana even vested train conductors and bus drivers with the authority to arrest passengers on possession charges. Alabama's strict law banned "any liquor, drink, or liquid made or used for beverage purpose" that contained any amount of alcohol, no matter how small. West Virginia outlawed "all liquids, mixtures, and preparations, whether patented or not, which will produce intoxication." In Vermont a person arrested for drunkenness could be jailed for refusing to name his liquor supplier.[25]

The Eighteenth Amendment didn't spell out exactly how concurrent enforcement would work, so it left the door open for disputes between Washington and the Statehouses. When Volstead began, the Treasury Department's Prohibition Unit took charge of federal enforcement. In keeping with the standard federal role in law enforcement, Treasury officials planned to focus on interstate commerce, illegal imports, and major criminal activity that crossed state lines. As Treasury saw the division of labor, the local police would be the workhorse of enforcement, doing the nitty-gritty daily task of stopping the illegal liquor traffic. Treasury's Internal Revenue commissioner stated that the federal government would "reinforce local efforts" as needed.[26]

The Statehouses didn't share the Treasury Department's vision of concurrent enforcement. State and local officials felt that Washington was dumping the responsibility for enforcement on them. They argued that the feds must provide most, if not all, of the money and manpower for enforcement. The states simply didn't have the money to pay for more lawmen, jails, judges, courts, and trials. The majority of Statehouses refused to appropriate any funds for Prohibition enforcement. Ohio, which spent the most on enforcement, appropriated less than $150,000 in 1927 — far from enough for a large state with numerous, well-organized bootleg gangs.[27]

Like most states, Pennsylvania appropriated no money to enforce Volstead in 1923. But there was nothing in state law to prevent private funding, so the Woman's Christian Temperance Union (WCTU) took a plan to Governor Gifford Pinchot, a prominent dry activist. The ladies volunteered to raise money for enforcement, and Pinchot gave his blessing. For several years, the WCTU donated enough money to pay for two deputy attorneys general and a small corps of undercover agents to fight the liquor traffic in the Keystone State.

During a U.S. Senate investigation, evidence revealed that Pennsylvania's undercover agents spent much of their time at speakeasies, buying and drinking liquor. Hanging out at bars was standard procedure because the lawmen needed to prove that liquor was being sold before they made an arrest. On average, a drink cost fifty cents in Pennsylvania, and each agent spent up to $10 per day — enough to get anybody drunk. The senators questioned whether this was an appropriate use of WCTU funds. A spokesman for the agents said they didn't get drunk because they spent most of the money "treating" other drinkers.[28] (If he saw any irony in spending WCTU money on booze, he didn't mention it.)

3. Body and Soul: Hospital Whiskey and Sacramental Wine

Read your Bible: Wine was served at the Last Supper.—Anti-Prohibition slogan

The U.S. Congress resisted the dry faction's pleas to outlaw the use of alcohol in two important sectors: religion and medicine. Millions of American Jews and Catholics drank wine as a traditional, integral part of their religious rituals. Thousands of doctors prescribed wine or distilled spirits to treat a wide variety of ailments. While denatured alcohol would suffice for industrial applications, potable alcohol was imperative for religious and medical purposes. Public sentiment favored the continued use of alcohol in worship and medicine, so Congress granted exemptions. Zealous dry leaders condemned these concessions and argued that no one needed drinkable alcohol for the body or the soul.

A Sure Cure

America's bonded warehouses held row upon row of barrels filled with premium, pre–Volstead liquor that could be used for medical purposes. The dry law allowed doctors, dentists, druggists, hospitals, and sanitariums with government permits to dispense "hospital alcohol" to their patients. Doctors most often prescribed whiskey or brandy, but the law also permitted the sale of wine and cordials for medical use. A few months after Volstead began, the Internal Revenue Bureau reported that sixteen thousand physicians had permits to write prescriptions for medical alcohol. The number of doctors with permits rose steadily, and nearly seventy thousand doctors were licensed to prescribe alcohol in 1929.[1]

Doctors found that patients asked for medical alcohol to treat a wide variety of ailments, both real and imagined. People wanted whiskey to cure indigestion, nerve disorders, chronic pain, insomnia, tired blood, and more. Doctors joked about their "pint patients" and the epidemic of "thirst-itis" that swept the country during the Great Drought. Upstanding citizens who would never set foot inside a saloon asked for prescriptions because a shot of whiskey was quite respectable when the doctor ordered it.

Drugstores could sell alcohol to fill prescriptions, but druggists hesitated to apply for the necessary licenses due to the burdensome red tape and recordkeeping. For starters, a retail druggist had to obtain two permits, one to buy liquor wholesale and another to sell it to consumers. Then he had to keep a record of every ounce of alcohol and every prescription that passed through his store.

Initially, only about ten percent of pharmacists applied for the permits to dispense hospital alcohol. Doctors worried that a lack of retail outlets would make it difficult for patients to fill their prescriptions. Public health officials urged pharmacists to do their civic duty and apply for permits. It only took a few weeks of Volstead to show druggists that medical whiskey was a moneymaker. They hurried to obtain the necessary permits. By July 1920 the government had licensed more than fifty-seven thousand pharmacists to fill alcohol prescriptions.[2]

Doctors prescribed roughly eight million gallons of medical alcohol during Volstead's first year. The initial demand was so high that Prohibition Commissioner Kramer felt it was excessive. He suspected widespread profiteering and fraudulent use of prescriptions. He noted one astonishing case where a doctor had signed 475 whiskey prescriptions in a single day! To restrict sales, Kramer ordered Prohibition supervisors to issue each physician only one hundred prescription forms per quarter. If a doctor needed to write more prescriptions than that, he had to request special permission from the Prohibition Unit.[3]

Due to the robust demand for medicinal whiskey, druggists charged a premium price, which led to consumer complaints. Only weeks after Volstead took effect, druggists in Brooklyn were charging up to $12 for a pint of whiskey. Buyers in other cities also reported price gouging, and doctors joined their patients in protesting the high cost. The Fair Price Commission recommended a top price of $2.50 per pint, but druggists generally charged as much as the market would bear. New York druggists were making up to six hundred per-cent profit on whiskey sales, according to a Prohibition official.[4]

The most expensive prescription for medical alcohol may have been filled by Helene Rabinoff, wife of opera impresario Max Rabinoff. The Rabinoffs were traveling in France when a mysterious ailment struck her. A French physician prescribed brandy. To protect her health, the Rabinoffs spared no expense. They bought French brandy distilled more than a century earlier for Napoleon's wine cellar. When they returned to the USA, they brought the costly medicine with them. Customs officials confiscated the brandy but soon returned it because Mrs. Rabinoff had a prescription.[5]

Helene Rabinoff wasn't the only patient who needed expensive French wine. The Pro-hibition Unit allowed the importation of French champagne as medicine, and wealthy con-sumers took advantage of this loophole. Department of Commerce figures showed a 332 percent increase in imports of French bubbly in 1920 compared to the previous year. Cynics said more of this champagne went to debutante balls than to hospitals.[6]

In Volstead's latter years, sales of hospital alcohol shrank substantially. In large part, the decrease was caused by new government regulations intended to plug loopholes and prevent fraud. In the mid–Twenties, Prohibition officials estimated the annual consumption of medical alcohol at three million gallons, significantly less than when Volstead began. In the late Twenties sales of hospital whiskey continued to fall, averaging less than two million gallons per year.[7]

Despite the falling demand, Prohibition officials saw a shortage of medical alcohol on the horizon. In 1926 Prohibition Director Lincoln Andrews announced that the nation's stock of hospital alcohol was so low it constituted an "emergency." In addition to the amount consumed by patients, many gallons disappeared each year due to evaporation and absorption. A substantial amount was also lost to thieves, despite diligent efforts to safeguard the inventory.

The government had the option of importing liquor to augment the supply, but Prohibition officials wanted to replenish it domestically because this would give them more control over the process. Andrews said it was crucial to authorize production without delay because the whiskey must age for several years "in order to acquire the qualities essential to a good brand of liquor."[8] And, presumably, the qualities essential to good medicine.

Dry leaders vigorously opposed expanding the nation's stock of potable whiskey, even for medical use. When Congress considered a bill to authorize the manufacture of more hospital alcohol, the drys mustered their forces to derail it. Due to the strong opposition, top officials at the Treasury Department decided to drop the matter, at least temporarily. In 1927 Treasury issued a statement saying that the existing supply of medical alcohol would be sufficient for several years due to the sharp decline in whiskey withdrawals from bonded warehouses.[9]

In 1929 Prohibition officials revived the plan to make medical alcohol and, surprisingly, encountered no real opposition from the dry camp. Washington decided to license the production of two million gallons annually; the new supply would be seventy percent bourbon and thirty percent rye. While the drys napped, the Treasury Department issued permits to distilleries in Kentucky to begin replenishing the supply of hospital whiskey.[10]

Legions of pint patients breathed a collective sigh of relief.

A Prescription for Trouble

Within the medical community, health care professionals debated the efficacy of medicinal alcohol. Many doctors argued that it had no therapeutic value whatsoever, but others felt it had valid medical uses. Under federal law, a doctor could prescribe up to one pint of distilled spirits for a patient every ten days, but state statutes were often more restrictive. Doctors who resented government regulation formed the Association against Impure Liquor (AAIL) and lobbied to remove all restrictions on medical alcohol. AAIL stated that each doctor had a "constitutional right to practice medicine unhampered by legislative tyranny and bureaucratic red tape." A New York doctor, with support from the American Medical Association, took a test case to the U.S. Supreme Court. The doctor argued that the legal limits on alcohol prescriptions had no medical justification and should be voided. The Supreme Court upheld the one-pint limit.[11]

Bootleggers coveted medical alcohol because they could sell the pristine, aged whiskey for top dollar. To obtain hospital alcohol through legal channels, liquor traffickers bought into legitimate pharmacies or wholesale drug companies. Bootleggers bought prescription forms from unethical doctors or paid physicians to sign counterfeit prescriptions. Bootlegging gangs opened their own drugstores, and a few set up bogus pharmaceutical firms that traded in nothing but alcohol. In New York nearly seven hundred new drugstores registered with the Board of Pharmacy in 1921-22.[12] Officials strongly suspected that a large percentage of these were mob-owned, but the board didn't have the resources to ferret out the bootleggers.

In 1931 federal agents in New York City broke up "the largest liquor-prescription syndicate ever uncovered in the United States." Roughly one thousand doctors and four hundred druggists were involved in a scam that netted millions of dollars for a bootleg gang. The doctors sold their signed prescription forms to the bootleggers, who used them to buy medical alcohol. Prosecutors couldn't take all the lawbreakers to court, simply because there were too many of them. Twelve physicians, thirteen druggists, and twenty-seven others were indicted for conspiring to divert medicinal alcohol into the illegal liquor traffic. When the court meted out justice, the guilty doctors were fined only $50 each — hardly a deterrent to crime.[13]

Counterfeiters found a healthy market for fake prescription forms for hospital alcohol. Bootleggers bought the bogus forms, and so did patients who wanted to bypass the doctor and self-medicate. Druggists used counterfeit forms to hide illegal sales to people without prescriptions. Officials in New York City said the town was "entirely flooded" with bogus prescriptions. Over a five-month period, Prohibition agents found a half-million counterfeit forms in NYC drugstores.[14] Despite the scope of the fraud, pharmacists were rarely arrested or indicted. Putting druggists in prison simply wasn't a high priority for the Prohibition Unit.

Sacrilegious Wine

Wine gained throngs of new devotees during Prohibition, largely due to loopholes in the dry law. Initially, the Volstead law had exemptions that allowed drinkers to consume medicinal, sacramental, and homemade wines. Sacramental wine could legally be used for the religious rituals and sacred holidays of all faiths. Doctors could prescribe wine for medicinal use, and the Prohibition Unit issued permits for home winemaking during Volstead's early years.

Wine drinkers who didn't want to pay bootleg prices could make their own vino at home. When Prohibition began, any citizen could get a government permit to make up to 200 gallons of wine tax-free if he didn't sell any of it. Wets loved this loophole, but the dry faction was determined to close it. The anti-alcohol lobbyists went to work, and in 1925 the federal government revoked all the permits for homemade wine. The do-it-yourself winemakers protested loudly, as did the grape growers, who didn't want to lose a big share of their market. After some bureaucratic wrangling, Washington decided that permit holders could still make wine at home, but they now had to pay taxes on their vino.[15]

The sacramental wine privilege allowed religious groups to follow their hallowed customs, despite opposition from dry activists who begrudged the faithful even a sip of vino. The drys argued that unfermented grape juice could be used in all sacred rituals. However, this idea was anathema to the vast majority of Catholics and Jews as well as some Protestants. Tradition and deeply-held beliefs won the day. Moderate dry leaders realized that taking sacramental wine away from true believers would make more foes than friends. Thus, dry attacks against the religious use of wine gradually fizzled out.

From time to time, Washington revised the rules for sacramental wine, but some form of the exemption existed until Volstead ended. Initially, the Prohibition Unit allowed any "duly-appointed religious leader" to obtain a permit to utilize the wine privilege. After securing his permit, the leader could buy, sell, or make wine "for his individual use or the use of his congregation." The government licensed stores to sell sacramental wine, and any individual with the proper permit could buy it at those outlets.

In Prohibition's first year, sales of sacramental wine grew by eight hundred thousand gallons over the final pre–Volstead year. Americans seemed to be taking communion with great regularity, but much of the wine never saw anything holier than a blind pig. When Lincoln Andrews was Volstead's top cop, he said the religious exemption made enforcement an "impossible task." He stated that sacramental wine stores ranked high among "the chief sources of the illicit liquor supply."[16]

In general, the sacramental wine stores sold to any buyer who had a permit, without trying to determine whether the document was genuine or fake. The shopkeepers weren't police officers, so they had no expertise in spotting forgeries. They were merely merchants trying to sell their inventory, and they weren't always picky about who bought it. In an undercover sting in New York City, a Prohibition agent bought wine at several stores that didn't even ask if he had a permit.[17]

Bootleggers often posed as clergymen to buy wine. They used counterfeit permits or real ones they had stolen or purchased from a corrupt Prohibition official. Since sacramental wine was never denatured, liquor traffickers could sell it immediately without the hassle of cleaning it. No one knew exactly how much sacramental wine was diverted into the illegal liquor traffic, but bootleggers easily obtained a large portion of the wine made for religious use. Wags suggested that the religious exemption should be called the "sacrilegious wine" privilege.

Catholics and Jews used sacramental wine differently, and the Jewish practices presented the bigger challenge for Volstead enforcement. The centralized, hierarchical structure of the Catholic Church helped the Prohibition Unit keep track of the wine sold to the dioceses. The unit held each bishop accountable for all the sacramental wine in his diocese. Under the bishop's supervision, an authorized church official bought the wine and doled it out to the parish priests and others who needed it. In contrast, the lack of a strong, central authority in the Jewish faith complicated matters for the Volstead enforcers. Rabbis had a great deal of autonomy, with less oversight than their Catholic counterparts. The individual rabbi bought or made a supply of sacramental wine and sold it to members of his congregation for use at home on religious holidays.

In Catholicism, the congregants drank the sacramental wine in public rituals at places of worship, which reduced the likelihood that it would be misused. Jewish families drank their wine at home, increasing the chance that it would be consumed for non-religious purposes. The rules allowed a rabbi to buy ten gallons of wine per year for each family in his congregation. In New York City a rabbi claimed a congregation of two thousand six hundred families, which allowed him to buy and resell twenty-six thousand gallons.[18] Of course, the typical rabbi had a much smaller flock.

Applications for sacramental wine permits flooded into the Prohibition offices in the big cities. Chicago appeared to be America's most devout metropolis since religious buyers there set the record for purchasing sacramental wine. The Windy City's licensed stores sold more than twice as much wine as New York City's, even though Chicago's population was smaller. According to a newsman, ninety percent of Chicago's sacramental wine stores were "bootlegging shops" that made "scant pretense of being anything else." Despite the vast scope of Chicago's illegal liquor traffic, the reporter blamed the wine privilege for Volstead's failure in the Windy City.

An investigation revealed massive graft in the issuance of wine permits in Chicago.

Bootleggers bribed officials to approve sacramental wine permits for nonexistent synagogues, temples, and churches. Religious wine permits were even given to athletic clubs. The number of permits issued to rabbis greatly exceeded the number of temples and synagogues in Chicago, but a bogus rabbi usually claimed that his flock met in a private home. By double-checking the records kept by wine retailers, investigators found numerous bogus sales. Store receipts showed many sales to clergymen and congregations that, in fact, had never ordered or received the wine.[19]

In San Francisco, Jewish leaders condemned the "mushroom congregations" that popped up to take advantage of the sacramental wine loophole. As few as two men could start a synagogue and select a third man to serve as their rabbi. Despite his tiny flock, the newly-minted rabbi could obtain a permit to buy sacramental wine. The Conference of Jewish Organizations (CJO) deplored this misuse of the wine privilege and vowed "to suppress the activities of fake congregations and pseudo rabbis" in the Bay Area. B'nai B'rith and California's Prohibition director empowered the CJO to review the credentials of all Jews applying for wine permits in the area, in order to weed out the fake rabbis.[20]

To stop the misuse of the wine privilege, Washington changed the rules governing sacramental wine in 1922. Under the new policy, the clergy could no longer make wine. However, a clergyman could supervise the production of sacramental wine in a bonded winery. In addition, a rabbi, priest, or minister of the gospel could own a winery licensed to make sacramental wine. The new rules reduced the annual wine allotment to two gallons per congregant. In 1923 the rules were revised again, reinstating the right of the clergy to make wine for religious use. Specifically, a clergyman could secure "a permit to manufacture enough wine to supply the ritualistic needs of his congregation for one year."[21]

In 1925 Prohibition officials reached an agreement with "a large number of rabbis" to curtail abuse of the wine privilege. Prohibition administrators were given a list of the names of rabbis "recognized as bona fide" by their peers. If an unlisted rabbi applied for a permit or tried to buy wine at a licensed store, the Prohibition Unit would investigate him. As part of the new agreement, Jewish sects, except the ultra-orthodox, agreed to reduce the annual wine ration to one gallon per adult. The ultra-orthodox allotment was five gallons per adult with the option of requesting more if needed.[22]

In 1926 New York's Prohibition administrator ordered his agents to close 210 retail stores deemed "responsible for flagrant abuses of the sacramental wine privileges." He also temporarily suspended all religious wine permits. He said that "misinterpretation of the regulations" had led officials to license wine stores. According to his reading of the law, sacramental wine must be delivered directly from the winery to an authorized religious official, eliminating the need for stores. He promised to institute a system that would do away with New York's stores while ensuring sufficient wine for religious needs. Subsequently, he adopted a system that entailed much paperwork and elicited many complaints from religious leaders. Under the new procedure, a clergyman who wanted to buy wine had to submit five copies of an application to withdraw it directly from a bonded facility. If he planned to resell the wine, his application had to be accompanied by an individual letter from each member of his congregation who wanted to buy a portion of the wine.[23]

In 1928 officials in Washington revamped the regulations for buying sacramental wine to simplify matters for Jewish groups. Under the new system, each rabbi approved all sales to his flock. Any Jew wanting to buy wine was allowed to withdraw up to five gallons from a licensed winery if he had an authorization card signed by his rabbi.[24] Thus, Prohibition officials threw up their hands and gave the rabbis full responsibility for dispensing sacramental wine to Jewish Americans.

To Your Health!

Although the Volstead law allowed physicians to prescribe wine, not all doctors did so. The medical community was divided on the issue of using alcohol as medicine, but the typical doctor wanted the freedom to use his own judgment. Dry leaders argued that wine had no curative powers and demanded a ban or, at least, very strict limits on prescribing wine as medicine. To their chagrin, Prohibition Commissioner Kramer decided that the medical profession should have free rein in the matter. He ruled that physicians could prescribe "such quantities of wine (vinous liquors) as they, in the exercise of their sound and honest judgment, deem necessary." The ASL condemned Kramer's decision and argued that the limit on distilled spirits, one pint per week, should also apply to wine. In 1923 Congress bowed to dry pressure and enacted stricter prescription limits. Doctors were restricted to prescribing one pint of distilled spirits for a patient every ten days. The ten-day limit for wine was one quart with a maximum alcohol content of twenty-four percent.[25]

To prevent abuse of medicinal wine, dry leaders thought it should be so distasteful that people wouldn't derive any pleasure from drinking it. To make it sufficiently unpleasant, they wanted to add quinine and/or cascara, an herbal laxative. Both doctors and patients rejected the idea of additives that might alter the taste of wine or produce undesirable side effects. Doctors most often prescribed port or sherry, and patients wanted them to taste like they did before Volstead.

Imported wines from Europe and Asia supplemented the stock of domestic vintages available for medical use. Cities with large Asian populations, such as San Francisco, imported vast quantities of medicinal wine from the Far East. The Oriental imports bore exotic names, like Dew of the Spring Months, Wine of the Three Serpents, Deer Horn Wine, Night Roaming Wild Goose, Monkey Delight, and Blackfoot Snake Wine.

Residents of San Francisco's Chinatown favored Ng Ka Py, commonly called opium in a bottle. In Volstead's early months, ships brought cargos of Ng Ka Py through the Golden Gate without any interference. Then the Prohibition Unit decided that the liquid didn't qualify as medicine and began seizing shipments. This led to a legal tug-of-war between the importers and the Prohibition office in San Francisco. After officials in Washington reviewed the matter, they ordered the return of a large quantity of Ng Ka Py to the importers — much to the delight of Chinatown denizens. Several months later, Prohibition Commissioner Kramer ordered the release of all confiscated Ng Ka Py in San Francisco with the proviso that it must be used as medicine, not as a beverage.[26]

Importers brought cargos of Chinese wine into the United States until 1922, when Washington reclassified it and removed it from the list of beverages approved for medical use. The Prohibition Unit gave importers a deadline for moving their Chinese wine out of the country; after that date it would be confiscated.

The New York Prohibition squad seized large shipments of imported Chinese wine and took them to the Brooklyn Navy Yard, where they were stored on a scow guarded by U.S. Marines. After a federal court ruled that the Chinese wine had been illegally imported, customs officials decided to dump it. On a brisk winter day, a tug attached a hawser to the liquor-laden scow and towed it out to sea. Customs inspectors did their duty, tossing 50,000 quarts of wine into the briny deep.[27]

Not all medicinal wine required a prescription. Drugstores, tobacco shops, and even restaurants sold over-the-counter wine tonics. Although these were marketed as nostrums, more than a few people drank them as table wine. A popular Tokay tonic was twenty percent alcohol with a modicum of pepsin so it qualified as an over-the-counter medicine. Other wine tonics had similar formulas that consumers could drink for pleasure if their taste buds weren't too finicky.

Of course, the easy availability of wine tonics led the dry faction to demand restrictions on them. Washington revised the regulations but never banned the tonics from the marketplace. In 1929 the Prohibition Bureau ruled that a wine tonic must contain not less than thirty percent solids "accomplished by the addition of bona fide drug material (such as sugar or glycerine)." The additives would "render the preparations practically worthless as beverages." Skeptics questioned whether the addition of sugar or glycerine would deter winos from guzzling wine tonics. Nontoxic additives might alter the taste, but they were unlikely to stop someone who really craved alcohol.[28]

The Brick with a Kick

America's vintners had the choice of closing their doors, operating illegally, or obtaining a license to make wine for medical and/or sacramental use. A substantial number of them straddled the line, making both legal and illegal wine. The U.S. wine industry was concentrated in California, where European immigrants had started numerous wineries. The typical Golden State winery was a family business built over generations, and the families fought hard to hold onto their land and their unique culture. New York also had a substantial number of wineries, but their output didn't equal California's in volume or quality.

Economists predicted Prohibition would cause the demise of the U.S. wine industry and inflict hard times on California's grape growers. Analysts forecast falling demand for grapes, so farmers in Southern California dug up their grapevines to make room for other crops. In contrast, growers in Northern California generally stuck with grapes because the region's sandy topsoil wouldn't support other crops. Due to the grapevine's unique root structure, vineyards thrived in Napa and Sonoma counties, making grapes and wine the area's economic bedrock.

When Volstead began, the typical Northern California winery obtained a government permit and made wine for the legal market, complying with all the regulations. Both licensed and unlicensed wineries secretly sold at least part of their output to bootleggers. Wine from Napa and Sonoma poured into San Francisco, where demand was especially strong in fine restaurants, luxury hotels, and private clubs.

To the forecasters' surprise, the dry law didn't decimate the demand for California grapes. Agents from cities in the East and Midwest traveled to California to place orders for railway carloads of grapes to sell to amateur winemakers. In 1921 a newspaper headline declared: "Home Winemaking Saves Grape Growers."[29]

When California's grapes reached the big cities, buyers flocked to the produce markets to purchase them. In New York City the wholesale market on West Street between Franklin and Park Place was "devoted almost exclusively" to the sale of grapes during California's harvest season. Shoppers crowded into the narrow aisles between stacks of crates, and the market buzzed with activity. "The casual passerby might easily mistake the cause of excitement for a street fight or something equally dramatic," an observer said. "In the fruit auction rooms bidding on these grapes reached a high pitch and wholesale prices jumped." The Alicante and Zinfandel varieties brought the highest prices.[30]

The proliferation of small wineries enhanced the demand for grapes in New York City. During the Great Drought the city was "simply dotted with wineries — all doing a tremendous business in every part of the city." Much of the wine was decidedly mediocre, but drinkers had to lower their standards during the Arid Era. The Lower East Side became an oasis in the Volstead desert, due to the area's high number of wineries and sacramental wine stores. Although some NYC vintners had government permits, illegal operations were the norm. Since Volstead enforcement was lax in the Big Apple, the winery owners had little fear of raids.[31]

By 1922 California grape growers were shipping so much product by train that railroads had a shortage of refrigerated cars, called "reefers." For that year's harvest, Californians used twenty-six thousand reefers, but they needed thousands more to get their perishable crop to market in good condition. The railway companies rushed to add more refrigerated cars to their rolling stock. In 1924 California grape growers shipped 55,000 railcars of product to markets across the country.[32]

Like all farmers, California's grape growers were at the mercy of the weather and the marketplace. They prospered in the mid–1920s but suffered serious setbacks in the latter half of the decade. Some years, bad weather produced poor crops. At other times, overproduction glutted the market and kept prices low. This was good news for consumers, but not for the grape growers. Even when the Napa-Sonoma growers had a superior harvest, they faced strong competition because farmers in other regions started selling grapes to the big city markets.

Grapes were a fragile fruit, so growers looked for ways to turn their harvest into products with a long shelf life. Concentrated grape juice and bricks of grape concentrate reduced spoilage and shipped easier than fresh grapes. Concentrates intended for the DIY market were sold under brand names like Vine-Glo, Forbidden Fruit, Vino Sano, and Moon Mist. Both liquid and brick concentrates came with instructions for making a nonalcoholic soft drink. The directions also explained the steps that would ruin the soft drink by turning it into an alcoholic beverage. In specialty stores, a helpful clerk would give the novice winemaker a tutorial in how to use the concentrate. To follow up, the obliging shopkeeper would send a clerk to the buyer's house to check on the wine's progress and offer advice. The market for grape concentrates was so strong that scammers sold "wine" bricks that were actually compressed sawdust or seaweed.

A California company marketed Vino Sano, the Brick with a Kick. The bricks of grape concentrate produced sherry, port, claret, and other varieties of wine. Vino Sano's label advised the buyer to dissolve the brick in water, add sugar, and consume within five days. Otherwise, the beverage might ferment, especially if it were kept in a warm place. The ASL pressured the Prohibition Unit to take action against the Brick with a Kick. At the ASL's behest, federal agents raided Vino Sano's Manhattan store, arrested the salesclerks, and seized truckloads of the grape concentrate.[33]

California's grape cooperatives merged to form Fruit Industries, which marketed Vine-Glo, a concentrate in brick form. Vine-Glo's advertising slogan was "Just Pull the Bung." The wine concentrate came in various flavors, including port, muscatel, sauterne, Riesling, and burgundy. The buyer was advised to put the Vine-Glo brick in a keg in his cellar and dilute it with water. After two months, he would have wine with an alcohol content of about fifteen percent. Vine-Glo ads assured buyers it was legal to enjoy this beverage at home, but they must not sell or transport it.[34]

The Virginia Dare Vineyards of New York advertised concentrated grape juice for making champagne. If the customer followed the directions and maintained the proper temperature, he could make his own bubbly in three to six weeks. The product came with a money-back guarantee if the customer didn't like the taste of the champagne — even if he had spoiled it through his own negligence. According to the ads, expert wine tasters rated the homemade Virginia Dare bubbly equal to vintage champagne.

Although the companies selling grape concentrates claimed they were a legal product, the drys disagreed. The companies argued that the concentrates contained no alcohol and were not intoxicating, which made them legal. However, the Volstead law prohibited the manufacture, sale, or possession of any product "designed or intended for use in the unlawful manufacture of intoxicating liquor." So there was a basis for prosecution based on illegal design and/or intent. But it would be a hard case to prove in court.

Federal prosecutors initiated a few cases to test the waters. A federal court in California ruled that making or selling bricks of grape concentrate did not violate the dry law. Juries in New York acquitted defendants accused of violating Volstead by selling grape juice concentrate. In St. Joseph, Missouri, a federal grand jury indicted the Ukiah Grape Products Company on multiple counts of possessing and selling grape juice concentrate. Ukiah was found guilty, but the all the charges were misdemeanors and the company paid only a small fine.[35]

Since the test cases garnered no major convictions, the federal Prohibition commissioner stated that his agency would pursue "no special drive against the sale of grape concentrates." Ukiah Grape Products withdrew its concentrate from the marketplace, but drinkers could still buy Vino Sano. Fruit Industries rebranded Vine-Glo and tweaked its sales strategy but continued to market wine concentrates. The DIY winemakers sipped their vino at the evening meal, confident that Prohibition agents wouldn't storm into the dining room.[36]

Pablo, Gozo, and Yip

Initially, the Volstead law had a medical exemption that allowed beer, like wine and whiskey, to be used as a curative product. But in 1921 the U.S. Congress passed the Willis-Campbell Act, prohibiting the use of beer as medicine. Naturally, there were protests from companies with government permits to make and/or sell beer for medical use. Several firms planned lawsuits to test the constitutionality of the beer ban. Piel Brothers brewery sued state and federal officials, in essence demanding the right to manufacture beer because it had legitimate medical uses. The company also claimed that the ban would inflict substantial monetary damages on Piel, which had invested large sums in updating its plant. The federal judge who heard Piel's case found no reason to overturn the ban. He ruled that the Willis-Campbell Act was constitutional because beer was not medicine. Malt liquor had "little or no value ... either as a therapeutic agent or as a galactagogue," he said.[37]

James Everard Breweries and Edward & John Burke, Ltd., also sued to void the ban, and they took their cases all the way to the U.S. Supreme Court. Everard had a government permit to manufacture intoxicating malt liquor for medical use and to sell stout wholesale to pharmacists. The Burke firm marketed Guinness's Stout in the U.S. "largely and predominantly for medicinal purposes." The Supreme Court heard the two cases together and, in a rare unanimous decision, upheld the ban on malt liquor. The ruling said, "Neither beer nor any other intoxicating malt liquor is listed as a medicinal remedy in the United States Pharmacopeia. They are not generally recognized as medicinal agents."[38]

A brewer couldn't make intoxicating malt liquors for medical use, but he could obtain a permit to make near beer. At first, the government specified that near beer must be made using the arrested fermentation process, which stopped the yeast action by manipulating the temperature, thereby keeping the alcohol content at the legal level. Then the regulations were changed, so the plants could brew strong beer and "de-alcoholize" it. Under the new rules, cereal beverage plants produced more than two hundred million gallons of real beer yearly. After the alcoholic content was diluted or drawn off, the product could be sold as near beer.

The Prohibition Unit inspected the near beer plants to ensure that they operated within the law. Nevertheless, a large portion of the licensees either fronted for a mob or actually belonged to one. Often, the licensed cereal beverage plant kept a small amount of near beer on hand to show the Prohibition inspectors. Meanwhile the high-octane brew was loaded onto trucks and sold to illegal outlets. In 1923 the federal government granted near-beer permits to seventy-two breweries in Pennsylvania. Governor Gifford Pinchot said few, if any of them, actually relied on near beer sales to stay in business.

Brewers marketed near beer under numerous brand names. The major ones were Schlitz's Famo, Stroh's Lux-o, Miller's Vivo, Pabst's Pablo, Anheuser-Busch's Bevo, and Budweiser Near Beer. Lesser-known brands included Chrismo, Graino, Barlo, Hoppy, Gozo, Singo, Golden Glow, Quizz, Yip, Mannah, and Mother's Malt. Near beer had a vast potential market. Because it was a soft drink, it could be sold to consumers of all ages at soda fountains, restaurants, grocery stores, ballparks, movie theatres, and so forth.

Anheuser-Busch spent years developing Bevo and began selling it during World War I. August A. Busch saw a market for near beer in the dry states, even if national Prohibition never became law. Bevo was an instant success, with sales reaching five million cases in 1918. The market soon expanded from the USA to Canada and the Hawaiian Islands. Eventually consumers could buy Bevo on five of the world's continents.

Despite Bevo's strong sales, Anheuser-Busch encountered problems when national Prohibition began. Volstead regulations required changes in the process for making Bevo. In addition, a shortage of residual yeast led to modification of the Bevo formula. During the first six months of Volstead, Bevo sales continued to be strong. Then sales fell sharply. Despite intensive advertising and sales campaigns, Bevo's free fall continued. By 1923 Bevo sales were adding little to the bottom line, but it remained part of the company's product mix until the end of the decade. Anheuser-Busch also marketed Budweiser Near Beer, which followed Bevo's trajectory: sales soared initially, then plummeted.[39]

The Yuengling brewery in Pottsville, Pennsylvania, accomplished a rare feat: it brewed a flavorful near beer that drinkers liked. At the onset of Prohibition, Yuengling invested in the latest technology, buying new equipment to make near beer using an "expensive vacuum distillation process." In this process the real-beer flavor was not lost during de-alcoholization but was preserved in the vacuum system, making Yuengling's near beer a close approximation of the genuine article.

Yuengling marketed near beer under several brand names, including Juvo, Por-tor, and Yuengling's Special. Por-tor, a dark brew with a hearty taste, was promoted as "a delicious and healthful drink" made from the best hops, malt, and "sparkling mountain spring water." Juvo was a cereal beverage intended for the whole family, including children. Yuengling's Special would probably fall into the lite-beer category today. In Volstead's latter years, demand for Yuengling's near beers rose because young consumers had grown up with them and liked their taste.[40]

PART II. THE TRAFFICKERS: WHEN LIQUOR IS OUTLAWED, OUTLAWS WILL HAVE LIQUOR

4. Everybody's Doing It: Breaking the Law for Fun and Profit

Papa's in the shed, mixing up the mash;
Junior's in the parlor, counting all the cash;
Mama's in the kitchen, washing out the mugs;
Sister's in the pantry, filling up the jugs. — Anonymous

The traditional rigid line between an honest citizen and a criminal became very fuzzy in the United States of Volstead. Disrespect for the law reached heights unheard of in American history. Hordes of citizens broke the dry law every day without feeling the slightest prick of guilt. Veteran criminals embraced liquor trafficking as the fast track to easy money. Throngs of Americans who regarded Prohibition as a joke or an injustice became enmeshed in crime for the first time. The ranks of the novice liquor traffickers included a vast number of women and teenagers who had no criminal records.

Innumerable citizens worked in or owned an illegal liquor business. Skilled master brewers and distillers, working in the only trade they knew, kept illegal plants running for Volstead's liquor lords. Moonshiners and alky cookers made booze, often working as independent contractors for the mob. Bartenders, waiters, and speakeasy hostesses served liquor in illegal saloons. Blue-collar workers toiled in plants that made bottles, kegs, caps, corks, and other supplies for the liquor trade. Counterfeiters turned out bogus labels, fake tax stamps, and phony government permits.

Urban mobs bootlegged on a grand scale, but almost anyone could start his own small operation as long as he didn't infringe on the big boys' trade. In apartment buildings, the super or the janitor kept a stock of liquor in the basement for sale to tenants. Train porters, cab drivers, hotel doormen, and bellhops sold whiskey to thirsty travelers. Delivery men driving their trucks or wagons around town added bootlegging to their daily routine. A driver could greatly augment his income by hauling a few bottles of booze along with the milk, ice, or coal.

The liquor lords ran glitzy speakeasies, but the typical illicit watering hole was not a grandiose martini palace. A surprising number were mom-and-pop operations. A household could make a decent living by turning the family home or apartment into a beer flat, buffet flat, or beer farm. Anyone with a modest amount of capital could open an illicit liquor outlet, such as a blind pig or a shinny joint. With so little investment required, illegal oases sprang up like weeds pushing through cracks in the sidewalk.

In a strange twist, the law intended to dry up America created jobs in the liquor industry. In unforeseen perverse ways, Prohibition stimulated private enterprise, the small business sector, and the informal economy. The new enterprises functioned outside the law, without government regulation or a conventional code of ethics. Although they mimicked legitimate business, they were predatory, lawless, and detrimental to society.

Leggers, Prohis, and Snake Charmers

During the Great Drought everybody talked about leggers, alky cookers, blind pigs, bathtub gin, and the Prohis. Wets elevated the leggers to pop culture heroes; drys demonized them. Wets hissed at the Prohis; drys admired them. Drinkers hung out at blind pigs, but a teetotaler never set foot inside one. The colorful Volstead slang was a combination of old and new terms, mostly related to the illegal liquor traffic. Americans communicated with code words that reflected everyday life under the Volstead law.

Consumers relied on bootleggers and rumrunners to deliver a steady supply of liquor that was usually safe to drink, even though it wasn't top quality. When Volstead began, the media used "bootlegger" and "rumrunner" interchangeably. Over time, the terms took on more specific meanings: a bootlegger trafficked on land while a rumrunner smuggled liquor on the waterways. Newspapers often shortened "bootlegger" to "legger" and "rumrunner" to "rummer." Headline writers trying to squeeze long words into small spaces probably coined these short forms. A few newspapers used "bootleggerette" or "bootleggeress" to designate a woman in the illegal liquor trade, but these terms didn't catch on. Flappers, who had their own special slang, called a woman legger a "snake charmer."

Smugglers hid bottles of liquor in their bootlegs long before the Eighteenth Amendment was ratified, but bootlegging reached its apogee during the Arid Era. Some historians believe the North American bootleg trade began at the eastern end of the Canada-USA border in the nineteenth century. On the Canadian side of the line, woodsmen and bushwhackers wore moccasin-like, oiled-leather boots called larrigans. The knee-high larrigans had wide tops, which allowed the wearer to slip a bottle or two into each boot. Canadians stuffed bottles of whiskey into their larrigans and crossed the border to sell them in Maine, where the demand was strong after the state began passing strict dry laws in the 1840s.[1]

The bootleg trade flourished in the United States in the second half of the nineteenth century. During the Civil War, peddlers hid pints of whiskey inside their bootlegs for sale to the soldiers. On the frontier, traders stuffed flasks of liquor into their boots when they went to barter with the Native Americans. By the 1880s the term "bootlegging" was in general use in the West and Midwest, but Easterners didn't always know what it meant. As late as 1897 a New York newspaper found it necessary to explain that a bootlegger was "one who sells whiskey out of bottles concealed in bootlegs."[2]

During Volstead bootlegging became the national pastime, and the federal Prohibition agents took the field to do battle with the leggers. Wets had a long list of derisive names for the Prohibition agents: cellar smellers, basement snoopers, mattress friskers, the sponge squad, and the mop brigade — to name a few. The press used "dry sleuth" to denote a federal agent or any other lawman who enforced Volstead. In the vernacular, "Prohis" was a collective term for the federal Volstead enforcers. When someone talked about the Prohis, he usually meant the federal dry agents who worked the streets. However, in some contexts, the term encompassed the entire Prohibition Unit (later the Prohibition Bureau).

When a special task force was needed to dry up a town, the Prohibition Unit assembled a "flying squad" of top federal agents from different districts. This elite squad of Prohis swooped down on the town to stage raids, confiscate liquor, arrest Volstead violators, and shut down illegal businesses. The operation was a show of force meant to intimidate both drinkers and liquor traffickers. When a flying squad came to town, the grapevine buzzed with the news and Volstead outlaws took cover. However, the impact was fleeting. When the flying squad moved on, the liquor traffickers returned to business as usual.

Blind Tigers and Mechanical Pigs

When Volstead closed the legal saloons, the dry activists expected drinkers to meekly forego the pleasure of socializing with others at public watering holes. But the drys failed to understand the importance of communal drinking in American society. Many people simply didn't want to drink alone because they valued sharing and interacting with others as part of the experience. No dry law could change that. To satisfy the need for public drinking spaces, Americans opened speakeasies, blind tigers, beer flats, rat dives, and other illicit liquor outlets.

Big city residents had a wide choice of public drinking spaces. For example, the Philadelphia police estimated that their city had at least eight thousand illegal watering holes in 1923. Five years later, Philly's mayor said the City of Brotherly Love had thirteen thousand illegal drinking spots. Boston had roughly four thousand speakeasies, including Cambridge's popular Gold Coast nightclubs — formerly a row of high-rent, private dorms for Harvard students. A Prohibition agent stated that Baltimore had twice as many speakeasies as pre-Volstead saloons. Many of the new places were in residential areas, which "scattered the evil" into neighborhoods previously without bars. According to a newspaper report, Chicago had at least four thousand bars openly selling drinks in 1921. Two years later Chicago's mayor said the city had six thousand soft-drink parlors that were selling far more booze than soda.[3]

Like bootleggers, blind pigs and blind tigers predated the Great Drought. They were retail establishments that sold liquor to be consumed on the premises; some also served food, but booze was the main attraction. Before Volstead, blind pigs and blind tigers thrived in local-option dry areas; during the Arid Era they cropped up everywhere. Their origins are so deeply buried in the past that no one is certain where they began. One explanation traces them back to the old custom of exhibiting exotic animals, such as tigers, in taverns. Another says that places serving liquor in a dry jurisdiction would charge customers to see an attraction, such as a blind pig, and give them free alcoholic drinks — thereby technically obeying the law.

Whatever the origin of "blind pig," dry activists said the term aptly described the illegal barrooms because the places resembled dirty, smelly pigpens. Drys extended the swine metaphor by accusing blind pigs of serving swill or slop. Similarly, they said that drunks bellied up to the trough. The cold water coalition wanted to strictly enforce the liquor laws to make the blind pigs squeal. Saying that someone had "looked at a blind pig too often" meant that he was very drunk.

In the mid–1880s the dry faction complained that blind pigs were a nuisance in the Midwest, especially in Minnesota. "An energetic blind pig has been doing a land office business at Minnehaha, and in East and South Minneapolis this variety of swine receives considerable attention," wrote a passenger on the Rock Island railroad. He noted that some blind pigs used clever contrivances. He had seen one where the buyer walked up to a trough and put his money in a mechanical pig, which then vanished. After a minute or so, the pig returned with liquor but without the money. (The traveler's description raises questions about exactly how the mechanical pig operated. Unfortunately, he didn't give any details.)[4]

A syndicated columnist wrote that he found a blind pig only "a few rods" from the famous Falls of Minnehaha. When he went inside to visit the "sightless swine," he saw "a sideboard of peculiar workmanship and mysterious attributes." He placed his money on a dumbwaiter, which briefly disappeared and then returned with a glass of liquor. An artist's sketch showed the sideboard with a semicircular slot for inserting coins and the dumbwaiter holding a stein of beer.[5]

Minnesota newspapers warned their readers to stay away from the blind pig at the state fairgrounds in Minneapolis-St. Paul. Drinkers complained that they had been fleeced out of their money when they patronized the place. A newspaper said this illegal bar should be closed, but the owner carefully hid his identity and "the vigilant authorities" couldn't track him down. The small Minnesota town of Anoka, which was notorious for its blind pigs, reportedly had seventeen of them in 1884. When a "dire conflagration" swept through the town, several blind pigs caught fire, along with numerous other buildings. Pious Prohibitionists didn't mourn the loss of the gin mills. They saw the hand of God at work.[6]

At least one of Minnesota's underground bars was literally below ground. A blind pig operated in a colliery hundreds of feet beneath the earth's surface at Chantler in St. Louis County. Miners hung out at the primitive bar — a wide plank resting on an empty powder keg and a pile of ore. When a deputy sheriff raided the place, he found an inventory of beer, moonshine, and cheap aged whiskey. He arrested the blind pigger, who was taken to Duluth for trial.[7]

There's no definitive explanation for the term "blind tiger," but one tale traces it to Capt. Dudley Bradstreet of London. During the eighteenth century, England endured the Gin Craze, a period when excessive gin drinking was rampant, especially among the lower class. To combat this substance-abuse crisis, the government imposed a high tax on gin and paid rewards to people who reported unlicensed barkeepers. The wily Capt. Bradstreet came up with a way to sell gin, keep his identity secret, and avoid paying the steep fee for a liquor license. He rented a room in Blue Anchor Court and covered the ground-floor window with a large wood sign depicting a cat. He cut a slot in the cat's mouth, and positioned a lead pipe to protrude through the cat's body. The drinker put two pence in the cat's mouth, stuck a tin cup under the pipe, and gin miraculously flowed into the cup. Bradstreet's device was a smash hit. Other barkeeps came up with variations on his idea, and the general concept was called a blind tiger.[8]

In the United States blind tigers flourished in the South before the Civil War. A man traveling along the Mississippi River wrote about an unusual house he saw in western Kentucky in 1857. The house had a hole cut in an exterior wall; above the opening hung a sign with big, bold letters: "BLIND TIGER, TEN CENTS A SIGHT." The traveler peeped through the hole and saw a man inside, using a stick to stir a kettle of liquid. The naive traveler gave the man a dime and asked to see the blind feline. The man handed him a glass of whiskey. The traveler learned that the blind tiger was "an arrangement to evade the law," which prohibited the sale of liquor by the glass. At that time, Kentucky law permitted sales by the gallon only.

In moonshine-soaked eastern Kentucky, log huts or cabins housed blind tigers where the seller and buyer didn't meet face-to-face. In the typical setup, an oblong box fit tightly into a hole in the cabin's exterior wall. When a customer knocked on the box, someone inside the hut pushed it open. The drinker put his money and an empty bottle into the box, which disappeared into the cabin. When the box reappeared, the bottle held moonshine.[9]

In 1885 a newspaper described a Georgia blind tiger, which resembled those in eastern Kentucky. "The blind tiger is a house where people can get whiskey but do not know from whom they buy it," the paper explained. An exterior wall of the Georgia house had a hole, and printed instructions were posted above it. After the buyer placed his money and an empty bottle in the hole, both quickly vanished. A few minutes later, the bottle returned, filled with whiskey. "No word is spoken, and not a sound is heard except the rolling of the bottle."[10]

In Fentress County, Tennessee, a pretty young woman known as Betty Smith ran a blind tiger in the 1880s. The customer entered the front hallway of Smith's cottage and pulled out a large drawer "neatly fitted into the wall." A menu pasted to the bottom of the drawer listed "beer, whiskey, apple brandy, peach and honey toddy, sour." The buyer laid a dime on his drink choice and closed the drawer. After a short wait, he carefully opened the drawer to claim his liquid refreshment.[11]

In 1887 a writer described a Kansas blind tiger that used a large wheel with compartments. Although he didn't give exact details, he indicated that the wheel was a turntable rotating through a hole in the wall. The drinker put his money and his order in a compartment and turned the wheel. After a short wait, the turntable revolved and the customer found his drink in one of the compartments. In the early 1900s when authorities in New York City decided to enforce the Sunday closing laws, barkeepers used a revolving "circular board" to sell drinks on the Sabbath. They called this revolving board a "Kansas speakeasy or blind pig."[12]

Speak Easy!

Americans fell in love with speakeasies during the Roaring Twenties. The trendy crowd flocked to lively nightspots that attracted a dazzling mix of celebrities, the super rich, the country club set, the new alcohol aristocracy, and Flaming Youth (AKA flappers and college boys). Upscale clubs usually featured a floorshow with a band, singers, and showgirls. The really hip speakeasies had live jazz, the decade's hottest music craze. Drinkers imbibed openly at most speakeasies, but some places made thinly-veiled attempts to hide the liquor. A favorite ruse was serving it in dainty teacups. Most speakeasies sold booze, but some clubs asked customers to bring their own. In BYOB clubs, the house sold mixers and setups.

In pop culture, the speakeasy is synonymous with the Roaring Twenties, but people drank at illegal bars long before the Arid Era. The name probably evolved from "speakaisy," a term used to denote a smugglers' den in Irish-English dialect in the nineteenth century. The obvious, underlying idea is that people should speak softly when doing something illegal, so they don't attract unwanted attention.

Due to a change in Pennsylvania's liquor laws, illegal drinking joints proliferated in Pittsburgh and Philadelphia in the late nineteenth century. Newspapers called the bars "speak-easy saloons," a term most Americans had never heard before. In 1887 the Pennsylvania legislature passed the Brooks High License Law, which markedly raised the price of a liquor license. The lawmakers intended to reduce the number of saloons by forcing sleazy gin mills out of business because the owners couldn't afford a license. The law backfired. Barkeepers who couldn't afford to pay the high license fee simply operated without one. In 1890 Pittsburgh had roughly 800 illegal speakeasies but only ninety-three licensed liquor dealers.[13]

An oft-told anecdote traces the term "speakeasy" to Kate Hester, a barkeeper in McKeesport, Pennsylvania. When the Brooks law went into effect, Hester couldn't afford a license for her bar, so she did business without one. Her customers sometimes became so rowdy that she feared a neighbor would summon the police. To quiet her patrons, "it was her custom to approach with warning finger upraised and an awe-inspiring look, and whisper: 'Speak easy, boys! Speak easy!' Soon the expression became common in McKeesport and spread to Pittsburgh."[14]

A Philadelphia newsman said that he first heard the term "speakeasy" in Pittsburgh. He attributed it to an elderly Irish widow who sold liquor without a license. When her customers became too loud, she would "raise her finger deprecatingly and say, 'Spake asy, now, the police are at the dure.'" The newsman stated that he was the first to use "speakeasy" in print in Philadelphia. "The term had an instantaneous success, being taken up by the people and the police, and it has been in universal use ever since," he wrote in a memoir. In 1891 a writer noted that "speakeasy" was not yet in Webster's dictionary, although it was used "all over the country" to denote a place where alcoholic beverages were sold illegally. He stated that editors had "accepted the term as filling a long-felt want."[15]

In the early 1920s, newspapers used the terms "speakeasy place" and "speakeasy establishment." As Volstead wore on, "speakeasy" stood alone because everybody knew what one was. Hipsters shortened the word to "speak" in both spoken and written English. Thus, a flapper and her sheik went to a speak to kick up their heels.

During the Arid Era, the amount of secrecy surrounding a speakeasy depended on its location. In some neighborhoods, illegal bars operated openly with little fear of the local police or the Prohis. In other places a speakeasy needed to hide behind a "front" or a legitimate business. A speakeasy façade might look like a barbershop, a bowling alley, a florist, a grocery store, or even a funeral parlor. In New York City, drinkers entered one popular watering hole through a telephone booth on Broadway. Some speaks shared a building with a legitimate business and operated in a backroom, in the basement, or on an upper floor.

A surprising number of speakeasies had no permanent location. Bootleggers turned limousines into compact mobile bars, selling liquor by the bottle or the drink. In a typical scenario, the driver parked his limo-speakeasy outside the football stadium before the big game and sold drinks. If he saw the cops coming, he simply hopped into his car and drove away. On Saturday night, limo-bars did a booming business on Fraternity Row. But college campuses weren't the only fertile ground for rolling bars. Limo-speakeasies near hotels prospered because guests often asked a hotel employee to direct them to the nearest liquor. At least one hotel doorman steered guests to a limo-bar parked across the street from his station at the front door. When someone asked for booze, he merely lifted his finger and pointed.

South of San Francisco in San Mateo County, dry activists formed the Veterans and Citizens Protection League. Members pledged to fight crime and to keep bootleggers away from the schools and the veterans' hospital. A legger who drove a "high-powered sedan, completely equipped for mixing cocktails" often parked outside the veterans' hospital and sold liquor to the patients. His mobility helped him elude lawmen for a time, but they finally caught up with him. When they searched his car, they found bottles of gin, wine, whiskey, and flavoring extracts.[16]

Buffet Flats and Beer Farms

Volstead created novel work-at-home business opportunities for anyone willing to turn his house or apartment into a saloon. Little capital was needed to transform the dining room into a cozy bar, the living room into a cocktail lounge, or the basement into a rathskeller. Homegrown speakeasies sprang up everywhere. In cities the new mom-and-pop liquor joints catered to a neighborhood clientele, much like the pre–Volstead saloon had done. In rural communities, the illegal watering hole was often an old farmhouse located on a country road, far from the nearest police station or sheriff's office.

Beer flats proliferated in apartment buildings in blue-collar neighborhoods where ethnic groups had a strong tradition of beer drinking. To a certain extent, the beer flat replaced the corner saloon because it served as a gathering place for the locals. As a general rule, strangers weren't welcome in mom-and-pop bars, so the patrons knew one another and the beer flat had an intimate, clubby feel. A discreet beer flat enjoyed a high degree of immunity from raids. The Prohis focused on shutting down the big speakeasies, and local cops invaded a beer flat only if the neighbors complained about the noise.

Although beer flats could exist anywhere, the Midwest had a special affinity for them. They thrived in Chicago, Milwaukee, Minneapolis-St. Paul, Kansas City, Indianapolis, St. Louis, and other Midwest towns. Minneapolis had hundreds of beer flats run by women who did more than serve liquor. Male customers could enjoy female company with their suds, and a quickie could be arranged if the guy didn't drink up all his money. In Cincinnati, the standard beer flat was a shoestring operation where the female family members, called "beer mamas," served the customers.[17]

Prohibition officials estimated that Chicago had five thousand beer flats in 1928. They saturated the West Side Badlands and the black neighborhoods on the South Side. The customers came for the beer — not the ambiance. Typically, the drinkers sat at card tables in the family's living or dining room, and the beer was served from a barrel in the kitchen.

When a law enforcement crusade closed many Chicago speakeasies in 1928, displaced drinkers flocked to the beer flats. To serve the larger clientele, new beer flats opened up, even in exclusive high-rent districts. The home watering holes were so numerous that city officials decided they were a public nuisance that must be curtailed. In a one-night sweep lawmen raided more than twenty beer flats scattered throughout Chicago. The dry sleuths complained that the flats were "by their very nature ... difficult to locate" because they were tucked away to avoid notoriety.[18]

Many drinkers kept a supply of beer at home, so law enforcement had to decide when a family crossed the line between having a stash of beer for personal use and having enough for a beer flat. In one case, the Chicago police raided a woman's apartment and seized seventy-five bottles of brew. In the courtroom, she denied running an illegal beer flat and said she had purchased the suds for an upcoming party. The judge didn't buy her story.

"Madam, no home can have seventy-five bottles of beer and not be a beer flat," he declared. "There is a beer capacity for homes, and that is reached at seventy-five bottles."

Nevertheless, the judge freed the woman because the police had entered her apartment without a search warrant.[19]

The buffet flat, first cousin to the beer flat, thrived in the black districts of Chicago and New York City. African Americans operated buffet flats before Prohibition, but they gained a wider clientele during the Great Drought. The buffet flat had a reputation as a rowdy, anything-goes place so it was a magnet for drinkers looking for more than a quiet, cozy bar. Women often ran the joints, which usually served food as well as liquor. During Volstead alcohol was the main attraction, but some buffet flats also offered gambling and/or prostitutes. Urban slang had many names for the beer flat, including Whist Club, Democratic Headquarters, and Good Time Flat. If a person said he was going to a parlor social, he was probably headed for a buffet flat.

By the late Twenties, buffet flats had spread from Harlem to other sections of the Big Apple. New flats opened to cater to niche markets in Greenwich Village, in Brooklyn, and on the Lower East Side. A society bootlegger was credited with popularizing the buffet flat among the upper crust. This well-dressed, genteel legger came from a prominent family and knew rich, influential people. After gambling away his inheritance, he found he could make a handsome income selling liquor to high society. When a friend needed a place to hold a party, the bootlegger opened his Fifth Avenue apartment for the event. The guests liked his home and his top-quality liquor. Seeing that he could make money as a host, he turned his home into a buffet flat. He ran his flat like a private club, catering to a wealthy, well-behaved clientele. He allowed his regular patrons to run a tab, and he sent out statements at the end of the month.[20]

Beer proved to be a profitable crop for more than a few farmers, especially in the Midwest. After a day's work in the fields, a farm family could earn a wad of cash by serving suds in the front parlor or on the back porch. However, beer farms were not always family enterprises. Sometimes a bootleg gang bought an isolated farm and turned the old homestead into an urban-style speakeasy. The gang usually converted the barn into a brewery or distillery to have a convenient, reliable source of booze.

Rural Minnesota had numerous beer farms run by hardworking country folk. A fellow could take his best girl to a beer farm, buy drinks, and enjoy the rustic ambiance. At some farms a couple could rent a room to enjoy a private drink or a toss in the hay. At a Congressional hearing, a witness stated that Minnesota's beer farms had revitalized the agricultural sector. "There's one reason you have not heard so much lately about farm relief," he said.[21]

Wisconsin bootleggers turned rural speakeasies into money machines. Every night up to fifty carloads of drinkers drove from the Milwaukee area to a beer farm near Nenomonee Falls. The city slickers could relax on the farmhouse's screened porch, slurping suds from a tin pail, instead of the traditional beer schooner. The beer farm had its own brewery, which packaged amber in bottles and barrels. When the brewery produced more beer than the farm needed, the surplus was sold to bootleg gangs.

In Milwaukee County, Prohibition agents raided what appeared to be an ordinary farmhouse. Inside, they found a spacious nightclub with two dance floors, a barroom, and a dining room. Dozens of customers were enjoying all the amenities available in a ritzy urban speakeasy. The Prohis seized a substantial quantity of beer from a wildcat brewery on the farm. When federal agents raided a beer farm near Mequon, Wisconsin, they found a crowd of merrymakers "amidst luxurious" furnishings in what had once been a humble farmhouse. The speakeasy offered a full drink menu, including beer, wine, gin, and whiskey. The Prohis confiscated twenty-four hundred quarts of bottled beer as well as sizeable quantities of wine and distilled spirits. They arrested the farm's owner along with her staff.

Beer farms dotted the countryside around Baraboo and Reedsburg, Wisconsin. For secrecy, the farmhouse windows were usually boarded up or heavily screened so the passerby couldn't see inside. The typical interior décor was Spartan, with rough-hewn tables and chairs for the customers. These beer farms attracted hordes of young people, including high school students. Although parents complained about the teenage drinking, the farms were rarely raided. Law enforcement blamed a shortage of personnel for its failure to police the places.[22]

Tipsy young women were vulnerable to sexual assault at the isolated beer farms, but the violence was rarely reported to police. An arrest was virtually unheard of even when the crime was reported. In one tragic case, an inebriated thirteen-year-old girl was lured into a car by a strange man at a beer farm near Elkhart, Indiana. Later she was found lying beside the highway, barely alive. She had been savagely attacked, and her neck was broken. Sadly, she died on the way to the hospital.[23]

The petting farm, a variation on the beer farm, was a passion pit for high school and college students. Typically, the young couple bought a bottle of liquor in the farmhouse and drank it in their car. For a private make-out session, the lovebirds could park their car behind the barn or beneath a shade tree far from the house. This new dating custom shocked adults who had grown up with the strict courting code of the pre-war era.

The WCTU's national headquarters cast a long shadow over the quiet, staid town of Evanston, Illinois. Despite the pervasive dry activism, rebellious local youth patronized a petting farm on the outskirts of town, a short distance from Evanston High School. Bootleggers converted the ramshackle old farmhouse into a blind pig with a player piano for entertainment. The teenagers bought bathtub gin and drank it in their cars, parked under trees in the orchard.[24] The Christian ladies couldn't even stop the flow of booze in their own backyard.

5. Hooch Haulers:
Roaring thru the Twenties

Bootleg money changed a multitude of convictions. — Edmund Fahey, bootlegger, Spokane, Washington[1]

Before national Prohibition, America's bootleggers smuggled liquor from wet jurisdictions to dry ones. With very few exceptions, America's major cities were wet, so bootlegging didn't become big business for the urban gangs until the 1920s. Before Volstead the typical bootlegger was a lone wolf who bought liquor from a wholesale source in a wet city and sold it in a small town. He carried a gun for self-defense and knew how to use it because every country boy could hunt. But his was a peaceful occupation. He rarely, if ever, had occasion to shoot at a lawman or another legger.

The pre–Volstead, small-town legger worked alone or hired a lackey to help with the heavy lifting. He didn't always get rich, but he escaped the daily grind and didn't have a boss breathing down his neck. He usually drove the fastest, most expensive car in town, which gave him a certain amount of prestige with the menfolk. He called the sheriff and the police chief by their first names because they had all gone to school together. The drys knew his line of business and condemned it, but he was a local boy so they tolerated him. The devout churchgoers prayed for him and felt sorry for his mother. If he had the good fortune to marry the right woman, he might repent of his sins before it was too late.

During the Great Drought, urban bootleg gangs dominated the illegal liquor traffic, but the independent operator still ruled in America's small towns. For the most part, the small-town legger personified rugged individualism. If his business grew too big for him to handle alone, he teamed up with a sidekick or a few local boys, but he wasn't an urban-style mob boss. He had several options for procuring a supply of liquor for his customers. He could buy whiskey from local moonshiners. He could make a connection with an urban liquor lord and buy booze that came from wildcat plants or cutting houses. He could go to Canada or Mexico, buy liquor, and smuggle it across the border into the United States. If he had enough capital, he could open his own illegal brewery or distillery and market the output under his own brand name.

While the lone-wolf legger thrived in rural areas, his urban counterparts formed gangs to dominate America's big cities. The urban bootleg gangs ruled the informal economy, making them major players in commerce as well as crime. Their beer wars turned American cities into battlegrounds, and the public tolerated the violence because they supplied a very popular product. As one legger said, "It was not really the rumrunner or bootlegger or corrupt official or gangster who made the defiance of Prohibition so profitable — and bloody. It was the honest, respectable citizens who wanted a drink at any cost."[2]

During the Arid Era, the proliferation of slang terms for "bootlegger" reflected his importance in society. Gin jogger, liquor runner, hooch hauler, and bootician were generic terms for anyone who delivered illegal booze to the marketplace. The bootlegger was called a moonlighter, because he usually worked at night, and an embalmer, because cheap whiskey was called embalming fluid. A bottle man delivered packages of bottled liquor to the buyer's home or office. A society bootlegger served an exclusive clientele of wealthy consumers. If a bootlegger smuggled liquor from Canada into the United States, he was called a border runner because he had to cross the international border. A land shark drove a car or truck to pick up liquor from rumrunning boats at the dock or on the beach. A land runner hauled booze overland in a car or truck, especially in the Northwest. In the South a driver who carried moonshine to market was a trip boy, a tripper, a transporter, or a ridge runner. Harkening back to earlier times, he was also called a blockade runner.

The Whiskey Six

A fast car was the most essential piece of equipment for the bootlegger who traveled overland to deliver his goods. Even more than his gun, he relied on his automobile. He used his car to haul liquor, and he depended on it to outrun the cops who chased him. In his expensive luxury car he projected an image of prosperity, power, and modernity — all highly respected traits in the Twenties. Roaring along in his high-powered auto, in synch with the tempo of the times, he was uniquely suited to his era — whether it was called the Lawless Decade, the Jazz Age, the Party of the Century, or another sobriquet.

On the open road the bootlegger needed a large, fast auto that could carry a sizeable payload and outrun lawmen or hijackers. The whiskey six, a powerful six-cylinder car that could go 60 mph or more on the highway, had everything a legger needed. Packard, Cadillac, Studebaker, Pierce-Arrow, and Auburn made the most popular whiskey sixes. Although these big cars were costly, a few good milk runs would pay for one.

Whenever a lawman spotted a bootlegger's car on the open road, a chase usually ensued. To escape lawmen in hot pursuit, the liquor runners developed special tactics, such as the famous bootlegger's slide (AKA the deluxe turnaround). The bootlegger's slide was a controlled skid that produced a quick 180-degree change of direction. A description of this maneuver said, "Let the cops get on your tail on a gravel road, get up your speed, then suddenly tromp on the brakes and swing the wheel hard over into a controlled four-wheel slide for about one-quarter mile until there is enough power to go forward again. The cops go east and the bootleggers west."[3]

Moonshine tripper Lloyd Seay, later a NASCAR driver, became an expert at executing the deluxe turnaround. He regularly drove white lightning from Dawsonville, Georgia, to Atlanta. In a typical deluxe turnaround, Seay was racing along at about 100 mph when he spotted lawmen blocking the road ahead. He hit the brake pedal and, with a violent jerk, slowed down to fifty mph. He took his foot off the brake pedal and reached down to tug on the emergency brake, which locked up the rear wheels. As the car spun around, it changed direction, lost traction, and slid slightly backwards. When Seay released the emergency brake and floored the accelerator, the car came to "a barely perceptible stop," then gripped the road, and shot forward. He quickly gained speed and left the lawmen behind.[4]

To execute a bootlegger's slide, the driver needed both nerve and quick reflexes. If he muffed it, he could expect a crash, a rollover, or a bumpy ride in the nearest ditch. He was likely to sustain serious or even fatal injuries. The deluxe turnaround "done properly at high speed ... would give the feeling of leaving the eyeballs looking south while the knees were headed north; done improperly, the driver was already dead."[5]

The smart bootlegger customized his car to improve his chances of outrunning the law. He had a choice of modifications ranging from simple to complex, from cheap to expensive. He could mount bright spotlights on his car's rear end and turn them on to blind pursuing lawmen. If he traveled on gravel roads, he could hang chains off the car's rear bumper. The dragging chains raised clouds of gravelly dust that reduced visibility and caused the pursuing lawmen to cough or choke. If the chains stirred up enough dust, the officers would give up the chase.

Customized whiskey sixes could produce a smokescreen to irritate the pursuing driver's eyes and respiratory system. When the smoke was thick enough, it greatly limited visibility, forcing the pursuer to stop. There were at least three ways to create a smokescreen. In the simplest, the legger or his passenger poured oil through a hole in the floorboard onto the car's hot muffler. This produced a sizeable cloud of smoke that billowed out behind the car. In a more sophisticated method, the auto was equipped with a switch on the dashboard to open a canister under the hood. When the bootlegger flipped the switch, the can opened, dumping a mix of oil and ammonia onto the hot manifold. A third method used a fire extinguisher with its nozzle connected to a tube running to the exhaust.[6]

During a chase, the bootlegger threw bottles of liquor out the car window, hoping the shattered glass would puncture the tires on the lawman's car. Similarly, the hooch hauler could carry a bucket of carpet tacks or nails and scatter them across road. Lawmen used a variation on this simple ploy to stop leggers. Long spikes were driven through a plank, which was placed on the road with the points sticking up. Then the cops hid and waited for an unsuspecting bootlegger to puncture his tires. In upstate New York lawmen studded a sheet of iron with spikes and attached ropes to it, so it could easily be pulled astraddle the road. Across the country dry sleuths fabricated their own variations on this design, and bootleggers called the spiked sheet a "whammy." To avoid stopping due to a puncture, some hooch haulers outfitted their cars with run-flat tires filled with a foamy material.[7]

The tires on a liquor runner's car endured a great deal of punishment. "Tires were put to the severest possible tests. Heavy loads, hauled over the toughest of roads, often at reckless speeds, kept the rubber on your car always under the utmost strain," a bootlegger wrote in his memoirs. "Therefore, the rum smuggler at all times used the best tires that could be bought.... Many a runner served time in jail simply because his rubber failed him at some critical moment." The legger recalled that he had suffered an astounding seven blowouts on his very first roundtrip from Spokane, Washington, to Fermie, British Columbia. Repairing the tires slowed him down, but he made it home without getting arrested. After "an extensive study of various brands," he bought new heavy-duty tires.[8]

A few inventive bootleggers equipped their cars with flanged wheels so they could drive

When an unlucky bootlegger wrecked his car, police officers came to the scene to arrest him and put him in the paddy wagon for the trip to jail (Library of Congress).

on railroad tracks. This tactic worked in the West where the tracks were often the best road-way across rugged terrain, but it wasn't feasible in urban areas with heavy train traffic. The flanged wheels allowed a car to speed along and to use railroad bridges that spanned hard-to-cross gorges and waterways. However, the legger ran the real danger of being run over by a train. A Great Northern freight train hit a car with flanged wheels and knocked it into a ditch near Springdale, Washington. Two bootleggers jumped out of the car, and the train crew watched them plod through the deep snow, escaping without serious injuries.[9]

One border runner who regularly carried booze from British Columbia to Washington State had to cross a railroad trestle bridge, without benefit of flanged wheels on his car. The gaps between the railroad ties guaranteed that the driver would have a bumpy ride. At an isolated spot on the Canada–USA border, the trestle bridge spanned the roiling Kettle River two hundred feet below. "To cross it in a car was a hazardous adventure, requiring utmost alertness on the part of the driver," the bootlegger said. "A single miscalculation with an automobile meant a drop into the churning river far below." The legger risked crossing the bridge because it spanned the international line and gave him access to a back road where he wouldn't encounter the U.S. border patrol.[10]

Naturally, the hooch hauler wanted to carry a large payload. With slight modifications, a whiskey six could hold hundreds of quarts of liquor in bottles or rectangular tin cans. Simply removing the backseat greatly increased the cargo space. False floorboards and storage areas could be added beneath a car to conceal bottles of liquor. Cloth-topped touring models could be fitted with a second top, so pint bottles could be stashed between the two layers. The stuffing and spiral springs could be removed from the car's seatbacks, making room for alcohol in tin containers.

Since a bootlegger's car hauled heavy cargo, he needed to equip it with "specially constructed" overload springs to "relieve the regular springs from excessive weight in the rear of the car." These springs kept the rear end from riding too low when fully loaded and reduced the risk of damaging the chassis on a rough, bumpy road. When a bootlegger's car wasn't hauling cargo, the springs caused the rear end to bounce and ride high, "like a cat in heat." To prevent this problem, a legger filled the trunk with sandbags or jugs of water when he had no liquor cargo. A gin jogger hauling water instead of booze was "running cold," as opposed to "running wet" with a load of liquor.[11]

In thinly-populated areas the liquor runner had to carry supplies to keep his car running. Gas stations were few and far between on the back roads used by bootleggers. The wise hooch hauler knew enough about cars to be a good roadside mechanic, and he planned ahead. For example, a legger making a roundtrip from Idaho to a liquor depot in British Columbia took cans of gasoline and motor oil with him. On the trip north he stashed some of these cans in safe places because he wanted to make room for more liquor, but he would need the supplies to keep his car running on the trek home.

To haul a bigger payload, a car's gas tank could be divided in half, with one part carrying gas and the other filled with alcohol. Of course, this entailed a certain risk because the legger might run out of fuel while being chased by the cops or hijackers. For this reason, the prudent bootlegger preferred extra gas over liquor and equipped his car with an auxiliary fuel tank. The typical hooch-hauling auto had an armor-plated gas tank to prevent damage from gunfire. In a chase, the lawmen usually shot at the tires and gas tank on the bootlegger's car. Meanwhile the guy riding shotgun in the legger's vehicle aimed at the radiator on the cops' car. To protect the radiator, a steel plate could be welded to the front of the car. Another option was relocating the radiator to the automobile's trunk.

More than one revenuer who chased bootleggers had a steel battering ram welded to the front of his car. If the agent caught up with a whiskey six on a curve and hit it at an angle with his battering ram, the legger's car would spin out. If the bootlegger anticipated the collision, he could engage in a little defensive driving. He could slow his car down a notch, wait for his pursuer to get very close, and then floorboard his gas pedal. He would spurt ahead while the lawman missed the target and ran off the road.

In the South inventive lawmen who chased trip boys attached a pincer, somewhat like a bear trap, to the front of their cars. The device was used to snag the rear fender of a whiskey-hauling auto to stop, or at least slow down, the vehicle. Since the trippers drove the faster cars, this pincer was most effective when the whiskey-laden auto had to slow down due to road conditions, like a sharp curve or a steep upgrade. The trippers quickly figured out how to neutralize the pincer. They removed the back fenders from their cars and reattached them loosely, often with wire coat hangers. When the pincer grabbed the tripper's car, the fender would snap off and bang against the lawman's car or get tangled up beneath it.[12]

Lawmen used various types of barricades and roadblocks to stop hooch-hauling cars on the popular bootlegging routes. When a legger spotted a roadblock, he might avoid it by racing across a field, jumping a ditch, or climbing an embankment. Lawmen often parked empty cars, usually autos seized from gin joggers, across a road to block it. The speeding legger was likely to crash into the empty cars, totaling his own vehicle. Lawmen sometimes stretched a heavy chain across the roadway. If the bootlegger hit the chain at just the right angle and the right speed, he might pull it loose and take it with him. Otherwise, the damage to his car's front end brought him to a sudden halt or, at least, slowed him down.

At night law enforcement used blinding lights as a way to stop hooch haulers. The lawmen set up one or more bright spotlights in the middle of the road. When they heard the roar of a whiskey six, they waited until just the right moment, then switched on the spotlights. If the blinded legger didn't drive into the ditch, he usually crashed into a tree or the lawmen's car. Of course, crashing a car didn't always lead to an arrest. If the legger had no injuries, he took off on foot, determined to outrun the law.

Although the whiskey six was ideal for bootlegging, not every legger drove one. In remote, mountainous areas, horses or mules were sometimes more reliable than automobiles. In the South, the trip boys who hauled moonshine favored Fords or Chevrolets because luxury cars aroused suspicion in the backwoods. A blockade runner could quickly make enough money to pay for a new Model A Ford. Trip boys liked the Model T Ford roadster because it held up to ninety gallons of whiskey. The 1929 Chevrolet touring car held an even bigger payload; it could be modified to hold 135 gallons. After Ford introduced its V-8 in 1932, trippers embraced it as "the best means of escape a southern boy could wish for." A Georgia bootlegger bragged that he could "climb a pine tree" in a Ford V-8 coupe.[13]

Taxicabs delivered countless bottles of liquor to combat the Big Thirst. In both cities and small towns, bootleggers owned cab companies. A taxi was large enough to hold several cases of liquor, and the cab company served as a legitimate business front. New York bootlegger/cab driver Larry Fay became a legend in the business. Mob lore had two versions of how he got started. In one tale, he was driving a cab and picked up a fare who wanted to go from New York City to Montreal, Quebec. The fare revealed that he was a bootlegger and told Fay how easy it was to make money in the liquor traffic. Mimicking his fare, Fay bought cases of Canadian whiskey, took them back to the Big Apple, and sold them for a huge profit. Alternately, Fay loved to play the horses and hit an amazing hundred-to-one shot at the Belmont racetrack. He invested his money in a cab company and saw that he could make money carrying booze as well as people.

Like taxis, hearses were well suited to bootlegging. By 1920 automobiles had replaced most of the horse-drawn funeral wagons, and the typical hearse was big enough to haul dozens of cases of liquor. Since a hearse was a common sight on the roadways, it aroused no special curiosity among lawmen. When the hearse driver closed the window curtains, people assumed he was carrying a corpse, but he might be hiding whiskey. According to mob lore, more than one bootleg gang staged a funeral procession just to transport liquor. Both the hearse and the mourners' cars held cargos of hooch. In the South a procession of cars led by a hearse, with all the vehicles carrying moonshine, was called a "wet funeral."

In upstate New York, hearses crossing the border into Canada were usually going to pick up a body. However, some hearses returned with Canadian booze instead of a corpse. In Chestertown, New York, two liquor hijackers waited near the border and shot at a hearse returning from Canada. When a bullet hit the hearse, the driver screeched to a stop. The hijackers ordered him to hand over the whiskey. He swore he had none. Disbelieving him, the thieves flung open the back doors. They froze when they saw two dead males, killed in a car-truck collision on a Canadian highway. The hijackers backed off and meekly apologized. Empty-handed, they disappeared into the night.[14]

The Long Haul

Bootleggers often traveled in convoys when driving long distances, especially in rural areas. A pilot or scout led the caravan, riding a motorcycle or driving a car. In either case, the scout carried no liquor. He went ahead and checked the road to be sure it was clear. If he saw a police roadblock or spotted hijackers lurking beside the highway, he used a pre-arranged signal to warn the leggers. Or, he made a quick U-turn and raced back to stop the convoy. In some cases, the scout played the role of "fixer." He carried a wad of cash and paid the lawmen to look the other way.

The last car in a bootlegging convoy carried no liquor, so it could function as a decoy or diversion. If a police car pursued the caravan, the decoy driver would lead it on a merry chase, turning onto a side road or cutting across a field. Meanwhile the bootleggers pushed their cars to the limit and raced away. After the decoy driver had led the police far afield, he surrendered, knowing he would be released because his car carried no liquor.

In the wide open spaces out West convoys encountered little traffic, but the topography could be challenging. Convoys sometimes found it necessary to ford rivers, either because there was no bridge or lawmen might try to trap the cars on the bridge. Isolated roads skirted rock formations where lawmen or hijackers could stage an ambush. The bootleggers relied on their scout to be sure no danger lurked in the shadows of buttes, mesas, or canyons. Ten Percent Norris, arguably the most famous scout, led booze convoys from Canada to the western U.S. He collected a commission from each bootlegger, making $1,000 or more on a long caravan.[15]

Like other bootleggers, the South's trip boys often traveled in convoys to deliver white lightning to the marketplace. In a typical moonshine caravan, the pilot led the way and warned the trippers if he spotted any trouble. The last vehicle was the block car, which carried no liquor and was driven by the blocker. If lawmen or hijackers chased the convoy, the blocker's job was to prevent them from passing his car and catching the trippers.

Mrs. Willy Carter Sharpe, a young Virginia woman who loved fast cars, became a moonshining celebrity during the Great Drought. She earned her fame by aggressively driving pilot and block cars for bootleg convoys in the Roanoke-Rocky Mount region. She was briefly married to a bootlegger, but she was very independent and, after getting a divorce, she ran her own show. A writer described her as "a rather handsome, slender black-haired woman." Another said that her "diamond-studded teeth caused a sensation." In fact, she had only one diamond-studded tooth, and it had to be extracted after several years.

On a typical trip, Sharpe drove the block car for a convoy of four to twelve vehicles traveling in close formation "like coupled railroad cars." She had her own speedy, customized roadster with steel-clad fenders to stop bullets. When asked why she had chosen such a dangerous job, she said, "It was the excitement that got me."

Sharpe's fans were so impressed with her driving exploits that they "made her a sort of superwoman." A Virginia man who watched Sharpe race through his hometown one night, with lawmen in hot pursuit, described the scene. "I saw her go right through the main street of our town, and there was a federal car after her," he said. "They were banging away, trying to shoot down her tires, and she was driving at seventy-five miles an hour! She got away."

Although Sharpe usually got away, she was arrested at least once and served a short term in prison. Author Sherwood Anderson interviewed her and found her to be a fascinating specimen of unconventional womanhood. He was so impressed that he used her as the model for his heroine in *Kit Brandon*, a novel about a female gangster involved in the bootleg trade.[16]

While bootleg convoys generally traveled at night without headlights, the mountain ridge runners didn't have that luxury because it was too dangerous to drive the narrow, winding back roads in the dark. Lawmen in the flatlands watched for car lights moving along the mountain roads. If they spotted a line of car headlights that looked like a convoy, they would anticipate the caravan's course and set up a roadblock to stop it at the bottom of the mountain.

A sheriff described a more or less typical confrontation he had with a trip boy hauling firewater from Cocke County, Tennessee, to North Carolina. The sheriff and his deputies waited on a road in North Carolina, watching the headlights in the distance. The lawmen "could see them coming for three miles, making those sharp turns around those mountain roads. Those lights kept swinging around ... swinging around those curves." The lawmen blocked the road with an old Ford and waited for the trip boy. "The usual method of the trippers, they'd come around a curve and see the road blocked, and they'd jump out and hightail it, and leave the car and the liquor," the sheriff explained.

On this particular night, the trip boy came around the curve and spotted the roadblock. He spun into a deluxe turnaround and headed back in the opposite direction. As he raced away, the sheriff shot at the car with a double-barrel shotgun. "I let both barrels go into the right-hand rear tire. It blew right off," the sheriff said. He jumped into the squad car with his deputies, and they took off after the tripper. Despite the tire damage, the tripper's car sped down the road until it careened around a curve and skidded into mud, where it mired down. As the sheriff's car rounded the curve, the men in the tripper's car hopped out and ran into the woods.

"We got the car and sixty-six gallons of white liquor," the sheriff said. "But we never did catch the men."[17]

In Wisconsin bootleg convoys from Milwaukee carried gargantuan cargos of alcohol hundreds of miles over highways and byways to Hurley, a wide-open logging town. Hurley served as the hub for liquor trafficking in northern Wisconsin and northwest Michigan. Bootleg convoys of twenty cars or more regularly made the long trip from the big city to the isolated logging town to help the woodmen survive the Big Thirst.

One night in October 1920, federal Prohibition agents hid in the woods beside a road leading into Hurley. They had information that armed men in autos would travel along that road bringing liquor from Milwaukee. When the Prohis heard the convoy coming, the agents ran to the road and drew their pistols, ready for gunplay. The Prohibition chief swung a red lantern to stop the whiskey sixes. The drivers braked to a halt. The leggers jumped out of their cars, firing their guns. Bullets flew in all directions, turning the road into a shooting gallery.

The bootleggers blasted away as they ran, escaping into the dense, dark timberland. The Prohis captured only one man, who had been struck by a bullet and died from the gunshot wound.[18]

After the deadly gunfight, the Prohis stayed in the area. Bootlegging convoys regularly passed that way, so the agents expected more action. They camped out beside a state highway south of Hurley and waited for cars to come barreling down the road. When they grew tired of waiting, they decided to break camp. As they prepared to leave, a Studebaker without lights sped past them. The Prohis jumped into their car and gave chase, firing their guns at the whiskey six. A few miles down the road, the Studebaker suddenly veered into the ditch and rolled over. Before the Prohis could reach the car, the leggers hopped out and ran off into the woods, making their escape.

Almost immediately, another whiskey six roared past the Prohis, who pulled out their guns and shot at the car while it was still within range. The legger riding shotgun returned fire. When a bullet hit the driver, the whiskey six swerved into the ditch. The shotgun jumped out of the car on the passenger's side and ran into the woods. He didn't stop to check on the driver, whose wounds proved to be fatal.

The Prohibition agents, who counted fifteen bullet holes in the leggers' car, found that it carried more than $30,000 worth of liquor. As they struggled to get this car out of the ditch, another whiskey six thundered down the road. The Prohis quickly hopped into their car, gave chase, and unleashed a hail of bullets. After a high-speed gunfight "in which a hundred shots were exchanged," the legger jumped out of his car, apparently unscathed. He fled into the woods, leaving his car and his whiskey behind.

The federal agents expected a long convoy, so they waited for more cars to appear. But they were disappointed. They saw no more hooch haulers that night. Later, they learned that a deputy sheriff in Mercer, Wisconsin, had stopped the leggers' convoy and warned the men that the Prohis lay in wait. Most of the liquor runners chose to take a detour through Michigan. Although Michigan state troopers had been ordered to patrol the alternate route, they didn't stop any cars. The leggers who detoured through Michigan reached Hurley's thirsty woodsmen with no trouble.[19]

The Cutting Edge

Not everyone in the bootleg liquor traffic drove a whiskey six. Many people worked in the shadows to produce alcoholic beverages for the marketplace. Although bootleggers claimed to sell high-quality liquor, they generally sold watered-down booze that merely imitated the premium brands. Only naïve consumers believed they were buying "the real stuff right off the boat" or "the good stuff" bottled before Volstead. As standard operating procedure, liquor traffickers cut, or diluted, genuine whiskey to create a bigger supply of their product. Typically, a gallon of aged whiskey and a gallon of grain alcohol were mixed with two gallons of water. Greedier bootleggers used even more water and less whiskey.

Disguising cut whiskey as the real thing required bottles, labels, tax stamps, and so forth. Across the USA cutting houses sprang up to water down booze and package it as the genuine article. When the real stuff came in from Canada or elsewhere, the cutters had methods of removing the expensive liquor from the bottle and diluting it. In one method, the cutter would take a red-hot wire and pierce the bottom of a bottle, opening a tiny hole.

The good liquor would be drained out and diluted. After the bottle was refilled with watered-down booze, the hole in the bottom was resealed with a heated glass rod. Because the bottle appeared to be intact, it fetched top dollar.[20]

After the cutting house refilled the original bottles, the rest of the diluted whiskey had to be packaged for sale. Glass manufacturers made and sold bottles exactly like those on the shelves before Volstead closed the liquor stores. Fastidious cutting houses bought new bottles, but some places reused old ones collected from illegal saloons. Bums wanting to make pocket change salvaged empty liquor bottles from the trash for sale to a cutting house.

Counterfeiters produced fake tax stamps for the bottles of diluted liquor. Printers replicated familiar pre–Volstead logos on bogus labels, which could be dipped in tea or salt water for the proper aged look. The condition of the bottle's cork testified as to the age of the liquor; when a cork was soft and dark, it had been in the bottle for a sufficient aging period. To give new corks the desired color and texture, the cutting houses soaked them in strong tea.

Despite the dry law, supply houses promoted their wares in magazine and newspaper ads. The Perfect Tinfoil Company advertised "bottles, cartons, corks and other essentials to go with doctored gin and whiskey." A Philadelphia plant filled orders for Pinch bottles and other distinctive shapes with trademarks blown into the glass. Bootleg products labeled Bacardi, Hennessey Three Star, and Martell Three Star were big sellers.[21]

According to Prohibition officials, Pittsburgh had twenty-five firms selling bottles, labels, caps, and wrappers for use in cutting houses. Chicago police raided a company that supplied bottles, labels, and counterfeit tax stamps to the Capone mob. The warehouse held more than a half-million bottles. Law enforcement in Syracuse, New York, found thousands of counterfeit tax stamps and fake Canadian whiskey labels in a printing plant. New York City had big operations that sold labels and bogus tax stamps to cutting houses across the country. At one of them, customs agents found twenty-five thousand strip stamps for use on whiskey bottles.[22]

Not all cutting plants operated onshore. Whenever a rumrunning ship left the Bahamas on its way to Rum Row, it became a mobile cutting house. In addition to a cargo of uncut whiskey, the ship carried grain alcohol, distilled water, tea, bottles, labels, corks, caps, corking and capping machines, paper wrappers, brushes, and paste. In fair weather when the ship practically sailed itself, the crewmen used their time to dilute the whiskey and repackage it. If they didn't finish their cutting chores at sea, they could complete the job while riding at anchor on Rum Row.

6. Jumping the Line:
The Canadian Connection

Four-and-twenty Yankees, feeling mighty dry,
Took a trip to Canada, to buy a case of rye.
When the case was opened, they began to sing —
To hell with Volstead, God save the king! — Anonymous

Canada and the United States, two friendly countries with much in common, took different approaches to liquor control after World War I. The USA had a federal Prohibition law for the entire country, while Canada's system divided control between the national government and the provinces. Under Canada's two-tier system, liquor was legally produced and sold in many locations across the country, but there were also wide swatches of dry territory.

Before the Great Drought, smuggling goods from Canada to the United States, or vice versa, was relatively easy because travel flowed across the border with few restrictions. Washington and Ottawa knew that smuggling went on, but neither regarded it as a major problem. The Volstead law set off a tsunami of liquor smuggling, which forced Washington to devote substantial resources to stopping the cross-border bootleg traffic. A Canadian magazine said "a new 'profession' ... that of professional smuggler" had emerged. "Previous to the enactment of Prohibition in the United States smugglers were, comparatively, isolated outlaws. A competent authority estimates, today on this continent, there are one hundred thousand men whose sole business is that of smuggling."[1] Of course, there were amateur, occasional smugglers as well as the professionals. An amazing number of Americans who never even jaywalked went to Canada and came home with whiskey.

Using virtually every form of transportation known to man, Americans smuggled Canadian liquor across the border — a feat known as "jumping the line." In the northeastern United States, Yankees yearning for forbidden potables traveled to Quebec or New Brunswick. With great regularity, convoys of American bootleggers drove north into Quebec and hauled the good stuff back to distribution hubs in Vermont and upstate New York. In Maine bootleggers had the choice of crossing the northern state line into Quebec or the eastern border into New Brunswick. In at least one location, Canadian beer jumped the line all by itself. A bootlegger in the Adirondack Mountains bought ale from exporters in Canada. The helpful

Canadians wrapped the bottles in cloth feed bags and dropped them into the St. Lawrence River at a place where the current would take them to New York. On the U.S. shore the bootlegger collected the wet bags to deliver to his customers.

The Canadian Way

Canada, like the United States, enacted wartime prohibition during World War I. Canada's federal cabinet passed an order-in-council prohibiting the manufacture of, importation of, and interprovincial trade in beverage alcohol until one year after the end of hostilities. When the order-in-council expired, each province could schedule a referendum on the liquor issue if the citizenry called for one. Thus, the voters could decide whether they wanted prohibition or another form of liquor control in their province. However, the national government restricted the provinces' regulatory powers in that Ottawa set the rules for manufacturing liquor and exporting it.

Due to the division of regulatory power in Canada, business could be tricky for the liquor companies. For example, a dry province could be home to a legal distillery if it exported its output to a wet province or another country. Thus, in the early 1920s, the dry province of Ontario had forty-four breweries, twelve wineries, and nine distilleries. Ottawa required these manufacturers to export their products or face legal sanctions.[2]

Canadian drys called Quebec "the barroom of America" because it had a sizeable wet majority that voted for the right to drink. In 1921 Quebec enacted a provincial law permitting the sale of liquor by the bottle in government-run stores as well as the sale of beer and wine with meals in licensed hotels and cafés. At the neighborhood level, voters decided if they wanted a local liquor store in their community. In order to buy liquor, a person needed a government permit, which could be revoked "for various good and sufficient reasons." A buyer shopping at a liquor store was allowed to purchase only one bottle per day, but he could patronize multiple stores on the same day.

Quebec's lawmakers didn't want disorderly saloons that catered to chronic drunks, so the law required liquor-by-the-drink outlets to serve food. Of course, some places wanted to sell drinks without the hassle of preparing food; so they offered only one menu item — a cheese sandwich. When a customer ordered beer or wine, the waiter would bring the drink and an old sandwich of stale bread and dried out cheese. No one ever ate the sandwich, and it would be served repeatedly until it became so disgusting it had to be thrown out.[3]

In 1920 voters in British Columbia (BC) adopted a new liquor control system to replace the wartime prohibition law. The province legalized the sale of beer and distilled spirits in sealed packages at government-owned stores. A buyer needed a permit to purchase liquor, but permits were easily obtained and there was no limit on how much alcohol a person could buy. Even foreign tourists could obtain a permit for only $2. In 1922 BC voters liberalized the law to allow the sale of beer by-the-glass at licensed establishments.[4]

Unlike British Columbia's voters, the residents of the Prairie Provinces favored strict liquor laws. In 1920 Alberta, Saskatchewan, and Manitoba held plebiscites on liquor control. All three provinces were dry and voted to remain dry. However, the prohibitory law was laxly enforced in many towns. In Alberta's legislature a speaker said that the vast majority of men "treated the law with neglect and contempt."[5] (He didn't address the issue of women breaking the dry law.)

Despite the wets' initial defeat in the Prairie Provinces, they didn't retire from the battlefield. They regrouped around the Moderation League, an organization that drew support from a wide spectrum of citizens, including military officers and World War I veterans. The wet activists relied heavily on a simple financial argument: taxes on legal liquor would provide badly needed revenue for the government. Prominent Tory politicos helped the wet faction mobilize voters for new plebiscites in Manitoba, Alberta, and Saskatchewan.

In Alberta's 1923 referendum the electorate approved both government-run liquor stores and the sale of beer-by-the-glass in hotel bars. The law required all bars to close at dinnertime so drinkers could go home to dine with their families. In order to purchase booze, a buyer needed a government permit, which allowed him to buy no more than three bottles of spirits, two gallons of wine, and a half-dozen bottles of beer per week. Persons on welfare couldn't buy liquor — at least not legally. Alberta's lawmakers, who seemed to feel that ladies must be protected from hard-drinking males, banned women from bars. Later the rules were changed so hotels could serve women but only in sex-segregated "beverage rooms."[6]

Manitoba voters chose to end prohibition by allowing the sale of liquor in government stores. A buyer had to have a permit, which cost $1 per annum. The buyer placed his order at the store, but he was not allowed to carry it away; the Liquor Commission delivered it to his home. In 1924 Saskatchewan voters approved liquor sales by the bottle in government stores but rejected beer-by-the-glass.[7]

Federal Prohibition agents used this sign at roadblocks and elsewhere to stop drivers in order to search cars for illegal liquor (Library of Congress).

In Ontario the wet forces failed in their first postwar attempts to repeal the provincial ban on alcohol sales. Drought relief didn't come until 1926 when Premier Howard Ferguson announced that his government would liberalize the liquor laws. Under Ferguson's regime, outlets were allowed to sell 4.4 percent beer, which grateful drinkers dubbed "Fergie's foam." Provincial authorities issued beer licenses to hotels, roadhouses, and other establishments with guest accommodations. Drinkers wanting beer for home consumption could buy it from wholesalers. "This is the first step in the direction of seeking greater temperance," Ontario's attorney general said. "I want to bring beer drinking out into the sunlight, rather than continue the system of consumption in cellars of poisonous concoctions which undermine the moral welfare and physical health of many residents...."

Several months after Ferguson legalized beer, the provincial legislature passed a new law giving individuals even more freedom to drink. Both residents and tourists could buy a variety of alcoholic beverages at government liquor stores. The buyer needed a permit, but there was no limit on how much he could buy. A resident paid $2 for an annual permit, while a nonresident could obtain one for $2 per month.[8]

In 1927 New Brunswick liberalized its liquor laws, and Nova Scotia followed suit three years later. Prince Edward Island remained a bastion of aridity, keeping its ban on alcohol until after World War II.

American bootleggers cared little about the finer points of Canada's complex liquor laws. To them Canada was a vast whiskey emporium sharing a long, porous border with the United States. The prospect of a big payday offset the slight risk a legger took when he jumped the line. For the Canadian liquor companies, Volstead created a win–win situation because they could make money selling to Americans while technically obeying their own laws. The cross-border bootleg trade fueled an amazing rise in Canada's annual per capita liquor sales. Before Volstead, Canadian booze sales averaged nine gallons of liquor per person per annum. During Volstead that average jumped to 102 gallons.[9]

Canada's Barroom

Living up to its reputation as Canada's barroom, Quebec proved to be a wellspring of liquor for the northeastern United States. Bootleg convoys sped along the highways that linked the USA with Quebec's wet towns. Pedestrians and horseback riders slipped across the border via narrow country roads or trails through the woods. Trains crisscrossed the border, hauling tons of freight and thousands of passengers every day. Boats from Quebec carried liquor to the USA via Lake Champlain or Lake Memphremagog.

In Volstead's early days American bootleggers drove empty cars to Quebec and returned with booze. They soon realized they could multiply their profits by carrying contraband in both directions. American tobacco products and textiles, especially silk, found a ready market in Canada. Luxury goods like furs and jewelry were also easy to sell. Although the illegal drug traffic was only a fraction of what it would become in the future, it paid big dividends. Gin joggers regarded narcotics as insurance because a small package of drugs was easier to hide than cases of liquor. Even if law enforcement stopped a bootlegger and confiscated his hooch, there was a good chance his drugs wouldn't be found.

Some bootleggers preferred to carry alcohol on both legs of a roundtrip. On the first leg, the legger hauled American moonshine or industrial alcohol to Quebec, where he took it to a cutting house to be flavored, colored, and bottled. Then the alcohol could be sold as genuine Canadian whiskey on either side of the border. In 1925 a New York State Police officer admitted that law enforcement had only recently learned that leggers were carrying alcohol to Canada. He said the northbound booze traffic was "about the most attractive thing in the smuggling line," due to the big markup on the ersatz aged whiskey.[10]

With very little effort, an American bootlegger could make a connection with a Canadian middleman who had liquor for sale. Canadian middlemen operating on a large scale bought booze wholesale through illegal channels. Small-time Canadian jobbers usually bought at retail from government liquor stores. Quebec's bottle-a-day rule complicated matters for them since a customer could buy only one bottle per day when he went into a store. However, nothing in the law kept him from visiting several stores on the same day. Since this was time consuming, middlemen hired bums to go from store to store buying liquor. At the end of the day, the tramps were paid a pittance or given a little whiskey.

A patient American bootlegger could buy his own booze and cut out the middleman. After crossing into Quebec, the Yankee stopped in a border town and bought a bottle at each local liquor store. If he had a flare for disguises, he changed his jacket, put on a toupee, or glued on a moustache; then he revisited each store for a second bottle. After buying all he could in one town, he motored on to another and repeated the process. When he reached Montreal, he hit the mother lode. Quebec's biggest city had roughly seventy liquor stores, making it a bonanza for bootleggers buying one bottle per outlet.[11]

Visiting American bootleggers filled Canada's liquor tax coffers. Sales soared at the government stores in Quebec's border towns. "A hundred bottles of whiskey would make the entire population of Granby, Quebec, drunk — but the sale per day is now six thousand bottles and climbing," a newspaper stated. Valleyfield, Quebec, had two government liquor stores, which averaged daily sales of $10,000 each during Volstead. Before U.S. Prohibition $200 per day had been typical.[12]

New York's Border Bootleggers

In the 1920s drivers had a choice of one thousand roads for transporting goods between Canada and the United States, according to the Law Enforcement Commission. Anyone driving into Canada from the USA was required to pick up a tourist permit at an official customs station and to show that permit at a station when he returned to the states. However, for the most part, compliance was voluntary. The U.S. customs stations were often located several miles south of the international border, giving smugglers plenty of leeway to avoid them. Moreover, long stretches of the border had no customs station at all. For instance, the State of Montana had only two border stations — at Sweet Grass and Gateway. Both stations were located at the western end of the state, leaving hundreds of miles of open border where a bootlegger could cross. Even if a liquor runner decided to go across at Gateway or Sweet Grass, the inspectors were busy with the railroad traffic and paid little attention to automobiles.[13]

Much of the Canadian liquor that crossed the border into upstate New York was destined for major urban markets, like Boston, Providence, and New York City. The bootlegging gangs hid their booze in secret spots until it could be moved to its final destination. They paid farmers to use barns as liquor warehouses, and they set up camps in wooded areas near the roads they traveled. They built garages to serve as transfer stations in central locations that served as hubs for the bootleg traffic.

The main roads from Quebec Province into upstate New York crossed the border near Mooers, Champlain, and Rouses Point. Although all three towns had customs houses, the inspectors rarely saw a bootlegger. During the day, drivers were expected to stop voluntarily and cooperate with the customs inspectors, who usually asked a few questions and had the authority to conduct a search, if necessary. At night, when bootleggers came roaring across the border, the customs houses were closed. On an average night, southbound cars passed through the village of Mooers at the rate of thirty per hour. Not even one stopped at the customs station.[14]

Law enforcement wasn't prepared to deal with the sudden explosion of smuggling caused by Volstead. In fact, the Prohibition Unit initially ignored it. In 1921 Volstead enforcement in upstate New York was directed by a Prohibition agent nearly three hundred miles away in Brooklyn. He emphatically stated that only a small amount of Canadian liquor entered via the state's northern border. "There is very little of it coming across the line just now," he said, "because all the roads are covered and the other ways of bringing it in are closely watched." Upstate residents, who saw the bootleg traffic every night, knew he was either delusional or ill-informed.[15]

To document the bootleg traffic from Quebec to upstate New York, a group of reporters spent several nights watching the roads suitable for liquor smuggling. Each night they counted fifty to 150 suspicious cars zooming along those roads. From reliable sources, they learned that each car carried 200–360 quarts of Canadian ale and whiskey, with ale predominating. The newsmen concluded that thirty thousand bottles of booze came across the border on a typical night. Based on their data, bootleggers drove up to four thousand five hundred hooch-hauling cars from Canada to upstate New York each month. In June 1923, a more or less typical month, federal lawmen captured only thirty-three of those cars! More than ninety-nine percent of the gin joggers escaped the law.[16]

After the press printed exposés of the liquor smuggling in upstate New York, Prohibition officials conceded that it was a problem, but they claimed the press exaggerated it. Upstate New Yorkers complained about the heavy bootleg traffic, so the customs service began keeping its Rouses Point station open at night. This had virtually no impact because the leggers took alternate routes or blew past the customs station without stopping. One night an observer counted 132 cars that passed the Rouses Point customs house as if it didn't even exist.[17]

By December 1923 the upstate liquor traffic had grown so huge that the Prohibition Unit could no longer ignore it. Officials admitted that "unprecedented quantities" of Canadian liquor were pouring into northern New York. To fight the traffic, federal and state agencies committed extra manpower to the region. Sixteen federal Prohibition agents were assigned to cover four counties in upstate New York. Fifty-eight Black Horse Troopers of the State Patrol were ordered to assist the feds. Enforcing Volstead was added to the troopers' other duties, so they were only part-time dry sleuths.[18]

Since the bootleg traffic dominated the roads at night, the lawmen often used roadblocks to plug up the main routes in hopes of stopping liquor convoys. Acting on a tip, one night law enforcement set up a roadblock between Mooers and Perrys Mills. The state troopers and federal agents parked empty autos across the road and waited. When the lawmen heard the roar of motors in the distance, they knew the convoy was coming. To avoid crashing into the roadblock, the leggers threw on their brakes and skidded to a sudden halt. The lawmen heard the screeching brakes and sprang into action. Both sides of the law whipped out their guns, blasting away with gusto. Amid the gunfire, the bootleggers jumped out of their cars and ran off. All the leggers escaped, but the lawmen had the satisfaction of confiscating thirteen autos and the booze.[19]

Plattsburgh, New York, became a major distribution hub for the liquor traffic, due to its convenient land and water arteries. A labyrinth of roads connected Quebec to Plattsburgh, but only a smattering of customs officers patrolled the area. Bootleggers rarely encountered any resistance as they roared along the roads. At least one garage in Plattsburgh was specially built as a liquor depot/transfer station. The bootlegger drove his car into this garage and stashed his contraband there until needed. On the edge of town, two hotels also served as liquor depots. A college professor, who saw that liquor trafficking paid better than academia, gave up teaching to run a busy transfer station in Plattsburgh.[20]

In Pine Plains near Syracuse, bootleggers used a heavily-wooded area as a transfer station and stored thousands of bottles of Canadian liquor there. The thick forest surrounded Pine Camp, a training site for National Guard artillery. During training exercises for the 106th Field Artillery of Buffalo, gunners aimed their howitzers at the woods and fired. They were surprised to hear the sound of shattering glass—and lots of it. A distinctive odor wafted through the air. Local bootleggers heard the canon fire and rushed to the woods. They found heaps of broken bottles, but the shells had missed several stashes in remote parts of the forest. They carted their treasure to another site for safekeeping until the artillery decamped.[21]

Vermont's Toughest Town

U.S. customs stations were scattered along the Vermont-Quebec border, but they had little impact on the bootleg traffic because they relied heavily on voluntary compliance. After a driver crossed the border into the USA, he was on his honor to stop at the nearest customs house and submit to a search if officials deemed one necessary. When it came to the hooch haulers, this policy had a serious flaw: bootleggers were not an honorable lot.

The bootleg traffic took advantage of the location of the inspection stations, which were not actually on the border. For instance, gin joggers leaving Quebec often crossed into the states on the road to Swanton, Vermont. U.S. customs inspectors were stationed at Highgate and Swanton, about four and ten miles, respectively, from the border. Before reaching the first station at Highgate, the bootlegger could unload his cargo, hiding it in the woods or stashing it in a friendly farmer's barn. He could also opt out of an inspection simply by driving past the customs stations, which didn't have the manpower to chase him down.

During Prohibition, Lyndonville had the dubious honor of being "Vermont's toughest town." Daring, reckless young men from New York, Massachusetts, and Rhode Island flocked to Lyndonville to join the local bootlegging gang. Two brothers ran the gang, which supplied Canadian liquor to markets in New England. According to local gossip, the gang sold the lion's share of its booze to Boston doctors who ran a racket selling medical alcohol. The leggers boosted Lyndonville's economy by spending money at the hotels, lunch counters, garages, poolrooms, barber shops, and boardinghouses. Initially, the townsfolk regarded the young gin joggers as harmless. However, as time wore on, the speeding cars, rowdy parties, and boozy brawls disrupted the sleepy little town. Parents worried because the strangers dated local girls and set a bad example for the teenage boys.

Lyndonville's two-man police force did little to impede the bootleg traffic, and honest citizens felt unsafe. A series of liquor hijackings raised fears of mob warfare between the local gang and rival bootleggers. In 1931 a bold daytime liquor heist showed how dangerous the town had become. One Sunday morning gangsters broke into the chief of police's home to reclaim a costly liquor shipment he had seized. Since law enforcement rarely confiscated any liquor, crime watchers wondered exactly what was going on. Had someone neglected to grease the proper palms?[22]

The brazen Sunday morning break-in finally roused Lyndonville's law-abiding residents to take their hometown back. Their initial efforts to oust the bootleggers met with mixed results, but they had overcome their inertia. They continued to battle lawlessness until Prohibition ended and Lyndonville relinquished its title as Vermont's toughest town.

Canadian whiskey on its way south often changed hands in Barre, Vermont, a major bootlegging hub. The legger who brought the booze from Canada drove his car into a special garage in Barre and parked in a bay. He left his liquor in the car, walked off, and hung around town for an hour or so. When he went back to the garage, his cargo was gone and his payment lay on the car seat. For driving a load to Barre from Highwater, Quebec, the standard pay was $125, the equivalent of three months' wages for many Vermonters.

Although hauling hooch in an automobile paid good money, not everyone could afford a car or truck. But every farmer owned four-footed transportation that could be used for bootlegging. More than one Yankee farmer led a string of horses into Quebec and strapped cases of liquor to their backs for the trip home. After a few trips, the farmer didn't have to lead the horses — they knew the way. If the farmer didn't want to use his horses as pack animals, a cow would do, although it couldn't be trained like a horse. One man regularly led his cow, with hay bales strapped to its sides, across the border and back home. After a time, a customs officer became suspicious. He searched the cow and found whiskey bottles hidden inside the bales.

A surprising number of bootleggers walked from Vermont to a roadhouse or loading station in Canada. Young men, even high school students, hiked into Canada, bought booze, and carried it home on their backs. One brawny man became a legend for routinely carrying four cases of beer on his back. Although walking was slow, the pedestrian could elude the law by taking trails through the woods. To shorten his trip, he could cut across farmland. In the winter the walking legger could strap on snowshoes and pull his load on a sled. More than one young man started out bootlegging on foot and earned enough money to buy a whiskey six. He lived the American dream, Prohibition-style.

The Maine Road

New Brunswick was legally dry until 1927, but this didn't stop the flow of Canadian liquor from the province to New England. Due to Canada's bifurcated liquor control system, exporting alcohol from the dry province was legal if the seller had a permit, which cost only $5. To funnel Canadian booze into the states, liquor export houses proliferated in New Brunswick. St. John City, a busy port on the Bay of Fundy, had twelve licensed liquor exporters plus a large number of unlicensed firms that sold to American rumrunners. Buildings on the waterfront had trap doors so booze could easily be loaded into the boats.[23]

At dusk in New Brunswick's southern ports, rumrunning boats picked up hooch for a fast sprint to the Pine Tree State. "Motorboats are running the booze from the New Brunswick side to the Maine side every night in Passamaquoddy Bay and in the St. Croix River," wrote a reporter. "Probably nowhere along the international boundary from the Atlantic to the Pacific is booze-running so rampant and so open as it is from New Brunswick into Maine."

Along New Brunswick's western border, the towns of St. Leonard, Grand Falls, Andover, Woodstock, and St. Stephen became bootlegging centers. On both sides of the border, lumberjacks and bushwhackers took up liquor smuggling. Despite Maine's bitter winters, rugged terrain, and country roads, the leggers regularly delivered the good stuff from Canada. An observer wrote, "Canadian liquor in quantities from one gallon to a truck-load is being hidden in the northern woods and distributed by automobile, sled and iceboat, on snowshoes and on skis." A newspaper reported "a heavy flow of firewater" from New Brunswick to Maine. "The liquor traffic in Aroostook County is getting to be a serious problem. In fact, it is not uncommon to hear of hundreds of quarts being smuggled in."

According to a "conservative estimate," at least one hundred cars per day were carrying whiskey from New Brunswick to Maine in 1921. New Brunswick bootleggers were supplying alcohol to at least three dozen rum rings in the Pine Tree State. Law enforcement was spotty in the sparsely-populated state, and the federal government didn't commit enough manpower to stop the cross-border liquor traffic. "The only obstruction worthy of the name is that offered by a small group of American customs agents," a newsman said. "About thirty men are assigned to patrol the three hundred miles of boundary."[24]

Despite the scarcity of Volstead enforcers, gunfights between liquor runners and lawmen were fairly common in Maine. Less than two months into Prohibition, blood stained the snow when a U.S. customs officer shot a bootlegger in the northern woods near Madawaska. The bootlegger bought liquor in Canada and loaded it onto a sled pulled by horses. He crossed into Maine on a logging road and was making his way through the dense forest. The customs officer, on the lookout for smugglers, spotted the bootlegger and ordered him to stop. The legger decided to make a run for it and snapped his whip at his horses. But before he could get away, the customs officer jumped on the sled. The officer pulled out his revolver and shot the legger at close range, killing him.

When Maine's gravel roads were dry enough for automobile traffic, U.S. customs officers lay in wait for liquor runners at the international border. Bootleggers knew this and expected a blood-stirring chase. When the legger spotted the customs patrol, he floored the gas pedal, hoping to leave the lawmen far behind. But the customs officers usually stayed on his tail. Neither the legger nor the lawmen shied away from gunfire as they raced along the country roads from one border town to the next. If the lawmen forced the legger off the road, he would have to surrender or abandon his car and hightail it through the woods.

Bootleggers often chose to cross the International Bridge that connected St. Stephen, New Brunswick, with Calais, Maine. U.S. law enforcement placed sharpshooters on the Maine side of the bridge to ambush the speeding hooch haulers. The bootleggers rarely, if ever, sustained fatal injuries from the volley of bullets. However, the snipers' bullets slowed the driver down, allowing the customs patrol to overtake his car and arrest him.

As Prohibition wore on, the opposing forces engaged in fewer gun battles in Maine. One historian has suggested two reasons for this. First, "the fanatics among the U.S. Prohibition enforcers had been weeded out." Second, the remaining lawmen lost their enthusiasm for chasing bootleggers and "settled down to a more or less amiable (and sometimes highly cooperative) coexistence" with the liquor smugglers. Why fight? The leggers were willing to pay the lawmen for safe passage. Nobody got shot, and everybody had a thick wallet.

In March 1932 the Royal Canadian Mounted Police (RCMP) took over law enforcement in the Province of New Brunswick in all areas without a municipal police force. When conditions warranted, the RCMP could also extend its jurisdiction to the areas with municipal police. The RCMP fought the American bootleggers with more vigor than was customary in New Brunswick. The Mounties were well-trained, professional lawmen. They had efficient communications, they blanketed the highways, they used aircraft for surveillance, and they didn't back away from a fight. The RCMP scored some impressive victories in their war against the liquor traffic, but they came late to the game.[25] The repeal movement was gaining steam, and Volstead's days were numbered.

Line Houses and Loading Stations

Line houses, buildings that straddled the Canada-USA border, played a unique role in the bootleg traffic during the Arid Era. The line houses and the land they sat on had a special attraction for smugglers because contraband could quickly be moved from one country to the other. During Volstead, the cross-border buildings were ideally situated to supply liquor to American tourists and bootleggers. Although a line house could exist anywhere along the land border, they were most common in the Northeast.

By stockpiling booze only yards away from the United States, Canadian liquor sellers made life easy for Yankee hooch haulers. Line houses and similar buildings near the border functioned as loading stations where bootleggers picked up their hooch. Normally the liquor was stowed in a garage or storage shed, but sometimes the cases were simply stacked high in the parking lot. To expedite matters for U.S. leggers, Canadian middlemen purchased booze, packed the bottles in burlap bags, and transported them to a loading station on or near the border. When a legger arrived to pick up his load, the middleman helped him put the bags in his car, so he was soon back in the USA.

U.S. Prohibition agents lacked the authority to venture into Canada to raid the cross-border liquor depositories. However, Washington and Ottawa agreed that the line houses facilitated smuggling, so they enacted regulations to stop the construction of new buildings straddling the border. Ottawa also allowed the Canadian customs service to close and raze any building where contraband liquor was found within three hundred feet of the international border.[26]

Although Washington and Ottawa made noises about closing the line houses, they flourished because Americans scooted across the border to patronize them. The Labounty Line House and the Canaan Line House straddled the Vermont-Quebec border. A newspaper reported that the Canaan watering hole attracted "more tourists than any other place in the vicinity." Spooner's Line House near Derby, Vermont, was a border-straddling oasis with a reputation as a rough place where barroom brawls broke out. The line house near Beecher Falls, Vermont, was very popular with city folk summering in the mountains.[27]

The Last Chance was a famous watering hole on the Canadian side of the border near Rouses Point, New York. It sat beside a busy bootlegging route with heavy nighttime traffic. To be safe, drinkers parked their cars in the ditch because vehicles sitting on the shoulder of the road might be sideswiped by leggers speeding down the highway. "When they come through here, they come a-runnin' and don't stop for nothin'. Get over in the ditch if you don't want to pick up your flivver with a shovel," one driver advised another at the Last Chance.[28]

Line houses and hotels near the Quebec border advertised in U.S. newspapers. The ads often included a map or driving directions from Vermont or New York. Automobile owners could drive themselves into Canada, but car ownership was far from universal in the Arid Era. Luckily for those without cars, taxis charged reasonable fares to go across the border. For example, a cab ride from the train station in Richford, Vermont, to an alcohol oasis in Abercorn, Quebec, cost only a quarter.[29]

The most famous loading station along the Quebec–New York line belonged to Toussaint Trombley (AKA Toussaint Twombley). Part of Trombley's property lay in Quebec while his house was situated astraddle the border near Mooers in Clinton County, New York. On the Canadian side of his property he had a long shed with space for several cars. A barn-like structure, used as a liquor warehouse, also sat in Canada. A bootlegger could drive into Trombley's shed and load up in five minutes; in another five minutes he could be several miles south of the border on his way to a distribution hub in New York.

Although U.S. authorities knew Trombley's was a loading station, they generally ignored the place. As late as 1929 no Prohibition agent was assigned to the border between Quebec and Clinton County, New York. The border patrol policed the area, but it didn't have enough manpower to seriously interfere with the bootleg traffic leaving Trombley's. Moreover, some of the patrolmen took bribes to ignore the liquor traffickers. In 1931 Canada deported Trombley to the United States, where authorities indicted him for conspiring with border patrolmen and bootleggers to violate the dry law. At trial he was convicted and sentenced to two years in federal prison. A legger who testified against him received a lighter sentence—four months in the county jail.[30]

Fortin's line house north of Fort Kent, Maine, was another notorious way station for Yankee bootleggers. On a frigid day in December 1922 U.S. Prohibition agents and customs officers set out to raid Fortin's place. Only one road led to the line house, and it lay on the Canadian side of the border, where U.S. lawmen had no jurisdiction. However, the Americans believed that the lack of access in Maine justified going into Canada, so they drove their cars across the border and bounced along the winding rural road to Fortin's. They raided the line house and seized a substantial quantity of liquor.

As the U.S. lawmen headed back to Maine in their drafty cars, they opened a few liquor bottles and sampled the contents to ward off the freezing weather. While the Americans were still in Canada, New Brunswick liquor inspectors spotted their cars and pulled them over. Although some of the U.S. lawmen were wearing their uniforms, the Canadian liquor inspectors were suspicious. After all, the strangers could be bootleggers posing as law officers. Several of them were obviously drunk, and their cars held cases of booze. The liquor inspectors arrested the Americans and took them to jail in Edmundston, New Brunswick. The story of the strangers' arrest spread quickly in the small town, arousing a great deal of curiosity.

The next morning the Americans were taken to a local magistrate's court. A crowd gathered outside, hoping to see the bootleggers who claimed to be law officers. While the legal process unfolded in the courtroom, someone outside noticed the Yankees' cars parked nearby. A cursory inspection revealed that the liquor was still in the cars. Moreover, the car doors were unlocked!

The Canadian judge listened to the U.S. lawmen tell their story and found them credible. However, before he released them, he gave them a stern lecture on how to conduct themselves in Canada. As he saw it, their major sins were drinking on the job and operating outside their jurisdiction. After the judge had his say, the humbled Yankees were eager to go home. They quickly discovered that their liquor had vanished, but they didn't take time to look for the thief. They were happy to escape jail and return to the states, even without their booze. The owner of Fortin's line house was never prosecuted — presumably because all the evidence disappeared down someone's gullet.[31]

Lillian "Queen Lil" Fleury (AKA Lillian Miner Shipley) owned a saloon/brothel astride the border in East Richford, Vermont. Queen Lil, who grew up on a farm in Vermont, ran away from home at a young age to marry a man who proved to be a scoundrel of the first order. The couple joined a medicine show and traveled around the country, trying to earn a dishonest living. When Queen Lil grew tired of her hectic life on the road, she settled down in Boston and ran a brothel.

One night, believing that her arrest was imminent, Lil fled Boston and returned to her hometown in Vermont. Later she bought a tract of land straddling the Vermont-Quebec border, an ideal site for an illegal business. Although the law prevented her from erecting a new building on the international line, a burned-out hotel sat on her land and she was allowed to rebuild on the old foundation.

Queen Lil's Palace had a saloon on the ground floor and bedrooms on the top floors. A train that ran beside her property dropped off passengers virtually on her doorstep. This was very convenient for railway workers, traveling salesmen, and others who wanted to hop off the train for a brief interlude. Like many people who sold illegal liquor, Lil supported Prohibition because it benefited her business. She made generous financial donations to the WCTU, and her largesse was reported in the local newspaper.

From time to time, U.S. or Canadian lawmen raided Lil's place, but they never found enough evidence to arrest her. She apparently paid an informant for advance warning of raids, so she could clean house before the lawmen arrived. After repeated raids without an arrest, frustrated U.S. and Canadian officials decided to work together to bust Lil. Somehow they managed to keep their plans secret, and a joint task force burst into Queen Lil's Palace. The lawmen found several unmarried couples in bed and arrested Lil. When her case went to trial, she pled guilty to keeping a bawdy house, paid a fine, and returned to her business. She ran her line house until the Depression economy left men with little money to spend on liquor and sordid thrills. She retired to enjoy her golden years on a farm in Vermont, returning to the rural lifestyle she had spurned decades earlier.[32]

The Drinking Man's Holiday

Countless Yankees traveled by car or train to a wet Canadian province to enjoy a respite from the Great Drought. As long as the American visitor didn't take a few bottles home with him, he had no reason to fear arrest on Volstead charges. On weekends "Beer Specials" left the train stations in Massachusetts, New Hampshire, and Vermont on the way to Montreal, where visitors could enjoy undiluted, safe liquor. In New York City passengers could board a train after dinner and eat breakfast in Montreal, complete with a high-octane eye opener.

In Montreal tourists slaked their thirst in hotels, restaurants, taverns, and private clubs. The Quebec Liquor Commission started a campaign to promote "civilized drinking, with food." To that end, every restaurant wine list included the commission's "lyric and impassioned little essay" on how to choose and serve wines. The wine fancier could begin "with a sherry and bitters, have a nice cool Chablis or sauterne with the fish, a red Bordeaux or burgundy with the roast, champagne with ... dessert, and port with the nuts." Neither pubs nor restaurants served cocktails, but American tourists who wanted mixed drinks could go to a private club or buy spirits at a liquor store and concoct their own.

Male tipplers who preferred suds could patronize one of Montreal's beer taverns, which by law served only men. An American visitor described the beer taverns as "plebian." None were located in Montreal's "better-class business section" or upscale residential neighborhoods. Although the typical tavern had an old-fashioned bar with a brass rail, drinkers were required to sit at tables. Conventional logic said that standing at the bar encouraged men to gulp down their suds, while sitting at a table was more civilized. Beer drinkers who didn't want to patronize a tavern could buy brew by the bottle, case, or barrel at a licensed store.

Montreal hotels tried to identify rowdy party animals when they checked in, so all the heavy drinkers could be segregated on the same floor or wing. This kept "less alcoholic visitors" from being "accosted in the halls by drunken and hilarious hotel guests." In warm weather, the drinkers shouted toasts out the open windows or congregated in the hotel courtyard for noisy parties.[33]

On Sunday night, after slaking their thirst, Americans crowded the Montreal railway station and boarded a train for the trip home. Many couldn't resist the temptation to hide a bottle or two in their luggage. Trains from Montreal stopped in Richford, Vermont, where U.S. customs officers climbed aboard for an inspection. To protect his contraband, more than one amateur legger tied a string around his bottle and dangled it out the window during the search. Customs soon caught onto this, so an inspector would walk along the side of the train, cutting the strings.[34]

7. Satan's Seat: Defying Volstead in New York City

Enforcement of the National Prohibition Act, particularly in the great City of New York, has been a tremendous problem, which at times seems well nigh hopeless....— Charles O'Connor, Prohibition official, New York[1]

Dry leaders called New York City "Satan's Seat." They had great disdain for the evil metropolis where unrepentant sinners frolicked with the devil. But New Yorkers viewed themselves as more sophisticated than sinful. Although Gotham had dry reformers who crusaded for sobriety, wets far outnumbered the arid activists. Wet or dry, everyone agreed that Prohibition had little public support in the city. Cocktails fit into the cosmopolitan lifestyle of New Yorkers who liked nightclubs, restaurants, Broadway, and Harlem. Drinking was linked to the cultural identities of ethnic groups who sipped wine with dinner or enjoyed family outings to the neighborhood beer garden. Prohibition simply felt wrong to throngs of New Yorkers.

Wets dominated local politics in Satan's Seat, where Tammany Hall still ran the show despite its ongoing, gradual decline. Opposing Prohibition was about the only thing all the major political factions agreed on. Gotham politicos condemned the dry law as the hayseed morality of chaw-bacons. They argued that New York City should not waste tax dollars or public resources trying to enforce an absurd, unpopular law. They steadfastly demanded the repeal of Volstead.

Mayors John Hylan (1918–1925) and James John "Jimmy" Walker (1926–1932) led Gotham's city government during the Jazz Age. Walker was a flamboyant, larger-than-life character who embodied the carefree spirit of the Roaring Twenties. His fans affectionately called him "Our Jimmy" or "The Nightclub Mayor." His critics preferred "Jimmy the Jester." Whatever people called him, his election was consistent with Gotham's disdain for Prohibition. Under his leadership, or lack of it, Volstead enforcement slid to its nadir in Satan's Seat. His Honor scoffed at the dry law and promoted the Big Apple's nightlife as one of its greatest assets. He made the rounds of the hotspots at night, slept late in the mornings, and treated the mayoralty as a part-time job. When he and his mistress were caught in a raid at notorious gambling joint, few New Yorkers were surprised or outraged.

Assistant U.S. Attorney General Mabel Willebrandt accused Mayor Walker of dereliction of duty when it came to Volstead. Walker defended himself and his police department by blaming the federal Prohibition Unit for haphazard enforcement. He said that the New York Police Department (NYPD) had notified the feds of twenty-nine thousand liquor violations and it was the Prohis' job to follow up. Walker's police commissioner declared that the NYPD had urgent duties that outranked Volstead. In a defiant letter to Willebrandt, he wrote, "I am not willing to have the men of the department, to whom our citizens look for protection of life and property, make an intensive crusade to enforce a Federal Act."[2]

Mayor Walker made one surprising concession to Volstead enforcement: he ordered Big Apple nightspots to close at two o'clock a.m. Club owners resisted the order, which "came as a shock" to habitués of the bright light district. But His Honor felt strongly that propriety and social justice mandated a curfew for nightclubs.

"There is no demand," Walker said, "on the part of respectable and decent people for such places which disgorge at seven or eight o'clock in the morning crowds of men in evening dress and women in flaming finery, which they flaunt in the faces of workmen on their way to their jobs. Such people create Bolsheviki."[3]

New York's Finest Crackdown

Only a minute percentage of New York City's police officers made a sincere effort to enforce the dry law. As a group, NYPD officers viewed Volstead enforcement as an onerous addition to an already heavy workload. Like every other worker, the cop on the beat resisted having new duties foisted upon him. He said he already had his hands full without hunting for people who were merely breaking the Volstead law. He had to deal with serious crimes, like robberies and shootings. Just as he ignored jaywalking, he had no qualms about looking the other way when he walked past an illegal bar.

As a general rule, the cops in Satan's Seat felt no obligation to obey Volstead in their personal socializing. When the Police Lieutenants' Benevolent Association held its annual dinner at the Commodore Hotel in 1921, liquid "cheerfulness ... entered the banquet hall in suitcases, handbags, and paper wrappers." The earsplitting "hilarity and general noise" reached levels typical of the clatter at a sopping wet pre–Volstead party.

Both New York City Mayor John Hylan and Police Commissioner Richard Enright attended the lieutenants' banquet. William Anderson, an ASL leader, publicly berated the city officials, saying they had presided over a "drunken orgy." In a stunning example of hifalutin rhetoric, Anderson called the mayor "a blatherskite monument to the political folly of the electorate."[4] (A blatherskite is a person who talks nonsense and lots of it. Although blatherskite is a noun, Anderson used it as an adjective. Outrage might account for his error.)

Only weeks after Volstead became law, NYC and federal officials met to work out the details of concurrent enforcement in the Big Apple. They agreed that federal Prohibition agents would take the lead in all matters relating to Volstead and would do all the "detective work." NYPD officers would make arrests when they saw liquor violations and would report "all rumors or suspicious appearances" to the feds. Thus, the NYPD wouldn't do undercover work or initiate Volstead investigations, except by passing information along to the federal authorities. The NYPD would make arrests for minor Volstead violations, when more urgent duties didn't demand their attention, but the feds had responsibility for shutting down the big operations.[5]

After Prohibition agents raided an illegal establishment in New York City, police officers watched as barrels of liquor were poured into the sewer system (Library of Congress).

From the very beginning, animosity between NYPD officers and federal Prohibition agents impeded enforcement. As a group, the federal agents considered themselves superior to local cops. Conversely, New York's finest regarded the feds as bossy, conceited amateurs because Prohibition agents weren't required to have previous law enforcement experience. Moreover, the federal dry sleuths were notoriously susceptible to graft. Although the NYPD took its share of payoffs, the city cops claimed to be outraged because the feds pocketed bribes from bootleggers.

In 1921 New York State passed a baby Volstead, the Mullan-Gage Act. The statute had strong backing from rural legislators and Governor Nathan Miller, a dry Republican. Politicos in the Big Apple didn't share Miller's enthusiasm for drying up New York. City officials feared that the new state law would spread NYPD resources too thin, allowing violent crime to flourish. A Gotham newspaper predicted Mullan-Gage would prove that the dry law simply could not be enforced. Another paper said Mullan-Gage was impractical because it would "require the placing of a policeman in every saloon" in Gotham. (Since Volstead outlawed the saloon, the city had none — in theory, anyway.)

Police Commissioner Enright seemed conflicted about the dry law. He didn't like Prohibition, but he argued that even a bad law must be enforced as long as it was on the books.

In the NYPD's annual report for 1921, Enright's inconsistency was apparent. He opined that the state's baby Volstead was a political tool passed by the dry lobby "for the sole purpose of embarrassing" the city government led by Mayor Hylan. He argued that if a serious effort were made to enforce Prohibition, "the effect on public sentiment would be to everlastingly damn those responsible for the attempt." He predicted "an extremely uphill fight in exacting obedience" to the dry law. "It will, however, be done," he vowed.

Despite Enright's pledge, the dry faction doubted his dedication to ending Volstead crime. When Governor Miller signed the Mullan-Gage Act into law, he singled out Commissioner Enright as the main reason for lax Volstead enforcement in NYC. Miller said, "I want the police commissioner of New York to understand ... that the law cannot be made a joke." The governor opined that the NYPD "with the right head would prevent what is now a public disgrace in the City of New York."[6]

Enright picked up the gauntlet and ordered a major crackdown on Gotham's liquor traffic, focusing on illegal bars and small-time bootleggers. Across the city, police invaded saloons and arrested bartenders for serving drinks. In Greenwich Village, officers made the rounds of the cafés, frisking patrons and looking for booze in teacups. Raids on Coney Island's liquor sellers left the amusement venue "absolutely dry." In the Theatre District, cops arrested "walking cellars," bootleggers who worked the streets, selling liquor out of bottles or flasks hidden in their clothing. Officers watched for men "wearing overcoats which gurgled or clinked." A deputy commissioner explained, "The police are not expected to go about slapping everybody's pockets, but if a man is suspected, they may jostle him."[7]

During the crackdown, police officers were stationed in popular cafés and nightspots with a reputation for violating the dry law. This took up to 750 police officers off the street. Of course, while the cops watched waiters to be sure they poured Darjeeling into the teacups, criminals were busy elsewhere. A judge said, "Men are stationed in restaurants to see no one steals a drink, while around the corner a holdup man is breaking into a jewelry shop." Since NYC was plagued with jewelry thefts at the time, this criticism rang true.[8]

Less than a month after the crackdown began, Enright estimated that the NYPD had seized $7 million worth of liquor, mostly from individuals or small retail outlets. The evidence storehouse could barely hold all that booze, and storing it cost roughly $20,000 per month, far more than the amount budgeted.[9] The long list of confiscated items included liquor in bottles, barrels, jugs, demijohns, flasks, and tin cans. The police also seized fruit presses, stills, cars, trucks, wagons, pushcarts, boats, suitcases, valises, trunks, handbags, glassware, barrels of mash, bags of hops, boxes of raisins, and buckets of suspicious corn mixtures. Confiscated horses had to be kept in stables, where feeding and caring for them added to the cost of the crackdown.

Commissioner Enright's dry offensive stretched the NYPD's personnel and funds to the breaking point. He asked the city for money to hire one thousand more policemen. He also needed $100,000 to gather evidence since plainclothes officers had to buy booze to have proof of liquor sales. After the alcohol was seized, it had to be tested, which strained the resources of the city lab where chemists analyzed the contraband.[10]

During Enright's dry crusade, the NYPD conducted 512 raids and made more than ten thousand arrests in nine months. While dry leaders applauded the effort, wets warned that the NYPD had gone overboard. Legal watchdogs worried that the police raids violated the citizenry's constitutional rights. Enright was subpoenaed to testify before a grand jury looking at search and seizure practices in the Bronx. The jurors were especially concerned about cops who had no search warrants but rummaged through bags, cars, and buildings anyway. Enright blamed Governor Miller for forcing the NYPD to adopt aggressive methods to enforce the state's baby Volstead.[11]

As the NYPD pursued its crackdown on Volstead violators, more citizens complained about illegal searches, wrongful arrests, and invasion of privacy. Mayor Hylan, never a fan of Prohibition, urged Enright to reorder the NYPD's priorities. The commissioner didn't need much prompting. Enforcing Volstead was a thankless task in Satan's Seat. Enright began withdrawing manpower and resources from the dry crusade and allowed it to peter out. On occasion he took disciplinary action against officers who were blatantly corrupt or lax in enforcing Volstead, but he no longer put Prohibition at the top of his agenda.

Despite the weak dry law enforcement in the Big Apple, Volstead cases clogged the courts. Each year, law enforcement in NYC received roughly one hundred eighty thousand reports of Volstead violations and made fifty thousand arrests. Low-paid service workers, such as waiters and bartenders, made up the vast majority of Volstead arrestees; hardcore criminals were less than one percent. Only ten to fifteen percent of New York's Volstead cases ever went to trial; the rest were thrown out, usually for lack of evidence.[12]

When U.S. Attorney Emory Buckner took office in 1925, he found a huge backlog of cases in the federal criminal courts in New York's Southern District. He estimated that there were three thousand untried Volstead cases plus six thousand criminal cases of other types. Defendants waited up to nine years to face a jury. When a Volstead violator finally had his day in court, the chances were good that the arresting officer wouldn't remember much about the case — if he even bothered to show up. In many instances, the evidence had been lost during the long delay. To unclog the legal pipeline, Buckner dismissed thousands of petty Volstead cases, which typically involved only a few ounces of alcohol.[13]

Judge John McIntyre of the Court of General Sessions urged dry law violators to plead guilty and forgo their right to a jury of their peers. His goal was avoiding jury trials, which would consume "much of the court's time and add expenses to the already overburdened taxpayers."[14] Only Volstead violators with bad legal advice chose to help the court system by pleading guilty. Lawyers knew that NYC juries were notoriously biased against the state in dry law cases. No matter how strong the evidence, defendants were rarely convicted of Volstead violations in Satan's Seat.

Forging Ahead

The premium, aged whiskey in America's bonded warehouses looked like an easy target to bootleggers. A few gangs specialized in robbing the warehouses at gunpoint, but boot-leggers with finesse used bogus permits to withdraw liquor safely and easily. Dishonest federal agents and office workers in the Prohibition Unit pocketed big bucks for helping leggers obtain bonded booze. Crooked Prohis sold valid withdrawal permits, which required the signature of a high-ranking Prohibition official. Since rubber stamps were widely used to sign documents, an official signature could usually be stamped on the permit. If not, a handwritten forgery would do the trick. For a few extra dollars, the helpful Prohis expedited the bootlegger's permit so it didn't get tied up in red tape.

Bootlegger Edward Donegan engineered one of the Arid Era's first withdrawal schemes. Donegan recruited Regina Sassone, "a girl clerk" in the Prohibition Unit, to aid him in a permit scam that led to the withdrawal of whiskey worth millions of dollars. Over a period of about five months, Sassone stole than one thousand valid permits and passed them along to Donegan. Sassone, a lowly clerk who worked for New York's Prohibition director, aroused suspicion by living large on her small paycheck. She wore expensive clothes and jewelry, lived at an upscale hotel, and was seen "taking automobile rides." At some point Donegan and Sassone became lovers, which added to the scandal when the scam was exposed. Respectable women were appalled when the girl clerk confessed that the bootlegger had "seduced" her. The cad!

After Sassone stole the withdrawal permits from her boss's office, Donegan used them to buy liquor from distilleries licensed to sell their pre–Volstead output for medical or industrial use. Before releasing any liquor, the distilleries sent telegrams to the director's office to verify the permits. Those telegrams crossed Sassone's desk, and she intercepted the ones for Donegan's withdrawals. He then sent a forged document that authorized the bonded facility to fill his order.[15]

Prosecutors charged Donegan with multiple dry law violations, bribery, and attempted bribery of employees in the Prohibition Unit. Sassone and Donegan were jointly accused of stealing government documents from the Prohibition director's office. They were also charged with "conspiracy to defraud the government by obtaining copies of telegrams inquiring as to the genuineness of withdrawal permits and by sending forged replies."[16]

At trial, the prosecution called a parade of credible witnesses, including federal agents, distillery officials, a bank auditor, Sassone's former boss, and clerks who had worked in the NYC Prohibition office. The evidence included telegrams from distilleries and forged documents found in Donegan's possession when he was arrested.

The state also presented a written, signed confession made by Sassone, who seemed genuinely remorseful. She admitted that she had intercepted telegrams for Donegan and he had paid her roughly $3,000. Summing up for the prosecution, the assistant district attorney called Sassone "an unfortunate tool in the hands of Donegan ... a low criminal type who for his own pleasure and profit ... misled the young woman." The attorney stated that Sassone's confession clearly proved Donegan's guilt as well as her own.

The defense called no witnesses but focused on attacking the prosecution's case. When the defense attorneys made their arguments to the jury, they called the state's case was "a fabrication of falsehoods." They claimed that the defendants hadn't stolen the withdrawal permits. Rather, defense counsel attributed the thefts to a former Prohibition Unit clerk, who had testified as a prosecution witness.[17]

After lengthy overnight deliberations, the jury found Donegan guilty on all counts. Sassone was acquitted of all charges, but the judge felt conflicted about the verdict. Speaking to the jurors, he said, "I am rather sorry, gentlemen, you found the girl not guilty on all counts of the indictment. She was guilty, of course, on her own admission, but I knew and you knew that she was but a tool of the man who debauched her."

The court fined Donegan $65,000 and sentenced him to ten years in the federal prison at Atlanta — an unusually tough punishment for permit fraud. He petitioned the court of appeals, which refused to reduce his fine or his prison term.[18]

Wanted: Music and Sweetness

Serving as federal Prohibition director for New York was a low-paying, stressful job with a high turnover rate. Judge Harold Hart was appointed to the post in May 1921. A city judge in Binghamton, Hart was a dry activist and "a militant law enforcer." Republican Party honchos had complained about the sloppy Volstead enforcement under his predecessor, a Democrat. They were certain Hart, a rising star in GOP politics, would do better. His new job paid only $5,000 per year, but it was "considered a big plum by the politicians because of the power involved."[19]

Hart had barely settled into the job when four hundred blank liquor withdrawal permits were "mysteriously removed" from a cabinet in his office. Up to four hundred thousand cases of whiskey, worth millions in the bootleg trade, could be purchased with the missing permits. All withdrawal permits were numbered serially, and regulations required them to be issued consecutively. The missing permits bore serial numbers much higher than those currently in use, so the bootleggers obviously hoped to make withdrawals before the theft was noticed.

Only days after Hart reported the theft to his superiors in Washington, a federal agent arrested a Philadelphia man who had one hundred of the missing permits. The following month the Prohibition Unit recovered about two hundred of the permits when buyers tried to purchase liquor with them. Lawmen arrested the would-be buyers, all of whom had connections to wholesale drug firms. The remaining permits couldn't be located so officials assumed that buyers had successfully used them to withdraw liquor before the theft was discovered.[20]

Less than five months after Hart took office, he abruptly resigned. His confidential assistant, who processed the withdrawal permits, also resigned. The grapevine hummed with rumors about the cause of Hart's sudden departure. He refused to comment, except to say that "the work was distasteful" and didn't pay enough. Although that seemed like sufficient reason, newshounds sniffed around, looking for more.[21]

A few weeks after Hart's resignation, a federal grand jury in NYC began hearing testimony about suspicious liquor withdrawals from bonded warehouses. The sales had been made to wholesale drug companies run by men who knew more about bootlegging than pharmacology. The jurors listened to numerous witnesses, including Hart. They returned indictments against sixteen individuals and four wholesale drug companies, accusing them of fraud and conspiracy to violate Volstead. A special indictment alleged that Hart had participated in the scheme. He was charged with conspiring to defraud the federal government and violate the dry law by issuing withdrawal permits for $10 million worth of liquor. He pled not guilty. His lawyer stated that the charges were "the result of agitation and sensationalism."[22]

At trial, the prosecution showed that suspicious permits from Hart's office had been used to buy liquor from distilleries in Kentucky and Maryland. The distillery managers had contacted Hart's office before the withdrawals, and someone on his staff had certified the permits as genuine. On the witness stand, distillery managers identified the wholesale druggists/bootleggers as the buyers who had used the permits.[23]

One of Hart's aides testified that at least seven hundred (not four hundred) withdrawal permits had disappeared during the director's short tenure. All the permits had been stored in a steel cabinet with only one key, which Hart himself kept. Another member of Hart's staff said that certain wholesale drug companies were given "special permits" and she was instructed to rush those through without any delay. A clerk in the Prohibition Unit stated that she had been demoted because she refused to certify "irregular permits."

The chief prosecutor stressed that Hart's staff, under his orders, had issued withdrawal permits to "upstart drug companies" run by men who knew nothing about the wholesale drug business. He condemned the conspirators' unlawful quest "to get rich, in two months to get millions of dollars' worth of liquor." He told the jurors that an acquittal would put the stamp of approval on bootlegging. "The eyes of the community are on you," he said.

Defense counsel argued that the evidence did not prove the existence of a conspiracy. Even if there had been a conspiracy, Hart hadn't been connected to the bogus drug firms. Moreover, the state couldn't prove that he had entered into an agreement with his codefendants. Hart's attorney said the former director had endured "the sufferings of the damned. This trial has taken all the sweetness and all the music out of his life. I ask you, by your verdict, to put back into his life that music and that sweetness."

The jurors obliged.[24] They found all the defendants not guilty, returning music and sweetness to everyone — except the prosecutor who lost the case.

A New Day

Ralph Day, a wealthy clothing manufacturer, became director of New York's federal Prohibition office in December 1921. Day was touted as an independent man who would lift Volstead enforcement "out of politics" and institute "a new era." Ironically, he was chosen because of his politics: he was a director of the National Republican Club and a close friend of New York's dry GOP governor. He had no law enforcement experience, but that wasn't unusual among top Prohibition officials.[25]

Day began with a personnel shakeup, getting rid of Prohibition agents who were known to be corrupt or otherwise derelict in doing their duty. His first day on the job, he dismissed seven agents and accepted the resignation of another. The agents had taken bribes and/or "were generally undesirable as members of the force." In the coming days, he continued his purge, discharging more than fifty agents. In a surprise move, he staged a raid on the restaurant across the street from his office because the eatery was "a loafing place" for Prohibition agents.[26]

Under Day's predecessors, the NYC Prohibition office had been plagued with scandals because withdrawal permits had fallen into the wrong hands. Day set out to rectify this problem by placing stricter controls on liquor withdrawals from bonded facilities. Nevertheless, on more than one occasion large quantities of liquor were illegally withdrawn from the Republic Storage Warehouse, a bonded facility in Manhattan. Investigators found evidence pointing to the Prohibition Unit, so six agents were suspended while a grand jury looked into the illegal withdrawals. The Prohis were accused of helping buyers use forged documents to remove more than 5,000 cases of whiskey and champagne from the warehouse.

Shortly after the agents were suspended, Day tendered his own resignation. After only ten months as director, he said that he must return to his clothing company for financial reasons. During his final days as director, he was subpoenaed to testify before the grand jury probing the illegal withdrawals from the Republic Storage Warehouse. He demanded immunity before he would agree to testify.[27]

Day was under suspicion because he had accepted improper loans during his tenure as Prohibition director. An investigator for a citizens' watchdog group told the grand jury that Day had borrowed $100,000 from a known bootlegger. Other witnesses stated that Day had refused to discharge an incompetent Prohibition agent because the director owned a sizeable sum of money to the agent's brother.[28]

The grand jury decided to inspect the financial records of Day's clothing company, but he refused to cooperate. After some bargaining, he agreed to comply with a subpoena for his financial data. His bookkeeper appeared before the grand jury and answered questions about the ledgers and other records. Day himself did not appear and steadfastly demanded immunity before he would cooperate. Due to his intransigence, he was held in contempt of court. Despite the grand jury's suspicions about Day's financial affairs, the investigation fizzled out. The contempt of court charge against him was dropped, even though he never testified.

The grand jury foreman, clearly frustrated with Day, sent a letter to Treasury Secretary Andrew Mellon. The foreman wrote that New York's Volstead enforcement under Day had been "conducted in an inefficient and disgraceful manner." He deplored the political patronage rampant in the NYC Prohibition unit. He said the squad was riddled with incompetence because politicos "secured appointments for their henchmen without proper regard for the qualifications of those chosen." He accused Day of showing favoritism to certain agents even though their work was substandard. He alleged that Day had allowed his agents to fraternize with bootleggers and saloonkeepers. He said that Day had undermined Prohibition by discharging agents "who exerted themselves to enforce the law."[29]

A few weeks after Day left his Prohibition post, the grand jury returned indictments in the Republic Storage case. The accused included millionaire bootlegger Mannie Kessler and the Prohibition agents suspended for their alleged role in the illegal withdrawals. At trial, the jury found Kessler and three Prohibition agents guilty; the other three Prohis were acquitted.[30]

Using government permits to withdraw alcohol from bonded storage facilities was a favorite tactic for the big city rum rings, especially in New York and Philadelphia. Although the scam didn't disappear until Volstead was repealed, it became less popular as Prohibition wore on. The amount of aged, pre–Volstead liquor in storage steadily declined as it was used for medical and industrial purposes. In addition, the Prohibition Unit tightened the controls on the bonded warehouses and made it harder to get a withdrawal permit. The big bootleg gangs found that operating their own wildcat distilleries was both easier and more profitable than manipulating the permit process to withdraw bonded alcohol.

Good Night, Baby Volstead

In 1922 New York voters resoundingly elected a wet governor, Alfred Smith. Several months after Smith took office, the legislature passed the Cuvillier Act, repealing the state's baby Volstead. Although Smith's sympathies lay with the wets, he didn't immediately sign the new law. The dry forces had substantial power in rural areas so it wasn't politic to ignore them. For nearly a month Smith professed to be studying the matter. Both wet and dry leaders pressured him to see things their way.

Ultimately Smith sided with the wet faction, and he invoked state's rights as his rationale for repealing the baby Volstead. He also gave his interpretation of the Eighteenth Amendment's concurrent enforcement clause, saying it "was not a command" but "an option."

Dry leaders greeted the repeal of New York's baby Volstead with their usual hysteria. The ASL spokesman foresaw "unbridled lawlessness" and called on dry voters to unite to oust Smith from the governor's office. The WCTU's Ella Boole warned that Smith's decision would give aid to the "rumrunners, smugglers, bootleggers, and violators of the Eighteenth Amendment." Sounding properly outraged, she said, "New York has stabbed the Eighteenth Amendment, and the wound will be felt all over the nation!"[31]

8. Speakeasy Heaven: Nightlife in the Big Apple

Successful Prohibition-era nightclubs in urban areas were a mix of high society, artistic wits, and seedy mobsters. — Christine Sismondo, historian[1]

The Big Apple didn't have a monopoly on speakeasies, but it certainly had more than any other American city. Estimates of the number of illegal bars in New York City ranged from a staggering twenty thousand to an astronomical one hundred thousand. In the late Twenties the NYPD put the number at thirty-two thousand. Speakeasies operated in virtually every type of urban real estate, including storefronts, brownstones, penthouses, basements, lofts, and office buildings. The illicit watering holes ran the gamut from grimy, stinky gin mills to glitzy nightclubs with live entertainment by top acts. Drinkers had their choice of plush palaces in midtown, jazz clubs in Harlem, beer gardens in the Bronx, tearooms in Greenwich Village, and more.

The Big Apple seemed to have a speakeasy for every affinity group and every consumer, from the richest to the poorest. The Cortlandt Club was a favorite with downtown businessmen, and stockbrokers patronized the Encore in the financial district. Journalists hung out at the Press Club or Jack Bleeck's Artists and Writers, next door to the *New York Tribune*. The Mummers' Club catered to the theatrical crowd, as did Paul and Joe's. Chorus girls and songwriters from Tin Pan Alley frequented the Ship Ahoy, while black performers liked Mexico's in Harlem. O'Leary's on the Bowery extended charity to any down-on-his-luck bum who wandered in.

Members-only clubs served drinkers who could afford a stiff initiation fee. Anthony Drexel Biddle Jr., an heir to banking fortunes, founded the Embassy Club, which charged an annual membership fee of $250. Drinkers paid $200 to join the Salon of the Great, which claimed to offer scintillating conversation along with top-quality booze. The exclusive Cloud Club, which occupied three floors in the Chrysler Building, offered a superb view of the city. Walter Chrysler and other moguls belonged to this all-male bastion, which had a bar, a stock ticker, and private liquor lockers.

Red-carpet speakeasies in midtown featured live entertainment, elegant décor, fine dining, and well-stocked bars. The Maison Doree, which occupied a big brownstone, had a cabaret, a dining room, a dance hall, and a clubroom. The reception hall was decorated with grand statuary, plush furniture, and costly rugs. At the Bernaise Restaurant, few patrons stopped to eat in the dining room; they hurried downstairs to the lounge, which was furnished with cocktail tables, overstuffed benches, and a jungle of potted palms. Jack and Charlie's (AKA Twenty-one) occupied an elegant house with dining rooms, bars, and game rooms. The wine cellars were hidden behind fortress-thick brick walls, which sprang open when a wire was inserted into a chink between certain bricks.

Greenwich Village was famous for tiny speakeasies with tons of character. "Village cabarets were relatively low-priced and were patronized more by college boys and girls out for a good time and less by 'sugar daddies' with chorus girls than were the midtown nightclubs," noted a sociologist. The Casual Club attracted a young crowd who called themselves "We Moderns." Art students and high-school girls hung out at the Jolly Friars, probably Greenwich Village's best-known speak. Chumley's had an unmarked, hard-to-find entrance, but that didn't stop it from being a favorite with the literary set. Both Harlem and Greenwich Village had speakeasies for the "temperamental element" (AKA homosexuals). The Jungle, the Red Mask, the Black Rabbit, and the Flower Pot were popular with the gay community.[2]

A speakeasy, like a theme restaurant, could create ambiance by using an evocative motif for its décor and menu. The Wild West, the Old South, the circus, and exotic places were typical themes. Ward's Sewanee Club, located in a cellar under the Apollo Theatre, had murals of cotton fields as well as small riverboats that moved along a track. The County Fair had a grandstand, picket fences, and kiddy cars that patrons could drive around the club. At the Pirates' Den, a doorman with a parrot on his shoulder greeted guests. Inside, the décor featured heavy chains, cutlasses, muskets, and old maps. The waiters and musicians dressed as buccaneers; Black Skull Punch was the house specialty. The Irish Veterans Association had Hibernian décor with shamrocks, Irish flags, clay dudeens, and blackthorn shillelaghs. Late at night, well-lubricated Irish tenors sang "Danny Boy" and "Mother Machree."

At the Aquarium, drinkers imbibed at a long glass bar/aquarium holding goldfish and other marine life. The signature drink was a goldfish cocktail (gin, French vermouth, and goldwasser). When federal Prohibition agents raided the Aquarium, they seized a case of liquor and "a few full jugs." Later a supervisor sent the agents back to confiscate the furnishings, including the bar/fish tank. While the bar/fish tank was stored in a warehouse, the Prohis had to deploy an agent to feed the marine life.[3]

Neighborhood bars sometimes resembled pre–Volstead saloons in terms of clientele, décor, and ambiance. Dan and Mort Moriarty's speakeasy looked much like their pre–Prohibition saloon, with added security to keep honest cops out. Located in the basement of a brownstone, the Moriartys' place had a Spartan interior and a plain, no-frills bar. To screen their clientele, the Moriartys looked through the Judas hole (AKA peephole) in the steel front door.

Pre–Volstead saloons had welcomed all comers, but speakeasies usually screened their clientele because they didn't want to admit anyone who might raid the place or file a complaint with law enforcement. Typically, a speakeasy required customers to show ID, use a password, and/or have references. "Buzz" was a common password, and the ubiquitous "Joe sent me" became a verbal symbol of the Roaring Twenties. Some speakeasies installed doorbells or buzzers; to gain entry, a patron had to know the code — a specified series of long and short rings or buzzes. Watering holes often gave regular patrons membership cards to show the doorman. A secret handshake was the magic signal at some exclusive clubs.

Extra-cautious bar owners installed more than one door. At the Sailors' Den near the Navy Yard, anyone wanting to enter had to rap five times on the front door and hold up three fingers. When that door opened, he could proceed to the second door where he held up two fingers and waited while someone peered through the Judas hole to give him the once over.[4]

Because the Big Apple had so many speakeasies, an owner sometimes chose an unusual name to draw attention to his club. Speakeasies with curious names included The Hyena Club, The Furnace, The Jail, The Eugenic Club, The Seven Deadly Sins, Peek Inn, Drool Inn, Ubangi, Hotsy-Totsy, Heigh-ho, and Ha! Ha! The Futuristic International Academy was a "hangout for internationalists of the modern school" who had radical ideas about almost everything. Russian artists and an occasional exiled aristocrat patronized the Cave of the Fallen Angels. Gypsy Land was famous for its semi-nude dancers; after the police shut it down, it reopened as the Hungarian Workmen's Home.

One of Gotham's most intimate bars was a joint on Pitkin Avenue run by Charles Papkus and his wife. On multiple occasions NYPD detectives saw drunken men staggering out of the Papkus establishment. Yet, strangely, police searches turned up no liquor. Then an observant officer noticed that Mrs. Papkus habitually wore a long, voluminous skirt adorned with ruffles — definitely a passé style in the Roaring Twenties. The officer also noted that Mrs. Papkus was very popular, always surrounded by men. A plainclothes cop joined the circle of men hovering around her to discover her secret. He saw that the ruffles covered pockets where she hid bottles of booze. The police arrested both Mr. and Mrs. Papkus on liquor charges.[5]

From time to time, an enterprising rumrunner opened a floating speakeasy accessible only by boat, but such places were not common. In one case, a newspaper described "a palatial floating barroom" off the coast of Long Island. The ship had an old-fashioned bar, a ballroom, and live music played by an Alabama jazz band. A "crude reproduction" of the Statue of Liberty stood on the poop deck. Private yachts and launches took drinkers out to the cabaret ship. New York's federal Prohibition director said the vessel lay outside his jurisdiction, so he had no control over it. The district Coast Guard commander questioned whether the cabaret ship actually existed. He said his men, who patrolled the water from Cape Cod to Cape May, had never seen it.[6]

Harlem's speakeasies were the hottest of the hotspots in Satan's Seat. Hordes of people came to join in the rollicking, pulsating nightlife fueled by jazz and booze. The show biz paper *Variety* said, Harlem's "nightlife now surpasses that of Broadway itself.... When it comes to pep, pulchritude, punch and presentation, the Harlem places have Broadway's nightclubs distanced." From midnight until dawn or later, limos and cabs brought visitors to Harlem's "sizzling cafes, speaks, nightclubs, and spiritual séances," said *Variety*. Among Harlem's most popular places were the Cotton Club, the Nest, Connie's Inn, Small's Paradise, Barron's, the Spider Webb, Saratoga, Ward's Sewanee, and Catagonia. Most Harlem speakeasies were segregated by race, but those known as black-and-tans catered to racially-mixed crowds.[7]

New York City had slipshod Volstead enforcement, and the liquor traffic in Harlem operated with even less interference than elsewhere in Gotham. In 1924 the NYPD commissioner said he had received more than one thousand complaints that the dry law "was being flagrantly violated in Harlem." He conceded that police officers "assigned to suppress speakeasies and vice and gambling resorts in Harlem had been particularly lax."[8] But he made only halfhearted efforts to correct the problem.

Connie's Inn, 7th Avenue at 132nd Street, was "the first stop on the route of the downtown night clubbers" who ventured into Harlem. "Walk down one flight of stairs and you are in this rendezvous, so low-ceilinged as to be cave-like. Around the dance floor is a three-foot barrier built in the semblance of a village — miniature bungalows and villas, and here and there a spired church, through the tiny windows of which comes the gleam of midget lights," a visitor wrote. "You can tell Connie's is a high-class joint as soon as you sit down because the waiter usually whispers that bottles should be carried in the pocket, and not be placed on the floor."[9]

The standard drink in a Harlem speakeasy was a "shorty," a four-ounce bottle of whiskey that cost fifty cents to a dollar in an upscale club. A shorty gave the drinker more bang for the buck than a mixed drink; a cocktail with an ounce of whiskey cost up to a half-dollar, so four ounces of whiskey cost two dollars if mixed. Harlem's whiskey connoisseurs preferred Mexico's Old 99, which was made locally, or Chicken Cock Whiskey, a pre–Volstead product from Kentucky.

Speakeasies were the most visible part of the liquor traffic in Harlem, but they were far from the only place to buy booze. *Variety* estimated that "five out of every seven cigar stores, lunchrooms, and beauty parlors in Harlem" sold liquor. Women's shops usually sold booze as well as dresses, hats, and hosiery. On average, there were two buffet flats "for every apartment building in the black belt," according to *Variety*. At a buffet flat, the cost of a shorty ranged from a dime to a dollar, but a quarter was the standard price, making it a real bargain.[10]

Tiny, dingy dives far outnumbered Harlem's swanky, expensive clubs. The NYPD estimated that Harlem had more than five hundred "colored cabarets of [the] lower ranks" in the late 1920s. It also had numerous "rat dives," sleazy saloons in basements. In the typical rat dive, the building's janitor ran the bar and sold corn liquor that he made himself. The basement booze had a reputation for being ultra strong. It drove "the drinker insane for an hour or two, then he passed out — dead to the world." A hangover from basement booze was reputed to be worse than the combined effect of reefers and absinthe.[11]

New York City had hundreds of dives called "hideaway speakeasies" where a man could knock back a few while being entertained by a hostess (AKA prostitute). The Committee of Fourteen, a watchdog group, reported that hideaway speakeasies "thickly dotted" Harlem and Yorkville. Unscrupulous cops demanded bribes from the hostesses and arrested those who didn't pay up. The shakedowns made the hideaway speakeasy "the largest single source of income of graft-seeking policemen."[12]

Members of the Committee of Fourteen visited speakeasies, purely for research purposes, of course. Based on their observations, the committee issued a report comparing the American hostess to the Japanese geisha. "The hostess of the nightclub and speakeasy is the American counterpart of the geisha girl," the report stated. "She is employed for the main purpose of increasing the sales of liquor, food, and other drinks; incidentally she is to provide esthetic, social, and sexual entertainment for the men customers. Her sex appeal largely accounts for her success."[13]

The Speakeasy Sting

From time to time, usually in response to pressure from the dry faction, the federal Prohibition squad in New York City set out to actually enforce Volstead. The Prohis routinely gathered evidence by hanging out at speakeasies, which led to the arrest of petty Volstead criminals, like bartenders and waiters. This clogged the courts with penny-ante cases but had no discernible impact on the bootleg traffic. To seriously disrupt the liquor trade, the Prohis needed to nab the booze barons who actually ran it. That required getting the inside dope straight from the guys in the know. The Prohis hit upon a novel scheme for gaining access to Gotham's bootleg bosses. If they opened a speakeasy, they could buy hooch directly from the bootleggers, collect evidence against them, and send them to prison. It was a great idea! It couldn't fail.

In Washington the chief Prohibition investigator approved the operation, and Bruce Bielaski, a special undercover agent, was chosen to head the task force in NYC. The feds rented space in a building on East 44th Street and paid a contractor to turn it into a comfortable, inviting speakeasy. They bought liquor, hired a staff, and went to Brooks Brothers to buy alpaca coats for the bartenders. Then they opened the redundantly-named Bridge Whist Club.

In the tradition of the old-time saloon, the feds' speakeasy offered a free lunch when the customer bought a beer. This proved to be immensely popular, and the place soon had loyal lunch patrons who returned at night. The Bridge Whist Club did "a roaring business at all hours of the day and night," according to a magazine article.[14]

The Prohis expected their bar to be a conduit to Gotham's major-league leggers. The undercover agents/barkeeps would make contact with the guys who sold the booze, gain their confidence, and learn about their racket. The liquor lords would drop in to check out the action, and the Prohis would subtly question them. To record conversations that could be used as evidence, the feds equipped the speakeasy with hidden, cutting-edge audio equipment (AKA Dictaphones).

The Prohis' ace agents were ready to snare big game, but they got off to a slow start. The agents/barkeeps dealt with mob underlings, mostly the clerks who took orders for booze and the truck drivers who delivered it. They needed time to cultivate those sources and gain access to the liquor lords. While they worked on using the lackeys as conduits, they made a decision that seemed logical but ultimately derailed the operation. Whenever a liquor delivery truck parked outside the club, the undercover agents alerted fellow Prohis, who quickly confiscated it. In fact, the Prohis seized so many trucks that the Bridge Whist Club got a bad rep in the underworld, and wary mobsters shunned it. In six months the feds' foolproof sting netted only one notable arrest, a mid-level bootlegger.

To cut its losses, the Prohibition squad decided to abort the operation. Bielaski sold the speakeasy, complete with its liquor inventory, at a fire-sale price. When news of the feds' fiasco leaked out, the Prohis took heat from all sides. The wets railed because Bielaski's task force had wasted nearly $45,000 of taxpayer money on a ruse that failed. The dry activists deplored the duplicity and criminality of the operation. They didn't want anybody selling liquor for any reason — even to catch bootleggers![15]

A Padlock on the Front Door

In the early 1920s law enforcement relied heavily on raids to close speakeasies and discourage people from opening new ones. By the mid–Twenties it was obvious that raids couldn't deliver the knockout punch because speakeasies simply restocked their bars and reopened after being raided. But law enforcement had other options for crippling the speakeasy sector. Padlocking was a legal action that could be used to close a public nuisance or illicit business temporarily or permanently. A padlock on a speakeasy's front door did more than shutter the business. It was a visible symbol of the government's power as well as a warning that there were substantial penalties for defying the dry law.

Predictably, wets and drys had different opinions about padlocks. Dry activists applauded padlocking and advocated wide usage of it to close saloons, distilleries, and breweries. But wets and civil libertarians worried about its overuse and abuse. Watchdog groups claimed that overzealous Volstead enforcers were padlocking legitimate businesses merely on suspicion of dry law violations. The critics pointed to drugstores and eateries that had been padlocked without hard evidence of illegal liquor sales. They accused officials of ignoring the legal rights of the citizens who owned those businesses. They argued that padlocks had a chilling effect on the retail sector and left honest workers without jobs.

In some jurisdictions, the courts had leeway to order "partial padlocking" to reduce the negative financial impact on a business that did more than sell liquor. When such a business was padlocked, only the part violating Volstead was closed. Thus, if a restaurant had a bar, the bar could be padlocked while the dining room remained open for business.

The Arid Era's most aggressive padlocking crusade took place in New York City in 1925-26. Emory Buckner, U.S. Attorney for the Southern District of New York, led the charge. Policy makers in Washington approved Buckner's padlock campaign and gave him the funds to form his own task force. He assembled an expert staff of top Prohibition agents to conduct investigations and lawyers to do the legal work. Across the USA, government officials watched Buckner's crusade to see if padlocks could be the key to fully implementing the dry law.[16]

Buckner expected padlocking to succeed because it targeted the wallets of the speakeasy operator, the employees, and the property owner. A shuttered speakeasy meant financial loss to everyone making money from the business. When the operator's cash cow dried up, he would be forced to find another way to make a living. The employees would lose their jobs and look for work elsewhere. The property owner would lose his rental income for months while he took legal action to evict his tenant and have the padlock removed. As more and more bars were padlocked, a ripple effect would spread across the city. Landlords would stop renting to speakeasies because they didn't want their property padlocked. Workers wouldn't take jobs in illegal liquor outlets because their paychecks might abruptly stop. The entire sector would be crippled.

With admirable vigor, Buckner set out to turn the Big Apple into a desert. He decided to use his own special squad to collect evidence, bypassing both the NYPD and NYC's federal Prohibition unit. Thus, he could be sure the evidence was collected properly and wasn't lost or tainted. After his squad gathered proof of liquor sales at a given address, his office would petition the court for an injunction, which would allow lawmen to padlock the place as a public nuisance. This would close the illegal liquor outlet for up to one year.[17]

Buckner's predecessors had tried using padlocks, with lackluster results. When he took over the U.S. attorney's office, he found a backlog of roughly four hundred padlock cases waiting to go to court. Some had been pending for up to two years. New York law allowed owners to keep their businesses open until they had their day in court, so they were in no hurry to go to trial. To correct the time-lag problem, Buckner persuaded the district court to establish a "special padlock court" that would devote one week per month to padlocking cases. He estimated that this special court would process up to fifty padlock cases per day, thereby ensuring speedy trials.[18]

Buckner launched his grand offensive with fanfare and headlines trumpeting the new era in Volstead enforcement. With surprising speed, he started court proceedings against more than one thousand liquor outlets. He targeted upscale clubs and speakeasies, rather than blue-collar saloons. By focusing on the high end of the sector, he hoped to stigmatize public drinking and persuade the upper classes to shun speakeasies. He wanted to remind drinkers that they were supporting a criminal venture that turned crooks into millionaires. Red-carpet speakeasies might be posh, but they were owned by criminals not far removed from pickpockets or safecrackers.[19]

Within two months Buckner padlocked fourteen of the Big Apple's busiest, most popular upscale speakeasies. For the most part, the proprietors decided it was smarter to bargain than fight. Nearly all consented to be padlocked after negotiating a short closure of a few weeks or months and signing an agreement to never again sell alcohol. Some speakeasy owners escaped even a short closure by putting up a bond to ensure future compliance with the dry law.[20]

In thirteen months Buckner padlocked more than five hundred illegal liquor outlets. Despite these closures, Gotham's drinkers found plenty of public watering holes. For every club Buckner closed, another seemed to spring up. *The New Yorker* noted that "each day brings new victims of Buckner's spies" along with new speakeasies. "The bigger the batch of places padlocked one month, the bigger is sure to be the hatch of their successors the next month."[21]

Speakeasy owners found ways to survive despite a padlock on the front door. After being padlocked some speaks quickly reopened at a new location, prompting *Variety* to say that the owners moved their clubs around like pieces in a game of Checkers. Proprietors who chose to stay put used various ploys. More than one ignored the padlock on his front door and let his customers in through the backdoor. At least one cut a hole in the front wall and made a new door next to the padlocked portal. Ironically, bar owners found that a padlock could be an asset because New Yorkers loved to thumb their collective nose at the dry law.

Although Buckner's padlocking binge didn't stop New Yorkers from going to illegal oases, it did change their options by reducing the number of glitzy red-carpet speakeasies. Barkeepers feared the financial costs of a padlock and closure, so they took steps to lower their expenses. When they opened new places, they focused on turning a quick profit. They spent frugally on décor and amenities because their investment might be lost. Small speaks in out-of-the-way places became the hot, new trend.

To protect their investment, speakeasy owners beefed up security to weed out undesirable guests. Cautious owners began to require their customers to call ahead to make a reservation. Doormen became more vigilant and more selective. Speakeasies regularly changed their buzz words and issued new membership cards. The tighter security created an aura of exclusivity that patrons enjoyed. A drinker felt a certain pride when the keeper of the Judas hole let him join the coterie in the inner sanctum.

Although U.S. Attorney Buckner pursued his padlocking crusade with uncommon resolve and energy, he wasn't satisfied with the results. By mid–1926 he had doubts about the viability of Prohibition. No matter how many speakeasies he padlocked, Satan's Seat never suffered a shortage of them. The consumer's demand for liquor showed no signs of shrinking. Maybe Volstead simply couldn't be enforced. The crusading attorney had a momentous change of mind; he joined the moderates who wanted to reform the dry law to give drinkers more choices. He argued that modifying Volstead to permit the sale of beer and light wines would be the best solution for New York City.[22]

After two years of frustrating attempts to dry up Gotham, Buckner needed a change and resigned from public service to work in the private sector. When he left, federal officials abolished his special investigative unit. The new U.S. Attorney for the Southern District announced that his staff would eschew detective work and focus on litigation. His office would not initiate Volstead investigations and wouldn't "supersede or replace any other departments or bureaus." The federal Prohibition director for NYC said his squad would work on stopping the supply of booze "at its source" and would give the responsibility for closing speakeasies to the local authorities.[23]

Since the NYPD generally ignored illegal saloons, speakeasy owners breathed easier. Padlocks might not disappear, but there surely would be fewer of them.

Pass the Buck, Please!

Gotham's barkeepers enjoyed the respite from padlocking, but they heard rumors of a new crusade when Maurice Campbell took over as the federal Prohibition administrator for New York in mid–1927. A relative newcomer to law enforcement, Campbell had pursued varied careers, including veterinarian, war correspondent, magazine publisher, press agent, and theatrical producer. He had also directed silent movies with suggestive titles, including "One Wild Week," "The Speed Girl," and "She Couldn't Help It."[24]

A dedicated dry, Campbell truly believed in the Volstead law and intended to enforce it. Prohibition agents routinely bought and drank liquor to collect evidence, but Campbell abhorred this practice. He formed a "padlock squad" of ten federal agents who would "do all the drinking to be done by the entire force" that worked under him. He vowed to summarily dismiss any other agent caught taking even a sip of booze. The padlock squad would visit speakeasies to collect evidence, but only on Campbell's orders. The agents would not "snoop around on their own initiative." Due to limited manpower, Campbell's unit would focus on padlocking the most popular drinking places — "the most flagrant violators of the resort class, the sore spots which are flashed continuously before the public eye."[25]

Despite Campbell's good intentions, his padlock crusade produced meager results. Then an influx of help from Washington added impetus to Volstead enforcement in New York City. In June 1928 the Prohis staged a splashy sweep in of raids in the Big Apple, invading twenty popular red-carpet speakeasies in one night.

Assistant U.S. Attorney General Mabel Willebrandt, a workaholic known for her attention to detail, personally planned the operation. To lay the foundation for the raids, she transferred twelve federal agents from other districts to New York City, where they weren't known to the liquor traffickers. These agents, "posing as wealthy men of leisure," visited the speakeasies Willebrandt planned to raid. They became regular customers, spending freely and getting to know the staff. After only a few visits, the speakeasy managers knew them as valued, trusted customers.[26]

On the night of the raids, a force of one hundred-plus lawmen assembled at federal Prohibition headquarters in NYC. To prevent news of the impending raids from leaking out, they were sequestered and couldn't use the telephones. Willebrandt knew that prosecutors often lost Volstead cases because the courts rejected the evidence collected in raids. To avoid this, she issued strict orders about collecting and preserving the evidence. Shortly after midnight, the dry sleuths divided into small squads and went to the speakeasies, where they posed as customers and bought liquor.

In each club, at the appointed time, a well-dressed man strode onto the dance floor, ordered the band to stop playing, and called for everyone's attention. In a no-nonsense voice, he declared that he was a Prohibition agent. "This place is now in the hands of the federal government," he said. "All guests must leave at once. Pay your checks before you go!"[27]

Willebrandt had targeted some of the city's busiest speakeasies, including Texas Guinan's Salon Royal, the Summer Home, the Blue Hour, Mimic, the Silver Slipper, Beaux Arts, the Ferndale Club, Frivolity, and Luigi's Restaurant. After clearing the guests out of the clubs, the agents collected and labeled the evidence. They interrogated dozens of workers, mostly waiters and bartenders. The lawmen arrested more than one hundred people and detained them at a police station for several hours until they could be arraigned.

To eliminate the standard time gap between raiding a club and closing it, the Prohis used temporary padlock orders to shutter the speakeasies. Government attorneys had obtained the orders before the raids even began. Lawyers for the closed clubs moved quickly to rescind the temporary orders. They argued that the padlocks were illegal because the speakeasy owners hadn't had their day in court and hadn't been found guilty of anything. Thus, they had been deprived of due process. A federal judge agreed that the temporary padlocks were illegal and ordered their removal.[28]

Both the prosecutors and the defendants began preparing for the upcoming trials. The Prohibition agents gave sworn affidavits about their undercover forays to the speakeasies before the raids. One agent stated that he had taken his wife to the Summer Home on several occasions and had also gone there with another federal agent. He had purchased whiskey, champagne, and other beverages, paying up to $15 per pint for the liquor. On two visits to the Silver Slipper, he had spent over $300 for food and drink. At Texas Guinan's Salon Royal, an agent had paid $141 for champagne, whiskey, and a cover charge. Other agents gave affidavits showing that they had also run up big tabs at speakeasies.

Based on the agents' expense reports and other data, the press estimated that the Prohis had spent a whopping $75,000 at the speakeasies. Both wets and drys were outraged because the agents had enjoyed costly food and drink at taxpayers' expense. In Washington the federal Prohibition commissioner tried to deflect the criticism. He said that the media's cost estimate was vastly inflated, and he put the total expenditure at roughly $9,000. Almost no one believed his number. The agents' own affidavits proved that they had gone on a boozy spending spree with tax dollars.[29]

The owners of the raided speakeasies had a choice: fight the padlocking action in court or accept a padlock without a trial. Even if the owner agreed to have his business padlocked, New York law limited the closure to no more than one year. The workers arrested in the raids could expedite matters by pleading guilty, but the vast majority chose to plead not guilty and go to trial. No matter which option the defendant chose, the punishment was light. The typical guilty defendant paid a small fine and was sentenced to a short, suspended jail term.[30]

Despite consuming much manpower and money, Willebrandt's June raids didn't catch even one major-league bootlegger. Although the raiders arrested speakeasy employees who played a vital role in the liquor traffic, the workers were minor cogs in a big machine. The press criticized the Prohis' speakeasy sweep as a waste of taxpayer money. An editorial said, "The raids do not touch the sources of supply. The gigantic traffic goes on, known to everybody."[31]

The visiting agents left Gotham after the June raids, so Campbell had to cope with his usual manpower shortage. In December 1928 a court decision promised to infuse new life into his padlock campaign, and he quickly seized the opportunity. The New York State Court of Appeals ruled that a speakeasy was subject to closure as a public nuisance under state statute. Campbell embraced this ruling as a way to use state and local law enforcement in his crusade. His staff was too small and the federal courts too busy to padlock all the speakeasies: state and local lawmen could do it.

Campbell envisioned a massive padlock drive in Gotham, with the NYPD doing most of the work. To get the ball rolling, he bundled up hundreds of complaints against speakeasies and sent them to NYC Police Commissioner Grover Aloysius Whalen. In effect, he told Whalen to buy padlocks and get busy. "If the police make raids and the several magistrates and district attorneys conscientiously do their duty," Campbell stated, "the speakeasies in New York will rapidly fade away."[32]

Alas, Commissioner Whalen did not embrace Campbell's grand plan. In fact, Whalen accused Campbell of shirking his duties: Volstead was a federal law and the Prohis must enforce it. The commissioner said his department didn't have the manpower or the resources to close Gotham's speakeasies. Using the NYPD to do the feds' work would require five thousand more police officers and an additional appropriation of $15 million per year. It was ludicrous to suggest that the city could afford such a costly crusade.

Whalen returned the bundle of complaints to Campbell with a letter saying that he would not allow NYPD officers to be used as Prohibition agents. Sounding snippy, he wrote, "If you are unwilling to discharge your sworn obligations to the federal government or wish to make a confession of your inability to effectively direct the activities of your department ... the admission should be made primarily to your superiors in Washington, instead of 'passing the buck' to the state law-enforcing officers."[33]

For months Campbell and Whalen engaged in a spirited verbal feud over Volstead enforcement in Satan's Seat. Commissioner Whalen declared there had been a "complete breakdown of the federal Prohibition machinery" in the city. He claimed that the NYPD initiated ninety-three percent of the Volstead cases in the southern and eastern districts of New York State. In his opinion, the inept Prohis were looking on while the NYPD did the heavy lifting.[34]

Campbell shot back, accusing both city and state officials of ignoring the dry law. He said, "Today, so far as state and city authorities are concerned, anyone can sell liquor whenever they like and to whomsoever they like. As a state and city, New York today has less prohibition than it had before federal Prohibition...." He urged city officials to crack down on speakeasies as a general crime-fighting tactic because the illegal bars nurtured disrespect for the law in all segments of society.[35]

NYPD Commissioner Whalen stated that the federal Prohibition enforcers were supposed to prevent liquor from entering the United States. Therefore, Campbell and other top Prohis "could settle the controversy by stopping at the border the illegal transportation of liquor which makes the speakeasies possible." If the Prohis did their job, illegal bars would close due to lack of booze. "Stop the liquor and there will be no speakeasies," Whalen said. "It is a function of the federal government in which the New York City police can only assist and for which they are not responsible."[36]

Other New York officials sided with Commissioner Whalen. Mayor Walker accused the federal Prohibition unit "of total lack of cooperation with the city" when it came to enforcing Volstead. Congressman Fiorello LaGuardia advised Campbell to "attend to his own business" as a federal official. District Attorney Joab Banton said, "If Mr. Campbell would talk less and work more, he would be a better Prohibition administrator."[37]

Although Campbell failed to get help from the city government, he didn't give up right away. He continued to argue that city officials should use the state nuisance statute to close the speakeasies. "A dirty city is a dirty city," he said, "and you can't expect Washington to clean up the streets of New York."[38] NYC officials seemed to think Gotham's streets were clean enough.

When Campbell finally realized that he would never persuade city officials to join his padlock crusade, he quietly dropped it to pursue other, equally futile ways of enforcing Volstead. Dens of liquid iniquity thrived in the Big Apple.

9. New York's Big Three: The Best of the Worst

The greatest single menace in the United States today is the Prohibition law. This is the most lawless country on the face of the earth, and Prohibition is the largest single factor in that condition. — Judge Alfred J. Tolley, Court of General Sessions, New York[1]

During the Great Drought, New York City supported an astounding number of bootleggers. As in all lines of work, a few of the leggers stood out as particularly smart, or ambitious, or charismatic. The strongest among them fought their way to the top, emerging as liquor lords who commanded battalions of mob soldiers. The bosses who controlled Gotham's illegal liquor traffic wielded vast power and made millions of dollars. When they fought for supremacy, violence and bloodshed rocked the underworld.

Gang wars and mob hits destabilized the criminal balance of power in New York during Prohibition. The reign of a mob boss was likely to be a short one, ending with a violent coup d'état. Nevertheless, beer barons Owney Madden, Dutch Schultz, and Waxy Gordon outlasted Prohibition. Shortly before the Great Drought ended, the *New York Times* called Madden, Schultz, and Gordon "the big three of the bootlegging era" in Gotham. The chief of the Treasury Department's Special Intelligence Unit didn't completely agree with that assessment. He called Schultz and Gordon "the men who owned the New York City underworld."[2]

Schultz, Madden, and Gordon had much in common. Each began his criminal career before Prohibition but reached the height of his power during the Arid Era. All three were born in poverty, spent little time in school, and became petty criminals before they were old enough to shave. They developed street smarts and keen survival instincts. They had the sociopath's deep cynicism about human nature and a profound distrust of mankind. Despite their similarities, each man had distinctive qualities that set him apart from the pack. Both Schultz and Madden had good business instincts and could have succeeded in lawful enterprises. Schultz, who appeared to have a high IQ, was more cerebral than the average gangster. Madden could be ruthless, but he was also charming, likeable, well mannered, and smooth. Gordon didn't have Schultz's intellect or Madden's finesse. He depended heavily on violence and brutality to get what he wanted. He seemed to function without a code of honor or a sense of ethics. In a profession without principles, he showed even less integrity than his peers.

Slightly below the big three on the mob ladder, Meyer Lansky and Lucky Luciano were street punks who became underworld superstars during Prohibition. Lansky was only seventeen years old when Volstead began, but he already had plans for building his own crime syndicate. Luciano was a cocky upstart with nothing but contempt for the old-style Italian mob bosses, derisively called "Moustache Petes." Luciano shared Lansky's vision of a modern mob that operated like a large corporation, wielding absolute power in the underworld. The restless young duo would play seminal roles in the rise of organized crime dominated by the Mafia. They warily coexisted with the old guard while waiting for the right moment to take over.

Owney the Killer

When Owen "Owney" Madden was born, only a truly gifted fortuneteller could have foreseen his future wealth and power. He survived grueling poverty, rose from two-bit hood to liquor lord, made millions, and died of natural causes. He even claimed the grand prize for immigrant mobsters: U.S. citizenship. During Prohibition, he owned speakeasies and a brewery, marketed his own brand of beer, managed prizefighters, and gambled for high stakes. Although he rarely talked to reporters or posed for news photographs, he became a gangland celebrity with a national reputation. Crime writers dubbed him "Owney the Killer," due to his involvement in high-profile shootings.

Madden was born in Leeds, England, in 1892. Although some crime writers label him an Irish mobster, he was a native-born Englishman. His parents were also born in Leeds, and both sets of his grandparents emigrated from Ireland to England. Owney's father, who worked as a cloth dresser in a flax mill, died at a young age. After his death, Owney's mother immigrated to New York and found work as a domestic. She left her children in England until she could earn enough money for their passage. Owney and his brother lived in an orphanage in Leeds until she sent for them and their sister in 1902.[3]

Mrs. Madden and her brood lived with her widowed sister in Hell's Kitchen, a tenement district in Manhattan. No doubt, Mrs. Madden dreamed of making a comfortable home for her children, but her meager wages barely put food on the table. Madden told a close friend, actor George Raft, that he began stealing soon after his arrival in New York. One day he went shopping with his mother, who was buying food from pushcarts on the street. She carried the groceries in a cloth bag as they walked home. A thief came up from behind, with a quick slash cut the string handles on the bag, and ran off with the food.

"You know, Georgie, when I saw what that kid got away with and how easy it was, I decided I was a sap not to do it myself," Madden said. "And I did. I was on the wrong side from there on."[4]

In choosing a life of crime, Madden followed in the footsteps of other poor boys in Hell's Kitchen. It was a noisy, sooty neighborhood with the Ninth Avenue el rattling overhead. Horrific accidents were common where the heavy train, car, and horse traffic converged on Eleventh Avenue, called "Death Avenue" by the locals. The area had many slaughterhouses and dingy saloons along the riverfront. The men who worked in the abattoirs handled knives with lethal precision, so knife fights settled disputes in the saloons and the back alleys.

Hell's Kitchen offered few good opportunities for adolescent males. The most enter-

Government storerooms held confiscated goods, such as these bags of sugar, jars of grain, and boxes of fruit jars intended for use in moonshining (Library of Congress).

prising youngsters hawked newspapers or worked as errand boys to earn pocket change. For recreation, the boys went swimming in the Hudson River or raised pigeons in coops on tenement rooftops. Raising a flock of Nun's Cap, Budapest Tiplitz, Hollanders, or another fancy breed gave the owner a great deal of prestige. As an adolescent, Madden found that he had a talent for breeding pigeons, and his flock became famous among bird hobbyists, even outside Hell's Kitchen.

Teenage boys commonly joined gangs, banding together for social and criminal pursuits. Madden joined the Gopher Gang, a notorious neighborhood mob that terrorized the law-abiding populace. The Gophers (pronounced "goofers"), who often fought with the rival Hudson Dusters, had a particularly violent track record. In addition to fighting outsiders, the Gophers fought amongst themselves, sometimes even to the point of death.

When the Gophers weren't fighting, they specialized in burglary, often looting railcars in the West Side train yards. Freight trains carried virtually every type of commodity, so the boxcars were a magnet for thieves. Young Madden made a name for himself as a daring, cunning thief who feared nothing. He led the Gophers as they broke into freight cars and outfoxed the railroad guards, who were reputed to be more aggressive and rougher than the NYPD.

Madden didn't confine his misdeeds to the railroad freight yards. He excelled at the criminal arts of sneak thievery, home burglary, and the stick-up. He also became proficient at extorting money from the owners of small businesses. His illicit talents so impressed his peers that he quickly rose to the top of the Gopher heap. Before he was twenty-one years old, the Gophers had become "Owney Madden's gang" in newspaper reports.[5]

A dapper dresser, Madden had blue eyes, sandy brown hair, and the slender, sleek physique that young men coveted in his era. Although he didn't look like a beefy street brawler, he relished fighting. With remarkable skill, he wielded the tools of gangland: the revolver, blackjack, slingshot, brass knuckles, and a lead pipe wrapped in newspaper. After a decade of gang crime, his rap sheet had numerous arrests but only four convictions — three for disorderly conduct and one for possessing burglars' tools. He did no prison time for these minor offenses.[6]

According to mob lore, Madden earned his nickname Owney the Killer by committing several murders while still in his teens. He probably committed his first murder at the tender age of fourteen when he used a heavy metal pipe to bludgeon a shopkeeper to death. Eyewitnesses saw him discard the murder weapon and run away. He was arrested, but the witnesses would not testify against him in court, so he escaped punishment.

At age eighteen, Madden shot and killed a member of the Hudson Dusters gang. He encountered the rival gangster on a street corner, pulled out his gun, and calmly squeezed the trigger. Witnesses saw Madden commit the cold-blooded murder, so the police arrested him. The prosecutor's office seemed to have more than enough evidence to convict him. However, before the case went to trial, key witnesses disappeared. Others refused to testify. The state's case fell apart, and Madden walked free.[7]

At age nineteen, Owney the Killer shot a romantic rival who dared to court a young lady Madden fancied. Owney spotted his competitor with the young woman at a streetcar stop, boarding a trolley. In a fit of jealousy Madden drew his revolver, thrust it through the bars of the streetcar gate, and shot his rival. Owney ran away before the police arrived, but eyewitnesses could identify him. Moreover, as the wounded man lay dying, he told a policeman that Madden had shot him.

For more than a week, detectives searched for Madden with no luck. Then, acting on a tip, they staked out an apartment building where they believed he was hiding. When he walked out the front door, he spotted them and took off running. The lawmen chased after him for blocks. The foot race ended when Madden ducked into a shack and barricaded himself in. The police surrounded the shanty, fought their way in, grabbed Madden, and took him into custody. When the case went to court, it was the same old story: the charges were dismissed because crucial witnesses wouldn't testify against Owney the Killer.[8]

One night in November 1912 the Gophers and their women were partying at the Arbor Dance Hall. It was a social occasion, so no trouble was expected. Madden escorted his wife to the upstairs balcony for a breath of fresh air. When she went downstairs to talk to a friend, he stayed on the balcony. The party was in full swing; Madden was relaxed and laid back. Suddenly he found himself surrounded by rival gangsters. As the band downstairs played a lively turkey trot, the men edged closer to him and drew their guns. He protested that he didn't have a weapon, but he would gladly fight if they gave him one.

The men closed in on Madden, aiming their guns at him. He stood his ground, practically daring them to shoot. They opened fire. Downstairs, the guests heard the gunshots;

the dancing and the raucous music abruptly ceased. The gunmen dashed down the stairs and out the door. Partygoers rushed upstairs, where they found Madden with blood spilling out of his abdomen. His wife knelt by his side, trying to comfort him. The partygoers hollered for the police, who ran to the scene from the nearby stationhouse.

On the way to the hospital, Madden's wife watched helplessly as he lost more blood. She wept when the doctor told her that Owney would surely die. The doctors removed several bullets from his body but decided not to extract all of them. The surgery was risky, and death seemed inevitable.

Despite the grim prognosis, Madden survived. The hospital staff marveled at his resilience as he grew stronger day by day. He acquired a new nickname—"Clay Pigeon." Gangland gossip said the Hudson Dusters had shot him, but he wouldn't confirm that. Obeying the code of silence, he refused to answer police questions about the attack. He preferred to let gangland justice run its bloody course. His buddies swore they would get revenge and hit the streets. Within a week, three prime suspects were shot, stabbed, or bludgeoned to death.[9]

Madden's top priority was regaining his health, but that wasn't the only thing he had to worry about. A former Gopher named Patsy Doyle was trying to take control of the gang. Doyle had a reputation as a crazed, bloodthirsty killer. He believed he could take over the Gophers while Madden was disabled, and he spread a rumor that Owney would be permanently crippled, a weakling unable to lead the gang. A faction of discontented goofers lined up with Doyle, ready to follow him as their new boss.

The Madden loyalists clashed with the malcontents. Profanity-laced shouting matches, fisticuffs, and rumbles added to the noisy chaos in Hell's Kitchen. Mayhem ruled the mean streets of gangland. A man attacked Patsy Doyle with a blackjack and left him lying unconscious in the street. Doyle survived and retaliated by stabbing one of Madden's closest pals, who suffered nonfatal wounds. Doyle was indicted for the knife attack, and the case followed the usual pattern. The stabbing victim didn't show up to testify in the courtroom, so the prosecution failed to convict Doyle.[10]

When Madden regained his full strength, he reasserted his control of the Gophers and resumed his criminal pursuits. In a curious case, he was arrested on burglary charges—specifically, pigeon rustling. One morning a poultry dealer found that someone had broken into his shop overnight. Two hundred pigeons valued at $1,000 were missing. The police immediately suspected Madden, but he swore he was innocent. He even offered to help the poultry man recover the lost birds. Nevertheless, the police arrested Madden for pigeon rustling, and he went on trial in a magistrate's court. Once again, he was acquitted. He suspected that wannabe mob boss Doyle had stolen the birds to frame him. He loudly accused Doyle of being a vile rat who cozied up to the police.[11]

A few weeks after the fowl episode, Madden sent his henchmen into a saloon where Doyle was hanging out. Madden waited on the street while his men confronted Doyle and shot the wannabe gang boss at close range. Despite his wounds, Doyle stumbled thru the saloon door onto the sidewalk, where he collapsed and died an ignominious death, sprawled in the gutter. Madden stood on the street corner, calmly smoking a cigarette as he watched his rival gasp his last breath.[12]

Although Madden didn't shoot Doyle, the district attorney believed he had planned the murder. A grand jury indicted the gang boss along with two of his henchmen for murder in the first degree. The state decided on separate trials for the trio. When Madden went on trial, the chief witnesses against him were two young women. A writer described them as gang molls or "camp followers — the flashy, paint and powder-dyed women of blatant laughter" who date gangsters. One woman testified that she hadn't witnessed the murder but Madden had told her he ordered the hit on Doyle. The other camp follower knew both Doyle and Madden intimately. She had been Doyle's girlfriend but left him to become Madden's paramour only days before the shooting. She stated that Owney the Killer had spent weeks planning Doyle's murder. When a lawyer asked her why she was testifying against Madden, she claimed her religion motivated her to tell the truth. "Because I wanted to go to Holy Communion on Easter Sunday and knew I could not go to confession without relieving my mind of the knowledge I had of Madden's connection with the murder of Patsy Doyle," she said.[13]

Madden's defense attorneys called several witnesses to establish an alibi for him. His sister, his button men, and even his barber claimed he couldn't have been at the shooting. The barber said that he had spent well over an hour cutting Madden's thick mane of sandy brown hair that evening. Other witnesses stated that the gang boss had suffered stomach pains and spent part of the evening at a hospital. Madden's henchmen who had also been indicted for Doyle's murder testified for their boss. Both denied that Madden had ordered them to shoot his rival.[14]

Madden took the stand to defend himself but proved to be less than the ideal witness. He became furious during cross-examination when the assistant D.A. caught him in a lie. He exploded and jumped up to leave the witness stand. Court attendants reacted quickly, grabbing him to restrain him. He struggled to break free, but they held onto him.

"For what I'm getting here, I might as well plead guilty. I'm not getting a fair chance!" Madden yelled. "You might as well take me out and kill me and have it over with!"

Madden refused to answer any more questions, so he was taken to the Tombs to cool off. Later that same day he returned to the witness stand and answered the assistant D.A.'s questions for nearly three hours. This time he stayed calm, but the jurors had already seen his hot temper.

The jury found Madden guilty of manslaughter in the first degree. When he heard the verdict, he smiled because he had escaped a first-degree murder conviction, which could've sent him to the electric chair. But he didn't smile when the judge handed him a tough sentence, sending him to Sing Sing state prison for ten to twenty years.[15]

After spending a few months in prison, Madden petitioned for a new trial, claiming he had been framed. Several witnesses, including the two camp followers, told the court they wanted to recant their testimony. Madden's gangster pals, confident that he would get a retrial, extorted money from businesses in Hell's Kitchen to pay for it. They also blackmailed "young men who frequented Broadway resorts" and feared "exposure to their employers."

To Madden's shock and dismay, the court denied his motion for a new trial. "The newly discovered evidence consists entirely in the statements of the people's witnesses impeaching and discrediting themselves and their testimony," the judge said. He deplored "the ease with which state witnesses may come into court and recant testimony in order to undo the conviction of criminals."[16]

Petition denied!

A Broadway Legend

Owney the Killer was paroled in 1923 after spending roughly seven years in prison. While he marked time behind bars, gangland changed. When he got home to Hell's Kitchen, he found that his old gang had broken up. Some of his Gopher minions were incarcerated; some had joined other mobs; some had been killed. The Volstead law had brought momentous change to gangland, opening up new career paths for ambitious young hoods. Like many guys his age, Madden embarked on a career in liquor trafficking. He began on a relatively small scale, stealing pre–Volstead liquor to be cut and repackaged.

In December 1923 Madden and two other men robbed a bonded liquor warehouse in New York City. After binding and gagging the elderly watchman, they stole two hundred cases of whiskey. NYC police caught up with the thieves as they made their getaway. After a car chase through the theatre district, the cops arrested the men. Like so many other Volstead cases, this one never went to trial.[17]

Only weeks after robbing the warehouse, Madden was in police custody again. State troopers arrested six men for stealing a large cache of pre–Volstead liquor from a country estate in Stockbridge, Massachusetts. When the troopers nabbed the men, they were driving a truckload of the stolen booze through Westchester County, New York. Madden gave an alias to the police, but they used his fingerprints to identify him. Two of the liquor thieves were extradited to Massachusetts; the others, including Madden, were held in New York on charges of receiving stolen goods.

At Madden's arraignment, he claimed that he had met the thieves more or less by accident. He was hitchhiking, and the truck driver stopped to pick him up. He was shocked when he learned that the truck was carrying stolen liquor. As improbable as this tale sounded, Madden managed to wiggle off the hook again.[18]

The New York County district attorney, outraged because Madden wasn't obeying the terms of his parole, wanted to send Owney the Killer back to the slammer. The D.A. wrote a letter to the state superintendent of prisons, arguing that Madden had violated his parole simply by associating with known bootleggers. The D.A. demanded that Madden be taken into custody to serve the remainder of his ten-to-twenty years for manslaughter. Despite Madden's repeated arrests, the parole board declined to act on the D.A.'s suggestion.[19]

Madden's initial, small-scale ventures in bootlegging showed him how lucrative illegal liquor could be. He wanted to play with the big boys, but a major obstacle stood in his way. To operate on a grand scale, he needed substantial capital. According to mob lore, he caught a lucky break: "Big Bill" Dwyer, the Czar of Rum Row, heard about Madden's post-prison exploits. The two men had grown up on the same street and knew one another by reputation but had never met face-to-face. The czar granted Madden an audience, and the two West Siders felt an instant rapport. Dwyer readily agreed to provide the seed money for Madden's new ventures.

A New York newspaper printed another account of Madden's post-prison rise, calling it "a Broadway legend." After leaving Sing Sing, Madden took a job as a strong arm for bootlegger Larry Fay, who owned a taxi company. Fay controlled profitable cab stands along Broadway, and his taxis transported booze as well as people. Owney the Killer was eager to be in the driver's seat. Using the money and the connections he made working for Fay, he started his own business. Madden "gradually grew in power until he loomed head and shoulders above his former employer."[20]

Madden tried to create an image as a smooth businessman, rather than a crude mobster. Like other rich liquor lords, he wore custom-made suits and spent lavishly on his wardrobe. But he aspired to dress like a wealthy gentleman, rather than a flashy mob boss. His signature look was a gray fedora hat, a dark suit, a black shirt, white tie, and white gloves. It wasn't clear why he wore the gloves; maybe he was afraid of germs or didn't want to leave fingerprints. Maybe he was merely making a fashion statement.

As Madden built his illicit enterprises, he managed to avoid the long arm of the law. Despite his growing power in the liquor traffic, he had only one notable indictment in the last half of the Twenties. In 1928 he was accused of being a kingpin in a rum ring that sold liquor in the Theatre District, the Financial District, Brooklyn, and the Bronx as well as on Long Island. The ring also operated speakeasies on Midtown's West Side.

NYC policemen and special Treasury agents teamed up to bust the rum ring, which was selling up to $50,000 worth of booze each day. Early one morning the lawmen raided a garage where they found more than three thousand quarts of hard liquor and two trucks loaded with barrels of beer. The garage was located on 50th Street near the waterfront, which made it easy for rumrunners to transfer hooch from their boats to the building. The police arrested all the men working in the garage.

Leaving a few lawmen behind to guard the garage, the raiders moved on to the Bosch Magneto Building, where the rum ring had offices. They rushed upstairs and burst into an office suite, surprising the workers. The suite had typical office furnishings plus "six telephone instruments," each connected to a separate line. After arresting the workers, the raiders answered the phones to gather more information about the business. In a short time, the lawmen took eighty calls, all from buyers ordering liquor in case lots.

Madden was not arrested during the raids, but he was indicted as one of the bosses who ran the syndicate. When the case went to court, he was tried along with fourteen other defendants. During the trial, the evidence and testimony incriminated low-ranking members of the rum ring. The bosses had protected themselves and left their minions holding the bag. Madden was acquitted, once more evading justice.[21]

The Phoenix Rises

In 1924 Owney Madden expanded his illegal operations by becoming a brewer. He took over a block-long brick building in Manhattan and opened the Phoenix Bottling Company (later renamed the Phoenix Cereal Beverage Company). Before Volstead the building had housed the Clausen-Flanagan Brewery, a well-known beer maker. When Prohibition forced Clausen-Flanagan to stop making high-octane brew, the company switched to near beer but couldn't sell enough to stay solvent.

Owney the Killer used the Phoenix plant to make Madden's Number One, a potent amber sold by the bottle and the barrel. The Phoenix brewery operated with little secrecy, and its trucks rolled along the city streets delivering beer. Payoffs to lawmen and politicos gave Phoenix a certain amount of protection, but the plant didn't enjoy total immunity from raids. From time to time federal Prohibition agents invaded the brewery to shut it down. As a rule, these closures didn't last long. Madden relied on payoffs and clever legal maneuvers to reopen his plant right away.

In September 1926, federal Prohibition agents raided Phoenix and seized one hundred thirty thousand gallons of beer. Major Chester Mills, the federal Prohibition administrator for New York, had ordered the raid as part of a new crackdown. The Prohis didn't arrest anyone, but they shuttered the brewery and placed it under guard.[22] Madden lost money while the plant was idle, but past experience had taught him how to manipulate the legal system and keep his brewery in business.

The Phoenix's next major clash with the law didn't come until 1930. During a routine inspection, Prohibition agents discovered that Phoenix had a concealed loading platform and a pipeline leading from the brewery to a nearby warehouse. The Prohis suspected that high-voltage beer was moving through the line to the warehouse for bottling and storage. Madden's workers refused to cooperate when the Prohis tried to investigate the matter. As a result, New York's federal Prohibition office revoked Phoenix's de-alcoholization permit, which allowed the brewery to make real beer and then reduce the alcohol content to the legal level. Without a permit, the brewery was forced to close.[23]

Only weeks after the closure, federal officials investigated a rumor that Phoenix was back in business. A squad of Prohibition agents and an assistant U.S. attorney entered the Phoenix plant for a thorough search of the premises. Determined to find proof of criminal activity, they made their way through a confusing maze of passageways and dark stairways. They ran into false doors and found a spiral staircase that led nowhere. They hammered on walls, listening for sounds that might lead them to secret rooms. On the brewery's top floor they found a door that led to the adjoining five-story warehouse.

Beginning on the top floor of the warehouse, the Prohis searched each story, working their way down to the sub-basement. They found bags of hops and other beer-making supplies but no beer. In the sub-cellar they found a hoist for lifting barrels to the street level. A subterranean brick wall looked strange to them, so they broke through it and found huge vats, which appeared to be empty. However, when they opened a faucet connected to the vats, beer trickled out, and they were able to collect a small amount before the flow stopped. The Prohis heard noises upstairs and looked for the source. They found a dozen workers busy cleaning the premises. Since the cleaning crew wasn't making beer, the Prohis didn't arrest anyone.[24]

The raid produced no solid evidence against Madden, but federal officials were convinced that Phoenix was making illegal beer. Beginning in August 1930, the Prohis kept the Phoenix plant under close surveillance around the clock. They saw nothing out of the ordinary during the day, but at night they observed a great deal of suspicious activity. During the stakeout, the feds rented a room across the street from the brewery gates and stationed a special agent there. He saw NYC police enter the brewery and watched them driving the escort cars when convoys of beer trucks left the site. It appeared that Madden had rogue cops on his payroll.[25]

After nearly a year of surveillance, federal Prohibition agents raided the Phoenix brewery. They obtained a search warrant based on the fact that they could smell the aroma of beer around the site. To gain entrance to the brewery's main building, they smashed through thick double doors. They found fermenting vats, several thousand barrels, a complete bottling plant, and 30,000 gallons of real beer in storage tanks. (In the cellar they encountered a mystery — an aquarium with hundreds of fish. This baffled them because it had no obvious connection to making beer. They decided to leave it alone because they could think of no compelling reason to confiscate or destroy it.)

They found that the beer vats in the cellar were connected to lines leading to the sewer system. "A river of beer" was gushing into the sewer because workers had opened the valves while the Prohis were battering down the front doors. The agents arrested the workers and, using a milk bottle, collected a sample of the flowing beer. The Prohis also confiscated the beer in Phoenix's storage tanks along with the boilers, bottles, refrigerating equipment, yeast, delivery trucks, and other property.

Madden expected to sustain losses due to raids, but the Prohis inflicted more than average damage this time. They put Phoenix out of business by seizing the expensive brewing equipment as well as the beer. Madden wanted retribution. His legal team petitioned the court for redress, claiming that the Prohis had used an invalid search warrant based on a false premise. The warrant had been issued because Prohibition agents smelled beer while on surveillance outside the brewery. Madden's lawyers argued that the Prohis had smelled near beer, not the real stuff. No one could determine the alcohol content of a beer simply by sniffing it from a distance.[26]

The court agreed that the search warrant was invalid and ordered the government to return the Phoenix's beer and equipment to Madden. In response, the U.S. attorney's office filed a motion asking for a stay, but it was rejected. Although the court ordered the feds to return Madden's property, the U.S. attorney refused to do so because he still had options for appealing the order. Subsequently, the Circuit Court of Appeals, Second Circuit, ruled that the search warrant had been issued without probable cause and the confiscated property must be returned to Phoenix. But the feds weren't ready to give up, so they continued their appeals in the "sniffing case," as the press called it.[27]

During the legal proceedings against the Phoenix brewery, the state secured a padlock order to close it for one year. However, this order couldn't be executed as long as the courts were considering the appeals. For nearly two years, a series of legal actions kept the sniffing case in the court system and left the padlocking order in limbo. As a result, the brewery was never padlocked. Madden replaced his confiscated equipment and had the brewery back in operation, producing illegal suds, well before Prohibition ended. The sniffing case finally became irrelevant when the dry law was modified to legalize beer in 1933.[28]

Shortly after beer regained its status as a legal product, the Phoenix brewery was sold to the Flanagan-Nay Brewing Corporation headed by Major Thomas Lanphier, a World War I hero who had commanded the First Pursuit Group of Selfridge Field. After the war Lanphier became a leading figure in the aircraft industry. More germane to the Phoenix brewery, Owney Madden had taken flying lessons from him.[29] It was widely assumed that Madden was the controlling partner in Flanagan-Nay and Lanphier would be the company's legal, public face.

Madden Speaks

New York City's multitude of speakeasies provided a ready-made, brisk market for Gotham's favorite brand of beer, Madden's Number One. The beer baron saw an easy route to even bigger profits if he opened his own nightspots. He entered into the speakeasy business with George Jean "Big Frenchy" DeMange, a yegg (safecracker) who also ran illegal saloons. In their youthful gang days, the two men had been enemies because DeMange was a top enforcer for the Hudson Dusters. As adults, they put aside the past because they saw advantages to teaming up in the liquor trade.

In short order Madden and DeMange built a lucrative business running some of New York's most popular speakeasies. Insiders knew who DeMange was, but he preferred to work backstage and his name rarely appeared in the press. Although Madden was also publicity shy, his name often popped up in the media as the owner of ritzy speakeasies. He cultivated an image as a wealthy powerbroker, and his polished veneer masked his ruthless nature. Sexpot actress Mae West described Madden as "so sweet and so vicious."[30]

Fun-loving crowds flocked to Madden's flagship speakeasy, the Cotton Club in Harlem. Located on Lenox Avenue, it was originally an entertainment venue with a theatre and a dance hall. When Madden decided to take it over, boxer Jack Johnson, a former world heavyweight champion, was managing it. Called the Club Deluxe, the place was struggling to stay open, largely due to Johnson's failure to secure a steady supply of decent liquor. Madden, DeMange, and Arnold "Big Bankroll" Rothstein put up the money to buy the club from Johnson, who stayed on as the straw man.[31]

Madden turned the Cotton Club into a trendy hotspot for hip, free-spending club goers looking for the latest sensation. He hired designer Joseph Urban to give the club's interior an exotic aura. Urban used jungle motifs and palm trees to create a surreal tropical landscape. The club's eclectic menu featured steak, lobster, and other basics along with Chinese and Mexican dishes, as well as Southern favorites, like barbecue and fried chicken. For serious drinkers, the main attraction was the better-than-average bootleg booze, which flowed like the Mississippi overtopping the levees.

When the Cotton Club first opened, it was segregated in that the clientele was white while the performers and staff were African Americans. Later, this policy was relaxed so the performers' families and friends could see the show. However, few blacks could afford the club's high prices so the patrons remained mostly whites, who came to listen to "real jazz" in Harlem.

The Cotton Club wowed its patrons with big-budget, Broadway-style musical revues starring famous singers, talented dancers, and shapely chorus girls. The sexy showgirls in their skimpy outfits pushed the boundaries of what was allowed onstage. The Twenties' trendy set loved jazz music, and the Cotton Club showcased some of the era's hottest jazz musicians. In the late 1920s, Duke Ellington and his Jungle Band played for the revues and also provided dance music. CBS Radio broadcast Ellington's music direct from the Cotton Club, greatly enlarging his audience. His "Cotton Club sound" gained national fame, and radio listeners far from NYC knew all about the speakeasy. The mere mention of the Cotton Club conjured up visions of night-on-the-town naughtiness. Tourists in the Big Apple put Harlem and the Cotton Club at the top of their must-see list.[32]

Madden promoted a somewhat less than respectable, yet safe, image for the Cotton Club. White folks could feel naughty and liberated going to a Harlem speakeasy run by a notorious beer baron. At the same time, they could be sure there was enough mob muscle on hand to deal with unruly drunks or other troublemakers. Anyone who stirred up trouble in the club quickly found himself on the sidewalk. "If one thing hallmarked Owney's clubs, it was an absence of fear," a lawyer said. "Anyone could visit the Cotton Club without the slightest worry of violence or intimidation.... Believe me, there were other places you felt lucky to get out of alive."[33]

Although Madden spent a great deal of money bribing policemen and city officials, law enforcement sometimes targeted his speakeasies. In 1925 a judge slapped a padlock on the Cotton Club, closing it for three months because the NYPD had received dozens of complaints about it. One complaint may have carried more weight than the others: NYC Mayor John Hylan was among those urging action against the Cotton Club. Normally, Hylan put little emphasis on enforcing the dry law. But it was an election year and he hoped to run for re-election, so he needed to bolster his crime-fighting record.

In addition to padlocking the Cotton Club, the judge levied a substantial fine against the owners. Madden was taken to court but, as usual, avoided going to prison. At trial the assistant U.S. attorney used Madden's criminal record to paint him as a public enemy, but Owney the Killer claimed he had reformed and was working to "make good." After the padlocking order expired, the Cotton Club reopened with a spectacular new revue. The legal troubles had given the club lots of free publicity, and crowds flocked to see the show.[34]

In 1929 a new speakeasy, the Plantation Club, opened on 126th Street in Harlem. It quickly became a favorite late-night hotspot for whites looking for a new watering hole. The decor, which evoked the Old South, included a showboat tableau, tiny cabins, and sentimental paintings of plantation life. The night-sky ceiling lit up with stars and moons that glittered above the parquet dance floor, which was surrounded by mirrors. For variety, a fog machine could create a cloudy-sky effect.

One morning, several weeks after the Plantation opened, employees were busy in the club preparing for the evening's business. The doorbell rang at the service entrance. When the watchman answered the door, a man wearing a white uniform said he was delivering laundry. He held what appeared to be a large bundle of clean linen. He pushed his way through the half-open door, followed by several other men, also dressed in white. Inside the club, they announced that they were federal agents searching for narcotics.

At gunpoint, two of the intruders herded the confused, scared workers into the cellar and stood guard over them. Meanwhile, the other invaders pulled crowbars, axes, knives, and picks out of the laundry bundle. With the knives, they vandalized the club, ripping open the seat cushions and the upholstered settees. They slashed paintings and tore the canvases out of their frames. They swung the crowbars at the ceiling, shattering the stars and moons. They smashed the spotlights and the cloud machine. With the crowbars and axes, they attacked the stage and tore up the parquet flooring. They destroyed the showboat tableau and shattered the mirrors around the dance floor. A man wielding a pickaxe struck the piano again and again, demolishing the keys and sounding board. For the grand finale, the gang broke into the backstage dressing rooms and slashed the costumes to ribbons.

Their rampage ended, the intruders dropped their tools and fled the club. Cautiously the workers ventured upstairs. They were stunned when they saw the costly fixtures reduced to rubble. They contacted the police, who came to collect evidence and dust the strangers' tools for fingerprints. Detectives theorized that the intruders were sent by a rival club owner who didn't like competition. Madden headed the suspect list.

The Plantation Club management announced that it would not be intimidated and would reopen as soon as repairs could be made. The club reopened while the police hunted for the wrecking crew. A few months after the attack, police officers arrested three conmen who were running a protection racket in Harlem. It was a simple scam: the trio demanded money from a club owner; if he didn't cough up the cash, they trashed his place. Suspicion shifted from Madden to this trio as the perpetrators of the carnage at the Plantation Club. However, law enforcement had no concrete evidence against anyone.[35]

The Royal Box

Because New Year's Eve was party night for countless Americans, the Prohis made a strong statement by raiding popular, busy speakeasies on December 31. Not only did the raids spoil the revelers' fun, they reminded the public that Prohibition was still the law of the land. They demonstrated the Prohis' power and got Volstead enforcement off to a strong start for the new year. Over the years the holiday raids became a sort of tradition that everyone expected. In the Big Apple, the New Year's Eve raids usually closed a half-dozen or so of the hottest, swankiest speakeasies.

On New Year's Eve 1931, Prohibition agents in NYC raided only one upscale speakeasy: the Royal Box. Beer baron Madden owned the controlling interest in the club, commonly called Zelli's because Joe Zelli was the straw man. A World War I army veteran, Zelli had run a Montmartre café popular with Americans in Paris. Then he moved to NYC where he worked for Madden and produced a Broadway play adapted from a British version of a French comedy based on a German novel. Perhaps predictably, it flopped in America.

The Royal Box, which catered to "the most expensive trade," had opened only weeks before New Year's Eve. The posh speakeasy occupied an entire five-story building on West Fifty-Sixth Street. The stone façade was adorned with blue-and-gold awnings, wrought-iron balconies, and colorful flower boxes.

The club's "modernistic" décor, which cost a quarter-million dollars, was "executed in exceptional taste in soft pastel shades." On the stairway landing between the bottom two floors stood the statue "Ease," a curvaceous life-sized, tawny nude female holding a bunch of plump grapes. The second floor had a massive circular bar made of exotic inlaid woods, with the outer rim edged in nickel. In the main dining room, banquettes lined the walls, which had frescoes with Oriental motifs. On the third floor, a mahogany-and-chrome bar stood at the head of the stairs. Here the walls "were of soft silver gilt," and a baby grand piano was "decorated in keeping with the rest of the room." The fourth floor had small rooms for private parties. On the top floor a movable wall concealed "an ingenious hideaway for drinkables."

Sixteen cooks worked in the club's oversized kitchen, which had the latest appliances. An array of "vast iceboxes" cooled the foodstuffs needed for serving gourmet meals. The well-ordered coolers held an impressive selection of foods, including "lobsters and fowl arranged in rows like battalions of soldiers."

On New Year's Eve the Prohis drove up to the Royal Box in taxis and rang the doorbell. Someone on the other side of the door peered out at them, didn't like their looks, and refused to let them in. The Prohis were not deterred. A physically-fit agent climbed up the façade of the building and crawled into the club through a second story window. Meanwhile, his associates took a more direct approach. Using an ax, they smashed their way through the front door.

When the Prohis invaded the speakeasy, the customers didn't panic or run for the fire exit. In fact, they seemed more amused than alarmed. The agents ordered them to leave — ladies first, followed by the men. Despite the command, most patrons stayed at their tables, either because they were still eating dinner or were enjoying the raid. While the Prohis tried to evict the diners, Royal Box employees fled through upper-floor windows to the roofs of other buildings. The agents rounded up and arrested all the staff they could find. The arrestees, including the manager and the captain of waiters, were taken to a nearby police station to be booked on Volstead charges. The Prohis confiscated the club's liquor but left the fancy furnishings to be trucked away later.

If the Royal Box's evicted patrons needed a drink to calm down after the excitement, they needed to walk only a short distance down the street. While Madden's speakeasy was being raided, reporters noticed "suspicious-looking bundles being unloaded with no effort at concealment" at a neighboring nightclub.[36]

Perhaps the other club owner's Christmas graft had been more generous than Madden's.

10. Feeling the Heat: Owney Madden

Millionaires and their ladies drank the Madden booze in many a joint. Gentlemen of the fancy sat at the ringside of Madison Square Garden and watched pugilists controlled by Madden. Other people sent their linen to Madden's laundry.— Stanley Walker, newspaper editor, New York City[1]

Throughout American history, small town folk have viewed big cities as centers of vice and lawlessness. They've idealized the small town as the safe, wholesome alternative to the urban cesspools. But not all small towns have lived up to the ideal. In fact, some have openly rejected the wholesome image, choosing to be a minor league Sin City. These places have cultivated and embraced the image of an open town where anything goes. They have promoted illegal gambling, prostitution, and other vices to lure tourists to town, thereby enriching the local economy. For many decades, one such place was Hot Springs, Arkansas.

Beginning in the early 1800s, warm waters flowing from springs on the western slope of Hot Springs Mountain attracted visitors who believed in the healing power of hydrotherapy. In the town of Hot Springs hotels and bathhouses were built to accommodate the visitors. The U.S. Congress created the Hot Springs Reservation to protect the area's natural resources. Over time, the tourist facilities were expanded and upgraded until the area became a popular resort/health spa. Seeking good health, people subjected themselves to mud baths, needle showers, steam rooms, and chill chambers. Hot Springs' boosters called it America's Baden Baden and proudly proclaimed "We Bathe the World." After the Civil War, illegal gambling vied with hydrotherapy as the area's chief attraction.

During Prohibition, Hot Springs became a mecca for tourists who wanted to drink and gamble in a wide open town. A-list mobsters, like Al Capone and Owney Madden, came to check out the action. The Belvedere was reputed to be the area's busiest gambling spot in the Arid Era. The upscale resort had comfortable rooms, good service, all the popular amenities, and a dining room that accommodated up to fifteen hundred diners. But not all Hot Springs gambling spots were swanky. Many were quite small and rather shabby.

According to local legend, Al Capone visited Hot Springs on a regular basis. Initially, he came to make deals with the moonshiners in the hills outside town. He kept returning because he liked the baths and the town's anything-goes attitude. He always brought a big entourage with him. He even purchased one of the older bathhouses and converted it into a gym so his men had a place to exercise.

Owney Madden first stopped by Hot Springs to visit a friend, an ex-boxer living there while he took hydrotherapy to treat his arthritis. Madden drove around town in his high-powered, bulletproof Duesenberg convertible, which turned heads wherever he went. Like other tourists, he stopped at a coffee shop/gift store run by Agnes Demby, the postmaster's daughter. Agnes was a gregarious young woman who made her customers feel right at home. Madden instantly liked her. He flirted with her and asked her for a date. At first she resisted his charms. He was a stranger from the big city — not a trustworthy local boy. Her small-town upbringing told her to be careful. But Madden's charm destroyed her defenses and she agreed to go out with him. Despite her better judgment, she soon fell hopelessly in love with the suave liquor lord.

Madden was a married man, but it was a marriage in name only. He and his wife had been estranged for many years. He chased actresses, showgirls, and any other woman who caught his eye. He found Agnes Demby to be a refreshing change from the hardened, worldly women he usually dated. He lingered in Hot Springs for more than two weeks, courting her. He didn't want to leave her, but he dared not neglect his criminal duties too long. Gangland was full of guys waiting for a chance to muscle in on another man's racket. Reluctantly, Madden decided to go home. As a parting gift, he handed Agnes an envelope with a train ticket to NYC.[2]

Like other beer barons, Owney the Killer was beginning to feel the pinch of hard times. The Great Depression had cast a pall over Gotham's nightlife. Financial problems were causing people to reassess their values and reorder their priorities. Hungry men "see things with new eyes," a journalist wrote in 1931. "The glamour has been stripped from the gangsters. Even the most stupid of us see them now as they are — yellow louts, red-handed plunderers. We have begun to realize that they have waged actual war upon us in this last red decade. Hunger has made us see the truth. We realize now that they have taken billions of dollars from us."[3]

In New York City, reform groups were working to stop the corruption that undermined both good government and legitimate business. The Citizens' Union was exposing graft in the NYPD, the court system, and the mayor's office. A rally at Madison Square Garden drew a capacity crowd of fired-up citizens who demanded the end of gang rule in Gotham. The crowd cheered wildly as speakers urged honest New Yorkers to reclaim their city from the racketeers.[4]

New York Governor Franklin D. Roosevelt cast his lot with the reformers. He promised to expose corrupt officials and to put the mobsters behind bars. He called on the legislature to pass emergency measures that would help prosecutors take the gangsters off the street. "A government which fails to take every reasonable precaution to protect the life of its residents from banditry is out of step with modern thought," FDR said. "Those who menace and prey on the community with ready revolvers and speeding automobiles must be pursued and eradicated."[5]

The public's new focus on law-and-order boded ill for men like Owney Madden. He had an almost magical knack for avoiding jail, but Gotham wasn't as hospitable to mobsters as it had been during the Roaring Twenties. In response to public pressure, the police began arresting Madden on minor charges and holding him in jail until his lawyer could spring him. In a relatively short time, dozens of arrests were added to his rap sheet. To avoid more nights in jail, he altered his lifestyle. He stayed close to home and rarely went to the Cotton Club or his other favorite haunts.[6]

In August 1931 Agnes Demby traveled to New York to sample life with Madden in his natural habitat. If she expected him to squire her around town and introduce her to VIP's, she was disappointed. He was feeling the heat from the cops and the reformers. He spent most of his time trying to be invisible. He had gone from strutting around like the King of New York to living like an outcast. Uncertainty clouded his future. Prohibition, his cash cow, seemed destined for repeal in the next few years. Moreover, he was widely regarded as a public enemy in his hometown. If he stayed in the Big Apple, he would probably end up in prison.

Madden welcomed Agnes to his home, but he relied on his female friends to show her around New York while he stayed out of sight. To make up for his lack of attention, he gave her pricey baubles from Tiffany's and tickets to Broadway's hottest shows. Then, without telling her, he abruptly skipped town, leaving her to her own devices. If a specific event or threat prompted him to flee, he didn't bother to tell her about it. Of course, she felt betrayed and lonely. Without her lover, she had no reason to stay in the big city. She boarded the train alone, headed back to Arkansas.[7]

To throw the cops off his trail, Madden's close pals told everyone that he had sailed to Europe. But he was actually driving to California in his bulletproof Duesenberg. The long hours on the road gave him time to think, to assess his options, and to figure out his future. After a brief stop in California, he traveled to Hawaii and checked into a Honolulu hotel. He was able to blend in there because he wasn't known in Hawaii.[8]

When Madden tired of the quiet life in Hawaii, he sailed to Los Angeles to visit actor George Raft, an old friend from Hell's Kitchen. The childhood pals had pursued different career paths. While Madden chose gangland, Raft set his heart on making it big in show biz. After years of being almost famous, he had found his niche playing mobsters in the movies. A handsome man with real star power, he had worked his way up from chorus line dancer to matinee idol. Women swooned over his good looks. Men liked his tough guy persona.

The movie star and the beer baron hung out at ritzy Hollywood speakeasies. Gossip columnists took note. So did law enforcement. When the L.A. district attorney heard that Madden was in town, he ordered the police to arrest the liquor lord. But someone probably gave Madden a heads up. When police officers arrived at Raft's home to take Owney the Killer into custody, they discovered he had moved on.[9]

Madden took up residence with another old friend, actress Mae West, who had moved from New York to L.A. to star in movies. Although Madden knew the police were looking for him, he decided to go to a nightclub one evening. A cop moonlighting as a doorman recognized the mega mobster from the Big Apple. Madden was promptly arrested and taken in for questioning. According to mob lore, sexpot West used her celebrated seductive charms to persuade the D.A. to release Madden. Whatever happened, Madden was released but was still unwelcome in the City of Angels. Lawmen escorted him to the city limits and bid him adieu, ordering him to stay out of L.A.

Madden traveled on, driving his customized Duesenberg to Mexico and Texas before heading north and reaching Hot Springs for a reunion with Agnes Demby. He turned on the charm, she forgave him for leaving her stranded in NYC, and their romance grew more intense. After spending two weeks with his lady love, Madden climbed into his Duesenberg, headed back home.[10]

Oh, What a Tangled Web!

Upon arriving in NYC, Madden heard alarming news. New York's state parole board was looking into allegations that he had violated the terms of his parole from Sing Sing prison. Although he had been out of Sing Sing for more than eight years, his manslaughter sentence didn't expire for roughly four more years. He could still be sent back to prison to finish serving his term.[11]

Mob watchers knew that Madden had repeatedly, routinely broken his parole. But the parole board needed proof of his misconduct, so it was proceeding with caution. The basic parole rules required Madden to "establish a home, be legitimately employed, and report when required to by the board." Official records showed that he had reported to the parole board when he first left prison. Then, in a routine procedure, the board turned his case over to a private agency, the Catholic Protectory, which worked closely with the state corrections department. The protectory found him so trustworthy that it required no personal interviews but allowed him to report by mail every three months.[12]

Madden claimed that the parole board had formally discharged him from all supervision on March 21, 1929. After that date, he no longer had to report to the protectory or anyone else. However, he couldn't prove his assertion. A formal discharge required a personal interview, but official records showed that he had not appeared before the parole board in person at any time after 1927. Neither Madden nor the Catholic Protectory could find his official discharge certificate. Therefore, in late 1931, the board decided that he must resume reporting to parole authorities on a regular basis.[13]

In February 1932 the state parole board met at Sing Sing to determine if Madden would return to prison. Madden was not present at the hearing, but he knew that his freedom was at stake. What seemed to be a minor prevarication proved to be the fatal lie for him. When questioned by state investigators before the hearing, Madden had claimed to be legally employed by the Hydrox Laundry & Dry Cleaning Company, a business closely tied to organized crime. The straw man at Hydrox was accustomed to covering up the company's mob ties. When officials talked to him, he emphatically denied that Madden worked for him or had any connection with the company. Moreover, Madden had never listed income from Hydrox on his tax returns.[14] Either he was lying about his employment or he was concealing taxable income. Or both.

At the hearing, the parole board reviewed all the evidence pertaining to Madden, including his fictional job at the laundry. While the board debated his fate, Madden wasn't the only person waiting anxiously to hear its decision. The NYPD commissioner and a squad of detectives also awaited the verdict, prepared to arrest him if necessary. The parole board issued an arrest warrant for Madden so he could be brought to Sing Sing for questioning. Along with several other warrants, the document was rushed by car from Sing Sing to NYPD headquarters. The commissioner instantly dispatched detectives to search for the crime lord, who was laying low because he anticipated the arrest warrant.

A three-day hunt for Madden ended when detectives staked out a building where he rented an apartment for his mother. When the lawmen spotted him entering the building, they nabbed him. He was placed under arrest and taken to the Tombs. Standard procedure called for him to stay in the Tombs until he could be moved to Sing Sing, where the parole board would question him and decide his future.[15]

Madden's lawyers immediately began legal maneuvers to free him. First, they filed a writ of habeas corpus demanding his release from "unlawful imprisonment." A New York State Supreme Court justice heard the arguments for and against the petition. Madden's lawyers claimed that the parole board had discharged him in 1929 and no longer had jurisdiction over him. His chief counsel stated that Madden was a law-abiding citizen. Since leaving Sing Sing, he had followed the rules and hadn't violated his parole. The lawyer insisted that Madden was not a crime lord but the victim of biased, sensational reporting by the media. The press had created a false public image of him as a vile, rapacious beer baron.[16]

New York's assistant attorney general argued against releasing Madden. He emphasized that the liquor lord had lied about being legally employed. "Madden violated his parole when he informed the parole board he was working, when as a matter of fact, he was not and has no legitimate employment," the attorney said. He stated that the crux of the case was the issue of whether the parole board or the court system had jurisdiction over paroled prisoners. He argued that the parole board — not the state supreme court — had the authority to discharge Madden or send him back to prison. He warned that the parole board would be eviscerated if the court overruled its decisions. "The board will be a joke," he declared.[17]

While waiting for the State Supreme Court justice to rule, Madden's lawyers filed a brief and an affidavit by the former supervisor of the Parole Department's Division of Protective Care. The affidavit stated that a "confidential agent of the prison department" had released Madden from the parole board's custody in 1926 and had given him permission to "go wherever he pleased." This bolstered Madden's assertion that he had been discharged, although he claimed the year was 1929.[18]

The assistant attorney general filed affidavits refuting Madden's version of events. In one affidavit, the chairman of the parole board stated that a thorough search of the records, conducted in the presence of Madden's counsel, had yielded no evidence of the purported discharge. In another affidavit, a member of the parole board unequivocally stated that Madden had never been discharged. Moreover, the official discharge letter sent from the board to the Catholic Protectory in 1929 did not list Madden among the discharged parolees.[19]

To the surprise of many legal experts, the Supreme Court justice found Madden's arguments convincing and released him from the custody of the parole board. The justice stated that the board had ordered Madden's arrest "on flimsy and highly technical grounds." Furthermore, his arrest was "an attempt to convict him ... for wrongs which cannot be brought home to him by competent evidence." The "common belief" or "common gossip" that Madden was a beer baron did not reach the level of credible proof. The justice scolded the parole board for sloppy recordkeeping and chided the state for failing to present a strong case.[20] Cynics said Madden had powerful friends and he knew how to wield his clout.

Governor Roosevelt, New York's attorney general, and other high-ranking officials strongly disagreed with the justice's decision. They applauded when the New York Appellate Division unanimously reversed his ruling. The appellate judges found "no evidence, either documentary or otherwise, of the slightest probative value" that the parole board had ever discharged Madden. Therefore, the liquor lord must return to Sing Sing, and the parole board would decide how long he must stay.[21]

Madden, understandably reluctant to go back to prison, went into hiding and managed to elude the police for several days. His Hot Springs flame, Agnes Demby, was visiting him in New York, and he wanted to spend time with her before going to Sing Sing. On July 6,

1932, he bowed to the inevitable, kissed Agnes goodbye, and took his leave. The lovers didn't know how long they would be separated. If the parole board kept Madden in prison until his manslaughter sentence expired, he would be there for three-plus years. However, if he didn't cause any trouble, he might get time off for good behavior.[22]

Madden joined two pals who were waiting for him in a car. With the window curtains drawn for privacy, the trio drove to the entrance of Sing Sing prison. Madden shook hands with his buddies, and the car pulled away. As Owney the Killer walked up to the tall gates, his old bullet wounds were bothering him, causing him to stoop over. He rapped on the massive door beside the gates. A small window opened and, through the metal grillwork, eyes stared at him. He identified himself as Owney Madden, but the guard didn't recognize him. Looking beyond the guard, Madden spotted a prison official he knew. He hailed his old acquaintance, who came over to welcome him back to Sing Sing.[23]

While Madden adjusted to life behind bars, his lawyers filed petitions, trying to get him out of Sing Sing on bail. The Court of Appeals in Albany quickly ruled that he must stay in prison. A few months later, the same court upheld the parole board's right to return him to prison "without red tape or court proceedings" because he had violated the terms of his parole. After the court affirmed the parole board's jurisdiction, the board members granted Madden an interview. After questioning him, they decided he must serve one more year in prison.[24]

Sing Sing's inmate population viewed Madden as a celebrity, but he avoided drawing attention to himself. In fact, he kept to himself so much that the other convicts called him Owney the Hermit. Initially, he was assigned to light manual labor on the yard crew because a chronic bronchial ailment prevented him from doing heavy work. Later he worked in the prison greenhouse near the Hudson River docks. Press releases about the prison's Easter services noted that Madden had grown the lilies on the altar. A newspaper called him Sing Sing's "quietest and best-behaved prisoner."[25]

In 1933 the parole board granted Madden an early release date. He would leave Sing Sing after serving slightly under a year for his parole violations. The conditions of his discharge included obeying the law, finding a job, and eschewing "evil associates and ways." Madden said he had a job waiting for him, working as a checker for the Champion Coal Company. The press reported that Champion had mob connections and operated less than ethically. The company routinely cheated customers by charging them for more coal than it delivered, a practice called short-weighting. However, the parole board didn't seem to be concerned about Madden's plan to work for a shady company.[26]

As Madden's release date neared, he prepared to leave Sing Sing. He declined both the customary free train ticket and the suit made by convicts in the sewing shop. The prison issued him a check for $51.52 — wages for his work in the greenhouse, the money in his prison spending account, and a gift from the rehabilitation fund. On July 1, 1933, he left Sing Sing in style, dressed in an expensive, natty suit and riding in a chauffeur-driven, luxury car sent by a friend.[27]

You Can't Go Home Again

Madden returned home to find that his criminal fiefdom had shrunk while he served time. Law enforcement had raided and shuttered some of his speakeasies. Others had closed due to lack of business because people in the throes of the Great Depression had little money to spend at nightclubs. The dry law had been modified so drinkers could buy legal beer and light wines, greatly reducing their dependence on bootleggers. Even the dry faction expected the repeal of the Eighteenth Amendment, which would make distilled spirits legal. The Big Apple had little need for an aging beer baron.

More and more, Madden was attracted to Hot Springs. His sweetheart lived there, and he rather enjoyed the folksy, unhurried Southern lifestyle. Arkansas' rural Sin City offered enticing opportunities for a man with his expertise. A big-city vice lord could turn the small-town rackets into a bonanza. The good ol' boys were making money, but Madden had national connections he could exploit. He could bring the real high rollers to town. There would be enough action to keep him from getting bored, and he could build a new life with his soul mate.

Owney the Killer had learned a little humility from his recent tussle with the parole board. Knowing that the board could still send him back to prison, he went through the formality of getting permission to move to Hot Springs. A doctor certified that he was in ill health and would benefit from a warm climate and hydrotherapy. The board parole put its stamp of approval on an extended stay in Hot Springs to improve his health.[28]

Madden traveled to Hot Springs to start over with Agnes Demby at his side. He settled into a comfortable, low-key lifestyle as a guest in the Demby family home. He planned to control the action in Hot Springs, but he couldn't ride in with guns blazing if he wanted to be accepted in the small town. He had to win the trust of the local nabobs. He must convince them that his national mob connections meant more money for everybody. He moved cautiously but resolutely. With finesse, he finagled his way into the good graces of the local powerbrokers and emerged as the new kingpin of vice. Gangland gossip said he paid a great deal of money to get in on the action. People who understood small Southern towns knew that money wasn't enough: Demby's family was the key to Madden's acceptance in Hot Springs.

While Madden enjoyed life in his new hometown, public outrage caused headaches for him in New York. His purported employer — the Champion Coal Company — was under scrutiny because it had bilked the City of New York out of money. Officials accused Champion of cheating the city by short-weighting and delivering coal with high moisture content. The grand jury looking into the scandal wanted Madden to testify, and the assistant D.A. asked him to simplify matters by voluntarily coming to New York.[29]

Madden hesitated to make the trip to testify before the grand jury. He didn't want to answer questions that could be incriminating and might even send him back to prison. While he pondered the problem, he received an official telegram: "Parole board decision is that you should return at once to appear before the grand jury." The new humble Madden, accompanied by his lady love, set out on the long drive from Arkansas to New York in the sweltering heat of summer. Upon arrival, he reported to a representative of the parole board.

On the day he was scheduled to testify, Madden dressed in a "tight-fitting indigo blue suit" and went to the Criminal Courts building. While he waited his turn, reporters and photographers swarmed around him, asking questions and taking pictures. He was visibly annoyed, especially by the cameramen. Parole board officers stayed with him in the grand jury ante-room and tried to shield him from the press.

Although Madden testified, he added little to the coal company investigation. He answered questions for the better part of an hour but, like a good gangster, divulged no secrets. His name appeared on Champion's payroll records, indicating that he had worked there for two months after he left Sing Sing. However, the entries were squeezed in between others and appeared to be recently added. It was questionable whether he had ever shown up for work at Champion. When he denied knowledge of company affairs, he was probably telling the truth.[30]

Although Madden's performance on the witness stand shed little light on Champion's affairs, he was subpoenaed for an encore. He returned to the courtroom for a second round of questions and again gave limited information. Since other witnesses were providing solid evidence against the coal company, his testimony wasn't essential to the investigation.

Madden looked relieved when he left the coal company hearing, but the legal system wasn't finished with him. He was ordered to appear before the New York County grand jury to answer questions about his release from Sing Sing. Specifically, authorities wanted to know if he had bribed members of the parole board or paid for special privileges. His early release and his move to Arkansas seemed suspect. The jurors heard testimony from members of the parole board and the prison physician who had treated Madden at Sing Sing. The witnesses agreed that the doctor had been concerned about Madden's health and had repeatedly asked permission for him to move to Hot Springs. That satisfied the grand jury.[31]

Madden wanted to wed Agnes Demby, but first he had to jump over some legal hurdles. He needed a divorce from his estranged wife before he could remarry. According to the rumor mill, he offered his wife a generous settlement of cash and property, including his Yonkers home and his yacht. She agreed to end what had become a sham marriage and moved to a hotel in Reno, Nevada, to establish residency for a quickie divorce. The couple had not lived together for at least ten years, which was more than sufficient grounds to dissolve a marriage in Nevada.[32]

After the New York grand juries finished with Madden, he returned to Hot Springs to focus on his new illegal ventures. He operated quietly, attracting little notice outside Arkansas. When he was summoned to appear before the parole board, he and Agnes traveled to New York. On June 15, 1935, he had his final personal interview with the board. At age forty-three, he was truly free of the New York prison system. In November, he married Agnes in a quiet ceremony at a resort in Mount Ida, Arkansas, the quartz crystal capital of the United States.[33]

Madden liked being the whale in Hot Springs' very small pond. His major venture was the Southern Club, a hotspot that offered food, drink, gambling, and live entertainment. In his leisure time he played golf and enjoyed his old hobby, raising pigeons. He joined the Chamber of Commerce, became a pillar of the community, and gave generously to local charities. He paid for hundreds of food baskets at Christmastime and bankrolled a fund that provided assistance to ex-cons on parole. He helped families who had been evicted from their homes and sent "tons of coal" to people who couldn't afford to pay their heating bills. He sponsored benefit concerts and paid performers to stage shows for convicts in prisons.[34]

The boy from Hell's Kitchen missed the action in the Big Apple and occasionally went back for a visit. But he was persona non grata in his hometown. Whenever the police spotted him in New York, they ordered him to leave. "Every time he is overwhelmed by nostalgia and creeps back to his old bailiwick, detectives throw him out again," wrote a crime reporter.

When Madden traveled to New York to watch the Baer-Mann boxing match at Madison Square Garden, cops nabbed him and took him to jail. He swore he was an honest mineral-water salesman, but the police knew otherwise. After a night in custody, he was put in a line-up and then taken to court, where he was arraigned on vagrancy charges. City officials told him to leave New York ASAP. He left because he had no clout in the Big Apple.[35]

During World War II, Madden decided to apply for U.S. citizenship. Years earlier he had attempted to obtain naturalization papers but Franklin D. Roosevelt, governor of New York at that time, made sure he didn't get them. Now Madden was living in Arkansas, where he cultivated an image as an altruistic, civic-minded businessman. His chances of becoming a naturalized citizen seemed good. According to mob lore, he went about obtaining his citizenship via his usual route: he spent a quarter-million dollars bribing officials, including a U.S. senator.

Madden hired Arkansas attorney Q. Byrum Hurst to argue his naturalization case before Judge John Miller. Hurst stated that Madden was an upstanding citizen, an asset to the Hot Springs business sector and the community at large. Agnes Demby Madden testified on behalf of her husband, portraying him in the best possible light.[36]

The Maddens waited a year to see if Owney the Killer had sanitized his image enough for citizenship. They were elated when Judge Miller signed the papers in 1943. When news of Madden's naturalization leaked out, many Americans were shocked that an immigrant career criminal had been given U.S. citizenship. Deportation seemed more appropriate. Judge Miller tried to absolve himself, saying, "I knew nothing of Madden's past." He claimed he had relied on the Naturalization Bureau's New Orleans office, which recommended Madden for citizenship. Madden declared he had revealed everything about his shady past to the authorities. "I omitted nothing," he said.[37]

In Washington, officialdom expressed dismay over Judge Miller's action and promised an inquiry into the allegations of bribery. But Washington had more pressing issues to deal with. The United States was at war, and Owney the Killer's heyday was long past. Although there were rumblings about taking away his citizenship, the feds had little interest in him. As long as he stayed in Hot Springs, he was definitely yesterday's news.

In April 1965, Madden died at age seventy-three. A heavy smoker, he had long suffered from respiratory ailments, including chronic emphysema.

Strange bedfellows rubbed shoulders at Madden's funeral. Big-city gangsters, Arkansas politicos, lawmen, and ordinary townsfolk came to say goodbye. When a spring downpour delayed the graveside service, the mourners huddled beneath the oak trees until the rain stopped. The soggy ground squished under their feet as they trooped to the grave. The sun popped out, "casting long shadows across a gentle eastern slope in Greenwood Cemetery, where Madden's casket was placed in its vault and lowered into the grave."

Madden's attorney, Q. Byrum Hurst, gave an elegant eulogy for his client/friend. "Page after page of sensationalism has been written about him, but when Owney Madden got off that train in Hot Springs, he became a truly different man and a real citizen," Hurst said. "I couldn't name all the people he helped. Every down-and-outer learned that a helping hand for those really in need could be found in Owen Madden.... If Owen made a dollar, it was rapidly given to someone else who needed it more.... We know not or care not what happened before he came to live with us in Hot Springs. We don't care what they say in New York, Chicago, or Washington. We simply know he was a kind, good man."[38]

Had Owney the Killer truly become Owney the Kind? Did his good deeds outweigh his life of crime? His lawyer answered, "Yes." Others weren't so sure.

11. Arthur Flegenheimer:
The Bronx Beer Baron

I may do a lot of lousy things, but I'll never make a living off women or narcotics. — Dutch
Schultz, beer baron, New York City[1]

Prohibition created many beer barons, but none deserved the title more than Arthur
Flegenheimer, an unlikely mob boss who became a one-man criminal conglomerate. Flegenheimer, commonly called Dutch Schultz or the Dutchman, made a fortune brewing and
selling illegal beer. He also owned a dozen or so speakeasies and a red-carpet nightclub.
Since drinking and gambling often went hand-in-hand, he diversified into the slot-machine
racket, placing his one-armed bandits in saloons, restaurants, and other venues. He had a
profitable sideline putting peanut vending machines in bars. He took over the insanely popular numbers game in Harlem, wresting control from the local policy bankers. He also operated a protection racket in the restaurant industry.[2]

Flegenheimer was born into a poor family in 1901 in Manhattan's Yorkville area. His father,
who ran a livery stable, deserted the family when Schultz was still a boy. Schultz, who never
quite recovered from this shattering rejection, told people that his father had died. He persisted
in telling this lie even as an adult, suggesting that he still felt the pain. Schultz's desperately
poor mother worked as a janitor to support her children. She also took in laundry — washing,
starching, and ironing clothes and household linens before "miracle fabrics" made the job easy.

Young Schultz liked school, especially history and composition. He had a keen mind,
but like many poor boys he spent more time hustling on the street than sitting in the classroom. He enjoyed reading, had a life-long love of books, and became a self-educated man.
During his reign as a liquor lord, he had a library card and even paid his overdue book fines.
As a child, he liked the novels of Charles Dickens and the formulaic success stories of Horatio
Alger, Jr.[3] (It's easy to see why he would've felt a kinship with the poor-boy protagonists created by Dickens and Alger. He may have felt a special empathy for Alger's typical hero, who
was raised by his widowed mom and struggled to make his way in New York City.)

As an adult, Schultz enjoyed books about history, geography, philosophy, and medicine.
He read Shakespeare and even quoted the Bard from memory — a rare feat for a mobster.
He was particularly fond of biographies; his favorite book was Stefan Zweig's biography of
Joseph Fouché, Napoleon's minister of police. He also liked Emil Ludwig's *Life of Napoleon*

and Fred Pasley's *Al Capone: The Biography of a Self-made Man,* written before Scarface became just another convict taking orders from the prison guards. Schultz once told reporters he was reading *Write It Right* by Ambrose Bierce and suggested they read it to improve their writing skills.[4]

Physically, the Dutchman did not stand out in a crowd. He was average height, somewhat shy, and neither fat nor thin. He had black hair, dark eyes, and a crooked nose that had been broken at least once. Although he rarely smiled for the camera, he didn't look like a bad ass mobster in news photographs. He looked more like a grocery clerk than a crime lord. "Why Schultz became so powerful was always a mystery," an observer wrote. "He was not physically brave, not the kind of man who could hold mastery of a group by his own personal prowess." His strength lay in his intellect and his aptitude for business management.[5]

While many gangsters took pride in their expensive tailored suits, Schultz was a sloppy dresser. His suits, which never fit well, tended to be crumpled and in need of dry cleaning. He both smoked and chewed tobacco, which gave his clothes a peculiar smell. A reporter said Schultz "managed to look like an ill-dressed vagrant. He seemed to have a special talent for looking like a perfect example of the unsuccessful man.... Even Schultz's lobbygows and errand boys managed to dress better than the boss."[6]

The Dutchman's pals tried to improve his appearance by giving him silk shirts and stylish ties. But the expensive shirts never looked quite right with his bargain basement suits. He thought his buddies were wasting their money on men's fashions. "Only a sucker will pay $15 or $20 for a silk shirt," he said. Mobster Lucky Luciano called Schultz "one of the cheapest guys I ever knew, practically a miser."[7]

Published photographs of Schultz indicate that his grooming and his fashion sense improved over the years. Photographs show him to be well dressed and neatly groomed in his later courtroom appearances. By that time he was married, so his young trophy wife may have taken charge of his wardrobe. Nevertheless, the press persisted in portraying him as a slovenly pinchpenny. He was well aware of his miserly public image and used it to his advantage on occasion. To avoid arrest, he rented a swanky penthouse in a building on Fifth Avenue, opposite Central Park, because he felt the police would never look for him in the high-rent district. The ruse worked for a while. Then the cops heard about the place and staked it out, using binoculars to spy on him.[8]

During his long criminal career the Dutchman used multiple names. His rap sheet showed arrests as Arthur Flegenheimer, Charles Harmon, Joseph Harmon, Arthur Funsfler, Arthur Schultz, and George Schultz—but never as Dutch Schultz. According to mob lore, his famous alias paid homage to a plucky street fighter who belonged to the Frog Hollow Gang during its heyday in the Bronx in the 1880s. Crime reporters speculated that he liked "Dutch Schultz" because it sounded tough. "Arthur Flegenheimer" seemed too wimpy for a mob boss. The Dutchman complained that headline writers liked his alias too much. "If I'd stuck to Flegenheimer, I'd never been in trouble like this," he said. "Schultz is a short word and swell for headlines."[9]

A Rough-Cut Diamond

As an adolescent Dutch Schultz dropped out of school and worked at various jobs, including newsboy and printer's apprentice. When he wasn't working, he hung out with a gang in the Mott Haven section of the Bronx. With his slacker pals, he spent considerable time in saloons and billiard parlors. He made extra cash as a pool hustler, and he had a reputation as a nimble fighter who knew how to handle a cue stick in a bar brawl. He had a good singing voice and enjoyed barroom harmonizing with the guys.

For a time Schultz worked as a roofer while also making money as a petty thief. He became adept at burglarizing apartments and snatching packages from delivery wagons. He found crime to be both easier and more lucrative than roofing, so he gave up honest work. However, he never quit the roofer's union. Even as a rich beer baron, he paid his union dues, carried his union card, and claimed to be a roofer when people asked his occupation.

At age eighteen Schultz had his first serious encounter with the criminal justice system. He was convicted of burglary and sentenced to Blackwell's Island prison in the East River. He proved to be an unruly inmate, so authorities transferred him to a tougher facility, Westhampton Prison Farms near Goshen, New York. After serving about fifteen months, he was released. Back on his home turf, he returned to thievery, and he drove a beer wagon for the Gass brothers, small-time bootleggers in the Bronx.[10]

In his early twenties Schultz joined a gang led by John Thomas "Legs" Diamond, a sleazy hood who trafficked in both drugs and liquor. The Dutchman rode shotgun on Diamond's liquor trucks to protect them from hijackers. On many runs, Schultz protected hijacked hooch from a second hijacking. Diamond specialized in stealing booze from other gangs, especially the Dwyer syndicate, a rumrunning ring that controlled a substantial portion of the illegal liquor traffic in New York.[11]

In gangland's panoply of sociopaths, Legs Diamond fit in as an unstable, dissolute mobster with a "lust for blood and torture." He had an unpredictable nature, sometimes polite and affable but more often violent and ferocious. An acquaintance called him a killer, a snake, a king cobra, and "a conscienceless rat." On one occasion Diamond blindfolded a man, tied him to a tree, stuck his index fingers into the barrels of a shotgun, and talked calmly about mob business.[12] One can only imagine the victim's anguish as he waited for Legs to pull the trigger.

In another gruesome incident, Diamond and his goons burned a man's bare feet with lit matches and paper tapers. Then they put a noose around his neck, threw the rope over a tree limb, and hoisted the helpless man off the ground. When the rope tightened around his neck, causing him to pass out, they let him down and threw buckets of cold water on him. After they revived him, they made him stand up while they fired bullets at his feet, barely missing. Then Legs and a flunkey drove the injured man to an isolated spot in the country and dumped him. Despite the open wounds on his feet, the victim limped along the road, suffering piercing pain with each step. With amazing fortitude, he walked until he found help.[13]

One of Diamond's peers described him as "a frail, tubercular little rat." He always looked emaciated because he was painfully thin, with angular features, dull gray eyes, and a pasty white complexion. He had dark hair, a sloping forehead, bushy eyebrows, and full lips. When it came to fashion, he had his own signature style: a chinchilla coat, a white silk scarf, and a wide-brimmed white felt hat.[14] He also liked to wear a three-piece suit with a golf cap — a rakish look popular with young mobsters. Even in his mug shots, he looked stylish — a lean, mean killer with a flair for fashion.

Diamond's peers gave several explanations for his nickname "Legs." Some said he earned it in his youth when he excelled as a truck bouncer, a thief who grabbed packages from delivery trucks and ran away. Others said it referred to his constant motion because he was always prowling around, never sitting still. His long, gangly legs and his nimble steps on the dance floor were alternate explanations. Bitter gang members said that "Legs" fit him because he ran out on his lieutenants and let them go to jail on bum raps.

When police officers were taking a Diamond militiaman to prison, a reporter asked, "What do you think of Legs now?" The gangster growled, "That no good son of a bitch double-crossed me!"

Another underling, also facing a prison term, claimed Legs had sabotaged his defense. "That Diamond fixed everything up!" the man said. "I got blamed for things I didn't even do. I hope he gets his head blown off!"[15]

A mob boss needed a strong personality, the respect of his men, and enough discipline to keep his minions in line. But Diamond couldn't control himself or his bruisers. He had a weakness for booze, and his behavior became more erratic as he aged because alcoholism took over his life. When he drank too much, his always bad temper became even worse. His explosive personality kept him from having a normal relationship with anyone over the long haul. Legs "brought grief to his father, ... abused and deserted his first wife, ... and went back on scores of men who had helped him." He showed his contempt for his second wife by moving his mistress into their home and expecting the two women to cater to his whims. He showed unwavering loyalty to only one person — Eddie Diamond, his brother and partner-in-crime, who died of tuberculosis at a young age.

Excessive drinking wasn't Diamond's only flaw. His egotism led him to seek the spotlight, unlike prudent crime lords who knew the benefits of anonymity. He fraternized with reporters, even though he was in a business where secrecy was vital. His name appeared in the headlines so often that his peers began to shy away from him. "He loved publicity, and his craze for public attention brought him so much to the attention of the police and the public that more canny racketeers and bootleggers began to avoid him. He was bringing trouble upon them as well as himself," a crime reporter wrote.[16]

In 1931 a botched international drug deal led to Diamond's exile from New York City. He was lucky to escape with his life after he lost mob money and the press exposed the whole fiasco. He settled in the Adirondacks and battled with local bootleggers to control the liquor traffic in the area. Two gunmen killed him one night after had he passed out drunk at a seedy boardinghouse in Albany. After the intruders used a key to unlock the door to his room, one put the muzzle of a pistol to his head and fired. Then, to be sure he was truly dead, one gunsel held Diamond's head still while the other put two more bullets in it.[17]

Judging by Diamond's newspaper obits, only his closest loved ones felt he had died too soon. "In the murder of Legs Diamond, society has not lost anything that it cannot very well do without," a journalist wrote. "Of all the racketeers whom postwar turbulence has thrown to the surface of society, he seems to have been one of the most despicable. Personal cowardice, colossal conceit, and mean cruelty — these seem to have been the chief elements of his character.... That his underworld enemies finally caught up with him is neither to be wondered at, nor regretted."[18]

Going Dutch

For a time, Dutch Schultz took orders from Legs Diamond, but that arrangement didn't last long. Schultz didn't like kowtowing to anyone. Moreover, he and Legs were polar opposites. The violent, impulsive Diamond forged blindly ahead, unable to foresee the consequences of his actions. He relished notoriety and cultivated a public image as a tough-talking, gun-toting mobster. The Dutchman took a deliberate, business-like approach to his illegal ventures. He stayed out of the spotlight, focused on his work, and built an efficient criminal organization.

After Schultz severed his ties with Diamond, he went into partnership with Joe Noe, a boyhood chum who ran a thriving saloon in the Bronx. Schultz and Noe assembled a gang of ambitious young hoods and set out to be big-time beer barons. They were selling an incredibly popular product, so they were able to expand quickly and aggressively. As their business grew, they made inroads into territory claimed by other bootleggers, notably Legs Diamond.[19]

One night in November 1928 Noe was sitting in his car in front of a nightclub when a Cadillac cruised along the street. The Caddy slowed down, and the passengers fired machineguns at Noe. Bullets punctured his body, inflicting serious wounds. Although he was badly injured, he lingered for a few weeks before dying. Both Noe's friends and the police assumed that the shooters belonged to a rival gang threatened by the Noe-Schultz expansion. Detectives believed that Legs Diamond had ordered the hit and had probably been one of the shooters. However, the police didn't have enough evidence to convict him in a court of law. Besides, gangsters liked to mete out their own brand of justice.[20]

After Joe Noe's death, the Dutchman took over as CEO of the growing criminal domain they had started. He wholesaled beer and enlarged his distribution network until he had absolute control of the beer traffic in the Bronx. Anybody who wanted to sell beer on his turf had to do business with him. Initially, he bought his beer from a brewery in Union City, New Jersey, and trucked it to New York. The trucks crossed the river via ferry, which involved a certain amount of risk and extra cost. To streamline his operations, he began buying beer from Owney Madden's Phoenix brewery in Manhattan and the State Cereal Beverage Company at Chicken Island in Yonkers. Later he bought the Chicken Island brewery and made most of the beer he sold.[21]

The Dutchman's fleet of delivery trucks rumbled along NYC streets in the wee hours of the morning, taking suds to his "beer drops"—big garages where he stored beer to be picked up by bootleggers and speakeasy owners. One drop, located near the railroad yards in Mott Haven, was known as "the Tins" because it had rows of metal garages. It also had at least one huge service elevator that could lower an empty truck underground and raise it after it was loaded.

The Dutchman, who had sound business instincts, saw the value of diversifying and having multiple revenue streams. Alongside his liquor business, he built an illegal gambling empire. He raked in tons of cash from the policy racket, or numbers game, in Harlem. He ruthlessly muscled his way into that racket, pushing aside the numbers bankers who had run the game for years. He installed slot machines in his speakeasies and in other outlets around the Big Apple. His one-armed bandits reportedly came with step ladders, so children could play. He ran protection rackets in the food service sector, extorting money from restaurant owners and the waiters' union. He even started legitimate ventures, such as a bail bond business and an architectural firm that specialized in renovating old breweries.

The Dutchman refused to traffic in drugs or women, and he felt morally superior to mobsters who made money in those rackets. On one occasion a drug dealer smuggled a million dollars' worth of heroin from Romania to New York and offered Schultz part of the action. The dealer wanted to use Schultz's connections to sell the heroin in Harlem, but the Dutchman flatly rejected the idea. He stayed true to his own code of ethics, which classified liquor trafficking and gambling as less reprehensible than narcotics and prostitution.[22]

The Mad Dog Bites

Brothers Pete Coll and Vincent "Mad Dog" Coll belonged to Dutch Schultz's inner circle. Schultz first met the Colls when they were boys growing up in the Morrisania district in the Bronx. Mad Dog Coll, the younger of the two, was a precocious child hoodlum who seemed destined to be a mob superstar. The court designated him a "disorderly child" at age eleven and sent him to the Immaculate Virgin Mission for rehabilitation. The mission couldn't reform the young troublemaker, and he was soon back on the streets. He continued on his wayward path and was arrested for burglary. This time the authorities sent him to a facility run by the Catholic Protectory, which failed in its efforts to change his unruly ways.[23]

As a young adult, Mad Dog Coll seemed to be caught in a revolving door in the justice system. On a more or less regular basis, he was arrested, served a short term in prison, got out, and returned to gangland. Despite his frequent enforced absences from the Schultz gang, he managed to become the Dutchman's trusted right-hand man.

Gangsters tended to look like thugs, but Mad Dog's appearance was deceptively clean-cut. He stood out in police lineups because the men around him seemed to be a lot rougher and tougher than he was. He "looked like a Harvard sophomore" or "a recent graduate of the University of Pennsylvania," according to newsmen. He was tall and lanky with thick blond hair, a deep dimple in his chin, and a bright, toothy smile. In photographs his sunny smile suggested a cheerful, friendly nature. But his wholesome appearance masked his true character. Despite his boy-next-door looks, he would always be a violent social pariah.[24]

In 1930 Mad Dog was arrested for murder after gunmen killed a dance hall hostess and a "slot-machine racketeer" in the Bronx. The murder victims had parked their car in a public garage and walked to the street corner. A big automobile pulled up to the curb; four men hopped out and opened fire. The victims ran in opposite directions. The woman, screaming for help, ran only a few yards before she tripped and stumbled. As she fell, two of the gunmen fired at her, shooting her in the back. The other triggermen chased the racketeer and cornered him on a ramp going upstairs at a garage. He was hit at least twice and died instantly. The gunmen hustled back to their car and drove away. Onlookers put the bleeding hostess in a taxi; she died on the way to the hospital.[25]

The police believed that the slot-machine racketeer had run afoul of Schultz, who had ordered the hit. In this scenario, Mad Dog Coll was the gunman who led the shooters. After the cops arrested and interrogated Mad Dog, he was charged with homicide and a felony violation of the Sullivan gun law. Once again, he was locked up behind bars. Subsequently, authorities dismissed the murder charges due to lack of evidence. But Mad Dog had to remain in jail on the gun felony until he paid $10,000 cash bail, which Schultz supplied, despite his reputation as a miser.[26]

Schultz was furious with his henchmen because, to his way of thinking, they had bungled the hit. The Dutchman read the riot act to them, calling the murders "crude" and unprofessional. Cornering a rival mobster and shooting him was okay in gangland. But the dance hall hostess, an unarmed woman, had been shot in the back. This was not standard operating procedure. After venting his rage, the Dutchman told the Coll brothers and two other gang members to hit the road! Pronto!

Predictably, the expelled hoods accused Schultz of betraying them. They had followed his orders and killed the slots racketeer. But the Dutchman didn't say "job well done." He sent them packing for no good reason. To show him who was really boss, they formed their own mob and set out to take over Schultz's beer business in Harlem and the Bronx. The beer baron reacted swiftly to protect his turf, and a gang war was on.[27]

Although Mad Dog Coll was busy battling Schultz, he found time to have an affair with the wife of another mobster. The woman fell in love with the handsome young hood and gave him thousands of dollars, which he used to open a speakeasy in the Bronx. Schultz viewed this as brazen, provocative trespass on his territory. He had ways of dealing with interlopers — some direct, others more circuitous. The police raided Coll's speakeasy and confiscated his liquor, shutting him down and costing him money he couldn't afford to lose. He felt certain that Schultz had arranged the raid, so the Coll gang retaliated by killing two of the Dutchman's soldiers.

Schultz didn't wait long to retaliate. Pete Coll, Mad Dog's brother, was driving his car down a city street one night, when an auto pulled alongside and gunmen shot at him. Several bullets shattered the windshield and hit Pete. His car crashed into a wall, and he died before rescuers could save him. The police suspected Schultz gunsels had fired the shots that caused Pete's death. Mad Dog agreed that Schultz had ordered the hit, but he believed it was a case of mistaken identity. Mad Dog thought he was the intended target and the shooters had killed the wrong Coll brother. He feared being gunned down if he attended Pete's funeral, so he stayed out of sight, watching it from a safe distance.[28]

Only days after Pete Coll's funeral, Mad Dog led his troops into a garage where Schultz stored trucks and equipment. The Coll gunmen surprised Schultz's men and got the upper hand. But the invaders took a big risk: they didn't tie up or shoot the Dutchman's soldiers. Instead the intruders ordered Schultz's men to use axes and sledge hammers to smash their boss's trucks, slot machines, bar fixtures, and vending machines. Schultz's soldiers followed orders and, surprisingly, didn't use the tools to attack the intruders.

Later that same night, the Dutchman heard about the attack and surveyed the damage to his property. Then he led his lieutenants on a hunt for Coll. When they caught up with Coll and his men, the two gangs fought a running battle in cars, racing along the city streets, firing at one another with pistols and machineguns. No fatalities were reported — presumably because shooting from speeding cars limited the gunners' accuracy.[29]

The mob war quieted down for a few weeks but heated up again when Coll's gun felony case went to trial. Mad Dog didn't show up in court, thereby forfeiting the $10,000 cash bail he had paid with Schultz's money. Coll's motive for being a no-show probably had more to do with Schultz than the gun charges. Causing the frugal mob boss to lose ten grand must've been sweet vengeance for Mad Dog. He struck the beer baron in a very sensitive place — his wallet. As for Schultz, the loss gave him another reason to loathe Mad Dog.

The war was on again and, despite casualties on both sides, showed no signs of cooling off. Coll's gang hijacked several of the Dutchman's beer trucks and killed the drivers. Mad Dog's goons also invaded the home of a Schultz underling and murdered him in his own bedroom. According to an informed source, the war claimed the lives of at least fifteen Schultz gangsters. Despite the beer baron's miserly reputation, he provided financial help for the families of his fallen soldiers.[30]

While the Dutchman feuded with Coll, he also had an occasional clash with law enforcement. In June 1931 Schultz and four of his henchmen fought a sidewalk gun battle with police detectives on Fifth Avenue in Manhattan. The shooting began when the Schultz contingent mistook the detectives for rival gangsters and ran after them. In the midst of the firefight, the Dutchman threw away his gun and sprinted down the street. The cops caught up and arrested him. Schultz wasn't wounded, but one of his lieutenants took a bullet in the abdomen and died later that night.

After Schultz was taken to the police station, he tried to buy his freedom by offering a bribe to two detectives; he proposed to give each of them a house and $50,000. They rejected his generous offer. At his arraignment, he was charged with attempted felonious assault on a police officer and violations of the Sullivan gun law. Bond was set at $150,000 — an outrageously high sum, even for a beer baron. At a subsequent hearing, his bail was reduced by half. Despite strong evidence against Schultz, the jury acquitted him at trial.

A surge in major crimes in Bronx County prompted law enforcement to crack down on racketeers, especially Schultz, in the early 1930s. The district attorney spearheaded a crusade to drive the beer baron out of the Bronx by seriously disrupting his business. Borough officials raided Schultz's Westchester Grill, which was more saloon than eatery, and stationed cops inside the building around the clock. The district attorney promised more raids and constant police surveillance of Schultz's speakeasies in the Bronx. He kept his word. Every day the police raided the speakeasy Schultz used as his headquarters — hitting it more than once on some days. After a time, the Dutchman closed that speakeasy and moved his headquarters to another location. The police staked out the new place and often barged in to check out the action. Law enforcement tapped Schultz's telephone lines and began confiscating his beer trucks. The Dutchman got the message. When Bronx officials ordered him to leave the borough, he moved his headquarters. Gangland sources said he set up a new command center in Manhattan.[31]

The Baby Massacre

On a sweltering dog-day afternoon in July 1931, the violent murder of an innocent child alarmed even blasé New Yorkers. In Harlem's Little Italy children were playing near a lemonade stand on the sidewalk on East 107th Street. Mothers, sitting on the stoops or looking out open windows, watched their children. Clumps of men stood on the street corner, smoking and talking. An open touring car cruised along the street. Suddenly shots rang out as gunmen in the auto opened fire with shotguns and pistols. Bullets tore through the air. Mothers ran to save their terrified, screaming children.

The gunners' target was a man standing in front of the Helmar Social Club, the hangout for a gang led by mobster Joe Rao. The human target hit the ground, kept his head down, and escaped injury. The youngsters didn't know the drill. Bullets struck four children playing on the sidewalk and a toddler napping in a wicker baby carriage. The shooting victims were rushed to nearby hospitals, but the doctors couldn't save five-year-old Michael Vengali.[32]

When the police arrived on the scene, they questioned the bystanders, but they couldn't find the male target, who had vanished in the chaos. Detectives believed the gunmen had intended to kill Joe Rao or a member of his gang. If so, the gunners in the car almost certainly belonged to the Coll gang. Underworld sources said that Coll had fought a gun battle with Joe Rao and his brother a few weeks earlier. Coll had suffered gunshot wounds but had recovered enough to return to combat in the mob wars. Joe Rao and Dutch Schultz were sometimes friends, sometimes foes. At present, they were partners in bootlegging and gambling ventures in Harlem. They were also allies in the war against Mad Dog Coll because both viewed him as an arrogant, reckless upstart who ought to be on a slab in the morgue.[33]

News of the drive-by shooting, dubbed "the baby massacre" by the press, spread at breakneck speed through New York City. Enraged, frightened citizens demanded that city officials do something ASAP! The NYPD beefed up its neighborhood patrols. Detectives armed with shotguns and tear gas cruised around Harlem. Plainclothes officers were deployed to stop and search all suspicious vehicles. If they saw anything strange about a driver or a vehicle — even a dirty license plate — they stopped the auto, interrogated the driver, and did a thorough search.[34]

More than fifty detectives were assigned to collect evidence and find mob bosses Coll and Rao. Despite the large task force, the police had trouble gathering information. Although many people had been present at the baby massacre, most couldn't or wouldn't help the police. Many potential witnesses weren't helpful because they had heard the shots but hadn't seen the shooters. Those who had seen the gunmen were, in general, afraid to talk to police. To motivate witnesses to come forth, city officials ordered a reward of $30,000.

Several days after the massacre, the police arrested a former member of the Coll gang, who admitted that he had been at the drive-by. But he denied being a shooter. In fact, he thought the gunmen had shot at him because he was on the sidewalk. He claimed he had scooped up a child and crawled to the hallway of a tenement, carrying the tot to safety. Like other witnesses, he couldn't or wouldn't identify the shooters.[35]

A major break came when the police arrested a robber a week after the drive-by shooting. Although his arrest had nothing to do with the baby massacre, he said that he had witnessed it. He wanted to bargain, and law enforcement agreed to drop the robbery charges in exchange for his information. The thief gave a description of the gunmen's car, including the license plate number. He also stated that he knew three of the shooters and all belonged to the Coll gang.[36]

Another eyewitness, Eskimo Pie salesman George Brecht, contacted the NYPD and said he could identify the gunmen because he had seen their faces. Moreover, he was willing to testify in court. The pieces were coming together. Prosecutors felt confident they could build a solid case against the Coll gang, so the NYPD stepped up the search for Mad Dog. Police informants said he was hiding in New York or New Jersey, so he hadn't gone far. Law enforcement launched an intensive manhunt, but he eluded capture.[37]

While the NYPD focused on the baby massacre, federal Prohibition agents turned up the heat on Dutch Schultz. The Prohis staked out the Majestic Garage, a Schultz beer depot on Westchester Avenue in the Bronx. One night in October they raided the garage and seized three truckloads of liquor parked near the rear exit. They were questioning Schultz's minions when a large stone crashed through a glass panel above the rear door. They barely had time to say "what-the-hell" before a bomb flew through the gaping hole. The explosive burst with a roar, shattering windows and waking people in nearby buildings. The Prohis ran outside in time to see a car racing away.[38]

Although the agents failed to get the license plate number on the bombers' car, an alert civilian wrote it down as the auto sped past him. This led to the quick arrest of the wheelman who had driven the getaway car. When detectives interrogated him, he admitted belonging to the Coll gang. He stated that Coll and his top lieutenants had recently come out of hiding and returned to NYC. He also revealed the location of the mob's hideout in upstate New York, where other gang members were keeping a low profile.

The NYPD moved swiftly to arrest the gang members in the city. Officers nabbed Coll at a NYC hotel, where he had registered on the day Schultz's depot was bombed. Since he was a wanted man, he had disguised himself by dyeing his hair, growing a moustache, and wearing glasses. He didn't resist arrest but did complain that he was being blamed for everything bad that had "happened in New York all summer."[39]

Based on information from the NYPD, lawmen in upstate New York stormed the Coll gang's headquarters at Averill Park near Troy. Predictably, both sides of the law opened fire. Dozens of shots were exchanged, but no one was injured. The lawmen rounded up the mobsters and took them to jail. The Coll gang was out of business — at least until the men could make bail.

The day after Coll's arrest, he was indicted on murder and gun charges related to the baby massacre. Everybody agreed that Coll had not acted alone, but investigators didn't know how many shooters had been in the car. Prosecutors decided they had a strong, convincing case against only two men — Mad Dog Coll and his lieutenant Frank Giordano, who was already under indictment for killing a member of the Schultz mob. Before the baby massacre case went to court, Giordano was tried for the mob hit and found guilty.

On December 17, 1931, Coll and Giordano went on trial for the drive-by shooting. Before testimony began, Mad Dog disavowed any role in the baby massacre. He issued a statement, saying, "I would like nothing better than to lay my hands on the man who did this. I would tear his throat out. There is nothing more despicable than a man who would harm an innocent child." Coll declared that he was the victim of "enemies, who have tried many times to assassinate me and have failed. Now they are trying to bring about my death through the law."[40]

Guards brought Giordano to the courtroom from the Death House at Sing Sing, where he was awaiting execution for the mob hit. The outcome of this new trial meant little to him. In the courtroom he looked bored and didn't seem interested in defending himself. For him, this trial was almost a nuisance. He already knew his fate.[41]

The prosecution's ace witness was ice cream salesman George Brecht, who had contacted police after the drive-by. A reporter called Brecht a "naïve hillbilly from Missouri" because he had recently moved to NYC from St. Louis. In the courtroom Brecht stated that he had never been in prison nor testified in a murder case. He didn't live in Harlem's Little Italy but happened to be there because he wanted to change jobs and had an interview at a belt factory. When he heard the shots, he was walking along East 107th Street. He saw a car with two men, one in the front seat and the other in the back, holding guns and shooting. In the courtroom, he positively, emphatically identified Coll and Giordano as the shooters.

Defense attorney Samuel Leibowitz attacked Brecht's credibility and accused him of testifying for money. Brecht admitted that the NYPD was paying his bills, including the tab for his hotel. The department was also giving him money to send to his wife. On top of that, the NYPD had given him tickets to ballgames at the Polo Grounds and prizefights at Madison Square Garden. However, he denied that he had come forward because he wanted the $30,000 reward.[42]

The prosecution called police officers and a ballistics expert to the witness stand to explain the evidence collected at the crime scene. Coll seemed to be affected only once: when the white wicker baby carriage, stained with the infant's blood, was brought into the courtroom, he looked away. The state's witnesses included two teenagers who had survived the drive-by and were brave enough to testify against the mobsters. The sister of the dead boy talked about her family's tragic loss. The former Coll gangster, who was probably the shooters' target, also took the stand. Like a typical mobster, he didn't remember much.[43]

The attorneys on both sides of the case knew that Brecht's testimony was crucial to a guilty verdict. Defense attorney Leibowitz recalled the ice cream man to the stand for another attempt to discredit him. Brecht held up well under the verbal assault, even though Leibowitz pointed out discrepancies between his testimony and that of other eyewitnesses. The most important inconsistency was the Missouri man's positive I.D. of Coll and Giordano. The teenage survivors agreed that the gunmen had pulled their hats low over their foreheads, obscuring their faces. Yet Brecht insisted that he had gotten a good look at their faces. He remained firm in identifying the defendants as the killers.[44]

When court convened on Christmas Eve morning, the baby massacre trial was winding down. The witnesses had testified, and the jurors had heard the evidence. But, to everyone's surprise, the trial ended with a dramatic twist. Defendants Coll and Giordano received an unexpected Christmas gift, courtesy of the ice cream salesman. A Brooklyn probation officer who knew Brecht had contacted the court with damaging information about the state's key witness. Defense attorney Leibowitz finally had the ammunition to discredit the Mad Dog's chief accuser.

Using the new evidence, Leibowitz proved that Brecht had a criminal record and had done time for stealing diamonds in Missouri. He had also spent time in a mental institution. Moreover, he was known as a "professional witness" in St. Louis. In at least one trial, the state and the victim's family had paid him to testify. He had also testified in a mob murder trial in St. Louis, giving testimony eerily similar to his statements in the present case. When Leibowitz questioned Brecht, the Missouri man admitted that he had come forward as a witness because he needed money. He also confessed that he had lied about his past.[45]

This left the state's case in shambles. The judge and the state's attorney agreed that Brecht was a "totally unreliable witness." The judge directed the jury to return a not guilty verdict for Coll and Giordano. Brecht was taken to the Bellevue Hospital psychopathic ward for observation.

Naturally, Coll was delighted with the directed verdict, but his joy was tempered by the fact that he wasn't a free man. Guards took him back to his jail cell because charges were pending against him for other crimes. After attorney Leibowitz obtained a writ of habeas corpus, Coll posted bail and was released on New Year's Eve.[46]

Although Mad Dog was free, he found himself under constant police surveillance. Cops staked out his home and followed him wherever he went. Twice in one week detectives arrested him and took him in for questioning. They also briefly took his wife into custody. The police scrutiny curtailed the Mad Dog's criminal pursuits, and he was reduced to working as a guard at crap games to earn a few bucks.[47]

Coll had to dodge more than the cops. The gangland grapevine said a $50,000 reward was waiting for the man who killed Mad Dog. There were conflicting rumors about who offered the bounty. The police believed Dutch Schultz would pay a hefty sum to get rid of his rival, but reliable sources said Owney Madden had put up the reward. According to gangland gossip, Coll had extorted money from Madden by kidnapping Owney's partner, Big Frenchy DeMange. Madden had paid the ransom, and now he wanted revenge.

On February 1, 1932, gunmen with automatic weapons invaded a dinner party in the Bronx and opened fire on members of the Coll gang. When the gunplay ended, two Coll lieutenants and a woman were dead. Another four individuals had gunshot wounds. Police said the gunsels had gone to the party looking for Mad Dog. But they missed him because he was not a punctual person and was running late, as usual. Detectives believed Schultz had sent the shooters.[48]

Only a week after the bloody dinner party, Mad Dog Coll was talking on the phone in a telephone booth at a pharmacy on West 23rd Street in Manhattan. He had arrived with another man, who was waiting for him at the soda fountain. He may or may not have noticed the police detective who had followed him from his home to the drugstore. A large sedan stopped at the curb outside the store, and three men hopped out. Two stood beside the car while the third walked quickly and resolutely into the pharmacy. As he pulled a Tommy gun from under his coat, he told the handful of clerks and customers to "keep cool." Coll's companion slipped out the front door. The gunman walked over to the phone booth and fired a barrage of bullets through the glass window. Mad Dog Coll died on the spot, his life over at age twenty-three.

The gunman strode out of the store and rejoined his buddies. They all piled into the big sedan and took off. The cop who had been shadowing Coll saw the car speeding away. He hailed a passing taxi, jumped on the running board, and ordered the driver to follow the sedan. At speeds up to sixty-five mph, the policeman hung onto the cab door with one hand while he fired his revolver at the getaway car. For about thirty harrowing blocks, the cab stayed close to the getaway car. Then the driver of the big sedan put on extra speed and pulled away, leaving the taxi behind.[49]

When bold headlines announced Coll's death, New Yorkers breathed a collective sigh of relief. Another vicious, bloodthirsty mobster had departed Gotham forever. Police detectives said they had promising clues that would lead them to the Mad Dog's killer. However, they soon hit the customary brick wall. Coll's wife refused to answer any questions that might help the police, but she did say that he had died broke, leaving her nothing of consequence.

The autopsy revealed that at least fifteen bullets had struck Coll in the head, chest, and arm. "There wasn't enough bone left in his right arm to make a toothpick out of," the medical examiner stated. After Coll's sister claimed his bullet-ridden body at the morgue, the family moved it to an undertaker's parlor in the Bronx. Only a handful of people came to pay their respects. Almost all of Coll's button men were in jail or on the lam. A curious crowd gathered outside the funeral home, and police were called to keep order. When strangers tried to enter the building to gawk at the notorious corpse, Coll's family asked the police to keep them out.

Due to the severe shortage of cash, Mad Dog's wife couldn't afford a lavish gangster funeral. Following a brief prayer at the funeral home, Coll was buried without fanfare at St. Raymond's Cemetery in the Bronx.[50]

Dutch Schultz didn't attend the funeral, but later a newsman asked him if he had been friends with Mad Dog.

The Dutchman grinned. "Sometimes," he said.[51]

12. Payback: The Tax Collector versus the Peculator

Let them come. I'm not afraid of anybody.—Dutch Schultz, beer baron, New York City[1]

Dutch Schultz spent the 1920s building his criminal fiefdom and enjoying the fruits of his illegal labor. Like other beer barons, he exploited the Great Drought to accumulate vast illicit wealth. During the Great Depression, the liquor lords felt the financial pinch along with everyone else, although not always to the same degree. Schultz thrived in the Roaring Twenties. In the Thirties he struggled to hold onto his power as his illegal income shrank and the federal government threatened to crush him. Washington chose tax fraud, rather than Volstead charges, to put him out of business. When the end came, the taxman proved to be kinder than his gangland rivals.

Trying Times

In the Roaring Twenties liquor traffickers had little fear of punishment. Until 1929 the standard sentence for a major Volstead conviction was two years in federal prison. With time off for good behavior, the bootlegger could expect an early parole. If he greased the right palms, he might receive a pardon. Even if he couldn't finagle a pardon, money would buy him special privileges inside the prison. He might even be allowed furloughs to attend to mob business or his personal affairs.

In order to send a bootlegger to prison, the state had to obtain a guilty verdict in a court of law, which could be a difficult feat during the Arid Era. Securing a conviction on Volstead charges was challenging for a variety of reasons—most notably, corruption and public apathy. The wise bootlegger budgeted a sizeable sum for payoffs to ensure that lawmen and government officials ignored his crimes. This generally kept him from being arrested. However, if bribery failed and the bootlegger actually faced a trial, a conviction was unlikely. Many citizens felt that selling liquor wasn't a crime and prosecuting Volstead violators was a waste of taxpayer money. They balked at incarcerating bootleggers for defying a minor, misguided law. They wanted the legal system to focus on serious crimes, like murder and armed robbery.

Given the public's feelings about the dry law, prosecutors found it frustrating to take

Volstead cases to court, especially in jurisdictions where there was general contempt for the dry law. Prosecuting attorneys learned that it was easier to convict bootleggers on crimes that did not deal directly with alcohol. Indicting liquor traffickers for tax fraud proved to be an effective tactic, putting many mobsters behind bars during Volstead's latter years.

In the 1920s the federal government relied on a new personal income tax to replace the funds lost when liquor taxes became a minor source of revenue. Naturally, it took time for the public to learn the finer points of the new tax code. Some people unintentionally broke the law; others willfully failed to report part or all of their income. To impress everyone with the dire consequences of tax evasion, the feds pursued tax fraud cases against famous people, especially movie stars. The press gave extensive coverage to these cases, which educated everyone about the high cost of lying to the Bureau of Internal Revenue (later the Internal Revenue Service).

The denizens of the underworld put their own spin on the new tax law. In gangland, conventional wisdom said that income from illicit sources, like bootlegging and illegal gambling, was not taxable. Of course, this was nothing more than wishful thinking. The federal government had the right to collect taxes on all income, whether legal or illegal. Nevertheless, bootleggers generally ignored the income tax law.

In the early 1920s court decisions laid the crucial groundwork for prosecuting the liquor lords for tax fraud. In *United States v. Yuginovich*, the U.S. Supreme Court ruled that the Congressional taxing power included the right to tax the owners of an illegal distillery. *United States v. Stafoff* combined three cases involving liquor traffickers. One of the defendants was Cincinnati's most notorious bootlegger, attorney George Remus. In the ruling, Justice Oliver Wendell Holmes Jr. said simply and empathically: "Of course Congress may tax what it also forbids."[2]

In another important case, the government charged the defendant with evading taxes on income gained by the illegal withdrawal and resale of medical alcohol. Although the defendant filed tax returns, he greatly under-reported his earnings. The defense argued that "the winnings of a professional gambler, the loot of a burglar, the bribes of a dishonest official, the wages of a prostitute, or the profits of any criminal commerce should not be regarded as income but, for reasons of public policy, be regarded as beneath the contempt of the law." Despite the clever argument, the court of appeals ruled that the income tax law pertained to gains, profits, and income derived from all sources—licit or illicit.[3]

United States v. Sullivan began as a simple rumrunning case but evolved to deal with a crucial constitutional issue: self-incrimination. Manly Sullivan and three accomplices were arrested for operating "a mammoth whiskey supply station" in Charleston, South Carolina. Federal agents confiscated Sullivan's rumrunning boat along with its expensive cargo of liquor. At trial, the defendants pled not guilty. Sullivan, a lawyer as well as a rumrunner, testified that the liquor on his boat didn't actually belong to him. He claimed that he had been arrested simply because the mayor of Charleston hated him. The case ended in a mistrial.[4]

Sullivan had won a victory of sorts, but the justice system wasn't finished with him. The state changed its strategy, indicting Sullivan for tax evasion because he didn't report his rumrunning income. In round one, he was found guilty in a federal district court. In round two, he appealed his conviction to the Fourth Circuit Court of Appeals. This time he argued that declaring income from a crime violated the Fifth Amendment protection against self-incrimination. Paying taxes on illegal income amounted to a criminal confession. The appeals court agreed, saying that paying taxes on illegal earnings compelled the lawbreaker "to keep a business record of his crime."

In the final round, Sullivan's case went to the U.S. Supreme Court. Assistant U.S. Attorney General Mabel Willebrandt argued that Sullivan had committed a crime by failing to report all his income on his tax return. The defense countered that Sullivan had a constitutional right against self-incrimination and, thus, a right to withhold inculpatory facts. Willebrandt disagreed, citing the established principle that "records required by law ... constitute an exception to the application of the Fifth Amendment." Moreover, the questions on the tax form did not actually compel Sullivan to disclose the specifics of his illegal business. The Supreme Court ruled that reporting income from illegal ventures did not violate the Fifth Amendment.[5]

In Volstead's early days, the Bureau of Internal Revenue (BIR) undertook to collect taxes from bootleggers in a scattershot fashion. A legger who spent lavishly and flashed big wads of cash was likely to attract the attention of revenue agents. His rank in gangland's hierarchy didn't matter; in fact, guppies were caught more often than whales. Income tax evasion carried serious penalties — up to $10,000 in fines and up to five years in federal prison plus the payment of back taxes. But the Treasury Department focused on collecting money, rather than sending tax evaders to jail.

The BIR issued press releases urging bootleggers to pay their taxes. The bureau seemed almost sympathetic to leggers "who, because of oversight, or lack of time, or pressure of business have neglected to file their income tax returns." The BIR called these men "peculators," a term denoting persons who dishonestly take money, especially public funds. The press releases assured bootleggers that they would not be turned over to the Prohibition Unit if they came to the BIR office to negotiate a tax settlement. By law, the BIR's files on a bootlegger's income were kept confidential and couldn't be given to the Prohis.[6] The wise bootlegger hurried over to the BIR to make a deal.

Justice on a Full Stomach

In June 1931 federal authorities revealed that they were opening a new front in the war against New York's most notorious public enemies. Prosecutions for tax fraud would be their weapon of choice and they would do more than collect money. They would send the guilty peculators to prison. The chief of the Treasury Department's Special Intelligence Unit would lead a squad of expert tax investigators to gather evidence "against racketeers who have grown wealthy from liquor, narcotics, and [the] operation of shady nightclubs." To no one's surprise, Dutch Schultz was on the short list.[7]

Only days after the Treasury Department announced its New York initiative, the Bronx County district attorney led a group of police detectives and federal investigators on a sensational raid. The men invaded the Bronx trucking company that fronted for Schultz's illegal beer distributorship. They seized ledgers, customer lists, and other documents from two safes in the office.

Schultz knew that the D.A.'s raiding party had seized incriminating records that could be used as evidence in court. No doubt, the Treasury's special squad would study those records and track down additional evidence to assemble an accurate, detailed picture of his finances. To stop the feds from delving deeper into his business, Schultz decided to pay his back taxes. On more than one occasion, he sent his attorneys to meet with federal officials and offer a cash settlement on his taxes if no criminal charges were filed against him.

The feds rejected all his offers because they wanted to put him behind bars as much as they wanted to collect his taxes. When asked about the Dutchman's overtures, U.S. Attorney George Medalie said, "My reply was that the federal government intended to prosecute Schultz and all others like him who evaded the law. First one attorney came, then another. But none of them got anywhere." In a proposal that truly smacked of desperation, Schultz offered to cough up $100,000 in back taxes plus $100,000 for Franklin Roosevelt's presidential campaign fund. Like his other overtures, this was a nonstarter.[8]

Schultz greeted New Year's 1933 knowing that the feds' plan to put him behind bars was gaining momentum. Prosecutors had already presented evidence about his finances to federal grand juries in New York. They had called roughly three hundred witnesses to testify, but not all had talked. Three of the Dutchman's top lieutenants had refused to answer questions; they were jailed for contempt of court.

On January 18, 1933, a federal commissioner signed an arrest warrant on a complaint charging Schultz with income tax evasion. The warrant was based on in-depth probes by revenue agents and a team led by Chief Assistant U.S. Attorney Thomas Dewey. Eight days later a federal grand jury voted a sealed indictment against Schultz for violating the income tax law.[9]

Shortly after the indictment, someone broke into the district attorney's office in Manhattan and stole much of the paper evidence against Schultz. Metal filing cabinets were jimmied open in a "rather primitive fashion." Sheaves of telephone invoices, business contracts, and grand jury records were taken. Also stolen were delivery receipts showing sales of gas and oil to Schultz's garages to keep his beer trucks running. There was no question about the motive for the break-in: only documents relating to Schultz were taken; all the other files were intact.

The theft didn't stop the probe, but replacing the lost documents slowed it down. The telephone company assigned "a corps of accountants and clerks to work" on reconstructing the phone records. Duplicates were available of most of the grand jury material, but copies of the contracts couldn't be found. Luckily for the prosecutors, the most important documents weren't stolen because they were stored at another office.[10]

To enforce the warrant for Schultz's arrest, lawmen began searching for him. They checked his usual haunts in Gotham but couldn't find him. The NYPD notified police departments across the country to watch for him. Gangland gossip said he had fled to a foreign country so he couldn't be extradited on tax charges. Law enforcement spent thousands of taxpayer dollars sending officers to check out leads in far-flung places, including Canada, Mexico, and Bermuda. At one point, the police believed Schultz had fled to Hawaii and then traveled from there to Cuba. Detectives flew to Cuba to nab him but arrived too late. He had boarded an airplane a few hours before they landed. (Fleeing to another country didn't necessarily mean freedom from prosecution. Although tax violations were not extraditable crimes, Washington could ask a foreign government to deport Schultz as an undesirable alien. If Washington applied enough pressure, the other government would allow U.S. lawmen to take Schultz back to the States.)[11]

The Dutchman may have briefly fled the USA, but he spent most of his time in New

York City. Despite his frugality, he rented three apartments so he could move from one hideout to another, as needed. To disguise himself, he wore spectacles and a wispy moustache. From time to time acquaintances spotted him on the street, in Penn Station, or at a popular steakhouse. Gangland sources said he made many visits to a famous brothel in Manhattan.[12] (Strangely, his code of ethics prevented him from owning a bordello but not from patronizing one.)

On one occasion police heard that Schultz was hunting on an estate near Newburgh, New York. A squad of federal agents and NYC detectives rushed to the scene but failed to find him. For a time, a Broadway actress sheltered Schultz at her home on Long Island. Then he moved to another Long Island address, living in a cottage at Idle Hour, a Connetquot River estate once owned by William Vanderbilt. On multiple occasions police detectives searched Idle Hour without finding the Dutchman. Hiding places were plentiful on the 900-acre estate, which boasted a Gilded Age mansion, cloistered walkways, an enclosed courtyard, gardens, tennis courts, a conservatory, a gatehouse, and a court for playing fives (a game resembling handball).

Underworld sources said that Schultz showed up at least once a week in Harlem to protect his interests there. Newspapers reported that he had attended a contentious no-holds-barred meeting to reassert his power over rebellious numbers bankers in Harlem.[13] If the press knew the Dutchman's whereabouts, why couldn't law enforcement nab him? Cynics said he was paying high-ranking officials not to find him.

Revenue agents arrested beer baron Waxy Gordon for tax fraud in June 1933. While the feds focused on prosecuting Gordon, they had less time to spend on Schultz. They let the Dutchman's case simmer on the backburner, but they didn't forget him. As soon as Gordon's trial ended in December 1933, finding Schultz became an urgent matter because the feds wanted to follow up with another front-page case.[14]

In January 1934, nearly a year after Schultz's tax indictment, the NYPD announced a new push to find him. At that time, reliable sources said he was living in Westchester, New York. "It is a disgrace to the police department that a man known to so many persons ... should be at large," said a high-ranking police officer. "The honesty, sincerity, and integrity of the department demand that he be apprehended." Two detectives "with a reputation for vigor in harrying members of Schultz's mob" were assigned to find the Dutchman.

The NYPD aces didn't have to carry the whole load. The head of the Internal Revenue's Bureau of Investigation handpicked a squad of federal agents to hunt for the sly Dutchman. Fifty thousand broadsheets describing Schultz, right down to the bullet scars on his forearm, were plastered like circus posters all over the country. Wanted posters with his mug shot and fingerprints were displayed in post offices, police stations, and federal buildings. The feds sent one hundred thousand circulars to police departments around the world. All this publicity led to unconfirmed Schultz sightings in places as far away as France, but he remained at large.[15]

In November 1934 Treasury Department officials and the mayor of New York City agreed to devote more resources to finding the elusive beer baron. Later that same month, newspapers reported that federal agents had Schultz under surveillance near Saratoga, New York.

The day before Thanksgiving, a sallow man in a baggy blue suit, a dark overcoat, and a gray felt hat walked into the U.S. Commissioner's office in Albany, New York. He introduced himself as Arthur Flegenheimer and said he was a wanted man. After nearly two years on the lam, he had come to surrender, accompanied by attorney James Noonan. The commissioner looked confused. Somehow he had missed all the publicity about Schultz, so the lawyer had to explain the Dutchman's case to the commissioner.

Within hours Schultz was locked up in Albany County's new $2 million, escape-proof jail. He spent a quiet Thanksgiving in his cell, reading and becoming acclimated to his new digs. Like his fellow inmates, he was treated to a special holiday meal — ham, potatoes, vegetables, pie, and coffee. The U.S. commissioner set the beer baron's bail at $50,000 and later doubled it.[16]

Schultz offered no public explanation for his decision to surrender. Mob watchers pointed to the new Department of Justice policy that empowered lawmen to shoot-to-kill when they confronted a notorious public enemy. In recent months, bullets had sent a surprising number of America's most wanted to the great beyond. The public had tolerated mobsters in the Roaring Twenties, but the ugly harshness of the Great Depression seemed to call for harsh law enforcement.

Federal officials planned to prosecute the Dutchman in New York City, but attorney Noonan had other ideas. For his opening gambit, he argued that Schultz's indictment was invalid because it was issued in New York's Southern District against a Bronx resident who was required to make his income tax payment to the Collector of Internal Revenue in New York's Northern District. Stated simply, Schultz claimed residency in the Bronx, which was in the Albany tax collection district.

Although this was a piddling jurisdictional issue, Noonan knew it could have a big impact on Schultz's fate. The Bronx beer boss made headlines with great regularity in New York City, but the state's rural newspapers gave him little ink. Upstate residents didn't know he was a mob overlord and a bona fide public enemy. His obscurity in upstate New York increased the likelihood of finding an impartial, even disinterested, jury there.

Federal prosecutors wanted to try Schultz in NYC to take advantage of his notoriety. Moreover, it would be cost-effective to have the trial in the city. The bill for prosecuting the Dutchman would soar if the government had to pay travel and living expenses for the lawyers and witnesses. The prosecutor's office argued that Schultz had recently rented apartments in Manhattan and his income came from rackets in Harlem and the Bronx. Although the Bronx was in the Northern District for tax purposes, it was in New York's Southern District as far as criminal prosecutions were concerned.[17]

In a remarkably short time, the feds dropped their efforts to keep Schultz's case in New York City. They were so eager to proceed with the tax trial that they meekly agreed to accept the change of venue. Federal attorneys went to the district court in Albany to obtain a new indictment that would move the trial to the Northern District. In short order, they had the new indictment, and Schultz was arraigned on tax charges in an upstate courtroom.[18]

On April 15, 1935, Schultz's long-delayed tax trial began in a Syracuse courthouse. He was accused of failing to pay roughly $92,000 in taxes on income derived from unlawful enterprises in 1929–1931. The state alleged that Schultz's beer business had grossed over $2.8 million in those years. The tax experts knew that the gross was actually much higher, but they had to build the case on provable numbers, so lowballing his income was prudent. As proof of Schultz's wealth, the state planned to present evidence that he had more than

$1.6 million in the bank accounts found by investigators.[19] Mob watchers assumed that he had other accounts the feds hadn't discovered.

With unusual efficiency, the opposing lawyers took only a few hours to choose a jury "of gray-haired, keen-faced merchants, farmers, and retired citizens." The juror who would serve as foreman told the court he was a bank appraiser, an insurance man, an auctioneer, a federal farm census taker, and the proprietor of a general store. A reporter called him a "rawboned giant" and "an upstate Will Rogers of heroic stature." During the trial the jurors would be sequestered at a hotel, to keep Schultz's goons from bribing or intimidating them.[20]

The prosecution had subpoenaed a long list of witnesses to testify against the Dutchman, but not everyone showed up at the courthouse. In keeping with the tradition of mob trials, about twenty reluctant witnesses "dropped out of sight rather than embarrass Schultz." The disappearance of Schultz's two bookkeepers left a hard-to-fill gap in the state's case. Of lesser import was the absence of Henry "Heinie" Zimmerman, famous third baseman for the New York Giants. During Prohibition he had owned a speakeasy with Schultz, and the pair had a joint bank account.

The prosecution opened its case with testimony by bank employees familiar with Schultz's accounts and financial transactions. Bank officers identified Schultz as a regular customer who often cashed big checks and withdrew large sums of money. The state submitted a mountain of signature cards, deposit slips, bank ledger sheets, and similar records pertaining to Schultz's accounts. Defense counsel "astonished everyone" by conceding that Schultz had signed bank signature cards under several aliases.[21]

Since the state planned to use wiretap evidence, counsel laid the groundwork by calling telephone company workers to the stand. The workers testified that Schultz had multiple phone lines, which were routed through a central switchboard at his headquarters. In an average month the switchboard handled more than one thousand calls.

Crucial testimony about Schultz's phone calls came from detectives in the NYPD's Secret Service unit. For almost ten months the unit had "supervised the Schultz telephone lines"—that is, listened to taps on his lines. With headsets clamped to their ears, the detectives eavesdropped and jotted down handwritten notes about what they overheard. The majority of callers to Schultz's numbers ordered beer or complained about receiving stale beer.

The Dutchman personally took phone calls from his henchmen, local politicos, and other mob bosses. He gave orders to his underlings and barked at them if they had done something to displease him. Other liquor lords called the Dutchman to ask for favors or to discuss business deals. Schultz often exchanged angry, foul-mouthed threats with his rivals, especially Mad Dog Coll. Taken as a whole, the wiretapping notes showed that Schultz tightly controlled the beer traffic in the Bronx. They also proved that he had substantial political clout and could be nasty when he was mad or threatened.[22]

Marguerite Scholl, a stenographer who had worked for Schultz's missing bookkeepers, testified for the state. Although she barely knew Schultz, she knew a great deal about his business because she had typed the payroll and sales records. In addition, she had access to a key that opened a hidden compartment in a filing cabinet where a secret ledger was stowed. She had given the secret ledger to federal lawmen after Schultz's office was raided.[23]

The prosecution and defense sparred over whether the secret ledger could be introduced into evidence. Defense counsel argued that it must be excluded because the lawmen had obtained it through illegal search and seizure. The judge ruled that the defense had failed to prove illegal search and seizure, but he left the door open for excluding the ledger on other grounds. He said that the ledger showed the profits of a business, but the prosecution had not proved that it belonged to Schultz. It could not "be considered as evidence" without stronger proof that it was, in fact, Schultz's ledger. So, for the time being, the prosecution could use the ledger, but he might rule it inadmissible before the trial ended.[24]

The prosecution called a federal agent to the witness stand to testify about the disputed ledger. His job was to identify the initials used in the secret ledger and explain the entries. Based on the numbers in the book, he calculated Schultz's profits for the jury. On cross-examination, defense counsel forced the agent to concede that he was relying heavily on conjecture. He admitted that the ledger did not contain the name Arthur Flegenheimer or any of his known aliases. The agent believed "sales of B" meant "sales of beer" but could not prove it. Likewise, he interpreted certain initials as standing for specific names, but he had no proof. Perhaps most significantly, the agent admitted that he knew little about accounting. In figuring Schultz's profits, he had not considered depreciation, maintenance, and other items normally taken into account.[25]

The defense attorneys focused on raising doubts about the secret ledger. Both the federal agent and stenographer Scholl admitted that their answers were highly speculative. Scholl had always been sent home when Schultz came to see her bosses, so she was not privy to any of their meetings. Only the missing bookkeepers and the Dutchman knew exactly what the ledger entries meant. Law enforcement couldn't find the bookkeepers, who were almost certainly dead or on the lam. If the men were found, they would face criminal charges, so they weren't likely to come forward voluntarily.

The prosecution called a number of nervous witnesses who didn't want to discuss their business dealings during Prohibition. All were barkeepers or restaurant owners who had bought illegal beer from Schultz. With reluctance, they answered questions about how much beer they had bought and what they paid for it. Some admitted calling Schultz to order beer and gave his phone number as proof. Others had foggy memories and couldn't remember details like his telephone number.

When the defense took over, counsel called only a handful of witnesses. Two were lawyers whom Schultz had hired to negotiate a tax settlement with the federal government. They produced "a sheaf of powers of attorney granted by the defendant to accountants and lawyers" who had met with officials in Washington. Schultz had offered to pay $100,000 in taxes and penalties, but the feds refused to bargain with him. A tax consultant testified that Schultz had sent him to Washington to pay all the taxes, all the interest, and all the penalties plus the interest on them. This consultant met with top Internal Revenue officials, who rejected Schultz's offer.

During breaks in the trial, the Dutchman talked to newsmen and seemed pleased with his defense. He claimed that the government was spending a million dollars trying to collect $100,000 from him. From a purely financial perspective, it made no sense.

"I offered $100,000 when the government was broke and people were talking revolution, and they turned me down cold," Schultz said. "You can see now that at least I was willing to pay.... Everybody knows I am being persecuted in this case. I wanted to pay ... but they wouldn't take it from me. I tried to do my duty as a citizen."[26]

Schultz's tax trial lasted almost three weeks. When the judge charged the jury, he said the case boiled down to two simple questions: (1) Did the defendant "have an income sufficient to call for tax payment?" and (2) "Did the defendant willfully attempt to evade and defeat the tax?" He instructed the jurors to rely on the secret ledger only if they were convinced that it belonged to Schultz and gave an accurate picture of his finances.

After hearing the judge's instructions, the jurors started their deliberations. Several hours later, they returned to the courtroom to ask a question. After a portion of the trial transcript was read to them, they went back to the jury room. When the jurors had been out for twelve hours, they seemed to be deadlocked. Courthouse gossip said some jurors were debating the case, but others were playing pinochle because they had made up their minds and refused to discuss it anymore. Shortly before midnight, the judge ordered the jury locked up for the night.[27]

The next day the jurors resumed their talks but made no progress. They were irrevocably deadlocked. Late that afternoon the judge dismissed the jury and declared a mistrial. Reliable sources said the jurors had taken a dozen ballots; the final count was seven for conviction, five for acquittal.

Schultz probably felt a measure of relief, but he knew that Washington wouldn't give up easily. Top federal officials wanted to put him in jail for tax fraud. The chief prosecutor immediately announced that the feds would ask for an early trial date to retry the case. "We're going to keep trying him until we get a conviction or an acquittal," the prosecutor said. "It is my opinion that the man is guilty, and we'll stick to the case. There will be no letting up, I can assure you."[28]

The venue for the retrial would be Malone, New York, because the federal district court rotated on a circuit from town to town. Before the retrial began, Schultz visited Malone, a village on the edge of the Adirondack Mountains in Upstate New York, not far from the Canadian border. The Dutchman staged a public relations blitz to show the townsfolk that he was a really nice guy — not a public enemy. Despite his frugal habits, he spent money like a drunken sailor. He patronized local businesses and handed out big tips to waiters, bellhops, and other workers. He bought flowers and candy for the sick children in the local hospital. He rented a dance hall and invited everyone in Malone to a big party with refreshments and music. He went to a baseball game with the mayor and other local bigwigs.[29]

Just about everybody in Malone found Schultz to be a swell guy. Congregationalist minister John Williams spoke for the minority when he objected to treating the liquor lord like royalty. The pastor chided the "men in high places" for fawning over the visiting mob boss. He said the local nabobs were dazzled simply because the Dutchman was spreading his ill-gotten wealth around town. He thought they should take a closer look at Schultz's character.[30]

As the citizens of Malone discussed the upcoming tax trial, the prevailing sentiment cast Schultz as a victim of government persecution. Due to his generosity and friendly gestures, the trusting townsfolk didn't view him as a violent, corrupt crime czar. The Dutchman hadn't caused any trouble in Malone, and the local consensus was that he should be acquitted. If he was a menace to society in New York City, he should be on trial in Satan's Seat.

While Schultz was living in Malone, he received good news that had nothing to do with his tax problems; his wife Frances had given birth to their first son in a NYC hospital. Frances Flegenheimer was a young beauty who had worked in speakeasies before she became the Dutchman's sweetheart. It wasn't clear whether the couple had legally tied the knot or simply had a common-law marriage. The new dad sounded excited when he talked about the blessed event, but he would have to wait to see the baby.[31]

The prosecution altered its strategy somewhat for the retrial. Instead of beginning with the financial evidence, the special prosecutor focused first on Schultz's criminal career. The state set up a display of New York City "rogues," a collection of mug shots of Schultz's underworld associates. On the witness stand NYC police officers identified the bad guys in the mug shots. They described the city's bloody mob wars and explained the Dutchman's pivotal role in them. Bronx police detectives testified about Schultz's beer business and his speakeasies. Officers who had listened to the telephone wiretaps summarized the phone conversations between Schultz and other mobsters. A former saloon owner told the jury how Schultz had muscled in and taken over his bar.[32]

In a rerun of the first tax trial, the prosecution called bank employees to testify about Schultz's finances. Internal Revenue officials explained technical details about the tax code and Schultz's financial records. The state's evidence included thick stacks of bank documents, such as checks and deposit slips. Hundreds of checks had to be entered into evidence one at a time — a tedious process that slowed the trial to a snail's pace. In the hot courtroom, everyone sweltered and fidgeted.

The prosecution called stenographer Marguerite Scholl, a star witness in the first trial, to testify about the secret ledger. The defense objected to admitting testimony about the ledger, arguing that law enforcement had seized it illegally. In a bombshell ruling, the judge agreed that the seizure had been illegal. He returned the ledger to the defense, and Schultz smiled broadly as the book changed hands. The prosecutors would have to regroup to make their case without the secret account book.[33]

The state called several of Schultz's henchmen to the witness stand. All of them invoked the Fifth Amendment and refused to testify. After the judge ordered them to answer the prosecutor's questions, they gave vague, often untruthful responses. One man said he had known Schultz for fourteen years but never knew that the Dutchman was a liquor trafficker. The judge sent four of the uncooperative witnesses to jail for contempt of court.[34]

The trial attracted crowds of upstate residents, but it wasn't an exciting, fast-paced show. "Country folk who came to town expecting to hear sensational details of the life of Dutch Schultz went away disappointed," wrote a reporter. "It was all too dull and dignified." The female spectators must've been even more disappointed than the males. The judge ordered the ladies out of the courtroom before a police officer testified about Schultz's spirited use of profanity.[35]

To prove the state's case, the prosecution put sixty-seven witnesses on the stand. When the defense's turn came, only four witnesses testified. The defense relied heavily on a "surprise witness"— Frank Wagner, a prominent citizen and tax consultant in Malone. Wagner stated that he had examined the records used by the government to calculate Schultz's income. Based on those records, he said it was impossible to determine Schultz's gross or net income. The defense's other witnesses were a tax specialist and two lawyers who had advised Schultz on tax matters.

In summation, defense counsel reminded the jurors that the case revolved around taxes — not bootlegging or racketeering. Hence, much of the prosecution's evidence was clearly irrelevant. A Schultz lawyer described the beer baron as a "kindly, good-natured man." He conceded that Schultz had defied the state and federal dry laws during Prohibition but so had many other New Yorkers. "It is a notorious fact that the laws were violated in the knowledge and tolerance of the officials of the City of New York. Federal officials also were there," he said. Echoing the sentiment in Malone, the lawyer declared, "A Franklin County jury should not be called upon to decide something that took place four hundred miles away."[36]

After the judge gave his instructions to the jurors, the "Adirondack woodsmen" retired to deliberate. Following lengthy debate, the jurors sent word to the judge that they were hopelessly deadlocked. The judge wouldn't let them quit. He told them to take a break for dinner and then resume their work.

After eating dinner, the jurors finished their job and returned to the courtroom with their verdict. Almost everyone in the room looked surprised when the jury foreman said, "Not guilty." The Dutchman gazed blankly at his attorneys as he processed what he had just heard. When the good news sank in, a wide grin spread across his face. The friendly locals who packed the courtroom clapped and cheered. The judge banged his gavel, demanding order in the court.

When silence returned, the judge glared at the jurors. "Before I discharge you, I will have to say that your verdict is such that shakes the confidence of law-abiding people in integrity and truth," he said. "It will be apparent to all who have followed the evidence in this case that you have reached a verdict based not on the evidence, but on some other reason." His eyes blazing with anger, he said, "You will go home with the satisfaction, if it is a satisfaction, that you have rendered a blow against law enforcement and given aid and encouragement to the people who would flout the law."[37]

Ironically, the jurors placed the blame — or the credit — for the acquittal on the judge's shoulders. They had asked him to declare a mistrial because they were deadlocked. He had refused and told them to eat dinner. A full stomach made all the difference. On the first ballot after dinner, they voted for acquittal.[38]

13. Famous Last Words:
Bet on Mom

I was proud of him, and I'll be proud to tell my children about their father. — Frances Flegenheimer, Dutch Schultz's wife[1]

Dutch Schultz barely had time to celebrate his victory in Malone before he faced a new barrage of legal hassles. The New York State Department of Taxation and Finance ordered him to appear in court regarding a tax warrant against him for $36,000 (later raised to $70,000). NYC Mayor Fiorello LaGuardia publicly ordered Schultz to stay out of the Big Apple. Special Prosecutor Thomas Dewey, a dedicated crime fighter, confirmed reports that he was leading a task force investigating Schultz's rackets. He planned to move quickly to present evidence to the grand jury. His task force included the Big Apple's first squad of "X-men," an elite group of police officers with special crime-fighting expertise.[2]

Law enforcement had multiple avenues it could pursue against the Dutchman in the post–Volstead era. In addition to the numbers game in Harlem, Schultz ran rackets extorting money from restaurants, unions, and trade associations. After evaluating the options, Dewey decided that prosecuting Schultz for the numbers racket would be his best bet. However, Dewey wasn't the only one who wanted Schultz in prison, and the feds moved first, once again opting for tax fraud.

A federal grand jury indicted Schultz on multiple misdemeanor counts of failing to file his income tax returns. Since his first two trials had been for felony tax fraud, these misdemeanors didn't constitute double jeopardy. The new trial would be in New York County, so prosecutors could choose jurors familiar with the beer baron's long criminal career, improving the odds for a conviction.[3]

After his success in Malone, Schultz paid secret visits to New York City, but he had to avoid arrest there to forestall the new tax trials. To be safe, he took up residence in a hotel in Bridgeport, Connecticut. An excellent horseman, he often rode his horse Suntan in the countryside around Fairfield. Local society embraced him as a celebrity, a very desirable guest at parties. One socialite called him "charming" and said it was "hard to believe all those horrid stories" about him.[4] Given his background, he probably knew nothing about high society except what he read in books. Apparently, it was enough to be a well-mannered guest.

When Schultz decided it was time to decamp, he moved to a hotel in Perth Amboy, New Jersey. The local deputy police chief received an anonymous tip that Schultz was in town and arrested him. After the Dutchman was charged with being a fugitive from justice, he was locked up. The next day he was taken to court for arraignment, and a federal attorney, armed with a bench warrant, took him into custody. The attorney, accompanied by federal agents, transferred the Dutchman to Newark, where the court set his bail at $75,000.

While Schultz's lawyers did their fancy footwork, he went to jail. His high-powered Jersey team, which included a former governor, moved quickly to obtain a writ of habeas corpus and a reduction in his bail. He paid up and left the hoosegow but stayed in New Jersey to avoid being arrested in his home state.[5]

On October 10, 1935, a federal judge in New York City issued an arrest warrant for Schultz on the tax misdemeanors. Because the State of New Jersey had technical jurisdiction over the Dutchman, an extradition hearing would be held before a judge in Newark. If the judge ruled for rendition, the government would move Schultz to New York for a new tax trial. But that wouldn't be the worst of his legal troubles. After all, he had beaten the felony tax rap twice and the new charges were only misdemeanors. What he really feared was being arrested on the racketeering charges brought by Special Prosecutor Dewey.

Schultz's Jersey lawyers delayed his extradition by questioning the judge's fitness to hear the case. The judge was not inclined to recuse himself, but he did take time to study the matter. On October 23, 1935, he issued a lengthy ruling that accused Schultz's lawyers of trying to manipulate the court system. He refused to recuse himself, and he seemed certain to send Schultz into the clutches of the special prosecutor.[6]

The Counterpunch

Dutch Schultz knew that Thomas Dewey's plan to prosecute him for the numbers game had the potential to completely change his life. A felony conviction for the policy racket would send him to prison for a long time. While he languished in the big house, his rivals would take over his rackets. When he got out, he would be a middle-aged man in a young man's game. He would have to assemble a new gang and defeat the young guns to regain his supremacy in the underworld.

Dewey was Schultz's most formidable foe ever, so the Dutchman had to find a way to stop him. Like other mob bosses, Schultz often resorted to bribing public officials. But Dewey was known as an honest, hard-hitting prosecutor who couldn't be bought. This created a quandary for Schultz: how could he stop a man who didn't take bribes? According to mob lore, the Dutchman decided to stop Dewey gangland-style: he would kill the special prosecutor.[7]

Sources who claimed to know the true inside story of the Dutchman's plan to murder Dewey told conflicting versions of how events unfolded. However, there was a common thread: Schultz sought the help of an organized crime outfit known as Murder, Inc. New York's most powerful mob honchos called the shots at Murder, Inc., which had a stable of professional guns-for-hire.

A squad of topnotch bodyguards protected Dewey, so Schultz knew he needed a real pro to rub out his nemesis. To find the right gunslinger, he met with the Murder, Inc. board of directors, including Lucky Luciano. He warned them that Dewey was a danger to every mobster in New York. If the crime-fighting special prosecutor could put Dutch Schultz in prison, he could bring down any mob boss. For everyone's safety, Dewey must be killed at once!

The Murder, Inc. board agreed that Dewey was a problem but opted for a cautious approach. As the first step, the board commissioned a sort of feasibility study. An operative was sent to shadow Dewey, learn his daily routine, and determine if a hit man could kill him without getting caught. In some versions of the story, a Schultz lieutenant followed Dewey. In others, homicide virtuoso Albert Anastasia stalked Dewey. Anastasia waited outside Dewey's apartment building each morning, posing as a father taking his child out for fresh air. In some accounts, Anastasia was pushing a baby girl in a perambulator. In others, he had a young son who was riding a tricycle, a velocipede, or a bike. Anastasia trailed Dewey and his bodyguards to a drugstore where the prosecutor stopped each morning. The bodyguards always waited outside while Dewey went in; so a hit man could kill the special prosecutor inside the store.

Although a hit was feasible, the Murder, Inc. bosses felt that it had the potential to backfire on them. Lucky Luciano, in particular, thought that killing Dewey would be bad for business. Murdering the famous crime fighter would bring too much heat down on the mob. The assassination would outrage the public and probably start a national crusade against organized crime. Besides, Schultz was exaggerating the danger posed by Dewey. The mob bosses had smart lawyers who could beat any rap. It was a proven fact that bribery and missing witnesses would derail even an airtight case.

The Murder, Inc. bosses worried that Schultz might actually cause them more grief than Dewey. Powerful legal forces were closing in on the Dutchman. He was clearly spooked and nervous. He might fold under pressure from the special prosecutor's office. He might make a deal with Dewey — save his own skin by turning state's evidence. If he ratted on his fellow mob bosses, he could send them up the river for a long time. He knew where the bodies were buried — figuratively and literally!

Luciano had his own special reason for wanting to see Schultz behind bars. Due to his tax troubles, the Dutchman had failed to keep a firm hold on his rackets. Although he managed to sneak into New York City from time to time, he was an absentee boss. He couldn't exercise the strong control needed to keep his operations running smoothly. Luciano had begun to take over Schultz's turf, muscling in on the Dutchman's rackets in Harlem and elsewhere. Lucky would have clear sailing if Dewey convicted Schultz and sent him to prison for a long stretch.

Luciano lobbied against killing Dewey, so the Murder, Inc. board vetoed Schultz's plan to assassinate the special prosecutor. When the Dutchman heard the verdict, he exploded. He wanted Dewey dead! And he didn't need Murder, Inc. to do it. He knew plenty of combat-tested gunmen willing to do the job. Defiantly, confidently, Schultz declared that he would get Dewey. The special prosecutor would be dead within forty-eight hours!

A Thousand Kim

On the night of October 23, 1935, Dutch Schultz went to eat dinner at the Palace Chophouse and Tavern in Newark, New Jersey. Since the chophouse was near the hotel where he was staying, he made it his unofficial command post. With his aides-de-camp,

Bernard "Lulu" Rosenkrantz and Abe Landau, Schultz took a table in a small, private back-room connected to the main room by a narrow hallway. After a while Frances Flegenheimer, the Dutchman's wife, joined them. Schultz's bail bondsman dropped by for a few minutes, then left. A short time later Otto "Abbadabba" Berman and another man joined the Schultz party in the backroom.

Later in the evening, everyone left except the Dutchman, Rosenkrantz, Landau, and Berman. In the quiet backroom, the quartet studied adding machine tapes and ledger sheets to calculate the profits from Schultz's rackets. Without the flood of cash from the bootleg liquor traffic, the bottom line had shrunk since the heady days of the Roaring Twenties.

After a time, Schultz took a break to go to the toilet, leaving his buddies at the table. It was a slow night at the chophouse. The barroom was deserted, except for the bored bartender leaning idly against the counter. Two men entered the chophouse through the front door. Their faces were barely visible because they had turned up their overcoat collars and pulled their hats low on their foreheads. They headed toward the backroom as if they were on a mission. When the strangers passed the bartender, one ordered him to hit the deck. As the intruder whipped a gun out of his shoulder holster, the barkeep dropped to the floor behind the counter, expecting to hear shots.

The gunmen didn't disappoint him. In the backroom, one intruder opened fire on the startled trio seated at the table — Rosenkrantz, Berman, and Landau. The other intruder pulled a sawed-off shotgun from beneath his overcoat and unleashed a barrage of lead. Bullets struck Rosenkrantz in his chest, abdomen, and right foot. Berman took hits in the neck, shoulder, elbow, and wrist. He tumbled out of his chair onto the tile floor. Blood oozed from his wounds, forming a puddle of sticky red fluid. Bullets tore through Landau's shoulder, his arm, and his wrist. Despite serious wounds, both Landau and Rosenkrantz drew their own guns and returned fire.

One of the intruders glanced around as if he were looking for something. He saw the men's room door, walked over, and kicked it open. He fired two shots at the unarmed man standing by the urinals. One bullet hit Dutch Schultz in his side just above his waist; it tore through his abdominal wall, large intestine, gall bladder, and liver before lodging in the floor near the urinals. The other bullet missed him and smashed into the bathroom wall.

While the gunner was shooting at Schultz in the toilet, his accomplice ran through the barroom and out the front door. A few seconds later, the gunman exited the lavatory and headed for the front door, dodging bullets as he fled. Landau, with blood spurting out of his neck, lurched along behind the intruder, firing wildly. Rosenkrantz also managed to shoot at the fleeing gunsel. The flying bullets shattered glassware, liquor bottles, the cigarette machine, the front door, and even a window in the building across the street. Bullets nicked the rear end of a bus turning into the driveway across the street. A stray bullet grazed the forehead of a man stepping off a streetcar at the trolley stop.[8]

Rosenkrantz collapsed on the barroom floor before he reached the front door. Landau stumbled out the door, still firing at the stranger, who ran down the street and vanished into the darkness. Landau reeled around unsteadily, then plunked down on a trashcan. His blue-black Smith & Wesson slipped out of his hand and clattered when it hit the sidewalk. Although he had emptied the clip, he hadn't felled the intruder.

Dutch Schultz, clutching his side, staggered out of the toilet, dropped into a chair at a table, and rested his head on the tabletop for a moment. Then he rasped, "Get a doctor! Quick!"

Despite multiple gunshot wounds, Rosenkrantz somehow summoned enough strength to stand up. Schultz's loyal servitor stuck his hand into his pants pocket, pulled out a quarter, and dropped it on the bar. With a weak, halting voice, he asked the stunned barkeep for change. Speechless, the bartender gave him nickels for the pay phone.

Inching along on unsteady legs, Rosenkrantz held onto the bar as he made his way to the phone booth. Leaning heavily against the booth to support his weight, he lifted the receiver and dialed "O." When the operator answered, he said, "I want the police. Hurry up!"

The operator put the call through. The police officer at the other end of the line heard a faint voice whisper, "Send me an ambulance. I'm dying."

When the cop asked the address, all he heard was the telephone receiver banging against the booth. Although Rosenkrantz was too weak to give the address, people who had heard the gunshots called the police station. Officers were soon on the scene. While they waited for the ambulances, the lawmen tried to interrogate the wounded men. All the gangsters stayed true to the code of silence and gave only vague, unhelpful answers. Schultz denied knowing the shooters, insisting they were "some fellows" he didn't recognize.

Rosenkrantz, despite his extreme weakness, showed his feisty side. When an officer asked him to name the shooters, Schultz's faithful minion growled, "Get the hell away from me! Go out and get me an ice cream soda."

The Newark City Hospital sent its entire fleet of three ambulances to pick up the wounded men. A policeman rode in the ambulance with Schultz, in case the mob boss decided to talk. At the hospital, the staff hustled to care for its new patients, but the facility was ill-equipped to treat multiple gunshot victims.

In the emergency room Schultz was given a dose of morphine to dull the pain. He asked to see Father Cornelius McInerney, a parish priest who visited prisoners in New Jersey jails. Two surgical interns, in charge of the emergency team, decided that Schultz's chances of survival were good and sent him to a ward to await his turn in the operating room. A police officer was assigned to stay with him. The Dutchman asked to see his wife and again requested a visit from Father McInerney. The cop asked the standard questions about the shooting; Schultz gave the standard non-answers.[9]

Abbadabba Berman lived only a short time at the hospital, dying in the wee hours of the morning. Abe Landau, who had a severed artery, died as dawn was breaking that same morning. Lulu Rosenkrantz survived longer but passed away the next day.

Schultz was finally wheeled into the operating room several hours after arriving at the hospital. The surgeons found extensive damage to his spleen, stomach, colon, and liver. He was hemorrhaging internally, and peritonitis had set in. Nevertheless, he seemed to rally after his surgery. In the recovery room, he talked to those around him and showed that he hadn't lost his sense of humor: whenever he wanted a dose of morphine, he asked for a bon-bon.

Schultz's wife and his mother spent time at his bedside. So did Father McInerney. The Dutchman said he wanted to die in the Catholic faith because his wife was a Catholic. The priest baptized him and gave him the last rites.[10]

As Schultz struggled to stay alive, he oscillated between lucidity and delirium. Words flowed from his mouth in a stream-of-consciousness monologue worthy of James Joyce. Police detectives hovered near his bed, asking questions and making notes. He rambled on, talking nonsense for the most part. However, the detectives sometimes recognized names and references to events in Schultz's past. Someone, probably the Newark police chief, decided a stenographer should record the Dutchman's words. Later, when detectives had time to analyze the transcript, it might help them find Schultz's killer or solve other crimes.

A secretary sat near Schultz's bed, making a shorthand record of his words until he fell into a coma shortly before he died. Among other things, he said:

> "I don't know who shot me, honest to God!"
> "These native children make this and sell you the joint."
> "George, don't make no bull moves."
> "No business, no hang-out, no friends, nothing. Just what you pick up and what you need."
> "Please, he eats like a little sausage baloney maker."
> "Oh, I forgot I am plaintiff and not defendant."
> "Please crack down on the Chinaman's friends and Hitler's commander."
> "You get ahead with the dot and dash system."
> "I would hear it, the circuit court would hear it, and the Supreme Court might hear it."
> "A boy has never wept [unintelligible] nor dashed a thousand kim."
> "I want to pay. Let them leave me alone."[11]

According to the death certificate, Schultz died at 8:35 p.m., October 24, 1935. Four days later he was buried in a simple, private service at the Gate of Heaven Cemetery in Hawthorne, New York.

The undertaker went to great lengths to keep the media and the public away from the service. On the day of the burial, a crowd estimated at two thousand gathered outside the funeral parlor, hoping to see a grandiose gangster-style sendoff. When a mahogany casket, followed by mourners, emerged from the funeral home, the crowd edged closer. The newsreel cameras rolled; the photographers snapped pictures. The crowd buzzed. Then a wave of disappointment swept over the onlookers when they heard that the gangster wasn't in the casket. Schultz's casket had been removed from the funeral parlor before dawn, so unwanted guests couldn't follow it to the cemetery.

At the Dutchman's graveside funeral, only five mourners were present: his wife, his mother, his sister, his brother-in-law, and his uncle. Father McInerney conducted "the customary Catholic burial service and offered a few simple prayers." At the request of Schultz's mother, a Jewish prayer shawl was draped over the coffin before it was lowered into a hillside grave overlooking the Bronx River Valley.[12]

Perhaps Mrs. Flegenheimer took comfort in knowing that her son, on his deathbed, had endorsed motherhood.

"Mother is the best bet, and don't let Satan draw you too fast," he said.[13]

The Getaway Car Got Away

Mob hits rarely resulted in a trial, and convictions were almost unheard of. But the murder of Dutch Schultz proved to be an exception to the gangland axiom that no mobster ever went to prison for killing a rival mobster. In 1941, more than five years after that bloody night in the Newark chophouse, a grand jury in Essex County, New Jersey, indicted Charles "the Bug" Workman for killing Schultz.[14]

In the underworld Workman ranked in the upper tier of elite hit men. The bosses at Murder, Inc. counted him among gangland's best contract killers. When he was indicted for Schultz's murder, law enforcement already had him in custody as a material witness in a probe of organized crime in Brooklyn. Mob informants had given the Brooklyn district attorney details about dozens of murders, including the Dutchman's. The D.A. turned the evidence about the Schultz hit over to New Jersey authorities.[15]

On the night Schultz was killed, torpedoes Charles "the Bug" Workman and Emanuel "Mendy" Weiss handled the artillery while Seymour "Piggy" Schechter drove the car. Weiss and Workmen were veteran gangland gunslingers who saw the Schultz hit as a more or less routine job. Piggy, a delivery truck driver in Brooklyn, aspired to be a mobster. He had never driven a getaway car before. This was his audition for gangland.

On the drive from Brooklyn to Newark, Piggy got cold feet. He wanted to turn around and go back home, but the gunmen ordered him to shut up and keep driving. He obeyed. When the trio arrived at the chophouse, Workman sent Piggy inside to scout the place. Although Piggy was nervous, he followed orders and returned to tell the gunmen that Dutch Schultz and three other guys were talking in the backroom. While the shooters went inside, Piggy sat in the car, with the motor running, like a good getaway driver.[16]

The gunmen went to the back room, where three men were sitting at a table. Without hesitation, the gunsels opened fire on the trio. But Piggy had seen four men. What had happened to the other guy? Workman knew Schultz because he had done jobs for the beer baron, so he realized that his primary target was missing. He saw the bathroom door, quickly deduced that the Dutchman was inside, and went in after him.

When Workman exited the toilet, two of the wounded guys shot at him. But Workman's own accomplices caused him more trouble than the bleeding men who couldn't shoot straight. While Workman was dodging bullets inside the barroom, Weiss and Piggy vanished. When the Workman got to the sidewalk, he couldn't believe his eyes. The getaway car was gone! His pals had ditched him! The police would arrive at any moment. He had to run for his life in a strange town.

In the darkness, Workman trotted down the street, ran through a park, and slogged through marshland. When he was too tired to keep going, he took a nap on top of a garbage dump. Before sunrise, he walked along railroad tracks until he made his way to the Hudson Tubes and back to Manhattan.[17]

Workman hid out at a friend's apartment so the police wouldn't find him. The Murder, Inc. bosses sent him money and told him to go to Florida for a while. He was mad as hell and wanted to beat the crap out of Weiss and Piggy — the bastards! But calmer heads persuaded him to leave town. He took his wife and baby to the Sunshine State for a vacation he definitely needed.

When Workman returned to New York City, he had unfinished business to take care of. He was determined to get even with Weiss and Piggy, the yellow bastards who had betrayed him. At a meeting of the Murder, Inc. board, Workman complained that the rats had left him behind to be shot or arrested. He demanded that they be severely punished. But Weiss defended himself, saying that Workman deserved to be left behind. He claimed that Workman had endangered everybody by going back into the toilet to steal Dutch Schultz's money and jewelry. Workman vehemently denied Weiss's accusation.[18]

The Murder, Inc. bosses had a dilemma on their hands. Weiss and Workman had proved their value to the organization. Topnotch torpedoes did a specialized job most men couldn't handle. Nevertheless, someone must be punished for leaving a gunman behind at a hit. Luckily, a scapegoat was waiting offstage. Murder, Inc. bruisers were dispatched to find the unsuspecting Piggy. They snatched the hapless delivery driver, tortured, and shot him. For an over-the-top finale, they set his corpse on fire. Thus ended Piggy's very short career as a mobster.[19]

If the Murder, Inc. bosses had investigated, they would have learned that Dutch Schultz wasn't robbed at the chophouse. In the ambulance on the way to the hospital an intern rode with Schultz, administering first aid. The beer baron reached into his pants pocket and pulled out a wad of bills. He handed $725 cash to the intern, saying, "Take care of me, buddy." After Schultz arrived at the hospital, the police impounded his gold wristwatch, his sapphire ring, and his switchblade knife.[20]

Would the facts have saved Piggy from an early grave? Probably not.

Alas, poor Piggy, he was expendable.

The Bug's Trial

Less than three months after Charles "the Bug" Workman was indicted for killing Schultz, he went on trial in a Newark courtroom. Two mob informants testified for the state. Although neither had been at the chophouse, both claimed to know the true story of the bloodbath. One testified that Workman had told him all the gory details when they were hoisting a few at a New Year's Eve party. A woman with mob ties testified that Workman had stayed in her apartment after the shooting and burned his dirty clothes in the building's incinerator. He had complained loudly about Weiss and Piggy leaving him at the scene of the crime.[21]

The Bug pled not guilty and claimed to have an alibi. He had been working at a funeral parlor in Brooklyn on the night Schultz was killed. Defense counsel called the undertaker to the stand to corroborate Workman's alibi. The undertaker, who had hired Workman to "ease out" his competition, said the mobster was helping him on the night in question. The witness seemed believable and even had payroll records with Workman's name on them.

Workman's defense got off to a good start with the undertaker's testimony, but it soon suffered a setback. The Brooklyn D.A., who was following the case closely, was convinced that the undertaker had lied under oath. The D.A. sent law officers to pick up the undertaker and bring him in for questioning. Under the D.A.'s intense interrogation, the man admitted he had lied on the witness stand. When the prosecutor cross-examined him in the courtroom, he publicly recanted his testimony. Without an alibi, Workman's chances of beating the rap plummeted.

The Bug decided not to defend himself any further and gave a written statement to his lawyers: "I, Charles Workman, being of the opinion that any witnesses called in my defense will be intimidated and arrested by members of the district attorney's office or police officials, and not wishing members of my family and other of my witnesses to be subjected to humiliation and embarrassment on my account, do hereby order you as my counsel not to call any witnesses in my defense, except myself...."

Workman's counsel urged him to let them call witnesses, but he insisted upon protecting his family and friends from harassment. He wanted to take the witness stand to defend himself, but his lawyers warned him that would be too risky. After considering his options, Workman changed his plea to *non vult*— in essence pleading guilty, which under New Jersey law meant that he could not be given the death penalty. The judge immediately sentenced Workman to life imprisonment.

Workman's failure to mount a defense puzzled observers. He repeatedly declared his innocence and claimed that he had been framed. Yet he opted for a plea that sent him to prison. After the trial, the Bug's lawyer said, "I always took the position that Workman did not kill Schultz. He changed his plea against my advice." The Brooklyn district attorney believed Workman chose *non vult* because he feared the electric chair. "The Bug changed his plea to beat the death penalty," the D.A. opined. Workman spent almost twenty-three years in prison for killing the Dutchman. A model inmate, he was allowed to serve most of his sentence in a "lenient institution" in Rahway, New Jersey.[22]

After leaving prison, Workman didn't renew his mob ties but worked in New York City's garment district, selling zippers and sewing notions. Hit man Mendy Weiss escaped punishment for Schultz's murder, but he didn't expire peacefully in his sleep. He died in the electric chair at Sing Sing after he was convicted of murdering the proprietor of a candy store.

Before Workman went to prison for Schultz's murder, he hinted that the mob informants hadn't told the whole truth about the chophouse slaughter. He even told a reporter that one day he might reveal the real story behind Schultz's death. If he did tell, it didn't make headlines. Maybe he never talked. Maybe it was ancient history, so the press didn't find it newsworthy.

14. Mr. Smooth: Waxy Gordon

Selling whiskey ain't no crime. It just happens to be against the law. —1920s cliché

Waxy Gordon ranked high among America's most wanted in the Arid Era, but he is usually overlooked in books and movies about Prohibition. He had a long, ignoble criminal career that lasted more than five decades. When Volstead began, he already had a lengthy rap sheet and had served substantial time behind bars. Although he committed a variety of crimes, he specialized in peddling illicit products, especially drugs and bootleg alcohol. When he made big money in the illegal liquor traffic, he spent lavishly, trying to build a façade of respectability for himself and his family.

Born in 1888 on Manhattan's Lower East Side, Gordon's real surname was Wexler (also spelled "Wechsler"). On legal documents his given name appeared as Irving, Isidore, or Isaac. Over the years Wexler used a remarkable number of aliases: Benjamin Lester, Benjamin Lustig, Harry Middleton, William Palinski, Benjamin Gordon, Harry Brown, Harry Gordon, and Harry Burns — to name a few. The surplus of aliases sometimes confused even Wexler. Once when he was in court on an assault-and-battery charge and was asked his name, he said he couldn't remember his current moniker. Of all his aliases, Waxy Gordon was the one that stuck with him. According to mob lore, "Waxy" referred to his smooth moves as a pickpocket. An alternate explanation was that his pals shortened "Wexler" to "Wexie," which became "Waxy."

Gordon dropped out of school at young age and worked as a bellhop. He also took up petty crime, becoming an adept pickpocket and purse snatcher. At an age when other boys were finishing high school, he was convicted of grand larceny and sentenced to the reformatory at Elmira, New York. Over the next eight years, he was in and out of prison, doing time in both New York and Pennsylvania. Between prison stints, he hung out on the streets with other hoods in Philadelphia and New York City.[1]

At age twenty-something, Gordon joined Benjamin "Dopey Benny" Fein's gang, which engaged in all sorts of crime and workplace violence. Under Fein's tutelage, Gordon learned the trades of labor goon, strikebreaker, bookie, burglar, drug pusher, and extortionist. When Fein was sent to prison, Gordon looked around for a dependable source of income. He hired on as a strong arm/debt collector for Arnold "Big Bankroll" Rothstein, a gambler who ran an illegal casino and did not deal gently with losers who owed him money. Working for Rothstein proved to be a temp job because the police arrested Gordon for assault and robbery. Following his conviction, he went to prison in 1915 but was paroled the next year.[2]

Upon his return to gangland, Gordon specialized in peddling drugs, principally cocaine, in New York and Philadelphia. He was not closely connected to any one gang but formed alliances with small clusters of pushers in Harlem, Manhattan, and Philly. He quickly became one of the busiest, best connected drug dealers in the Northeast. When Volstead began, he added bootleg liquor to his line of risky products.[3]

The Dirty Duo

For many years, Gordon's closest ally was gangster "Big Maxie" Greenberg, whom he met in New York during World War I. Although Greenberg moved around, his primary residence was St. Louis, where he hung out with a local mob known as Egan's Rats. With other gang members he committed assorted felonies, including hold-ups, bank heists, train robberies, and torch jobs (arson to defraud an insurance company).[4]

Like many of his peers, Greenberg had high hopes of getting rich as a liquor lord. However, his bootlegging career got off to a bad start when he rashly double-crossed Rats boss Willie Egan. With Egan's money, Greenberg bought a load of whiskey from a rumrunner in New Orleans, put it on a barge, and sent it up the Mississippi River. When the liquor failed to reach its destination, Greenberg told Egan that the barge had sunk, taking its cargo to the bottom of the river. The story sounded fishy to the mob boss. He suspected that Greenberg had sold the whiskey and pocketed the money. Determined to know the truth, Egan arranged to have the sunken barge raised. It was weighted down with sandbags; the liquor had vanished. Egan vowed to get his money back or get revenge.

To escape Egan's wrath, Greenberg fled to Detroit, where he dabbled in the cross-border liquor traffic until he felt it was safe to return home. Back in St. Louis, he had tense face-offs with mob boss Egan. The confrontations stopped short of gunplay, but Greenberg knew he had a target on his back. One night Egan called Greenberg, a lawyer, and a mutual acquaintance together for a meeting about the missing liquor cargo. Egan demanded to be repaid for the lost hooch, but Greenberg stubbornly refused to cough up the cash. After the meeting broke up, Greenberg and the lawyer were standing on a street corner when gunfire shattered the peace. Both men were struck by bullets. A stray bullet grazed Egan, who was standing a short distance behind them. The lawyer's wounds proved to be fatal. Greenberg sustained serious injuries but survived.[5]

After the shooting, Greenberg spent more time in New York City, always looking for a chance to score big in the rackets. He teamed up with his friend Waxy Gordon to run the Fourth Avenue Hotel, which was more bordello than hostelry. The duo also trafficked in narcotics and alcohol.

Gordon wanted to get into rumrunning on a grand scale, hauling cargos of booze from foreign ports to New York. He needed a sizable amount of money to acquire a suitable ship, so he approached Rothstein, his former employer. Rothstein, an underworld entrepreneur as well as a gambler, was called the Big Bankroll because he put up capital for criminal ventures. Since liquor trafficking was the proverbial sure thing, he was investing heavily in it. He was already financing the bootlegging schemes of Meyer Lansky, Dutch Schultz, and other rising mob stars.

Rothstein agreed to help launch Gordon's rumrunning business. In addition to providing the seed money, the gambler introduced the mobster to major players in the international liquor traffic. Gordon's new connections helped him buy large cargos of liquor, including premium Scotch whiskey, in the British Isles. His rum ring prospered and expanded, importing costly cargos of booze from Canada and the Bahamas as well as Britain. To supplement his import business, Gordon bought a brewery in Paterson, New Jersey, and a distillery in Elmira, New York.[6]

Only Two Vices

With his ill-gotten wealth, Waxy Gordon embraced the lavish lifestyle of a *nouveau riche* liquor lord. Conspicuous consumption could've been his hobby. He bought expensive things that he enjoyed owning, and he also purchased items that he felt would elevate his status in life by giving him respectability. When an attorney asked Waxy about his extravagant spending, he modestly said, "I guess I've got only two vices. One is for beautiful clothes, and the other is for a beautiful home."[7]

Gordon lived with his wife and children in a luxurious ten-room, four-bath apartment in a posh building in Manhattan. A staff of five waited on the family. The apartment had an impressive walnut bar well-stocked with the best brands of liquor. A colorful stained-glass window with "drinking figures of poured, leaded glass" paid homage to the source of Gordon's money. The handsome library had custom woodwork and shelves filled with leather-bound books that Gordon rarely, if ever, opened. When he bought the books, he told the bookseller they were for his wife and kids.

Gordon, in keeping with the adage that clothes make the man, spent huge sums on his wardrobe. Like other alcohol aristocrats, he treated himself to custom-made suits in the latest styles. His closet held more than two hundred suits plus silk ties, pleated shirts, linen collars, tuxedos, and overcoats. He even bought custom-tailored golf knickers and monogrammed silk boxers. He preferred ties made of French airplane silk and custom-made shirts with soft collars that didn't irritate "his sensitive neck."[8]

To show off his wealth, Gordon drove big, costly automobiles. He traded cars often and particularly liked Pierce-Arrow, Lincoln, and Buick autos. When he traveled, he booked first-class accommodations on trains and ships. He took his wife on luxury cruises, which combined business and pleasure because he went ashore to arrange shipments of alcohol and narcotics. He owned a spacious summer cottage at Bradley Beach, NJ. Like Al Capone, he wintered in Florida.[9]

When Gordon began raking in piles of misbegotten money, he followed orthodox business advice and diversified. He reportedly paid $300,000 to buy the Philadelphia franchise for the General News Bureau, a horse-racing wire service that monitored tracks around the country and quickly telegraphed race results to off-track betting parlors. He invested in licit ventures in real estate, energy, and show business. He owned fifty percent of the Paramount Hotel Corporation, which built the Piccadilly Hotel in the Big Apple's theater district. The Piccadilly was noted for its Georgian ballroom, which had dazzling crystal chandeliers, still-life murals, and Victorian-style portraits in ornate frames. Gordon also owned interests in the Allied Hotel Construction Company and the Mansing Coal Corporation.[10]

Gordon provided major financing for at least two Broadway musicals, *Forward March* and *Strike Me Pink* starring Jimmy Durante.[11] Financing Broadway plays and burlesque shows gave mobsters an entrée to the glittery world of show biz. It also endeared them to sexy female performers who otherwise might rebuff their advances.

When Gordon met stripper Gypsy Rose Lee, they formed a strong bond. Both had grown up poor, were uneducated, lacked social graces, and craved the respectability that seemed to lie just beyond their reach. As a stripper working in burlesque, Lee was accustomed to men who had more money than finesse, so she didn't find Gordon too crude. In fact, she was intrigued by his tough mobster persona, which made him more exciting than the average drooling burlesque fan. She felt safe with the liquor lord, and he protected her, ordering one of his goons to be her bodyguard whenever she needed one.

Although Gordon rarely showed empathy for others, he shared his good fortune with Lee and wooed her with gifts more practical than romantic. The ecdysiast was self-conscious about her smile because her teeth needed straightening, so he paid a dentist to fix her teeth. He also gave her a massive Mission-style, oak dining room set with thirty chairs for her suburban home in Queens. (She eventually lost the house because she couldn't make the mortgage payments. He should've given her cash.)

Gordon promoted Lee's career by getting her an audition with Flo Ziegfeld, who produced musical extravaganzas. At her audition, Lee wore a swimsuit that showed off her shapely legs — an asset Ziegfeld valued highly. He hired her on the spot. Because she wanted respectability so badly, she took a gigantic pay cut, reportedly giving up $1,000 per week in burlesque for $60 in Ziegfeld's classy revue, "Hot Cha!" Insiders said Gordon was one of the revue's financial backers.

Perhaps Gordon's strangest show biz venture was staging a musical revue at Great Meadow Prison (AKA Comstock) in Upstate New York. He hired stripper Lee, an orchestra, and other performers for the event. He transported them to the prison via train, feeding them a lobster dinner en route. Although Lee was ready to bump and grind across the stage, the show went on without her. Prison officials wouldn't allow the stripper to perform because they feared she would corrupt the convicts' morals.

The moral guardians had no objection to repeat-offender Gordon. He sat beside the warden to watch the show.[12]

Greener Grass in the Garden State

In April 1925 *S.S. Nantisco*, a three-masted schooner, sailed from Nova Scotia to New York City carrying a load of timber for builders in Queens, where the housing market was booming. Lumber was piled high on the schooner's decks, but customs officials suspected that the ship held more than building supplies. Federal agents had evidence linking it to the illegal liquor traffic. Customs inspectors boarded the schooner and searched carefully, even crawling through narrow openings between piles of lumber and the vessel's ceilings. After hours of looking, they found five hundred cases of Scotch whiskey hidden amongst the timber.

The owners of rumrunning vessels falsified official records to hide their identity, so law enforcement couldn't make any arrests until they traced *Nantisco's* ownership. U.S. Attorney Buckner's special detective squad followed the twisted paper trail, which eventually led them to Waxy Gordon's rum ring. A federal investigator went to Nova Scotia, where he mingled with the rumrunners to obtain evidence about Gordon's smuggling ventures.[13]

In New York City the Gordon syndicate used real estate offices in Times Square as a front. To collect evidence against the ringleaders, a squadron of city police, Prohis, and agents from the Bureau of Investigation raided the realty offices. A search of the premises yielded bottles of Scotch whiskey and stacks of documents, including liquor price lists, sales records, and ocean charts. The lawmen also found a code key used for sending messages to rumrunning ships and an apparatus for testing the alcohol content of liquids. The confiscated sales records showed that the Gordon ring routinely filled orders for vast quantities of liquor. Financial documents revealed that the ring had deposited a fortune in its bank accounts.

The raiders arrested thirteen men, including Maxie Greenberg, who was out of jail on bail after being indicted for the possession of stolen bonds. Waxy Gordon couldn't be found because he had taken his wife on a luxurious ocean voyage aboard the cruise ship *Majestic*. When Gordon's lawyer learned about the raid, he assured the U.S. attorney that Waxy was not on the lam and would return to New York City after the cruise. Since the mobster was sailing in international waters, it would be difficult for U.S. authorities so arrest him, so they allowed him to return voluntarily. After a month's vacation, he came home to face the music.[14]

Following Gordon's return, a federal grand jury indicted him and other members of his rum ring on Volstead conspiracy charges. In preparing its case, the prosecution used information gathered by the special squad working for U.S. Attorney Buckner. But the most crucial evidence came from two informants, Mr. and Mrs. Hans Fuhrmann.[15]

Hans Fuhrmann was a sailor who worked on rumrunning vessels owned by the Gordon ring. To Mrs. Fuhrmann's disgust, her husband always came home drunk and broke after his rumrunning trips. She went to see his bosses, told them about the problem, and asked them to always give his paycheck to her. They refused. In fact, they laughed at her. (Perhaps they had never heard about the fury of a woman scorned.)

Enraged by the way the men had treated her, Mrs. Fuhrmann decided to expose the rum ring. She told her story to a Brooklyn newspaper, and officials at the Department of Justice (DOJ) heard about her. When approached by DOJ agents, she claimed that her husband was being held hostage on a rumrunning ship. Law officers raided the ship, "freed" Fuhrmann from the rumrunners, and took him into custody. Later, it appeared that Mrs. Fuhrmann had lied about his being held hostage because she didn't want him to be arrested as a rumrunner. Most likely, he was working on the ship of his own volition.

Hans Fuhrmann cooperated with the Prohis, giving them the inside dope about Gordon's rum ring. To reward him and ensure his loyalty, the New York Prohibition office put him on its payroll as an investigator. Law enforcement officials feared that Gordon might offer the Fuhrmanns a bribe or even have them killed. To ensure their safety, the government held both of them in protective custody. When Mr. Fuhrmann testified at a preliminary hearing, deputy U.S. marshals guarded him in the courthouse. As soon as he finished his testimony, the deputies whisked him away to a secret location.

Despite being in protective custody, Mr. Fuhrmann was found dead in his bed in a hotel room. He had been shot in the head and was holding a gun in his hand. The medical examiner concluded that Fuhrmann had killed himself, although he left no suicide note. Mrs. Fuhrmann believed that her husband had been murdered to keep him from testifying against Gordon in the upcoming trial. She claimed that the rum ring had put a bounty on her husband's head and he had survived an earlier attempt to kill him. To her bitter dismay, top Prohibition officials agreed with the examiner's verdict of suicide.[16]

Hans Fuhrmann's death gutted the state's case against Gordon's rum ring. The prosecution's most compelling evidence died with the star witness. Mrs. Fuhrmann could testify, but she had only secondhand knowledge of her husband's rumrunning voyages. Gordon escaped the rumrunning charges and, if he did in fact order a hit on his former underling, he also got away with murder.

Gordon and Greenberg continued to traffic in liquor, but by the late Twenties the Big Apple seemed hostile to the dirty duo. Turf wars roiled the waters in the city's underbelly. The violent young bloods were taking charge, and the old guard was an endangered species. Moreover, Gordon and Greenberg felt hemmed in because law enforcement was keeping close tabs on them in New York. The tight surveillance made it hard for them to conduct their nefarious enterprises. They looked around, spied greener pastures in New Jersey, and began shifting their business across the state line.

New Jersey wasn't exactly a sea of tranquility, but the dirty duo saw opportunity there because an epidemic of mob hits had created openings in the top echelons of gangland. Police believed that the Jersey mobs were battling among themselves and also warring with New York gangs. The sudden demise of several high-ranking Jersey mobsters had left a power vacuum in the Garden State. Mob watchers speculated that Gordon and Goldberg had played a major role in creating that void, which presented a golden opportunity for the pair. They moved quickly to grab control of the beer business in North Jersey.[17]

15. New Jersey's Triple X: Max, Maxie, and Waxy

> Max Hassel took an unusual route to becoming a big-time beer bootlegger.... He never carried a gun and didn't use typical Jersey strong-arm tactics.... By all accounts, he was just an honest gentleman conducting an illegal business in a world of violent gangsters. He believed that his reputation and business savvy could lead him to success and keep him out of harm's way.—Michael Pellegrino, attorney and author[1]

Small-town beer baron Max Hassel operated breweries in rural Pennsylvania and New Jersey. He hired expert brew masters, made first-rate beer, and took pride in his product. More businessman than mobster, he was a respected member of the community in his hometown of Reading, Pennsylvania. His illicit, but first-rate, breweries churned out so much beer that law enforcement targeted them for closure.

Philadelphia, the biggest city in Pennsylvania, was awash with bootleg booze. Even dry leaders, when they were being realistic, knew the City of Brotherly Love would never be a desert. Compared to the big-city liquor traffic, Hassel's small-town operations looked like an easy enforcement job. Sending the rural beer baron to prison would be a badly-needed triumph for Volstead enforcement in the Keystone State.

For several years, federal Prohibition agents and Pennsylvania state troopers repeatedly raided Hassel's breweries, smashed his equipment, and emptied his vats. When he saw his bottom line shrinking, he decided to change course—but not to go straight. He downsized his operations in Pennsylvania and expanded his holdings in New Jersey. He moved from the sideshow to the big tent when he teamed up with Waxy Gordon and Maxie Greenberg.

The Millionaire Newsboy

Max Hassel (AKA Mendel Gassel) was born in Latvia, and as an adolescent he immigrated with his family to Reading, Pennsylvania. Even as a youngster, he showed promise. He had more than the standard measure of ambition, fortitude, confidence, and dedication. In his new hometown, he became a familiar sight because he worked as a newsboy, hawking papers on street corners. After he made a fortune selling illegal beer, the press dubbed him "the Millionaire Newsboy."

As a teenager, Hassel stood out as a serious, polite young man with the potential for great success in business. He had intelligence, people skills, street smarts, and a work ethic that put the Puritans to shame. He was a hustler in the respectable sense of the word, always looking for a good business opportunity, always striving to get ahead. He had the advantage of growing up in a tight-knit, religious family with a stable home life. Unlike the typical Volstead gangster, he grew up with good role models and was never arrested as a juvenile.

Hassel was only nineteen years old when Volstead began, but he already knew how to run a business. In his early teens he had dropped out of school, rented a workroom, and started a hand-rolled cigar business with a friend. After a time the teenage partners expanded, running two wholesale cigar companies and opening a retail smoke shop in Reading.[2]

Hassel had what it took to succeed in legal ventures, but he also had the impatience of youth. He chose liquor trafficking as his shortcut to wealth. For his opening gambit, he exploited Volstead's legal exemptions for sacramental wine and industrial alcohol. With an older businessman as his partner, he set up the Schuylkill Extract Company, ostensibly to make flavorings and extracts. The older man put up most, if not all, of the money, but young Hassel took charge. He quickly obtained government permits to buy sacramental wine and withdraw distilled spirits from bonded warehouses. With these permits he bought large quantities of liquor, purportedly for use in manufacturing food flavorings.

The Philadelphia Prohibition squad, which monitored the permits, noticed that Hassel was buying more liquor than his small extract company could possibly use. The suspicious Prohis investigated and found that he had falsified the shipping records for his business. When the Prohis confronted him, he voluntarily surrendered his liquor permits. Because he cooperated, the feds didn't prosecute him. In fact, the government refunded $20,000 he had put up as bond when he received his permits. It wasn't clear exactly what had happened to the liquor he purchased. Presumably he resold it to bootleggers.

Hassel had hit a pothole in the fast lane, but he hardly noticed. He was soon operating a chemical company with a government permit to buy and use special denatured alcohol in manufacturing. His company was also licensed to buy and sell alcohol for medical use. Hassel's entry into the chemical business aroused the curiosity of the Philadelphia Prohis, who had decided to keep an eye on the busy hustler. When the lawmen questioned him, he couldn't remember essential facts, such as the formulas used in his plant or the name of his company chemist. The Prohibition Unit revoked Hassel's permits and cited him for Volstead violations but didn't incarcerate him.[3]

The young entrepreneur took this latest setback in stride because he had a grand vision for the future. He planned to make a fortune by taking over the beer traffic in southeastern Pennsylvania. His hometown wasn't a big city, but it had several pre–Volstead breweries and good railway connections to Philadelphia. He could reopen Reading's breweries and sell his beer in Philly as well as nearby small towns.

In the early 1920s Hassel built a prosperous illegal brewing business in the boondocks. Hiding behind straw men, he bought, leased, operated, and sold breweries. Relying on his charisma and sales skills, he persuaded a remarkable number of ghost owners to sign deeds and mortgages to hide his holdings. He recruited friends, relatives, employees, and even his haberdasher to serve as front men for him. He blazed a confusing paper trail that was virtually impossible to follow.[4]

By 1928 Hassel owned part or all of at least twelve breweries. One of his properties was the Seitz Brewery in Easton, Pennsylvania, across the Delaware River from a rural area in New Jersey. To secretly move beer from Seitz's waterfront plant to Jersey, Hassel laid a pipeline across the river bottom. On the Jersey side, the line terminated at a garage/gas station, where the beer was packaged in barrels and loaded onto trucks.[5]

Hassel used a similar pipeline at the Reiker Brewery in Lancaster, Pennsylvania. Hoses from the brewery snaked through the city sewers to another building at a lower elevation some distance away. According to local lore, Hassel hired "midgets" to drag the hoses through the sewers. When the Reiker brew reached the second building, it was packaged and loaded onto trucks. Night after night Lancaster residents heard the Reiker beer trucks rumbling along the streets on the western side of town. They saw Hassel's spotters standing on the street corners, checking the route to be sure neither lawmen nor hijackers lay in wait for the trucks.[6]

Hassel's breweries made him a rich young man who could afford virtually anything he wanted. Government investigators said he was a millionaire by age twenty-four. He enjoyed his prosperity but didn't flaunt his wealth. The son of a tailor, he dressed like a conservative businessman. He had a thin, lithe body, and he wore his coal black hair in the slicked-down style popular in the Roaring Twenties. He owned a closet full of custom-made suits, dress shirts, silk ties, and expensive stickpins. According to an admirer, his clothes were "the personification of refinement, culture, conservatism, and grace." For headgear, he preferred a straw boater or a fedora with a snap brim, worn at a rakish angle. He had a passion for hats and bought hundreds of them. He liked bling, particularly diamond rings, but didn't overdo it. He preferred an elegantly understated look in jewelry.[7]

Hassel enjoyed golf and gambling, especially a friendly card game with his buddies. He also liked betting on dice. He hated violence, never carried a gun, and tried to keep his name out of the crime news. He was well liked in Reading, where his neighbors viewed him as an honest man making an illegal, but popular, product. He empathized with low-income working families like his own. With his brother, he endowed an interest-free loan fund that lent money to needy Jews. In addition, he made generous donations to Reading's local charity drives. At Thanksgiving he gave hundreds of food baskets to poor families.[8]

Hassling Hassel

Pennsylvania Governor Gifford Pinchot (1923–27, 1931–35) was a staunch dry activist, truly outraged by the unbridled flow of alcoholic beverages in his state. He put pressure on law enforcement to crack down on all segments of the illegal liquor industry. Under his regime, both the state police and the Prohis stepped up their raids and arrests. Because Max Hassel was more visible and less violent than the big-city beer barons, he was a frequent target for the Volstead enforcers. Raids, arrests, and padlocks became almost routine for him. He grew accustomed to hearing that lawmen had invaded one of his plants or stopped one of his delivery trucks and arrested the driver.

The tug-of-war between the law and the rural beer baron followed a predictable pattern. After raiding one of Hassel's breweries, the government would go to court seeking permission to padlock the plant and/or dismantle the brewing equipment. The brewery was allowed to stay open until the case was decided, so Hassel's legal team used delaying tactics to keep the case from being resolved. Some cases dragged on for years while the breweries operated full blast, making illegal suds with little secrecy.

On one occasion lawmen invaded Hassel's Reading Brewery, opened all the vats, and emptied about twenty-eight hundred barrels of high-voltage brew into the city sewer. As thousands of gallons collected underground, the pressure built up, sending manhole covers airborne. "One by one, the lids on the manholes were hurled into the air, while the foaming beer gushed forth in a torrent." Nearby residents heard the uproar and brought pails to collect beer as it spewed out of the manholes. (A quick trip through the sewer didn't ruin free suds!) A giant puddle of beer collected in the street, up to a foot deep in spots.[9]

With great regularity, lawmen raided the Fisher Brewing Company in Muhlenberg Township, Pennsylvania. In 1924 the straw-man owner, acting with Hassel's consent, agreed that the government could dismantle Fisher's equipment, confiscate the raw materials, seize the inventory, and padlock the plant for one year. Since the brewery had a large inventory of beer, the U.S. Marshal's office decided to leave it at the plant and hire guards to protect it. Hassel saw this as an opportunity to circumvent the padlock. He offered bribes to the guards and found that the underpaid men were happy to take his money. The guards simply didn't notice when Hassel's trucks loaded up with beer and drove away from the plant.[10]

After the padlock expired, Hassel revved up his brewing operations at the Fisher brewery. Law enforcement almost certainly knew what was happening but didn't try to stop it. Hassel probably doled out wads of cash as insurance against raids. After a hiatus of nearly two years, the Prohis raided Fisher and seized $120,000 worth of beer. Government lawyers went to the federal court in Philadelphia to get a new padlock order for Fisher. To their dismay, the case was dismissed because the Prohibition agents didn't show up to testify. Cynics assumed that Hassel had bribed them to stay away.

The Fisher brewery kept churning out beer, so Prohibition officials made another effort to close it. One night a squad of Prohis hid in a marsh near the brewery, watching for illegal activity. Fighting off the mosquitoes kept them alert and awake all night, but they saw no action at the plant. Then at dawn, the brewery gates swung wide open; two railcars rolled down a siding and were coupled to a locomotive. The agents moved quickly, climbed aboard the locomotive, and prevented it from leaving. Then they seized the beer in the boxcars.[11]

The Prohis needed a search warrant to enter the brewery. While an officer went to procure the document from a magistrate, the dry sleuths had to wait outside the building. While they stood idly by, brewery workers emptied thousands of gallons of beer from the vats into the storm drains. When the agents entered with their search warrant, they found no beer inside the brewery. Hassel's industrious employees had foiled the feds. They made no arrests that morning.[12]

Law enforcement continued to target Hassel's breweries in Reading and succeeded in padlocking most of them by the spring of 1925. The beer baron found this inconvenient but not catastrophic. Two of his padlocked breweries had ice plants, which were allowed to operate because they were making a legal product. Hassel took advantage of this to produce beer and move it offsite in the ice trucks. If the Prohis suspected that the breweries were making more than ice, they ignored the situation. More than likely, Hassel had some corrupt federal agents on his payroll.

One autumn afternoon in 1925, the Pennsylvania State Police raided Lauer Brewery, which Hassel leased from its owner. Lauer, one of Pennsylvania's oldest breweries, had a license to make near beer, but the lawmen knew it was brewing the real stuff. The state troopers used pickaxes to break through heavy doors inside the plant. Behind the doors they found working vats and rows of storage tanks filled with beer. After arresting the brewery workers, they waited for the boss to show up. Capturing Hassel at his own brewery would be a real coup and almost guarantee his conviction when the case went to court.[13]

As the afternoon wore on, the lawmen became frustrated and angry because Hassel was a no-show. In a collective snit, they opened the tank valves and smashed dozens of vats on the brewery's upper floor. Neighbors heard the commotion and ran to the plant to see what was happening. Roughly ten thousand barrels of beer gushed out of the tanks and vats, flooding the upper floor. The foamy brew seeped out the windows and through the air vents. It flowed down the stairs and the elevator shaft. As the beer streamed into the gutter, the neighbors used cans and pails to scoop up the grimy suds.[14]

Flooding the brewery relieved the tension for the raiders, but they didn't get their man. The beer baron never showed up.

Although Hassel escaped the clutches of the law at the Lauer raid, he had plenty of legal headaches and multiple cases pending in court. In one indictment the federal government accused him of bribing Prohibition agents. He claimed entrapment. At trial he swore that the Prohis had asked him for money and threatened to raid his breweries if he didn't pay up. The U.S. commissioner dismissed the charges, agreeing that the federal agents had entrapped him.

In a similar case, Hassel and his brother went on trial for bribing corrupt Prohis to allow them to transport beer made at the Fisher Brewery. The U.S. District Court in Philadelphia dismissed the case after the judge ruled that the Prohis had lured the Hassels into a trap. "The law will not stand for the conviction of a man who was induced to commit a crime by federal officials," the judge said.

In yet another case, Hassel and two associates were charged with bribing a state trooper and conspiring to violate the dry law. It took prosecutors three attempts to get this case into the courtroom. Two trials were derailed because the state's star witness vanished. At the third trial, the prosecution went forward without the witness, and the jury reached a verdict of not guilty for all the defendants.[15]

In 1926 the federal government opened a new front in the attack on Hassel: a tax evasion case. Although the beer baron paid income taxes, he underreported his earnings to reduce the tax bite. After experts analyzed Hassel's finances, the Treasury Department issued a $1.24 million lien against him. The Millionaire Newsboy agreed to pay his back taxes but wanted to negotiate a lower number. When the negotiations failed, the government prosecuted Hassel for perjury and tax fraud. After court hearings, the government seemed to have doubts about winning the case and offered to settle for $150,000. Hassel agreed to pay that hefty sum plus a $2,000 fine. As part of the bargain, the government expunged all the legal records pertaining to his criminal activities.[16]

After paying his back taxes, Hassel enjoyed a long hiatus from raids. Then in March 1928 a joint force of Prohibition agents and state troopers invaded his Reading Brewery. Once again, neighbors spotted the raiders and came to watch, bringing cups and buckets. When the lawmen opened the storage vats, beer poured onto the floor, covering it with two feet of amber liquid. Beer flowed out of the building into the street. The onlookers scooped up beer, but their fun didn't last long. Hassel's lawyer rushed to court for an injunction to keep the raiders from draining all the beer out of the vats. When the sheriff showed up to enforce the injunction, the raiders reluctantly turned off the spigots. The drinkers were as glum as the lawmen; the judge had spoiled everybody's fun.

Several days after the raid, government attorneys persuaded the court to lift the injunction. Law officers hurried over to the Reading Brewery and once again opened the spigots. Beer lovers rushed to the scene, ready to corral the suds. This time they weren't disappointed. They filled dozens of buckets with gallons of beer, and the street party went on even after the gutters ran dry.[17]

The U.S. District Court in Philadelphia issued padlock orders closing both the Fisher and Reading breweries in 1928. Hassel complied with the orders and abandoned the plants. After the padlocks were removed in 1929, the rumor mill said that Hassel had the breweries up and running again. A Prohibition administrator and a state official inspected the plants. They found no evidence of illegal activity. "Why, these breweries couldn't operate if they wanted to," the administrator said. "Our inspection trip was most thorough, and we found that the brew kettles had been taken out, that they had been broken up with acetylene torches, and sold by the sheriff."[18]

New Jersey Beckons

The raids, padlocks, and trials drove up the overhead at Max Hassel's illicit breweries, causing him to reassess his options in the late Twenties. A few of his Pennsylvania breweries were making money, but he had been forced to close others and didn't expect to reopen them. He needed to move his headquarters to a new location where he could operate with more freedom. He was already doing business in New Jersey, so he knew that Volstead enforcement was very lax there. The Garden State held the promise of a more profitable future for him.

Hassel acquired the Camden County Cereal Beverage Company in New Jersey, across the river from Philadelphia. In his new plant Hassel produced near beer in plain sight for the government inspectors to see. He also made high-octane beer that he didn't allow them to see. He used his favorite ploy to move the real stuff underground, piping beer from the plant via a pipeline in the city's sewer system to a garage blocks away.[19]

Hassel wasn't the only Pennsylvania liquor lord who wanted to relocate. Philly mob boss Mickey Duffy had also suffered significant losses due to the crackdown in the Keystone State. Like Hassel, he thought New Jersey would be a more hospitable place. He had his eye on the Camden County Cereal Beverage Company, but the Millionaire Newsboy got there first. Duffy felt he had been cheated, and he didn't plan to give up gracefully. One night he took a dozen of his henchmen to confront Hassel, who was working alone in his office at the brewery. Duffy's men brandished their guns and threatened to shoot Hassel, who never carried a firearm. Then the thugs roughed him up, dragged him outside, and dumped him on the sidewalk. In no uncertain terms, Duffy told Hassel to get lost and stay lost. The Camden County Cereal Beverage Company had a new owner.

The typical gangster would've started a bloody mob war to get his property back, but Hassel was more accountant than mobster. He hated violence; he loved to bargain. After licking his wounds for a while, he made a daring move: he went to talk to Duffy. Hassel insisted that he owned the Camden County brewery, but he was willing to make a deal. They could be partners if Hassel had complete control and Duffy's goons did the dirty work. Surprisingly, the two rivals struck a deal. Even more surprising, they worked well together. Their joint venture thrived, and they made tons of money until law enforcement padlocked the Camden County brewery in 1930.[20]

Max Hassel and Waxy Gordon were in the illegal liquor business and had mutual friends, so they became acquainted, probably in Philadelphia where both had business interests. When they met, neither man made his headquarters in New Jersey, but each had reason to be looking for a new home. The beer barons were unlikely pals, given their very different personalities. Hassel was polished, disciplined, and humane. He was a suave operator who swayed people with words and numbers. Gordon had rough edges that kept him from being socially acceptable outside gangland. A violent man, he relied on brute force to get what he wanted. Gordon was known and respected in the underworld, where Hassel was an outsider and needed allies.

Hassel joined forces with Gordon and his faithful sidekick Maxie Greenberg to create a powerful liquor syndicate in New Jersey. In gangland they were known as the Jersey Trio. They branded their beer Triple X, presumably because each man's name had an "x" in it. The Jersey Trio ran a chain of at least sixteen breweries in New Jersey, Pennsylvania, Maryland, and New York.[21] Beer with their Triple X brand was distributed from coast to coast via truck and railroad. Their crown jewels were two New Jersey plants: the Eureka Cereal Beverage Company in Paterson and the Union City Brewery in Union City.

Hassel hired experienced brew masters at his plants and gave them free rein in making the beer. He took pride in marketing a superior product, but Gordon cared nothing about quality. At the brewery in Paterson, Triple X hired a brew master with decades of experience. The master brewer told Gordon that it took four to six weeks to make good beer, which should then age in the vats for two to three months, depending on the weather and other factors. Gordon didn't have time for quality. He ordered the brew master to leave the beer in the vats for exactly two days![22]

To transport beer from the Paterson brewery to the packaging point, the Jersey Trio used the tried-and-true method: an underground pipeline. The beer was forced through a network of pipes to a machine shop beside the brewery. From there, the pipes led to a house, where a detachable hose connected to Paterson's sewer system. After the hose was attached to a line inside the sewer, the beer was sent several blocks to a garage, where it was pumped into barrels. When lawmen learned about the garage, the Trio rented another building a few blocks away and snaked another length of hose through the sewer.[23]

After the 1932 Presidential election, as the end of Prohibition neared, America's beer barons plotted to survive. Hassel was better positioned than most because he wasn't closely associated with organized crime. Moreover, as part of the settlement in his tax evasion case, the government had expunged his criminal record. Of equal importance, he understood the arts of bribery and friendly persuasion. Over the years he had cultivated friendships with powerful politicos, bureaucrats, and businessmen. Now those friends could help him secure the permits he needed to make legal, post–Volstead beer.

Several weeks before beer rejoined the roster of legal beverages, Hassel traveled to Washington, D.C. So did a member of the New Jersey Beer Control Commission, who enjoyed Hassel's hospitality in the nation's capital. Around the same time, Triple X's Maxie Greenberg went to Washington and paid $100,000 in bribes to a high-ranking official at the Alcohol Licensing Department.

The Jersey Trio's costly graft paid off. Federal officials approved post–Volstead permits for the Triple X breweries in Harrison, Paterson, and Newark, New Jersey. In addition, Hassel secured licenses that would allow him to operate at least two breweries in Pennsylvania.[24]

Being a licensed brewer in a legal industry promised to be a dream-come-true for the Millionaire Newsboy. At last, he would have his own legitimate business with vast earning potential. He wouldn't have to dodge the Prohis or hire a lawyer to stop the government from padlocking his plants. He could be proud of his product and make his mark in the world, selling premium beer with his brand name on the label.

Sadly, the Millionaire Newsboy never lived his dream. Less than a week after beer became legal, he met the typical gangster's death. Hassel and Greenberg were fatally shot in a hotel suite in Elizabeth, New Jersey. Police found Greenberg seated at a roll-top desk, slumped over in a chair, his hand touching a loaded revolver in his jacket pocket. He had been shot several times in the head. Hassel, unarmed as always, lay sprawled on the floor, face down. He had three bullets from a .38 caliber "police special" in the back of his head. A brick-size piece of concrete lay on the floor beside his body. Bottles of liquor and eight half-full glasses of whiskey sat on a table.[25]

When news of Hassel's violent death reached Reading, residents were stunned. They remembered a polite, amiable guy who was decent and trustworthy, despite his illegal vocation. Everybody seemed to have only good things to say about him. Hassel's barber called him "the greatest guy I ever knew." The bootblack who shined his shoes said, "There'll never be another like him." The Taxpayers' Protective League, a group of unemployed workers, voted to send a wreath to his funeral. The group's leader spoke for his comrades, saying, "Max Hassel was the workingman's friend."

Hassel's body was sent home in a humble pine box and transferred to an expensive casket for burial. Thousands of people filed past his impressive casket to pay their last respects to a hometown boy who made good. More than one hundred cars joined the funeral procession that carried him to Reading's Green Tree Cemetery, where he was buried beside his parents.[26]

Mob hits usually went unsolved, but the police expected to find Hassel's killers, who had left significant evidence behind, including the murder weapon. The gun was found in the hotel's rear stairwell where someone had tossed it away, presumably as he ran down the stairs. The police soon named several suspects, all with mob ties and all capable of cold-blooded murder.

The police interrogated Waxy Gordon to learn where he had been when his partners perished. He claimed that he had been in the hotel room across the hall when the shots were fired. He denied gangland rumors that he was having sex with a prostitute during the shooting. He said he had heard a loud noise that "sounded like breaking glass or someone dropping dishes." The noise spooked him and he fled the hotel because he was scared. He swore that he didn't know the identity of the shooters or their motive.

Gordon didn't have a finely-tuned sense of ethics, but he seemed to realize that he had failed his pals by running away when they were under fire. He defended his reaction by arguing that he had to save himself. "I'd have got the works, same as they did," he said. "They was both good friends of mine."[27]

Less than a month after the Hassel-Greenberg murders, the case was presented to the grand jury in Elizabeth. New Jersey Supreme Court Justice Clarence Case told the jurors they were "in the front line of battle" against organized crime. "Disabuse your minds of the thought that perhaps those men are better off dead and the world better off without them," he said. "That spells the way to destruction of society. You must see to it that, so far as it lies within your power, the perpetrators of this crime are brought to justice."[28]

Despite the judge's dramatic words, the grand jury failed to indict anyone for the Hassel-Greenberg murders. The case was filed away but not forgotten. Almost three years after the shooting, an indictment was finally issued in Union County, New Jersey. A grand jury decreed that Frankie Carbo (AKA Frank Tucker, Jimmy the Wop) would stand trial for the hit. Carbo, a boxing promoter/manager and one of the usual suspects in mob hits, was reputed to be a top triggerman for Murder, Inc. Over the years, he was accused of killing at least nine of his peers.[29]

New York City police arrested Carbo at Madison Square Garden, where he had gone to watch a fight. After his arrest, he languished in jail for months, waiting to go on trial for the Hassel-Greenberg murders. Then, as often happened in mob cases, he was freed, due to insufficient evidence. Prosecutors simply didn't have the proof needed to convict him.[30]

Hassel's criminal enterprises seemed to expand after his death. The U.S. Secret Service alleged that he had bankrolled and masterminded a forgery ring, which counterfeited both money and stock certificates. He was also accused of kidnapping the Lindbergh baby, a sensational crime that made headlines around the world. Given everything known about Hassel, the first accusation seemed plausible. The second sounded truly preposterous and was quickly disproved.[31]

After a few weeks of posthumous infamy, Hassel sank into an obscure corner of crime history. The probe into his murder died a natural death in the cold case files. No one was ever convicted of killing the Millionaire Newsboy.

The Waxy Hijacking

During his long criminal career Waxy Gordon victimized many people. In a case of gangland poetic justice, he got a taste of being the victim when hijackers stole a shipment of whiskey intended for him. The daring, bloody crime set off a mini-mob war and, through a circuitous route, helped the feds send Gordon to prison. The hijacking became a mob legend that has been recounted in movies, books, and TV shows.

On a road outside Atlantic City, New Jersey, high-strung young guns Meyer Lansky and Bugsy Siegel led a group of thugs who set a trap for a bootleg convoy expected later that night. The hijackers chopped down a small tree and laid it across the road, as if it had fallen there. They took cover in the darkness and waited. In the wee hours of the morning, they heard the convoy of liquor trucks rumbling down the road. When the first truck driver saw the tree, he slammed on his brakes. The other drivers braked to a halt. The bootleggers on the trucks jumped out to move the tree, and the hijackers opened fire. In only seconds, gunshots killed three bootleggers and seriously wounded several others. The outgunned leggers surrendered.[32]

If the bootleggers hoped to be treated humanely, they were out of luck. The hijackers were in a nasty mood. Using their fists, feet, and wood clubs, they beat the bootleggers to near death. Then, leaving the wounded leggers beside the road, the hijackers jumped on the liquor trucks and drove away with their loot.

The battered bootleggers who survived the ordeal didn't talk to the cops, but the tale of the hijacking kept gangland abuzz with gossip. At least one of the leggers had recognized Lansky during the brutal beating, and the underworld hummed with the news. Waxy Gordon soon knew who had stolen his booze.

The bloody hijacking set off a feud between Gordon, a middle-aged liquor lord, and Lansky, a rising mob star. With typical gangster braggadocio, the two men engaged in shouting matches, cursing at one another and making vile threats. Lucky Luciano, Lansky's close friend, tried to play peacemaker, with little success. On at least one occasion the verbal sparring between Gordon and Lansky led to fisticuffs, and Luciano had to physically separate the pair. He defused the situation temporarily, but the simmering hatred between Gordon and Lansky needed only a little heat to boil over.[33]

Although Luciano acted as peacemaker, his sympathies lay with his pal Lansky. When Luciano and Lansky heard a rumor that the feds were investigating Gordon's finances to build a tax fraud case, they were overjoyed. They decided to help the feds take a public enemy off the streets. With the right evidence, prosecutors could send Gordon to the slammer for a long stretch. Lansky recruited his brother to secretly feed damaging information about Gordon to the Internal Revenue office in Philadelphia.[34]

Dewey Wins

If Waxy Gordon read the tea leaves, or the newspapers, he must've known that his future held a trial for tax fraud. The federal government's assault on tax cheats was filling prisons with the crème de la crème of mobsters. Only days after Gordon's Triple X partners were shot to death at the hotel, Waxy was indicted for tax evasion. According to the Internal Revenue accountants, he owed nearly $383,000 on an income of more than $1.5 million for 1930-31. He had reported a total income of only $40,000 for those years.[35]

When Gordon heard about the indictment, he decided he'd rather run than fight, so he went on the lam. Law enforcement quickly launched a nationwide search for him. He hid out with relatives for a time and then rented a hunting lodge on White Lake in the Catskills. He docked a speedy motorboat on the lake, in case he needed to make a fast getaway. His loyal minions, including Joey the Fleabag, stood guard at the lodge.

Gordon's goons failed to be the faithful, alert watchdogs he needed. They were asleep when treasury agents arrived to arrest him early one Sunday morning. Hoping to fool the agents, Gordon loudly claimed to be an innocent man. He swore he was William Palinski, a tobacco executive. But the T-men didn't believe him for even a nanosecond. As usual, he was wearing monogrammed silk drawers: the agents knew "IW" stood for Irving Wexler.[36]

After the agents arrested Gordon, he was arraigned on the tax charges. He was incarcerated in the Federal House of Detention in New York City until he posted bond.

At the time of Gordon's arrest, Thomas Dewey was serving as Chief Assistant U.S. Attorney for the Southern District of New York. The young attorney had quit a private law practice to head a special squad assigned to expose "the lush underworld of the East." Waxy Gordon and Dutch Schultz were the squad's primary targets due to their preeminent roles in Volstead crime. Law enforcement captured Gordon first, so the U.S. attorney's office gave his tax trial top priority, leaving Schultz's case for a later date. Under Dewey's supervision, six investigators worked full-time collecting evidence against the lone Triple X survivor. As Gordon's trial date drew nearer, six lawyers and twelve revenue agents were added to the task force.[37]

In keeping with time-honored mob tradition, potential witnesses against Gordon began to disappear soon after his indictment. Three men who could testify against him met violent deaths. His chauffeur, a bodyguard, and a man who played "an important part" in running his rackets were murdered. In the following months, at least eight witnesses disappeared, either due to foul play or fear of reprisal if they testified.[38]

Gordon's minions weren't content with witness tampering. To expunge the paper trail, they destroyed some of his financial records and altered others. They broke into business offices to steal pertinent documents to reduce the paper evidence against him. Legitimate business people who had dealt with Gordon had reason to fear both Waxy's henchmen and the Internal Revenue auditors. Some business owners revised their ledgers to hide transactions and minimize their dealings with him.

Gordon's North Jersey bankers, due to fear or loyalty, helped him hide evidence. Ledgers "almost too large for men to carry walked out of banks in New Jersey." At some banks, the managers stonewalled Dewey's investigators while "Gordon's men would arrive from nowhere, withdraw all the money in the accounts, and make away with all the evidence." At a bank in Paterson, the investigators spent hours combing through thick bundles of deposit slips. They found not a single slip for Gordon's accounts because someone had meticulously removed all of them. When federal agents went to a Hoboken bank, the local police showed up and arrested them. The cops accused the feds of using forged credentials and detained them until Gordon's records could be spirited away.

Gordon also had bank accounts outside New Jersey. Fortunately for Dewey's task force, New York bankers were made of sterner stuff than their Jersey colleagues. Bank officers in the Empire State didn't succumb to bribery or threats. They kept Gordon's records intact and turned them over to law enforcement.[39]

Gordon's tax fraud trial began on November 30, 1933, in federal court in New York City. Two days into the trial, Dewey was appointed Acting U.S. Attorney for the Southern District of New York. He would serve in his new post for only five weeks, but the Gordon trial would establish his credentials as a fierce foe of organized crime.

In the courtroom Dewey methodically pieced together the fragments of evidence to construct an accurate picture of Gordon's finances. He presented days of testimony about Gordon's bank accounts, money transfers, business transactions, insurance policies, and so forth. Even though some evidence had vanished, the state submitted a mountain of ledgers, account books, debit sheets, transcripts, deposit slips, cancelled checks, and toll slips for phone calls. Dewey's team set up a display of charts to visually reinforce the financial data heard by the jury. Before Dewey rested his case, the state called 131 witnesses and presented 939 exhibits![40]

In order to verify Gordon's tax debt, the prosecution had to make a reasonable estimate of the Jersey Trio's profits. A revenue agent stated that two of the Trio's chain of breweries, Eureka and Union City, had a combined net profit of more than $4.5 million in 1930-31. He had computed this number based on bills of lading, the number of truck drivers employed, the number of outlets selling Triple X beer, the price of the beer, and production figures supplied by the brew masters.[41]

Testimony about the Jersey Trio's truck fleet showed that Triple X beer had wide distribution. A truck salesman stated that he had sold fourteen vehicles to the Trio in only one year. "A gray-haired, gray-faced man" in a wheelchair also testified about the truck fleet. A former agent for the New Jersey Motor Vehicle License Bureau, he stated that the Trio operated at least forty big trucks on routes along the East Coast.

A man who sold beer-making ingredients testified about his business transactions with the Triple X breweries in New Jersey. He had first met Waxy Gordon when the beer baron came to his office and paid him $100,000 owed by two mobsters who had just been murdered. Gordon said he was taking over their business. Soon after that, the Jersey Trio had the Union City and Eureka breweries running at full capacity.[42]

A handwriting expert identified Gordon's signature on checks that were submitted as evidence. Although Gordon used aliases on his bank accounts, on a few occasions he had carelessly signed his real name when endorsing checks. At other times he had remembered to endorse his checks with an alias. The expert showed that the handwriting was consistent on all the endorsements, regardless of the name.

Although Gordon claimed to have limited income, bank documents showed that he had enough financial surety to obtain large loans. Records showed that he had personally guaranteed a hotel construction loan for $1 million, and he had signed another note for $795,000.[43]

After listening to the state's carefully crafted case, Gordon took the stand to defend himself. To look like a respectable businessman, he had chosen to wear a conservative gray suit, a white shirt, and a gray-and-white knit tie. For several hours, he answered questions put to him by his own attorney. Despite his many previous appearances in court, he seemed nervous. He squirmed in the witness chair and spoke softly, his lips barely moving. He confessed that he had made youthful "mistakes" and had served time in prison, but he denied running the Triple X syndicate in New Jersey. He claimed he was "only a cog" in a big machine — an underpaid lackey who answered to the real bosses, Max Hassel and Maxie Greenberg.

Gordon said his job was finding distributors for Triple X beer. His tightfisted bosses paid him from $125 to $300 per week plus an occasional dividend. He drove a company car, but he made so little money that his wife had to sell her jewelry to pay the rent on their luxury apartment.

During cross-examination, Dewey pressed Gordon for answers about the ownership of the Triple X breweries. The mobster insisted that he didn't own an interest in the Union City brewery or any other. As far as he knew, Hassel and Greenberg never owned any breweries either. He believed they had bought their beer from a supplier in Pennsylvania. When Dewey suggested that Gordon knew more about the syndicate's business than he would divulge, Waxy said, "There's something you don't understand, Mr. Dewey. We never ask questions in the beer business."[44]

After only an hour of Dewey's questions, Gordon seemed exhausted, too weak to go on. His face was ghostly white, and he looked so sickly that Dewey's assistants urged their boss to end the interrogation. They were afraid a lengthy, hard-hitting cross-examination would cause the jurors to empathize with Gordon. Dewey took their advice, wrapping up the session with a series of straightforward questions about Gordon's finances.[45]

In Dewey's summation to the jury, he emphasized that his case was built on fragments of evidence because many documents had been destroyed. Despite the missing pieces, the records proved that Gordon was a tax dodger. "The defendant, by his own admission, is a cheat, a fraud, a robber, a pickpocket, a professional criminal and also a man so low that, although he must have had a colossal income ... he paid the government a pittance and left the support of the government to the honest citizens of the United States...," Dewey said.

The jurors didn't need lengthy deliberations to reach a verdict. They quickly found Gordon guilty on four counts of tax evasion. When the verdict was read, Gordon took the news calmly, but his wife sobbed. The judge, after calling Gordon "a gang leader of the worst type," sentenced him to ten years in federal prison and fined him $80,000. Gordon's attorney announced that he would petition the U.S. Court of Appeals to overturn the verdict.[46]

Only days after Gordon's conviction, he suffered a shocking, devastating blow much worse than what he had endured in the courtroom. His son, Theodore Wexler, was killed in a horrific accident when a train crushed his car at a railroad crossing. The beer baron had shielded Theodore from gangland, sending him to a military prep school and then to the University of North Carolina, where he was majoring in pre-med. Gordon had envisioned a great future for his son. He truly believed that Theodore would excel in an honest career and be a valuable member of society. Perhaps in some way, that would be redemption for Gordon's own wickedness.

The heartbroken father begged the judge for permission to attend his son's funeral. "That boy was my one hope. I counted on him. Everything I did centered around him," Gordon said.

Shackled to a U.S. marshal, Gordon didn't look like a tough, powerful mobster at his son's funeral. Tears streamed down his cheeks while "like a man in a dream" he mumbled the words of the traditional burial *Kaddish*. A man in a nightmare might've been a better description.[47]

After the funeral Gordon marked time behind bars while his legal team appealed the guilty verdict. The appeal claimed that Dewey had made inflammatory remarks to the jury and repeatedly asked questions about the missing witnesses, implying that Gordon had engineered their murder or disappearance. Moreover, Dewey had implied that Gordon was somehow involved in the bloody mob-style murders of his Triple X partners. Nearly two years after the trial, the U.S. Circuit Court of Appeals upheld Gordon's conviction.[48]

Gordon was sent to Lewisburg Federal Penitentiary in Pennsylvania to serve his sentence. Even though he had done time before and knew the routine, he created problems at Lewisburg. Far from being the ideal inmate, he repeatedly broke the rules and antagonized the guards. This prompted the Bureau of Prisons (BOP) to transfer him to the federal facility in Atlanta. His bad behavior continued, and the BOP moved him again—this time to Leavenworth, Kansas.

After serving less than seven years, Gordon applied for a parole, even though his prison record indicated that he was an unrepentant troublemaker. Thomas Dewey strongly opposed Gordon's parole, saying that the beer baron was "commonly known as New York's public enemy number one." Nevertheless, the parole board granted the mobster a conditional release from Leavenworth.[49]

A few days after leaving prison, Gordon returned to New York City. He declared that he was going straight, and he vowed to find honest work as a salesman. A wire service quoted him as saying, "Listen, Waxy Gordon is dead. There's no more Waxy Gordon. It's Wexler, Irving Wexler, I'm interested in."[50]

While in prison Gordon avoided paying his back taxes and the fines he owned because, like most convicts, he took a pauper's oath. Now that he was back in New York, a federal judge ordered him to appear at a court hearing to determine the status of his finances. The hearing and the subsequent attempts to collect what Gordon owed the government yielded nothing. He steadfastly claimed he was broke and, until the day he died, hid his assets from the IRS. (Two years after his death, his name appeared on a list of delinquent taxpayers; the IRS said he still owed nearly $1.4 million in taxes and penalties.)[51]

Almost no one believed Gordon's public proclamations that he had given up his felonious ways. Lawmen dogged him wherever he went and arrested him on minor charges. When he visited San Francisco, authorities suspected that he had come on a criminal mission. Police showed up at his swanky hotel and arrested him for vagrancy. When he was hauled into court, the judge strongly suggested that he leave the City by the Bay — ASAP. Taking the hint, he flew to Los Angeles, where FBI agents, local police, and the district attorney's investigators met him at the airport. The DA's chief investigator told Gordon he would be wise to leave within twenty-four hours. The unwelcome mobster quickly departed the City of Angels.[52]

During World War II Gordon was indicted for falsifying ration bank deposits. He pled guilty and was sentenced to one year in federal prison. After serving his time, he traded in military surplus on the black market. The U.S. Senate's War Investigating Committee called him to Washington to answer questions about his shady business. He "explained carefully that he had no funds, that he had not worked regularly since 1933, that he lived on the kindness of friends."[53]

After World War II Gordon specialized in drug trafficking, a racket he had dabbled in for decades. Police learned that the paunchy, balding mobster was a kingpin in an international narcotics ring. Reminiscent of his rumrunning days, he imported drugs on ships sailing into U.S. ports from Europe and Asia. He had accomplices across the country, selling the dope from coast to coast.

To gather solid evidence about kingpin Gordon, lawmen followed him everywhere. They set up a successful sting in which an informant bought drugs from him in New York City. But they felt they needed more ammunition for an ironclad case, so they continued to shadow him. Late one night federal agents and NYC police followed him to a street corner on Manhattan's East Side. They watched him furtively accept a bundle, wrapped in newspaper, from a man in a car. The package held uncut heroin, part of a large shipment his henchmen had picked up on the waterfront in Jersey City. The lawmen swooped down on Gordon and his goons.

Falling to his knees, Gordon begged one of the police officers, "Please kill me.... Shoot me! I'm an old man and I'm through. Don't take me in.... Let me run, and then you shoot me!"

The police officer ignored Gordon's pathetic plea. One of Gordon's henchmen took two diamond rings off his fingers and offered them to the cops. There were no takers. Then the young hood said he would pay them $25,000 to let "Pops" Gordon go. But these were honest lawmen. They wanted to nab the drug boss more than they wanted money. (The published reports of Gordon's arrest read like bad fiction, but reliable sources said the mobster did in fact sob and beg to be shot.)[54]

After Gordon's arrest, prosecutors had a choice of federal or state charges. Under New York state law, he could be sentenced to a prison term of twenty-five years to life as an offender with four felony convictions. If given a life sentence, he would almost certainly die in jail — an outcome many people would applaud. Federal prosecutors agreed to defer action so he could be tried under the state law. If he wiggled off the state's hook, the feds would open their own case against him.

Gordon was indicted in New York County and pled guilty to two felony counts of narcotics trafficking. In court, he said he understood that his guilty plea could send him to prison for the rest of his life.[55]

Following the established procedure, Gordon was given a jury trial to determine whether he was in fact a four-time felon. This trial should've been a formality, but Gordon decided to put up a defense. His lawyer argued that a conviction for theft in Philadelphia, way back in 1909, didn't count as a felony because Gordon had snatched a woman's purse worth only $3.25. Although this was a felony in Pennsylvania, in New York it was petty larceny, a misdemeanor. The prosecutor disagreed, arguing that purse snatching was "larceny from the person," a felony in both states.

The judge dismissed the jury, saying the felony or misdemeanor question was a technical issue that couldn't be resolved by laymen. Subsequently, a New York court ruled that Gordon was subject to the four-felony penalty. A judge sentenced the habitual offender to a prison term of twenty-five years to life. He said Gordon's long criminal career had been "a malignant cancer, weakening the dignity and good order of the community."[56]

After a brief stay in Sing Sing, Gordon was transferred to Attica State Prison. But this wouldn't be his last move. A federal grand jury in California indicted him along with his accomplices who sold illicit drugs in Reno, Phoenix, Portland, and San Francisco. After some legal formalities, New York State agreed to turn Gordon over to the feds for trial in California. Law enforcement moved the ageing drug pusher to San Francisco, where he was arraigned on narcotics charges.[57]

At age sixty-three Gordon had serious heart problems and needed regular medical attention. After a short stay in the San Francisco jail, he was moved to the federal prison hospital on Alcatraz Island. On June 24, 1952, the career criminal died of a massive heart attack while talking to a doctor at Alcatraz.[58]

In his long lifetime of crime Waxy Gordon had victimized countless people, peddled addictive substances, killed rivals to get what he wanted, and never reformed. He remained a gangster to the very end.

16. Smedley and Boo Boo: Prohibition in Philadelphia

Philadelphia is sopping wet, and there are more speakeasies around than statues and pictures of Benjamin Franklin. Up and down Broad Street, along Market and just around the corner, thirst relief stations are stacked one on top of the other. It is a quarter of a mile between nightclubs, but there always is a speakeasy within a funnel's throw where one can fill his hip flask for the journey.—Tom Pettey, newspaper reporter[1]

Before Volstead, Philadelphia was so quiet and staid that it was called the City of Seven Sundays. During Prohibition a visitor said, "It isn't that kind of a town at all." Philly had more saloons during Volstead than before, and numerous cracked ice emporiums catered to the hip-flask crowd. The city had a dozen or so trendy nightclubs with jazz bands and A-list performers. The "street level bars" were wide open, and "any good conversationalist" could talk his way into the most exclusive speakeasies. "In Philadelphia the Liberty Bell is more than a symbol," a reporter wrote. "It pleases these citizens to assume they still have the right to conduct themselves as they desire.... They do both their drinking and church-going in the shadow of Independence Hall."[2]

Philadelphia's liquor lords relied on graft to keep the spigots open. Corruption pervaded the police department, and local lawmen did little to aid Governor Gifford Pinchot's state-wide dry crusade. A pandemic of malfeasance infected city hall. Philly's corrupt political machine was an "invisible dictatorship" comparable to the regime of Benito Mussolini, according to one writer. The reigning Republican politicos "ran things with a level of corruption that made Al Capone's operation look honest."[3]

In Prohibition's early years, Philly's illegal watering holes suffered little interference from law enforcement. Governor Pinchot seethed with anger because saloons operated openly in Philadelphia. On a fact-finding tour he visited several speakeasies, including one where drinkers stood "four deep" at the bar. He said the place "was easy to find, for there was as little secrecy about it as there is about the Washington Monument."[4]

During the Arid Era, the City of Philadelphia mounted only two protracted offensives against the illegal liquor traffic. A Marine Corps general was appointed director of public safety in 1924, with a mandate to clean up the City of Brotherly Love. In 1928, a special grand jury led a probe into bootlegging and gambling in Philadelphia. Both initiatives had

161

earnest support from civic groups and received a great deal of favorable press coverage. Both brought about some change, but neither lived up to the hype.

Old Duckboards

When Freeland Kendrick ran for mayor of Philadelphia in 1923, he made an always popular campaign promise: he would wipe out crime and corruption. After his election, he decided to hire a military man to lead his anti-crime offensive. He chose a local hero, USMC Brigadier General Smedley Butler, who had grown up in nearby West Chester. Butler was known as a fiery, shoot-from-the-hip guy who got things done. Equally germane to his selection, he had personal connections to the Republican political machine in Philadelphia. His father was U.S. Representative Thomas Butler, an influential GOP Congressman from Pennsylvania.[5]

The Marine Corps, with President Coolidge's permission, granted Butler a year's leave of absence so he could serve as Philadelphia's director of public safety, in charge of the police and fire departments. The loquacious Butler was a blustery, zealous Teddy Roosevelt type. During his military service, he earned colorful nicknames, including "the Fighting Quaker," "Old Gimlet Eye," "Hell's Devil Butler," and "Old Duckboards." He proudly wore an array of military awards on his chest, including two Medals of Honor, the Distinguished Service Cross, and the Marine Corps Brevet Medal.

Butler began his career in the Spanish-American War and went on to lead Marine units in several countries. During World War I he served in France. During the Banana Wars he was credited with capturing Fort Riviere, Haiti, and Veracruz, Mexico. In Haiti, he commanded U.S. Marines and Haitians who built highways so troops and equipment could be deployed quickly. In Nicaragua an enemy general with two thousand troops surrounded Butler's force of only 180 Leathernecks. Legend says Butler met the opposing general face-to-face, stuck a pistol in his midriff, and pulled on the man's whiskers until he let the Marines go.[6]

Butler, who had a king-sized flare for the theatrical, grabbed the spotlight as Philly's top cop. A short man with a prominent Roman nose and a strong jaw, he wanted to create a superhero image to intimidate the bad guys. He dressed in an eye-catching blue uniform with lots of gold braid, topped off with a showy blue cape lined with red silk. He carried a gun and fired it in more than one shootout. He traveled around town in a Packard limousine, its siren blaring much of the time.[7]

Butler launched his war against Philadelphia's criminal miscreants in January 1924. If empathic public statements could get the job done, Old Duckboards couldn't fail. On January 2, he said, "I am going to enforce the law if I am torn apart in the attempt." Two days later he declared, "The lid will be closed down tight in forty-eight hours." The following day, he said, "In forty-eight hours the lieutenants of the districts have got to have them clean." On January 11, he proudly crowed, "The town's clean!" Five months later, he said, "Philadelphia is thirty percent clean." After another three months, he announced, "Our object is to clean up this town, and we are going to do it!"[8]

Undeniably, Old Duckboards started off with a bang. During his first five days in office, he closed more than eighty percent of the city's estimated twelve hundred illegal saloons. Later, he commanded a citywide dragnet that nabbed more than eleven hundred saloonkeepers, gamblers, and prostitutes. On one occasion, he shut down every speakeasy in town for forty-eight hours, a much-hyped feat that produced banner headlines. (Surely he missed a few bars, but the press gave him the benefit of the doubt.)

Butler's raids made headlines, annoyed barkeepers, and interrupted the liquor traffic. But the impact was temporary. The watering holes usually reopened soon after being raided. For instance, Butler's raiders hit the Venice Café seven times in one week; this disrupted business but didn't actually close the place. Despite the raids, the bartender at the café readily confessed to a reporter that he was still serving beer. Other newsmen found that strangers got the cold shoulder in saloons that had been raided, but trusted customers were still being served. While the illegal bars became more secretive and selective, they didn't go out of business.

Butler revamped the police department's structure and procedures in an effort to improve results. He created an elite squad, Enforce-

A police official in Philadelphia smashed a barrel of beer from the truckload of confiscated booze behind him (Library of Congress).

ment Unit No. 1, which he staffed with top-ranked police officers. Before he took over, the police department had routinely notified the mayor when raids were in the offing. Word of the plans would leak out, so the raids would net little liquor and few arrests. Butler adopted what he called his "pounce policy"—staging lightning-fast raids without notifying the mayor's office beforehand. Old Duckboards didn't like sitting behind a desk, so he was a hands-on commander who spent a lot of time on the street with his men.[9]

Under Butler's regime the number of liquor-related arrests rose, but the conviction rate was rather low for Volstead offenses. In 1924 Philadelphia's city courts had a conviction rate of forty-eight percent in liquor cases. The next year that rate fell to thirty-three percent. Butler complained that the city magistrates weren't doing their part to enforce the dry law. The magistrates blamed the Snyder Act, Pennsylvania's baby Volstead, because it didn't clearly specify the standards for search warrants and admissible evidence. The jurists said this ambiguity greatly complicated their job.[10]

Of course, many magistrates objected to enforcing Volstead simply because they disliked Prohibition. Magistrate Edward Carney, known as "the dancing judge," openly defied Volstead by patronizing nightclubs. When Philadelphia's city solicitor told Carney that finding liquor in a private residence was "prima facie evidence of an intent to violate the law," the dancing judge exploded. "If that's so, we're all breaking the law, from the mayor on down. I know I've got liquor in my house, and heaven help the cop who tries to get it!"[11]

Philadelphia's magistrates sided with dancer Carney. At a meeting they voted to reject the city solicitor's argument that finding liquor in a private residence was prima facie evidence of criminal intent. They agreed to require lawmen to show substantial cause before granting a search warrant. They would disqualify any evidence that had been collected without strict adherence to the rules for search and seizure. They also agreed to greatly limit the use of John Doe warrants in enforcing Volstead. (A police officer could request a Joe Doe warrant if he suspected someone of a crime but didn't know that individual's name.) Civil libertarians lauded the magistrates for protecting sacred constitutional rights. Dry leaders protested that the magistrates were aiding the liquor traffickers.

General Butler reluctantly honored the magistrates' strict guidelines. He ordered his officers not to seize stills without a warrant, not to search private homes without concrete evidence, and not to destroy private property during raids. Showing his sensitivity to local politics, he said, "Guard against anything that will embarrass Mayor Kendrick's administration." He also strongly cautioned his staff against being overzealous in raiding saloons. "I must admit that I have sinned in this latter respect more than any of you," he said, "and the only excuse I have to offer is that I was unduly excited and enthusiastic."[12]

Although Mayor Kendrick had chosen Butler to be his anti-crime czar, he seemed conflicted about the general. In public His Honor was usually supportive, but in private he worried that Old Duckboards was too aggressive. The two clashed often, especially over personnel matters in the police department. Butler wanted to totally reorganize the department, reducing the number of districts from forty-two to twenty-two. Each police district roughly coincided with a political ward, which allowed the local GOP boss to exert a lot of influence in police affairs. Butler's plan would reapportion the political power because each new police district would include parts of at least two political wards.[13]

Cynics said Mayor Kendrick was upset because Butler was doing his job too well: he was actually cleaning up Philly when all Kendrick wanted was a whitewash. Realpolitik dictated that the mayor stay on good terms with the saloonkeepers and their pals because they turned out the vote on Election Day. Philly's GOP politicos viewed Old Duckboards as a liability because he raided too many saloons. The city treasurer declared, "This country, as well as the Republican organization, would be a hell of a sight better off without Butler."

As the political pressure mounted within the GOP, Kendrick became more critical of Butler. He publicly admitted that he was displeased with the general and had no "rapport" with him. The mayor issued a mild threat, saying, "If I can't have a man who will cooperate with me, I'll put in another." In response, Butler's fans organized a show of support to keep him on the job. A public meeting drew thousands of Philadelphians who liked his approach to law enforcement. Civic and business leaders lauded his work. The crowd passed a resolution demanding that the "intrepid soldier, fearless officer, and devoted servant of the people be retained until his work is fully completed."[14]

The public show of support for Butler made an impression on Mayor Kendrick. Both men realized that the citizenry wanted them to stop bickering and work together. Butler publicly apologized for failing to confer and coordinate with the mayor. His Honor bowed to public sentiment and asked President Coolidge to extend Butler's military leave of absence for three more years. Church groups and the Pennsylvania Law Enforcement Association also appealed to Coolidge to allow Butler to continue his crime-fighting crusade.

After due consideration, the President granted a second year's leave of absence to Butler but emphasized that he would not consent to a third. As Old Duckboards embarked on his second year as Philly's chief crime fighter, he sounded pessimistic. He compared his job to slow, excruciating torture, saying, "Drops of water have been dripping on my head since I have been here." In a particularly glum speech, he groused, "You have taken me and kicked me and dragged me to death." His regime had produced a substantial drop in the number of felonies, but he had hit a brick wall when he tried to enforce Volstead. "Either I am unpopular, or the enforcement of the liquor laws is unpopular in this city," he wryly observed.[15]

Butler felt besieged by both wets and drys when he tried to set the priorities for Volstead enforcement. Upscale restaurants and hotels generally had illegal bars or allowed customers to bring their own booze. City officials told Butler not to raid these businesses because they were important to the local economy. On the other hand, dry activists criticized him for raiding hole-in-the-wall saloons while ignoring the liquor purveyors at posh hotels and restaurants. Butler formed a "soup and fish squad" of young, socially-acceptable police officers to infiltrate formal events and gather evidence of Volstead violations.[16]

Butler decided to show his independence by defying the politicos and raiding the city's best hotels. By closing down million-dollar hotels, he would prove that he could not be intimidated. He ordered raids on several places, including the Ritz-Carlton, the Walton Hotel, and the Bellevue-Stratford. In a highly-publicized raid city officials invaded a debutante's coming out party in the ballroom at the Ritz-Carlton Hotel. The lawmen seized bottles of wine, champagne, and Scotch whiskey. After police chemists confirmed that the confiscated liquids were intoxicants, Butler resolved to padlock the Ritz-Carlton. "Something must be done to teach these big fellows that they must obey the law as well as the little fellows," he declared.

Butler went to Mayor Kendrick with a plan to padlock two large hotels, the Ritz-Carlton and the Bellevue-Stratford. The mayor flatly refused to order the city solicitor to padlock the hotels, which were among the city's busiest, priciest hostelries. Butler ranted and raved. He threatened to contact dry Governor Pinchot, who could order the state attorney general to padlock the hotels. But there was no guarantee the Republican governor would pull rank on the Republican mayor. Besides, Butler belonged to a political family and knew he must not start a feud within the GOP. Mayor Kendrick and Old Duckboards had reached an impasse.

As Butler neared the end of his extended military leave, Mayor Kendrick made a pro forma plea to President Coolidge, requesting the general's services for another year. Privately, His Honor probably hoped that Coolidge would deny the request. The President stuck to his earlier decision, and Butler was slated to return to the Marine Corps at the end of the year. The general seemed eager to go back to military service. With Butler's approval, Kendrick announced that he had already chosen the man who would replace Old Duckboards. The mayor barely hid his joy over the general's imminent departure.[17]

General Butler, who had a reputation for doing the unpredictable, stayed true to form. He changed his mind about leaving Philadelphia. Without consulting the mayor, he resigned from the Marine Corps and announced that he would stay on as Philly's director of public safety. His abrupt volte-face made headlines in the morning newspapers. Kendrick fumed over the bombshell and demanded the general's resignation. Old Duckboards refused. Kendrick wasted no time: he instantly, unequivocally fired Butler.

Butler had abruptly lost both of his jobs. He had nowhere to wear his general's stars or his crime-fighting cape. He cast about for a face-saving option. General John Lejeune, head of the Marine Corps, came to his rescue and gave him permission to withdraw his resignation from the military. Butler quickly did so and headed out to California to command the Marine base at San Diego.

Butler fired some parting shots, turning his verbal big guns on Mayor Kendrick. He accused Kendrick of running a corrupt city, interfering in police matters, and preventing the police department from enforcing Volstead. In a speech to a dry group, Butler called Kendrick "a disloyal chief" and said he regretted that he had not "pulled the mayor's nose." He urged the public to demand clean government and take a stand against corruption in the City of Brotherly Love. "Pennsylvania can't afford to have a cesspool at its doorstep," he said. "That's what Philadelphia is."[18]

While serving in California, Butler had time to reflect on the unfairness inherent in Prohibition. In a speech, he denounced the dry law as "class legislation" that penalized the poor and "favored the rich man." He stated that Volstead was designed "to keep liquor away from persons without influence, and doesn't apply at all to those with influence and the money to pay for it." He said, "It's a case of enforcing the law in some places and bluffing at enforcing it in others."

Comparing his military and civilian careers, Butler declared, "Trying to enforce the law in Philadelphia was worse than any battle I was ever in."[19]

King Boo Boo

One night in February 1927, gangster John Bricker was leaving Philly's Club Cadix with Mickey Duffy, the mob boss who owned the speakeasy. As the two men and Mrs. Duffy exited through the club's front door, a sedan drove slowly down the street. Sudden blasts of machinegun fire rang out. Mrs. Duffy's car was parked at the curb, so she ducked inside. She escaped injury, but Bricker, Duffy, and the Cadix doorman weren't as lucky. The doorman took a bullet in the leg, and Duffy suffered multiple gunshot wounds. Several bullets struck Bricker in the head and neck, killing him instantly. He had the dubious honor of being the first Philadelphian murdered by machinegun.[20]

Mob boss Duffy was taken to Hahnemann Hospital, where he had the best care money could buy: a private room, nurses, and doctors "constantly in attendance upon him." Only Duffy's wife was permitted to visit him, but the waiting room was crowded with "scores of callers, hard-faced men in flashy raiment, for the most part." Florists delivered dozens of huge bouquets for Duffy, and the hospital switchboard was flooded with calls asking about him.[21]

Mob watchers attributed the Cadix shooting to an ongoing gang war that seemed to be getting hotter. Police arrested two men who had bought machineguns a few days before the drive-by, but they were later released. After several weeks in the hospital, Duffy was discharged, healthy enough to return to his shady endeavors.

The machinegun drive-by at the Cadix raised mob warfare to a gorier, deadlier level in the City of Brotherly Love. Police believed that the warring mobsters included Chicago gunmen as well as homegrown hoods. Philly had an array of active mobs, including Duffy's gang, the Zanghi brothers, the O'Leary brothers, the Lanzetti brothers, and the American Blackies. The city also had an active but low-profile Mafia family led by Salvatore Sabella. During the Arid Era, Philly's Mafioso specialized in loan sharking, bootlegging, and the protection racket. The press dubbed the Lanzetti brothers Philadelphia's "First Family of Crime" because the clan ran the numbers game as well as trafficking in drugs and alcohol. "We have picked up the Lanzettis one hundred times!" a police official declared. But the Lanzettis consistently "beat the rap."[22]

Philadelphia police recorded twenty-five gangland murders in two years of mob warfare. In all probability, other mob killings went unreported. Nobody knew how many bodies were secretly dumped in Bandits' Cemetery, a bog gangsters favored when disposing of inconvenient corpses. A newspaper wire service called Philadelphia "the machinegun belt of the East." Despite occasional arrests, only one killer was convicted for a gangland slaying during the mob war.[23] Philly mobsters, like their peers elsewhere, didn't cooperate with the police in murder probes. Instead, they bought guns and bulletproof vests and sallied forth to ambush the enemy.

At first Philadelphians seemed to take the mob warfare in stride. However, as fatalities mounted, the citizenry became alarmed. Judge Edwin Lewis of the Quarter Sessions Court decided the problem must be addressed. In 1928 he ordered the August grand jury, then in session, to investigate organized crime in the city. "Philadelphia shall not become a second Chicago," he vowed. "The police not only can but must break up organized crime, bootlegging syndicates, organized banditry, and thuggery."[24]

District Attorney John Monaghan took charge of gathering the evidence and presenting it to the grand jury. He vowed to expose the ties that closely linked organized crime, corrupt cops, and dishonest city officials. He told the grand jury that "a steady stream of gold" poured from the mobs' coffers into "the eager hands" of crooked public servants. He said that "enormous sums of money were paid police and officials for services rendered" to the mob.[25]

Monaghan zeroed in on Max "Boo Boo" Hoff as the probe's central target. A boxing promoter who ran Philly's biggest liquor syndicate, Hoff was widely known as the city's bootleg king. His rum ring was often called the Seventh Street Gang because he had offices in a building on South Seventh Street. Boxing fans knew Hoff as a flamboyant promoter who set up prizefights with big purses and lots of ballyhoo. An admirer described him as "a born promoter" with "charming manners" and "a generous, thoughtful disposition." Critics called him cocky and devious. He was a short, slight man with thin lips, bushy eyebrows, and a receding hairline. Beefy boxers accompanied him everywhere to protect him.

Hoff's nickname was a hand-me-down from his older brother, Lou. When Lou was a child in South Philly, his mother would holler "Bo" (Yiddish for "come") when she wanted him to hightail it home. His playmates teased him by calling him "Boo Boo." When Max began playing with the boys, he became "Little Boo Boo." After Max became a powerful liquor lord, no one dared call him "little." But Boo Boo stuck with him until the day he died.[26]

While Hoff had financial ups and downs in the fight game, the liquor traffic always produced profits. Alone or with partners, he owned three firms with government permits to deal in alcohol: the Quaker Industrial Alcohol Company, the Glenwood Industrial Distilling Company, and the Consolidated Ethyl Solvents Company. These companies bought and sold millions of gallons of denatured alcohol. Hoff's syndicate also owned licensed distilleries that produced grain alcohol for industrial use. This alcohol could easily be diverted into the illegal liquor traffic, before or after denaturing. Informed sources said the ring owned or controlled fifteen distilleries in Pennsylvania, New Jersey, Maryland, Ohio, Indiana, and Kentucky.[27]

Hoff funneled much of the syndicate's income through two financial firms that he controlled: the Franklin Mortgage & Investment Company and the Union Bank & Trust Company. Lawmen hunting for evidence confiscated a sizeable cache of Hoff's financial records from the Union Bank & Trust. The documents showed that his rum ring had multiple bank accounts under various names, and at least $12 million was deposited in those accounts in 1927. When investigators tried to question the account holders, they learned that the depositors had phony addresses. One depositor's address proved to be a vacant lot. Other account holders resided in cemeteries. A man who claimed to live in a stable had nearly $500,000 in his account.

Hoff's financial records showed that he made monthly payments to a long roster of lawmen, including top police officials. Some officers had received expensive cars and "palatial homes" as well as money. At Christmastime, Hoff played Santa Claus, spending about $250,000 on gifts for the friendly cops on his "turkey list." He even bribed members of Smedley Butler's elite Unit No. 1. According to Hoff's records, he had paid men in the special squad from $50 to $500 per month until it was disbanded after Old Duckboards left Philly.[28]

At the grand jury hearing, District Attorney Monaghan called a long list of witnesses to testify about Hoff's rum ring. The jurors listened to distillery workers, truck drivers, bootleggers, alky cookers, speakeasy waiters, gun dealers, police officers, bankers, vendors, realtors, convicted felons, and a handwriting expert. When the witnesses' answers were pieced together, they furnished a graphic picture of Philly's illicit liquor traffic and Hoff's central role in it.[29]

Soon after the grand jury inquiry began, the rumor mill said that GOP politicos were determined to stop it. The D.A. assured the public that political pressure would not force him to abandon it. "The truth is coming out," Monaghan said. "This investigation will never be stopped now until this whole rotten system of corruption, bribery, bootlegging and murdering is opened to public view and then smashed as it deserves to be smashed." Although the D.A. was a registered Republican, he assured the public that he was an independent prosecutor. "I am not affiliated in any way, shape, or form with any man or set of men," he said. "This investigation cannot be stopped by anyone."[30]

While the grand jury investigation continued, Mayor Harry Mackey, who had replaced Kendrick at city hall, began his own anti-vice crusade. He ordered the police department to make a "real and not perfunctory" effort to "clean up Philadelphia." Accordingly, police officials planned a massive, citywide sweep to close illegal saloons, gambling clubs, and vice dens. They chose September 3, 1928, as the night when each police district would dispatch squads of raiders to shut down all the illegal establishments in the city.

On the night of the raids, city officials reported spectacular results. They were especially excited about a district where the police had closed thirty-seven speakeasies and cafés. But a little investigative journalism revealed that the vice sweep had a fleeting impact. Only hours after the raids, a newsman toured the city and found that many illegal places had already reopened. In center city, business owners had received advance warning of the raids so they had taken precautions. Most had posted lookouts or simply stopped serving liquor for the night. Several police districts had staged no raids at all, because they failed to procure search warrants.

The morning after the raids, Mayor Mackey reiterated his commitment to curbing crime. He met with top police officials and ordered them to shut down "any places given over to lawlessness." He also told them to cooperate with the grand jury investigation. He called upon all citizens "to support the government by self-sacrifice." Specifically, he asked Philadelphians to stop patronizing speakeasies and bootleggers. He pointed out that the purveyors of illegal liquor supplied a demand and would go out of business if consumers stopped buying booze.[31]

Despite Mayor Mackey's public statements about fighting crime, cynics said he was lukewarm about helping Monaghan clean up the city. Although the mayor and the D.A. were supposed to be Republican allies, informed sources said they distrusted one another. Each wanted to get the upper hand and control the GOP machine that ruled the City of Brotherly Love. Of course, the mayor denied any conflict. When asked if politics was hampering the clean-up drive, he declared the crusade had "no political aspects at all."[32]

After a month of the grand jury hearings, D.A. Monaghan conceded that the liquor traffic hadn't dried up. He said that "heavy motor trucks with cargos of beer and alcohol" were still rolling along Philadelphia's streets. He laid "the blame ... at the door of the police department" because the cops were taking at least $2 million annually in bribes from Hoff's liquor syndicate.[33]

The press reported that the anti-crime crusade was producing limited change in the liquor traffic in the central business district. Some center city saloons had closed, but hooch was still for sale in the area. Strolling vendors were working the streets with pints stashed in their pockets and/or gallon "body tanks" full of booze strapped to their chests. Some walking vendors were selling liquor by the drink and carrying a glass to serve it.[34] (No doubt they washed the glass between customers.)

The grand jury hearings took a dramatic turn when D.A. Monaghan showed the jurors two books chockfull of data about the underworld: a little black book and "the Blue Book" of Philadelphia mobsters. Federal Prohibition agents had seized one of the colorful tomes in a raid; county detectives had found the other.[35]

The Blue Book was, in essence, an address book for the underworld. The book's owner had recorded the names and addresses of bootleggers, gunmen, hijackers, and mob utility men in Philly, Pittsburgh, Cleveland, and New York City. It also had lists of police officials, special investigators, and attorneys with mob ties. The Blue Book even listed mob wives and sweethearts who weren't above getting their hands dirty if the men needed help.

The little black book was a ledger that reinforced the evidence found in other financial records and account books confiscated by lawmen. The books listed the names of Philadelphia police officers and the amount of money the rum ring paid them. To take advantage of this startling evidence, D.A. Monaghan gave Boo Boo Hoff a reprieve and focused on police corruption. He ordered the arrests of a police captain, seven sergeants, two detectives, and twelve patrolmen. Some of the lawmen readily confessed to being on the take. All were arraigned before the grand jury on charges of extortion, bribery, and/or conspiracy.[36]

Looking for more proof of malfeasance, Monaghan's staff culled through a mountain of bank records. In less than two months, the evidence led to the arrests of more than thirty police detectives and patrolmen. In addition, the grand jury found 138 policemen to be "unfit for service." The names of the corrupt cops were published in the newspapers for all Philadelphians to see.[37]

The *nouveau riche* lawmen offered plausible, if somewhat improbable, explanations for the extra money in their bank accounts. Some claimed they had padded their wallets by playing craps, breeding dogs, selling canaries, betting on horse races, dabbling in real estate, or playing the stock market. Others said they had inherited money or married a rich woman.

When D.A. Monaghan finished with the corrupt cops, he returned to the investigation's original target: Boo Boo Hoff. But the long side trip had diverted attention from the liquor lord and given him time to regroup. Crucial witnesses against him had disappeared, voluntarily or otherwise. The district attorney's case against him seemed disjointed and incoherent without those witnesses. Monaghan called minor mob players to testify, but they failed to provide enough evidence to nail Boo Boo.

Over the course of the inquiry, Monaghan put Hoff on the witness stand eight times and pressured him with tough questions. A court watcher noted a gradual deterioration in Hoff's cocky demeanor on the stand. "Boo Boo at first had the same bearing of nonchalance as did many of his lieutenants and servants who were called," the observer wrote. "But subjected day after day to the District Attorney's crossfire of questions, the little leader became a mental wreck. He lost his savoir faire. He worried. He lost his strut." But Hoff was no stranger to the courtroom, and he knew how to survive an interrogation. Even without his strut, the bootleg king left the courtroom with only a few scratches on his underworld armor.[38]

After calling 748 witnesses for the grand jury probe, D.A. Monaghan declared victory and withdrew from the battlefield. He announced that the grand jury investigation had decimated the liquor traffic in Philadelphia. He stated that 1,185 saloons had operated in the city before the hearings; now "every one of them" was closed. The lid was screwed down "as tight as it has ever been and I guess as it ever can be," he said. "There is no longer any importation or exportation of liquor, although before this, millions of gallons were shipped yearly from Philadelphia."[39]

The special grand jury issued a final report declaring the investigation a total success. The summary claimed that the probe had (1) eliminated the corner saloon, (2) reduced the number of speakeasies, (3) decreased the production of industrial alcohol, (4) crippled organized gambling, (5) shattered "the system of protected commercialized vice," (6) made "substantial progress in ridding the police department of grafters," and (7) broken the "unholy alliance" of police, politicians, and gangsters.[40]

Without question, Philly's illegal liquor traffic had suffered setbacks, but history suggested the impact would be short term. Local production of liquor had virtually stopped. Law enforcement had padlocked two breweries and one industrial alcohol plant; other brewers and distillers saw the wisdom of taking a vacation. Bootleggers were scrambling to fill the void by importing liquor from Canada and New Jersey. Since many speakeasies had closed, drinkers phoned their orders in to the bottle men who delivered booze to homes and offices. Due to the shortage of top-quality whiskey, medical alcohol was the hottest commodity in town. Honest bootleggers were buying it from pharmacies and wholesale drug companies. Their less ethical brethren were stealing it.[41]

Three months after the grand jury investigation ended, many of Philadelphia's shuttered saloons had reopened their doors. To prevent raids and closures, bar owners increased security and admitted fewer people. Trusted customers used elaborate systems of signaling for admittance. Strangers were turned away. Lookouts watched for honest lawmen and warned bartenders when to dump the liquor — pronto!

The grand jury probe failed to rid Philly of its speakeasies, gambling parlors, and vice dens over the long term, but District Attorney Monaghan seemed happy with what it did accomplish. "The stranglehold of the crook on Philadelphia has been broken, and the city is once more master of its fate," he said. "It is not ruled by thugs!"[42]

Boo Boo's Downhill Slide

The district attorney admitted that his efforts before the grand jury had fallen short in one respect. He and his staff had spent countless hours culling through Boo Boo Hoff's financial records, hunting for enough evidence to send him to prison. The D.A. had interrogated the bootleg king multiple times, on and off the witness stand. The grand jury had heard testimony from many of Hoff's business associates and underlings. Yet Monaghan couldn't gather enough solid evidence to prosecute him. Philadelphia's supreme liquor lord cleverly hid behind straw men, lawyers, agents, and dupes who formed a solid wall of protection.

Law enforcement didn't bring Hoff down, but challenges from younger, hungrier mobsters took a toll on him. Over the years, power struggles loosened his hold on Philly's underworld. His share of the liquor traffic shrank, and he spent more of his time promoting prizefights. In 1929 he ran afoul of Al Capone, a most egregious misstep in gangland. He divulged a great deal of damaging information to an undercover federal agent who worked for the task force preparing to indict Capone on tax charges.[43] Hoff probably didn't intend to betray the incredibly powerful Scarface, but intentions meant nothing in gangland.

Hoff's downhill slide accelerated in the 1930s due to the Great Depression and the repeal of Prohibition. Lavish spending, gambling losses, and lawsuits over boxing contracts depleted his coffers. The IRS accused him of tax fraud, and most of his assets were sold to pay back taxes or other debts. He spent his last years running the Village Barn, a juke-box, jitterbug joint that catered to college kids in West Philly. At the relatively young age of forty-six, Hoff died in his sleep. An empty bottle of sleeping pills was found on his bedside table, but the autopsy pinpointed heart failure as the cause of death.[44]

17. Washington, D.C.: The Capitol Hill Bootlegger and the Amphibians

Nothing has done more to disgust honest men and women than the hypocrisy of the wet-drinking, dry-voting Congressmen. — Mabel Willebrandt, Assistant U.S. Attorney General[1]

Blaming politicians is a favorite American pastime, and Prohibition provided lots of ammo for the blame game. Both the wet and dry factions blasted the politicians, especially the U.S. Congress, for causing all the ills that came along with Volstead. Politics was "the greatest handicap in the enforcement of Prohibition" and "most responsible for its failures," said Assistant U.S. Attorney General Mabel Willebrandt. Using an apt metaphor, she declared, "Politics and liquor are as inseparable ... as beer and pretzels." She rightly attributed many of Volstead's defects to the rampant graft and the unholy alliances between politicians and bootleggers.[2]

Whenever Congress voted on liquor legislation, the lawmakers divided into three blocs. Without fail, Capitol Hill's bone-dry teetotalers gleefully voted for Prohibition. Openly wet Congressmen, often called "the beer bloc," voted for the citizen's right to make a personal choice. A third group of lawmakers, nicknamed "the amphibians," straddled the Prohibition issue, voicing one opinion in public and another in private. They voted dry even though they drank and/or believed that each person had a right to make his own decision. These members of Congress represented dry districts and felt compelled to vote in synch with their constituents. Whether this was hypocrisy or pragmatic politics depended on one's point of view. Disgusted wets said Capitol Hill should be renamed Hypocrite Hill.

Despite the dry law, more than a few members of Congress kept liquor in their offices and served drinks to their visitors. "Bootleggers infest the halls and corridors of the Capitol and ply their trade there," Willebrandt said. A dry Congressman from Georgia groused that "scores" of his colleagues acted as if Prohibition didn't even exist. Wet lawmakers entrusted their flasks to the waiters in the Senate dining room so they could be served drinks at mealtime. A magazine writer who attended a dinner party with more than thirty members of Congress reported that all but one of them consumed an alcoholic drink. Senator William Bruce (D-MD) said that all the non-drinking U.S. senators could fit into one taxicab.[3]

Washington's liquor traffickers sold a variety of alcoholic beverages, ranging from rotgut to aged whiskey and imported, vintage wine. The best alcohol in town was the embassy or diplomatic liquor, which was imported, usually from Europe. Possession of diplomatic liquor was legal as long as the alcohol stayed on embassy property, which technically was foreign soil. An invitation to an embassy party was highly coveted by drinkers thirsting for genuine, uncut potables that tasted like liquor should taste.

Virtually every D.C. bootlegger told his customers that he obtained his hooch from an embassy. "It's the bootlegger's chief selling point," said an observer. Although a fraction of the embassy booze did make its way into the illegal liquor traffic, as a rule it was carefully guarded because it was an expensive, hard-to-get commodity. From time to time, a member of a foreign legation was accused of bootlegging or stealing liquor from the embassy cellars, but such incidents were rare.[4]

Washington's illegal distillers produced alcohol within sight of government buildings. Lawmen found three stills in an elegant, but rundown, home opposite the House Office Building. The alky cookers were distilling fruit-flavored mash into brandy. Lawmen also uncovered an operation with nine stills a few blocks from the Treasury Building. A government official estimated that Washington had at least fifty stills producing ardent spirits at any given time. Two D.C. metal shops did a land office business fabricating stills.[5]

Countless Washington residents, including more than a few Congressmen, made liquor at home. Representative Nicholas Longworth (R–OH) and his wife Alice, who was Teddy Roosevelt's daughter, defied the dry law with gusto. The Longworths bought grapes and experimented with making their own wine. They owned a small still, which their butler used to make gin. Their greatest DIY success was the "really good beer" they made in their cellar. When they needed liquor for parties, they found that the bootleggers had ample stocks of booze and would deliver to their home. Mrs. Longworth, a moderate drinker, didn't like drunks or teetotalers. "The fanatics on both sides were just about equally distasteful to me," she said.[6]

A Maryland highway was called Bootleg Boulevard due to the heavy traffic of vehicles hauling liquor, especially moonshine, to Washington. The backwoods distiller drove his product to the highway, where he met up with a legger who put the booze in his whiskey six for delivery to outlets in D.C. A gin jogger who delivered to Capitol Hill had a steady demand for shine, mostly from Southern Congressmen who liked the outlaw brands from just below the Mason-Dixon Line. "Hardly a day passes that either police or Prohibition agents do not make a sizable seizure of moonshine liquor flowing in from the stills in nearby Maryland and Virginia," Willebrandt noted.[7]

Washington police discovered that the U.S. Treasury owned a Pennsylvania Avenue building used "as the rendezvous of numerous bootleggers." Treasury leased the building to tenants who ran a round-the-clock diner that leggers used as their unofficial headquarters. They took orders for booze over telephones in the building and cooperated in "a delivery system ... efficient to the highest degree." The Treasury Department asked the diner's proprietors to stop the bootleggers from taking phone orders and using the building as their base. The proprietors replied that they weren't paid to enforce Volstead.[8]

On a slow news day, three parched *Washington Times* reporters went looking for refreshments and data for an exposé of the liquor traffic. In the name of investigative journalism, they bought drinks at forty-nine speakeasies. Their sensational report set Washington abuzz.

When a grand jury tried to get more information from them, they refused to incriminate the barkeepers. The judge found them in contempt of court, but they stuck to their journalistic guns.

A reporter estimated that five hundred bootleggers operated "within rifle shot of the White House" in 1923. According to a Congressional probe, "at least two thousand bootleggers were doing business in the District of Columbia" in the late Twenties. At a Congressional hearing in 1930 a witness said that Washington was infested with seven hundred speakeasies and four thousand bootleggers. A year later the D.C. police department estimated that the city had sixteen hundred illegal liquor outlets, compared to 325 licensed saloons before Prohibition.[9]

Officials at the Prohibition Bureau stated that the number of Washington bootleggers was in the hundreds, not the thousands. In 1929 the Bureau estimated that the city had three hundred leggers. A federal grand jury report cast doubt on the sensational news stories about Washington's wetness. The report stated that D.C. was "not the vice-ridden, lawless community" depicted by the media. "While there are numerous violations of the Prohibition law in the District of Columbia, conditions are certainly no worse, and are probably better, than those existing in other sections of the United States."[10] Faint praise, indeed.

Prohibition agent Izzy Einstein discovered that it could be hard for a stranger to buy booze in Washington. Einstein kept a record of how long it took him to find a drink when he arrived in a new city. His fastest time was thirty-five seconds in New Orleans. His longest was two hours, eight minutes in Washington. When Einstein got off the train in New Orleans, he slid into a taxi and asked the driver where he could get a drink. The driver handed him a bottle. He found Washington to be more challenging. After almost two hours of trying to buy a drink, he gave up and went to a barbershop for a shave. After the shave, the barber suggested a splash of bay rum. Einstein said he would rather have a drink, and the barber sold him a bottle of booze.

The SOB Bootlegger

The press delighted in writing articles about the bootleggers who sold booze to the nation's lawmakers on Capitol Hill. Wets found the stories amusing. Drys found them infuriating. Dry leaders firmly believed that Congress had a moral obligation to obey the law and set a good example for John Q. Citizen. The dry legislators fumed and fussed about their colleagues who belonged to the beer bloc or the amphibians. The dry bloc held committee hearings and loudly demanded that law enforcement put an end to the liquor traffic on Capitol Hill. Despite an occasional arrest, the trade went on because the leggers had steady, paying customers in the halls of Congress.

In keeping with the solemnity of Congress, Capitol Hill bootleggers usually went quietly about their business and respected the dignity of the institution. In a rare breach of Congressional decorum, two bootleggers had a spirited fistfight in the House Office Building (HOB). It began when one legger, who regarded the building as his personal territory, attacked a competitor for horning in. Even in the halls of Congress punks fought to protect their turf.[11]

George Cassiday, the busiest bootlegger on Capitol Hill, had a sterling reputation for honesty and reliability. Because he often wore a green felt homburg to cover his bald head,

Lawmen pose with a moonshiner's still and other illegal items confiscated in Washington, D.C., in 1922 (Library of Congress).

reporters dubbed him "the Man in the Green Hat." Cassiday, a military veteran who had served in World War I, didn't belong to a mob. He claimed that he bootlegged simply because he couldn't find any other job. He had grown up in a dry family and attended Sunday school at a Methodist church. His mother belonged to the WCTU, and his father was a teetotaler. Cassiday himself was an occasional drinker who disapproved of Prohibition because it infringed on personal freedom.[12]

A few months after Volstead started, Cassiday was looking for a job and a friend said he could make good money bootlegging on Capitol Hill. Cassiday didn't know any Congressmen, so his friend introduced him to two representatives who wanted to buy whiskey. Cassiday began delivering liquor to these men, who recommended him to other lawmakers, and his business grew apace. He visited the HOB daily, filling twenty to twenty-five orders on an average day. He found that, for the most part, the lawmakers were moderate drinkers, and he encountered few alcoholics. Some of his best customers were teetotalers who kept liquor on hand for their visitors, particularly their wet constituents.

Cassiday found it easy to procure moonshine, but most Congressmen wanted aged, imported whiskey — or a convincing facsimile. He needed a reliable source of high-quality liquor. Luckily, he knew a former federal agent who had contacts with big-time liquor traffickers. The agent took him to New York City and introduced him to the proper people. He established a routine, buying from a liquor wholesaler who catered to the "suitcase brigade" — that is, bootleggers who rode the train and carried their bottles in a valise. Cassiday found that he could carry up to forty quarts in two suitcases. The wholesaler had "watchers" stationed along the route from his business to Penn Station, ready to spring into action if a thief tried to grab a suitcase of liquor. Cassiday made regular trips to New York for a time; then he switched to a supplier in Newark, then Baltimore, and finally Philadelphia.

To prevent the theft of government property, the Capitol Hill security guards routinely searched briefcases and packages being carried out of the office buildings. However, they didn't search bags coming in, so Cassiday had little to fear when he entered the HOB with bottles of liquor. To be extra safe, he would enter when most people were leaving for the day so the guards were busy looking for stolen office supplies. He discovered that he could also enter at night without being noticed.

At first Cassiday stored his liquor inventory at his house, but this meant slow deliveries because he took orders and went home to fill them. In order to give faster service, he needed to keep his stock near his buyers. A steady customer solved the problem by giving Cassiday the key to a small storeroom in the HOB. He began keeping liquor there so he could fill orders without leaving the building. Caucus nights were especially hectic for him because caucusing seemed to make the lawmakers extra thirsty and he would be busy until midnight. He preferred to sell uncut liquor, but spot shortages of the good stuff sometimes forced him to dilute his whiskey. As the Great Drought dragged on, these shortages occurred more often.

A group of Congressmen and staffers who called themselves the Bar Flies Association relied on Cassiday for their liquor. At impromptu parties in the HOB the group "would have a few rounds of drinks, sing a few songs, and have a general good time." Cassiday also furnished liquid refreshment for card players in the HOB's poker room, a secret haven in the basement. The hideaway had comfy swivel chairs and a mahogany table with a green felt top.

Cassiday had his first brush with law enforcement in 1922. A Prohibition agent posed as the brother-in-law of a Congressman and asked the bootlegger to deliver an order to his apartment. When Cassiday arrived at the apartment, he was arrested. After being indicted, he returned to bootlegging but was extra cautious about selling to strangers. Like so many Volstead indictments, Cassiday's case hung in limbo for years without going to trial.

In 1925, a Congressional committee exposed the liquor trade on Capitol Hill, raising public awareness of the problem. Around the time of this exposé, a policeman accosted Cassiday one morning as he entered the HOB with a briefcase full of liquor. When the officer wasn't looking, Cassiday set the briefcase down by a desk. He tried to walk off and disown it, but the policeman didn't fall for that trick. After Cassiday was arrested, he was indicted and his old case was joined with the new one. He pled guilty to all charges. The judge sentenced him to twenty days in the district jail, where he worked as a doctor's orderly in the drug room.

After Cassiday's second arrest, dry Congressmen were determined to bar him from the HOB. With the Speaker's consent, the House of Representatives adopted a special rule banning him from the building. When Cassiday got out of jail, he couldn't work in the HOB, so he had to rethink his career. He moved his bootlegging business to the Senate Office Building (SOB).

Cassiday set up his business in the SOB stationery room and enjoyed brisk sales, although the senators were more cautious than the representatives. Whereas the representatives dealt directly with him, his Senate customers normally used their secretaries as go-betweens. One senator kept his bottles of liquor on a shelf in his bookcase, next to bound copies of the *Congressional Record.* When he wanted to buy booze, he would tell his "librarian" (AKA Cassiday) that he needed some "new reading matter."

Cassiday spent so much time in Congress that he became a political junkie. When he had free time, he sat in the gallery and listened to the debates. He became especially interested in farm relief, taxes, and the soldier's bonus bill. When Congress was in recess, he had time on his hands so he could travel outside the city. During one recess he traveled to the Midwest to work in a senator's re-election campaign. He distributed posters and campaign literature, attended ward meetings, and made "curtain raiser" speeches at rallies.

On Halloween 1929 policemen stopped Cassiday, who was wearing a grey hat instead of his customary green homburg, as he strode up the steps to the SOB. He was carrying a bottle of whiskey wrapped in a newspaper, and the police found more bottles in his car. Then they raided his house, where he had stashed 266 quarts "intended to slake the thirst of American statesmen." The police arrested him and confiscated his black book with the list of his customers. Several weeks after the arrest, a grand jury indicted him for dry law violations. He lucked out. Due to a legal technicality, his trial was postponed indefinitely and he was set free on bail. He resumed his bootlegging routine in the SOB.[13]

On a busy day in February 1930 lawmen arrested three gin joggers who were delivering hooch to Congress. Cassiday and his assistant were nabbed as they entered the SOB carrying six quarts of Scotch whiskey. Politics usually lurked behind a bootlegging bust on Capitol Hill, and these arrests followed an upturn in public criticism of President Hoover's lackluster record on Volstead enforcement. The highly-publicized busts proved that Hoover was cracking down on leggers, even those with friends in high places. Cassiday was specifically targeted because the dry bloc had complained to the vice president about his use of the SOB stationery room.[14]

Soon after the February arrest, Cassiday was indicted on multiple Volstead charges. The judge dismissed one charge, ruling that Cassiday had been subjected to illegal search and seizure because the arresting officers had no warrant. But he ordered the legger to stand trial on the other charges. At trial the jury convicted Cassiday of possessing and transporting liquor. His lawyers appealed but failed to get his conviction overturned.

The judge sentenced Cassiday to eighteen months in jail. However, he never actually spent a night in the slammer. He was allowed to sign into the jail in the morning, spend a few hours in custody, and go home. This enabled him to enjoy a family dinner and a good night's sleep in his own bed.[15]

The Man in the Green Hat wrote his memoirs in 1930. He declared that he had quit bootlegging forever. "I want the world to know that I am through with working on Capitol Hill, or anyplace else, in the kind of business that has engaged me for the last ten years," he said. Although some bootleggers made millions, he claimed he wasn't rich. "The truth is that I never made more than a good living to support myself and my family," he wrote. "That was because I never went in for any of the sidelines of Prohibition, and never will."

The Capitol Hill bootlegger described some of his Congressional clients "as mighty good fellows" and others as "not so good." He said, "I learned right off the bat that when it comes to eating, drinking, and having a good time in general, they are as human as other folks."

The Senator's Smelling Party

On Capitol Hill the beer bloc viewed Senator Smith Brookhart (R-IA) as a meddle-some, Puritanical bluenose. The Iowan delighted in scolding his liberal colleagues, especially those who took a nip or two. A militant teetotaler, Brookhart eagerly testified before a grand jury investigating a dinner party hosted by a rich stockbroker at a posh Washington hotel. Roughly twenty Senators went to the bash, where the guests were invited to help themselves to silver flasks discreetly hidden behind a curtain.

Brookhart, who attended the party, was irate because several senators had taken flasks. With outrage in his voice, he revealed that he had smelled the contents of a flask and "had enough experience in the chemical laboratory to know that it had a heavy content of alcohol." Despite the senator's reputation for absolute honesty, the grand jury declined to indict any-one based on his olfactory. The press had a field day with the story, dubbing the affair "Brook-hart's smelling party."[16]

When returning to the United States from a trip abroad, members of Congress could choose one of two privileges to expedite their re-entry at customs. "Freedom of the port" allowed them to pass through customs with no baggage search. "Free entry" essentially moved them to the front of the line but didn't exempt them from the luggage search. It was com-monly believed that these privileges entitled them to bring liquor into the country, even during Prohibition. Strictly speaking, that was not true. Nevertheless, members of Congress usually sailed through customs even if their luggage held a few suspicious bottles.

During Congressional recesses, parched lawmakers headed to foreign ports that just happened to be wet. On the return trip, they brought bottles of the good stuff home with them and skipped the customs check. Generally, customs inspectors didn't challenge a rep-resentative or senator if he refused to open his luggage for a routine search. However, a few unlucky Congressmen had problems getting their booze to Washington.

Congressman Alfred Michaelson (R-IL), who voted dry, took a trip to Cuba and Panama. He re-entered the United States through Key West, Florida. His six trunks passed through customs without inspection and were loaded onto a railway car. At the train station in Jack-sonville, Florida, a porter noticed liquid trickling out of a trunk. It smelled like booze, so he deduced that a broken bottle was inside. He notified the authorities, who decided to investigate. Federal agents opened Michaelson's baggage and found liquor in two of his trunks. The agents allowed the trunks to travel on to Washington, where the Congressman claimed them — only to have them seized by lawmen who had been notified to watch for them.

Based on the contents of the baggage, a grand jury indicted Michaelson for illegally importing "six quarts of John Haig whiskey, two quarts of crème de menthe liquor, one quart of Taffel Akavait, one quart of crème de cacao, one quart of cherry brandy, and one keg of plum Barbaucourt."[17] ("Plum Barbaucourt" may have been a typo for "Rhum Bar-bancourt," a popular Caribbean rum.)

When Michaelson's case went to trial, his defense counsel called Walter Gramm, a Chicago coal dealer, to the witness stand. The Congressman identified Gramm as "just a dear friend," but they were also brothers-in-law. Gramm testified that he had traveled with Michaelson on the junket and the liquor-laden trunks actually belonged to him. When the prosecutor asked Gramm if he had told the Congressman about the trunks' illegal contents, the coal dealer refused to answer.

Gramm was a very convincing witness, and the jury acquitted Michaelson. But Gramm would soon have reason to regret his testimony. Only hours after the acquittal, police arrested the star defense witness. After all, Gramm had confessed to a crime on the witness stand. He was indicted for conspiring to violate the dry law. At trial, his lawyer argued that the coal dealer's actions did not rise to the level of an illegal Volstead conspiracy. His error "was just a social one" with "no commercial aspect." Although Gramm was guilty, the judge said he "had no desire to wreck a man's life with a prison term" for a minor infraction. So he limited Gramm's punishment to a fine of $1,000.[18]

The jurors who acquitted Representative Michaelson of the Volstead charges were kinder than the voters. He did not win re-election to another term in Congress.

Representative Edward Everett Denison (R-IL), another dry voter, also had leaky luggage. Prohibition agents were called to Washington's Union Station to inspect a damp, smelly suitcase addressed to a man in care of Denison. The Prohis checked the express records and found that the shipment included a large trunk as well as the fragrant suitcase. Since the trunk had already been delivered, federal agents went to the Congressman's office to examine it. Denison claimed he didn't have the trunk key but would try to locate it, so the agents left. When they returned, Denison said he couldn't find the key because the trunk didn't belong to him. The exasperated agents broke into it and found bottles of gin and whiskey.

Both Denison and the addressee, who was the Congressman's former secretary, were accused of breaking the dry law. The addressee said he knew nothing about the trunk. Denison also disclaimed the trunk, saying it had been delivered to him by mistake. His own trunk had been lost on the dock in New York City during a blizzard, and he didn't realize the mistake until the Prohibition agents opened the strange trunk in his office. Despite the tenuous evidence against Everett, the voters found him guilty and he was defeated in his bid for re-election.[19]

They Tried to Crucify Me

The transgressions of Congressman John Wesley Langley (R-KY) went far beyond hiding a few bottles of booze in his valise. Langley came from a state famous for its smooth, aged bourbon, so perhaps it wasn't surprising that he had a weakness for fine whiskey. Even though he shared the name of Methodism's dry founder, Langley was arrested for public drunkenness more than once. But his occasional bender was trivial compared to his Volstead felonies. Ironically, he voted dry and represented a bone-dry Fundamentalist constituency in Eastern Kentucky.[20]

Langley was indicted on multiple counts of tax fraud and conspiracy to violate the dry law. The indictment alleged that a group of individuals, "known and unknown," had entered into a plot to buy, withdraw, and transport whiskey from a bonded distillery warehouse in Cheswick, Pennsylvania, to a drug company in Pittsburgh. The conspirators were also accused of failing to pay the liquor tax on the whiskey.

For his part in the conspiracy, Langley used his political wiles to entice Prohibition officials to issue withdrawal permits for liquor from the Cheswick warehouse. He met with low-ranking officials and offered them generous bribes, promotions, and "tenure" in return for the permits. He convinced at least two low-level functionaries to join the plot. He also tried to enlist the help of Prohibition Commissioner John Kramer, and it appeared that he had done so. The commissioner sent telegrams authorizing the sale and removal of four thousand cases of whiskey from the Cheswick warehouse. (Kramer later stated that he had only pretended to go along with the plot, in order to gather evidence. He was never indicted in the case.)[21]

The Cheswick conspiracy wasn't the only episode where Langley used his political clout. A rum ring obtained a permit to withdraw fourteen hundred cases of whiskey from the Belle of Anderson Distillery in Lawrenceburg, Kentucky. In order to move it to Philadelphia for resale, a transportation permit was also needed. When the ringleaders asked Kentucky Prohibition Director Sam Collins for a permit authorizing the transport, he refused. They asked Langley to intervene, so he went to Kentucky to meet with Collins. After that meeting, the rum ring obtained the permit.

A federal grand jury indicted Langley and five other men for Volstead conspiracy and tax fraud after the whiskey was removed from the Belle of Anderson Distillery. Langley's codefendants included the acting Prohibition director at Philadelphia but not Kentucky's Sam Collins.[22]

The Belle of Anderson trial, which went to court first, began in May 1924 in Covington, Kentucky. The state alleged that the conspirators had illegally secured a withdrawal permit, had transported the whiskey from the warehouse to other locations, and had evaded paying the liquor tax. In explaining the nature of the conspiracy, the district attorney said, "The government will not prove any written agreement or contract existed between the defendants, but we will prove that they were banded together and knew what was going on."

According to the D.A., three of the conspirators had gone to the Belle of Anderson distillery and arranged "to take over all the liquor in the warehouse." They led the distillery owner to believe they wanted the liquor for medical use, "but they actually had no idea in mind other than to sell it for beverage purposes at bootleg prices." The D.A. stated that Langley had become rich in public office and had secret, illicit sources of income. Although his Congressional salary was only $7,500 per year, he had deposited $115,000 in bank accounts in only three years. This total was merely what investigators could verify. It was likely that he had large amounts of cash and/or bank accounts under aliases.[23]

Two of Langley's codefendants turned state's evidence and testified against him. They said the rum ring had paid Langley large sums to obtain the government permits. When he demanded more money, the ring gave him "loans" that he didn't have to repay if he succeeded in his part of the conspiracy. Witnesses also testified that Langley had attended meetings where arrangements were made to truck the whiskey from the Belle of Anderson distillery to Philadelphia and other cities.

Kentucky Prohibition Director Collins testified that Langley had pressured him to issue the permit needed to transport the whiskey, but he had refused. He said the Congressman became angry and threatened to "break him politically" if he didn't play ball. Collins didn't cave in to the threat.[24]

Langley took the witness stand in his own defense and denied any wrongdoing. He stated that he had discussed the liquor permit with Prohibition Director Collins merely "to learn from a man whom he considered a friend what was, or would be, Mr. Collins' attitude and action" in such a situation. When Collins said he would not authorize such shipments, Langley "dismissed the matter from his mind" and gave it no more thought.

Langley confessed that he had accepted a loan from the rum ring because he needed cash. He also admitted that he had met with a Washington operative who had ties to the rum ring. On cross-examination, he confessed he had never repaid the loan from the ring. He said a portion of it had been a campaign donation, which he turned over to the Republican Party. Prominent elected officials took the stand as character witnesses for their political ally. Two Congressmen and the governor of Kentucky testified that Langley was an honest man and an excellent legislator. They agreed that he had only one serious flaw: sometimes he drank too much.[25]

After hearing all the evidence, the jury returned a guilty verdict for Langley. Before the judge imposed sentence, the Congressman read a self-serving statement proclaiming his innocence. The judge was unmoved. He sentenced Langley to two years in the federal prison in Atlanta. Langley's attorney immediately stated that he would file an appeal, and Langley was released on bond.[26]

Only weeks after the guilty verdict, Langley began campaigning for another term in Congress. When he won the GOP primary, he called it a "vindication" by his constituents. In November 1924 he was again vindicated by the voters, winning re-election by a landslide.

In January 1926 his legal appeal finally reached the U.S. Supreme Court. The justices denied him a writ of certiorari, removing his last hope for overturning his conviction. He resigned from Congress and embarked on his mandatory vacation in Atlanta. After he settled into the routine behind the bars, he edited *Good Words*, a magazine published "for the encouragement and educational advancement of the prisoners."[27]

Langley had been forced to retire from politics, but his wife hadn't. She announced that she would run to replace her husband as U.S. representative for Kentucky's Tenth Congressional District. To her dismay, the GOP nominating convention chose another candidate. But she was determined and had enough political savvy to get her name on the primary ballot. She took to the campaign trail, courting the support of the "mountain folks," especially women. One of her opponents claimed she was a hypocrite who actually "felt she was above mountain people."

Mrs. Langley won the primary in the heavily Republican district and went on to become the first female to represent Kentucky in the United States Congress. Prison officials allowed Mr. Langley to send her a congratulatory telegram. "I am supremely happy," he wrote. "Even these grey prison walls seem to shine with the luster of our beloved Cumberland and Blue Ridge. Mine eyes have seen the glory of the coming of the Lord.... My love and greetings to the first Congresswoman of the old Commonwealth."[28]

A few days before Christmas 1926, Langley was paroled although he had served only eleven months. Mrs. Langley said, "It will be indeed a joyous Christmas in the hills of old Kentucky among the many friends who know us best." She denied a rumor that she would take her husband to Washington to be her secretary, but she did have plans for his future. She persuaded President Coolidge to pardon her husband, thereby restoring all his legal rights.[29]

Mr. Langley returned to work as a lawyer, and he wrote his memoirs, *They Tried to Crucify Me: or the Smoke Screen of the Cumberlands*. He said the book was his true story and his "final defense." Critics said the book contained little truth and no convincing defense, final or otherwise.[30]

The Congressman's Beer

When Volstead began, there seemed to be a consensus that homemade beer wouldn't be a popular way of circumventing the dry law. A spokesman for the U.S. Brewers Association said few people would attempt to make their own beer because home brewing was "troublesome and messy, and not very successful." The chief chemist at the Treasury Bureau confidently stated, "It's too much trouble for uncertain results. They may try it once or twice, but not more."[31]

These experts greatly misjudged the tenacity of beer lovers. Although brewing beer required patience and skill, many drinkers diligently made batch after batch until they mastered the art. The experts also overlooked the shortcuts people would take to make a reasonable facsimile of old-fashioned beer. U.S. Representative Fiorello LaGuardia (R–NY), leader of the beer bloc in Congress, brazenly defied the dry law by publicizing his own quick and easy recipe for making beer.

Congressman LaGuardia represented a very wet, multiethnic district that included East Harlem. In debates in the House of Representatives, he vociferously clashed with dry lawmakers. He argued against the passage of the Volstead act because he foresaw how complicated enforcement would be. "I maintain that this law will be almost impossible of enforcement," he said. "And if this law fails to be enforced — as it certainly will be … it will create contempt and disregard for law all over the country."

LaGuardia stated that temperance was "a matter of education and not of legislation." He pointed to the WCTU's educational programs as the right way to produce a sober nation. "By proper education, by proper training — if you really have the interest and welfare of this country at heart — you can train the people so the next generation will not use alcohol and will not require any law of this sort."[32]

After Volstead went into effect, LaGuardia didn't condemn drinkers for breaking the dry law because he didn't regard drinking as a crime. "An act which is inherently wrong, an act which involves moral turpitude, an act which indicates depravity cannot be compared to an act which for eight thousands years has been legal and is now prohibited by statutory law," he said. He argued that Prohibition was class warfare because it handicapped the working class more than wealthy Americans. Rich people could buy expensive safe, imported liquor while the working class could afford only cheap, risky rotgut.[33]

Because LaGuardia was a masterful political showman, the press liked him and gave him a great deal of favorable ink. When he announced that he had his own method for turning near beer into real suds, reporters were intrigued. When he dared to demonstrate his method publicly in East Harlem, the media came to watch.

Standing at the corner of Lenox Avenue and 115th Street on a summer day, LaGuardia attracted a sizeable crowd of curious onlookers. As newsreel cameras rolled, he mixed two legal products, near beer and Liebig's Malt Extract, to make an illegal drink. The extract, which had three percent alcohol content, was labeled "for medicinal purposes" and could be purchased at drugstores without a prescription. LaGuardia's recipe called for one-third near beer and two-thirds extract, which made his brew weaker than pre–Volstead suds but stronger than the legal cereal beverages.

LaGuardia proudly gave samples of his brew to the onlookers for a taste test. Most rated it an average beer, among neither the best nor the worst they had ever tasted. When the cop on the beat happened by, he pushed his way through the crowd to see what was going on. Although LaGuardia readily admitted that he was making beer, the policeman didn't arrest him. The federal Prohibition agents were supposed to enforce Volstead. "Let them do it" was the cop's attitude. But the feds didn't come to arrest LaGuardia. The chief of NYC's federal Prohibition squad told reporters that he had no interest in the Congressman's stunt. So the lawmen let LaGuardia openly defy the National Prohibition Act.[34] His wet constituents were amused and delighted. The Congressional drys fumed.

18. Country Cousins:
Dew Boys and Alky Cookers

Rightly or wrongly, the mountaineer was never able to discriminate between corn turned into pork and corn turned into whiskey.—Francis Pridemore, retired moonshiner, West Virginia[1]

Long before Prohibition, making moonshine was a hallowed tradition in rural America, especially in isolated, hard-to-reach spots where the corn stalks grew tall. Illegal alcohol fueled the economy in the Moonshine Belt, which included Appalachia, the Smoky Mountains, the Ozarks, the Alleghenies, and the Blue Ridge Mountains. The moonshiners passed their expertise down from generation to generation, and their distilling wisdom paid off during the Great Drought. But not all of Volstead's white lightning came from the boondocks. Illegal stills operated in every corner of the United States, making powerful potables guaranteed to pack a punch. Alky cookers, the urban version of moonshiners, produced oceans of alcohol for the bootleg trade in America's cities.

While rural and urban moonshiners did essentially the same job, they felt little kinship. The North's urban alky cooker no more resembled the South's dew boy "than a rat bears resemblance to an eagle," wrote an observer.[2] The backwoods moonshiners were proud of their craft and their product. They felt superior to the alky cookers who took shortcuts to speed up distillation, with no concern for quality. The dew boy scoffed at the alky cooker's "sugar head," so called because it had a high sugar content that caused severe headaches.

The dew boys and the alky cookers came from different worlds. The Southern moonshiner, like others born and bred in isolated rural communities, tended to be a nativist. He was proud of his ancestors and his "pure" bloodlines. He distrusted the urban alky cooker whose ethnic heritage differed from his own. In turn, the urbanite looked down on the rural moonshiners because he knew them only from pop culture, which depicted them as ignorant, ne'er do well slackers.

In the early 1920s, top officials in the Prohibition Unit regarded moonshine as a minor, isolated problem. Traditional moonshiners lived in remote areas and operated on a small scale. To them, moonshining was their birthright as well as a defiant gesture—a protest against taxes and government interference in their business. For the most part, they peddled their goods to their neighbors and relatives. They had a loyal, but limited, clientele—called the

Federal Prohibition agents inspect an alky cooker's still in a private residence in Detroit (Walter P. Reuther Library, Archives of Labor and Urban Affairs, Wayne State University).

fruit-jar trade because moonshine was sold in glass jars made for home canning. Country folk said that the true moonshine lover had a ridge across his nose caused by drinking from a fruit jar.

During the Arid Era, the moonshine business boomed. Demand for white lightning soared in places where people had once spurned it as a jerkwater joke. In the early Twenties moonshine moved from the backwoods barn dance to the speakeasy. Across the USA, people were drinking it as never before, either because they liked it or because they couldn't find anything else.

In 1926 Prohibition czar Lincoln Andrews declared war on moonshine because a half-million people were involved in the trade, making it a major sector of the illegal liquor traffic. Andrews formed a special "moonshine squadron" of experienced revenue agents to lead the offensive. Despite countless raids on illegal distillers, he estimated that law enforcement had shut down less than ten percent of the country's small stills. In public statements, he warned that most corn liquor contained poison. Strangely, he endorsed moonshine from Kentucky, Tennessee, and North Carolina as being "a better quality."[3]

After three years of the war on moonshine, a top Prohibition policy maker stated that it remained a high priority. Bootleggers were selling more white lightning than ever before, primarily because the supply of genuine aged whiskey continued to shrink. To serve the city markets, highly-organized, well-financed urban gangs had opened more illegal distilleries in residential neighborhoods and business districts.[4]

By the late 1920s the nature of rural moonshining was changing to meet the strong demand for white lightning. The rural moonshiners began to imitate the urban liquor lords, and the lone mountaineer making small batches became an endangered species. The new-fangled moonshine boss owned multiple stills and paid hired hands to keep them running. Profits trumped taste, so the moonshine boss cut corners, like the urban alky cookers did. To curb competition, he terrorized his rivals and stole their stills. Moonshining became less tradition and more cutthroat crime in the United States of Volstead.[5]

Stump Juice and Monkey Rum

Mountain moonshiners used a colorful jargon to communicate with one another. Laymen learned the lingo when moonshine moved from the bush league to the big city during Prohibition. Moonshine connoisseurs coined dozens of nicknames for their favorite beverage: shine, moon, mountain dew, pack, stump juice, mountain dynamite, monkey rum, ruckus juice, tiger spit, and panther sweat — to name only a few. Moonshine was also called jackass because it had a hell of a bite and a hell of a kick. The most popular sobriquet was white lightning. According to folklore, lightning comes in two colors: white and red/blue. When white lightning strikes, the fire cannot be extinguished.

In the South, the moonshiner was called a shiner, a stiller, or a dew boy. Shiners with tongue-in-cheek called themselves "independent distillers." The moonshiner's nemesis was the revenuer, a Treasury Department agent who hunted down distillers for failing to pay the taxes on their alcohol. During Volstead, mountaineers used the term "revenuer" for all the lawmen who enforced Prohibition. The revenuers searched the backwoods for stills and confiscated or smashed the equipment. Whenever possible, they arrested the moonshiners, but the stillers usually eluded the law because they were experts at hiding in the woods.

When a dew boy talked about his pot, he meant his still. Some pots had a distinctive shape and were named accordingly, such as a coffin still or a submarine still. Generally, a small still was called a mountain teapot. A person who made moonshine was stillin' (or stilling in Standard English).

Moonshine made by a clan or in a specific location often acquired an informal brand, and drinkers asked for it by name. Minnesota Thirteen was the generic name for moonshine from Stearns County, Minnesota. Cocke County, Tennessee, was famous for its Silver Cloud brand. In Washington, D.C., the posh Willard Hotel sold the St. Mary's Sampler, an assortment of moonshines from Maryland. In Richmond, Virginia, hotels favored Nomini Mix, a popular outlaw brand named for a creek that fed into the Chesapeake.

A moon drinker might buy his favorite outlaw brand under the counter at a crossroads store, but many dew boys let the customers come to them. In a time-honored method of selling mountain dew, the stiller placed a large container of his product on a stump. Then a family member, often a child, hid nearby to keep an eye on it. A buyer would come, pour some of the alcohol into a small container, and leave his payment on the stump. In a variation on this, the moonshiner hung a bell or a bugle on a tree limb; the buyer rang the bell or blew the bugle — one ring or blast for each quart he wanted to buy. Then he waited. A horse would amble out of the woods, with a sack of jugs strapped across its back. The buyer took his jugs, stuck his money in the sack, and pointed the horse down the path toward home.

Fightin' Whiskey

For most drinkers, white lightning was an acquired taste due to its potency and lack of aging. Backwoods shine packed a wallop that tended to burn all the way down. A raconteur said moon burns "with all the restless fires of hell" and the bouquet "comes shearing through like a rusty can opener, to smite us between the eyes." One moonshiner claimed that he gave every customer a whisk broom, so the drinker could brush himself off after he got up from the floor. Humorist Irvin Cobb tried to capture the essence of shine, saying, "It smells like gangrene starting in a mildewed silo, it tastes like wrath to come, and when you absorb a deep swig of it, you have all the sensations of having swallowed a lighted kerosene lamp. A sudden, violent jolt of it has been known to stop the victim's watch, snap his suspenders, and crack his glass eye."[6]

Kentuckians called moonshine "fightin' whiskey" while aged bourbon was "courtin' whiskey." A Kentucky politico said white lightning would "make a rabbit spit in a bulldog's face." Likewise, moonshine "would make a circuit judge fight a wildcat." One stiller said he had taken his gun and a jar of moon when he went squirrel hunting on a crisp winter day. When he spied a squirrel on a tree limb, he laid down his gun, chugged the moonshine, shimmied up the tree, and caught the animal with his bare hands. A sociologist who studied feuds among Kentucky clans said that "three drinks of mountain dew cause, on average, one fight."[7]

Over the generations, moonshiners refined their distilling methods, although the basic chemical reaction was immutable. An Arkansas schoolteacher wrote a detailed account of stilling in the Ozarks in the 1880s. First, the dew boy filled cloth sacks with shelled corn and soaked the sacks in water for a day or two. Then he spread the corn kernels on a flat surface, such as a plank, to sprout. After the corn sprouted, he ground it into small particles called "chops." He did this by hollowing out a hole in a solid stump, pouring the corn in, and pounding it with a pestle. Or, he placed the corn kernels on a flat rock and crushed them with another rock.

Mash, moonshine's basic ingredient, must ferment to produce alcohol. To make the mash, the Ozark shiner dumped bushels of coarse-ground cornmeal into a heavy oak barrel, added a bushel of chops, and let the mixture stand for a few days. When the mash had the right smell and consistency, he poured it into his pot, started a fire, and regularly added wood to keep it burning. The steam from the cooking mash escaped through a tube into a pipe that lay in a trough of cold water and emptied into a jug. The steam in the pipe condensed into a liquid, called "sanglin's" or "singlings," which dripped into the jug. When the condensation stopped, the singlings were poured back into the pot, cooked again, and condensed again — producing drinkable alcohol. The moonshiner inspected his product. If he decided it was too weak, he put it back in the pot, added more mash, and distilled it again — producing a more potent beverage.[8]

Additives, called "kickers" or "ticklers," could be used to accelerate fermentation. Dew boys preferred animal manure, especially chicken droppings, as a kicker. Urban alky cookers added large amounts of granulated sugar to the mash. They also used urea, either alone or combined with disodium phosphate, dead yeast, or calcium sulfate. Other popular but risky additives were lye, chlorine bleach, paint thinner, rubbing alcohol, canned heat, turpentine, embalming fluid, formaldehyde, glycerine, and fertilizer.[9]

While moonshine fans liked its raw taste, the average drinker preferred a smooth, aged whiskey. To make raw moon look, if not taste, like aged whiskey, the shiner had a choice of shortcuts. In one method he charred wood chips and mixed them with unburned chips in a barrel. Then he poured his raw whiskey into the barrel for several days of aging and tinting. In "toasting" or "kiln aging," the distillate was poured into a charred barrel and stored in a very hot, closed room for a brief period of time. Alternately, the distiller poured his moonshine into empty barrels that had held Coca-Cola syrup. The alcohol soon darkened and gained a distinctive sweet taste many people liked.

To add color, the stiller could pour granulated charcoal into a barrel of alcohol and shake it until the liquid darkened. An ingenious way to stir the contents was setting the barrel in a rocking chair and assigning a child to rock it back and forth. Or, the barrel could be placed in the rumble seat of a car that was driven over the back roads. For an ultra-quick tint, the stiller simply added brown sugar, food coloring, or pokeberry juice to his raw whiskey.[10]

Volstead's Alky Cookers

To increase the supply of alcohol while keeping costs low, urban mobs hired alky cookers who ran small stills in their homes or apartments. As pre–Volstead liquor disappeared from the market, this cottage industry flourished. In big cities, ethnic neighborhoods like Little Italy, Little Bohemia, and Little Jerusalem teemed with poor men desperate for jobs. To them, making alcohol wasn't a crime because they saw Volstead as an irrational law imposed on them by crazy do-gooders. If they could pay their bills by distilling a few gallons of alcohol, they were happy to do so.

In South Philadelphia the Lanzetti Brothers supplied stills to row-house residents and bought the alcohol they made. Brooklyn mobster Frankie Yale paid home distillers $15 a day for their output. In Chicago the Genna Brothers hired Little Italy residents to make alcohol. The Gennas supplied everything needed for distilling spirits and showed the alky cooker how to save money by tapping into the city gas and water lines. Making alcohol for the Gennas paid up to $105 per week — a fortune for a poor family. Alky cooking was so prevalent in Chicago's slums that a delivery man said, "You walked down Taylor Street and you could damn near get drunk on the fumes."[11]

Alky cooking tended to be a family project for people living in crowded tenements. Although the man of the house dealt with the mob, he might put his wife or son in charge of the actual distilling. When police detectives in New York arrested a twelve-year-old boy, they called him "the city's youngest bootlegger." They found the boy alone in an apartment on Avenue A, running a still and selling liquor. He offered drinks to the detectives and sold them a pint of gin. The police confiscated his still, mash, and other alky-cooking necessities. Juvenile authorities took custody of the boy.[12]

Another New Yorker, "master moonshiner" Simon Nosowitz, was convicted of manufacturing stills, selling them, and "teaching the principles of whiskey making in the home." The judge sent him to jail for one day. Later both Simon and his son were convicted of building stills. They appealed, and the Circuit Court of Appeals ruled in their favor, saying that the law did not ban the manufacture of stills.[13]

Nosowitz had a good business selling stills, but many home distillers built their own. Any adult who could use a few basic tools and follow directions could assemble a still. An alky cooker could learn his new trade by reading a book or getting on-the-job training from another stiller. For those who wanted formal training, master distillers offered classes and coaching. In Pittsburgh, a two-week course in distilling cost $50—a sizable sum for a poor man but a good investment. The new alky cooker could quickly recoup the price of the course and his still.

An alky cooker needed a certain level of skill to avoid blowing himself up. An overheated still could explode, start a fire, and cause deaths. In big cities, firefighters knew the dangers of home distilleries all too well. In congested slums, exploding pots often started fires that spread to adjacent flats or houses. One horrific night in Brooklyn eight stills exploded, and five firemen suffered serious burns fighting the blaze.[14]

Fire wasn't the only hazard associated with alky cooking. In some instances, noxious vapors caused illness or death. When a Brooklyn man was found dead beside his still, officials attributed his demise to the inhalation of deadly vapors. In Benton Harbor, Michigan, two brothers died while operating a large still. Their bodies were found in a fermentation vat. Authorities theorized that fumes had knocked one brother unconscious and he had fallen into the vat. His brother tried to pull him out, fell into the vat, and suffocated to death in the mash.[15]

Still Hiding

U.S. Senator William Cabell Bruce (D-MD) said that before Volstead, moonshine stills were found in "a few crude, sequestered localities," but during Prohibition they were everywhere—"in swamps, in mountain fastnesses, in dense thickets, on rivers, in attics, in basements, in garages, in warehouses, in office buildings, even in caves and other underground retreats." He could've added gas stations, mom-and-pop stores, abandoned factories, Turkish baths, campgrounds, houseboats, stables, and chicken coops. The Prohis found stills in almost every conceivable place, including at least one church building.[16]

The typical urban alky cooker didn't have a lot of space to work in or a wide choice of hiding places. If he owned a house, he might put his still in the attic or basement, but most often it sat in his kitchen. Rural moonshiners had more choices. A farmer could put his still in the barn, the smokehouse, the chicken coop, a lean-to, or another outbuilding. If he wanted to go farther afield, he could hide his pot in a tobacco field, an orchard, a grove of trees, or the underbrush beside a creek.

Beside a narrow wagon road in Virginia, federal agents found an underground still on land owned by a prosperous farmer. Brush and tree limbs screened the entrance to an enormous dugout, an underground chamber with roughly sixteen hundred square feet. Heavy timbers, like those used in coal mines, supported the ceiling. The chamber held thirteen medium-sized stills and a steam boiler. The boiler smokestack was vented through a hollow tree stump. To anyone passing by, it appeared that the stump had been set afire and was smoldering—a fairly common sight on farms.[17]

A gang of Kentucky moonshiners set up their still in a coal mine. They used a pipe to ventilate the place and take away the distinctive odor produced by stilling. When Prohibition agents sniffed the familiar smell wafting through the air, they searched for the source and found the pipe. The crafty agents plugged up the pipe and waited. When the fumes backed up in the mine, the shiners came running out the entrance, coughing and gasping for air. The Prohis quickly arrested them.[18]

In Ohio, New Straitville (also Straitsville) became famous for Straitville Stuff, a shine distilled underground in deserted coal mines. Subterranean fires smoldered in the old mines, giving the area its sobriquet: the Valley of Ten Thousand Smokes. Fumes seeped up through fissures in the rock, polluting the air and the groundwater. Little vegetation grew; sink holes pitted roads and yards. The dark, deserted mine shafts were ideal for hiding an illicit business. According to a local bootlegger, about one thousand stills were operating at any given time. "The mines are done for, and you can't farm in this country," he said. "It's either make corn liquor or starve."[19]

In southeastern Kansas, moonshining thrived in the Balkans, a depressed mining region that stretched across Crawford and Cherokee counties. During Volstead, shine sales kept the area's stagnant economy from total collapse. Stills were scattered throughout the counties, with many operating in abandoned mines. Deep Shaft, the generic name for moon made in the Balkans, had wide distribution, even outside of Kansas because big-city mobs bought much of it. The Balkans' shiners took their product to a common collection point, where bootleggers picked it up and hauled it to Kansas City or another urban market.

The Balkans' bootleggers operated openly in places like Carona, Camp Forty-two, Roseland, and Frontenac. Locals claimed that bootlegging went on in every third or fourth house in Frontenac. They liked an oft-repeated anecdote about their hometown: a stranger stopped a Frontenac resident and asked where he could buy a bottle of Deep Shaft. Pointing at the U.S. Post Office, the local said, "Anywhere but there."[20]

A lead and zinc mine at Picher, Oklahoma, housed "an elaborate, electrically-equipped distillery 250 feet underground." The moonshiners, who entered the mineshaft through a garage, used an electric hoist to reach the mine chambers. The plant included four huge copper stills in the mine's lower drift. Electric pumps forced the distillate into a cooling tank in the upper drift. The distillers secretly siphoned off their water supply from the town's public water system.[21]

Colorado lawmen found a heap of dead animal carcasses half-buried near the entrance to a cave. Moonshiners had set up a still and were relying on the repulsive stench of rotting critters to keep people out of the cave. The repugnant odor also masked the distinctive aroma of mash. Despite the revolting stench, the lawmen moved heavy brush away from the cave entrance and seized the still.[22]

Sutro Tunnel originated at Virginia City, Nevada, and ran for about six miles. Federal agents discovered a sizeable moonshine plant in the abandoned tunnel, which had been built to provide drainage for the Comstock Lode mines. They arrested the men running the plant and confiscated several stills, each with a capacity of more than one hundred gallons. The agents also seized hogsheads and barrels filled with moonshine and brandy.[23]

Across rural America farmers jumped on the moonshine bandwagon to boost their income. As a general rule, making shine was a seasonal job for a farmer. During warm weather, he had to work in the fields. After the fall harvest, he could devote his time to moonshining until spring. If he didn't need his wife to help in the fields, he might turn the still over to her during his busy farming season and have a year-round sideline.

Iowa farmers hid so many stills in their cornfields that revenue agents in airplanes flew over the crops looking for pots. On the Iron Range in northern Minnesota, "every homestead" had a still producing moon. According to testimony before the U.S. Congress, one-fourth of North Dakota's farmers made moonshine.[24]

North Dakotan Nels Hanson had a reputation for making topnotch moonshine, but lawmen couldn't find his still when they searched his farm. After some coaxing, Hanson agreed to show it to them. He led the lawmen to his pigsty and scraped away the pig litter. With a claw hammer, he opened a trapdoor and went down a ladder to an underground chamber. The room, which was lined with tarpaper, held a pot and barrels of mash. The pigs played a dual role: the pigsty odor masked the smell from the still and the swine consumed the leftover mash. Even though Hanson cooperated with the lawmen, he was prosecuted, fined, and sentenced to a short jail term.

In Montana's Hill County the farmer-rancher battled for survival. He struggled to grow crops without adequate rainfall, and he usually reaped a sparse harvest. If he raised poultry and cattle, he could sell his extra eggs and cream. He could join other men in rabbit round-ups and sell the pelts. He could also make moonshine for extra income. "Farm moonshining became so common it was a standard joke to ask how many gallons—rather than how many bushels—a field ran to the acre," wrote an observer. In Montana's Milk River Country, stills hummed in the Bear's Paw Mountains as well as on the ranches. A bootleg gang furnished the stills and paid the shiners with food and supplies. In tiny Bear Creek in southern Montana, making moon was "everybody's pastime" because it was a reliable source of cash.[25]

An influx of newcomers from Kentucky stimulated the growth of Wisconsin's moonshine trade in the Arid Era. The owners of a big timber company targeted Kentucky mountaineers as a market for its cutover lands in northern Wisconsin. The sales campaign prompted a substantial number of Kentuckians to move to the Badger State. Some of the new arrivals farmed, but others pursued the business they knew best—making moonshine.

Wisconsin's Forest County became a major supplier of moonshine to the bootleg trade in Milwaukee, Minneapolis, and Chicago. At least fourteen distillers had large operations, and hundreds of people ran gasoline-can stills. Kentuckians in Forest County owned and operated "the three largest stills ever uncovered in Wisconsin," according to a 1922 report. The stills, hidden deep in the woods, were housed in log cabins. The shiners used steam heat to warm their mash.

In Superior, Wisconsin, the sheriff said a "whole regiment of officers could not round up the moonshiners in the county." The shiners were well-organized and always seemed to have advance warning about raids. On several occasions, lawmen searching for stills spotted a man on a black horse loitering in the woods. When the lawmen approached, the horseman rode off in a hurry. Soon the lawmen heard two shots, which were answered by shots farther away. The two-shot warning system was a tradition among moonshiners, and the stillers from Kentucky probably introduced it to Wisconsin.[26]

Although California lay far outside the Moonshine Belt, countless stills made white lightning for drinkers in the Golden State. On the banks of the Alamo River near Brawley, an enterprising moonshiner hid his distillery underground. A manhole in the riverbank led to a cavern where he operated the still. To prevent a cave-in, he used thick timbers to reinforce the chamber walls and ceiling. He piped his water supply into the cavern from an irrigation ditch. Another pipe took away the leftover mash, dumping it into the river.

On a goat farm in Riverside County, bales of hay were stacked up in a field to make a giant rectangle. A snoopy Prohibition agent discovered that the bales formed a wall hiding a substantial building. Inside the building the agent found everything needed to distill ten thousand gallons of liquor per day. The surprised farmer said he didn't know a distillery lurked behind his bales. He couldn't imagine how it got there!

California's moonshine trade thrived in a most unlikely place — the Mojave Desert. At first glance, the desert seemed ill-suited for making white lightning. However, it had the essential elements: water, isolation, and men who needed money. The Mojave River flowed across the desert, often underground, providing water. Even when the riverbed appeared to be dry, water lurked just below the surface. Stills could be hidden in the thickets of willows, mesquite, catalpa, and cottonwood that grew along the riverbank. The region's high unemployment rate ensured an ample supply of men willing to tend stills.

Bootleggers from Los Angeles recruited Mojave residents for the moonshine trade. The leggers furnished the stills and bought their output. More than one city rum ring leased a ranch, set up multiple stills, and hired locals to keep them running. Across the region, isolated ranches and deserted mines housed illicit distilleries. Sand dunes hid caches of alcohol. The shiners planted small flags in the dunes to mark the hiding spots so they could easily retrieve the liquor.

The Prohis focused on enforcing Volstead in the bigger towns near the Mojave, turning enforcement in the desert over to the local constables. The constables' ties to the community complicated their job because the shiners were often men they had known since boyhood. One constable admitted that he didn't even try to round up the moonshiners. "I didn't go out looking for them," he said, "or I would have had to arrest all my friends and neighbors."[27]

The Pride of Arkansas

Arkansas, a state saturated with mountain dew, had many notoriously wet spots. Among the wettest was Garland City, "a hamlet of perhaps one hundred white people, situated on the west bank of the Red River" near the Texas-Arkansas border. The tiny business district had a handful of offices and shops, which closed in the afternoon while the proprietors went hunting or fishing. Garland City's economic engine lay outside town in the swamplands, so ideal for moonshining that they might've been created just for that purpose. On tiny islets, the dew boys fired up their stills amongst the cypress knees that poked up out of the shallow, muddy water. The stillers made Garland City Pride, an outlaw brand of corn liquor that sold briskly as far away as Dallas and Little Rock.

Garland City's moonshine business, which had deep roots, assumed new importance at the end of World War I. Falling cotton prices and rampaging floods impoverished local farmers, especially the sharecroppers. Starvation threatened many families. Moonshine always found a market, and the trip boys who hauled it to the cities brought outside money home with them. Locals joked that they had their own farm relief plan, funded by bootleggers.

At night Garland City bustled with traffic. Drivers in speedy cars picked up loads of shine at the edge of the swamp and sped along the town's unpaved, dusty streets toward the highway. Many were headed to Texarkana and points west. Other trippers eased their cars down the boat slip and onto the ferry, the first leg of the trip to El Dorado, the oil capital of Arkansas.[28]

Men who worked in the oil fields made good wages and spent freely on vices, especially moonshine and soiled doves. The bars typically served moon in used Coca-Cola bottles, which were virtually indestructible and could be refilled countless times. The oilmen kicked up their heels in rowdy barrel houses in El Dorado, Shotgun Valley, Pistol Hill, and Upland. ("Barrel house" denoted a bar where the bartender ejected a drunk who had run out of money by putting him in a barrel and rolling him out the door. A quick spin is just what a drunk needs!)

When Prohibition began, local lawmen naively believed they could enforce Volstead by shutting down the stills around Garland City. They made numerous forays to seize stills in the swamplands outside town. They threw the confiscated stills in a pile behind the county jail, and the heap grew until it reached eight feet tall. But the raids failed to stop the shiners. For every confiscated still, the dew boys seemed to fire up two new ones. Shrewd shiners used the raids as an excuse for raising their prices, claiming that they had a shortage of product due to the seizures.

Despite raids and arrests, Garland City's stillers spent little time in jail because juries rarely convicted them. In a more or less typical case, a young farmer was arrested for possessing mash and distilling equipment, including copper pots. At his trial in Texarkana, he testified that he used the copper pots to cook sweet potatoes for his hogs. He said he had learned in school that yams were good pig feed if they were boiled for easy digestion. He claimed that the mash fermenting in barrels in his barn was also hog feed. The jurors approved of his swine-feeding regiment. They acquitted him.[29]

Kentucky's Moonshine Wars

Eastern Kentucky's rugged, mountainous terrain created a moonshiner's paradise. Steep slopes, dense woods, isolated hollows, and narrow, unpaved roads discouraged visitors from the flatlands. Sinkhole pockets, ravines, and underground streams dotted the perilous karst. This treacherous terrain was ideal for the stillers, who operated in secret, trusted only their kin folk, and didn't cotton to strangers. They had few visitors, and they liked it that way.

The name "Kentucky" was derived from an Indian word "kaintuck," meaning dark and bloody ground. That name seemed apt during Prohibition when the Moonshine Wars claimed many lives in the Bluegrass State. Kentucky's stillers didn't hesitate to shoot at one another or at the lawmen trying to enforce Volstead. Like other mountaineers, the stillers regarded guns as essential tools for killing game, settling disputes, and protecting their property. Winchester rifles, large-caliber pistols, double-barrel shotguns, and magazine-loading repeater shotguns were favorite weapons in the hills of Kentucky.

During Volstead at least thirty-five federal agents were killed in Kentucky's Moonshine Wars. Dozens of state and local lawmen also lost their lives. Law enforcement in Letcher County suffered an unusually high death toll: sixteen deputy sheriffs killed in only four years. No one kept a count of how many moonshiners died in the gun battles. However, based on news reports, dead outlaws clearly outnumbered the dead lawmen. Sadly, the gunplay also killed a number of innocent bystanders.[30]

In January 1921 Governor Edwin Morrow stated that the Prohibition law was "being brazenly, notoriously, impudently, and openly violated in Kentucky." He issued a formal proclamation urging Kentuckians to "assist in suppressing moonshiners and bootleggers." He warned that the shiners, the leggers, and their allies were striking "at the source of all public authority," which could lead to a total breakdown of law and order.[31]

Despite the governor's plea, shootouts between the outlaws and the lawmen continued to claim lives. Only a month after the governor's proclamation, moonshiners in Carter County shot at the sheriff's squad and wounded five deputies. When a posse of federal agents and Breathitt County lawmen went hunting for moonshiners, they followed a gang into Knott County. The gang lured the posse into an ambush and "a rain of bullets" poured down. A deputy sheriff and a teenager riding with the posse were shot to death. A lawman and three bootleggers died in a gun battle in Leslie County. During two days of fighting in Harlan eight people died of gunshot wounds.[32]

In Hindman, a tiny village in Knott County, shiners fought a series of gun battles with the sheriff's forces. One moonshiner was killed; three stillers and a deputy sheriff were wounded. Also in Knott County, two deputy sheriffs were indicted for killing a moonshiner and were found guilty at trial. The other deputies felt their comrades had been unjustly convicted. They went on strike and demanded that Governor Morrow pardon the duo. Their plan worked. The governor issued a pardon, and all the deputies returned to work.[33]

When members of an infamous moonshining clan were imprisoned in the Breathitt County jail, masked men stormed the building, determined to free the prisoners. In the ensuing gunplay, three innocent people were shot; both the jailer's wife and nephew died from gunshot wounds. Despite the bloodshed, the masked men left empty-handed because officials had anticipated the rescue attempt and moved the prisoners to another jail.[34]

Near Hazard, federal Prohibition agents ventured into the Lost Creek area hunting a gang of moonshiners. The feds tromped through the dense thickets until they reached an isolated valley surrounded by tall mountains. At nightfall a deep, eerie darkness descended on the wildwood valley. Suddenly, shots rang out. The agents returned fire but couldn't see their enemy. They shot at flashes of light and took aim at telltale noises. For several hours, bursts of gunfire crackled in the quiet darkness. After midnight a sheriff's posse, familiar with the terrain and the moonshine gang, came to reinforce the Prohis. The posse quickly gained control and arrested several stillers. Despite all the gunfire, no one was injured because the shooters couldn't aim accurately in the darkness.[35]

A brutal battle between lawmen and the notorious Ballard moonshining clan raged for days in Menifee County. The Prohis targeted the gang because it was supplying large amounts of white lightning to the liquor trade in Cincinnati, Ohio. The Ballard brothers, reputed to be fearless fighters and crack marksmen, were armed and ready for combat at their mountain fastness. Led by agent Bob Duff, a squad of Prohis that included Duff's sons, set out for the Ballards' stronghold. On the way, the agents encountered and captured a member of the gang.[36]

When the Prohis reached the Ballards' place, they found that the gang had built a sturdy, fort-like log cabin at the entrance to a cave. The gang had used "chimney cliffs," ledges of rock that can be pried up as smooth slabs and cemented together to form chimneys. The cabin's outer log walls were reinforced with chimney-cliff slabs; behind this stone barrier was another wall made of thick oak boards. Even armor-piercing bullets couldn't penetrate this multi-layer wall.

Agent Duff hammered on the door of the cabin/fort, ordering the moonshiners to surrender. The door abruptly swung open, a barrage of bullets struck Duff, and he fell to the ground. The door snapped shut. The Prohis ran for cover and opened fire. Agent Duff died where he had fallen while his horrified, helpless sons watched. For several hours the lawmen and the Ballard clan exchanged shots. As long as the Ballards stayed inside their cabin/fort, the Prohis had virtually no chance of capturing them. Finally, the Prohis retreated, leaving their fallen comrade behind. The Ballard gang stripped the dead man of his valuables, stealing his money, pistol, watch, and badge.[37]

The next day a squad of federal agents and a sheriff's posse went to the Ballards' stronghold, hoping to capture them and retrieve agent Duff's body. The moonshiners weren't home, but the lawmen suspected the dew boys were nearby, hiding in the dense woods, watching every move the posse made. The lawmen destroyed the gang's still and emptied the containers of mash and moonshine. Then they searched for the Ballards.

Treating the lawmen like targets in a shooting gallery, the Ballards hid in the mountains and shot at the posse. When the posse headed in the direction of the shots, the Ballard gunmen moved to another location. After a brief, silent respite, gunfire rang out from the rim of a tall cliff. A bullet hit a member of the posse, lodging in his neck. He fell to the ground, mortally wounded. The lawmen headed toward the cliff, spotted the Ballard shooters, and trailed them until darkness stopped the search.[38]

While the lawmen hunted for the Ballards in the woods, Kentucky's Prohibition director and other officials huddled in strategy sessions. They considered various options, including air power. After the Prohis sent an airplane on a scouting sortie over Menifee County, they decided against using military planes to drop bombs on the shiners. Instead, they sent a squad of Prohibition agents to stage another assault on the Ballard stronghold. The agents stopped at all the houses along their route and handcuffed the male residents to trees to prevent them from joining in the fight.[39]

When the Prohis approached the Ballards' cabin/fort, agent Guy Cole, armed with a rifle, led the way. Gunmen inside the stronghold opened fire. In an eerie replay of the earlier gun battle, a bullet struck Cole, who fell near the front door. The door flew open; hands attached to unseen bodies reached out and dragged the dying officer inside, then slammed the door shut. Bullets zinged through the air. The gunfight was on. In the heat of the battle, a daring Ballard gunman jumped out a cabin window. Running and shooting, he made his way to a waiting horse, hopped on, and galloped away.

The lawmen continued to shoot at the fort/cabin, repeatedly emptying the magazines on their Browning rifles. When the return fire ceased, they ran to the barricaded door, battered it down, and rushed in with their guns drawn. Moonshiner Bob Ballard lay unconscious on the floor, beside the slain Prohibition agent. The rugged mountaineer had multiple gunshot wounds but was still breathing. He appeared to be the lone living soul in the cabin.

The tired, hungry lawmen smelled the inviting scent of home cooking. They found that someone, presumably Ballard, had cooked a hearty meal. A fire smoldered in the iron stove, and a pot of beans was waiting to be eaten. A pan of warm cornbread, a skillet of fried side-meat, and a pot of coffee completed the menu. The lawmen settled down to enjoy a tasty repast while they waited for their host to expire. Bleeding and struggling to breathe, Bob Ballard survived for about an hour.

The lawmen believed that Bob's brother, Charles Ballard, was the shooter who had escaped on horseback. Aided by bloodhounds, they set out to track him down. Although Charles had bullet wounds in his shoulder and both legs, he made his way north to Bath County and hid out there. After a few days the law caught up with him, and he was arrested.[40]

Charles Ballard was indicted for killing Prohibition agents Cole and Duff during the shootouts. He first stood trial for murdering Cole, and the jury acquitted him. In the second trial he was prosecuted for the murder of agent Duff. The state built its case around the testimony of a Prohibition agent who had been present at the gun battle. When questioned by defense counsel, the agent admitted that he had taken cover when the shooting started, which somewhat limited his credibility as an eyewitness. The defense produced alibi witnesses who claimed that Charles Ballard had not even been at the scene of the shootout. The jury took only five minutes to find Ballard not guilty. The courtroom crowd gave the moonshiner a standing ovation for being "the defender of mountain liberty."

As news of Ballard's acquittal spread, "cheers resounded up and down the valley for hours afterwards." He was the guest of honor at "a great banquet ... at the home of a well-known and much feared moonshiner." The mountain dew flowed like champagne while the guests celebrated Ballard's victory over the legal system.[41]

As one headline put it: "Killing Dry Agent Is No Crime in Kentuck."[42]

19. Motor On:
High-Octane Fuel for Detroit

I can say without reservation that Detroit is the wettest city I have been assigned to. I have worked in several parts of the country and observed conditions carefully, and I can say without hesitation that nowhere else is the law so openly violated....—A.B. Stroup, deputy administrator, Federal Prohibition Unit[1]

When Volstead became the law of the land, Detroit's liquor traffickers needed a dependable supply of booze for the thirsty masses. Luckily for them, reservoirs of liquor lay just across the border in Canada. Like a seductive mermaid, the Detroit River beckoned to rum-runners because a speedboat could race from Ontario to Michigan in only a few minutes. The river, less than a mile wide in places, separated Motor City from several Ontario ports — notably Windsor, Walkerville, Amherstburg, and LaSalle. Ontario had at least two dozen government-licensed export docks on the Detroit River where a smuggler could pick up a cargo of booze for the quick trip to Motown.

Detroit's close proximity to Canadian liquor guaranteed that, despite the Big Thirst, Motor City drinkers would never have parched throats. Both amateur smugglers and organized mobs found it easy and lucrative to deliver booze to Motown. A Detroiter who couldn't find a drink wasn't really trying. In addition to keeping Motown wet enough for hip boots, Detroit's liquor traffickers supplied booze to bootleg gangs throughout the Midwest, including Al Capone's Chicago Outfit.

In every corner of the Wolverine State, defiant drinkers and bootleggers showed their contempt for Volsteadism. Commander Roy Vandercook of the Michigan State Police said, "We could not enforce the Prohibition law in Michigan if we had the United States' standing army. As long as the people maintain their present attitude toward Prohibition, the law is unenforceable."[2]

Any Which Way

Detroit's enterprising smugglers showed amazing ingenuity in transporting liquor by foot, boat, car, and truck from Canada to Michigan. Both seasoned career criminals and amateurs embraced rumrunning as the fast track to a wallet full of whip-out. The career

197

criminals tolerated the neophytes because the Detroit market was monstrously huge; there was enough business for everybody. Some liquor runners jumped the line with thousands of bottles; others carried a dozen or less. Whatever the size of the cargo, a liquor smuggler was more likely to be foiled by an accident than an arrest.

When the waterways were navigable, an armada of booze boats sailed each day from Ontario to Michigan. The big operators used fast, streamlined motorboats that held substantial payloads. A smuggler operating on a shoestring made the trip in a canoe, a rowboat, or anything else that would float. The rumrunners landed their cargoes on the waterfront in Detroit and nearby small towns, especially Ecorse, Wyandotte, and Monroe.

Although rumrunners worked the nightshift in most ports, booze boats operated round-the-clock on the Detroit River. A combination of graft and reconnaissance kept the liquor boats safe. The rummers had a simple but effective way of knowing when the government patrol boats were waiting for them. An alert sailor/spy in a speedboat cruised along the Michigan shore. Using signal flags in daylight or flashing lights after dark, he told the rumrunners when the coast was clear. According to gangland gossip, Canadian liquor companies paid for the boat and the spy.[3]

One rumrunning gang stationed a lookout at the tip of Peche Island near the Canadian shore where the river opens into Lake St. Clair. The lookout used binoculars to follow the movements of boats on the Michigan side of the watery border. When he saw nothing that would impede a quick trip to the U.S. shore, he stood up. If he stayed seated or left his post, the rumrunning boats remained in Canadian waters and waited for him to signal "all clear."[4]

One rumrunning operation used modern technology — namely, the telephone — for reconnaissance. Lookouts were stationed around the clock on the sixth floor of an abandoned office building in Detroit. Peering through binoculars, they watched everything that happened at the U.S. Customs Service headquarters on the riverfront. To communicate quickly, the lookouts used a dedicated phone line to call the rumrunners in Windsor without going through the central exchange. "The American customs service on the Detroit riverfront cannot even drag out a boat to wash it without word of their move flashing instantaneously to the Canadian side," wrote a reporter.[5]

The rumrunners often hired teenagers as lookouts, spies, or messengers. A police officer said that the young spies, who "spread out along the waterfront" at strategic points, were "very awake and diligent." The more daring teenagers weren't content to be lookouts or messengers. They graduated to liquor smuggling. Police arrested a fifteen-year-old boy who was delivering a truckload of liquor to a downriver saloon. The earnest lad stated that he never skipped school but only worked nights and weekends. In February 1923 lawmen arrested two high school boys pulling a load of beer on a sled across the frozen Detroit River. The teens said that "lots of fellows" their age made money hauling liquor.[6]

Like the mailman, the booze runners delivered the goods even in bad weather. During Michigan's frigorific winters, when the water froze solid, the normal boat traffic ceased. Hundreds of tire tracks marred the ice as bootleggers convoyed across the frozen water in cars and trucks. Some leggers drove jalopies with bolts protruding from the tires to provide traction. Other drivers removed the front tires from their vehicles and replaced them with oversized skis. A vehicle's doors could be removed, so the driver could bail out if his automobile broke through the ice. For a bigger payload, a motor vehicle with a cargo of liquor

In 1929 lawmen discovered this cable system, which was used to smuggle liquor across the Detroit River from Canada to Michigan (Walter P. Reuther Library, Archives of Labor and Urban Affairs, Wayne State University).

could pull a sledge or sleigh also carrying booze. The drivers worried more about thin ice than about getting arrested. "What we are really afraid of is the ice," a driver said. "Anytime it may give way beneath and let one of us through."[7]

One bitterly cold February morning a *Detroit News* reporter watched dozens of bootleggers leave the Amherstburg, Ontario, docks driving cars with liquor cargos. The leggers convoyed across the solid ice headed for Michigan. Some cars went straight to Motown, but most stopped at Grosse Ile in the Detroit River. There the liquor was stored or transferred to camouflaged trucks, which crossed the bridge to the U.S. mainland. Grosse Isle was the site of vacation homes inhabited by wealthy folks in the summer. In the winter the big homes served as liquor warehouses — sometimes without the owner's knowledge.[8]

On breezy winter nights, iceboats with sails skimmed across the frozen water carrying liquor. In the moonlight the canvas sails, stretched taut by the wind, shimmered with a silvery hue. "A gust of flying snow and perhaps now and then a trace of silver canvas in the wind, and the boats were gone," an observer wrote. Smugglers wearing ice skates pulled their liquid cargo on sleds. Spiked "ice creepers" were another footwear option, but the bootlegger moved faster on skates. In snowy weather, a legger could go "ghost walking."

He draped white sheets over himself and his sled-load of liquor. Against the snow, the white bed linens made him virtually invisible to everyone, including lawmen watching for smugglers.[9]

Horses could pull substantial liquor cargos on cutters across the frozen waters. One glacial February morning Prohibition agents spotted a horse and cutter, without a driver, crossing the ice on the St. Clair River. The Prohis headed off the wandering nag and seized it along with the sleigh and the cases of Canadian whiskey. The Prohis weren't sure if the horse began the trip with a driver or if the bootlegger trusted the nag to find its way across the river without human help. In any case, someone soon stole the horse from the stable where the agents put him for safekeeping.[10]

Boatyards fabricated custom sled-boats for hauling booze on partially-frozen waterways. Small boats were fitted with runners so they could either float on the water or be pulled across the ice. Booze runners routinely used sled-boats to cross from Petite Cote, Ontario, to Ecorse, Michigan. Typically, a lookout with a whistle left Petite Cote ahead of his comrades. If he didn't encounter any problems, he blew his whistle, signaling that it was okay to cross. A swarm of rumrunners pushed their sled-boats onto the ice along the Petite Cote shore. When they reached water, they hopped into the sled-boats and rowed to the solid ice along the far shore. Trucks were waiting when the amphibians arrived at Ecorse.

"There before our astounded eyes were the boats on runners, loaded down to the gunwales with kegs and cartons of beer," wrote a man who saw the sled-boats. "They were spaced out at approximately hundred-yard intervals. We soon counted twelve, and more were shooting out from the shelter of the canals on the Canadian side. The men who were dragging and shoving them across the ice looked like pirates in their toques and high rubber boots."[11]

Inventive bootleggers rigged up sturdy cables to carry Canadian liquor to Michigan. An underwater cable, attached to windlasses onshore, stretched from Ecorse to Mud Island in the Detroit River. Boats carried liquor from Canada to the island, where the hooch was stashed until it could be moved to Ecorse. The windlasses were hidden in a boathouse on the island and a garage on the mainland. The cable pulled a sledge weighted down with liquor to Ecorse, where a diver unloaded it at the water's edge. When the cable system was in use, customs inspectors saw "an apparently inactive waterfront and reported 'all quiet' in the rum war."

A more advanced cable system operated between Detroit and Peche Island at the juncture of Lake St. Clair and the Detroit River. A motor-driven windlass, hidden in a house on the Detroit waterfront, pulled a submerged torpedo-like metal container filled with cases of whiskey. After each trip to Detroit, a rowboat towed the empty cylinder back to the island. One day a customs inspector noticed a suspicious rowboat and followed it in his own boat. The oarsman, seeing the inspector, cast off his tow. Later the customs inspector saw someone retrieve the container. He waited until the cable started moving and followed it to the house on the waterfront. The men running the operation escaped, but law enforcement confiscated the windlass, motor, and cable.[12]

An informant told federal agents that "electrically operated torpedoes loaded with whiskey" crossed the Detroit River from Canada to Michigan each day. He claimed that the copper torpedoes carried ten to twenty-five gallons per trip. Each torpedo had a propeller powered by electric storage batteries. Traveling one hundred feet underwater, the device crossed the river in about five minutes. The Prohis investigated but didn't find any evidence to verify that these submarines existed.[13]

According to mob lore, beer was pumped across the Detroit River via a pipeline from a brewery in Ontario. This bit of gossip was repeated so often that people regarded it as gospel truth, but law enforcement denied that such a pipeline existed. Prohibition Commissioner Roy Haynes called the claim "one of the many bootlegger canards."[14]

In the late 1920s the ferries running between Detroit and Windsor carried twenty million passengers and one million automobiles each year, according to official estimates.[15] Many ferry riders couldn't resist the urge to smuggle a little liquor for their personal use or for sale in Motown. Customs officers called these amateur bootleggers "casuals" and didn't hassle them as long as they carried only small quantities.

Workers who commuted from Windsor to Detroit could stash liquor in their lunchboxes or under their clothes. Male customs officers made only cursory searches of women, so ladies could carry "girdle whiskey"—a half-pint or flask tucked into their underclothes. A few ladies wore religious garb to fool the inspectors. A woman wearing a nun's habit didn't always belong to a religious order; she might be hiding a few pints under her long skirt. A woman pushing a baby carriage could hide a flask or bottle under the baby blanket. In some cases, the carriage had been modified so the baby lay on top of a compartment that held several bottles.

A man could wear an oversized coat to hide a hot water bottle or a rubber chest protector filled with alcohol. Smugglers sewed secret pockets into the lining of their overcoats to hold pints or half-pints. A carpenter's apron with deep pockets could hide a flask or bottle. Ferry riders lugged heavy briefcases, valises, steamer trunks, and tool chests onto the vessel. More than a few of these had false bottoms that concealed bottles of booze. A pet owner who often rode the ferry always took his dog in a cage-like carrier. A customs official became suspicious and searched the carrier; he found a false bottom hiding bottles of Canadian whiskey.[16]

U.S. Customs agents who searched the ferries found booze in hollowed-out baseball bats, potatoes, loaves of bread, and wood sculptures. One unhurried smuggler chose to fill eggs with liquor. He made a tiny hole in each egg, emptied it, filled it with booze, and sealed it. A customs agent discovered this ploy when the smuggler dropped his basket of eggs, cracking some open. Strangely, this man was not the only liquor-egg smuggler. A "frazzled Ukrainian housewife" tried the same ploy. When a customs officer picked up an egg from her basket, it broke in his hand and liquor oozed out. The average ham-handed bootlegger couldn't pull off this ploy, but Ukrainians had a tradition of decorating eggs, which might explain the woman's *modus operandi*.[17]

Booze boats crossed the border from Canada into the United States at numerous locations, but the rumrunning traffic was especially heavy on the Detroit River. In 1927 a Canadian customs study found that $40 million worth of liquor had been shipped from Windsor, Ontario, to the USA in only one year. Given Windsor's proximity to Michigan, it was obvious that most of the booze boats had landed at Detroit or a nearby small town.[18]

Washington's Prohibition administrators complained that Canadian authorities weren't doing their share to stop the rum boats on the Detroit River. But Ottawa saw the situation differently. Since liquor exports were legal, Canadian customs routinely issued clearance papers to vessels with whiskey cargos bound for foreign countries, including the United States.

Ottawa argued that Canadian customs agents were paid to enforce Canada's trade regulations, not the USA's dry law. From Ottawa's perspective, the U.S. authorities weren't doing enough to enforce Prohibition. Washington had no right to expect Canada to take up the slack.

William Euler, Canada's minister of national revenue, created a stir when he revealed that he had ridden on a booze boat carrying a cargo of liquor across the Detroit River. Standing on the dock in Ontario, Euler could see the U.S. customs office across the water in Michigan. He said, "I could see that it was not difficult to detect any boats that left the Canadian shore to go to the American side." When the minister asked the rumrunner how he would evade U.S. customs officers, the man said, "Well, it just happens they aren't there when we get across."[19]

In June 1930 Ottawa finally acceded to Washington's repeated calls for stricter control of the rum boats leaving Canada. Ottawa ordered Canadian customs to "refuse clearance to all vessels with liquor cargos destined for the United States and refuse any other official documentation covering such liquor." Since this did not outlaw liquor exports per se, Canadian vessels could transport hooch to countries other than the USA after posting a bond. As a practical matter, Canadian officials had no control over a vessel after it left Canadian waters.[20]

Several months after Canada implemented the new system, Washington admitted it "was having but little effect in stopping the flow of liquor." Small speedboats didn't need clearance papers, so they could haul booze without worrying about the red tape. Bigger rum boats declared that they were going to Cuba or Mexico, posted bond, left Canada with the requisite clearance papers, and returned an hour or so later. Clearly, they hadn't made a roundtrip to Cuba or Mexico, but everybody accepted the fiction.[21]

Not all Canadian liquor entered the Wolverine State on a boat. A small percentage arrived via the highways or the railways. The amount of Canadian hooch hauled to Michigan in motor vehicles rose sharply with the opening of the Ambassador Bridge in 1929 and the Detroit-Windsor Tunnel in 1930. In fact, so much booze passed through the tunnel that locals called it "the Detroit funnel." In 1931 the toll-free Wayne County Bridge, a converted railroad bridge, began carrying automotive traffic between Grosse Ile and the mainland, providing another option for bootleggers.

Purple Power

During the Arid Era at least six major gangs vied for power in Detroit. By the mid–Twenties the Purple Gang had emerged as the city's dominant mob, with a finger in every illegal pie in Motown. The gang began in an area called Little Jerusalem, part of the teeming, multi-ethnic boiling pot on Detroit's East Side. Many children in Little Jerusalem were native-born Americans whose parents or grandparents had emigrated from Eastern Europe. Poverty was endemic, and every young person hoped to find a way out. Many boys were attracted to street life as the path to survival — and maybe riches. At a young age, these boys began their on-the-job training in gangland, running errands for mob journeymen, stealing from street vendors, and terrorizing other youngsters.

A mob called the Sugar House Gang operated out of a sugar warehouse on Oakland Street. The thugs' main rackets were making moonshine, selling supplies to alky cookers, and running a protection scheme. These mature hoodlums, who hired young toughs to do the menial jobs, taught the criminal ropes to their protégés. They discovered that the youthful Bernstein (also Burnstein) brothers — Abe, Joey, Izzy, and Ray — were fast learners. In a remarkably short time, the brothers graduated from apprentices to old hands. They joined forces with two other sets of siblings — the Keywells and the Fleishers — to form the nucleus of a new mob that would become Detroit's most notorious gang in the Volstead Era.

Somewhere along the way these ruthless young hoods became known as the Purple Gang. Several sketchy tales have been put forward to explain the colorful name, but it remains a mystery. When an incarcerated Purple was asked, he disclaimed any knowledge of the name, saying that he and his comrades never called themselves the Purple Gang. One plausible tale traces the sobriquet to the gang's involvement in a protection racket that extorted money from dry cleaners and dyers. If a dyer or dry cleaner refused to pay for protection, mobsters wrecked his place of business, poured purple dye on the clothes in his shop, and hijacked his delivery trucks.[22]

The Purple Gang quickly grew into a criminal syndicate, trafficking in liquor, drugs, prostitution, and stolen goods, especially jewelry. The gang distilled and cut liquor, operated blind pigs, and hijacked booze shipments from other mobs. The gang's rumrunning subsidiary, the Little Jewish Navy was also known as the Third Avenue Navy because its booze boats landed liquor at the railroad yards between Third and Fourth Avenues. The rumrunners worked out a signaling system with the railroad men, who used train whistles to tell the rummers when government patrol boats were nearby.[23]

As criminal jacks-of-all-trades, the Purple gangsters dabbled in contract killings, bombings, kidnappings, and insurance fraud, especially fake accidents. They also extorted protection money from both legal and illegal businesses. By the late 1920s, the Purple Gang dominated illegal gambling in Motown because it controlled the wire service that reported horse races.

Naturally, the Purples didn't get to the top of the gangland heap by being nice guys. A jazz musician who knew many mobsters said the Purples were "a hard lot of guys, so tough they made Capone's playmates look like a kindergarten class." According to mob lore, the Purple bosses stood up to Scarface when he tried to muscle in on their turf. Capone took a scouting trip to Detroit because he planned to take over the liquor traffic there. The Purple bosses didn't blink. They told Capone that they controlled the waterfront and he would have to buy from them. They were so fierce that they put the fear of God in Big Al and he became their best customer.[24]

As in other large cities, Detroit's gangs coexisted uneasily, and turf wars broke out from time to time. In the late Twenties the Purples battled with other mobs, especially the Italians, to control gangland. For the most part, law enforcement ignored the violence and gunplay. Detroit's police commissioner publicly declared that he would not assign extra officers to investigate mob killings "so long as they confine their shootings to their own kind." Mayor Charles Bowles said, "It is just as well to let these gangsters kill each other off, if they are so minded. You know the scientists employ one set of parasites to destroy another."[25]

Detroit's mob warfare contributed to the city's high murder rate, which climbed to 18.6 per one hundred thousand residents in 1929. In contrast, New York City's murder rate was 7.1 for that same year. On the Canadian side of the Detroit River, Windsor's was only 3.8. In less than two weeks in July 1930, gang warfare claimed the lives of ten Motor City mobsters. Crime watchers, who called the month "Bloody July," said Motor City should be renamed Murder City.[26]

Despite the Purple Gang's power and dominance, its golden age soon passed. An underworld bloodbath played a decisive role in the Purples' decline. In September 1931 Purple gunmen killed three unarmed mobsters known as the Third Avenue Terrors. Detroit's crime bosses allowed the threesome to operate their own rackets as long as they didn't interfere with other gangs. But the incredibly reckless trio double-crossed both the Purples and an Italian mob. In an apartment on the corner of Twelfth and Collingwood streets, the Purple triggermen shot the Third Avenue Terrors, leaving them face down on the bloody floor.

The triple homicide, dubbed the "Collingwood Massacre," alarmed Detroit's citizens, just as the infamous St. Valentine Day's slaughter had outraged Chicagoans. The public demanded a swift response from city officials, and the police moved quickly to arrest key Purple mobsters. In a departure from the norm for mob hits, the state prosecuted three Purple gangsters for murdering the Third Avenue Terrors. They were convicted and sentenced to life in prison.[27]

In the aftermath of the Collingwood Massacre, the Purple Gang slowly disintegrated. The Purple mobsters who didn't end up in prison usually met a violent death. Disputes over money and power led to internecine murders. The Purples lucky enough to survive the intramural mayhem faced the very real possibility of being killed by another gang. The smartest of the Purples saw that their future lay in pledging allegiance to one of the emerging organized crime syndicates. As the surviving Purples blended into the bigger mobs, Motor City's most notorious gang sank into the dust bin of history.

School Pigs and Saloons

Illegal liquor outlets prospered in all sections of Detroit, catering to every socioeconomic class. Consumers could buy liquor in drugstores, barbershops, meat markets, ice cream parlors, confectionaries, feed and seed stores, beer flats, bootleg stands, tire stores, and at least one Turkish bathhouse. An irreverent Detroiter even opened a blind pig in a church basement. Illicit saloons thrived in shacks and boathouses along the waterfront between Detroit and River Rouge. Blind pigs operated near the factory gates in the industrial towns of Fordson, Hamtramck, and River Rouge.

Many Detroit eateries served liquor during the Great Drought. Generally, the bar was moved to a backroom, the basement, or the second floor, and a bouncer stood guard to see that only trusted patrons got in. However, on Grand River Avenue watering holes made no effort to hide their old-fashioned bars, and passersby could see the drinkers hoist their glasses to defy Volstead. A popular tavern, Nick Schaefer's, was located across the street from police headquarters. Cops and newsmen were among Schaefer's loyal customers, who enjoyed the "free" lunch that came with the purchase of beer. Farmhouses along Six, Seven, and Eight Mile roads were converted to speakeasies that, in general, had a dubious reputation because they attracted rowdy drinkers.[28]

Motown's upscale speakeasies usually offered food, dancing, and gambling as well as liquor. Sam Kerr and Sam Cohen, known as "the Two Sammies," operated some of Detroit's most popular red-carpet speakeasies. They had strong connections to the Purple Gang, which guaranteed a steady supply of liquor for their ritzy clubs. Nightlife lovers flocked to the Sammies' K&C Club, where the patrons rubbed elbows with politicians, mobsters, and high-ranking police brass.[29]

The typical liquor control system specifies the legal drinking age in order to keep alcohol away from children and teenagers. But Volstead had no regulations to prevent under-age drinking because, theoretically, there was none. However, parents knew that teenagers and even younger children could get their hands on liquor despite Prohibition. Dry leaders often exaggerated the sins of the liquor trade, but they were rightly outraged when they railed against blind pigs that served youngsters. In Detroit, drinking among students was so prevalent that educators warned parents about the "school pigs" that catered to youngsters. These blind pigs, which were located near schools, opened in upper middle class neighbor-hoods as well as blue-collar areas. Teachers reported cases of drunkenness even among ele-mentary school students.

The principal of the Franklin School told the mayor that blind pigs near his school routinely sold liquor to students. At Cass Technical High School students were required to bring lunch from home or buy it in the cafeteria. Under no circumstances were they allowed to leave the premises during their noon break because they might patronize the nearby school pigs. The principal of the Lyon School said that five blind pigs were located on the same block as her school. She stated that "slow learners" in the special education classes were especially drawn to them. Administrators at the Florence Crittenton Home, a facility for unwed moth-ers, said that underage drinking at blind pigs was "the principal contributing cause" for a dramatic increase in home's caseload after Volstead began.[30]

In Detroit, as in other jurisdictions, raids were a major tool against blind pigs and other illegal liquor outlets. Generally, saloon owners relied on payoffs to local officials to prevent raids or at least buy them a forewarning. U.S. District Attorney Earl Davis stated that Detroit's liquor sellers received advance notice of impending raids, but he didn't attribute this to bribery. He believed that mobsters constantly shadowed the Motor City Prohis and knew their plans. "Despite every precaution we have been able to take," Davis said, "boot-leggers recently have been given full information regarding our proposed raids, even before the search warrants have been drawn up." When raids were imminent, lawyers appeared at the federal building to represent men not yet in custody. Likewise, bondsmen waited at the courthouse to furnish bail for men who expected to be arrested.[31]

Since raids weren't having the desired impact, D.A. Davis decided to use padlocking as a weapon against Motown's illegal saloons. Special Prohibition agents from New York City were sent to Detroit to conduct an undercover investigation to lay the groundwork for the padlock cases. In June 1923 Davis announced that deputy sheriffs and Prohibition agents would serve padlock notices on fifty places, mostly in Hamtramck. "This is the biggest Pro-hibition drive ever attempted in Michigan," an official said. "Now it is our purpose to put on the padlock more tightly than it was ever before applied in any place in the United States."[32]

Despite the padlocking drive, Detroit's illicit watering holes prospered and proliferated. In 1923, the year Davis started his padlock crusade, the Detroit police department said Motown had three thousand blind pigs, but a news report put the number at ten thousand. Two years later Detroit's chief of police said Motor City had at least fifteen thousand illegal liquor outlets. In 1928 *Detroit News* put the number of blind pigs in the sixteen to twenty-five thousand range. According to the newspaper, in some poor neighborhoods every house was either a bootleg stand or a blind pig. The paper's reporters found 150 blind pigs in a single block, but that was well above average. In a twenty-block area, they found roughly five hundred — enough to ensure that a drinker didn't have to walk far for potent refreshment.[33]

Life for a Pint

Michigan was among the wettest states in the Union, even though it had unusually harsh penalties for repeat offenders, including Volstead violators. Michigan's criminal law code had a habitual offender statute that enumerated a long list of minor felonies entailing a life sentence for the fourth violation. During Prohibition, the statute was commonly known as the life-for-a-pint law because four convictions for liquor offenses could send someone to prison for life, even if very small amounts of booze were involved.

Under Michigan's habitual offender statute at least six people received life sentences for Volstead violations. Fred Palm had the dubious distinction of being the first. When Lansing policemen went to Palm's home with a bench warrant for his arrest, a cop spotted a pint bottle of gin, about half-empty. Palm had a serious felony on his rap sheet plus two previous Volstead convictions for possessing small amounts of liquor. The Ingham County Court sentenced him to life in prison.

The harsh punishment outraged the leaders of the Association against the Prohibition Amendment (AAPA), which offered Palm legal and financial aid. With the help of an AAPA attorney, he appealed his conviction. He argued that the police had acted without a search warrant and that his life sentence was cruel and unusual punishment. The Michigan Supreme Court ruled against him, saying, "Experience teaches that the fear of severe punishment is more likely to rid the State of professional criminals than any effort looking to their reformation."[34]

Two other life-for-a-pint prisoners grabbed the public's attention because their rap sheets had only minor Volstead convictions. Channie Tripp, a small-time bootlegger, paid a fine or served a short jail term for his first three liquor offenses. At his fourth trial the jury found him guilty but recommended leniency. The judge stated that the court had no leeway; a life sentence was mandatory under the habitual offender law.[35]

Etta Mae Miller was convicted of a fourth offense on evidence that seemed less than conclusive. Two policemen had staked out Miller's house because she was known to bootleg on a small scale. They saw her hand something to a man in a parked car. When the man drove away, the cops followed him until they saw two pint bottles tossed out the car window. The police retrieved the discarded bottles and charged Miller with selling liquor. At her trial, the car's driver and his passenger were called to the witness stand. They testified they had been too drunk to remember where they bought the booze.

After deliberating only thirteen minutes, the jury found Miller guilty of selling two pints of moonshine. The judge sentenced her to life in the Detroit House of Correction. In contrast, on the same day in the same court, a defendant pled guilty to manslaughter and was freed after paying a fine of only $400.

The press portrayed Miller as the kindly mother and grandmother of a large brood. But rabid dry leaders had no sympathy for her. "Our only regret is that the woman was not sentenced to life imprisonment before her ten children were born," said a high-ranking

Methodist churchman. "When one has violated the Constitution four times, he or she is proved to be an habitual criminal and should be segregated from society to prevent the production of subnormal offspring."[36]

Although the dry fanatics applauded Michigan's habitual offender law, the public in general favored a modification of the statute. In 1929 Michigan Governor Fred Green signed a law removing many minor felonies from the list of crimes that carried a life sentence for four offenses. Under the new law, fifteen years was the maximum sentence for a fourth Volstead violation. In January 1930 Green commuted the sentences of Etta Mae Miller and five others imprisoned under the life-for-a-pint law.

The governor's commutation reduced Miller's sentence but did not void it, so she faced the prospect of another six and one-half years in prison. She appealed to the Michigan Supreme Court, which decreed that she was entitled to a new trial due to an error by the judge who had sentenced her to life. In 1930 Miller was released on bond, pending further legal action. A few weeks later, rulings by the Michigan Supreme Court and the Circuit Court ensured that she would remain free and would not face another trial on the liquor charges.[37]

Miller's fifteen minutes of fame weren't quite over. Her name popped up in the press when her attorney, Seymour Person, ran for U.S. Representative in Michigan's Sixth Congressional District. In the GOP primary Person went up against the incumbent, who was a militant dry and former superintendent of the Michigan Anti-Saloon League. Prohibition was the major issue in the urban district that encompassed a large section of Detroit. Person's wet supporters held a controversial campaign dinner where "wine tonic, bought at a drugstore, was served as a legal beverage containing twenty-two percent alcohol." The arid activists went ballistic, and Prohibition officials promised to investigate the matter. However, most Motown voters didn't share the drys' outrage over a little wine tonic. Attorney Person won the primary and the general election.[38]

20. Detroit's Downriver Rumrunners

In the past there was lively gunplay between smugglers and hijackers, but arms were seldom used against government forces. Now the day has passed when Prohibition officers can shoot with immunity. Rumrunners carry automatic rifles and machineguns — and use them. — James C. Young, reporter[1]

The Detroit River, one of the world's busiest waterways, carried virtually every type of watercraft known to man. Freighters delivered consumer goods and products for industry, especially raw materials for the factories and automobile plants in Motor City. Barges hauled essential goods, like coal and timber. Recreational boaters used the river for pleasure, and fishermen pulled in their catches. Detroit shared the shoreline, roughly twenty-eight miles long, with small towns where many residents relied on the river for their income.

During the Arid Era, a line of buildings called Smugglers Row stretched for several miles downriver from Detroit. Few of these buildings were sturdy, conventional structures. The jerry-built places seemed to pop up on demand along the shore near the downriver towns south of Motor City. Covered piers and underground channels proliferated because the rummers needed places to unload and stash booze. Over time the riverbank became "burrowed as though it were a rabbit warren."[2]

The Detroit River's rumrunners, like their comrades elsewhere, carried guns to fight off hijackers and law enforcement. With scary frequency, shootouts disrupted the waterborne traffic. "After nightfall the river is a no man's land where honest folk seldom venture," wrote a newsman. "It is a dull night when the crack of shots and the flash of pistols fail to mark the great international game of smuggling." The rapid, staccato fire of machineguns became a familiar sound to anyone living or working on the waterfront. When the crew of a booze boat spotted a government patrol boat on the river, the rumrunners sprayed the water with machinegun fire. This kept the Volstead enforcers at bay while the booze boat swung around and raced back into the safe Canadian waters.[3]

When the combatants in the rum war shot at one another, civilian boaters might be caught in the crossfire. Pleasure boaters traveled on the Detroit River at their own risk. Fishermen feared the government patrol boats more than the rumrunners. They complained that the federal Volstead enforcers fired on them without warning. They claimed they were willing to stop for a search, but the trigger-happy feds wouldn't give them a chance to do so. They learned to keep a sharp lookout for the patrol boats and take cover in a hurry.

Liquor poured out the windows when Prohibition agents smashed the contents of an illegal distillery (Walter P. Reuther Library, Archives of Labor and Urban Affairs, Wayne State University).

Naturally, the residents of waterfront towns found the gunplay troubling. Many of them felt that the Volstead enforcers should not shoot at booze boats because the rumrunners were only smuggling liquor. The mayor of Wyandotte stated that Prohibition enforcement was endangering the public and causing great inconvenience. He accused the federal lawmen of lacking both "common sense" and "common courtesy." He said, "Innocent people should be able to use their river without being in constant fear for their safety." The mayor of Trenton also expressed concern, saying there were "too many enforcement boats on the river for the safety of Trenton residents."[4]

The hair-raising gunplay wasn't confined to boats on the water. Sometimes a shootout occurred on the streets or sidewalks near the riverfront. In one incident, rumrunners and border patrol agents fought a running gun battle along Detroit's waterfront. Six federal agents captured a large booze boat from Canada near the terminus of the Ambassador Bridge. The rumrunners, who greatly outnumbered the agents, drew their pistols and fired. The agents shot back. The rummers fled on foot. The combatants exchanged many rounds, but the rummers escaped. In a getaway worthy of an urban legend, several rummers hopped into patrol cars belonging to the U.S. customs service and sped away. Law enforcement later found the cars but not the rumrunners.[5]

Downriver Rumrunning

A large portion of Detroit's rumrunners made their headquarters in Ecorse, a small downriver town. By motorboat, Ecorse lay less than four minutes across the river from Canada. The village had a European flavor due to the high number of immigrant residents who spoke little or no English. Exotic aromas from ethnic cafés wafted through the air and mingled with the acrid sooty smell of Detroit's industrial smokestacks. Shanties and makeshift piers dotted Ecorse's marshy, horseshoe-shaped shoreline. Fishermen and factory workers lived in waterfront cottages and houseboats on the river.

Anybody with a boat and a little nerve could join the rumrunning fleet, which had its "general staff headquarters in a shack at Ecorse." Generally, the rummers picked up their cargo at the liquor export docks in LaSalle, Ontario. Fighting Island lay in the middle of the river on the Canadian side of the border, so a rummer could stop there if he spotted a U.S. government boat patrolling the area. Many of the rumrunners were experienced smugglers who liked to haul booze because it was a low-risk, high-profit commodity. "Before Prohibition these smugglers were bringing in Chinese at from $300 to $1,000 each. But they have ceased smuggling Chinese. Everything else has given way before the great American demand for booze," a newspaper reported.[6]

Ecorse's rumrunners operated with "no more secrecy than if they had been dealing in groceries." In the early Twenties, they routinely sprinted across the river in the daytime, making little attempt to hide their illegal activity. An adventurous reporter rode with a rumrunner carrying a load of whiskey from Ontario to Ecorse in an open boat in broad daylight. At the dock, the newsman helped to transfer the liquor to a bootlegger's automobile. Then he rode with the legger all the way to Chicago. The bootlegger drove on major highways in Michigan, Indiana, and Illinois "without hindrance from any source."[7]

From time to time the federal Volstead enforcers cracked down on Detroit's liquor traffickers. During these drives, Ecorse's rumrunners became more cautious and sailed at night. In the darkness, the rummers waited in Canadian waters for signals from a lookout in Ecorse or on an island in the river. One signaling method relied on whistles, with the sound modulated to convey either a warning or an all-clear message. Another method used red and green lanterns to mimic Morse code. A series of slow and quick flashes told the rummers when to start across the river. Prohibition agents learned the code so they could use lantern signals to confuse and trap the rummers.

Ecorse functioned as a sort of kerb market for the liquor trade. Local men acted as brokers, setting the price for liquor by the bottle, case, or boatload, based on supply and demand. The prices fluctuated from day to day or even from hour to hour. When conditions were very unstable, the prices might change from minute to minute. If bad weather kept the boats from sailing or the Prohis came to town, the supply of booze shrank and prices soared. Even a barroom brawl could raise prices if local authorities called in the state police to prevent more violence. The normal flow of booze was disrupted because the rummers laid low until the state troopers left town.[8]

At night Ecorse's waterfront district, the Half-Mile of Hell, transformed into a lively bright light district where people acted as if Prohibition didn't exist. A trip to the Half-Mile of Hell was "an unforgettable experience, for no gold camp of the Old West presented a more glamorous spectacle," wrote a visitor. "It was a perpetual carnival of drinking, gambling, and assorted vices by night and a frenzied business-like community by day. Silk-shirted bootleggers walked its streets, and it was the Mecca for the greedy, the unscrupulous, and the criminal of both sexes."[9]

Half-Mile of Hell boathouses held saloons that attracted hordes of drinkers, who often arrived by boat. "The odors of beer and liquors ... were more than enough to offset the smell of brackish water that came off the nearby mud flats," a journalist wrote. He went into a boathouse with "a fully equipped bar, with all the ancient traditional furniture of such an institution and the wide variety of drinks that were carried in stock in the days of the legal saloon." To his surprise, the saloon even offered "the time-honored free lunch." He found one thing the old-time barroom never had: "women who roamed the place at will."[10]

Rumrunners and other shady characters hung out in dives on Hogan's Alley, a narrow street that led to the riverfront. The denizens of the underworld drank, gambled, and whored in the dimly-lit shacks along the alley. Rumrunners made deals and sealed them with shots of bootleg whiskey. No one shied away from fisticuffs or gunplay. Hogan's Alley regulars were armed "with ever-ready automatics" and had "no conscience," said a frightened visitor.[11]

Lawmen assumed more than normal risk when they entered Hogan's Alley because the slightest spark might ignite the powder keg. One night in 1928 a full-scale battle broke out between police and rumrunners. About thirty lawmen waited in cars and boats, planning to capture booze boats arriving at the pier near the alley. When a rumrunning boat pulled up to the pier, the law officers rushed the crewmen and arrested them. The arrestees yelled for help. Hogan's Alley regulars, always ready to take on the law, hurried over to rescue their comrades. A mob of thugs threw rocks and bottles at the lawmen. Another group pushed cars across the alley entrance, trapping the gendarmes between the barricade and the river. The lawmen banded together, rushed the barricade, and broke through. They outran the frenzied mob to reach a safe haven. Despite the chaos, both sides of the law showed amazing restraint; no shots were fired that night.[12]

During the Arid Era, Ecorse gained a national reputation as a wide-open, lawless rumrunning center. Civic leaders worried about the village's bad image, so they tried to discredit the press reports about the liquor traffic. "Any statements about rumrunning on a large scale are bunk," declared the village president. Ecorse's chief of police agreed that any rumrunning was strictly bush league. He stated that not more than forty "professional" rumrunners worked along the entire Detroit riverfront.[13] (He didn't say how much booze one had to smuggle to qualify as a professional.)

In July 1923 Prohibition officials decided to stop the downriver liquor traffic by confiscating boats that didn't comply with all government regulations. When the Prohis began seizing boats, furious rumrunners swarmed down to the riverbank. They shouted loud threats, taunting the agents. Fights broke out in several locations, and clusters of lawmen tussled with gangs of hoodlums. The most serious battle occurred on a wood bridge that led to a boat-well where the rumrunners had stashed cases of liquor. Federal agents blocked access to the bridge and tried to fend off the rum pirates. But the rumrunners didn't give up. They attempted to dynamite the bridge, then tried to demolish it with crowbars, and finally set it on fire.

After the riot subsided, the federal agents proceeded with their plan and seized roughly two hundred motorboats in Ecorse, Wyandotte, and Trenton. After customs service seals were affixed to the motors, the boats were towed to shore and placed under guard. Authorities stated that they would hold the boats until the rumrunners agreed to comply with all pertinent regulations. They ordered the rummers to register their boats, so law enforcement could keep tabs on them.[14]

The federal Prohibition director for Michigan pronounced the mass confiscation of boats a complete success. He boasted, "We are satisfied we have the rumrunners on the run at last." He warned the rummers that he would "run every unregistered boat out of American waters." But, like so many enforcement drives, this one had only temporary impact. Some of the rum pirates reclaimed their boats, while others bought new, faster vessels.[15]

In the late Twenties, one of the periodic enforcement crusades made it risky to store liquor in Ecorse. Rumrunners had to quickly unload their cargo, so it could be moved out of town. Generally, bootleggers were waiting in cars or trucks at the dock when a booze boat arrived from Canada. In only minutes, the entire cargo was offloaded to a vehicle that would take the liquid gold to a safe location outside town.

In 1928 Ecorse's most notorious rumrunners were indicted for bribing U.S. border patrolmen. To escape prosecution, the rummers fled to Ontario, where they lived in exile and continued their smuggling from their new home base. The mass exodus didn't magically end crime in Ecorse, but the criminal element was greatly reduced. Smugglers Row became a ghost town after the rummers abandoned their riverfront shacks and warehouses, which were subsequently razed. In the late 1930s trees blossomed in a new county park on the riverfront, replacing the last vestiges of Ecorse's infamous Smugglers Row.[16]

Flagging Zeal

In 1929 *Detroit News* published a photograph of rumrunners landing liquor at a dock only blocks from the headquarters of the U.S. Customs Border Patrol. The photograph, taken with a hidden camera, showed men moving Canadian booze from a speedboat to waiting automobiles. The rummers worked smoothly and quickly. They knew the routine well: it took them roughly three minutes to race across the water and transfer their cargo.

After the booze was loaded in the vehicles, the drivers were ready to roll. One of the rumrunners played traffic cop, stopping all the autos on the cross streets to clear the way for the liquor convoy. When a driver complained about having to wait for the bootleggers' caravan to pass, the ersatz traffic cop threatened to blow up his car.[17]

The newspaper's report clearly showed that the U.S. Customs Service wasn't doing its job on the Detroit waterfront. The public asked why. Customs officials said that the service was understaffed and didn't have enough equipment to enforce the dry law in Motown. A few weeks after *Detroit News* published the sensational photograph, Detroit's collector of customs resigned, citing the agency's tight budget as a major reason for leaving. "I have been faced with many difficult problems, one of the most serious being the lack of funds made available to properly equip the customs border patrol," he said.[18]

The Prohibition policymakers in Washington took note of the dire situation on the Detroit River and, soon after the collector's resignation, announced a new offensive against Motown rumrunners. The national Prohibition commissioner vowed that the illegal liquor traffickers would be forced off Detroit's waterways. "We need only adequate numbers of men and boats, responsible authority, unflagging zeal. All of these needs are about to be supplied," he said.[19]

For the new push, the feds planned a formidable show of force. They would deploy more than forty boats and five hundred enforcers, including Coast Guards and border patrolmen. Approximately two hundred veteran Prohibition agents and inspectors would be transferred from other cities to Motown, where they would operate onshore to support the Volstead enforcers on the waterways. If this buildup proved inadequate, Assistant Secretary of the Treasury Seymour Lowman promised that units of U.S. Marines would also be sent to Detroit.

Lowman, who called the waterways between Lake Erie and Lake Huron the "sore spot" of Prohibition, went to Detroit to put his personal stamp on the crusade. He approved a centralized, modern communications system that enabled the commanders to quickly deploy and regroup their forces as needed. To provide up-to-the-minute intelligence, lookouts were stationed onshore and aboard vessels to monitor the movement of the booze boats. By coordinating the water and land patrols, the commanders expected to capture any rumrunner foolish enough to cross from Canada into Michigan waters.[20]

The rumrunners watched the buildup of government forces on the waterfront and paid informants for the skinny on it. While law enforcement planned its strategy, the rummers schemed to stay in business. Their favorite landing spots would be under surveillance, so they set up new loading and unloading stations at strategic points along the shore. They devised their own intelligence network so they would know where the Volstead enforcers were deployed. If the dry forces blockaded the Detroit River, the rummers would have the option of hauling booze across Lake Erie or Huron. Rumrunners who could afford new boats upgraded their fleets, buying larger, sturdier vessels suitable for the rough waters of Erie and Huron.[21]

When the crackdown began, the dry forces claimed to have "five lines of defense" that were "bristling with weapons" to prevent rumrunners from landing in Detroit. The Coast Guard cutters had machineguns and one-pound cannon ready for battle if needed. The majority of the government cutters were deployed to form a blockade in U.S. waters near Ecorse and Wyandotte. Heavily-armed dry sleuths camped out in the weeds and marshes along the shoreline, watching for booze boats. Other lawmen patrolled the riverfront in cars to nab any rumrunners who came ashore. "From Lake Erie to Lake Huron the patrols cooperate and interlock, turning what was one of Michigan's greatest recreation areas into a battlefield covering 102 miles of water frontage," reported a newspaper.[22]

Due to the dry offensive, prudent rumrunners deserted the Detroit River. They found it safer to ferry their cargos across the St. Clair River or Lake St. Clair, Erie, or Huron. Because the government had transferred boats and manpower to the Detroit riverfront, much of the Great Lakes coastline was unguarded. Along Lake Erie's unprotected shore, rumrunners found it easy to land liquor in Cleveland, Buffalo, Erie, and Conneaut.[23]

Unlike their cautious brethren, the toughest, heaviest-armed rum smugglers vowed to meet the government forces head on. They itched for action, confident they could outrun and outshoot the dry navy. For the first few days of the offensive, the rumrunners and the lawmen stayed on opposite sides of the Detroit River. They engaged in a war of nerves, watching one another, waiting for something to happen. Since the dry navy couldn't cross the border to fight in Canada, the opening gambit must come from the rumrunners.[24]

The first skirmish shattered the peace along the waterfront on June 19, 1929. An hour or so before sunrise, a booze boat sped across the invisible line in the river. When it was only a hundred feet from the Detroit shore, the crew saw a customs border patrol boat cruising downstream. The rumrunners shot first, blasting away at the customs cutter. The border agents returned fire, and the rummers took cover behind cases of whiskey stacked on the deck. With guns blazing, the two boats raced around the tip of Belle Isle. Rummy bullets hit the customs cutter, puncturing the prow above the water line, causing substantial damage. The rummers rushed back to Canada, firing at the customs cutter as they left it behind.[25]

The rumrunners didn't reach Detroit, but they did escape with their boat and their booze. They could ride at anchor off the coast of Ontario while they waited for another chance to jump the line. They couldn't return to Ontario because Canadian regulations forbade them to enter a Canadian port with their liquor after they had cleared for the United States. Their cargo was too valuable to toss overboard without an urgent reason, so they waited offshore. If they were patient, they would find the right time for a mad dash to Detroit.

For two weeks, the dry navy focused on keeping the blockade tight to prevent the alcohol armada from entering U.S. waters. Nevertheless, on multiple occasions, booze boats raced across the river to Detroit. Some landed their liquor and sped away. Others were hemmed in by the Volstead enforcers. The rumrunners generally escaped, but the lawmen seized several boats and substantial amounts of liquor. "Most of our seizures take place on land," explained a customs border patrol officer. "We spot the boats as they pull into the shore. The men on them jump into the river and abandon the craft." He stated that the primary objective was to keep the rum boats from crossing the border. "Our main purpose is to bottle up the stuff in Canada — keep it from coming across. We aren't primarily interested in making seizures. Capturing one or two loads in itself doesn't mean much. It's actually keeping it on the other side that gets results," he said.[26]

On the Fourth of July, safety-minded boaters stayed off the Detroit River because law enforcement predicted the rumrunners would try to deliver booze for the holiday festivities. The dry navy massed its vessels along the waterfront in Motor City. On the Canadian side of the river, eighteen booze boats cleared Amherstburg and lay just offshore, waiting for the right moment to dash to Michigan with the good stuff for Independence Day celebrations. Tension mounted in both camps as everybody anticipated the upcoming battle. If the rumrunners crossed the invisible border into U.S. waters, they would be chased, shot at, and possibly captured.

As the day wore on, four rumrunning crews grew tired of the waiting game. Their nerves stretched to the breaking point, the crewmen dumped their liquor overboard and cruised back into Amherstburg. One booze boat had engine trouble and caught fire, prompting the crew to abandon ship. A boat dashed across the line and tried to land at Ecorse. The

Coast Guard captured the vessel, but the crew escaped. The remaining booze boats bobbed aimlessly in the water, caught in limbo between Canada and the United States. Independence Day was drier than usual in Detroit.[27]

On July 7, fourteen large boats with liquor cargos were tied up at the quayage in Amherstburg. The crewmen watched the movements of the dry navy, knowing they couldn't return to Canada if the Volstead enforcers kept them from landing in Michigan. While the bigger boats waited for an opening, audacious lone seamen ran the dry blockade in skipjacks, rowboats with outboard motors. The skipjacks could outrun the dry fleet in open water and could navigate in water too shallow for the patrol boats. A skipjack carried a small payload, but it could make two or more trips each day.

At night stealthy rumrunners used canoes, painted black, to slip silently across the water and maneuver through marshes where the big boats couldn't operate. "Small loads and lots of them is today's slogan," wrote an observer. "Thousands of small boats are now darting like so many mosquitoes out from the Canadian side of the Detroit River and over to the American side with their loads," an official admitted.[28]

On July 13 the customs border patrol made what it called "the largest liquor seizure ever" on the Detroit River. In keeping with the new normal on the river, no big vessels were involved. Border patrolmen captured a canoe, eight rowboats, and three speedboats in the wee hours of the morning. They arrested five rumrunners, but other men escaped by diving into the river and swimming away. The border patrol estimated that the boats carried ninety-six hundred cases of booze — a remarkably large amount given their size.[29]

Soon after the big seizure, Prohibition officials announced that the dry offensive had eradicated the waterborne liquor traffic around Detroit. This surprised many observers; reliable sources insisted that ten to fifteen large boats were landing their liquor cargos every night. Still, this was a major victory for the Volstead enforcers because 200–300 booze boats had crossed the river daily before the crackdown. Congratulations seemed to be in order. "A few dozen boats, a few hundred men — and a determination to clean up: that was what the situation called for, and as soon as the job was begun in earnest, it proved successful," a newspaper stated.[30]

Just when the Detroit River offensive seemed to be working, Washington eviscerated it by abruptly shifting manpower and vessels to other areas. The reasons for this change weren't clear. Volstead enforcement was always underfunded, and politics played a big part in setting Prohibition priorities. Maybe the Detroit crusade was using too much of the scarce funding. Maybe Detroit politicos didn't want an arid city, or dry leaders were clamoring for Volstead enforcement elsewhere. At any rate, the highly-hyped crackdown petered out about six weeks after it began.

By August 1929 Motown's illegal liquor traffic was once again running smoothly. The rumrunners were routinely landing liquor "at Detroit docks in the heart of the city" in the daylight. Armed men met the boats to transfer the contraband to waiting automobiles. Remarkably, the booze boats were arriving on a regular schedule at 7 a.m., 10:30 a.m., and noon each day. Waterfront workers grew accustomed to seeing the uneventful, routine landings. In mid–August riverfront observers said the liquor runners had been following the three-a-day schedule for weeks with no interference from law enforcement.

After a reporter watched a booze boat unload one morning, he questioned the acting collector of customs about it. The acting collector accused a picket boat crew of disobeying orders and leaving their post to take their boat into the base for fuel. During the boat's absence, the rumrunners had slipped across the river. The acting collector didn't explain why the dry navy was allowing the rumrunners to operate on a regular schedule.[31]

Massive graft was the most likely explanation for why officials didn't stop the liquor traffic on the Detroit River. An informed source estimated that half of the illegal liquor from Canada came into the USA "with the connivance of the customs officials." The customs border patrol in Detroit seemed to be especially amenable to bribery. On a typical night a rumrunner could bribe a customs officer to ensure that no patrol boat bothered him. Sometimes the rummers banded together to buy a "free night" for $500. On a free night, the booze boats jumped the line with no fear of encountering the customs service border patrol.[32]

Periodically, Washington launched investigations that exposed bribery on a monumental scale in Motor City. The Treasury Department sent Lawrence Fleischman, a chief petty officer in the U.S. Navy, to work undercover on the Detroit waterfront. Posing as a federal Prohibition agent, Fleischman collected hundreds of dollars each week in bribes from rumrunners. As a result, in 1928 law enforcement arrested twenty-three customs inspectors, and nineteen rumrunners were indicted for their part in the graft scheme. Most of the rummers fled to Ontario to avoid prosecution, but two of them stood trial and were sentenced to the federal prison at Leavenworth. At trial, all of the customs inspectors were found guilty of accepting bribes.[33]

After the exposé of corruption in Detroit's customs border patrol, the unit was reorganized. Nearly all the border patrolmen resigned or were discharged. In hiring the new patrolmen, the customs service listed honesty and trustworthiness as the top criteria. The new hires were chosen because they showed strength of character and enough backbone to resist bribery. Nevertheless, in less than two years, forty percent of the new inspectors resigned rather than fight allegations of corruption.

In November 1930 federal authorities accused half of Detroit's customs inspectors of accepting bribes or extorting money from rumrunners. Federal officials decided to prosecute thirty inspectors and to terminate forty-five men, who would lose their jobs but would not be indicted. It was alleged that some inspectors did considerably more than take bribes; they actually helped rumrunners transport liquor and load it onto trucks. At arraignment, nine of the customs inspectors pled guilty to conspiracy charges. They were not sent to jail because they agreed to testify against the rumrunners in upcoming trials.[34]

21. Mob Mayhem in the Wicked City

In all the seven seas and the lands bordering thereon, there is probably no name which more quickly calls up thoughts of crime, violence, and wickedness than does that of Chicago.— R.L. Duffus, journalist[1]

More than any other city, Chicago has come to symbolize the bloody, lawless years of the Volstead Era. Pop culture has etched an image of Chicago's violent, rapacious gangsters into America's collective consciousness. Countless books, magazines, movies, and TV shows have told and retold the saga of Al Capone, Bugs Moran, Dion O'Banion, and Chicago's other larger-than-life mobsters. In both fact and fiction, Chicago's gangs were ruthless, brutal, heavily-armed urban warriors. They rode roughshod over the city, using guns and graft to silence anyone who threatened their rule. Graft of gargantuan portions polluted city hall and the police force. Cops on the take seemed to outnumber honest policemen, and dishonest public officials overshadowed those who couldn't be bought. Despite brief periods of reform, Chicago deserved its slot on the top-ten list of corrupt cities. During the Arid Era, the press aptly branded Chicago the Wicked City.

In the final days before Prohibition began, Major A.V. Dalrymple, the top Volstead official in Chicago, sounded confident about drying up the city. "We have made final arrangements to take over the work of nailing down the lid," he said. He would command a force of 250 federal Prohibition agents hired to enforce the dry law in the upper Midwest. He knew he would encounter some resistance, so he expected enforcement to be difficult but not impossible.[2] He had no crystal ball to forewarn him of the crime tsunami that would sweep over the Windy City during the Great Drought.

After eight years of Prohibition, the Illinois Association for Criminal Justice released an extensive study of crime in Chicago. The research proved "the existence of a powerful union of gambling, bootlegging, vice, and political interests" that had turned the city into a mobocracy. Organized crime in Chicago was "powerful in the making and unmaking of public officials." The "real leaders of organized crime" had greater longevity and, in general, more clout than elected officials. "Administrations come and go," the study said, "but the overlord of vice continues in power."[3]

A Joke in Chicago

William Hale "Big Bill" Thompson was firmly ensconced in Chicago's mayor's office when Prohibition began. His critics called him a corrupt buffoon, liar, and malefactor. While those were harsh words, even Big Bill's supporters knew that he would never be voted states-man of the year — unless the election were rigged. Cronyism and backroom deals had long dominated Chicago's rough brand of politics, and Thompson embraced that tradition. He paid lip service to the idea of clean government, but he never pursued reform with any con-viction. Although he had little interest in enforcing Volstead, he said what he was expected to say and publicly vowed to boot Demon Rum out of Chicago. Only the very naïve believed him.

In November 1920 Chicago's superintendent of police resigned due to charges of ram-pant corruption in the force. Federal authorities were investigating reports that city police officers had sold confiscated liquor and had extorted money from barkeepers. Mayor Thomp-son promoted his secretary, Charles Fitzmorris, to the post of police superintendent.

Fitzmorris, who had no law enforcement experience, tackled his duties with the enthu-siasm of an earnest, energetic novice. He vowed to improve the police force by weeding out corrupt, incompetent cops. He declared that "Bolsheviki and loafers" would be "given the gate unless they change their ways." He warned that a major shakeup was in the offing. "There are five hundred cops who won't work for me," he said. "Let them grab their hats for they are going for a rough ride."[4]

After only days on the job, Fitzmorris ordered a city-wide sweep of saloons, poolrooms, and disorderly houses. Squads of police officers spread out across the city to arrest lawbreakers and close dozens of illicit businesses. At the end of the day nearly one thousand people had been arrested. They were packed like sardines into patrol wagons for the trip to the nearest police station. The following night Fitzmorris ordered another round of raids, which pro-duced more than one hundred arrests.[5]

Although Fitzmorris hit the ground running, he soon became frustrated because dif-ferent groups applied pressure on him. He singled out the "reformers and moralists" as the sharpest thorn in his side. The moral watchdogs demanded that Fitzmorris shut down Chi-cago's gambling dens and brothels. They mobilized public pressure until he was forced to assign more than half of his police officers to vice details, mostly in the "black belt." This left him with limited manpower for his top priority, fighting violent crime.

Fitzmorris complained that the criminal justice system didn't help him put felons behind bars. He accused the judges of being too lenient with criminals and allowing them to go free on legal technicalities. He alarmed the legal community by lauding police officers who shot and killed reputed felons instead of arresting them.[6]

Fitzmorris, like many of his fellow police chiefs, felt lukewarm about enforcing the dry law. In Chicago, as in other big cities, local officials tended to ignore the concurrent power clause of the Eighteenth Amendment. When it came to the Volstead law, Chicago's police department delegated the heavy lifting to the federal Prohibition agents. "My policy has been to aid the federal authorities in every way," Fitzmorris said, "but the police cannot be expected to enforce Prohibition. That is a matter for the federal people."[7]

After less than a year on the job, Fitzmorris admitted that Volstead was failing in the Windy City. "Prohibition enforcement in Chicago is a joke," he said. "In Chicago there is more drunkenness than there ever was, more deaths from liquor than before Prohibition, more of every evil attributable to the use of liquor." Despite his efforts to reform the police department, he admitted that his own men were sabotaging Volstead enforcement. He estimated that half of Chicago's five thousand cops were "bootleggers" who expended more energy on their illegal ventures than their police work.

Fitzmorris declared that corrupt city officials aided the liquor traffic, saying the police force was "not the only body implicated in violations of the Prohibition law in Chicago." He also blamed the public for thwarting Volstead enforcement. "Thousands of Chicagoans are violating Prohibition laws every day," he said. The huge number of violators made enforcement impractical in America's urban centers. "Prohibition is not a fact, but a fallacy, not only to Chicago, but to every city of which I have knowledge," Fitzmorris said.[8]

As 1921 drew to a close, Mayor Thompson issued one of his periodic edicts ordering the police department to enforce the dry law. When a reporter asked Fitzmorris why the mayor had abruptly elevated Volstead to top priority, the chief said, "The police department has been busy reducing major crimes. That is done, and now we have to take up this new burden." The real reason for Thompson's change in priorities was probably pressure from the cold water coalition.

In accordance with Thompson's directive to dry up Chicago, Fitzmorris ordered his police force to tighten the lid "until it squeaks." He vowed that he would strictly enforce Illinois' baby Volstead, which was even more stringent than the federal law. He said Chicago would be "so dry that a sponge can be wiped across it without picking up a drop of liquor."[9]

Only weeks after the mayor issued his edict to enforce Volstead, federal Prohibition Commissioner Roy Haynes visited Chicago. He invited Thompson and Fitzmorris to a meeting to make a blueprint for tough enforcement, but they snubbed him. They didn't even show up for the powwow. Hayes forged ahead without them. He promised the Chicago Prohibition unit a larger staff, including fifty more federal agents. "As far as the federal authorities are concerned, we shall stop following the man up the alley who has a pint bottle on his hip," Haynes said. "We are going to go after the source of the stuff, the man who loads up a thousand gallons on a truck and drives off." Under his plan the local police were relegated to lesser Volstead tasks. "The small offenders will be left to city and state authorities," he said.[10]

In 1922 the Chicago police force expended little energy on Volstead because a wave of violent crimes monopolized the department's resources. Shootings, bombings, arson, and labor unrest made headlines with scary regularity. Much of the violence was due to an ongoing war among labor bosses, who recruited "wrecking crews" to intimidate or kill rival union leaders. The overworked police force also had to deal with an epidemic of armed robberies. Chief Fitzmorris stated that he simply didn't have enough police officers to combat the reign of terror.

To beef up the police force, the city council authorized Fitzmorris to hire one thousand additional officers. But it took time to bring them aboard, so Chicago had to wait for better law enforcement. Even after the new officers joined the force, Fitzmorris felt no urgency about enforcing the dry law. As far as he was concerned, solving serious crimes far outranked arresting bootleggers.

Largely due to the crime wave, Chicago's voters decided it was time to shake up city hall. Democratic reformer William Dever became mayor in 1923, supplanting Thompson.

Dever approved of "good, wholesome beer at moderate prices." However, he felt that his duty to enforce the law trumped his own personal views on drinking. He vowed to protect Chicagoans from "poisonous green beer, deadly hooch, or moonshine." He pledged tough Volstead enforcement, arguing that "the only way to get rid of a bad law is to strictly enforce it." He promised to stop Chicago's illegal liquor traffic and keep the city dry until the Volstead law could be repealed or modified.[11]

Mayor Dever appointed a new police chief, Morgan Collins, a veteran lawman with many years of experience. Collins promptly announced the usual "crusade against vice, bootlegging, and graft in Chicago." He stated that any police officer who failed "to suppress commercialized vice, gambling, and bootlegging" would be summarily dismissed. The press reported that "scores of vice dens, saloons, and gambling houses" closed in anticipation of Collins' strict regime.[12]

In enforcing the dry law, Collins drew a sharp distinction between liquor traffickers and consumers. "The Chicago police department has enough to do without stopping citizens to search them for hip flasks and to smell their breaths for an alcoholic odor," he said. "We are too busy dealing with crime to fool with that sort of thing."[13] Chicago drinkers liked his sensible approach. Moderates agreed that he had his priorities straight.

Shortly after Collins became police chief, Mayor Dever's administration cooperated with federal officials in an "injunction campaign" to padlock speakeasies and other illegal liquor outlets. The city had tried padlocks before, but the new strategy called for vastly expanded use of them. In less than three months the U.S. attorney secured injunctions closing five breweries and 135 liquor retailers for up to one year. In addition, city authorities shuttered fourteen hundred illicit businesses of various types. Landlords voluntarily closed many other illegal places, ejecting the tenants in order to avoid a padlock on the property.[14]

At city hall officials congratulated themselves on the successful padlocking campaign, but it was evident that injunctions had the whack-a-mole effect. When one speakeasy closed, another popped up. A Chicagoan who discovered a padlock on his favorite watering hole usually found a familiar face behind the bar at the new oasis down the block. Drinkers suffered only brief spot shortages of powerful potables in the Wicked City.

In 1925 Washington's top Volstead policymakers decided to take a new stab at turning Chicago into the Gobi. A veteran federal agent and administrator, E.C. Yellowley, was appointed to serve as Prohibition director for the Chicago district, which encompassed Illinois, Indiana, and Wisconsin. Yellowley, known as "the ace of mop men," began by cleaning house. He dismissed more than forty federal agents in Chicago and brought in new undercover operatives not known to the local liquor lords.

Yellowley assured Chicagoans that he would go after the bosses who controlled the illegal liquor traffic. "I'm going to concentrate on the sources of supply," he said. "In making the district dry, we'll first get after the manufacturers and quantity distributors. The diversion of industrial alcohol, which is one of the greatest problems, will get early attention.... Same way with withdrawals of bonded liquors — we'll clamp down on them harder than ever. Beer will get plenty of attention, too, right at the source of supply."[15]

Yellowley used raids sparingly, despite their popularity as an enforcement tool. On New Year's Eve, Chicagoans expected the Prohis to stage raids because they had become a holiday tradition in the United States of Volstead. But Yellowley ordered only one raid — on a drugstore where an agent bought pints of gin for a New Year's Eve party. In lieu of the customary raids, Yellowley deployed his agents to visit nightclubs and arrest revelers guzzling alcoholic beverages. But his agents were so easy to spot that drinkers behaved like WCTU teetotalers. Incredibly, the Prohis saw no one violating the dry law and made no arrests.[16]

To reduce the supply of liquor, Yellowley focused on the permit system whereby individuals and companies were licensed to produce, sell, and/or buy alcohol for legal purposes. He revoked the permits of doctors and druggists suspected of prescribing or selling hospital alcohol for non-medical use. He also cancelled the permits of every near-beer brewery and distillery licensed to make industrial or medical alcohol in his district. In order to get a new license, the facility owner had to submit to an investigation and agree to strict terms specified by Yellowley.[17]

Despite Yellowley's pledge to go after the guys at the top of the supply chain, he nabbed minor players in the liquor traffic — mostly doctors, retail druggists, and straw men who fronted for the real owners of the breweries and distilleries. While the Prohis crossed the t's and dotted the i's on the liquor permits, the booze barons did business as usual — keeping Chicago as wet as Lake Michigan.

Chicago's dry leaders and honest officials criticized the Prohis for arresting only minor figures in the city's vast liquor traffic. Federal Judge James Wilkerson complained that petty cases monopolized his court. He chided prosecutors for focusing on "the poor, the friendless and the ignorant, while the big violators get away." The judge was especially annoyed by the prosecution of an elderly farmer who had a small still in his cellar. "I'm not going to send this old man to jail for such an offense while the big violators are running around untouched," Wilkerson said. He sentenced the farmer to one day in the custody of a U.S. marshal.

Judge Wilkerson sounded impatient and frustrated. He wanted to hear important Volstead cases that didn't waste his time and the taxpayer's money. "[T]he Prohibition enforcement officers have brought nobody but the poor, the friendless and the ignorant into this court," he said. "Let them go after the big fellows."[18]

The time would come when Wilkerson would have no reason to complain about the small-fry cases. When the feds finally had enough evidence against Al Capone, the judge would preside over the trial of the biggest big fellow.

Talcum Cheeks

Gabriele and Teresina Capone migrated from a village near Naples, Italy, to Brooklyn, New York, circa 1894. They brought two young sons with them, and their family continued to grow until the poor immigrant couple had nine children, including Alphonse or Al, born in 1899. To support his offspring, Gabriele worked in a grocery store and later opened his own barber shop. Teresina earned money as a seamstress.

After dropping out of school at a young age, Al spent time on the streets, hanging out with other adolescent males who would never be Rhodes Scholars. He joined the James Street Boys, a group of apprentice hoods led by Johnny Torrio, who had natural leadership skills that put him at the head of the pack. In time, both Capone and Torrio graduated to the older, more lethal Five Points Gang.

Capone's friendship with Torrio would last for decades and would be the reason for his move to Chicago. While the boys were growing up in New York, Giacomo "Big Jim"

Colosimo was busy building a vice empire in Chicago's Levee district. Brothels and gambling dens paid for Colosimo's flashy diamond rings and the leather bags full of loose diamonds he carried around. In addition to his illegal enterprises, Big Jim owned Colosimo's Cafe, a nightspot famous for its Italian food and lively atmosphere. Opera singers, showmen, politicians, prizefighters, athletes, and gangsters frequented Colosimo's. Enrico Caruso, George M. Cohan, Luisa Tetrazzini, and John McCormack were among the stars who wined and dined at Big Jim's place.

When Colosimo needed a tough, loyal young man to watch his back, his wife suggested that he hire her nephew, Johnny Torrio, who lived in New York but was willing to move to Chicago. Torrio quickly became Colosimo's top lieutenant. He managed Big Jim's brothels and also opened his own vice den, a combination saloon-casino-bordello. On May 11, 1920, Torrio failed to do his duty as Colosimo's protector. The vice lord was shot to death at his own restaurant. Although the police had several suspects, the murder was never solved. According to one scenario, Torrio himself ordered the hit on Colosimo because the old timer's thinking was too antiquated for the modern criminal world. Big Jim was holding Torrio back.[19]

Around the time of Colosimo's death, Torrio decided to enlarge his vice operations and expand his stake in Chicago's liquor traffic. He needed a partner, so he asked his buddy Al Capone to join him. By the time Capone arrived in the Windy City, he had a long, disfiguring mark on his cheek, which he didn't like to talk about. More than one tough guy claimed that he had etched the scar on Capone's face. He probably acquired it as a young man in a fight at Coney Island's Harvard Inn, where he worked as a bouncer. The press called him Scarface or Talcum Cheeks because he wore talcum powder in a futile attempt to cover the cicatrix. His pals were more politic. They called him Snorkey, slang for a well-dressed man-about-town.

Torrio and Capone saw that Prohibition would be a gold mine for men bright enough, strong enough, and ruthless enough to exploit it. They set about forming a syndicate to control vice and the bootleg traffic in Chicago. Torrio had an aptitude for management, and he wanted to conduct his illicit ventures as a business. He planned to build a crime syndicate far more organized, disciplined, methodical, and efficient than anything the underworld had ever seen.

In a remarkably short time, Torrio's vision of an efficient, powerful crime syndicate took shape. In 1922 the Windy City's police chief warned, "We have in Chicago today an organization of criminals that is becoming better organized every day. How long the police department and other agencies of law enforcement ... can hold this organization in check is a matter that should be of immediate and deep concern."[20]

As Torrio and Capone pursued their criminal vision, their mob grew, and somewhere along the way it came to be known as the Chicago Outfit. The Outfit wasn't the only gang in the Wicked City, but it brutally muscled aside the competition until its power far surpassed that of any other mob. The Outfit forcefully protected its turf, using as much violence as necessary to keep its rivals boxed into small areas of the city. Mobsters who challenged the Outfit lived to regret it, if they had enough time for that luxury before being gunned down.

When Mayor Dever took over, he ordered an all-out war on crime as the keystone of his reform agenda. With newly-appointed chief Collins at the helm, the police force embarked on a series of raids and dragnets to clean up the city's vice zones. In two sweeps, the cops arrested roughly thirteen hundred people at brothels, gambling dens, and other vice venues. Another round of raids on disorderly houses and gambling dens yielded 450 arrestees. To stop illegal liquor sales, the city closed more than four thousand saloons, soft drink parlors, and drugstores in less than two months.[21]

As the arrests and closures mounted, Mayor Dever's supporters lauded him for taking thugs off the streets. However, his critics voiced a familiar complaint: the police were arresting only low-rent hoods. "Jails and station cells already are filled to overflowing with a malodorous crew of cheap thieves, panders, gamblers and small-fry crooks of every description. But the big fish continue at liberty," a newspaper stated. On the rare occasion when a mob boss was arrested, he made bail and walked free in a matter of hours or even minutes.[22]

Despite the criticism, Dever and Collins continued the citywide dragnets. One night in November 1924, the police arrested more than one thousand people in a massive roundup. In a replay of previous sweeps, the dragnet snared no mob bosses. "No one prominent in gun or hijacking circles was taken," a newspaper reported. While the police were busy catching the minnows, criminals committed at least fifteen armed robberies as well as a kidnapping and numerous burglaries in the Wicked City.[23]

Mayor Dever's tough-on-crime policy didn't work miracles, but it did have an impact because it hit the vice lords where it hurt the most — at the cash register. Their illegal profits fell as their clientele went off to jail and had to spend their money on lawyers and bail. The downturn in business prompted Torrio and Capone to seek greener pastures for their illicit ventures. They moved their headquarters west of Chicago's Loop to suburban Cicero, a gritty factory town riddled with illegal bars and gambling dens. A minor mob boss ruled Cicero's underworld until the Outfit arrived. When the hometown hood saw the city mobsters moving in, he decided that Wisconsin would be healthier for him. He beat a hasty retreat, letting the Outfit take over the blue-collar burg, which was soon nicknamed Gangster Town.

Using a combination of bribery and threats, Torrio and Capone convinced the Cicero police to shut down the town's small, dingy gambling dens. Then the Outfit opened its own gambling spots, which offered casino games and off-track betting for horse races around the country. Due to Mayor Dever's crackdown on vice parlors in the city, Chicago gamblers flocked to Cicero to lose their money at the Outfit's new clubs.[24]

Say It with Guns

The Sieben brewery was among Chicago's oldest beer plants, dating back to the 1860s. When Prohibition came, the Sieben family leased the property to a company that claimed to make legal near beer. Lurking offstage, Johnny Torrio and Al Capone ran the Sieben brewery in partnership with Dion O'Banion, a mob boss who controlled the liquor traffic on Chicago's North Side. The brewery operated full blast, more or less openly. Workers went about their business, making beer and loading delivery trucks. Policemen from the local precinct knew about it, and many of them were on the take.

Torrio and O'Banion had a long, tangled history. Torrio had given O'Banion his start in the rackets and then felt betrayed when the Irishman broke away to start his own gang. Even after O'Banion left the Torrio fold, the men continued to have business dealings, which were complicated by mutual distrust and suspicion. O'Banion was an extroverted, aggressive hood who wanted more than his fair share of the illegal pie. His oversized greed and his penchant for violence offended Torrio, who believed in being low-key, tactful, and businesslike. While O'Banion blustered his way through life, Torrio preferred finesse.

When O'Banion offered to sell his interest in the Sieben Brewery to Torrio for a half-million dollars, the two quickly struck a deal. After the sale, the uneasy business partners would go their separate ways. O'Banion talked about starting anew in another state. He said he might quit the rackets and move to Colorado. Torrio salivated at the prospect of adding Chicago's North Side to the Outfit's fiefdom.

On May 19, 1924, Torrio and O'Banion went to the Sieben Brewery for a face-to-face meeting, probably to discuss the impending sale. The meeting proved to be more eventful than expected. Mayor Dever's anti-crime crusade was underway, and graft was no guarantee against a raid. Under orders from police chief Collins, Chicago cops staked out the Sieben brewery while the two liquor lords were inside. The police saw lots of activity around the loading dock, where workers were putting beer barrels on trucks. When the caravan of trucks started to drive away, the lawmen pounced. They seized ten trucks, seven cars, and a large quantity of beer. They also arrested thirty men, including Torrio and O'Banion.[25]

According to mob lore, O'Banion had set up the raid or at least knew about it in advance. His motive was to send Torrio to prison. O'Banion had no prior Volstead violations so he expected to pay only a small fine when his case went to court. Torrio, however, had been found guilty of liquor offenses in an earlier case. With those violations on his rap sheet, he would receive a substantial prison term at trial.[26]

Although gangland gossips repeated this tale as gospel truth, they overlooked salient facts. Not only had O'Banion been arrested for hijacking liquor a few months earlier, he had even more recently been indicted on Volstead charges and was awaiting trial. When the police searched O'Banion during the raid, they discovered that he was carrying his "little black book" which listed the people on his payroll. The list included police officers, politicos, and federal Prohibition agents. If O'Banion had expected the raid, surely he would've left this sensational evidence at home. The bail situation added another question mark. After the liquor lords were arrested, Torrio paid $7,500 cash bail from a wad of whip-out. O'Banion didn't have cash and had to wait for a bail bondsman to spring him. If O'Banion expected the raid, why didn't he have the money to pay his bail?[27]

After the Sieben raid, police chief Collins dramatically accused the liquor lords of "a plot of diabolic cunning to lead dry raiders into a lethal chamber and perhaps to death." A pipeline had been set up to move ammonia from the brewery's refrigeration plant to a room where the windows were hermetically sealed. The cocks on the pipeline were arranged so that "a single jerk of a lever in an outlying part of the plant would flood the room" with ammonia. The brewers planned to trap the police in the sealed room and subject them to noxious ammonia fumes. Upon hearing about the plot shortly before the raid, chief Collins had ordered his men to stake out the plant but not to invade it. Thus, they watched from a safe distance and didn't arrest anyone until the trucks started to roll.[28]

After shutting down the Sieben brewery, the police department's top brass zeroed in on the names in O'Banion's little black book. Three policemen were fired immediately. Many others found themselves under investigation. A federal grand jury indicted thirty-eight people, including several politicians, for conspiring to violate the dry law. A separate indictment accused O'Banion, six police detectives, and twenty other men of Volstead conspiracy.[29]

If O'Banion had cooked up the Sieben raid to send Torrio to the slammer, he didn't get instant gratification. Although both liquor lords were indicted, prosecutors didn't rush their cases to trial. Both were free on bail, so they resumed their daily lives. As they went about their mob business, their mutual distrust and hatred intensified. Mob watchers expected fireworks. Bloodshed seemed certain; the only question was whose blood would be spilled first.

O'Banion had a number of eccentricities, including an unusual hobby for a mobster: he liked to arrange flowers. He could often be found puttering around the florist shop he owned with a partner. On November 10, 1924, as O'Banion was working on a floral arrangement for a funeral, three men entered his shop. O'Banion, who seemed to recognize the men, welcomed them to his store. As he shook hands with one man, the others whipped out their guns and fired. Bullets penetrated O'Banion's chest, throat, and face. Blood splattered on the beautiful, sweet-smelling flowers he loved so much. His lifeless body fell to the floor. The killers exited through the front door.

As a rule, the murder of a liquor lord ushered in mob warfare and more killings, so city officials braced for mayhem. They expected O'Banion loyalists to avenge his death, sooner rather than later. Mayor Dever tried to get control of the situation by ordering "every known gunman in the city to be arrested immediately." He said, "It is time to determine whether organized outlaws shall continue to shoot and rob with impunity or whether decency and order will prevail."[30]

Following the mayor's lead, police chief Collins declared "a war of extermination" on Chicago's mobs. He announced a shake-up in the detective bureau and the formation of "a strong-arm squad of twelve picked fighters." He didn't expect the new squad "to bother with taking prisoners to court but rather to deal out summary justice in the alleys, gang headquarters, soft drink parlors, or wherever they find the most convenient place to fight gangsters with their own methods." Officials predicted there would be "less work for the courts and more for the surgeons and undertakers." Collins' new strategy was branded his Blood-and-Iron policy. The Chicago police force had a new, unofficial motto: "Say It with Guns."[31]

The police investigators assumed that a rival kingpin had ordered the hit on O'Banion. They interrogated the usual gangland suspects, including Torrio. An informant pointed the finger at Frankie Yale (also Uale), a Brooklyn mob boss known to be good friends with Al Capone. Yale happened to be in Chicago and had been spotted at the train station. Police detectives rushed to the train depot to look for him. They nabbed him and a bodyguard as the duo tried to leave town on the Twentieth Century Limited.

Yale, who admitted being in Chicago when O'Banion was shot, said he had come to attend a friend's funeral. The police showed Yale to witnesses who had seen the shooters entering or leaving the flower shop. But the eyewitnesses didn't recognize Yale or his bodyguard. The Brooklyn mob boss claimed he had an alibi for the time of the shooting, and the police had no real evidence against him. They had to let him go—at least temporarily.[32]

Despite the lack of evidence against Yale, mob sources said that he had been one of the gunmen at the florist shop. His accomplices were John Scalisi (also Scalise) and Albert Anselmi (also Anselmo, Anselino, Anselni), hardened sociopaths who had immigrated to New York after running afoul of the law in Italy. The vicious duo had briefly pledged allegiance to Frankie Yale before moving to Chicago. In the Windy City they found robust demand for their killing skills. They worked mostly for the Genna brothers, a family of mobsters with no love for O'Banion.[33]

In gangland Anselmi and Scalisi were famous for the "handshake hit." Anselmi would extend his hand to the victim for a friendly handshake. When the man took it, Anselmi would entrap both of the victim's hands in a vise-like grip and prevent him from reaching for his gun while Scalisi shot him. With a hint of both respect and fear, mobsters called Anselmi and Scalisi the Homicide Squad or the Murder Twins.

Although O'Banion's murder sounded like a textbook example of the handshake hit, law enforcement didn't find enough evidence to prosecute anyone for it. A notation in the Cook County coroner's file said, "Slayers not apprehended. John Scalisi and Albert Anselmi and Frank Yale suspected, but never brought to trial." Most likely, Torrio or the Genna brothers had ordered the hit and Yale had helped the Murder Twins execute the North Side boss.[34]

About eight months after the raid on the Sieben brewery, Johnny Torrio went on trial for the charges related to it. He put up a flimsy defense, and in a departure from the standard scenario for a mob trial, the jury found him guilty. The court imposed a hefty fine and sentenced him to nine months in jail. He was temporarily released on bail so he could get his affairs in order before serving his time.[35]

On January 24, 1925, Torrio went shopping with his wife, and his chauffeur drove them home to their posh South Shore apartment. Mrs. Torrio stepped out of the car first and walked into the building. As her husband exited the car, another auto pulled up beside him. Two men leapt out and opened fire with pistols and sawed-off shotguns. Torrio was hit multiple times, suffering wounds to his jaw, neck, chest, stomach, and arm. The gunmen hopped back in their car, and the driver sped away. Mrs. Torrio somehow lifted her bleeding spouse enough to drag him into the vestibule while they waited for the police.[36]

When the emergency vehicles arrived, Torrio was taken to the Jackson Park Hospital. The police theorized that the shooters were O'Banion associates, avenging his untimely death. Detectives interrogated Torrio in his sickroom, but he suffered the usual case of gangster amnesia and couldn't remember anything. His wife also stonewalled the cops. However, the police obtained some information from Torrio's neighbors who had seen the shooting.[37]

The police believed that the triggermen were George "Bugs" Moran and Hymie Weiss (AKA Earl Wojeciechowski), members of O'Banion's North Side gang. They surmised that Vincent "Schemer" Drucci, another O'Banion henchman, had driven the car. The police arrested Moran but didn't have enough evidence to keep him in custody. As usual, the investigation soon hit a dead end. The police couldn't gather the evidence needed to convict Moran or anyone else of shooting Torrio.[38]

Although Torrio's doctors expected him to die, he slowly recovered. He appeared to be chastened by his brush with death. He showed a new, humbler attitude toward the law. Without fanfare, he went to serve his time at the Lake County Jail in Waukegan — perhaps because it was a safe haven where the North Side gunmen were unlikely to get a good shot at him. He surprised everyone by declaring that he would embark on a new life after finishing his jail term. He planned to move to Italy for a fresh start.

To some extent, Torrio carried out his plan. After serving his time, he lived in Italy for a while, but he didn't make the move permanent. He returned to his old stomping grounds in New York City, where he carved out a niche as a low-profile, yet powerful, player in organized crime. Torrio, in effect, abdicated his throne in Chicago's underworld. Capone filled the vacuum, taking over as the Outfit's head honcho. Torrio never tried to regain control of his old mob. Most likely, Torrio stayed away from Chicago because he both feared and respected Scarface.

Whose Turf Is It Anyway?

Corpses piled up in the Wicked City as roughly a dozen gangs fought for turf in the mid–1920s. The powerhouses were Capone's Chicago Outfit, the Genna brothers, the McDonnell clans, O'Banion's old North Side mob, and the Saltis-McErlane gang. Although the North Side mob declined after O'Banion's death, it still controlled a respectable portion of the bootleg traffic. The two O'Donnell clans were small in number, but they caused a great deal of havoc in gangland. In the early Twenties the South Side O'Donnells, led by Spike O'Donnell, were closely allied with the Outfit and took their marching orders from Capone. Then they declared their independence and set out to wrest turf from both the Outfit and Saltis-McErlane. The West Side O'Donnells, led by Miles and Klondike O'Donnell, earned Capone's eternal wrath by undercutting his beer prices.[39]

On an autumn day in September 1926, a brazen, reckless machinegun attack rattled Scarface to the core. At noontime a convoy of touring cars drove slowly down a city street past the Hawthorn Inn, Capone's headquarters in Cicero. Machine gunners inside the cars fired a fusillade of bullets, strafing the inn and an adjacent building. Windows shattered; bullets ricocheted off walls; pedestrians screamed and dived for cover. Capone, who was eating lunch at the inn's restaurant, hopped up when he heard the commotion. He started for the front door, but his bodyguard tackled him and threw him to the floor. A shooter jumped out of a car and strode defiantly to the restaurant door. Sparks of light flashed from his machinegun as he fired into the room where Capone hugged the floor. When the shooter emptied the canister, he ran back to his car and the convoy raced away.[40]

Although Capone ducked the bullets, he was both shaken and furious. Miraculously, no one was killed in the machinegun barrage, but at least two bystanders suffered injuries.[41] Gangland sources said that the shooter who led the rampage was Hymie Weiss, O'Banion's successor as North Side chieftain. Chicago's mob world and the police force braced for more gunplay. It didn't take a crystal ball to know that Capone would retaliate in the near future.

Three weeks after the machinegun attack at the Hawthorn Inn, Hymie Weiss was walking along the sidewalk with two gangsters, a defense attorney, and a private investigator. In front of the stately Holy Name Cathedral, they paused before crossing the street. Suddenly, a cloudburst of bullets rained down on them. The gunmen were shooting from windows in a boardinghouse across the street. The bullets killed Weiss and one of his henchmen. The other men were wounded but survived.[42]

The police suspected that Capone had sent his gorillas to assassinate Weiss. Of course, Scarface had an ironclad alibi to prove that he wasn't anywhere near the Holy Name Cathedral when the shots were fired. Police interrogations and a coroner's inquest made no headway in finding the gunmen who had killed Weiss and his lieutenant. With gangsters shooting at one another on the city streets, Chicago residents didn't feel safe going about their daily business. In response to public outcry, police chief Collins stepped up efforts to stop the open warfare. He mobilized an army of seventeen hundred policemen and "thirty high-powered cars" to patrol the city streets. He also put the department's "207 flivver details" on standby to help as needed. "If we can put enough policemen in automobiles," Collins said, "sooner or later they will run into an actual gunfight. When they do, they'll be able to get somebody that maybe we can make tell us something." Getting a mobster to talk was a long shot, but Collins seemed to think it was his best bet.[43]

As the corpses stacked up, even Al Capone grew tired of the unrelenting violence. To reassure the public, he held an almost maudlin press conference to share his feelings with reporters. Speaking to newsmen at a Cicero hotel, he claimed that he hated the "butchery" and had tried to convince his rivals to stop the killing. "I don't want to die in the street, punctured by machinegun fire," he said. Holding up a photograph of his young son, he talked about how much he loved his family. He invited his fellow mob bosses to come to a peace conference. "I'll tell them why I want peace — because I don't want to break the hearts of the people that love me. And maybe I can make them think of their mothers and sisters, and if they think of them, they'll put up their guns and treat their business like any other man treats his — as something to work at and forget when he goes home at night."[44]

After Capone's touchy-feely press conference, events moved quickly. About a week later, Chicago's top mob lords met to impersonate diplomats. They agreed on a truce in the gang war, divided the city into territories, and pledged to stay on their own turf. They vowed to keep the peace by forgoing revenge for past murders or shootings.

To a large extent, the mob bloodshed abated. Yet, gangsters don't forgive and forget easily, so neither the one-way ride nor the concrete kimono totally vanished. Despite the truce, "individual sniping and murder continued," wrote a criminologist. The mob chieftains "did not, and probably could not, prevent many conflicts arising among their followers." Guerrilla warfare and rearguard actions replaced Chicago's full-scale mob war.[45]

Truce or no truce, it was always open season on Al Capone. To protect himself, he traveled in a custom-built, armor-plated, bulletproof Cadillac. At least one bodyguard accompanied him wherever he went, and his militiamen patrolled the lobby of the hotel where he lived. Guards stood watch at night while he slept, and he kept loaded pistols under his pillow. According to mob lore, Capone triggerman "Machinegun" Jack McGurn stopped eight would-be assassins in less than four months.[46]

In 1927 former mayor "Big Bill" Thompson returned to the forefront of Chicago politics. He won the mayoralty election, ending Dever's bid for another term to implement his reform agenda. Big Bill, who ran on "a wide-open platform," liked to say he was "as wet as the middle of the Atlantic Ocean." During the election campaign he vowed, "We'll not only reopen places these people have closed, but we'll open ten thousand new ones." With Thompson in charge at city hall, crime flourished and became "steadily worse," according to a report by criminologists. Al Capone found Big Bill's policies to be favorable to his business, so he moved his headquarters back into the city of Chicago, leaving his vassals in charge of Cicero.[47]

In November 1927, roughly a year after the mob lords had agreed on the peace pact, Chicago police noted a hot flareback of gang warfare. They attributed it primarily to a struggle for "gambling supremacy" between Capone's Outfit and the North Siders, now led by George "Bugs" Moran. Capone was also fighting to keep control of the Unione Siciliana, an Italian fraternal order with strong ties to organized crime.

When the underworld truce broke down and gunfire shattered the peace, Chicagoans called on law enforcement to stop the renewed mob war. City officials vowed to take decisive action. Chicago's chief of police detectives announced the formation of ten machinegun squads "to drive the gangsters from the streets."[48]

The police offensive didn't put an end to the mobs, but other factors caused the violence to subside. Most importantly, prosperity seemed to breed content. While the police talked tough, the illegal liquor trade went on as usual and netted huge profits, even for the small bootleg gangs. With everyone making money, gangland enjoyed a new Era of Good Feeling and a rosy glow spread over the Wicked City. Despite Capone's ongoing feuds and the occasional gunfight, Chicago's underworld was almost placid.[49]

Chicago's mob wars proved to be cyclical, with intervals of peace interrupted by periods of violence. In autumn 1928 the police noted a sudden upturn in mob mayhem. Much of it revolved around Capone, who had multiple enemies trying to assassinate him or, at least, cut him down to size. Scarface regarded rival mob boss Ralph Sheldon as the primary threat to his crime-land throne. He kept close tabs on Sheldon, a former ally he no longer trusted. According to gangland gossip, some of Capone's own men were plotting to oust him and elevate Sheldon to boss of the Outfit.[50]

On Chicago's South Side, mobsters Joe Saltis and Frank McErlane had a falling out and parted company, splitting up their gang. Spike O'Donnell and his South Siders poached on turf claimed by Saltis, known as the Beer Baron of the Stockyards. The O'Donnell and Saltis gangs engaged in a series of deadly clashes, gunfights, and bombings. McErlane joined the fight against his ex-partner Saltis, forming an alliance with O'Donnell.[51]

Spike O'Donnell, who seemed to have more lives than a cat, survived at least four attempts to kill him, including a drive-by shooting at his home. In one gunfight, shooters in a convoy of four cars strafed a garage where Spike and his brother were hanging out. When the convoy stopped in front of the building, the O'Donnells returned fire. The cars sped away, then came back, and the gun battle raged on. A bullet struck Spike in his arm, and two bullets somehow made holes in his clothes without puncturing his body.[52]

Spike O'Donnell outlasted Saltis, who had legal problems that removed him from gangland for substantial periods of time. When Saltis was convicted of carrying a concealed weapon, he went on the lam to avoid going to jail. After hiding out for about seven months, he reappeared and served his jail time. Soon after being freed, he was sent back to jail on Volstead charges. After regaining his freedom, he "retired" to an estate in Wisconsin and announced that he had quit the rackets. The police believed he was still involved in liquor trafficking, but his lengthy absences greatly reduced his power in gangland. By 1930 Spike O'Donnell sat atop of the South Side pyramid as the ruling beer baron. But Capone remained the supreme dark power in the Wicked City.[53]

22. Valentine's Day, Chicago-Style

If people did not want beer and wouldn't drink it, a fellow would be crazy for going around trying to sell it. — Al Capone, liquor lord, Chicago[1]

On February 14, 1929, Chicago mobsters turned a holiday devoted to love into a gory bloodbath. The triggermen delivered bullets instead of fancy Valentines, bouquets of long-stemmed red roses, and heart-shaped boxes of chocolate bonbons. The multiple murder repudiated everything the holiday stood for. In the weeks after the massacre, police and crime reporters put forth various scenarios. For the most part, they dealt in speculation. They couldn't identify the shooters or the diabolical mastermind who had planned the hit. Although the motive seemed obvious, they couldn't even be certain about that until they found the killers.

On St. Valentine's Day a black Cadillac, resembling the sedans driven by Chicago police detectives, cruised down North Clark Street about 10:30 a.m. The driver stopped on the street near the SMC Cartage Company, an unremarkable commercial building with a brick facade. Since SMC wasn't a real trucking business, the front window had been painted black to prevent passersby from peeking inside. The front door opened into a garage with a small office and a much larger space used for vehicle storage and maintenance. Wide garage doors opened onto a back alley. The cartage served as a liquor depot for the North Side mob led by George "Bugs" Moran, who had claimed the top spot more or less by default. His predecessors, including Dion O'Banion and Hymie Weiss, had died of gunshot wounds, leaving a leadership vacuum.

After the Cadillac driver parked the car on North Clark Street, four men — two in police uniforms and two in plainclothes — climbed out. The uniformed cops carried sub-machine guns; the plainclothes detectives had stubby shotguns. The driver stayed in the sedan.

The policemen entered SMC Cartage through the front door and saw seven men, presumably members of Bugs Moran's gang, loitering inside. The cops lined the men up along the back wall and ordered them to face the wall. An Alsatian shepherd, tied up in the corner, barked at the strangers. He yanked on his rope and lunged at the intruders, trying to free himself.[2]

Windy City bootleggers knew that Chicago's finest might appear at any time for a shakedown or a token raid. As Bugs Moran's minions stared at the brick wall, they probably assumed the police had come for a payoff or a *pro forma* bust. Like a sudden thunderclap, the cops' guns spit out a barrage of hot lead. Bullets punctured the victims' flesh; blood spurted through the torn skin. The expert marksmen knew to aim at the head and the vital organs. Only a few bullets missed the human targets and lodged in the brick wall. Bodies riddled with bullets sank to the floor. Blood oozed from the gunshot wounds and ran in jagged rivulets on the concrete floor, mingling with the grease and oil stains. One of the wounded men moved slightly. A volley of bullets ripped his head off above his ears. His blood and brains splattered all around him.

Dead were gangsters Peter Gusenberg, Al Weinshank, James Clark (AKA Albert Kachellek), and John Snyder (AKA Adam Heyer, Arthur Hayes, and Adam Myers). The other corpses were John May, a safecracker/auto mechanic, and Dr. Reinhart Schwimmer, an optician/gambler who liked to hang out with mobsters. Despite multiple bullet wounds, gangster Frank Gusenberg was clinging to life by the thinnest of threads.[3]

Outside the garage, several people heard gunfire and looked around in time to see two men in overcoats holding their hands up in surrender as they walked to the Cadillac sedan. They were followed by policemen with their guns aimed at the duo. The cops and their prisoners climbed into the squad car; the driver sped away. It appeared to be another routine arrest in Chicago's never-ending game of cops-and-leggers.

Only one person who heard the commotion ventured over to the garage to investigate. Jeanette Landesman, who lived in the apartment building next door to SMC Cartage, went to check it out. She couldn't see through the blacked-out front window; nor could she open the door. She ran back to her building and asked a male neighbor for help. He muscled open the SMC's front door. Inside the dimly-lit garage he saw a gory tableau: five dead bodies lay on the concrete floor; one crumpled corpse leaned against a chair. The lone survivor was struggling to crawl across the floor.

Landesman composed herself enough to phone the nearest police station, but she sounded far from calm. The desk sergeant who took her call had his doubts about her hysterical tale of dead bodies piled up in a garage. Nevertheless, he told an officer to go check out the building. No squad car was available, so the officer hitched a ride with a telephone repairman who happened to be in the station. Another man who liked to ride along on police calls went with them.[4]

When the police officer arrived at the crime scene, he found Frank Gusenberg still breathing but near death. The officer questioned the mobster while they waited for the emergency vehicles to arrive. Gusenberg managed to articulate a few words as he gasped for breath. After he was transported to the Alexian Brothers' Hospital, another policeman interrogated him. Reports differed as to what Gusenberg had told the police officers. Some claimed he said that cops had shot him. Others said he stayed true to the mobster's code and answered no questions. Everyone agreed that he died without giving the police enough facts to solve the multiple homicide.[5]

Mob boss Bugs Moran wasn't in the garage when the shooting occurred, but police theorized that he had been the primary target. Gangland gossip said that Moran had barely missed being killed. His men were waiting for him at the cartage, but he had stopped at a barbershop for a haircut and arrived at the garage in time to see the phony cops go inside. He beat a hasty retreat to avoid arrest.

Police detectives let their mob contacts know that they wanted to question Moran. The mob boss refused to venture out of his hiding place, but he sent an emissary to the police. The go-between said that Moran "did not know and could not guess either the identity of the killers or their reason." Consistent with the code of silence, the messenger quoted Moran as saying, "We're facing an enemy in the dark."[6]

Despite Moran's guarded message to the police, some newspapers reported that he had accused Al Capone of ordering the hit. A crime writer quoted Bugs as saying, "Only one gang kills like that — Capone's." When Scarface heard this quote, he quipped, "They don't call that guy 'bugs' for nothing." (If Moran did accuse Capone of the massacre, it was a serious breach of mob protocol that he later tried to recant. In 1930 he empathically told reporters he had never blamed Capone for the slaughter.)[7]

Because of the bad blood between Capone's Outfit and Moran's North Side mob, police believed Scarface had ordered the massacre. Capone was wintering in Florida, so he had an ironclad alibi for February 14. However, that didn't preclude his planning the hit. Investigators pieced together a crime timeline and compiled a long list of gunmen who could've been in the firing squad. They interrogated dozens of gangsters and checked out countless leads. Within two weeks, law enforcement issued arrest warrants for at least seventeen men. The police station became a revolving door as the suspects were brought in, questioned, and released.[8]

The Murder Twins, Anselmi and Scalisi, were logical suspects anytime a Capone rival died of unnatural causes. At least three members of Detroit's Purple Gang had been seen in Chicago only hours before the massacre, putting them on the suspect list. Also on the list were several Egan's Rats, who had moved north from St. Louis to join Capone's Outfit. Scarface called them "the American Boys" because they were Midwesterners who didn't fit the mobster stereotype common in pop culture.[9]

The morning after the Valentine's Day massacre, the Cook County coroner hastily convened a blue-ribbon panel to begin an inquest. His investigation showed that the killers had fired roughly two hundred bullets; more than half of them had hit their human targets. Based on the bullet patterns, the coroner concluded that two killers with shotguns stood between two shooters with machineguns. Autopsies revealed that up to twenty bullets had pierced each corpse.[10]

Eight days after the massacre, firemen called the police to a smoky garage on a back alley. There detectives found the smoldering remains of a 1927 Cadillac, like the sedan driven by the phony cops on Valentine's Day. A man, or possibly two, had been using an acetylene torch to disassemble the car, which caught fire and exploded. Witnesses had seen a man run away from the garage. Police learned that he had gone to a nearby hospital, so they rushed over to nab him. They arrived too late; the hospital staff said the man had bolted before his burns were treated.[11]

Although the police didn't find the injured man, they were excited because the garage held promising clues. In addition to the charred car, police found an acetylene torch, a hacksaw, a Luger pistol, a piece of another gun, a siren, an overcoat, and a man's hat. The officers knew the Cadillac could be traced to the dealer who had sold it. They could use the tag on the acetylene tank to identify where it had been purchased and by whom. The owner of the garage could identify the man or men who had tried to disassemble the car. The clues seemed so significant that one law enforcement official boasted the case would "be solved by morning."[12]

Based on information from the hospital, the police identified the man burned in the explosion. The acetylene tank led them to the man who had rented the garage and then sublet it to someone else. All these men had mob ties, but the police didn't accuse them of being the firing squad. They were only minor players, destroying evidence that could incriminate guys higher up the mob ladder. Yet, they had inside information and could lead detectives to the killers.

Only days after the Cadillac exploded, police in suburban Maywood found another charred wreck, a black Peerless sedan. Someone had tried to demolish this car with dynamite but hadn't used enough; the damage was confined to the front end. Like the Cadillac, the Peerless resembled a police squad car. Someone had equipped it with a gun rack and a gong like those found on squad cars. The first three digits of the Peerless license plate matched those on vehicles used by the police detective bureau. Inside the damaged car, investigators found a small notebook with handwritten records of beer sales. It also contained the names of two mobsters, one of whom had been killed in the massacre.[13]

Although the Peerless had been modified to look like a squad car, investigators didn't agree on its relation to the crime. In one theory, the Peerless had not been used in the massacre but was part of an elaborate ruse. The charred Peerless, "a clumsy attempt to confuse the police," had been "planted" as evidence to throw the investigators off the track. Another theory, which posited a two-car scenario, said the Peerless had been parked in the alley behind SMC Cartage during the bloodbath. This fit the stories told by two eyewitnesses who had seen a second police car at the crime scene. The police traced the Peerless through several owners and discovered that the current one had given a vacant lot as his address.[14]

To shorten the lengthy suspect list, police officers showed mug shots of Scarface's henchmen to the eyewitnesses. Based on their reaction to the photographs, the cops hunted for three Capone operatives: "Machinegun" Jack McGurn, Rocco Fanelli, and John Scalisi of the Murder Twins. After the police arrested McGurn, two eyewitnesses looked him over and positively placed him at the crime scene. As Capone's top torpedo, McGurn played a pivotal role in the mob wars, both as a shooter and a target. He had a strong motive for murdering the Gusenberg brothers because they had tried to kill him on more than one occasion.[15]

In a public statement, a mob lawyer defended McGurn and Fanelli, saying they were "goats selected to allow the police to make a showing." An assistant state's attorney disagreed; he declared that the state had an airtight case against Fanelli and would take the mobster to trial within thirty days. But he spoke too soon. Only two weeks later prosecutors admitted that "the charges against Fanelli could not be substantiated." The court formally dismissed the case against him.[16]

A week after arresting McGurn, the police caught Scalisi, half of the Murder Twins. Both gangsters were taken to court to be formally arraigned for the St. Valentine's Day massacre. On a subsequent trip to the courtroom, both entered pleas of not guilty. They were initially denied bail, but after a brief period in jail they were released under $50,000 bond.[17]

While McGurn awaited trial, he denied being part of the firing squad. He argued that he could not have been a shooter because the Gusenberg brothers would've recognized him, whipped out their guns, and blasted away. Veteran crime reporters agreed with him. They said the Gusenbergs would have known McGurn even if he wore a police uniform. The brothers would not have turned their backs and meekly faced the wall, waiting for Machine-gun Jack to execute them.

Of course, McGurn could have planned the massacre and sent other gunmen to do the dirty work. Many mob watchers subscribed to this theory of the crime. Machinegun Jack was a cunning killer, a virtuoso of mob hits, capable of plotting a horrific multiple murder. However, if he only wrote the script for the bloodbath and wasn't at the crime scene, the state might find it difficult to build a strong case against him.

The Wistful Boy Gangster

Jack McGurn was a living legend in gangland, revered as Capone's master hit man, "the professional killer's killer." He generally carried a revolver, but he was called "Machine-gun Jack" or "the Machine Gunner" because he was ambidextrous with a Chicago chopper, shooting it with lethal precision either right- or left-handed. Both his mental and physical reflexes operated at lightning speed, giving him an advantage in any gunfight. He was physically fit but not muscle-bound. He wore three-piece business suits and slicked his wavy hair down in the popular Twenties style. A crime writer dubbed him "the wistful boy gangster," adding an aura of vulnerability to his tough-guy image.[18]

McGurn was born Vincenzo Gibaldi (also Gebardi or Gebhardi), most likely in Licata, Italy, in 1902. At age four he came with his mother to the United States, according to a ship's manifest of alien passengers submitted to immigration officers at Ellis Island. However, as an adult McGurn claimed to be a native-born U.S. citizen. When interrogated by the head of the U.S. naturalization bureau, he stated that he was born in Chicago in 1903. He said his father was an Italian immigrant who became a naturalized U.S. citizen. The naturalization bureau didn't take McGurn into custody and he was not deported, so he may have had some documentation to support his claim. Confusion about the names of immigrants entering the USA was commonplace at Ellis Island, so all manifests were suspect in that respect. The most compelling evidence that McGurn was born in Italy was a brief birth notice that appeared in an Italian newspaper, but that was not an official document.[19]

McGurn was blessed with natural athletic talent that gave him more options than the average boy living in the tenement district. In his teen years, he learned the basics of boxing and golf. Boxing was a popular activity for poor boys, but golf was a country club sport too costly for the lower class. Most likely, McGurn learned to play golf by working as a caddy. Gifted prizefighters earned fame and fortune, so McGurn focused on that sport as his road to wealth. Because he had real potential, he was lucky enough to find a sponsor to help him get started in the fight game. Since Irish boxers were respected in the ring, he changed his name to Jack McGurn. He trained and fought in the Chicago area in the early 1920s, before he found his true calling.

According to mob lore, McGurn's stepfather, an alky cooker and small-time bootlegger, was targeted by Black Hand goons. A trio of Black Hand thugs demanded money from the stepfather and threatened to harm his family if he didn't pay up. When they came to collect the money, he defied them and refused to pay. He was gunned down on the street. Young McGurn stepped up to the plate as the new male head of the household. In accordance with Sicilian tradition, he swore to avenge his stepfather's death. He bought an air rifle, learned to shoot, and graduated to a revolver with dum-dum bullets. He spent months stalking his stepfather's killers, waiting for the right moment to shoot them. One at a time, he took them out.

Chicago newspapers reported the three homicides and stated that police had few clues and little hope of finding the shooters. Al Capone read the articles about the murders of the three Black Hand hoods. He realized that the killings were connected and were the work of a single, very talented gunman. When he made discreet inquiries in the underworld, he learned that McGurn had reason to kill the Black Hand trio. Scarface sent for McGurn and offered him a job as a hired gun.

Although this mob tale is intriguing, a look at the early careers of the two mobsters suggests a more prosaic, and probable, connection between them. In the early 1920s the sports pages of Chicago newspapers identified Al Capone as a boxing manager/promoter. During this same timeframe McGurn was trying to make it as a professional boxer. With both of them in the fight game in the same city, their paths undoubtedly crossed.[20]

Regardless of how McGurn became part of Capone's Outfit, he soared to mob stardom by being a remarkably accurate, cunning assassin. He earned an underworld halo as a gutsy, never-fail torpedo. He could've been dubbed the "Teflon torpedo" if the nonstick coating had been invented in the Twenties. Although he was reputed to be Chicago's busiest hit man, he had a very short rap sheet and spent remarkably little time in jail or in the court-room. Based on a report by the Cook County coroner, a crime writer deduced that Machine-gun Jack had killed twenty-two of his peers by 1930. Yet he had never been convicted of murder.[21]

McGurn was both a topnotch hit man for Capone and a high-value target for other mobs. More than one jealous rival wanted to see Machinegun Jack's name on a tombstone. In the spring of 1928 he survived two very public attempts on his life. In the first, he was chatting with a pal in the smoke shop at the McCormick Hotel. Two armed men, one carrying a submachine gun, stormed into the shop and began firing. McGurn flattened his body against the wall and jerked two revolvers out of his coat. Before he could shoot, bullets hit him in the arm and chest. He suffered serious wounds and the shooters got away, but he survived.

Only weeks after the attack in the smoke shop, McGurn was driving along a city street when he heard the familiar sound of machinegun fire. Believing the bullets were meant for him, he slouched down in his car seat, keeping his head out of sight until the gunfire stopped. Frightened bystanders called the police. When the cops arrived, they found McGurn's car riddled with bullets, but he had fled the scene. Since he was able to run away, the police assumed he had only minor wounds.[22]

Although McGurn grew up in a poor family, he fit into middle-class America better than most mobsters. In some respects, he led a double life. He dressed stylishly, but not flamboyantly, and looked more like a young businessman than a gangster. Somewhere along the way, perhaps while working as a golf caddy, he picked up the polish needed to mingle with the country club set. He owned part interest in a golf course, played well enough to enter tournaments, and talked about "turning pro." According to some sources, he played under an alias in at least one U.S. Open Championship.

Police once arrested McGurn while he was competing in a golf tournament as Vincent Gebardi. A police detective reading the sports page saw Gebardi's name among the golfers in the Western Open Championship at Olympia Fields in Chicago. He knew Gebardi was a variation of McGurn's real name. He also knew there was an outstanding arrest warrant for McGurn under the "criminal reputation law," which allowed police to take known mobsters into custody on petty charges, like vagrancy. A squad of policemen headed out to the golf course to arrest Machinegun Jack.

The cops found McGurn on the seventh green, one under par for the first six holes. He listened calmly as a police lieutenant read the warrant to him; then he politely asked if he could finish the round. As he headed for the next tee, the police fell in behind him. He shot a double-bogey six on the seventh hole. At the eighth hole, a newspaper photographer moved in close, snapping pictures. McGurn, clearly annoyed, shot a humiliating seven over par on that hole.

Grabbing the photographer's shirt, Machinegun Jack growled, "You've busted up my game!"

The photographer backed off. Having vented his anger, McGurn regained his composure and played well on the remaining holes. However, he scored too high to make the cut.

On the eighteenth green, McGurn said good-bye to his golfing buddies. With two cops squeezed into the rumble seat of his car, he drove himself to the highway police station. Reporters followed his car and crowded inside the station, where he was booked and held for interrogation.

While chatting with reporters, he quipped, "Just put it down that I'm booked for carrying concealed ideas."[23]

Jack's Blonde Alibi

When Chicago policemen went to arrest Jack McGurn for the Valentine's Day massacre, they found him at the upscale Hotel Stevens, where he had been living for about two weeks. He was sharing a luxury suite with his girlfriend, Louise "Lulu Lou" Rolfe. The hotel staff said that McGurn rarely went out and they had never seen Rolfe leave the hotel. The cocooning couple lived quietly, treated the staff politely, and ordered their meals from room service.[24]

The police questioned the couple about their whereabouts on February 14. The lovebirds said they had spent a romantic Valentine's Day in their suite. McGurn claimed he had been there all day on February 14; Rolfe agreed that he hadn't left her side. (Later they changed their story slightly, saying that McGurn had left the suite in the afternoon. Some hotel workers remembered that he had gone out on Valentine's Day, but they couldn't pinpoint the time.)

The police arrested McGurn for the Valentine's Day slaughter and took Rolfe into custody as an accessory to murder. McGurn was locked up in the Cook County jail, and Rolfe was held in the women's quarters at the police station. Investigators had no evidence against her, but holding her put extra pressure on Machinegun Jack. He would have more than his own skin to worry about.

When reporters heard that Machinegun Jack's girlfriend was in police custody, they rushed to interview her. She clearly charmed one newsman, who described her as "modish, sophisticated, slender, and bejeweled." He wrote that the young divorcée carried "herself confidently" without being brash. Her makeup was subtle and her fashionable frock was modest, not at all revealing. She wore a simple black crepe dress with a white lace collar and "touches of white at the wrists." Her jewelry consisted of a string of pearls, an emerald-cut diamond ring, and a delicate gold ankle circlet, called a "slave bracelet." The reporter said she was "not the mother type" although she had "a touch of wistfulness that is not so alien to motherhood." (In fact, she had a young daughter but spent little time with the child.)[25]

After being arraigned, Rolfe paid her bail and left the courthouse. She was never indicted on any charges related to the St. Valentine's Day massacre. However, she was important because she could testify for McGurn if the case went to trial. The press branded her the gunslinger's "Blonde Alibi" since she had been with him on Valentine's Day.

Hop Toad and the Murder Twins

Just before daylight on May 8, 1929, police in Hammond, Indiana, found a ditched car at Spooner's Nook, an isolated lover's lane on the outskirts of town. Inside the auto they discovered two dead bodies wrapped in blankets. A third battered corpse lay nearby in the underbrush. The victims had bullet wounds as well as broken bones and numerous deep bruises. Reporters who came to cover the story identified the dead men as Joseph "Hop Toad" Guinta and the Murder Twins, Scalisi and Anselmi.[26]

The coroner found that the dead men had been shot and severely beaten with a long weapon, such as a club or baseball bat. He stated that up to four attackers had surprised the victims, giving them no chance to defend themselves. "The three men apparently were seated at a table when their killers surprised them," the coroner said. "Scalisi threw up his left hand to cover his face and a bullet cut off his little finger and crashed into his eye." Another bullet lodged in his jaw, and he tumbled out of his chair.

The killers had quickly crippled Anselmi and Guinta "with bullets in the body," the coroner said. When the victims fell on the floor, their assailants stood over them and fired several more shots into their lifeless bodies. Someone transported the corpses to Spooner's Nook. Two were left in the abandoned car, and the third was tossed out like a bag of garbage.[27]

As usual, there were multiple theories of the crime but little evidence. Police began their investigation with the most obvious scenario: North Side mob boss Bugs Moran had avenged the Valentine's Day slaughter by killing a trio of Capone captains. Although this was the logical starting point, investigators had few clues to pursue. They didn't even know where the crime had happened. Hammond was near the Indiana-Illinois state line and the victims were from Chicago, so the murders could have occurred in either state.[28]

One theory of the crime posited robbery as the motive for the killings. The three victims had been soliciting money from individuals and businesses for a $100,000 fund to pay for Scalisi's defense in his upcoming trial for the Valentine's Day massacre. Since the trio had collected a sizeable amount of cash, the killers might've been after that money. In a variation on this scenario, the victims had roughed up someone who refused to donate to the defense fund; this person retaliated by killing them. Another explanation said the murders were "evidence of goodwill toward Chicago police" because the three mobsters would no longer plague the city. Who made this gruesome goodwill gesture was unknown.[29]

In Chicago's Little Italy, mob watchers favored a scenario that focused on the constant tug-of-war over the Unione Siciliana. In the beginning, the Unione Siciliana was a benign ethnic association, similar to fraternal orders like the Elks or the Odd Fellows. However, over time, it was subverted by mobsters who used it as a front for their illegal ventures. Al Capone was Chicago's supreme crime lord, but he could only be the power-behind-the-throne in the Sicilian club because Naples was his ancestral home. The Sicilian Aiello clan, led by Joe Aiello, fought Capone for control of the Unione because they didn't want Scarface's puppet in charge.

Murder victim Hop Toad Guinta was a newcomer who had moved to Chicago less than two years before his death. Capone had imported the young man from New York to groom him to run the Unione Siciliana at some point in the future. As often happened in gangland, gunfire created sudden vacancies in the executive office suite. So Guinta's promotion to the Unione's top spot came sooner than expected. During his tenure, Scalisi and Anselmi served as vice-presidents of the Unione.

Several months before his death, Guinta had represented the Chicago chapter of the Unione at a mob summit in Cleveland. Dozens of top-tier hoods from New York City, Buffalo, Detroit, Chicago, St. Louis, Tampa, and New Jersey assembled for the conclave. The meeting was a sort of strategy planning session for the future of the mobs. Gangland sources said the delegates divided into two factions — those who wanted a strong, national organized crime syndicate and those who favored a decentralized structure where the local gangs had autonomy. The summit was derailed when Cleveland police learned about it and arrested nearly two dozen visiting mobsters. The hoodlums quickly made bail, and everybody left town in a hurry.

Guinta and the Murder Twins firmly opposed the idea of a unified national crime syndicate. Their resistance netted them powerful, ruthless enemies willing to kill to further their agenda. On the night of the murders, the three victims were lured to an Indiana road-house by associates who saw them as obstacles to a strong national crime cartel. Their hosts "greeted them with kisses of brotherhood and welcome." All the mobsters sat down at a table laden with good food and fine wine. While the unsuspecting victims were feasting, one of the killers gave a signal to his co-conspirators. The murderers attacked their victims first with their fists, and then the guns roared.

In yet another theory of the crime, an agreement among Chicago mob bosses led to the savage triple homicide. Capone wanted to negotiate a new peace treaty for gangland, but the other mob chieftains refused to bargain until Anselmi, Scalisi, and Guinta were rubbed out. The three had to be eliminated because they had violated past peace pacts and couldn't be trusted. Under gangland's code, their own mob had to execute them. At a meeting of Chicago's most powerful crime lords, Scarface agreed to sacrifice his underlings. Only days later, the bloody deed was done, with Capone's blessing.[30]

In a scenario akin to a Shakespearean tragedy, unbridled ambition spawned the triple murder and Capone himself beat the victims to death. Anselmi, Scalisi, and Guinta were cunning professional criminals with visions of grandeur. Capone expected Guinta to do his bidding, but Hop Toad had an independent streak. Guinta met with Joe Aiello, Capone's rival in the Unione Siciliana, to plot a coup. When Scarface heard about the scheme, he invited Guinta and the Murder Twins, along with his other top henchmen, to a party at the Hawthorn Inn. After the guests drank generous amounts of the Outfit's best booze, Scarface accused Scalisi, Anselmi, and Guinta of betraying him. While his minions prevented the three from running away, Capone beat them to death with a baseball bat.[31]

With so many theories and so little evidence, prosecutors couldn't take the case to court. No one was ever convicted of killing Hop Toad and the Murder Twins.

And Then There Was One

After Scalisi's sudden death, McGurn stood alone as the only man indicted for the Valentine's Day massacre. From law enforcement's perspective, the importance of convicting Machinegun Jack could hardly be overstated. Capone's top gun had an aura of invincibility. He dodged bullets and the police with the greatest of ease. Despite all the notches on his gun, he had never faced the gallows or even a long prison term. Shattering his invincible shield would prove that law enforcement had the upper hand. The police would have something to crow about. Chicago would be a safer city. Congratulations, and boldface headlines, would be in order when the state's attorney sent McGurn to prison.

The state's attorney's office sounded very confident about the evidence against McGurn. An assistant state's attorney declared that Machinegun Jack's alibi for the morning of February 14 had been "smashed." In response to questions from the press, he gave few details. However, officials admitted that law enforcement had tapped telephones used by the Capone mob. The intercepted calls included conversations between McGurn and other men, including Capone. The mobsters used code words to transmit messages, but the police said they had cracked the code and the tapped calls disproved McGurn's alibi.[32]

Although the state claimed to be eager to prosecute McGurn, the legal process moved slowly. His case was repeatedly slated for trial, but at each hearing the state asked for more time to prepare. McGurn's lawyers objected to the delays, citing the Sixth Amendment right to a speedy trial. In October 1929, the prosecution asked the court for another continuance. The judge granted the state's request and rescheduled the trial for December. He also empathically warned that no further delays would be tolerated.[33]

On December 2, 1929, an assistant state's attorney told the court that he didn't have enough evidence to convict McGurn. He said the prosecution's case revolved around Scalisi and McGurn acting together. Due to Scalisi's death, the state had no choice except *nolle prosequi*, a Latin term meaning that the prosecution wouldn't pursue the case any further.

With a smile lighting up his face, McGurn bounced out of the courtroom! His invincible shield had worked again.[34]

Skeptics said the prosecution had used Scalisi's demise as an excuse for its own ineptitude. The state had simply failed to build a provable case against McGurn. The police had interrogated dozens of mobsters and scores of potential witnesses. They had collected and analyzed evidence, using the most advanced technology available. However, they had gathered little evidence that would stand up in court. Crime reporters wrote that law enforcement had no hope of solving the Valentine's Day massacre. They predicted that no one would go to prison for the horrendous crime.

Déjà Vu, Valentine

On February 14, 1929, a gang of gunmen delivered a brutal, bloody Valentine to Bugs Moran's North Side mob. Seven years later someone who didn't bother to sign his name gave Jack McGurn a Valentine's Day card reflecting the hard times of the Great Depression.

On the card's cover, a man and woman stood in their underwear in front of a house with a "sold" sign. Inside the sentiment read:

> You've lost your job.
> You've lost your dough, your jewels and cars, and handsome houses.
> But things could still be worse, you know —
> You haven't lost your trousers.

Police found this card, soaked with blood but still readable, beside Machinegun Jack's dead body. The unsigned card was addressed to McGurn. It might have been given to him earlier in the day, or it might have been left by his killers to add a touch of black humor to the hit.[35]

McGurn always enjoyed sports, and in the 1930s he added bowling to his favorite pastimes. He joined a bowling league and became a regular at the Avenue Recreation Rooms on Milwaukee Avenue. Shortly before midnight on February 14, 1936, McGurn and two other men arrived at the bowling alley on the second floor of the building. All the lanes were being used, so they signed their names to a score sheet and waited. A short time later, three men entered and made a beeline for McGurn.

"Stick 'em up!" one of the newcomers barked, brandishing a gun. "Stand where you are!"

McGurn stood still, his back to the intruders. Without warning, they opened fire with .45 caliber pistols. Bowlers scrambled for cover, although they weren't really in danger. The shooters had only one target—Machinegun Jack. A bullet struck him behind the right ear; another lodged in his lower neck. He collapsed in a crumple on the floor. The shooters backed away; then ran down the steps into the darkness. Nearly all the bowlers followed them, leaving the crime scene virtually deserted.[36]

Before joining the mass exodus, McGurn's two companions straightened out his lifeless body, leaving him face-up on the floor, with blood oozing from the back of his head to make a crimson halo. As his pals headed for the door, one of them grabbed the score sheet with their names on it.

When the police arrived, the bowling alley was as quiet as a morgue. McGurn, always a snazzy dresser, seemed to be waiting for the press photographers. Although his head rested in a pool of coagulating blood, the front of his clothes had no splatters or rips. Stretched out on the floor, he looked eerily dapper in his gray vest and slacks, linen dress shirt, red tie, red suspenders, and pearl gray spats.[37]

The owner of the bowling alley told police that his customers had fled as soon as the shooting stopped. He said that McGurn was a regular but the gunmen were strangers. He didn't recognize McGurn's companions or the shooters. Police suspected that McGurn's pals were "finger men" who set him up for the hit. After all, no one shot at them.

Seven men had been killed in the St. Valentine's Day massacre, and seven years later McGurn was shot to death. However, if the killers meant to hit him on Valentine's Day, they were a little late. The coroner's report pinpointed the time of death as 12:02 a.m., February 15, although some sources stated that it was closer to 2 a.m.

McGurn's violent death surprised almost no one because he had made lots of enemies in gangland. Many men wanted to kill Machinegun Jack to avenge the death of a pal or a family member. There were "plenty of people with reason to bump him off," a police captain said bluntly.[38]

McGurn's wife and mother were mourners-in-chief at the simple funeral attended by his family and a cluster of friends. His body was buried at Mount Carmel Cemetery in suburban Hillside. His final resting place already sheltered the remains of several gangland friends and foes, including one victim of the St. Valentine's Day massacre. McGurn was afforded an honor many gangsters didn't enjoy. He had never been convicted of a serious crime, so his body was buried on consecrated ground in the graveyard.[39]

The men who shot the professional killer's killer were never brought to justice. It was the same old story: the police had few clues and the investigation petered out. Perhaps McGurn would've wanted it that way. He believed in personal revenge, and he had little respect for the police. His career seemed to prove the impotency of the criminal justice system. He killed people but never faced a jury on homicide charges. He spent brief periods in jail, but he never served hard time. Unlike most Volstead Era gangsters, he never did time in a federal prison. All in all, he fared well for a professional gunslinger in the Wicked City.

McGurn started out to be a famous boxer but became a gangland celebrity instead. Ironically, after his death, sports fame finally came his way. The press gave the nickname "Machinegun Jack McGurn" to an outstanding Big Ten football player, a fullback named George McGurn. It's a safe bet the original Machinegun Jack would've smiled to see his name in the sports headlines.

Gunpoint

No one ever went to prison for the St. Valentine's Day Massacre, but police did have strong ballistics evidence against one suspect. On December 14, 1929, in St. Joseph, Michigan, a drunk driver rammed another car. The accident happened near the police station, and an officer hurried over to investigate. The driver who was hit demanded five dollars to repair his car. The drunk refused and drove away in his Hudson coupe. The cop jumped on the running board of the other car, and the driver took off, chasing the Hudson. When he caught up with the Hudson, he forced it to the curb and the police officer approached the drunk driver. What seemed like a minor incident suddenly turned deadly. The drunk pulled out a pistol and shot the lawman at close range.

The shooter sped away, leaving the wounded officer on the street. On a sharp curve the drunk lost control of his Hudson, crashing it into a telephone pole. He continued on foot until he was able to hijack a car at gunpoint. A little farther down the road, he hopped out of that car and hitched a ride with an acquaintance who happened to drive by. The police officer died a few hours after the shooting.[40]

Law enforcement set up roadblocks and launched an all-out search for the drunk driver. A deputy sheriff found the wrecked Hudson coupe, and papers inside the car led him to a residential address. When lawmen searched the house, they discovered that gangster Fred Burke, an exile from Chicago, lived there. Burke stood out as the smartest, and probably the deadliest, of Al Capone's American Boys. His pals called him "professor" because he was interested in science, especially chemistry and metallurgy. He spent a great deal of time reading science textbooks. He also liked detective novels and treated them as crime texts, underlining the criminal's blunders and writing notes in the margins. He had specialized criminal skills, including safecracking and wiretapping. When committing a crime, he liked to wear a disguise or a costume, such as a police uniform.

Lawmen searching Burke's home forcibly opened a locked closet door. Inside they found a small arsenal of guns, hand grenades, bulletproof vests, and teargas bombs. The cache included two Thompson machineguns plus clips and drums. The search of the house also netted nitroglycerin and nearly $320,000 in stolen bonds.

Burke was a suspect in the Valentine's Day massacre, so the guns and ammo were sent to Chicago for ballistics testing in the city's new cutting-edge crime lab, which had opened a few months after the slaughter. Colonel Calvin Goddard, the nation's foremost ballistics expert, fired hundreds of test bullets from Burke's guns. Using a recent innovation, the comparison microscope, Goddard contrasted the markings on the test bullets with those extracted from the massacre victims.[41]

When Colonel Goddard finished his analysis, the coroner convened a jury to hear the expert testimony. Goddard stated that Burke's machineguns had been used in the Valentine's Day bloodbath. Based on the ballistics, he could say, with certainty, that Burke's guns had killed Dr. Schwimmer and gangster James Clark.[42]

The Chicago police had good reason to arrest Burke, but so did other jurisdictions. He was wanted for roughly a dozen murders, including a mob hit in New York City and the death of the police officer in St. Joseph. He was a suspect in major robberies in Ohio, Kentucky, Indiana, California, New Jersey, and elsewhere. Spurred on by the new evidence against Burke, law enforcement ramped up a nationwide manhunt for him, with a large reward for his capture.

Burke, who had extensive experience in evading the police, wasn't easy to find. Acting on a tip, lawmen finally nabbed him in Milan, Missouri, in 1931, more than two years after the Valentine's Day massacre. He was hiding out in a farmhouse with a teenage girl he had recently wed. Michigan's attorney general quickly filed extradition papers, beating other states to the punch. The governor of Missouri turned Burke over to Michigan authorities so he could be prosecuted for killing the police officer in St. Joseph. The other jurisdictions would have to wait their turn.

Investigators from Chicago traveled to Michigan to interrogate Burke about several crimes, most notably the Valentine's Day murders. They obtained no useful information from him. He gave flippant answers and even denied knowing Al Capone. At his Michigan trial he pled guilty to second-degree murder and was sentenced to life in Marquette Prison. He died of heart failure in 1940, although arguably his heart had failed much earlier. He never made a confession or any other public statement about his role in the St. Valentine's Day massacre.[43]

In 1935 bold newspaper headlines trumpeted "the true story" of the massacre. The reports were based on tales told by Byron Bolton, a former Capone lackey who was in FBI custody on a kidnapping charge. Bolton confessed to playing a minor role in the slaughter. Before the massacre, his superiors had given him mob money to buy a Cadillac touring car. At the time, he believed the auto would be used for hauling whiskey, but it was really needed for the massacre. Bolton claimed that buying the car had been his only role in the crime, but he was probably lying. Soon after the massacre, Chicago police had found evidence that lookouts, including Bolton, had watched SMC Cartage from across the street. They had given the firing squad the green light when the Moran mob went into the garage.[44]

Bolton identified Capone operatives Fred Burke, Ray Nugent, Bob Carey, Fred Goetz, and Gus Winkler (also Winkeler) as the men who committed the massacre. Bolton's account generally rang true, although some parts contradicted known facts. The most glaring error was his assertion that the killers didn't wear police uniforms. He claimed that they had police badges but were dressed as civilians; yet eyewitnesses stated that two of the men wore police uniforms.[45]

Consistent with the FBI policy of refusing to comment on investigations, FBI officials wouldn't confirm media reports that Bolton had confessed to the Valentine's Day massacre. The FBI stayed focused on its kidnapping investigation and showed no interest in the old murder case. Chicago officials complained that the feds weren't helping them find the Valentine's Day gunmen, but in actuality they showed scant interest, too. Burke was locked up for life. Goetz and Winkler were dead, shot in what appeared to be mob hits. Carey had killed himself and his wife in a murder-suicide. Nugent had disappeared in Florida, and authorities believed he was dead.[46]

The cold case went back into the deep freeze. From time to time, crime writers, amateur detectives, and gangland sources claimed to know the identity of the gunmen who killed the North Side mobsters. But it was far too late to prove the case in court and punish the shooters. The St. Valentine's Day massacre will always be the perfect crime in the sense that the perpetrators got away with it.

23. Uncle Sam versus Scarface

Who's Al Capone? To me, he's just a fat little guy in a mustard-colored suit. — Elmer Irey, Special Intelligence Unit, Department of the Treasury[1]

By the late 1920s Al Capone ruled the underworld as the king of liquor lords. He had power, money, and fame. Virtually every American knew his name. Many upstanding citizens regarded him as a necessary evil who supplied outlawed, but popular, alcoholic beverages to the drinking public. His fans viewed him as a modern Robin Hood, defying an unjust law for a just cause. Yet Scarface seemed disillusioned with fame and wealth. Being a crime lord didn't guarantee happiness or a long life. Prison and an early death were occupational hazards: prosecutors wanted him behind bars; his rivals wanted him in a casket.

Capone expressed deep discontent when he talked to the press. In December 1927 he told reporters that he would winter in Florida. "Let the worthy citizens of Chicago get their liquor the best they can," he said. "I'm sick of the job — it's a thankless one and full of grief." He whined that he didn't get the respect he merited. "I've been spending the best years of my life as a public benefactor," he said. "I've given people the light pleasures, shown them a good time. And all I get is abuse — the existence of a hunted man. I'm called a killer." He deserved better treatment. "Public service is my motto," he said. "Ninety-nine percent of the people in Chicago drink and gamble. I've tried to serve them decent liquor and square games. But I'm not appreciated."[2]

Capone summed up his predicament in another public jeremiad in 1929. "I went into the racket in Chicago four and a half years ago," he said. "During the past two years I've been trying to get out. But once in the racket, you're always in it, it seems. The parasites trail you, begging you for favors and for money, and you can never get away from them, no matter where you go."[3]

Pay Up!

In the early 1920s the Treasury Department tested the judicial waters to see if tax fraud cases could be proved against illegal liquor traffickers. The department began by targeting minor league beer barons. In an early tax case, Treasury agents investigated Lawrence "Butch" Crowley, a flamboyant bootleg boss in northern Illinois. Crowley, the son of a dogcatcher, had served in the army, driven a cab, and worked as a mechanic. When Volstead began, he took a job delivering beer for bootleggers. He saw that his bosses were getting rich, so he decided to start his own operation and make his own fortune.

Crowley's bootlegging business took off like a rocket. With his profits, he bought his breweries in Elgin and Pekin, Illinois. He also made legitimate real estate investments and built a mansion in Joliet. He became famous as the bootlegger with gold doorknobs because his home sported gleaming hardware that appeared to be made of the precious metal. He wore a flashy diamond ring, a platinum watch fob, and a diamond-studded watch. He owned a fleet of cars, including several Cadillacs, a Pierce-Arrow, and a Locomobile. When his mother died, he paid $25,000 for her elaborate tombstone.

The Treasury Department accused Crowley of income tax fraud, claiming that he owed taxes and penalties totaling more than $135,000 on an income of $1.5 million. Federal officials decided to shelve the tax charges because they had a stronger case against him for bribing a Prohibition agent. In a plea bargain, he copped to the bribery charge and agreed to let the feds dismantle his brewery in Elgin. He received a light sentence — six months in jail plus a $10,000 fine.[4]

When Crowley was released from jail, he claimed to be a new man and vowed to make an honest living. To avoid another trial, he bargained his tax liability down to $65,000, which he immediately paid. He began working in real estate and undertook an ambitious project to rescue a failing summer resort. He bought a nightclub in Joliet and, with a Methodist minister as his partner, purchased a radio station, WWAE (later WJOB). At night Crowley hosted a radio show with live dance music from his nightclub. On Sundays the station broadcast the minister's sermon, followed by an organ concert.[5] It appeared that the bootlegger had learned to run an honest business.

In 1923 Internal Revenue officials investigated Terry Druggan, an Illinois bootlegger who attracted their attention when he spent a fortune for an estate at Lake Zurich. A newspaper called Druggan "a gunman who was able to run a shoestring into a million with the aid of a Smith & Wesson, the Volstead Act, and not too much conscience." Before Prohibition, Druggan had belonged to a gang of hoods who terrorized the Valley, one of Chicago's poorest neighborhoods. When Volstead came along, he moved into bootlegging on a grand scale. His assets included five near beer breweries that actually made the real stuff.[6]

The Internal Revenue office in Chicago subpoenaed the beer baron to question him about his failure to file income tax returns. But the tax probe was placed on hold while prosecutors pressed Volstead charges against Druggan and his partner, Frank Lake, a former Chicago fireman. At trial, the two received sentences of a year in jail for Volstead violations.[7]

After Druggan and Lake finished their jail terms, the feds pursued tax charges against both of them. Revenue agents estimated that the pair had raked in roughly $15 million in four years. However, the government could prove a total income of only $3 million. The duo said they were willing to pay their back taxes and told their lawyers to negotiate a settlement, based on an income of $1.5 million. After months of haggling, the government placed the pair's tax liability at nearly $518,000. They failed to pay up, so officials filed tax liens on property belonging to the beer barons, who owned racehorses, luxury cars, and assorted real estate, including a farm and an apartment building. Druggan also owned an estate in Florida, which the government seized and sold at auction.[8]

Both Druggan and Lake were indicted for their "willful failure" to file income tax returns for 1924-25. Revenue agents estimated their income at more than $1 million for those two years, but prosecutors took a cautious approach and set out to prove a lower number in court. The beer barons entered "conditional pleas of guilty" for attempting to "cheat, swindle, and defraud the United States." (The court allowed the conditional pleas because similar tax fraud cases were in the appeals process, headed for the U.S. Supreme Court. When the high court ruled in those cases, Druggan and Lake would have the option of changing their plea if they would derive any benefit from doing so.)[9]

The high court rulings didn't open any new legal avenues for Druggan and Lake, so they were headed to jail. Both men were sentenced to two years in the federal prison at Leavenworth, Kansas. Druggan caused trouble at Leavenworth, so he was transferred to the Atlanta federal prison. Lake, on the other hand, followed the rules and his good behavior earned him an early release. Claiming he wanted to go straight, he moved to Birmingham, Michigan, where he built a new life as a businessman and an active church member.[10]

By the late 1920s federal officials saw tax fraud charges as a viable strategy for breaking Al Capone's grip on Chicago. Everybody knew that Capone raked in millions, but his exact income was unknown. His financial paper trail was almost nonexistent. He dealt in cash and held no bank accounts or real estate in his own name. To protect his assets, he often put them in his wife's name or his mother's. He paid cash for big ticket items, even his yacht and his mansion in Florida. He hired bookkeepers to conduct the daily financial business of his illicit empire but kept them in the dark as much as possible — for their safety as well as his own.[11]

To test the waters, federal prosecutors initiated tax cases against Capone's top henchmen. Gathering evidence against his lieutenants would shed light on Capone's finances by exposing the Outfit's inner workings. Moreover, the cases would be a sort of dress rehearsal that would reveal how juries reacted to the evidence. The Treasury Department's Special Intelligence Unit (SIU) was assigned to ferret out the nitty-gritty financial details necessary to convict the Outfit bosses.

Ralph "Bottles" Capone, Al's brother, was indicted on multiple counts of income tax fraud in 1930. Revenue officials said Ralph owed roughly $300,000 in taxes and penalties. Ralph claimed to be an insolvent "racehorse man," but evidence showed that he had used aliases to deposit more than $1.8 million in a bank in Cicero. Cancelled checks connected him to illegal brewers, who testified that he regularly ordered large quantities of beer. Saloon owners told the jury that they bought their beer from Ralph. The jurors found Ralph Capone guilty of tax fraud, but he appealed the verdict. The U.S. Circuit Court of Appeals issued a mixed ruling that voided some charges but upheld his conviction on the major counts. He was sentenced to prison at Leavenworth and ordered to pay his back taxes plus a hefty fine.[12]

The Guzik brothers and Frank Nitti ranked high among Capone's myrmidons. Scarface called Jack "Greasy Thumb" Guzik his "financial secretary" because he signed the checks and kept Capone's finances in order. Greasy Thumb garnered a five-year sentence after the state proved he hadn't paid taxes on more than $1 million of ill-gotten personal income. Tax offenses also sent his brother Sam Guzik to prison for a year-and-a-day. Frank Nitti pled guilty to failure to pay income taxes on nearly $159,000 and was sentenced to eighteen months in prison.[13]

Civic Betterment

In the mid–1920s the Outfit ruled Cicero with an iron fist, and Capone treated the town as his personal fiefdom. Scarface, who frowned on insubordination, expected city officials to do his bidding. He exploded if they didn't. Once when Mayor Joseph Klenha failed to follow Capone's orders, Scarface knocked his honor down the steps of city hall and savagely kicked him as he scrambled to get up.[14]

Although Cicero's top officials kowtowed to Capone, the town had a small group of reformers who wanted a safe, family-friendly city. These activists formed the West Suburban Ministers and Citizens Association to fight crime in Cicero and nearby towns. They galvanized public opinion and demanded that law enforcement do its job. Whenever public pressure built up to the point that officialdom couldn't ignore it, the police would raid a few Outfit establishments. The Outfit would shut down the raided places and quickly open new ones nearby. "Within an hour after they were raided in one place, they were going full blast in the next place," an attorney said.[15]

Cicero's elected officials failed to fight the Outfit with real zeal, so the reformers staged their own raids. On several occasions the gutsy do-gooders secured search warrants and succeeded in shutting down vice resorts in both Cicero and Stickney.

On Kentucky Derby Day in 1925, a busy Saturday for off-track betting, the Reverend Henry Hoover led a group of reformers and deputy sheriffs on a raid at the Hawthorn Smoke Shop, an illegal gambling joint/saloon run by Capone. Bettors could wager on roulette, blackjack, horse races, craps, chuck-a-luck, and other games. Before the raid began, Hoover and an associate went inside to gamble, so they could describe what went on at the smoke shop, if called to testify in court. About an hour later, the citizen-raiders and the deputy sheriffs burst in to shut the place down.[16]

A citizen-raider was stationed at the Hawthorn's front door, with orders to let no one in or out. A burly man rushed out of the hotel across the street from the smoke shop. He was unshaven and sloppily dressed, his pajamas showing beneath his street clothes. Huffing and puffing, he made a beeline for the Hawthorn's front door. When the citizen-raider refused to let him in, he growled, "I'm the owner of this place." He shoved the door open, forcing his way inside.

The citizen-raider recognized the famous face with the scar. "Come on in, Al," he said, "we're waiting for you."

Capone rushed upstairs to where the raiders were busy dismantling the gambling equipment. He paused to confront the Reverend Hoover and issue a thinly-veiled death threat. Staring the minister in the eye, Scarface declared, "This is the last raid you will ever pull!"

The minister didn't blink. He knew he held the high ground. Capone went to the backroom, where he grabbed money out of the cash register and stuffed it in his pockets. Hoover followed him into the backroom.

Capone said, "Why are you fellows always picking on me?"

Hoover replied that his group was merely trying to enforce the law and make the suburbs safer. Scarface cleaned out the till, hurried down the stairs, and exited the building. The citizen-raiders continued dismantling the equipment, carrying it downstairs, and loading it onto trucks.

After a short time Capone, clean shaven and neatly dressed, returned to the smoke shop. This time he approached Hoover in a friendly, conciliatory manner.

"Reverend, can't you and I get together? Come to some understanding?" he asked. "If you will let up on me in Cicero, I'll withdraw from Stickney."

"The only understanding, Mr. Capone, you and I can ever have is that you must obey the law or get out of the western suburbs," the brave parson replied.

Pastor Hoover then asked the sheriff's deputies to arrest Capone. The lawmen said they would need an arrest warrant to take him into custody. Since they didn't have a warrant, they stood aside and let Scarface leave the building.[17] The citizen-raiders had put the smoke shop out of business, but Capone still controlled Cicero. Realists knew that the gambling joint/saloon would reopen soon.

Balancing the Books

Nearly a year after pastor Hoover led the raid on the Hawthorn Smoke Shop, police stormed the place, looking for evidence in a murder case. An assistant state's attorney had been killed, and the police believed Capone had ordered the hit. The cops confiscated everything that might prove useful, including a ledger from the office safe. The homicide detectives found no murder clues in the ledger, so it was filed away. When the Treasury Department investigated Capone's finances, an agent stumbled across the ledger in a pile of documents stored in an evidence safe. He glanced at the numbers and quickly realized that this book would be crucial in building a tax case against Capone.[18]

Federal agents carefully compared the handwritten ledger entries with handwriting samples from Capone's underlings. They found that the entries had been made by three employees at the Hawthorn Smoke Shop; the majority belonged to head cashier Leslie Shumway, who had kept meticulous records. Shumway knew all the nitty-gritty financial details of the business. He could identify the "investors" in the Outfit's illegal enterprises and could testify that Scarface was, in essence, the senior partner. He could verify the ledger entries and show that enormous sums of money flowed through the smoke shop. His testimony would be crucial in verifying Capone's immense income.[19]

The federal agents needed to interrogate Shumway, but he had disappeared from Chicago. His whereabouts were unknown. He might be on the lam or he might be rotting in a shallow grave, his corpse riddled with machinegun bullets. After searching for months, the feds found him living in Miami. Lawmen questioned him and urged him to testify against Capone. He reluctantly agreed to cooperate with the feds, knowing that his life would be in danger when Scarface found out. He gave a sworn statement in Miami and then returned to Chicago to testify before a grand jury. Law enforcement provided tight security to protect him from Capone's goons.[20]

While the Treasury Department delved into Capone's finances, law enforcement opened up another front against Scarface. A special squad of young lawmen fought a guerrilla war against the Outfit. Originally called the District Attorney's Squad, the group became famous as the Untouchables led by Eliot Ness. They were a giant thorn in Capone's side, disrupting his business and costing him money. They repeatedly, relentlessly raided his booze-making plants. They harassed the Outfit militiamen, smashed countless barrels of Capone's booze, and confiscated dozens of his trucks. To taunt Scarface, the brash young lawmen once drove a convoy of his confiscated beer trucks past the hotel where he lived.[21]

When Capone heard that Treasury agents were gathering evidence for a tax case against him, he didn't panic. He believed he could buy his way out of the tax trouble, so he sent his lawyers to talk to Treasury officials. He volunteered to pay $4 million to settle his tax liability — an offer Washington flatly rejected. Publicly, federal officials stated they wouldn't bargain with Scarface because they were determined to smash the Chicago mob. Privately, they debated the advantages of a plea bargain. They had no guarantee Capone would be convicted at trial. He had a high-priced, talented legal team who would put up a good defense. As a fail-safe, he could bribe or intimidate the jurors. Witnesses in mob cases often vanished before the trial began, gutting the state's case. Maybe it would be prudent to negotiate with Capone.[22]

After a great deal of speculation about Capone's taxes, the press reported that Scarface had made a "secret" deal with federal prosecutors. He would plead guilty to minor tax charges and be sentenced to a short term in prison. He anticipated spending less than three years behind bars. Moreover, he expected to pay only part of his delinquent taxes because he had few provable assets.[23]

On July 30, 1931, Capone showed up in federal court, looking confident and prosperous. The smiling, pudgy liquor lord wore an expensive custom-made suit. He held his head high and seemed unworried, even upbeat. He was ready to take his slap on the wrist. The court was called to order, and the legal formalities began. Then Judge James Wilkerson veered off-script. Sounding annoyed, he questioned the attorneys about Capone's guilty plea. The judge didn't seem eager to rubber stamp Capone's not-so-secret plea bargain. As the liquor lord listened to the legalese, his good mood ebbed away. A "wilted," worried look replaced the smile on the famous Scarface mug. He began to sweat and to fidget. "His ear-to-ear grin was displaced by a scowl as he puffed in distress."[24]

Judge Wilkerson sternly questioned both the U.S. attorney and Capone's defense lawyer. The U.S. attorney said he endorsed the plea bargain because the state's witnesses feared for their lives and he couldn't be certain they would testify when the time came. A few had already disappeared, presumably taking mob money to leave Chicago and lay low until after the trial.[25]

The U.S. attorney noted that the plea deal would send Capone to prison immediately. However, if Scarface were convicted and sentenced to a long term, he could afford legal appeals that would keep him out of prison for years. Maybe permanently. The U.S. attorney said that his superiors in Washington approved of the plea bargain, and he showed the judge a confidential letter from the U.S. Attorney General.

Capone's defense attorney, Michael Ahern, said he had advised his client to plead guilty because he believed the U.S. Attorney's office was acting in good faith. It was his understanding that top officials in Washington had sanctioned the deal. "We were led to believe that the recommendations would be approved by the court," Ahern said.[26]

Judge Wilkerson didn't like what he heard. He expected to call the shots in his courtroom. He said that he would listen to counsels' recommendations, but he had the discretion to honor or to reject any plea deal. Given the circumstances, the judge suggested that Capone might want to reconsider his strategy and file a motion to recall his guilty plea. Attorney Ahern said he would do so. Several weeks later, the court officially allowed Scarface to change his plea to not guilty. The stage was set for Capone's big trial.[27]

When the trial began, the prosecution called the Reverend Hoover and members of his reform group to testify about their raids on Capone's vice dens. However, the financial evidence was the crux of the case. The prosecution relied heavily on Leslie Shumway, the former head cashier at the Hawthorn Smoke Shop. He described his job and explained the bookkeeping routine at the illegal joint. Based on his numbers, the smoke shop profits totaled roughly $588,000 for June 1924–May 1926. Capone took home fifty-two percent of the profits in 1925-26. This was his take from only one small part of his criminal empire, but it was provable income, which made it important for tax purposes.[28]

The prosecution called another Outfit cashier, Fred Ries, as a hostile witness. Ries had testified in earlier tax evasion cases against Ralph Capone and other Outfit honchos. Then he had disappeared. Gangland sources said he feared for his life, so he had gone to South America. Ries actually stayed closer to home, but he moved from place to place, trying to be invisible. Federal agents caught up with the reluctant witness in St. Louis. He was taken before a judge and jailed in Danville, Illinois, to ensure that he didn't disappear again. The federal agents knew he has afraid of insects, so they made sure he had a bug-infested jail cell. After a few days his nerves were stretched to the breaking point. To get away from the cockroaches and other creepy pests, he agreed to help the feds.[29]

At Capone's trial, Ries testified that he had worked at illegal joints in Cicero, including the Ship (AKA the Hawthorn Smoke Shop). Ries routinely purchased cashier's checks with the "surplus cash" from the Ship. He used aliases to buy the checks and turned them over to a trusted Capone aide. Ries identified a series of cancelled checks, including one actually endorsed with the signature "Alphonse Capone."[30]

A Florida hotel owner, who was friends with Scarface, admitted that he had negotiated the purchase of Capone's Palm Island mansion and held the title in his name for a while. The hotelman conceded that he often cashed large Western Union money orders for Scarface. The manager of a Western Union office in Miami Beach testified that she knew Capone and recognized his handwriting. She verified his signature on a series of wire transfers, and another Western Union employee identified bank drafts endorsed by Capone.

Since a person's expenditures are usually an indication of his income, the prosecution wanted jurors to hear about Capone's extravagant spending habits. The manager of a Chicago hotel testified that Scarface had been a long-term guest, occupying a large corner suite. His hotel bill ran up to $1,500 per week, more than the typical renter paid for a year's lease on an apartment. For one big party, Capone had paid $3,000 to rent the hotel banquet room. (To put that number in perspective, a consumer could buy a new car for less than $600.)

Furniture salesmen presented records showing that Capone had spent more than $29,600 on home furnishings. A car salesman testified that he sold the liquor lord two McFarlane automobiles for $25,000. A jeweler said that one holiday season Capone had paid $8,250 for diamond-studded belt buckles to give away as Christmas gifts. Another jeweler stated that Scarface spent nearly $6,000 at his store, buying jewelry and silverware.

Capone's telephone bills were astronomical compared to the average American's. Making or receiving a long-distance call was not an everyday event in the typical household, due to the high cost. But Scarface liked to keep in touch. While living at the Lexington Hotel in Chicago, he spent a whopping $38,939 on long distance in less than two years. Records from Southern Bell Telephone and Telegraph Company showed that he also chattered away in Florida. His Miami phone bill totaled more than $6,200 when he vacationed there for a few months.

Several witnesses described Capone's lavish lifestyle in Florida. When he came for the winter, he brought an entourage with him and spent extravagantly to entertain his guests. He often threw dinner parties for forty or more people. A butcher testified that the liquor lord spent up to $1,400 monthly for meat.

Capone took pride in his attire and spared no expense in clothing himself. A decent off-the-rack suit cost less than $50, but Scarface routinely paid $135 for tailor-made. An employee in the custom tailoring department at Marshall Field & Company stated that Capone was a regular customer. In addition to buying for himself, he sometimes ordered suits for his favorite henchmen. The tailors were instructed to make the mobsters' suits with large, reinforced pockets to hold revolvers.[31]

In addition to wowing the jury with Capone's lavish lifestyle, the prosecution wanted to present evidence gained during the plea bargaining process. Capone's attorneys cried foul and tried to suppress the documents, arguing that they had been part of confidential negotiations. After listening to spirited debate on the issue, Judge Wilkerson refused to bar the evidence, which included a letter to the IRS written by a lawyer who had formerly represented Capone. The letter admitted that Scarface had "large taxable income," that he was "a principal" in a "syndicate," and that he received one-sixth of that syndicate's profits.

The defense tried to blunt the impact of the letter, but the document spoke for itself. The prosecution had Scarface "nailed to the cross now," as a defense attorney put it.[32]

On October 17, 1931, after lengthy deliberations, the jury returned its verdict on the tax fraud charges. Neither prosecution nor defense was completely satisfied. The jurors found Capone guilty on five counts — two misdemeanors and three felonies. They acquitted him on eighteen counts. Judge Wilkerson sentenced Scarface to eleven years in federal prison. In addition to his delinquent taxes, he was ordered to pay $80,000 in fines and court costs.[33]

Capone's attorneys quickly started the appeals process. While the petitions progressed through the system, Scarface was held behind bars at the Cook County jail in Chicago. His visitors included his wife, priests, and cowboy humorist Will Rogers. In February 1932 the Circuit Court of Appeals upheld the sentence imposed by Judge Wilkerson. Three months later the U.S. Supreme Court rejected Capone's petition for a review of his case. His future looked bleak.[34]

A Smile for Everyone

The day after the Supreme Court refused to hear Capone's appeal, reporters flocked to the Cook County jail to cover his departure for prison. They expected Capone to be taken to the federal pen at Leavenworth, but there was a last minute change. The Justice Department announced that Scarface would be locked up in Atlanta, to keep him separated from other Chicago mobsters already at leisure in Leavenworth.

At dusk, lawmen handcuffed Scarface to another prisoner who would ride on the same train. The other man would be transported to Florida, where he was accused of automobile theft. The press and hundreds of spectators waited outside the jail to see Capone. Reporters, photographers, and newsreel cameramen were poised to record the momentous departure.

As Scarface exited the jailhouse, he paused to take in the scene. "You'd think Mussolini was passin' through," he quipped.

A phalanx of Prohibition agents and cops put the two prisoners in a car waiting inside the jail-yard fence. The big gates swung outward, parting the crowd; the car spurted into the street. A convoy of police vehicles, with sirens shrieking, sped toward the Dearborn Street Station of the Chicago & Eastern Illinois Railroad. Cars filled with the press corps joined the motorcade, speeding to keep up.

At the train station passengers and railroad workers bustled about. A crowd of curious onlookers awaited Capone's arrival. The police squad cars screeched to a halt, and the officers jumped out. The lawmen "had considerable difficulty" getting the prisoners out of the car. The twosome struggled with their shackles, and Capone's obese body seemed to anchor both of them to the car. The scene could've been in a Keystone Kops movie, but Scarface wasn't laughing.

When Capone finally squeezed out of the car, he stood on the curb and smiled at the crowd. The spectators included some of his mob pals, who waved and shouted, wishing him well. Flashbulbs popped; newsreel cameras rolled; reporters fired questions at Capone. Someone asked him how he felt.

"I am glad to get started," Scarface said.

As Capone and his police escort made their way to the train shed, they squeezed through the mass of humanity — onlookers, passengers, conductors, porters, reporters, photographers. Scarface grew impatient and snapped at the cops, ordering them to walk faster. His eyes flashed with anger. He plunged ahead, dragging "the automobile thief along behind him." The harried procession lumbered past a long line of Pullman coaches to reach the prison car. The two criminals, with three guards, climbed aboard the Dixie Flyer.[35]

When Capone arrived at the Atlanta penitentiary, he became inmate number 40886. The prison staffers feared he would be a troublemaker, but they were pleasantly surprised. He quickly adjusted to being just another con. He exchanged his tailored suits and silk jockey shorts for the convict's denim uniform and coarse underwear. He traded a diet of rich food at fancy restaurants for simple prison fare, and he soon began losing weight. He went from running a criminal empire to working in the sewing shop, where he cut fabric to make overalls. Later he was transferred to the shoe factory.

Although Capone was accustomed to issuing orders, he had to take them in the big house. He proved to be quite docile. He cooperated with the prison staff and caused no trouble. By mid-summer officials were calling him a model prisoner. An attorney who visited him reported that he worked hard, was "generally well liked," and had "a smile for everyone."[36]

Nuttier Than a Fruitcake

After slightly more than two years at Atlanta, Capone was transferred to the federal prison on Alcatraz Island near San Francisco. Known as "The Rock," Alcatraz had a long history as the site of a fort, a military prison, and a detention center for conscientious objectors. During Prohibition, the Federal Prison Bureau urgently needed more cells to house liquor traffickers and violent offenders. The bureau acquired Alcatraz and converted it to a maximum-security facility for "defiant and dangerous criminals" — the worst of the worst. Despite Capone's record as a model prisoner, his infamy earned him a cell at Alcatraz.[37]

Scarface was one of forty-plus inmates moved from Atlanta to Alcatraz on a special train with armed guards and heavy security. Word of the special train leaked out, so crowds gathered along the route to catch a glimpse of the outlaws. Despite tight security, officials worried that mobsters might try to free their comrades in crime. The train was shunted several times to foil any plots. At Tiburon, California, heavily-armed federal agents and prison guards met the train. The railway cars were loaded onto a barge, which was then towed to the island. Prison vehicles took Scarface and the other convicts up the steep road to their new home atop The Rock.[38]

Although Alcatraz prison had electric lights and modern plumbing, inmates didn't live the good life. They followed a strict regimen and enjoyed few privileges. They were not allowed to listen to the radio or read the newspaper. They were permitted to read magazines only after prison officials had censored them. At mealtime, a convict was required to eat all the food on his plate. If he didn't clean his plate, his punishment was missing a meal.

The tight security included an "electric eye" that searched for weapons hidden on the convict's body. Inmates were permitted to talk to one another only on Saturday afternoon in the prison yard. If they were caught whispering or using signals, they were punished. Capone, like many of his fellow inmates, found the no-talking rule very irksome. In his first year at Alcatraz he was sent to solitary confinement several times for talking. Despite his occasional slip-up, prison officials did not view him as a problem.[39]

As early as 1931 Capone tested positive on the Wasserman test used to diagnose syphilis. Exactly when he had contracted syphilis was unknown. He worked in brothels as a young man and was sexually promiscuous so he was exposed to sexually-transmitted diseases on a more or less routine basis. To treat the syphilis, his doctors gave him "intramuscular, antiluetic injections." The disease seemed to go into remission, but medical science had no cure for syphilis.

By 1938 prison officials noted that Capone's mental and physical atrophy showed signs of acceleration. Doctors diagnosed his primary problem as paresis, or mental deterioration caused by syphilis. (At various stages, paresis entails partial paralysis, muscular weakness, slurred speech, and dementia.) Capone's syphilis was manifesting itself in memory loss, irrational behavior, and skin disease.

Capone sometimes threw childlike temper tantrums. At other times, he was silent and withdrawn and refused to leave his cell to go to the dining hall or his job. At least once when he was acting up, prison officials put him in a straitjacket to restrain him. On another occasion he fell into a coma and had to be hospitalized. To gauge his mental regression, he was given the Revised Stanford Binet Intelligence Test. Results showed that he had a mental age of eight years eleven months, placing him in "the middle-grade moron group."[40]

Rumors about Capone's poor health abounded inside and outside Alcatraz. The press reported that he had gone "stir crazy." This prompted the Department of Justice to issue a statement saying, "His condition is in no wise due to his confinement, but grows out of conditions originating prior to his incarceration." His health became so bad that he was admitted to the prison hospital as a permanent patient, with no real prospect of ever returning to his cell.[41]

Naturally, Capone's loved ones worried about his declining health. His family asked the government to release him or move him to a facility where he could get better health care. His lawyers argued that the harsh life and limited medical resources at Alcatraz were exacerbating his health problems. In response, the Justice Department pointed out that he had paid only a small portion of the fines and costs he owed the federal district court in Chicago. His family got the message. In January 1939 a lawyer paid the court nearly $38,000 as an installment on what he still owed. Only days later, Scarface was transferred to Terminal Island Federal Prison near Long Beach, California.[42]

With time off for good behavior, Capone would be eligible for parole by 1940 if his family satisfied Uncle Sam's demand for another payment on his debt to the government. His family claimed financial hardship, but the feds stood firm. In November 1939, a lawyer paid the court an additional $20,000 to ensure Capone's release.[43]

Later that same month a prison doctor and two guards escorted Scarface from California to Lewisburg Penitentiary in Pennsylvania. Without fanfare, the entourage traveled across the country via train. To avoid calling attention to their famous prisoner, the guards didn't handcuff Scarface, whose poor health virtually guaranteed that he couldn't escape. When Capone reached Lewisburg, he was paroled after serving seven and one-half years of his sentence. From prison he went directly to Baltimore's Union Memorial Hospital to be treated for paresis.

At the Baltimore hospital Capone stayed in a two-room suite with a connecting bathroom for $30 per day. Federal agents guarded his suite around the clock, and local police watched the hospital. His wife, his mother, and a younger brother were allowed to visit him. Although hospital officials refused to discuss the details of Capone's illness, they confirmed that a syphilis specialist was treating him.[44]

After several weeks in the hospital, Capone moved to a "secluded residence in a quiet, fashionable section of Baltimore" to stay near his doctor. His caregivers acknowledged that he was "chronically ill, in need of rest and quiet and continued medical treatment." Although he was only forty years old, he seemed to become weaker every day.

In March 1940 Capone returned to his Florida estate to live with his family, who cared for him and catered to his whims as if he were a petulant child. That summer he enjoyed a brief period of good health and normalcy. He practiced his golf swing, swam in his pool, and fished from a pier. Miami Beach residents spotted him in restaurants and nightclubs. But this proved to be only a brief respite in his unstoppable decline.[45]

As time progressed Capone became sicker, both mentally and physically. His family spent large sums of money to ensure that he had the best medical care, but the doctors couldn't cure him. His dementia worsened, and his skimble-skamble behavior became more noticeable. "Al's nuttier than a fruitcake," mobster Jack Guzik said, with more candor than sensitivity.[46]

On January 25, 1947, Capone died after suffering an "apoplectic stroke." His body was taken to Chicago, where his family and friends held a private wake and memorial service. The police and the press corps kept a low profile during the mass at Holy Name Cathedral. On February 4, Capone had a public burial in the family plot on consecrated ground at Mount Olivet Cemetery. Msgr. William Gorman, who had known the family for many years, conducted a simple graveside service. Fewer than forty people braved the blustery, frigid weather to watch the gravediggers lower Al Capone's bronze coffin into the ground.[47] Scarface died a broken man who had outlived his shameful glory years as the Scourge of the Nation.

24. Whiskey-Six Cowboys: The Boozorium Trail and Beyond

A greatly different air seemed to surround the runner when he was once over the line and in Canada. In the Dominion, he was looked upon by the gentry as a bona fide business-man engaged in legitimate affairs. In the States, he was a felon, hunted by officers of the law.— Edmund Fahey, bootlegger, Spokane, Washington[1]

The Wild West attracted strong, trail-blazing men and women willing to take big risks. Ideally, the Westerner was a rugged, fiercely independent individual who had cast off the shackles of urban society. He believed in personal liberty and had little need of, or respect for, the government. He wanted to live his life with a minimum of rules, regulations, and social conventions. In his view, the Volstead law definitely fell into the category of unneeded, onerous regulation. True to character, the Westerner who liked his whiskey ignored Prohibition with no disquiet or guilty feelings.

Border runners kept the Canadian liquor flowing across the plains and the badlands. Although a few organized rum rings operated in the West, the typical border runner had only a trusty sidekick to help him. "Every man hauled for himself and himself only," said a former bootlegger. "There was no organized racket running the smuggling in our area. On several occasions some guy tried to move in and be a big shot, but, in true western fashion, his ambitions were always curtailed." The border runners didn't belong to a mob, but they formed a sort of fraternity or brotherhood. One runner described his peers as "a decent type" of men. "They'd give you the shirt off their backs," he said. If hijackers stole a border runner's cargo or the police confiscated his car and booze, he could count on his bootlegging brothers to help him. They would lend him a car and enough money to buy a load of Canadian liquor, so he could get back in the game.[2]

The West's border runners bought their booze in Saskatchewan, Alberta, or British Columbia. Saskatchewan Province was legally dry when the Great Drought began in the United States. Despite the provincial prohibition law, Canada's national law allowed merchants to stockpile liquor in dry Saskatchewan and sell it for export. Before Volstead, Saskatchewan's liquor merchants sold their products by mail order to customers in Canada's wet provinces. As the USA prepared for the Big Thirst, Saskatchewan's liquor purveyors saw dollar signs across the border. To profit from the coming drought, they filled their storerooms with popular brands of aged whiskey from Scotland, the USA, and elsewhere. These well-stocked warehouses, called "boozoriums," were powerful magnets drawing U.S. bootleggers across the international border.

The Boozorium Trail began in small Canadian towns near the U.S. border and extended north to Saskatoon. After crossing into Canada, a bootleg convoy drove to Moose Jaw, Gainsborough, Carnduff, Carievale, Assiniboia, Estevan, Tribune, Bienfait, Govenlock, or Maple Creek to buy liquor from an exporter. Border runners from Montana, North Dakota, and other states kept the cash registers ringing at the boozoriums. Most of the bootleggers had a list of regular customers waiting on the south side of the international border.

The Boozorium Trail could've been called the Golden Road because Saskatchewan's liquor purveyors made enormous profits. The Bronfman family, prairie-town entrepreneurs, aggressively moved into the liquor business and opened several boozoriums. In the run-up to the Great Drought, the Bronfmans used all the cash and credit they could muster to buy railcar loads of booze. The investment paid off. Sales at the Bronfmans' small liquor depot in Bienfait averaged $500,000 per month in 1922, and that was only one of their outlets.[3]

A few months after Volstead began, a high-ranking lawman in Saskatchewan said the bootleg traffic was booming. "Especially from Estevan, Saskatchewan, to Minot, North Dakota, has whiskey smuggling into the United States assumed huge proportions. Minot alone contains enough whiskey to float a ship," the officer stated. After the Canadian liquor arrived in Minot, much of it traveled on to Minneapolis, where it sold for top dollar.[4]

Bottineau County, North Dakota, served as a friendly gateway for Canadian liquor headed to South Dakota, Nebraska, Iowa, and Minnesota. The whiskey sixes usually traveled in a convoy with a "feeler" or "tow" car leading the way. By prearrangement the Canadian liquor seller sent a feeler car down to North Dakota to escort the convoy to the boozorium. After the leggers loaded their cargo, the feeler escorted the caravan several miles back across the border into North Dakota. If Bottineau County lawmen were waiting for the convoy and suspected that the first car was a feeler, they would let it pass and then try to stop the other vehicles. The lawmen were armed with Browning machineguns, but they were vastly outnumbered by the bootleggers, who had their own guns. Despite all the firepower, shoot-outs were rare because North Dakotans generally tolerated the liquor traffic and saved their bullets for more important matters.[5]

Saskatchewan's boozoriums didn't have a monopoly on selling Canadian whiskey to bootleggers from the American West. In Alberta and British Columbia liquor exporters ran garages where U.S. leggers picked up cargos of hooch. The coal mining town of Fernie, British Columbia, had an oversized garage that held a liquor depot with "a store of booze big enough to make an anti-saloon leaguer swoon." The place also had a car repair shop and cots where tired leggers could snooze.[6] In Alberta garages served as liquor depots for the bootleg traffic in Lethbridge, Medicine Hat, Blairmore, and the grain-elevator towns near the Montana border.

In the early 1920s, the West's border runners found it easy to jump the line because the U.S. had few border inspection stations. When the government opened more stations to beef up its anti-smuggling efforts, the bootleggers had to deal with the U.S. border patrol. Canada's liquor exporters came to their aid. When a bootlegger bought hooch at a boozorium or a liquor export house, he also paid protection money. The Canadian exporter used this money to bribe U.S. patrol officers to ensure that the border runners could jump the line without being arrested. Each U.S. border patrol unit had a supervising officer who assigned his subordinates to watch certain roads at certain times. In return for the bribe money, the supervisor guaranteed that certain routes would be unguarded so the bootleg convoy could pass through. This system of organized graft ensured that each border runner paid his fair share and wasn't overcharged or double-crossed by the patrol officer.[7]

The average bootlegger had a cynical view of lawmen, but even some leggers were surprised by the corruption in the U.S. border patrol. The officers' "utter disdain for a law they had sworn to uphold was at times perplexing and even shocking to the rumrunner," said a bootlegger. "When an officer ... let a caravan of seven or eight cars together jump the line a stone's throw from a customs house, travel down a main highway, and drive right through the center of the border patrolmen's headquarters town, it made a rumrunner feel like an amateur in crime."[8]

Automobiles carried the vast majority of Canadian hooch across the border, but the western liquor runners sometimes used rafts, horses, or railcars. A bootlegger could buy a small cargo of liquor at a boozorium, drive it to a stream near the international border, and put it on a raft. He or his sidekick would guide the raft across the border while the other man drove the empty car to their meeting site. The wise bootlegger went rafting at night and chose a secluded site to transfer the liquor to his car. If he didn't, he "was liable to find himself facing searchlights and guns in mid-transfer."

Pack horses could carry heavy loads on rough trails in the mountains and woods far from the nearest highway, border patrol station, and sheriff's office. Farmers who lived on or near the international border could make easy money leading a string of horses across the line. The border runner bought a load of whiskey at a boozorium and hauled it to the farm. Five or six cases of whiskey were diamond-hitched to each packsaddle, and the farmer usually led a string of eighteen to twenty horses. The bootlegger or his sidekick rode with the farmer to guide the horses while the other man drove the empty car across the border to their meeting site. Since the pack animals stayed off the beaten path, the men traveling with the horses were rarely arrested. If the farmer did get arrested, the honorable bootlegger paid all the legal expenses and, if need be, hired someone to tend the crops until the farmer got out of jail. In general, judges meted out light punishment to farmers because they weren't full-time bootleggers.[9]

Shipping illegal liquor across the border by railcar was an expensive proposition because the bootlegger had to bribe all the train crews along the route. Nevertheless, leggers used railcars, especially when the border patrol or another enforcement unit cracked down on the liquor runners. The standard pay-off to a railroad crew was $25 for each man working on the train or in the freight yard. This could add up to a substantial amount of money, but only a foolish bootlegger skimped on the pay-offs. If a disgruntled crewman ratted on the legger, he would be arrested and his cargo would be confiscated.

Long freight trains carrying tons of coal crossed the international border every day. At Rexford, Montana, a spur from the mainline ran into Fernie, British Columbia. The border runner bought his booze in Fernie and informed the liquor exporter that he wanted it shipped on the railroad. The exporter arranged for the cargo to be moved to the railway yard and hidden in a load of coal. The bootlegger hung around the freight yard to see his precious cargo loaded onto the coal car, and he kept an eye on it until the train left the station.

When the train pulled out, the bootlegger hopped in his car and followed the railroad route so he would know when his cargo got sidetracked. After the coal car with his booze was left on the sidetrack, he hung around the freight yard until dark. Then he took a shovel and climbed into the railcar to retrieve his liquor. When he finished, he was "black as an eight ball" because he was covered with soot from head to toe. In the nearest stream he washed the soot off himself and his cargo. Then he hid his booze in the underbrush by the freight yard and waited for a train headed to his destination.

When the right train stopped at the station, he talked to the conductor and they agreed on a price. The conductor pointed out a railcar and gave the bootlegger ten minutes to load his cargo. When the liquor reached its destination, the border runner had a truck waiting in the freight yard. The booze was quickly transferred to the truck and rushed to safe storage.[10]

The Boozorium Boys

On a typical day in Govenlock, Saskatchewan, the bootleggers from Montana arrived in mid-afternoon in their big cars. The Americans hung out at the billiard parlor until dusk, playing pool or poker. At sunset they went to work. They backed their cars, which had auxiliary leaf springs to handle extra weight, into the boozorium warehouse. They removed the sandbags that had kept the rear end from riding too high on the trip north. Then they loaded up with cases of whiskey and/or burlap bags holding bottles of beer. The typical whiskey six held a liquor cargo that would net about $2,500 in the States.

The border runners started their homeward trek after nightfall. While they were in Saskatchewan, the provincial police and the Mounties kept an eye on them. The Canadian lawmen followed the leggers out of town and often trailed them all the way to the border to watch them jump the line. The gendarmes wanted to be sure that the liquor left Saskatchewan and wasn't resold in the dry province. Their jurisdiction ended at the U.S. border.[11]

Farmers grew accustomed to hearing the bootleg convoys rumble along the back roads at night. "The unmarked trails past our homestead, mere wagon tracks across a sea of grass, witnessed ... a remarkable lot of traffic in Marmons and Hudson Super Sixes, tightly side-curtained and so heavily loaded that their rear springs rode clear down on the axles," wrote a man who lived near the border. "They drove mainly at night or in foul weather. We could see their lights far out across the plains, groping toward Montana ... and we met them sometimes in the rain, traveling when no one else would risk the gumbo."[12] On rainy nights it was not uncommon for a whiskey six to get mired down in the mud. The leggers had to push the car out of the mud or find a friendly farmer who would lend them a mule to pull it out.

Farmers traveling on horseback or by wagon were grateful that their horses were attuned to the sound of automobile engines. When the farmer's horse or team acted up, he knew it was time to move off the road and wait for the whiskey sixes to roar past. But the bootleggers didn't always stay on the beaten path. When a legger was evading the law, he might take a shortcut across farmland or drive into a barn if the door was open. A bootlegger tearing across the countryside might crash into a fence or drive through it, leaving a sizeable gap. On at least one occasion, bootleggers trying to outrun the law in Montana set fire to a wood bridge to keep the officers at bay.

Although gun battles between leggers and lawmen weren't commonplace, they did happen from time to time. One night in Montana a deadly shootout occurred when bootleggers hauling booze from Canada reached the Milk River, where a boat was waiting for them. When they began transferring their whiskey to the boat, lawmen pounced on them. Shots were fired, and bullets struck a bootlegger. The leggers fled across the river, taking their bleeding, dying comrade with them. They reached a car waiting on the other riverbank, hopped in, and sped away. The next morning a farmer who lived near the river found an unwanted guest in his haystack — a dead bootlegger. The deceased man's comrades had deposited him there, for unknown reasons. Maybe they just wanted to lighten the load.[13]

During warm weather the typical border runner made at least four trips per month to Canada. In the winter bootleggers crossed the border less often, and severe weather sometimes brought the liquor traffic to a total standstill. In the summer a legger driving to Canada might take a woman along as his passenger or relief driver. Lawmen were less likely to shoot at a car driven by a woman, even if they suspected it carried liquor. In the winter months, the male leggers left their women at home because the trip might be perilous.

During the worst winter weather, impassable roads stopped the parade of bootleg convoys. The Bronfmans had invested heavily in boozoriums and other liquor ventures, so they couldn't afford long disruptions in the bootleg traffic. Because they depended on sales to the U.S. market, they shipped booze via railway express to stations near the border, where Americans picked it up. This made the bootlegger's life easier and kept the booze flowing southward. At the end of 1922 Ottawa stopped the railway shipments of liquor, which reduced sales to bootleggers during the winter months.[14]

Canada's border towns welcomed the injection of liquor money into the local economy, but some residents didn't approve of the American bootleggers with their swagger and their guns. In general, the Americans came only to buy liquor and behaved themselves while taking care of business. However, bootleggers were outlaws, and a few committed serious crimes in Canada. The boozoriums had lax security and Canadians didn't share America's obsession with guns, making the liquor depots soft targets.

In November 1920 a gang of armed robbers from North Dakota burst into a boozorium in Tribune, Saskatchewan. They held the Canadians at gunpoint and stole two carloads of liquor. In a similar incident, masked gunmen invaded a liquor depot in Carnduff. A gunman stood guard over the employees while his cohorts loaded hooch into several cars. After the thieves tied up the employees and a nosey passerby, they drove away, headed for the USA. As they raced along, they scattered tacks and bent nails on the road behind them to disable other cars. The simple ploy worked. They escaped.[15]

In another violent crime, unknown persons in Bienfait, presumed to be American bootleggers, stole $6,000 in cash from a boozorium and killed a man who worked there. The outlaws also hijacked a truckload of whiskey that the man had just sold to a customer. Authorities in Regina responded by equipping the provincial police with machineguns for use along the international border.[16]

In 1921 changes in Canadian law greatly restricted the export of liquor from Saskatchewan to other provinces but not to the United States. The boozoriums lost a large portion of their domestic sales, making the U.S. trade even more important. Later, in a move to reduce the U.S. bootleg traffic, Saskatchewan restricted liquor export houses to cities with a population of at least ten thousand. More than thirty boozoriums closed, but those in Regina, Saskatoon, and Moose Jaw remained open. Closing the boozoriums nearest the border added many miles to the U.S. bootlegger's drive, which was especially irksome when the roads were icy or muddy.[17]

The Havre Bunch

Havre, Montana, barely a speck on the map, became a wide-open conduit for illegal liquor during the Arid Era. Local leggers kept Havre well supplied with hooch, and countless bootleg convoys passed through the village, headed to towns throughout the West. Cowboys traded their horses for whiskey sixes because bootlegging was easier than punching cattle and it paid better. Moreover, the typical cowboy got a high from defying Prohibition, driving a fast car, and outrunning hijackers or lawmen.

In Prohibition's early years the United States had no border station on the road that ran from Havre into Canada, so bootleg convoys had clear sailing. A smattering of border patrolmen and customs officials watched Montana's highways and back roads, but they were outnumbered and outgunned by the bootleggers, cattle rustlers, and smugglers. Havre's residents saw no harm in a little vice, so the feds couldn't expect help from local lawmen. "The town of Havre is a major smuggling headquarters. Everybody profits by it. Nobody wants it stopped, and booze sleuths have no friends in Havre," a federal officer stated.[18]

Like their peers in the big cities, Havre's liquor lords formed a syndicate to control the illicit liquor traffic in their area. Businessmen, farmers, ranchers, and illegal saloon owners held a meeting to put Havre's whiskey syndicate on a sound footing. "Investors were found, leadership elected, lawyers engaged, and a secret service formed," reported a newspaper. The financing came from local bankers and businessmen. "None of the banks in this burnt-out, worm-eaten country could stay open if it wasn't for the bootleggers and whiskey runners," a newsman said.[19]

The whiskey syndicate, called the Havre Bunch, ran its own secret service to gather intelligence and stay ahead of law enforcement. The Bunch hired "detectives of national stature" to keep tabs on the federal agents assigned to enforce the dry law in Montana. Local residents were eager to help their neighbors and the "famous Eastern detectives." Townsfolk and farmers watched the federal agents and reported their movements to the bootleggers.[20]

The Havre Bunch recruited "custom cutter" Pat Thomas to lead the syndicate's bootleg convoys. Thomas traveled all over Montana and the Dakotas in a crew that cut and threshed wheat for farmers at harvest time. He had a reputation as a fearless broncobuster and barroom brawler. Although he was no choir boy, he generally operated within the law, so he had his doubts about bootlegging. The Bunch honchos convinced him to try it, and he found his true love. He thrived on driving fast, taking risks, calling the shots, and outfoxing the law. Moreover, for the first time in his life, he had plenty of money.

Thomas piloted convoys of border runners who hauled Canadian liquor to the western states. After he led a convoy out of Canada, he often traveled along the mainline of the Great Northern Railway through Montana and then took the old cattle trails that went all the way to Texas. His convoys delivered booze to distribution points in Montana, Wyoming, Colorado, and Texas. According to mob lore, the Havre Bunch had strong links to Al Capone's Outfit, and Thomas led long convoys to Chicago several times each year. When Thomas ran afoul of a gang in Denver, he was kidnapped and tortured. Capone reportedly ordered the Colorado gangsters to lay off the Montana bootlegger. Thomas had no more trouble in the Centennial State.[21]

Like other bootleggers, Thomas avoided arrest by driving on remote back roads whenever possible. But it was impossible to dodge the law all the time, so he was armed and ready. He survived more than one shootout with lawmen, and he went to jail from time to time. Canadian police once arrested him because he walked out of a theatre while "God Save the King" was being played. Other encounters with the law entailed more danger. On a snowy night with low visibility he was leading a convoy of four vehicles on a long haul. The convoy picked up liquor at Fernie, British Columbia, and an informant warned Thomas that customs patrol officers would be waiting for him in Montana.

Thomas stopped in Comrey, Alberta, to stash part of his liquor for safekeeping. When he jumped the line, he was carrying a small load of whiskey and three men in his car. Customs officers in a Studebaker pulled out from behind a grain elevator to follow him. His passengers quickly threw the remaining cargo, bottles of whiskey in gunny sacks, out the windows. The well-packed sacks landed softly on the snow, without breaking the bottles. The Studebaker closed in on Thomas, and the cars locked bumpers. The patrolmen opened fire with a machinegun. Thomas and his passengers pulled out their weapons and shot back. Thomas ordered his men to bail out. Then he drove on, with the Studebaker on his tail. His men gathered up the jettisoned cargo and buried it in the snow. They made their way to a friend's cabin on the Milk River and later retrieved the hooch.

After giving his men enough time to run away, Thomas jumped out of his car. He slogged through the deep snow until a railroad right-of-way fence blocked his path. As he climbed over it, the patrolmen fired at him and hit his leg. Blood spurted from his leg, and he knew he couldn't outrun the lawmen, so he surrendered.

Thomas was taken to the hospital to be treated for his gunshot wound. While he was in the hospital, the court convicted him and sentenced him to eight months in jail. He would be under house arrest until he fully recovered from his injury and that time would count toward serving his sentence. When his wound healed, he decided he'd rather be in a comfortable bed than a jail cell. He persuaded his doctor to put a fake cast on his leg, and he pretended to be in recovery until his jail sentence expired.[22]

Thomas spent little time in the hoosegow, but buying the wrong car put him behind bars for a while. Black was by far the most popular color for automobiles. In fact, many models were available only in black. But Thomas wanted something flashier than basic black, so he bought a bright red Cadillac. His crimson car stood out in traffic, and lawmen found it easy to spot him on the road. One day he was driving along when he saw a police roadblock near Great Falls, Montana. He tried to drive around it, but the lawmen recognized his Cadillac and pulled out their machineguns. When the gunfire stopped, the red Cadillac looked like a target at a shooting range, but Thomas was okay. The episode earned him a short stretch in the Cascade County jail.

Marge Thomas, Pat's young daughter, accompanied her father on many bootlegging trips. Like her dad, Marge loved the adventure of the open road. On one trip lawmen shot at their car when Pat ran a police roadblock. The radiator was damaged, so Marge climbed onto the fender and poured beer on the radiator while her dad drove to a garage where the car could be fixed. Marge suffered from a chronic disease diagnosed as "blood eczema," and her treatment included X-ray therapy. Since no X-ray equipment was available in Havre, Pat Thomas used some of his whiskey money to buy a machine for her doctor's office.[23]

Although Havre was a small town in a remote location, the Bunch had a national distribution network. With a touch of local pride, Havre's liquor lords bragged that they delivered whiskey to every state in the union, except Maine, which had "too many toll gates." The Bunch took orders via telegraph and telephone. Urban mob bosses who needed large quantities of hooch traveled to Havre to haggle over the price. Railroad conductors and porters served as whiskey salesmen, picking up written orders as they crisscrossed the West on trains.

The Havre Bunch needed sizable, secret storage facilities to warehouse its booze. The syndicate stashed hooch underground in abandoned coal mines and in tunnels beneath buildings in town. A few miles from town the Bunch had a "chicken ranch" where whiskey was stored in the barn and poultry roamed around the property for authenticity. The Bunch stored liquor in the basement of a one-room school and gave the teacher a new car in exchange for her silence. Ranches north of Havre sheltered both booze and bootleggers. If a legger with a carload of hooch saw lawmen on the road, he could make a mad dash to a ranch and hide there. The farsighted bootleggers erected hollow haystacks on ranches to conceal their cars if necessary.[24]

Since many liquor convoys passed through Havre, hijacking booze from other gangs was a profitable sideline for the Bunch. If Havre men hijacked a convoy from a nearby town, they extended a sort of professional courtesy: they stole only half of the liquor. Convoys from farther afield lost all their booze when they dared to drive through Havre. To avoid being hijacked, wise bootleggers prepaid the Bunch for safe passage through town. The toll was high, but the liquor traffickers could pass the cost along to the consumer. A lone-wolf legger took a huge risk if he drove through Havre because he was an easy target for the local hijackers.

The Bunch wasn't the only hijacking hazard in Havre. The underpaid local lawmen supplemented their wages by stealing liquor from convoys passing through town. A scarcity of automobiles complicated matters for the gendarmes. They didn't have any squad cars, so they had to commandeer a taxi whether they were fighting crime or committing one. Taxis weren't plentiful in Havre, but somehow the cops managed to catch an occasional outlaw and rob a few liquor caravans.[25]

In 1924 the federal government beefed up its presence in northern Montana in order to curtail all types of smuggling. The U.S. Border Patrol established the Havre District Headquarters with ten patrolmen and two inspectors. In addition to enforcing the dry law, the unit was supposed to stop smugglers and keep illegal aliens out of Montana. The poorly-equipped federal lawmen drove old Model T Fords, which were no match for a bootlegger's souped-up whiskey six. "It was like sending a man out with a wheelbarrow to overtake a fast horse," an observer said.[26]

In the late 1920s the federal government assigned more Prohibition agents to Montana to fill the void created when the state repealed its baby Volstead law. The federal agents took over because the state and local lawmen withdrew from dry law enforcement. The feds earnestly set out to stop the bootleg traffic from Canada to Big Sky Country. They placed "spotters" with binoculars on rooftops to watch for bootleg convoys on the roads. They developed an intelligence network and put informants on the federal payroll. In many cases, when a Montana bootlegger left a Canadian liquor store, an informer called or wired the feds so they could be waiting when the car crossed the border. In a single month federal lawmen arrested 180 people, confiscated thirty-five stills, and seized nearly 2,900 gallons of liquor in Montana.[27]

When the feds made it harder to jump the line, Montana's booze barons sold more local moonshine and homemade concoctions. A popular formula for bathtub gin combined "cleaned" rubbing alcohol, juniper oil, gin oil, and distilled water. With colossal nerve, the liquor traffickers affixed labels for premium British brands to this sad imitation of gin. Beer was plentiful in Havre because an illegal brewery operated in tunnels beneath a shady establishment known as the Honky Tonk. The Prohis raided the brewery, smashed the bottles, and wrecked the equipment. This raid drastically reduced the supply of beer until local men opened a new brewery in the basement of a farmhouse.

In 1929 the Prohis staged numerous raids in Havre, and authorities padlocked fifty-two places involved in the illegal liquor trade. Some of the business owners were allowed to reopen under bond if they pledged to operate within the law. The stricter Volstead enforcement didn't put Havre's liquor traffickers out of business, but it did force them to operate on a smaller scale with greater secrecy. The handful of honest, hardworking Prohibition agents in northern Montana brought a modicum of law and order to the outlaw town, even though they failed to banish all the bootleggers.[28]

25. Seattle's Bootleg King and LSD's Johnny Appleseed

The gregarious Olmstead was known to the business and political elite of Seattle, and he found a ready clientele in a market that depended on personal connections. At its peak, Olmstead's business was delivering over two hundred cases of liquor daily to Seattle residents, hotels, and restaurants. — Richard F. Hamm, historian[1]

When Roy Olmstead was twenty years old, he joined the Seattle police force as a rookie cop walking a beat. A tall, extroverted man with a quick mind, Olmstead stood out in any crowd. His forceful, yet affable, personality made him a natural leader. People valued his opinion and trusted him to steer them in the right direction. He loved police work, excelled at it, and began moving up in the ranks. At age twenty-three he became a desk sergeant in the booking room. Ten years later he was promoted to lieutenant, the youngest man with that rank on Seattle's police force.[2]

Olmstead's job gave him an insider's view of bootlegging in the Emerald City. Like other cops, he observed the workings of the illegal liquor traffic and learned the tricks of the trade. He knew that bootleggers carried big wads of money, drove luxury cars, and whipped out cash to pay their bail. Obviously, liquor trafficking paid much better than the police department. The lure of easy money led Olmstead to a life-changing decision that would radically alter his future.

Olmstead's decision had unforeseen consequences, and he became the central figure in a groundbreaking legal case. In the Roaring Twenties, Americans took the telephone for granted as an everyday marvel; yet there were unresolved legal issues about the modern technology. Law enforcement used wiretaps to gather evidence, but legal experts disagreed over whether such evidence should be admissible in court. Did wiretapping violate the Fourth Amendment protection against unreasonable search and seizure? Did it violate the Fifth Amendment guarantee against self-incrimination? After the federal government used wiretaps to convict Olmstead of Volstead conspiracy, his case went all the way to the U.S. Supreme Court to resolve the legal issues.

Phonies

Shortly after Volstead began, federal Prohibition agents suspected that rumrunners were landing liquor on the Browns Bay shore near Edmonds, Washington. One night the Prohis checked out Browns Bay and saw men loitering on the shore. Assuming that the men were bootleggers, the agents barricaded the road to the shore and waited. In the wee hours of the morning they saw a tugboat stop in the shallow water. Hiding behind their barricade, the Prohis watched the leggers transfer cases of liquor from the boat to cars. Before the bootleggers could drive away, the agents opened fire. The leggers surrendered. The federal agents seized nine men, six automobiles, and nearly one hundred cases of whiskey. One quick-thinking bootlegger escaped by jumping into his car and driving around the agents' barricade. But the fugitive wouldn't evade the law for long. The feds knew him because he was a Seattle police officer nicknamed "the Baby Lieutenant."[3]

When Roy Olmstead was arrested, he glibly explained why he had been on the waterfront. He had gone to arrest the bootleggers, but the Prohis beat him to the punch. Although his story sounded plausible, it simply didn't hold water. Browns Bay lay outside his jurisdiction, and his superior officers denied any knowledge of his activity. He was dismissed from the police force and arraigned in federal court. He pled guilty, paid a $500 fine, and strolled out a free man.[4]

Now Olmstead could devote all his time to his moneymaking ventures. He had a grand vision of his future as a liquor lord. In order to dominate Seattle's liquor traffic, he formed a syndicate with eleven other men. He put up $10,000 in capital while the others contributed $1,000 each. Olmstead would be the CEO and would receive half of the rum ring's profits. He rented offices and garage space in the city. Outside town, he leased a farm, where his lackeys dug a huge underground storeroom to hold thousands of cases of whiskey. To transport liquor, he bought trucks and rumrunning vessels, both seagoing and small craft. He planned to operate on a large scale, so he hired truck drivers, mechanics, sailors, salesmen, collectors, lookouts, swampers, and a dispatcher. He even put an attorney on retainer because he anticipated an occasional clash with law enforcement.[5]

Olmstead's rum ring soon ruled the illegal liquor traffic in the Emerald City. Syndicate sales totaled more than $2 million per year in the early 1920s. Most of Seattle's bootleggers either joined Olmstead's ring or left the business. To keep gangland peaceful, the former cop didn't allow his men to carry guns. Hijackers occasionally stole a load of his liquor, but he just wrote it off as the cost of doing business. His policies created a tranquil underworld where mob hits were rarer than a sunny day in Seattle.

Like other West Coast liquor lords, Olmstead bought booze from exporters in British Columbia. Typically, an American placed his order for liquor with an export house in Vancouver and wired his payment to the exporter's Canadian bank. To hide the transaction, the merchant officially exported the liquor to Mexico, but the buyer arranged for it to be delivered to one of the tiny, isolated islets just north of the U.S. border. Industrious Canadian boatmen did a steady business delivering cargos of whiskey FOS (flat on the sand) to Discovery, Saturna, and D'Arcy islands. Olmstead favored the heavily-wooded D'Arcy Island, which attracted few visitors because it was home to a lepers' colony.[6]

Olmstead's rum ring sold directly to speakeasies, private clubs, restaurants, and individuals who ordered in bulk. Anyone buying only a bottle or two had to patronize a middleman.

Customers placed their orders via telephone to the dispatcher, who manned a desk with three phones. When a customer called, the dispatcher took the order, relayed it to a syndicate bootlegger, and followed up until it was delivered.[7]

The idea of using wiretaps to expose Olmstead's rum ring didn't originate with the Prohibition Unit but with a private detective who had an ax to grind. He had a personal grudge against Seattle's mayor and wanted to prove that His Honor was in cahoots with Olmstead. The detective and a telephone technician used micro-wires to tap into one of phone lines used by Olmstead's dispatcher. The technician had the expertise for the caper because he was a professional eavesdropper; he had learned his craft at a telephone company where his job was listening in on employees' calls.

The wiretapping duo soon collected a thick file of damaging evidence against Olmstead. The private detective knew he could parlay this information into cash if he found the right buyer. It could be used to prosecute Olmstead, so he went to the federal Prohibition office in Seattle and offered to sell the evidence for $1,000. Administrator William Whitney said the Prohis couldn't afford to pay that much. He offered a mere $50—far too little for the avaricious detective. Unable to make a deal with the feds, the private eye decided to try blackmail. He arranged a meeting with Olmstead and attempted to extort $1,000 from the bootleg king. But the former cop wasn't intimidated. He walked out of the meeting after telling the detective to get lost.

The private detective had failed to strike a deal with the Prohis' William Whitney, but he had planted an idea in the administrator's mind. Whitney was a dedicated public servant who took his duties seriously. Yet, like a surprising number of officials sworn to enforce Prohibition, he was a drinking man. In fact, he was reputed to be an alcoholic who consumed up to a quart of liquor per day. Despite his weakness for demon rum, he was a law-and-order proponent who firmly believed in enforcing Volstead. Convicting Olmstead would be a major coup for him — one that he would greatly relish.

After talking to the private detective, Whitney was convinced he could use a wiretap to collect enough evidence to send Olmstead to prison. He sought out the private eye's telephone technician and offered the man a job. The expert eavesdropper joined the federal payroll as a Prohibition agent.[8]

The Prohis rented an office near the garage where Olmstead's telephone dispatcher worked. To help with the eavesdropping, Whitney recruited his wife, an ace stenographer. On a daily basis Mrs. Whitney and/or a Prohibition agent listened to the dispatcher's incoming calls and made notes. Later she typed the notes, went over them with the agent and her husband, made corrections, and typed a clean copy. The wiretaps were yielding exactly the kind of evidence Whitney needed. In fact, he was so pleased with the results that he expanded the operation, tapping into other lines used by the rum ring, including Olmstead's home phone. The pages of transcripts mounted up, becoming a thick volume of evidence.

Olmstead became suspicious when he heard strange noises and static on his telephones. He believed someone was using a wiretap to eavesdrop on him. To find out for sure, he hired a telephone repairman to check the lines used by his dispatcher to take orders. The repairman found and removed two wiretaps. The next day Olmstead did his own inspection and discovered that the taps had already been replaced. He was dealing with a very determined snoop. He gave his operatives code names to use on the telephone and told them to be cautious because someone was listening in.

Olmstead assumed that the eavesdroppers were Prohibition agents, so he tried to mislead them. He went to a pay telephone to make important calls and gave out misinformation over his home phone. He especially liked to send the agents on wild goose chases to isolated beaches on cold, rainy nights. For his own amusement, he slipped barbs about Whitney into the conversations. He also mounted a counterattack, placing a wiretap on Whitney's office phone. When this tap produced little useful information, he removed it because he didn't want to get caught.[9]

Although bootlegging kept Olmstead busy, he found time for romance. A married man with children, he had an illicit affair with a young woman named Elise. A certain amount of mystery surrounded Elise, an Englishwoman who had moved to Canada after World War I. According to some sources, Olmstead met her while in Vancouver on rum-running business. Others said she was an undercover Prohibition agent who took a job as his bookkeeper in order to spy on him. Regardless of how they met, the bootleg king fell in love with her.

Olmstead and Elise had to delay their marital bliss until he could divorce his wife. While they waited for the legal process to run its course, they set up housekeeping without benefit of wedlock. He bought a lovely, spacious home in Seattle's exclusive Mount Baker district. With Elise's help, he furnished it with expensive furniture, Oriental rugs, and a grand piano. The kitchen boasted the latest conveniences, including an electric icebox by Frigidaire. After his divorce became final, the lovebirds tied the knot.[10]

In the Roaring Twenties, Americans went gaga over a new gadget — the radio. For the first time, a family could gather around a box in the living room, twist the radio knobs until they heard a station, and listen to music or other programming. Across the USA radio stations popped up like mushrooms because the public loved the amazing new medium. The Olmsteads used part of their wet wealth to start the American Radio Telephone Company in Seattle. They wanted to cash in on the latest trend, but they probably had an additional motive. Olmstead needed to communicate with the skippers on his rumrunning ships, and he could use his radio station to broadcast coded messages.

To supply the technical expertise needed for a radio station, the Olmsteads hired Alfred Hubbard, a purported science whiz. Known as "Seattle's Boy Inventor," Hubbard had achieved local fame for devising "an atmospheric power generator" that used radium. He claimed his device could generate heat, power a car or boat, furnish the electric current for a large home, or "illuminate a moderate-sized office building." He wowed the locals with a demonstration, using his invention to propel a boat around Portage Bay on Lake Union. He also talked of his plans to build a "vision radio machine." But the young inventor had little formal education and no special credentials in science. While he impressed the average Joe, the scientific community dismissed him as a blowhard.[11]

Although the chubby, boyish Hubbard looked harmless, he had a truly dark, duplicitous nature. A facile liar, he charmed many people, including Olmstead, who certainly wasn't naive or easy to fool. The manipulative young man quickly became more than an employee to the Olmsteads, who failed to see his true character. They treated him like a son, and he moved into their home, bringing his pregnant wife with him.

The Olmsteads built a long-range radio transmitter and a commercial broadcasting studio for their new station, KFQX. They also used their spare bedroom as a studio in order to have the convenience of broadcasting from home. KFQX had a strong signal that could be heard offshore and as far away as New Mexico. Like most early stations, it broadcast only at night. The programming consisted of news, weather reports, bedtime stories, and concerts by a local orchestra. Elise Olmstead read the children's bedtime stories before the orchestra played. The Prohis believed that she wove code words into her stories, telling Olmstead's skippers when and where to land their liquor cargos.[12]

One night in November 1924, after Olmstead's phones had been tapped for several months, he heard a loud knock on his front door. Elise was in the bedroom, reading a children's story on KFQX, so he went to answer the door. When he opened it, he saw sixteen Prohibition agents, led by William Whitney, on his front porch. They carried pump-action shotguns and a sledgehammer, in case they had to smash the door or shoot their way into the house. When Whitney flashed a search warrant, Olmstead politely invited the Prohis inside.

The agents searched the house from top to bottom, turning everything topsy-turvy, but they found no liquor. Whitney was determined to arrest Olmstead, so he tried another tactic. Using phone numbers gleaned from the wiretaps on Olmstead's phones, Whitney began calling the liquor lord's associates, trying to lure them to the house. Imitating Olmstead's voice, Whitney invited people to come over for a BYOB party. He proved to be quite persuasive. Over the next few hours, the Olmstead home filled up with people, including bootleggers, KFQX employees, and a bewildered orchestra leader. When the guests arrived with their liquor, the Prohis confiscated it and at gunpoint herded them into the living room. It was no party, but the Olmsteads felt an obligation to entertain their visitors, so Elise told her cook to fry ham and eggs for everyone. After the repast, the Prohis arrested Olmstead, Elise, and ten others. Everybody else was free to leave.[13]

After the raid at Olmstead's house, the Prohis made a concerted effort to put his syndicate out of business. Prohibition agents arrested dozens of his associates. They also raided his attorney's office and seized legal files that could be used as evidence at trial. In January 1925 a federal grand jury returned indictments against ninety people, including Roy and Elise Olmstead, for conspiring to violate the dry law. With so many defendants, the attorneys on both sides of the case needed extra time to prepare; the court scheduled the trial for January 1926.[14]

Due to the indictments, Olmstead's rum ring fell apart, leaving him without a steady income. Because he no longer had a reliable cash flow, he was forced to sell his radio station, losing money on the deal. For income, he joined with a former partner to start a new bootlegging business, far less ambitious than his defunct syndicate. The partners formed a small gang to smuggle whiskey from British Columbia into Washington via railcar, barge, and speedboat.[15]

Without the radio station, Al Hubbard had no job, so Seattle's Boy Inventor changed vocations. He joined the bootlegging fraternity as an order taker/salesman for Olmstead's new business. Over time he graduated to office manager, taking charge of deliveries, collections, and bookkeeping. He preferred the safety of office work, so he turned down repeated invitations to go on rumrunning trips. When he finally summoned up enough nerve to sail with one of Olmstead's best skippers, he found it exhilarating. He loved skimming across the open water at high speeds. The danger inherent in delivering an illegal cargo was an added thrill. He began sailing regularly, and he used his mechanical skill to increase the speed of Olmstead's booze boats.

Although the Olmsteads treated Hubbard like a beloved son, the young man showed no loyalty to them. With perfidy befitting Judas, Seattle's Boy Inventor went to the federal Prohibition office and offered to betray his friend and employer. He promised to help the Prohis convict Olmstead in exchange for a job as an undercover agent. His intimate knowledge of Olmstead's business would virtually guarantee a guilty verdict and a stiff prison term for the bootleg king.

The Prohis hired Seattle's Boy Inventor as a sort of double agent to help them nail Olmstead. In his new role, Hubbard continued his illegal activities and also met regularly with a Prohibition agent. He gave the feds information about Olmstead's illicit business and passed along pertinent documents, such as bank deposit slips. He also met with a stenographer, who took dictation from him and turned his words into typed reports that would be useful in building a case against Seattle's bootleg king.[16]

In the mid–1920s, the Coast Guard beefed up its operations on the Pacific Ocean, making rumrunning more perilous along Washington's coast. In response, Olmstead changed his modus operandi. His boats from Canada delivered their cargo to the western side of Whidbey Island, a long land mass situated in U.S. waters, separated by Skagit Bay from mainland Washington. Olmstead's swampers met the booze boats, carried the liquor ashore, loaded it onto trucks or wagons, and moved it to a cove on the eastern side of the island. When Olmstead needed the liquor, the swampers transferred it to fishing boats that carried it down the Saratoga Passage to Everett or Seattle.[17]

After a year of waiting, Olmstead finally went to trial on the Volstead conspiracy charges. Dubbed "the Whispering Wires" trial by the press, this case would make judicial history as a landmark decision on using wiretaps to obtain evidence. Although ninety people had been indicted, only half of them went on trial. Some of the accused had already pled guilty and/or turned state's evidence to curry favor with the federal prosecutors. Thirty-two defendants had absconded to Canada, which did not extradite U.S. citizens in liquor cases. Several defendants were excused during the trial, mostly due to dismissal for lack of evidence.

The prosecution called dozens of witnesses who described every phase of the Olmstead syndicate's operations, from buying liquor in British Columbia to selling it in Washington. Former bootleggers gave detailed testimony about the nitty-gritty of liquor trafficking in the Emerald City. Insiders testified that they had bribed Seattle policemen to ignore the syndicate's operations. Documents showed the acquisition of boats, trucks, and other equipment needed to transport booze. Prominent Seattle residents, including aircraft mogul William Boeing, took the stand and admitted buying liquor from Olmstead.[18]

The state's chief witnesses were Olmstead's former dispatcher and Prohibition administrator William Whitney. The wiretaps had produced an astounding 775 pages of transcribed phone calls, which had been bound into a heavy tome dubbed "the Doomsday Book." The prosecution and the defense sparred over admitting the Doomsday Book into evidence. Olmstead's lawyer objected to using the transcripts because wiretapping was a misdemeanor in Washington. The prosecutor pointed out that the federal courts were not bound by state statutes. Moreover, the Washington law did not explicitly ban the use of wiretap transcripts in the courtroom. The judge straddled the issue. He ruled that witnesses could use the Doomsday Book to refresh their memories but must not quote it verbatim. Thus, the evidence gleaned from the wiretaps was admissible, but the Doomsday Book itself was not admitted as evidence.[19]

The jurors endured nearly five weeks of testimony by more than 100 witnesses. Then the judge gave his instructions to the jury. Although he spent nearly two hours summarizing the case, he brushed over the wiretap evidence. It appeared that he was having second thoughts about the taps' admissibility and felt it wise to emphasize other aspects of the case. He stated that he believed the prosecution had proved Olmstead's guilt beyond a reasonable doubt, but the jurors must decide for themselves.

After being sequestered overnight, the jurors returned with their verdict. They found Olmstead and the other ringleaders guilty. They also returned guilty verdicts against the operatives who had played an active role in transporting the liquor, including the boat skippers and the truck drivers. The jury acquitted Elise Olmstead and five defendants who had played only minor roles in the syndicate. The court sentenced Roy Olmstead to four years in the federal prison on McNeil Island.[20]

Olmstead and two groups of his codefendants filed separate appeals contesting the admissibility of the wiretap evidence. Olmstead remained free while the Whispering Wires case made its way through the appeals process. To pay his legal expenses, he sold his house and its contents — even the prized electric icebox. He also resumed rumrunning on a limited scale. His boats carried small cargoes of Canadian liquor across the Strait of Juan de Fuca to Discovery Bay, where it was loaded onto trucks for the trip down the Olympic Peninsula. He shipped hooch from Vancouver to Seattle on railroad tankers that carried gasoline from the United States to Canada, were drained, and returned "empty" to Washington.[21]

The top men in Seattle's Prohibition unit worried that the appeals court would reverse the Whispering Wires verdict and void Olmstead's sentence. So they began making plans for another, grander Olmstead trial. The Prohibition chiefs planned to expose a vast liquor trafficking network of bootleggers and corrupt lawmen, including Seattle police officers, deputy sheriffs, and Coast Guardsmen. This time the prosecution wouldn't rely on wiretap evidence. The case would be built around eyewitness testimony, with the double-dealing Al Hubbard as the star of the show. The emphasis on corruption would distinguish this case from the Whispering Wires trial.

In May 1926 a federal grand jury heard evidence against several bootlegging gangs in Seattle, including Olmstead's. Although scores of witnesses testified, the state's big gun was Hubbard, who seemed willing to betray anybody who had ever trusted him. After the jury issued indictments, the police arrested bootleggers, lawmen, bankers, ranchers, and government officials. They also nabbed unlucky Canadian liquor exporters who had chosen the wrong time to visit Washington. Many of the indictees fled the state, but Olmstead went to the U.S. marshal's office and turned himself in.[22]

In October 1927 the new case began, with the bribery and corruption charges taking center stage. This trial covered Olmstead's illegal activities during the period when Hubbard had served as his right-hand man. Some of Olmstead's codefendants were familiar figures because they had also been part of the Whispering Wires case. But there were new faces, including Olmstead's allies in the police department, the sheriff's office, and the U.S. Coast Guard. Olmstead himself was conspicuously absent — a fugitive from justice. Even though he had surrendered to the marshal, he disappeared shortly before this new case went to court.[23]

Before the trial began, the never trustworthy Hubbard was suspended from his job as a Prohibition agent because he was caught taking bribes from bootleggers. Despite this latest black mark on Hubbard's record, he was the state's marquee witness because the case would fall apart without him. Under oath, he said he had become a Prohibition agent because he grew disgusted with the "whole rotten business of bootlegging." He described Seattle's illegal liquor trade and explained his role as Olmstead's trusted lieutenant. He admitted he had spied on Olmstead while keeping up the masquerade of being close friends with the bootleg king.

After five days of testimony, the judge turned the defendants' fates over to the jury. Whether consciously or unconsciously, the jurors divided the accused into two groups — bootleggers and lawmen. They acquitted all the law officers and found all the bootleggers guilty. This simplistic, biased approach to justice angered the leggers and their families. A bootlegger's wife was so mad that she caught up with Hubbard outside the courtroom and punched him in the face.[24]

Shortly after this trial ended, Olmstead resurfaced in Seattle. Law enforcement quickly locked him up in the King County jail because he had yet another trial on the court docket. There appeared to be no way the prosecution could lose this upcoming case because the bootleg king had been caught red-handed. In November 1925 Prohibition agents had nabbed Olmstead, Hubbard, and some other men on an isolated beach as they transferred a cargo of liquor from a boat to trucks. This would be a simple, straightforward case for the prosecution. Surely the verdict was a forgone conclusion. Nevertheless, Olmstead pled not guilty.

Testimony and arguments lasted only two days in this trial. Hubbard, who had turned state's evidence, was the prosecution's chief witness. He emphasized Olmstead's role as boss of the bootleg gang. He claimed that he had pretended to be part of the gang so he could collect evidence against the liquor lord. Elise Olmstead testified for the defense. She stated that Hubbard had actually owned the liquor cargo the men were unloading at the time of their arrest. Hubbard asked Olmstead to help him transfer the cargo, and she believed Hubbard set her husband up to be arrested. The jurors found her more truthful than Hubbard. They acquitted Olmstead.[25]

In November 1927 the U.S. Supreme Court refused to hear Olmstead's appeal regarding the Whispering Wires trial. The case seemed to be over. Only days later Olmstead traveled to McNeil Island, where he would serve his time. Reporters came to see him off. As he talked to the newsmen, he sounded contrite. "You can't tread on live coals without getting your feet scorched," he said. "I violated the law. That is always wrong. And now I am going to pay the penalty."[26]

To everyone's surprise, the U.S. Supreme Court did a volte-face, an extremely rare event for that august group. The last of the three Whispering Wires appeals reached the high court, and the justices reevaluated the issues. Although each case alone did not merit review, combining the appeals raised weighty constitutional questions. The court announced that it would hear the Whispering Wires case, merging all the appeals into *Olmstead v. U.S.* Roy Olmstead had reason to be ecstatic. At least, he would be out of prison for a while; at best he would never go back. He was released from McNeil Island, pending the Supreme Court's decision.

The U.S. Supreme Court heard *Olmstead v. U.S.* on February 20, 1928. In June the court issued its ruling, written by Chief Justice Taft. He focused on the Fourth Amendment, saying, "There is no room in the present case for applying the Fifth Amendment, unless the Fourth Amendment was first violated." Nevertheless, he noted that the defendants were not compelled to incriminate themselves; they had voluntarily used the telephone in a criminal enterprise.

Taft's ruling looked at the Fourth Amendment protection against the seizure of tangible, material objects. Did this protection extend to intangible, immaterial things — like voices? Capturing a voice over a telephone wire was obviously not the same as seizing a person's tangible communications, like letters. Moreover, the wiretappers had not invaded Olmstead's home or office. The taps had been placed on outside wires leading into his house and in the basement of an office building. "There was no searching. There was no seizure," wrote Taft. "There was no entry of the houses or offices." Thus, wiretaps did not constitute search or seizure within the meaning of the Fourth Amendment. Outside telephone wires were not part of an individual's home or office "any more than are the highways along which they are stretched." The Supreme Court let Olmstead's conviction stand.[27]

The high court had given law enforcement the green light to use wiretaps. Nevertheless, top officials took a cautious approach to wiretapping. U.S. Attorney General William Mitchell publicly stated that wiretapping should be eschewed "as a general practice" and must be "used only under exceptional circumstances." The preponderance of public opinion agreed with the attorney general. A leading newspaper called wiretapping a "dirty business," and another said the Olmstead ruling "made universal snooping possible." Many editorial writers warned that wiretaps were a threat to individual liberty. Even an ASL leader argued against using taps to enforce Volstead. In response, the U.S. Congress passed legislation that the Supreme Court would later use to require federal agents to obtain a warrant before setting up a wiretap.[28]

Two High Roads

In Olmstead's early days at McNeil Island Federal Penitentiary, his job was harvesting the driftwood that washed up on the beach. Later he was promoted to chief clerk in the administrative offices. Ironically, his duties resembled those he had performed as a desk sergeant in the police department. In his leisure time he read voraciously, delving into books on philosophy, religion, and psychology. An inmate lent him *Science and Health*, the basic text of the Christian Science faith. Mary Baker Eddy's writings answered his most profound questions, and soon he became a devout Christian Scientist.

In the midst of the Great Depression, Olmstead was released from McNeil Island, after serving thirty-five months. Although he had run the Northwest's biggest liquor syndicate, he vowed to start a new, honest life. He struggled to keep his head above water in the stagnant economy. He sold pesticides door-to-door and, for a discount on his rent, fumigated apartments for his landlord. Later he juggled two jobs, working at a furniture store and running his own exterminating business.[29]

Law enforcement kept an eye on Olmstead but found no evidence that he was involved in crime. In fact, he showed no outward signs of being a rough character. An FBI report noted, "The subject does not drink, smoke, or use harsh language." He devoted much of his leisure time to religious pursuits. On Christmas Eve 1935 President Franklin D. Roosevelt granted Olmstead a pardon, restoring his full citizenship rights. The government also refunded the money he had paid in fines and court costs.[30]

At the time of his pardon, Olmstead was working at a retail credit bureau in Seattle.

He thanked his wife Elise for the pardon, saying that she had worked diligently on his behalf. "It was because of her loyalty and unceasing efforts that I have started life anew. My slate is clean now," he said. Despite his gratitude to Elise, they had serious marital problems and ended up in divorce court.

In his later years Olmstead became a full-time Christian Science practitioner. He regularly visited inmates at the King County jail, sharing his faith and urging them to become law-abiding citizens. "My life is now dedicated to God," he said. "I realize that I was lawless, that lawlessness is a state of mind. Nobody makes you lawless. You do it yourself by wrong thinking."

Olmstead died in 1966 at age seventy-nine, leaving a legacy of voluntarism and faith along with a modest estate for his children.[31]

Like Olmstead, Al Hubbard spent years searching for the right pathway, but his quest took a bizarre turn. In 1936 he was arrested as a "key figure" in a rum ring that smuggled liquor from Mexico to California even after the repeal of Prohibition. Once again he showed no loyalty to his comrades and turned state's evidence, trying to avoid prison. However, this time the double-crosser was convicted and served a term at McNeil Island federal prison.

Hubbard left prison before the United States entered World War II, and he later told exciting tales about his exploits during the war. He claimed he had been an agent for the Office of Strategic Services and had worked on the Manhattan Project. He smuggled millions of dollars to finance covert operations in Europe and carried weapons into Canada for transfer to Britain. In his wartime fantasy, he flew airplanes and captained ships as part of his cloak-and-dagger work.

Hubbard actually did serve in the military during the war, but his fantastic tales have never been verified. In 1945 his citizenship rights were restored in a blanket Presidential pardon granted to thousands of ex-convicts who had been inducted into the U.S. military and had served at least one year.[32]

After World War II, Hubbard lived on Dayman Island, off the coast of British Columbia, where he hoped to build a cutting-edge research lab. He started grandiose ventures to market radium and radioactive products around the world. He also experimented with producing electrical power directly from radioactive sources.[33]

Hubbard seemed destined to spend his life dabbling with radioactive materials, but a vision sent him in another direction. While he was hiking in the woods, an angel appeared to him. She said that something supremely important to the future of mankind would happen soon and he would play a crucial role in it. Although she offered no specifics, he knew he was destined for greatness. Subsequently he stumbled across an article about lysergic acid (LSD) in a scientific journal. Intrigued by the drug's potential, he procured some and took his first acid trip. *Voilà!* He understood the angel's prophecy. He was destined to be an LSD evangelist. He would spend the rest of his life helping people turn on and tune in.

Hubbard became a psychiatric researcher, thanks to a PhD picked up by correspondence from a diploma mill. He specialized in aviation physiology and pilot stress. In the name of medical research, he gave flyers hallucinogenic drugs — mainly mescaline and LSD — to reduce stress. He also experimented with LSD as a cure for "irretrievable alcoholics." He gave large doses of LSD to chronic alcohol abusers to see if the drug would induce "a drastic and permanent change in the way they viewed themselves and the world."[34]

Hubbard worked as a consultant at the International Foundation for Advanced Study (IFAS) in Menlo Park, California. The group conducted clinical studies on the effects of LSD and mescaline until the 1965 Drug Abuse Control Amendment placed severe restrictions on LSD. Shortly before the United States criminalized LSD, Hubbard borrowed a large sum of money and purchased a supply — purely for research use, of course. When interrogated by the FBI, he claimed that he kept his stash in Canada, far beyond the reach of U.S. law enforcement.

Hubbard became a special investigator for the Stanford Research Institute, gathering data on drug abuse, student unrest, and radical political groups. He fraternized with psychiatrists and scholars who studied psychedelic drugs, but he may have been more drug peddler than researcher. By the late Sixties hallucinogenic drugs were extremely hard to procure. Yet Hubbard supplied his friends with mescaline, psilocybin, and Sandoz LSD-25. On one occasion law enforcement nabbed him in Switzerland with a large supply of LSD; he claimed to be a Canadian citizen and was released.

In 1982 Hubbard died at age eighty-one in Casa Grande, Arizona. He was destitute and living alone in a trailer park. Yet he was a celebrity of sorts — revered in the Drug Culture as the "Johnny Appleseed of LSD."[35]

26. Dutiful Wives and Desperate Mothers

Every woman can find lasting romance — even the lady moonshiner if a man loves her still.
— Anonymous

Women's groups, especially the WCTU, worked arduously to enact national Prohibition. In contrast, women played a very minor role in the groups that tried to prevent Prohibition. This meshed with the general perception that men drank but ladies didn't. Men hung out at saloons while their womenfolk waited at home, keeping dinner warm. Men competed in the rough-and-tumble real world while ladies led sheltered lives dedicated to family, home, and church. In the Roaring Twenties, daring women smashed these gender stereotypes to smithereens. The rebellious gals wore short skirts, smoked cigarettes, drank bathtub gin, and danced the Charleston. A shocking number also worked in the illegal liquor traffic.

The WCTU ladies were appalled because the Volstead law drew many women into criminal ventures. In general, these female offenders had no criminal record before the Great Drought. Yet they couldn't resist the lure of making easy money in the illicit liquor trade. Court records indicate that most female bootleggers were desperate mothers, dutiful wives, or both. The desperate mother, often a widow, worked in the liquor traffic to support her family. The dutiful wife acted as her husband's accomplice in crime, either voluntarily or under duress. More than one obedient wife truly believed in Prohibition but was coerced into bootlegging by her spouse.

The majority of women bootleggers worked in tandem with a man, but a small portion operated alone or in partnership with other women. The typical distaff Volstead violator divided her time between her family and her moneymaking ventures, much like a modern business woman. She worked in the illegal liquor traffic while also fulfilling her role as wife, mother, and homemaker. A stay-at-home mom could double as an alky cooker, a beer-flat hostess, or an order taker for a bootlegger. Female Volstead violators who did "public work" were likely to run a cafe, grocery store, or other business where selling liquor was a logical adjunct. In some neighborhoods even ladies' dress shops sold hooch.

The epidemic of Volstead crime among women surprised and alarmed the public. The criminal justice system struggled to deal with the sudden influx of female offenders. Extenuating circumstances often led judges to be lenient with women, but the basic principle of equal justice seemed to mandate comparable punishment for the sexes. When Volstead began, Prohibition Commissioner John Kramer declared in favor of stiff penalties for female offenders. "Women who violate the national Prohibition law may expect no leniency from the enforcement officials because of their sex," he promised.[1]

A woman was the defendant or codefendant in one-fourth of all Volstead trials, according to Prohibition official Roy Haynes. "It is bad enough for the men of the country to become lawbreakers in large numbers, but when the women follow in their footsteps, things seem to be getting in rather bad shape," Haynes said. "If it were just the women of the lower classes it would be bad enough, but 'society' women are doing it. Even the young girls are taking up the practice ... I declare it is a problem that seems to be getting worse as the days go by."

Haynes urged law enforcement to get tough with the ladies. "It is high time that women find they cannot get away with things just because they are women," he said. "The law must be enforced, and social climbers and silly girls will begin to realize that being arrested is no joke, but a disgrace."[2]

In the Roaring Twenties the dry law and the Harrison Narcotic Act led to the arrest of women in record numbers. The federal prison system had no females-only facility, which restricted the options for incarceration. Women's groups, including the WCTU, lobbied Congress to fund a progressive, up-to-date facility for female offenders. The need for such a facility was undeniable, and Congress appropriated money for it.

The Federal Prison Camp for women opened in Alderson, West Virginia, in 1927. The minimum-security prison, nicknamed "Camp Cupcake," looked like a college campus. A brick

A woman's boot might be a flask holder as well as a fashion statement (Library of Congress).

structure with stately columns dominated the complex. The inmates lived in cottage dormitories, and guards were on duty only at night. Most of the women worked in the sewing and knitting shops. Inmates could take academic or vocational classes, and emphasis was placed "upon the value of music as a therapeutic measure."[3] (Decades after Prohibition ended, Camp Cupcake would be in the news as the home of a famous prisoner — domestic doyenne Martha Stewart.)

The Quality of Mercy

In the early years of the Great Drought, judges were often sympathetic to women arrested on Volstead charges. Although chivalry was dying, it wasn't quite dead and nearly all judges were male. Like other men of their generation, they believed in protecting ladies from such sordid places as jail. Some male judges simply refused to send a woman to prison for anything less than murder or a very egregious felony.

Attitudes toward female offenders hardened over time because many of them tried to exploit their gender to escape punishment. A frustrated Prohibition official urged judges to stop coddling women. "We realize that the sight of a woman with six or seven children being dragged into jail is not very inspiring," he said, "but the laws were made for women as well as men. The male bootleggers ... have taken advantage of the situation by attempting to hide behind petticoats." A judge in Brooklyn declared, "I am getting tired of husbands who let their wives do bootlegging for them ... and send them to weep in court. I shall deal more severely with such cases in the future." In another New York court the judge said he would show no leniency to female leggers because the city offered "plenty of honest work for women." He sentenced three distaff alky cookers to the gloomy, forbidding, rat-infested Tombs (AKA the Manhattan House of Detention).[4]

At the federal Prohibition office in Los Angeles, the supervising agent announced that his men would no longer treat females with kid gloves. "We have found it necessary to use more drastic measures toward women defendants because of the fact that bootleggers are taking advantage of previous lenient measures to use women more extensively as agents and decoys," he said. "No matter how comely or pitiful women bootleggers caught by our men may be ... we propose to make them face the same sort of prosecution as that meted out to the men."[5]

A Texas judge agreed that female offenders deserved harsher treatment. "I'm tired of women appearing before me and begging for mercy simply because they are women," he said. "From now on, I'm going to treat them as men. They smoke cigarettes, hold men's jobs, and otherwise act as men." In Santa Ana, California, a judge rejected the jury's recommendation of leniency for a woman convicted of bootlegging. "The jury's sympathy may have been won by the fact that she is a woman," said the judge, "but that cuts no figure with me." He sent the lady legger to the country jail for the maximum sentence, six months.[6]

Arkansas officials stated that distaff bootleggers dominated the liquor traffic in the Wonder State. "Seventy-five percent of the bootlegging in this state is being carried on by women," stated a Prohibition administrator. In 1929 the Prohis planned a crackdown that would put hundreds of Arkansas women on trial in federal court. Although the judges were usually lenient with the ladies, a Prohibition official declared that the "days of Southern chivalry" had ended for female leggers. "Previously we have had to pay little attention to

Two Navy nurses, who were accused of smuggling liquor from Cuba to Virginia, posed with their attorneys in 1925. They were acquitted at their trial, the first court martial for women in the history of the U.S. Navy (Library of Congress).

the women because we had no place to confine them," he said. "Now that the new reformatory at Alderson, West Virginia, is completed, we have a place for them and intend to treat them rough."

The Prohis did extensive undercover work to prepare for the crackdown in Arkansas. The sweep began with raids and arrests in Miller County on the Arkansas-Texas border. On the first day, lawmen arrested fourteen women, equally divided between whites and African Americans. They also arrested six men. A Prohibition official said, "We have data to show that fifty percent of the women engaged in peddling liquor in Arkansas are doing so as agents for their husbands or men friends." He scornfully accused the males of hiding behind the ladies' skirts.

As part of the Arkansas crackdown, more than twenty female offenders were arraigned in Texarkana. A grand jury indicted sixteen of them for possessing and/or selling liquor. Eleven of them pled guilty. An elderly, "bent and gray" father appealed for clemency for his three daughters. One of them was "a helpless cripple" due to an auto accident that had occurred after her arrest. Her husband had deserted her, leaving her destitute. The old man's other daughters were widows with a total of nine children between them. They depended on liquor money to support the kids. Another father appealed for leniency for his daughter, a runaway child bride married for only a few months. The girl pled not guilty, even though dry agents swore that they had purchased whiskey from her. The prosecution agreed to dismiss her case after she promised to obey her father, give up her wanton ways, and never sell whiskey again.[7]

Tales of Woe

In courts across the USA, tearful women told sad sagas of being forced into the liquor trade because they had to support their children or a sick husband. Although the tales of woe had the same plotline, the details varied from case to case. The female offenders almost always cited poverty as their reason for breaking the law. Women had few career choices and even fewer opportunities to earn a high salary. A woman lucky enough to find a job usually took home a tiny paycheck, far too little to support her family. Predictably, the prospect of making money in the informal economy drew desperate women into the illegal liquor traffic.

When the needy woman's case went to trial, she claimed hardship and begged for leniency because her family depended on her. How she fared varied from court to court. Her story might fall on the ears of a sympathetic judge and jury who would acquit her or find her guilty yet mete out light punishment. But it might fall on deaf ears.

In Mount Holly, New Jersey, Mary Storline told the judge she bootlegged to support her sick spouse and five children. Despite her hardship, the judge fined her $350 and sent her to jail because she couldn't pay it. Kind neighbors cared for her family while she languished in the hoosegow. A Sunday school teacher tried to raise the money to pay Storline's fine but scraped together only $250. The judge agreed to reduce the fine, and Storline was released after six months in jail.[8]

Irma Lackman, who claimed to be a reluctant bootlegger, was arrested in New Orleans. In court she admitted her guilt. "I would rather be dead than violate the law," she said. "We have two young children though, and I was forced to sell liquor or see them go hungry and without clothes." Because her husband was serving a jail term, she was the head of the household. For months she had looked for a job without success. In desperation, she began bootlegging. She said that she sold liquor to friends "who were willing to buy to help me support my children." The judge gave her a suspended sentence plus five years' probation.

Odelia Ray, an African American woman in New Orleans, sold booze to provide for her seven children. In court she testified, "Some men told me that they had to have two gallons of liquor a week and would buy it from me to help me support my family. I was selling only to them." In pleading her case, she promised she would never break the law again. The judge, who seemed to find her sincere, gave her a suspended sentence plus probation.[9]

In Oakland, California, J.J. Catelini and his wife Florence were arrested for selling wine. In court Florence held her youngest child, a babe-in-arms, while her case was heard. After the couple pled guilty, the judge fined J.J. $250 and Florence only $1. He warned the couple that "their family of six little ones" would not be a mitigating circumstance if they were arrested again.[10]

Californian Louise Casella claimed she sold booze to pay college tuition for her daughter, a sophomore at the University of California. "The only reason she sold liquor was to get money to send me to college," Casella's daughter told the judge. "It was all my fault." A Prohibition agent accused the mother of being a virago who "put up the hardest fight I ever saw in my life." He said, "It took four of us to put the handcuffs on her." The judge ordered Casella to pay a fine and also sentenced her to six months in jail.[11]

Mrs. Vincent Ponic of Chicago ran a beer flat to pay her son's law school expenses at Notre Dame University. At her vacation home on Lake Fox, she took in nearly $5,000 during the summer season. When she and her lawyer-husband got a divorce, the court heard testimony about her illegal business. "My wife makes more money selling beer than I make practicing law," her husband said. "She turned my home into a beer flat and ruined my reputation as an attorney."[12]

Widow Women

Poor widows made up a sizeable portion of the women trying to earn a living in the illegal liquor trade. As a group, they elicited empathy, even from hardened cops and judges. J. Carroll Cate headed the federal Prohibition unit in East Tennessee, a region rife with moonshiners. "I've turned many a widow woman loose and never made a report," Cate admitted. "I did it because ... her children would have had no food."[13] A significant number of lawmen joined Cate in refusing to arrest impoverished widows. However, others felt their duty to enforce the law barred any special treatment for poor women.

In Jonesboro, Arkansas, the widow of a deputy sheriff was given a suspended sentence for selling liquor. Her late husband had stored a large quantity of confiscated liquor in an outbuilding on their property. Over time, she sold the booze in small amounts to support her children. Widow Rebecca Hirschman was arrested on Coney Island and charged with carrying a gallon of whiskey in a satchel. She told the grand jury that this whiskey was the only thing of value her husband had left her and she was selling it to pay some bills. The jury didn't indict her.[14]

Acting on a tip from a group called the Volstead Vigilantes, Prohibition agents in New Orleans raided widow Marie Hoppe's home, where they seized 130 bottles of homemade beer. At Hoppe's arraignment, she told the judge that beer was a healthy, nutritious drink. She believed it was "vital for a child's muscle development." She faithfully gave each of her children a daily glass of beer and drank her own dose of three glasses per day. The judge believed she was selling part of her homebrew, so he ordered her held for trial. Sadly, the widow died before her trial, leaving her children orphaned.

A widow was arrested for selling whiskey in her small hotel on Bourbon Street in New Orleans. She pled guilty and asked for leniency because she was the mother of three daughters. The judge wasn't in a lenient mood. When he sentenced her to the parish prison, she collapsed and needed assistance to stand up. The judge showed that he was not totally insensitive to her plight. He didn't impose a fine, and he gave her time to arrange for childcare before going to prison.

Mary Rourke, a widowed mother of nine, was arrested for selling liquor at her boardinghouse in New Orleans. After her arrest, she stopped selling booze and tried to make an honest living. Sadly, without the liquor sales, she couldn't make enough money to provide for her children. At her trial, a Prohibition agent testified on her behalf, saying that she was destitute without the liquor money. The judge placed Rourke on probation and told her to find another source of income.

Widow Albertine Durine ran a restaurant in the French Quarter in New Orleans. When she was arrested for serving liquor, she claimed financial hardship. Her husband had been dead for several years, and the restaurant produced a meager income. She admitted that she was "technically guilty" of selling liquor but didn't feel she had committed a serious crime. "I merely had it on hand for those patrons who still like a drink with their meals," she told the court. She claimed that most of her drinking patrons were personal friends. Prohibition agents testified that they had found only a tiny amount of liquor in Durine's restaurant. Nevertheless, the court fined her $200 and sent her to the parish jail for three months.[15]

In Barre, Vermont, the granite industry employed many men in hazardous workplaces where they inhaled dust that caused chronic diseases. These diseases, combined with the Spanish flu epidemic, produced a large number of widows in Barre after World War I. The women had few job choices. Some tried to make ends meet by babysitting, doing laundry, or cleaning houses. Others took in boarders or found low-paying jobs in stores or offices.

A few enterprising Barre widows scraped together enough money to buy a supply of booze and turn their homes into bars. After work, men would come to enjoy a drink and play a friendly game of cards. "Men in Barre were thankful for the widows," a local resident said. "It gave them a place to drink, hang out with friends, and play cards. The widows didn't get rich, but they made enough money to pay their bills.... There wasn't any stigma about running such a house because most people realized the women didn't have any other choice."[16]

In the frontier town of Butte, Montana, homes buzzed with activity as independent, self-reliant women made and sold alcoholic beverages. More than one Butte mother confessed to making alcohol in her kitchen so she could work at home while caring for her children. Nora Gallagher was a widow raising a houseful of kids. When the police raided her home, she admitted that she was running a still in her kitchen. She was trying to earn enough money to buy Easter outfits for her children. In Butte's Dublin Gulch neighborhood, women who ran boardinghouses made wine to serve their boarders and to sell for a little extra cash.[17]

Texanna Chappell, a Virginia mother with six children, became a widow when her husband died suddenly. At his funeral, a relative told Chappell that many people were earning money as alky cookers and she could, too. Later, the helpful relative sent her a recipe for making corn whiskey. One day when Chappell's children were crying due to hunger, she decided to become an alky cooker. She bought the components for a still, assembled it herself, and set it up in her home. She was afraid to fire up the still because she nervous and apprehensive about breaking the law. But she calmed down, made her first batch, and sold it to a neighbor who bootlegged.

"With that first money, I gave a party for the youngsters," Chappell said. "We had chicken, and ice cream and cake, and everything that the kids could think of."

After Chappell had been making alcohol for several months, acquaintances told her that the police were planning to raid her house. She disposed of her mash, dismantled her still, and poured all her whiskey down the drain. She knew that bootleggers routinely bribed the cops to stay away, but she didn't know how to arrange that. "All the while I was making whiskey, I never even got up nerve enough to talk to a cop, much less offer him any money to lay off me," she said.

For about three months, Chappell refrained from making moonshine because she feared a raid. But she police didn't bother her, so she decided to fire up her still. She had a grand plan; she would make moon until she had enough money to open a boardinghouse. Unfortunately, before she could earn enough, the vice squad invaded her home. She was arrested, convicted, fined, and sentenced to a month in jail in Norfolk, Virginia. At the end of her sentence, she vowed to quit the liquor trade and show her children "that the straight way is the only really happy way to live."[18]

Young Offenders

In terms of age, female Volstead violators ranged from young teens to senior citizens. The teenaged girls often worked in family operations, although a surprising number struck out on their own. Lawmen, to their astonishment, sometimes found older teen girls calling the shots in small gangs. These girls had leadership and management skills they could've used in an honest career, but for various reasons they were drawn into liquor trafficking.

Fourteen-year-old Mary Squeglis was among the youngest Volstead violators in New York City. She was arrested for selling whiskey to a customer in her mother's shop on Coney Island. Her mother was also arrested and charged with "impairing the morals of a minor." In a similar case, young Bertha Johnson was charged with selling whiskey in her mother's store in Burlington, New Jersey. The teenager said she sold booze to pay for her school clothes. She was sentenced to forty-five days in the county jail because she couldn't pay a $300 fine. She went to jail but spent only a few days there. Helpful friends and neighbors raised enough money to pay her fine.[19]

In Springfield, Massachusetts, sixteen-year-old Sarah Levyl ran a moonshine business, supported her siblings, and managed to save a sizable nest egg before she was arrested. The court gave her a suspended sentence and ordered her to move away "from her present home, in a locality where much moonshining has been brought to light." Levyl promised to make an honest living in the future.[20]

Prohibition agents accused Helen Ross, age nineteen, of leading a band of bootleggers in Los Angeles. She dressed in men's clothing, and the male gang members took orders from her. In Kansas City, lawmen arrested a group of girls "who were vamping doctors" to obtain prescriptions for medical alcohol. Evidence indicated that the girls were selling the hospital whiskey, but the judge let them go, after giving them a stern warning.[21]

Ida Lebeau, a poor farm girl in her early teens, ran her own bootlegging business in northern Vermont. She got her start when a man at the local blacksmith's shop offered to pay her if she would ride her horse to a moonshiner's farm to pick up a jug of stump juice. Although it was a bitterly cold night, she couldn't turn down the five dollars he promised her. She mounted her horse, made her way through the snow to the moonshiner's place, and picked up the jug. She returned to the blacksmith's shop — frozen to the core but happy to earn money.

Lebeau's family barely eked out a living on the farm, so her payday was a welcome windfall. Seeing her pathway to riches, she decided to go into the bootlegging business. In small towns, residents parked their horses and buggies in sheds while they shopped or took care of business. The sheds also served as a meeting place where men hung out, talking and drinking. In Orleans, Vermont, Lebeau scoured the shacks for discarded liquor bottles, which she took home and washed. She bought moonshine, poured it into her bottles, and packed them in a burlap sack. Then she climbed onto her horse and rode off to sell the shine to thirsty men.

She quickly built up a good business, often riding her horse to logging camps deep in the woods. As a group, loggers were heavy drinkers, and they worked up a mighty thirst using handsaws and axes to fell trees. Between sales trips Lebeau stored her liquor in her father's barn, burying the bottles in the haymow or grain bin. She netted a respectable profit, contributed to the family coffers, and saved enough money to buy every teenager's desire — her very own car.

Lebeau usually bought her liquor from a moonshiner, but one year at Christmastime she tried making her own. The venture turned out to be little short of a disaster. She recruited her uncle to help with the moonshining. They rigged up a still, made mash, let it ferment, and started distilling. For quality control, her uncle decided to taste their output. He liked it so much that he drank nearly all of it and got totally smashed. In a huff, Lebeau read the riot act to her uncle. Then she threw the leftover mash out into the yard, where the farm animals lapped it up. Soon the chickens and ducks were squawking and staggering around the barnyard like drunken sailors.

Lebeau's parents didn't approve of her illegal job and nagged her to quit because they feared for her safety. She might be waylaid and robbed on a back road. They warned her that she might be arrested, and they vowed they wouldn't bail her out of jail. But Lebeau didn't fear arrest. Lawmen generally ignored her as she went about her business, probably because she was so young and didn't look like the typical bootlegger.

Ironically, Lebeau's only arrest had nothing to do with bootlegging. One night when she was driving a friend's car, state troopers stopped the vehicle and arrested her because she had no driver's license. They took her to jail, but it wasn't set up for young women, so she spent the night at the sheriff's home. In the morning her father came to pay her bail. Although the bail was only $13, he was so mad that he yelled at her and hit her. The sheriff threatened to arrest him if he didn't cool down. Since he had hay to "get in," he calmed down, paid the money, and took his daughter home to work in the fields.[22]

The Buettner family ran a moonshine business on their farm near Schoeneck, Pennsylvania, in bucolic Amish Country. Violet, an older teen, delivered the moon made by her younger brother, who tended the still. Police stopped Violet's car more than once as she sped down the Lincoln Highway, the area's major thoroughfare. One day she was involved in an auto accident while delivering moonshine. Before the police arrived, Violet and her passenger, also a young woman, dumped one hundred gallons of whiskey in the field beside the highway. Even though they ditched the evidence, Violet was indicted and served a month in jail.

Schoeneck's dry activists complained that Violet's escapades besmirched the reputation of their small town. "The church people of the village are objecting to Violet always giving her address as Schoeneck when she is arrested for rumrunning," a local man told a reporter. The justice of the peace agreed that the god-fearing folks were "much offended" by Violet's shenanigans. "Despite the fact that there are a number of moonshiners operating in the hills around here," he said, "the church people of this community resent the publicity and notoriety resulting from Violet Buettner's alleged activities."

Newsmen took note and moved Violet to the town of Stouchsburg — in print if not in reality.[23]

Never Too Old

Illegal liquor provided income for a surprising number of older women who urgently needed money, usually to deal with family troubles. The enterprising seniors showed remarkable strength and fortitude as they craved out a niche in a cutthroat business run by mobsters. Judges sometimes sent older women to prison, which may have been a blessing in disguise for the frail, elderly ladies who struggled to keep the wolf from the door.

Prohibition agents caught Rosa Fontana, age eighty-three, making and selling wine in New Orleans. She was a fragile, doddering woman who needed help to walk. She claimed that she was making medicinal wine for her gravely-ill husband. The couple had run a profitable grocery store in the Garden District, but his illness had depleted their savings, leaving them penniless. Following Rosa's third arrest, she pled guilty to manufacturing and selling liquor. The judge, who sent Fontana to Alderson prison for fifteen months, seemed to think Camp Cupcake wouldn't be a hardship for her. "You will be as well off in Alderson as you are here," he told her.

Lawmen arrested sixty-something Dominica Cortono for making wine in her home in New Orleans. She told the court she was selling wine because she wanted to help her daughter buy a wedding trousseau. She was released on bond, and the charges were later dropped. Elsewhere in the Big Easy, lawmen nabbed a grandmother for operating a blind pig in her boardinghouse. She pled guilty but asked for leniency because she had custody of her grandsons. "I will die before I give my children up," she said. "I can take care of them, and I am going to!" The judge sentenced her to three months in jail with the stipulation that she would only serve thirty days. Her grandsons were placed in an orphanage while she did her time.[24]

Prohibition agents found more than eight hundred bottles of beer at the home of Lena Severance in Crawfordsville, Florida. Severance, age sixty-three, was running a restaurant of sorts in her house, trying to support herself and her sickly husband. She admitted owning the beer but claimed she had never sold any. "I did not sell the beer. I sold cheese and crackers and gave the beer to drink with the sandwiches," she said. "I have never been arrested for any violation of the National Prohibition Act."[25]

In Sausalito, California, a Prohibition agent suspected Annie Louder, age eighty, of selling liquor. He searched her soft-drink shop and found a quantity of wine. Then he searched her home, where he discovered nearly five hundred quarts of homebrew. Looking further, he found a substantial stock of jackass brandy. When he tried to seize Louder's personal stash of jackass brandy, she attacked, punching and scratching him. Although she inflicted ugly scratches on the agent, he did his job. A newspaper said Louder held "the old-age bootleg championship."[26]

Maggie Bailey of Harlan, Kentucky, probably set a record for longevity among moonshine purveyors. In 1921, at age seventeen she began selling moonshine and continued to do so until a few years before she died at age 101. Initially, she drove her horse and buggy far out into the woods in Harlan County to buy moonshine at the stills. Later, her sister, who had an old Dodge touring car, drove her to the stills.

Over time, Bailey built a thriving retail business and also sold moonshine wholesale to bootleggers. She was arrested and indicted many times but usually beat the rap because jurors liked her and refused to convict her. Her warm personality, her candor, and her generosity made her popular in the community. She became a sort of David bootlegger fighting the Goliath revenuers. Her only major bust came during World War II when she was persuaded to sell moonshine to an undercover federal agent. The feds raided her place, and she served time in a prison camp for women.

In later decades Bailey was "hauled into court at least one hundred times," according to a lawyer who represented her. "I don't care what the evidence was, the juries would not convict her," he said. One hectic day, Bailey had six trials in three different courts and was acquitted in all of them. A federal judge said, "I always thought she was a delightful lady. She was an expert on the Fourth Amendment. She knew the laws of search and seizure as well as any person I've known."[27]

Just Following Orders

More than a few women used the obedient wife defense to explain why they had broken the dry law. The obedient wife tried to minimize her guilt by claiming that circumstances forced her to become her husband's accomplice. Often the couple had money problems and turned to bootlegging to pay their debts. Generally, the woman felt she was honoring her marriage vows by doing what her husband expected her to do. She was simply fulfilling her duty as his helpmate. In the twenty-first century, the obedient wife defense seems absurd, but juries often found it reasonable in the 1920s.

Lawmen arrested Anne Foster for selling beer to a Prohibition agent in New Orleans. In court she pled guilty and said that obeying her husband was a higher duty than obeying the law. "I'll admit I got the bottle of liquor and gave it to the man," she said, "but my husband told me to, and I have to do what he tells me." The judge gave her probation and sent her husband to jail for ninety days. An observer approved of the judge's ruling, saying that "the court took cognizance of her allegiance to the marriage vows and dealt with her lightly."[28]

Young, blonde Gladys Bonicard was arrested when Prohibition agents stopped her car and found gallons of liquor, which she was delivering to an illegal saloon in New Orleans. In court she told the judge that she was helping her husband, a well-known liquor trafficker. She declared that "a woman should help her husband, even in bootlegging." The judge disagreed. He fined her $200 and sentenced her to sixty days in jail. Later the court also confiscated her car.[29]

In Brooklyn a woman was arrested for owning a still and making whiskey in her home. She told the grand jury that she made the alcohol for her husband, a Russian "accustomed to a regular ration of a quart of whiskey a week." She believed that making the liquor was one of her wifely duties, and she intended to honor her wedding vows. The grand jury didn't indict her.[30]

A jury in Detroit heard the case of Eleanor Lukitch who was accused of selling liquor to a policeman. The officer stated that he had consumed alcoholic beverages at Lukitch's house on several occasions and had bought a bottle from her. Lukitch claimed that she had never sold any liquor to the cop. However, she had given him free drinks because her husband told her to and she felt honor-bound to obey her hubby. The jury took only minutes to acquit Mrs. Lukitch.[31]

One More Time

Like their male counterparts, female bootleggers tended to be repeat offenders. A woman had a good chance of receiving light punishment for her first Volstead violation, but the penalties varied for subsequent convictions. For the most part, the sentences reflected the judge's own attitude toward women and how they should be treated. Some judges felt that justice required stiff penalties for repeat offenders regardless of their gender. Other judges felt that the fair sex couldn't withstand the harsh punishment meted out to men.

New Orleans resident Johanna Roberts was arrested twice within three months for selling liquor at her home. At her first arraignment, the single mom said she was selling only enough liquor to provide for her children. Her first husband had died, and the second had deserted her. The judge gave her a suspended sentence. When she was arrested again, the judge was decidedly unsympathetic. He sent her to jail for seven months.

When Marie Troia and her husband were arrested for bootlegging, they took their six children to the arraignment in a New Orleans court. The judge set the parents' bail onerously high at $4,000. The couple didn't hesitate to exploit their children, pushing the youngsters forward to appeal to the judge for leniency. The ploy worked, and the judge lowered their bail. Several years later the Troias were again arrested on Volstead charges. This time Mrs. Troia took all the blame. "My husband had nothing to do with the liquor," she said. "He works ... but we didn't have enough money to care of the kids, so I just kept on selling it." The charges against her husband were dropped. She paid a fine and was sentenced to the Alderson prison camp, far from her children.

Wilhemina Normandale, described by dry agents as a "quiet and well-mannered woman," sold liquor in a back room in her grocery store in the Irish Channel section of New Orleans. Lawmen raided her place and found an enormous stock of liquor. The court fined her $500 and sent her to jail for two months. Alas, jail failed to rehabilitate her. She returned to the liquor trade, so the authorities padlocked her store. Wilhemina was the mother of Harold "Dutch" Normandale, a notorious, oft-arrested gangster known as the "bad boy of New Orleans." Dutch had a long rap sheet for homicide, narcotics, auto theft, and other crimes. But he was never arrested for bootlegging. That was Mom's racket.[32]

One Christmas Eve a police detective spotted a well-known woman bootlegger driving along a street in Dallas, Texas. She sped away, with the officer in hot pursuit. He caught up, forced her to stop, and found forty-two gallons of whiskey in her car. The woman seemed resigned to her punishment. "Well, I'll just have to spend Christmas in jail," she said. "This is the third time I have been caught, and there's no use in wasting any money on a lawyer."[33]

In Los Angeles, Josefa Campo endured three trials for the same minor Volstead offense. Campo sold a pint of moonshine whiskey to a county Prohibition agent who worked in the sheriff's department. Campo's first two trials ended with hung juries. In the third, prosecutors finally convicted her and she was sentenced to a short term in jail. Critics said county officials had spent $3,000 to convict Campo for selling one pint while they ignored big-time bootleggers who sold thousands of pints.[34]

Not So Poor

The media stereotyped female Volstead offenders as indigent lower class women who belonged to ethnic or racial minorities. But this stereotyping overlooked a substantial segment of women in the illegal liquor trade. "Many people suppose that only the foreign-born women or the worst sort of colored women are engaged in selling or making liquor, but it is not so," said Prohibition official Roy Haynes.[35]

Haynes noted that society women figured prominently in the liquor traffic in Washington, D.C. The embassies in Washington were technically foreign soil, so liquor could be stored and served there. Imported wines and whiskies, highly coveted due to their scarcity, somehow made their way from embassy cellars to Washington's society bootleggers. A roundup of leggers peddling embassy liquor snagged several women who supplied hooch to tenants in posh apartment houses "in the fashionable Northwest section."[36]

Fashionably-dressed women bootleggers plied their trade at tourist sites in Florida. The ladies sold their intoxicating wares at hotels, beaches, parks, race tracks, and other touristy places in Miami. A woman could blend in with the travelers and carry a few pints or half-pints in a roomy purse or a beach bag. "Ladies in the smartest of summer costumes" sold booze at band concerts in Miami's Royal Palm Park.[37]

Katherine O'Connor, the daughter of a wealthy businessman, belonged to Denver's elite society. The community was shocked when O'Connor was indicted along with a Catholic priest serving at the Shrine of St. Anne. The two were accused of using forged withdrawal permits to obtain barrels of wine and whiskey from bonded facilities. They claimed they planned to give the liquor to a senior citizens' nursing home for medical use.

When the priest suddenly left Denver and dropped out of sight, officials launched a nationwide search for him. He surfaced in Pennsylvania and arranged to surrender to law enforcement. At trial, he was found guilty of Volstead offenses and sentenced to prison. Katherine O'Connor, his partner in crime, pled guilty to the charge of illegal possession and paid a fine. The priest appealed his conviction but lost and served his time in Leavenworth federal prison.[38]

In Berkeley, California, Kathryn Hayward made a niche for herself as a popular hostess who threw first-rate parties. Her husband was reputed to be a wealthy man, so her friends were surprised when she began selling liquor. Her faithful clientele included many college students at UC Berkeley. "It seems almost impossible that such a woman would stoop so low, but stoop she did," a Prohibition official said, "and [she] had almost ruined the morals and manners of hundreds of students ... before we realized how things were going there."

Two frat boys told law enforcement that Hayward was selling booze. At her trial, the boys testified that she had sold them pints of whiskey. They had also seen dozens of bottles of wine at her house. Hayward admitted selling booze "but said she made no profit and only wanted to accommodate the students so they could have liquor for their parties." The judge sentenced her to six months in the county jail but didn't require her to serve her time.[39]

Hayward wasn't the only bootlegger supplying booze to collegians. To almost no one's surprise, the illicit liquor traffic boomed around college campuses. Mary Elizabeth Hill, an attractive redhead, owned Betty's Place, a speakeasy popular with college students in uptown New Orleans. Prohibition agents checked out the place during a rowdy victory party for the

Tulane University football team. After the agents chose a table, Hill threw toy crickets on the tabletop and told the men to "make much whoopee." The Prohis, who claimed to be fanatic football fans, enjoyed the festivities for a while. Then they arrested Hill, her bartender, and her servers.

The raid briefly disrupted Hill's life, but she soon reopened Betty's Place. When the Prohis heard that she was back in business, they invaded the speakeasy and arrested her again. Her trial attracted lots of media attention, partly because she hired a female lawyer, a rarity in the Deep South. Attorney Claire Ernest Loeb argued that Hill was merely the speakeasy hostess, an employee rather than the owner. Loeb also asserted that the raid had been conducted without a search warrant.

The jurors deliberated for several hours before returning a verdict. They found Hill guilty of possessing liquor and maintaining a nuisance. However, they deadlocked on the charges that involved selling liquor, so those counts were dismissed. Before the judge pronounced sentence, a probation officer spoke on Hill's behalf. He insisted that she had quit the liquor business. He painted her as a chastened, reformed woman with serious family problems. She was getting a divorce and had lost custody of her children, who were living in an orphan asylum. The judge seemed unmoved by Hill's troubles. He imposed a $200 fine and sentenced her to six months in jail.[40]

In Madison, Wisconsin, Jennie Justo dropped out of the university and opened a speakeasy in the basement of her parents' house. Since the house was in the city's Greenbush area, locals called Justo "the Belle of the Bush." A reporter described Justo as "pretty and vivacious" and said she catered to "the better class of the student business." Her clientele included hip young faculty members as well as Joe College and Betty Coed. Her speakeasy was the "rendezvous for many a collegiate whoopee party." The place had a private room that was often reserved for parties, especially fraternity blowouts.[41]

Although Justo had an occasional brush with the law, she avoided prison in the Roaring Twenties. In June 1931, federal Prohibition agents and local cops raided her place. They seized a sizeable quantity of beer, wine, and bonded whiskey. At trial Justo pled guilty to violating the dry law. The judge fined her $500 and sentenced her to six months in the Milwaukee House of Corrections followed by probation. Authorities padlocked her basement speakeasy but allowed her family access to the furnace and coal bin.

After serving her time, Justo was released on probation and returned to Madison. But she violated the terms of her probation and was sent back to the Milwaukee facility. In March 1934, after Prohibition had ended, Justo was released. She went home to Madison and married a local sports star. For decades the couple operated supper clubs in and around Madison. Justo's cooking skills brought her renown among the townspeople. Customers raved about her sensational food and forgot about her shady past. She lived a full life, dying at age eighty-three, a respected member of the community.[42]

Her Highness, Queen of the Bootleggers

The press tended to bestow the title of queen on any woman who made a name for herself in the bootleg trade. Since Prohibition opened new doors for women in crime, the bootleg queens were rarely hardened criminals. Many were young, pretty flappers who wore bobbed hair and stylish clothes. They were modern women in that they were strong, independent, and willing to compete in a man's world. They drove fast cars, outran the police, and didn't wilt when they faced danger.

New Englanders called Hilda Stone the Queen of the Border Rumrunners. Authorities said she was "one of the chief field lieutenants" of a rum ring headquartered in Greenfield, Massachusetts. When she jumped the line, she drove a car "with skillfully devised" secret compartments for hauling liquor. On one occasion lawmen stopped her and found an astonishing 560 bottles in her car. She was fined $500. She crossed the international border so often and so easily that Customs officials suspected she had help. They accused a U.S. customs inspector of being her accomplice. When asked to resign, he quit and began a new career in bootlegging.[43]

In the Mid-Atlantic region, the Queen of the Bootleggers was Nettie Martin, "a young, petite blonde of the flapper type." She and her husband George led a daring, ruthless gang that stole whiskey from bonded distilleries. Nettie was known for her high-speed, daredevil driving when she drove the getaway car to escape the police. George was reportedly the "brains" of the outfit, but federal lawmen said Nettie was "as clever as her husband." Her name was "mentioned with mingled admiration and wrath by dry agents."

Law enforcement officials alleged that the Martins staged at least seven distillery robberies in Maryland and Pennsylvania. In one daring heist, the Martin gang, with Nettie in charge, invaded the Foust Distillery in Glen Rock, Pennsylvania. Brandishing sawed-off shotguns, they disarmed the security guards and loaded more than 180 barrels of whiskey onto trucks.

The Martin gang pulled off multiple robberies at the Outerbridge Horsey Company Distillery in Maryland. George, Nettie, and eight gang members were arrested and indicted for stealing eleven hundred cases of whiskey from Outerbridge in September 1921. George was the first to be prosecuted. Although the state presented a strong case with several witnesses who identified George, he was acquitted. The state's attorney dropped the charges against Nettie and conceded that he had no real hope of convicting the other gang members.[44]

The media called Agnes Szabo the Queen of Indiana Bootleggers. She began her legging career as a teenager, driving "her nifty little motorcar" from South Bend to Chicago to pick up liquor. A reporter described her as "pretty, modishly dressed" with "the carriage and poise of the honor pupil of a select finishing school." He praised her language skills, saying she "speaks English in keeping with her appearance."

After multiple arrests, Szabo was convicted of Volstead offenses. She agreed to testify for the prosecution in a sensational corruption case against government officials in Gary, Indiana. A writer covering the trial called her "clever and pretty." Another said she was "a smart dresser and appeared to take great delight" in exposing the corrupt officials. The jury returned guilty verdicts for fifty-five people, including Gary's mayor, a city judge, an attorney, a former sheriff, and a prominent GOP politico.[45]

Los Angeles police called K. Onio the Queen of the Bootleggers. She specialized in selling sake, mostly in the Japanese community. Police officers raided a house in Wilshire where they found Onio and gallons of sake. They intentionally allowed her to escape, hoping she would lead them to her accomplices. They trailed her to another house and, when they searched it, discovered a trapdoor under a bed. Below the trapdoor they found the room where the rice liquor was brewed. The officers seized a substantial quantity of sake and arrested Onio along with three men.[46]

In New York City, twenty-something Frances Cannistraci was called the Queen of the Bootleggers. Cannistraci sold liquor she obtained from the Olivet Distributing Company, which held a government permit to process alcohol for industrial use. A master saleswoman, Cannistraci routinely sold Olivet's entire output plus alcohol she procured from other sources. She grossed up to $2,800 per day. A federal grand jury indicted Cannistraci, her "girl book-keeper," and twenty-three men for breaking the dry law by diverting industrial alcohol into illegal channels.[47]

On Long Island, Bootleg Queen Helen Smith was prosecuted along with three men on theft charges — specifically, hijacking two carloads of liquor in Montauk, New York. On the witness stand in court, Smith admitted that she sometimes purchased liquor and carried it in her automobile.

"Then you admit you are a bootlegger?" asked the prosecutor.

"Well, I don't know whether I am or not," Smith said. "I have never been caught."

The attorney asked her if people called her the "bootleg queen."

"Only by hearsay," she answered.

Although the state had some strong evidence against the hijacking gang, the jury dead-locked. The prosecution failed to dethrone Queen Helen.[48]

Untimely Death

Distaff bootleggers, like their male counterparts, ran the risk of being killed on the job. A lady legger might be shot by a gangland rival who wanted to take over her territory. She might be wounded in gunplay during a hijacking or a shootout with the cops. Working with her spouse or a male partner didn't necessarily make her life safer since he might turn against her and harm her. If she had a romance with her partner, she was especially vulnerable because strong emotions came into play. More than one lover's quarrel between leggers turned deadly.

In Grand Rapids, Michigan, a woman bootlegger was found dead in her car parked beside the road. Her body was badly bruised, and her skull was bashed in. The car held seventy gallons of liquor, which she had picked up shortly before her murder. Police believed the killer had lured her from the car and bludgeoned her to death, then dragged her lifeless body back to the car. The sheriff arrested her boyfriend, who admitted being in the car with her but denied killing her. He claimed she had accidentally fallen out of the auto.[49]

In Baltimore, bootlegger Camilla Farraco's body was found in bushes beside the golf course at the Rolling Road Club. A newspaper described her murder as "brutal in the extreme." Investigators believed she had been kidnapped in Martinsburg, West Virginia, and driven to Baltimore. Police in Martinsburg said she knew she was "a marked woman" and had made "desperate efforts" to persuade Prohibition officials to protect her. Shortly before her death, a motorcycle policeman saw her riding "in a large car with a man of foreign appearance." When the cop stopped the car, the man claimed Farraco was his wife. Farraco said they had been arguing, but she declined to have her companion arrested. She was never seen alive again.[50]

Acting on a tip from an informant, the police in Decatur, Illinois, were watching for a carload of liquor to reach town. When they spotted Mary Didrago's car on a downtown street, they hurried over to investigate and found that she was hauling liquor. They tried to arrest her, but she pulled out her revolver and shot at them. They returned fire and exchanged shots with her until her gun jammed. A police bullet lodged in Didrago's breast, and she died after being taken to the hospital. Police arrested her husband "as her accomplice in a big liquor traffic scheme."[51]

Lawmen stopped "titian-haired" Louise Horton and her driver on a country road near Herington, Kansas. The officers, who were led by the sheriff, had been tipped off that Horton would be passing through with a carload of booze. When the lawmen tried to question Horton, she ordered her driver to "floor it." The sheriff leapt onto the running board of her car and hung on as it careened down the rough, bumpy road.

Horton pulled out her revolver, stuck it against the sheriff's ribs, and told him to jump off or she would "blow him to hell." Tenaciously he clung to her car. Hanging on with one hand, he somehow reached his gun and "fired from his hip," sending a bullet into Horton's chest. She slumped over, slid onto the floor of her car, and died.

The lawmen, who found forty gallons of liquor in Horton's car, arrested her driver. In less than twenty-four hours a coroner's jury convened to investigate the shooting. Horton's driver said his stylishly-dressed boss lived in the "country club" district in Kansas City. She was a newlywed, having married a bootlegger several weeks earlier. The driver said Horton, who was probably drunk, "appeared crazed" when the sheriff jumped onto the running board. The other lawmen testified that she had cursed at the sheriff and seemed to be "liquor-crazed."

The coroner's jury quickly exonerated the sheriff. The verdict said he had "shot lawfully in the discharge of his duty in the defense of his life." With moist eyes, the sheriff said he regretted having to shoot her. "A liquor-crazed woman with a pistol is a combination which cannot be treated lightly," he said. "It was my life against hers, and I was quicker with my pistol. Of course, I am extremely sorry it happened. It's unpleasant and distasteful enough to shoot a man."[52]

It Takes a Woman

Dry leaders, especially the women, favored harsh penalties for female liquor traffickers. The righteous sober ladies wanted their wayward sisters punished. They complained that lawmen coddled the bad girls because the distaff gin joggers vamped the men. The dry ladies argued that female Prohibition agents were needed. "Some of the meanest bootleggers in America are women," said a WCTU leader. "They are too smart for the male enforcement officers. You need a woman officer to catch a woman bootlegger."[53]

Despite the perceived need for women in Volstead enforcement, males dominated the Prohibition squads. The Prohibition Unit hired a handful of token women agents, but very few of them worked the streets. In general, the girls stayed in the office, doing paperwork. The male agents sometimes took a secretary along on a raid to make notes that could be used as evidence. When the Prohis tapped a phone line, a stenographer listened in to record the calls in shorthand. When a male agent went to gather evidence at a speakeasy, he might take his wife or a female agent along, so they could pose as a couple out for a night on the town.

Daisy Simpson was an exception to the rule that female agents did paperwork. She liked excitement too much to let the men have all the fun. Simpson led raids, worked undercover, shadowed bootleggers, and chased the bad guys on the streets of San Francisco. Newspapers called her the "lady hooch hunter" and, rather awkwardly, the "feminine nemesis for boot-leggers." She did most of her crime fighting in California, but she also worked on special assignments in Chicago, Milwaukee, Baltimore, New York, and Great Falls, Montana.[54]

In her youth Simpson reveled in the seamy side of life in San Francisco. She hung out in dingy dives, dated tough guys, and experimented with illicit drugs. She became addicted to narcotics because, if gossip can be believed, a tragic love affair caused her great pain. In a relatively short time, she found Mr. Right, married him, and got divorced. She also mustered the strength to sober up. During World War I she began a career in law enforcement, joining the morals squad of the San Francisco police department. Her life experience combined with her knowledge of the city's underbelly solidly qualified her for the risky job. She investigated the illicit drug traffic and sales of illegal alcohol to soldiers. When Volstead began, joining the Prohibition squad was a logical step for her.

Simpson could've been the plucky, sexy heroine of a dime novel. "She was eye-filling, her presence stimulating," said an admirer. She knew how to lure bad guys into the traps she set for them. A wire service reporter described her as pretty and petite. He said this was important because attractive women could coax bartenders to serve them cocktails. "If they can display a pair of dainty feet and trimly turned ankles, all well and good.... But if they are a bit heavy on the hoof, near beer is the best they can get," the sexist wrote.[55] Since Simpson often persuaded men to sell her liquor, her ankles must've been acceptable.

Like fictional detectives of the era, Simpson often wore disguises. She could convince people that she was a charwoman, a society matron, a chambermaid, or an opium addict. Her experience with drugs helped her realistically "simulate the droop and twitch" of an opium eater. "She was a mistress of make-up, even in the detail of the angle of the eyebrow," an observer wrote. "She entered into all her characters with a grace and perfection that would have aroused the envy of a finished actress."

When Simpson worked undercover, she often pretended to be a weak, harmless old lady. She dressed in appropriate out-of-date attire, including a sunbonnet and a plaid shawl. She always carried a gun and handcuffs hidden in her clothing. In one incident she went to check out "a particularly vicious bootleg establishment on lower Folsom Street" in San Francisco. She arrested five men and "with a brace of guns" held them at gunpoint until the police were called and arrived to take the miscreants to jail.[56]

Simpson's superiors once sent her to single-handedly raid a raucous "booze party." She crashed the party, identified herself as a federal agent, and seized two bottles of wine to use as evidence against the hosts. Angry guests confronted her, trying to reclaim the bottles of vino. Simpson whipped out her gun and fired shots into the wall, startling everyone and alerting the police that she needed help. Although she was outnumbered, she trained her gun on the partiers and kept the situation under control until the cops arrived. The hosts were arrested on possession charges.[57]

To gather evidence, Prohibition agents had to frequent places that sold liquor. Often this meant spending an evening at a speakeasy or a restaurant, eating and drinking. Critics accused the agents of using their expense accounts to indulge in the high life. A newspaper charged Simpson with wasting money on the "epicurean joys of dry sleuths." To collect evidence against a San Francisco tavern, Simpson and her male escort ate dinner there, spending $15 on squab, artichokes, and green peas. In addition, they gave the waiter a princely tip, trying to induce him to serve them wine. The waiter never brought any wine, so Simpson and her escort left the tavern. But they didn't give up. They returned on another night, ordered wine, and were served. They signaled to their backup agents, who were waiting outside the tavern. The dry sleuths confiscated all the liquor they could find and arrested several employees.[58]

The San Francisco Prohibition squad's jurisdiction extended beyond the city to the small winery towns in northern California. The Wine Country vintners cringed whenever they heard that Simpson had been spotted in Napa or Sonoma. Local newspapers warned their readers if she had been seen or was expected to arrive soon. As one paper put it: when Santa Rosa's bootleggers heard a rumor that Simpson was in town, they took it "as an omen of impending disaster."

In a major coup, Simpson secured evidence that led to the dumping of more than 8,000 gallons of prewar vintage at a winery in Healdsburg. The local vintners mourned the loss and found another reason to fear her. When she led federal agents on a series of raids in Santa Rosa and the Valley of the Moon, the vintners complained about entrapment. They claimed she persuaded "unsuspecting residents who had wine to sell her some, and afterwards she turned witness against them and had the dry law violators placed under heavy bond." From Simpson's point of view, she was merely doing her job.[59]

Like other dry sleuths, Simpson nabbed low-rent hoods more often than liquor lords. Judge George Borquin didn't like what he called trivial "helldiver cases" (a reference to a diving waterfowl better known as a grebe). The judge chastised Simpson for arresting a man when she found a demijohn with traces of moonshine in his car. "These more or less accidental and insignificant dregs of whiskey adhering to a jug ... do not rise to the eminence of intoxicating liquor possessed and transported within the intent and meaning of the Volstead act," the judge explained. He dismissed all charges against the defendant.

Borquin wasn't the only official to question Simpson's judgment. Judge Frank Rudkin didn't like the way she procured liquor from a hotel bellboy. After she checked into the hotel, she tipped the bellboy generously and told him she had terrible stomach pains. She stated that she needed whiskey to numb the pain but had no prescription. The bellboy left the hotel, bought liquor, and delivered it to her room. Although this incident was typical of how the San Francisco Prohis operated, Judge Rudkin reprimanded Simpson for setting a trap. Moreover, she had netted only a helldiver, not a whale.[60]

In November 1925 Simpson resigned from the Prohibition squad because illness was keeping her bedridden. Subsequently her health improved and she traveled to El Paso, Texas. In West Texas she became involved with drug traffickers and was arrested on narcotics charges. It appeared that she had relapsed into drug addiction and was selling narcotics to support her habit. The police took her to jail. She couldn't pay her bail, so she sent telegrams to the husband she had long ago divorced, begging him to send money. She also contacted friends, asking for help.

When she received no financial aid, she became despondent. She wrote a suicide note addressed to her former husband, saying, "I can't stand jail, and the shame has broken my heart. Dearest, if you don't want me, the only one I depended on, I am ready to die." As always, she was carrying a pistol hidden in her clothes. She took out the gun and shot herself in the abdomen.[61]

Simpson was taken to a hospital, where she hovered near death for weeks. Despite her serious condition, the legal process went forward and court officials came to her sickroom so she could enter her plea. Lying in the hospital bed, she pled not guilty to the drug charges. Her health gradually improved, and she was able to borrow money to pay her bail. She finally recovered enough to go home to California. When it was time for her trial, she traveled to the Lone Star State to face the music. She changed her plea to guilty and was given a suspended sentence.[62]

Daisy Simpson, the famous hooch hunter, retired from the public scene to live a quiet life outside the media spotlight.

27. Winging It: Flying Bootleggers

> The yellow Rio Grande and the terrestrial barricades held by law enforcement agents on the Canadian border are all the same to these rumrunners of the air. They hop north, south, east, and west at mile-a-minute speed, scorning the minions of the law who may be plodding along on their trail, but rarely get within sight of the quarry. — Howard Mingos, newspaper reporter[1]

During the Great Drought most liquor traffickers moved their illegal products via automobile, boat, or train. But a few cutting-edge traffickers used airplanes to smuggle booze. The typical airborne bootlegger learned to fly military aircraft during World War I and loved the thrill of flying. He couldn't imagine life without it. After the war he bought a military surplus airplane at a bargain basement price and set out to earn his living as a pilot. Commercial aviation was in its infancy, so it offered few jobs. Barnstorming and flying circuses provided plenty of adventure, but they didn't guarantee a steady paycheck. Piloting a plane filled with a cargo of illegal liquor offered thrills plus a big payday.

Aerial bootlegging, a curiosity in the early Twenties, became more common in Volstead's latter years. However, the amount of liquor carried by airplanes was always a tiny fraction of the illegal traffic. The typical plane held fewer than fifty cases of whiskey; some could carry only ten cases. The bootlegging pilot had to fly many trips to get rich, but air traffic was virtually unregulated and he stood only a minute chance of getting arrested.

In general, flying bootleggers operated along the international border, making short flights to haul booze from Canada or Mexico into the United States. A few pilots flew seaplanes and landed on the water near Rum Row. The seaplane pilot bought liquor from a rumrunning ship and delivered it to a nearby airport or improvised landing strip. Most runways had only natural lighting, so daytime flying was the norm for legal ventures. Nighttime landings were dangerous, but the airborne bootlegger routinely took the risk of flying after dark, due to his need for secrecy. If bootleggers were waiting to pick up his liquor cargo, they might improvise lighting to help him get his bearings. They could park beside the runway and turn on their headlights or signal with lanterns.

Flying leggers usually worked for a mob or rum ring, but a few were lone wolves who ran a one-man show. Whether the bootlegging pilot worked for himself or someone else, he occupied a special niche as a bold, elite Volstead outlaw. His flying skills separated him from the typical thuggish urban gangster. He was more soldier of fortune than mobster. He was also a unique type of aviation pioneer.

Smugglers in the Sky

In the early 1920s federal Prohibition officials stated that airplanes were active in the liquor traffic in New York State. According to their intelligence, one rum ring had at least eleven airplanes that made regular trips to smuggle hooch from Canada to Long Island. Each carried a payload of thirty to forty cases of Canadian liquor. A very active New York syndicate operated twenty-one airplanes "for the purpose of openly and flagrantly violating the Eighteenth Amendment." Some of the planes carried liquor from Montreal, Quebec, to airfields near New York City. This ring also used seaplanes to ferry whiskey from ships at sea to Rockaway and Montauk Point, Long Island. The Prohis claimed that the bottoms of the aircraft had trap doors, which could be opened to dump the liquor at sea if necessary. Booze-smuggling seaplanes from Quebec often landed on Lake Champlain in upstate New York, and hydroplanes were sometimes spotted on the Hudson River.[2]

In Lockport, New York, the customs patrol learned that a gang was using an airplane to bring in Canadian booze as well as an occasional illegal alien. Customs officers patrolled several airfields in the vicinity of Niagara Falls, hoping to spot the aircraft. One day they happened to be at the right airstrip at the right time. As the gang's plane landed, the patrolmen bombarded it with "gas bombs," blinding the pilot. The lawmen arrested him and seized his load of ale and whiskey. He carried no illegal immigrants on that run.[3]

On Rum Row off the coast of New York City, a pilot called "Music" (possibly aviation pioneer Ed Musik) was a regular visitor. He flew his seaplane to pick up booze from a vessel on Rum Row, making the shore-to-ship roundtrip in an hour or so. Since he could carry only twenty cases per trip, he made multiple runs each day. Music liked to tease the Coast Guard by flying low over the patrol boats and waving at the Coasties. One morning, after he put a load of booze on his seaplane, he tried to lift off but the motor malfunctioned. It wouldn't put out enough power to get the plane airborne, so Music had to skip along on the water. He was moving so slowly that the skipper of a Coast Guard cutter decided to chase him. Music quickly dumped his liquor overboard. The cutter overhauled him and towed him into the harbor. After a search, the authorities freed him because they found no liquor on the plane.[4]

Music wasn't the only flying bootlegger who had trouble lifting off. A pilot with a small plane that held a dozen cases made regular runs from Rum Row to Atlantic Highlands, New Jersey. On one trip he loaded up and pulled away from the rumrunning ship but couldn't lift off. He tried to taxi into port, but his seaplane developed more mechanical problems. Finally, he was forced to abandon his craft, leaving it and his liquor behind to be retrieved later, if the Coast Guard didn't find it first. To save his own hide, he dived into the water and swam ashore.

Like their colleagues who traveled on land, flying bootleggers feared hijackers. One night a pilot with a cargo of booze landed near a deserted dock at Atlantic Highlands. Strangers materialized out of the darkness and surrounded him. One of the strangers stuck a gun against the pilot's ribcage and told him they would take care of his cargo. While the other hijackers unloaded the plane, the gunman marched the pilot down a dark road and then allowed him to run away. When the fly boy dared to pause and look over his shoulder, he saw flames leaping into the sky. The hijackers had torched his plane! Soon they sped past him in a car, making off with his liquor. He lost his valuable assets, but he lived to fly another day.

The rum rings used aircraft for reconnaissance as well as smuggling. Mob planes flew over the ocean to keep track of the Coast Guard patrol boats and inform the rumrunning crews of the Coasties' whereabouts. Frequently, the vessels on Rum Row had to change positions to evade the patrol boats. Sometimes Rum Row was off the coast of lower New Jersey; at other times the ships moved to Long Island or even farther east. When a syndicate's rumrunning ship or ships moved, a pilot would fly a "rum spotter" over the ocean to find the new location. The spotter knew exactly which ship to look for. When he spotted it, he would inform the syndicate where to send the motorboats that picked up liquor on Rum Row.[5]

Russell "Curly" Hosler, a World War I flying ace, headed a squadron of booze-running pilots who flew nightly trips from airfields near Windsor, Ontario, to isolated landing spots around Detroit, Michigan. Bootleggers waiting for the contraband liquor lit the runway for the pilots. When the leggers were expecting a plane, they parked their cars on the edge of the airstrip and waited. When they heard the aircraft engine, they turned on their headlights. After the plane landed, the men quickly loaded the whiskey into their cars and sped away.

In 1930 Hosler was arrested for smuggling liquor and illegal aliens into the United States. A federal grand jury indicted the war hero along with thirteen other men; all were accused of being part of smuggling rings that flew contraband from Canada to remote airstrips in Michigan. Law enforcement seized twelve of the thirty airplanes used by the smugglers. After Hosler's arrest and conviction, he did a short stretch in the federal prison at Leavenworth, where he passed the time by building a glider. According to the cons' grapevine, he planned to escape in it by soaring off the roof of the prison shoe factory. Prison officials confiscated the homemade glider, even though it was too small and flimsy for an escape flight. After the Big Thirst ended, Hosler built experimental aircraft and competed in air races.[6]

In the late 1920s Prohibition officials heard about a gang of flying bootleggers who smuggled liquor from a private airport at Amherstburg, Ontario, to airstrips near Detroit. The booze was offloaded onto trucks that carried it to Detroit, Chicago, and other cities in the Midwest. The flyers operated on a relatively small scale but had plans for expansion. Federal agents infiltrated the group and collected enough evidence to arrest the ringleaders before they could expand their racket.[7]

Military pilots stationed at Selfridge Field, north of Detroit, regularly made the round-trip to Ontario on maneuvers. Some of the flyers augmented their income by hauling Canadian liquor for bootleggers in Motor City. In late 1929 law enforcement confiscated five civilian planes that had landed liquor in or near Detroit. In one instance, customs patrolmen seized a rum-smuggling airplane that landed in a field at Dodge Park near Detroit. The customs men saw the plane in the sky and wondered why it was landing at the park instead of the airport. They hurried to the landing site and questioned the pilot. When he acted suspicious, they searched his plane, found the liquor cargo, and arrested him.[8]

In mid–1920s Manitoba's provincial police stated that airplanes were transporting

Prohibition agents confiscated the liquor cargo from this airplane after a bootlegger landed it in Michigan (Walter P. Reuther Library, Archives of Labor and Urban Affairs, Wayne State University).

Canadian liquor from Winnipeg to Minneapolis, Minnesota. American customs officials confiscated two of the planes, which were equipped with skids for landing on ice in the winter. Canadian officials investigated an "airplane smuggling system" headquartered in Kingsville, Ontario, and learned that the flyers were carrying large amounts of liquor to cities in Midwest. In November 1929 Ontario's provincial police staged a series of raids on the liquor export docks along the Detroit River, to put the airborne smuggling system out of business.[9]

The denizens of gangland knew Frank Parker as "the crown prince of automobile thieves" in Illinois. During World War I Parker was found guilty of stealing cars and imprisoned at Joliet. When he was released in 1921, he had no money, but he did have big plans for going into the liquor business as a flying bootlegger. He put his plan into action, and five years later he had amassed more than $5 million selling illegal hooch. His assets included a chain of breweries and a fleet of airplanes. Although his enterprises required secrecy, Parker liked publicity. He made news when he flew supplies to a group of fishermen trapped by a blizzard on South Fox Island in Lake Michigan. He became a sports celebrity as the guarantor of a highly-hyped boxing match, the Carpentier-Gibbons fight at Michigan City, Indiana.[10]

Ralph Capone, Al's brother, bought aircraft and hired pilots to fly hooch from Canada to Illinois. Gangland sources said Capone had a fleet of twenty planes, but federal agents could document only two in 1930. One was a tri-motor Fokker monoplane that could carry fifty cases of liquor. The other plane carried a payload of only twenty cases. The planes made daily runs from Windsor, Ontario, to an airfield near Cicero, Illinois. The aircraft traveled together, and one would circle above the field while the other landed. Trucks waited beside the runway to pick up the cargo, which was removed via a sliding door in the fuselage. Federal agents estimated that the two planes landed $1.4 million worth of booze in only eight months. According to gangland gossip, Capone's airplanes carried narcotics as well as liquor, but the federal agents couldn't verify this.[11]

Mob hits were a workplace hazard for liquor traffickers in Chicago, and flying bootleggers weren't immune. Irving "Sonny" Schlig piloted a plane between Chicago and Canada on a regular basis. Police believed he was smuggling liquor and perhaps drugs or jewelry. In the underworld he was reputed to be a "stick-up man" as well as a master jewel thief who had pulled off big heists. During the Arid Era, he added flying bootlegger to his résumé. Initially, he flew for the Torrio-Capone mob, but after a time he decided to go it alone so he could be the boss. He showed a truly reckless, egomaniacal streak when he flew Canadian liquor into Chicago and sold it on the Outfit's turf without permission.

Although Schlig chose a life of crime, he seemed to have no illusions about its rewards or his prospects. "In this racket about the best you can do is pay the rent for a prostitute," he said. "You don't trust her, and she doesn't trust you. You drift away from her and pick up someone no better." Despite his cynicism, he spent freely to keep his mistress in "a lavishly fitted love nest." He gave her precious gems, beautiful gowns, exquisite lingerie, plush furniture, and "soft Chinese rugs."[12]

Late one night the bodies of Schlig and an accomplice were found at the edge of the Illinois Aero Club's Ashburn Field. A leafy, spreading oak tree formed a funereal canopy for the corpses. Each victim had taken a bullet in the back of the neck. A small black suitcase, believed to be Schlig's, lay near the bodies. Bloody handprints stained the bag's contents. Police theorized that someone had rummaged through the bag, looking for drugs or other contraband. Schlig's car, riddled with bullets, was found a short distance away in a lagoon.

When Sonny Schlig's parents learned of his murder, his father stated that corrupt cops had threatened to kill the flying bootlegger. He also said that Sonny had vowed to quit the gang and "go straight." Like many a gangster's mother, Mrs. Schlig said, "He was a good boy at heart — but wild."[13]

At the inquest into Schlig's death, both his father and his mistress testified, but they couldn't or wouldn't identify his killers. Schlig's mother found the inquest so painful that she fainted and didn't testify. The coroner's jury returned a finding that Schlig had been killed by unknown persons. A police captain theorized that a gang feud lay behind the murder. "When thieves or bootleggers fall out nowadays," he said, "there's usually a killing. Schlig must have double-crossed someone, either on a whiskey deal or in the division of loot from a jewel theft." The captain felt Schlig's death was no loss. "Whoever killed the wretch ought to get a medal," he declared.[14]

In the South, along the Gulf Coast, bootleggers used seaplanes to transport liquor from rumrunning ships to isolated spots where the booze was transferred to cars or boats. In a typical operation, a seaplane landed near a rumrunning ship, picked up a cargo of liquor, and flew away. The loaded seaplane usually followed the course of the Mississippi River to a prearranged meeting place in a remote rural area. The bootleggers waited on the riverbank and signaled the pilot, so he would land at the right spot.

West End, the largest community on Grand Bahama Island, was only sixty miles from West Palm Beach, Florida. West End served as the base of operations for hooch-hauling airplanes as well as rumrunning boats. Bootlegging pilots could buy or lease vacant land on the West End to use as an airstrip. At least one Bahamas liquor wholesaler owned a private runway for his customers' use. Approximately twenty pilots used his runway on a regular basis, making multiple roundtrips each day.[15]

On a typical liquor run from the Bahamas, the pilot headed to a remote destination in South Florida. He took off from an island airstrip after dark, flying low over the water. In Florida he landed on an isolated runway, a cattle farm, a dry lakebed, or a road far off the beaten path. His comrades waited to transfer the liquor to a car or truck. One pilot who made regular runs landed at the head of Lake Worth channel, where his accomplices waited in a boat. They would transfer the liquor to the boat and deliver it to waterfront restaurants in Palm Beach County.[16]

In the Pacific Northwest flying bootleggers attracted unwanted attention because air traffic was relatively rare, especially at night. Only three weeks after Prohibition began, police in Portland, Oregon, suspected that flying leggers were bringing in Canadian booze. Residents reported that they had heard airplane noises at night and had seen moving lights in the sky. The police believed that seaplanes loaded with liquor were landing along the Willamette and Portland rivers. By 1921 a bootlegging gang was operating seven planes in Portland, smuggling large quantities of Canadian liquor into the city. The leggers ran a flying school as a front.[17]

One afternoon in Everett, Washington, deputy sheriffs standing on a city street noticed "a strange looking plane" flying over the water. They hurried to the harbor and watched the seaplane land. When they searched it, they found liquor and arrested the pilot. Subsequently he was indicted, tried, and found guilty of violating the dry law. However, Washington's state Supreme Court overturned his conviction because the deputies had acted without a warrant and without probable cause, thereby trampling on his constitutional rights.[18]

Bootlegging pilots in Spokane, Washington, enlisted the aid of Doukhobors, a sect of Russian religious dissenters who lived in a colony along the border in British Columbia. The Spokane bootleggers ordered liquor from a Canadian exporter, who delivered the booze to a Doukhobor farm. The pilots flew to the farm and landed in a field to pick up the cargo. Since the fields weren't proper landing strips, an airplane sometimes sustained significant damage. If the plane wasn't safe to fly, the pilot would make an urgent call to the Spokane airport to request a mechanic. The repairman would load his tools and spare parts on an airplane and fly to the Doukhobor farm to fix the problem.[19]

A few American mobs owned distilleries in Mexico and hauled their output across the border into Texas or California, but Mexican plants produced most of the liquor "exported" to the USA during Prohibition. Since lax security was the norm along the international border, countless smugglers crossed the line from Mexico into Texas. Liquor and drugs were the most popular payloads for traffickers flying across the border into the Lone Star State.

Along the Rio Grande, bootlegging was a very dangerous game. If a pilot left his plane unguarded, he could say good-bye to his cargo, tires, and instruments. To protect his airplane, the outlaw flyer usually slept outdoors under the wings. "They're a bunch of double-crossers out here," a flying bootlegger told a reporter. "When I go to sleep, I have a gun in one hand and a cord tied around a finger of the other." The cord, which was attached to the plane, acted as a kind of alarm system to wake the pilot if anyone tampered with his aircraft. "I've never killed a man yet," the fly boy said, "but I winged one who was trying to lift a tire."[20]

In San Antonio an ex-military flyer managed a fleet of twelve planes that ferried contraband across the border. The Texas pilots usually carried ammunition and explosives to Mexico. They returned with "the wicked concoctions which the Mexicans sell as hard liquor."

A member of San Antonio's flying bootleg gang crossed the border into U.S. airspace one night, returning home with a load of Mexican liquor. His plane sputtered as it ran out of fuel. He quickly switched on his emergency tank, only to find it plugged up. He made an emergency landing in the nearest field. A constable materialized, seemingly from nowhere, and came running toward the plane. The pilot suspected that someone had tampered with his aircraft to set him up for an arrest. When the constable tried to arrest him, the quick-witted aviator insisted that his machine was a mail plane. He ordered the constable to get him some fuel, so the mail could go through.

The pilot's bluff worked. The constable drove away in his flivver and soon returned with the fuel. The bootlegger's plane lifted off just as a squad of Prohibition agents arrived at the field. The pilot later learned that his boss, the ex-military flyer, had double-crossed him as part of a deal with the Prohis. His boss had agreed to let the agents arrest one pilot while his other planes landed their liquor hassle-free at another spot.[21]

In California at least one flying bootlegger picked up white lightning from moonshiners in the Mojave Desert. At night, the desert was eerily dark, but people living near Harper Dry Lake could see car headlights around the lakebed. The car lights blinked on and off. Flashing lights answered from the hills in the distance, near Black Canyon. Residents heard the hum of an aircraft engine. Then a plane landed on the dry lakebed. Men hopped out of the cars and hurriedly put jugs of moonshine on the aircraft. After a few minutes, residents heard the plane take off and saw the car headlights disappear down the road. The light show had ended. Quiet returned to the desert.[22]

Forced Landing

Unless a flying bootlegger was seriously injured in a crash or forced landing, his chances of being nabbed were minuscule. In case of an emergency landing, the flyer usually jumped out of his plane and ran away, hoping to escape with his life if not his hooch. If he had no major injuries, he could find a secure hiding place or hustle down the road before law enforcement arrived at the scene. Rarely did a crash send a flying bootlegger to jail.

A Curtiss biplane crashed into the side of a heavily-wooded hill in Croton-on-Hudson, New York, in 1922. The pilot climbed out of his disabled plane, leaving a load of whiskey onboard. Witnesses who rushed to the scene saw a car pick up the limping flyer and speed away. In all probability, the driver had been waiting to transfer the booze to his car.[23]

Troopers from the New York State Constabulary came to the crash scene to investigate. They decided to confiscate the aircraft, so they removed the plane's wings and propeller. Despite the trees and the steep upgrade, they managed to hoist the fuselage onto a truck.

Then they moved the wreckage, along with the booze, to the constabulary barracks. Losing the aircraft was a major mischance, but the pilot escaped arrest.[24]

A bootlegger flying along the Hudson River one night had engine trouble, so he looked for a good landing spot. He circled over farmland near Newburgh, New York, and picked out a field. Meanwhile, the plane's hot exhaust was spitting out sparks, visible for miles around. Farmers heard the sputtering engine, looked up at the sky, and saw flashes of light. Several of them heard the plane crash and went to investigate. They found the wreckage of the airplane, including a wing that had been ripped off during the forced landing. The pilot ran away, leaving one hundred quarts of liquor behind. Lawmen spent weeks trying to track down the bootlegging airman but finally gave up.

Mechanical problems forced an unlucky pilot down in a small town in North Dakota. As his plane rolled through a field of tall grass on the edge of town, he saw an excited group running toward him, shouting and waving. He wasn't sure what this welcoming committee had in mind. Would the townsfolk be happy to share his liquid cargo? Or, were they dry fanatics who would grab him and drag him to the nearest jail? He didn't wait to find out. He hopped out of his plane and sprinted away from the townsfolk as fast as he could.[25]

A forced landing off the coast of southern Maine led to the arrest of two men in a seaplane in June 1922. The plane was on its way to deliver whiskey to a rumrunning boat, which was waiting near Halfway Rock Lighthouse to take the liquor ashore. The seaplane faltered only miles from its destination. Lawmen arrested the pilot, E. Kenneth Jaquith, and his passenger. Jaquith, a famous daredevil pilot and flying instructor, admitted that he had picked up his liquid cargo in Canada. Despite his confession, U.S. authorities couldn't hold him because he had landed in international waters. When his plane was repaired, he was free to fly away.

Jaquith had another brush with the law in 1925. This time he was flying off the coast of New Jersey in *Lorraine II*, a large Curtiss seaplane. The crew on the Coast Guard cutter *Mojave* spotted *Lorraine II* alongside *D.D. MacKenzie,* a rumrunning ship. When *Mojave* approached *Lorraine II*, the seaplane took off, skimming over the water. The Coast Guard cutter followed closely behind. After traveling several miles, the seaplane stopped near another rumrunning schooner. The Guard cutter caught up and fired at *Lorraine II*.

Jaquith and his passenger surrendered. The Coast Guards took them into custody and seized the seaplane. Treasury agents identified Jaquith's passenger as a notorious rumrunner who had served time in federal prison after being convicted in a high-profile trial. The U.S. attorney's office questioned both the arrestees and the Guards who had nabbed them. Jaquith claimed he had made a forced landing due to a leaking radiator and hadn't bought liquor from the rumrunning ships. It appeared that Jaquith was telling the truth, so the U.S. attorney released both arrestees, due to insufficient evidence.[26]

Airborne Enforcers

During the early days of the Great Drought, law enforcement rarely captured a booze-running aircraft. Prohibition officials mostly ignored sky smuggling because they had their hands full trying to stop the more conventional liquor traffic. As flying bootleggers grew in number, law enforcement made sporadic attempts to stop the airborne smugglers. But the efforts, which were never a top priority, lacked sufficient funding. Despite the limited scope of the airborne liquor traffic, the Volstead enforcers simply didn't have the resources to stop it.

In February 1922 newspapers trumpeted "the first dry law air-raid at sea," which occurred on Jewfish Creek in the Florida Keys. To combat flying bootleggers in the Southeast, the federal government deployed a squadron of eleven airplanes at bases between Miami, Florida, and Charleston, South Carolina. To command the new unit, Stanley Hubbard was appointed chief of the Prohibition Department's Air Service. Each government plane carried weapons, including a machinegun, and at least one gunner. Using information from scouts on government ships, pilots stationed in Miami found the rumrunner *Annabelle* on Jewfish Creek. With their guns pointed at the schooner's deck, the roaring planes swooped down to buzz the boat. The stunned sailors immediately surrendered.[27]

A few months later, Hubbard piloted a seaplane that exchanged gunfire with a rum-running vessel off Cape Florida Lighthouse near Key Biscayne. Sitting at the controls of his seaplane, Hubbard floated on the water off the cape, watching for rumrunners. When he spotted a suspicious boat, he ordered the skipper to pull alongside his plane. The boat's crewmen opened fire, and a bullet lodged in Hubbard's hand. The seaplane's gunners quickly hit the boat with dozens of rounds. Nevertheless, the rummers' boat sped away, eluding both Hubbard's plane and a Coast Guard cutter.

Even though Hubbard's flying squadron scored some successes in Florida, it had a brief lifespan. In 1924 a newspaper reported, "There is more talk about what government enforcement agents are doing with aircraft than the facts warrant." At that time the Coast Guard, which had primary responsibility for stopping liquor smugglers at sea, owned no airplanes. Some observers blamed politics for the early demise of the Prohibition Department's Air Service.[28] As a general rule, political priorities determined how and where enforcement money was spent.

In 1926 the U.S. Congress appropriated a sizeable sum to buy aircraft for the Coast Guard (CG) to use in enforcing the dry law. The CG spent the funding to purchase Loening OL-5 amphibian aircraft and Chance-Vought UO-1s observation planes. The flying enforcers focused on stopping the liquor traffic at sea along the Northeast and Southeast coasts. In the Northeast enforcement flights originated at Cape May Coast Guard Airbase in New Jersey, Squantum naval air station in Boston Harbor, or Ten Pound Island, north of Boston. Four hydroplanes were assigned to the naval station at Pensacola "to constitute an aerial fleet for suppression of rumrunning" in the waters around Florida.[29]

In 1928 the Coast Guard stationed two airplanes at Fort Lauderdale to stop the smuggling of liquor and illegal aliens into Miami from nearby islands. Flying bootleggers were easy to spot in the daylight, so the air squadron had great success in stopping the daytime traffic. In fact, daylight liquor flights to Florida from Bimini and other islands ground to a halt. The bootleggers were forced to make their runs at night when flying was riskier. Despite the Coast Guard's seeming success in Fort Lauderdale, the airplanes were moved to other bases. As usual, politics was blamed for changing the mission.[30]

In 1929 the head of the customs service announced plans for using aircraft to combat rumrunning on the Detroit River, Lake Erie, and Lake St. Clair. He envisioned a large Prohibition Air Force, but initially it consisted of only two airplanes, which had been confiscated from smugglers. A third confiscated plane was soon added to the fleet. Despite a promising start, the grandiose plan for a Prohibition Air Force fell by the wayside. In 1930 the customs patrol along the Michigan–Ontario border had only one airplane, which was used to uncover the "new bases and tricks of smugglers." After that plane crashed, it was replaced with a confiscated "pursuit-style biplane." The used biplane didn't have a mounted gun, but the pilot was licensed to carry a revolver.[31]

Given the massive scope of the liquor traffic around Detroit, a lone flyer with a revolver had roughly the same impact as a clown with a water pistol.

PART III.
CHOICE VERSUS PROHIBITION:
THE CYCLE OF HISTORY

28. Preserving God's Bounty

If barley be wanting to make into malt,
We must be content and think it no fault.
For we can make liquor to sweeten our lips,
Of pumpkins, parsnips, and walnut-tree chips.
— Rhyme popular in Colonial America

Beginning with the arrival of the first European settlers, alcohol played a major role in everyday life in the American colonies. The Europeans brought potent potables with them for very practical reasons. Before mechanical refrigeration, people had few ways of preserving summer's bounty for winter consumption. They relied on fermentation and distillation to convert fruits and grains into liquids with a long shelf-life. The colonists had limited medical resources, so they used potent potables for medicine as well as for nourishment. Alcohol dulled pain, aided digestion, soothed the nerves, induced sleep, warmed the body, and chased away "the blues." Fear of New World water was another incentive for drinking alcohol. The settlers believed that the streams were contaminated and drinking the water would cause illness.

The American colonists drank potent potables at home, at taverns, and in the workplace. Even uptight Puritans prized alcoholic beverages as "the good creatures," valuable gifts from an omnipotent God. The typical colonist consumed alcohol with every meal — including breakfast. In most families, even children drank wine, hard cider, and "small beer" with low alcohol content.

Weddings, baptisms, funerals, church dedications, ordinations, and other special occasions called for libations. Alcoholic beverages flowed freely at sporting events, such as horse races, cockfights, and wrestling matches. Men drank heavily on Election Day and at militia musters. Taverns doubled as courthouses, so the judge, jurors, and litigants usually drank during trials and legal proceedings.

For a vivid illustration of the role alcohol played in the civic and social lives of Americans, consider July 4, 1788. On that date, the City of Philadelphia hosted an all-day event to celebrate the ratification of the U.S. Constitution. The festivities began with a parade of bands, military units, dignitaries, and workers in various trades, including carpentry, millinery, and butchery. A group of brewers marched under a banner proclaiming: "BEER, ALE, PORTER — PROPER DRINK FOR AMERICANS."

The parade ended at Bush Hill estate, where the crowd enjoyed food and drink, especially tankards of beer and hard cider. The festive patriots drank a series of toasts, each announced by a trumpet fanfare and followed by ten artillery shots. They toasted the American people, the Constitutional Convention, the states that had ratified the Constitution, General George Washington, America's foreign allies, The Netherlands, the king of France, and the heroes who had fought the Revolutionary War. They also lifted their mugs to salute American agriculture, manufacturing, and commerce. They drank to pledge that "reason, and not the sword, [will] hereafter decide all national disputes." Finally, the patriots who were still able to raise their mugs toasted "the whole family of mankind."[1]

Early and Often

As a group, colonial Americans consumed prodigious amounts of alcohol of all types. Although precise consumption figures do not exist, historical documents indicate that beer and hard cider were the most popular colonial quaffs. Other favorites were rum, whiskey, brandy, cordials, applejack (distilled cider), mead (distilled honey), and perry (fermented pear juice). For special occasions the proper colonial hostess served concoctions like eggnog, syllabub (wine, milk, and sugar), Sampson (warm cider and rum), and tiff (small beer, rum, and sugar, with a side dish of buttered toast).

More often than not, the colonists drank homemade liquor, which they produced using wild or cultivated plants. The Virginia settlers used wild hedge grapes to make wine, "which was neere as good as your French British wine," according to Captain John Smith. The Virginians also made alcoholic beverages using Indian corn, barley, sassafras, molasses, potatoes, maize stalks, pumpkins, wild persimmons, and Jerusalem artichokes. The Pilgrims made wine from wild grapes and brewed beer using Indian corn, tree roots, and spruce twigs.[2]

In the beginning, trans–Atlantic shipping was slow and unpredictable, so imported goods didn't arrive on a regular schedule. When imports were available, they cost dearly and only the richest colonists could afford them. A prosperous man showed off his riches by stocking his wine cellar with pricey liquors. For example, South Carolina planter John Rutledge filled his large cellar with barrels and bottles of Madeira, claret, port, Lisbon, schnapps, sauterne, porter, and ale. His expensive cache also included demijohns of imported brandy, whiskey, and rum. Rutledge, like many wealthy Southern men, routinely drank two bottles of wine each day. His close friend Henry Laurens was known as an abstemious man because he consumed only one.[3]

Even after trade with Europe grew more common, the typical colonial family consumed homemade liquor. Many households owned a malt mill, a fruit press, a limbec (small still), or other equipment for making alcoholic beverages. The female head of the household usually took charge of concocting the potent potables. A male colonist wrote disdainfully of women who didn't make good liquor, calling them "negligent and idle ... sloathfull and carelesse." He warned, "[T]hey will be adjudged by their drinks, what kinde of housewives they are."[4]

Settlers typically started their day with strong drink, but the beverage of choice varied. New England colonists often began the day with a tankard of hard cider or beer at breakfast. Along the Atlantic coast, the favorite eye-opener was bitters mixed with rum, gin, or whiskey. Fishermen called this morning snort a phlegm-cutter, fog cutter, or anti-fogmatic. "The great utility of rum has given it the medical name of an anti-fogmatic. The quantity taken every morning is in exact proportion to the thickness of the fog," reported a newspaper. Southerners tended to start the day with peach or apple brandy, commonly called "Virginia drams." They might also drink a julep at breakfast, to protect themselves from malaria. Virginians "from the hoary-headed father to the little child, partook daily of the morning 'dram' and the noontide 'grog' or 'toddy,'" wrote a minister.[5]

Alcoholic refreshments were standard fare at work parties, such as a corn husking or barn raising. At harvest time, the farmer pulled the ears of corn off the stalks. Then he carried them to the barn to be stacked in piles for the husking party. The guests were treated to food and drink; in return, they shucked the corn. In some communities, only young singles were invited to the party. This gave them the freedom to flirt and steal a kiss or two. A New England poet described a husking party he attended with a lively group of high-spirited guests. He claimed that "kisses and drams set the virgins on flame." The girls "tumbled about on the husks," mussing their hair and clothes. The evening climaxed with "scenes of vile lewdness" with young couples "tussling" on the floor. (The poet didn't say if this was typical behavior at husking parties, but his tone sounds more amused than shocked, so it may have been the norm.)[6]

Erecting a building was often a community project that depended on volunteer labor, and liquor kept the workers happy. In Litchfield, Connecticut, the Congregational church decided to replace its meetinghouse with a new structure. As was customary, men volunteered to help with the "raising." However, the church didn't provide the customary free whiskey. Only small beer was available. The men insisted on the hard stuff. To get the job started, a doctor went to his private stash and brought back bottles of rum and whiskey. With distilled spirits to spur them on, the men cheerfully pitched in. To ensure a full crew when the spire was raised a few days later, the church provided large tubs of rum punch.[7]

In colonial America the stereotypical preacher was a stern, wrathful prophet of hellfire and damnation. But even the crapehangers enjoyed the cup that cheers. At the Reverend Lyman Beecher's ordination in Litchfield, the visiting clergy consumed seventeen bottles of wine, nine bottles of distilled spirits, and a bowl of spiked punch. At an ordination in Plymouth, the clergy drank copious amounts of "all the kinds of liquors." The meeting room looked and smelled like "a very active grog-shop," Beecher said.[8]

A funeral was supposed to be a somber occasion, but the colonists didn't hesitate to hoist their mugs to honor the deceased. The bereaved polished off a barrel of wine and two barrels of hard cider at the funeral of the Reverend Thomas Cobbett in Ipswich, Massachusetts. At a funeral in Boston, mourners consoled themselves with more than fifty-one gallons of "the best Malaga wine." Since drinks were customary at funerals, the local government supplied alcoholic beverages for a pauper's burial.

Although many funeral goers looked forward to the free libations, some people questioned the propriety of imbibing on such a solemn occasion. Families with strong objections to funereal drinking sometimes refused to serve potent potables, but they were a minority. In 1742 the General Court of Massachusetts forbade drinking wine or rum at funerals but did not ban beer or cider. By the mid–1770s Quaker custom decreed that the jug could be passed around only twice at a Friend's funeral.[9]

Farmers and tradesmen kept potent potables on hand for themselves and the hired help. In the South work stopped at 11 a.m. for the "elevens," usually a gin sling or a toddy with rum or whiskey. In northern villages, a bell rang at 11 a.m. and 4 p.m., reminding workers to stop for a quaff. In 1762 the Massachusetts General Court noted that "many refuse to work" without a daily allowance of wine or another alcoholic beverage.[10] Without heavy equipment or moving assembly lines, drinking on the job involved little risk. If the cobbler nodded off at his bench, his work waited for him.

The village tavern played an essential role in everyday life in the American colonies. In addition to being a way station for travelers, the pub functioned as a community center where villagers met to socialize and conduct business. On Election Day the tavern served as a polling place, which led to a close association between drinking and voting. A wise candidate budgeted a generous amount of money for buying liquor. When George Washington ran for Virginia's House of Burgesses in 1758, his campaign budget was thirty-seven pounds; he spent thirty-four of them treating voters to drinks on Election Day.[11]

The Scarlet D

The extremes of drinking habits — never imbibing and chronic drunkenness — were both outside the realm of normal behavior in the American colonies. A teetotaler was a true rarity, likely to be called "crank-brained" because he wasn't enjoying the wondrous benefits of alcohol. At the other end of the drinking spectrum, the chronic drunk endured public disdain and punishment. The colonists condemned the habitual drunkard for misusing God's good creatures, for failing to pull his weight in the community, and for being a liability to his family.

While the colonists forgave sporadic intoxication, they viewed chronic drunkenness as a debilitating character flaw. A person who regularly drank to excess was called a "common drunkard" or a "habitual drunkard." In general, alcohol abuse was viewed as a bad habit arising from personal weakness or moral defects. The habitual drunkard drank too much simply because he liked alcohol and chose to get drunk. Evangelist Jonathan Edwards said that the drunkard always had the power to "keep the cup from his mouth" but he chose to drink because it "appears most agreeable to him, and suits him best." The concept of compulsion or addiction didn't enter into the equation. The term "alcoholism" wasn't part of the vernacular, and only a few enlightened thinkers wondered if drunkenness might be a disease.[12]

Due to lack of data, historians don't know what percentage of the population fell into the habitual drunkard category. Some scholars argue that alcoholism must've been widespread because liquor was ubiquitous. Others say chronic drunkenness was rare because social norms forbade it and the colonists usually drank low-alcohol beverages. While legal records show that the courts routinely dealt with drunkards, they do not provide enough data to quantify the problem. Thomas Jefferson said that whiskey "kills a third of our citizens and ruins their families." By the end of the eighteenth century, "almost every American family, however respectable, could show some victim to intemperance among its men," according to Henry Adams.[13]

In today's society it's hard to imagine the intimacy, interdependence, and cohesiveness of a colonial settlement. The colonists' very survival depended on being a tight-knit community. They had to erect shelters, protect themselves from wild animals, and adapt to a strange environment while they cleared the land, cultivated crops, and built a village. Pioneering in a new land left little room for eccentric or unproductive behavior. Survival demanded both individual diligence and unified group effort. The colonists' daily lives were so tightly intermeshed that abnormal behavior was both intolerable and hard to hide.

Chronic intoxication had a ripple effect that spread from the individual to the group. The habitual drunkard failed himself, his family, his community, and God. The Puritan Work Ethic placed great emphasis on the value of labor and the rewards for working hard, both on earth and in heaven. Working was part of God's plan for mankind and an essential element in salvation. People labored to honor God; in turn, He rewarded their hard work with wealth. Prosperity was a sign of God's favor, so chronic drunkenness was especially shameful when it led to poverty. A poor souse disgraced his family as well as himself.

Religious doctrine classified chronic drunkenness as a gateway sin that debased human nature and led to more sinning. In general, religious leaders viewed habitual intoxication as a satanic choice as well as a grave personal flaw and a despicable weakness. Society prescribed prayer, Bible reading, and self-discipline to reform the chronic inebriate. If he failed to give up his vice, then society must punish him. Penalties for drunkenness varied from place to place, but sots were often sentenced to jail time, the stocks, and/or the lash. Fines were also common.

The humiliation of being confined in the stocks or whipped in public was intended to shame the drunkard into sobriety. Both punishments caused a degree of physical pain, but public embarrassment was the crux of the penalty. If the stocks or the lash didn't cure the drunkard, harsher punishment was called for. Courts in New York sometimes forced the sot to drink three quarts of salted water laced with lamp oil. In Massachusetts, the court could disenfranchise a drunkard and sentence him to wear a scarlet D on his shirt or a bib around his neck. In extreme cases, a hot branding iron was used to burn a D into the toper's skin.[14]

A Virginia statute called drunkenness an "odious and loathsome sinne" as well as the cause of "other enormous sinnes." Yet the punishment for drunkenness was relatively mild in the Old Dominion. For a first offense, the drunk was privately reproved by his minister. For a second offense, the minister would publicly rebuke him; for a third, the drunk had to pay a fine and spend twelve hours in the "boltes" or stocks. A Virginian guilty of drunkenness might be confined in the stocks at church during the Sabbath worship service. Presumably, this focused his attention on the sermon.[15]

In the southern colonies, fines for drunkenness were often paid in tobacco. For example, chronic drunkenness carried a penalty of one hundred pounds of tobacco in Maryland in the 1640s. When a drunk was convicted because someone turned him in, the informant received half of the tobacco. For a second offense in Maryland, the habitual drunk was publicly flogged or fined three hundred pounds of tobacco. If convicted a third time, he was "adjudged infamous and disenfranchised for three years."[16]

To prevent public drunkenness, lawmakers regulated alcohol sales in taverns by setting the price, the closing time, and so forth. Generally, taverns were forbidden to sell alcohol to indentured servants, apprentices, and Negroes. Some jurisdictions limited a drinker's consumption to one half-pint or less per tavern visit. On Long Island in the 1650s, "youths or such as are under other men's management" could buy only two ounces of liquor per pub visit. In the 1630s innkeepers in the Plymouth Colony could sell only two-pence worth of liquor to each customer, except "strangers just arrived." Both New Jersey and Connecticut banned drinking in taverns after nine p.m.[17]

To prevent rowdiness, colonies passed laws to ban drunkards and troublemakers from the taverns. Village officials sometimes posted a list of known drunkards in the taverns to be sure they weren't served. In Boston a tavern keeper could be punished for selling liquor to "such as were drunk." In at least one case, Boston church officials seized all the liquor belonging to a taverner who had served drunks; the confiscated booze was used "for the benefit of the poor."[18]

Local governments sometimes appointed a supervisor of drinking to monitor the inns and taverns. In 1638 a visitor to Boston noticed a drinking supervisor with his eyes riveted on a tippler at an inn. The supervisor moved close, "thrust himself ... uninvited" into the toper's company, and watched like a hawk. When the supervisor judged that the sot had drunk enough, he told the drinker it was time to quit. When the toper ordered another drink anyway, the supervisor countermanded the order. The tippler had to go elsewhere for his next snort.[19]

In Boston a person could be punished for drinking with "disreputable associates," especially if he failed to lecture them on the evils of excess. A Boston magistrate punished Benjamin Hubbard because he was seen "drinking of the strong-water bottle" with a group of chronic drinkers and didn't try to reform them. The First Church of Boston "admonished" Temperance Sweete for entertaining "disorderly company and ministering unto them wine and strong waters even unto drunkenness."[20] (Apparently, Temperance's parents had mis-named her.)

As early as 1633 lawmakers in the Plymouth Colony forbade drunkenness in private homes. For decades, little was done to enforce this law. Then, in 1675 officials decided to put some teeth in the statute by creating the position of tithing-man. Each tithing-man "diligently" monitored ten to twelve families. (Shades of Mrs. Grundy!) The tithing-man reported liquor violations to local officials, who turned the cases over to the court for prosecution. Some citizens objected to being spied on, but officials argued that it was okay because the tithing-men were appointed by the town selectmen and they didn't hide their identity. In 1679 the Reforming Synod extended the tithing-men's power, authorizing them to report infractions of any kind.[21] (Historical records do not reveal how many souls were saved by the neighborhood spies.)

The Georgia colony, founded as a haven for debtors and the "worthy poor," greatly restricted the liquor trade. Georgia's trustees feared that drunkenness would perpetuate poverty by distracting the settlers from the hard work that must be done to establish the colony. They believed that banning distilled spirits would benefit the morals of both the immigrants and the Native Americans. However, they didn't ban all alcoholic drinks. They gave each settler a generous ration of beer and allowed the colonists to buy additional beer as well as Madeira wine. To reinforce the trustees' policy, the British Parliament passed a law banning rum and brandy in Georgia.

Predictably, drinkers looked for ways to circumvent Georgia's ban on hard liquor. Colonists in South Carolina, seeing a golden opportunity to make money, smuggled rum into Georgia. Enterprising Georgians set up stills and opened illegal taverns; public officials accepted payoffs for ignoring the lawbreakers. After nine years, the colony's trustees conceded that the ban on ardent spirits was impossible to enforce. They set up a system for licensing taverns and allowed merchants to import rum. A few years later, an official report said that drunkenness had markedly decreased under the new, more permissive law.[22]

29. Whiskey and Rum: America's New Favorites

> Most men are so bewitch'd or delighted with the beloved strong rum (rumbullion or kill-devil...) that they think no liquor comparable thereto. — John Norris, author[1]

In the late seventeenth century colonists along the Atlantic Seaboard, from Massachusetts to the Carolinas, developed a taste for rum. European settlers in the West Indies probably invented this distilled spirit, which was also called rum-bullion or kill-devil because it was "hot" and "hellish." Initially, American colonists drank cheap Caribbean rum that arrived via ship. But the rum trade was destined to become a booming industry in New England, due to the strong demand and the steady profits it generated.

Exactly when domestic production began is unknown, but records show that a Boston distillery was making rum in 1657, using molasses from plantations in the West Indies. By the early eighteenth century distillers in Massachusetts, Connecticut, and Rhode Island were producing so much rum that the price plummeted. In 1750 Massachusetts had sixty-three distilleries making rum from molasses, according to an official report sent to His Majesty's Treasury. In the late 1760s Newport, Rhode Island, had thirty distilleries. The city's distillers were exporting large amounts of rum to the African coast, where it displaced French brandy as the favorite ardent spirit.[2]

The demand for rum was so great that domestic distilleries couldn't satisfy it and Americans continued to import a significant amount. In 1770, the American colonies imported four million gallons of rum in addition to the five million gallons of domestic production. The abundance kept the price down. In fact, rum was so cheap that a common laborer could earn enough in one day to stay drunk for a week. Hordes of working-class men became addicted to rum and were "fonder of it than ... their wives and children."[3]

The American colonists drank rum straight, spiced, or mixed. They combined it with a long list of ingredients: rum mixed with hard cider was called stonewall; rum and beer made bogus; rum and molasses made blackstrap. Bombo contained rum, sugar, water, and nutmeg; mimbo was bombo minus the nutmeg. A popular drink called meridian combined rum, lime, water, and sugar. On cold nights, the colonists warmed up with hot buttered rum, eggnog spiked with rum, or rum mulled with egg yolk and allspice. Another winter favorite was made by mixing rum, beer, and sugar in a mug and then plunging a red-hot fireplace poker into it.

During the Revolutionary War, the British navy blockaded American ports, disrupting the flow of rum and molasses from the West Indies. To offset dwindling rum supplies, the colonists distilled more whiskey. In addition to the civilian market for whiskey, the military demand was strong because soldiers in the Continental Army received a daily liquor ration. When the war disrupted agriculture and created a shortage of food grains, the Continental Congress considered a ban on the distillation of corn and wheat. But Americans liked their whiskey so the proposal didn't muster enough support.[4]

After the Revolutionary War, an influx of Scotch-Irish immigrants boosted the upward trend in whiskey production. The newcomers included experienced, skillful distillers who made top-quality spirits. James Anderson, a Scotsman with distilling expertise, convinced George Washington to open a distillery at cash-strapped Mount Vernon. The operation proved so profitable that Washington soon authorized a major expansion of the business. The Father of His Country wholesaled whiskey, bartered it to pay bills, and reserved the best for his personal use. Although Washington profited from whiskey, he advised against drinking too much of it. "The benefits arising from the moderate use of strong liquor ... are not to be disputed," he said. But overindulgence could cause problems.[5]

In the late eighteenth century bourbon whiskey was "invented," giving American drinkers a wider choice of beverages. Several legends purport to tell the true tale of bourbon's origin. According to one, lightning struck a barn where barrels of whiskey were stored. The lightning charred a barrel, imparting a dark color and rich flavor to the liquid inside. Another story says that a Kentucky farmer didn't have enough crocks to hold all his whiskey, so he stored a portion in a charred barrel. When he opened the barrel months later, he found that the whiskey had an unusual amber hue. He was afraid to drink it due to its strange color, but a slave offered to taste it in exchange for his freedom. The bargain was struck, and the slave pronounced the whiskey to be the best he ever tasted.

The best-known tale about bourbon's origin credits Elijah Craig, a Baptist minister, with making the first batch in 1789 at Royal Spring in what later became the Commonwealth of Kentucky. The preacher accidentally charred the white oak staves he was using to make a barrel. Being frugal, he didn't want to waste the staves, so he finished the barrel and stored whiskey inside. When he opened that barrel after several months, he loved the whiskey's rich, mellow taste.[6]

Kill Men for the Devil

When Americans began consuming large quantities of rum and whiskey, attitudes about alcohol started to change. People observed that ardent spirits had a harmful impact on drinkers who consumed too much of them. Conventional wisdom said that ardent spirits endangered society by creating chronic drunkards who led unproductive lives. Compared to sober men, these habitual drunks were more prone to violence and crime. Worried civic and religious leaders called attention to the dangers of America's new drinking customs. Influential opinion-makers promoted temperance as a safeguard against the evils of alcohol, especially distilled spirits.

For generations the Mather family wielded great influence in New England. In 1673 pastor Increase Mather, famous for his role in the Salem witch trials, published two temperance sermons titled *Wo to Drunkards*. With forceful language, he condemned "that worse than brutish sin of drunkenness." He said, "Drink is in itself a good creature of God ... but the abuse of drink is from Satan; the wine is from God, but the drunkard is from the devil." He lamented the abundance of cheap distilled spirits that allowed the poor and the weak to get drunk. He feared that God would punish society for tolerating the sin of excessive drinking.[7]

Cotton Mather, Increase's son, warned that excessive drinking had begun to "drown Christianity." In 1694 he joined other ministers in petitioning the Massachusetts General Court for stricter regulation of taverns and ordinaries. While he endorsed moderate drinking, he believed that the rising consumption of rum threatened orderly, lawful society. He blamed drunkenness for abetting crime, poverty, gambling, and prostitution.[8]

In the early 1700s, clergymen continued to raise warning flags about the dangers of intemperance. Puritan divine Samuel Danforth stated that habitual drunkenness had dire consequences, both secular and spiritual. Topers, more often than sober men, suffered debilitating poverty, injuries, and ill health. In addition, drunkards were "by nature or custom inclined" to commit many sins that would count against them when they tried to enter the Kingdom of Heaven.[9]

Almost forty years after the first publication of *Wo to Drunkards*, it was reprinted with a new preface and revisions. In this new edition, Increase Mather wrote that public drunkenness had become a shameful epidemic in New England. Widespread abuse of hard cider and "a spirit extracted" from cider plagued society and ruined lives. Increase claimed that rum imported from the Sugar Islands had proved to be "the most fatal" of liquors. He said colonists called rum "kill-devil," but "kill men for the devil" better described its impact.[10]

In 1771 Methodist evangelist Francis Asbury arrived in Philadelphia to preach the gospel. Like the other Methodist circuit riders, he would travel around the country on horseback, spreading John Wesley's religious doctrine. Asbury believed that all distilled liquors must be banned, but he was not a teetotaler. He approved the moderate use of low-alcohol beverages and sometimes drank beer or wine for his health. He called drunkenness "the prime curse" of society. In his first American sermon he strongly denounced whiskey, and he preached against it until the end of his life.

Asbury's first job was convincing his fellow circuit riders to stop drinking distilled spirits. Like most Americans, the circuit-riding preachers consumed alcoholic beverages as part of their regular diet. In general, they didn't see any danger in ardent spirits and weren't motivated to change their drinking habits. But Asbury placed a high priority on converting the circuit riders to his way of thinking. He tirelessly espoused the virtues of sobriety and abstinence from hard liquor. Two young Methodist preachers, James Axley and James Finley, were among the first to join his crusade. Both traveled widely, preaching fiery sermons against the evils of whiskey. The zealous Axley didn't stop with verbal volleys; he attacked taverns with a hammer, smashing bottles and bar fixtures.

In 1780 Asbury convened a conference of Methodist ministers and convinced them to pass a resolution against the distillation of liquor. The pastors pledged to "disown" their friends and parishioners who refused to stop distilling and/or drinking hard liquor. Four years later, when Asbury was elevated to bishop, the Methodist Discipline was revised to explicitly ban the consumption of distilled spirits, except for medical use.[11]

The Methodist Church wasn't the only religious force for temperance. The Philadelphia Society of Friends called for a ban on the sale of distilled spirits and urged consumers to drink

beer instead of hard liquor. The Friends' Yearly Meeting warned Quakers not to drink exces-
sively but didn't set any firm rules about the type or quantity of alcohol that was permissible.
In 1789 the General Assembly of the Presbyterian Church voted to use its influence "to make
men sober." The 1812 General Assembly appointed a committee to find methods of "restrict-
ing the use of intoxicants." In 1827 the General Assembly urged the presbyteries "to cooperate
in every possible way with the American Temperance Society."[12]

The Church of the United Brethren in Christ added pro-abstinence language to its
Book of Discipline in 1814. Two years later, the newly-formed African Methodist Church
adopted a strict policy against distilled spirits and drunkenness. The New York Synod of
the Dutch Reformed Church urged its ministers and members "to abstain entirely from the
use of spirituous liquors and to promote, by precept and example, the cause of strict temperance." The General Associations of Congregational Churches in New England branded the
liquor trade "as immoral and inconsistent with a profession of the Christian religion."[13]

Lyman Beecher, a Congregational minister, embraced temperance because he saw the
harmful effects of heavy drinking on the people around him. He first questioned the wisdom
of drinking when he saw his drunken classmates misbehaving at Yale. He found their profanity, gambling, and "licentiousness" to be repulsive. After he became an ordained minister,
he felt that many of his colleagues and parishioners failed to fulfill their potential because
they drank too much.

In 1811 Beecher moved to Litchfield, Connecticut, where a local temperance society
had been active for more than twenty years. Farmers had started the society because they
viewed overindulgence as a "pernicious practice" that caused "a train of evils." The members
agreed to a personal ban on "distilled spirits as an article of refreshment." In lieu of ardent
spirits, they served their guests wholesome drinks made from fruits grown on their farms.
They provided only low-alcohol beer and cider for their hired hands.[14]

After arriving in Litchfield, Beecher became a charter member of the Connecticut Society for the Promotion of Good Morals. He believed it was imperative to protect respectable
citizens from the immorality of Sabbath-breakers, rum sellers, "tippling folk, infidels, and
ruff-scruff." In a series of written sermons, he called excessive drinking "the sin of our land"
and warned that it threatened the stability of the nation. He condemned wine and other
low-alcohol beverages because they seemed harmless but enticed drinkers to try hard liquor.
He argued that routine moderate drinking was very harmful, saying that "habitual tippling"
was riskier than an occasional binge. The daily use of ardent spirits was "deeply injurious,
though its results may be slow and never be ascribed to the real cause." The habitual drinker
did "violence to the laws of his nature," putting his "whole system into disorder." Beecher
called drunkenness a disease as well as a crime. Although the ravages to the physical body were
serious, moral ruin was the worst consequence of drunkenness.

Beecher implored every American to stop drinking alcoholic beverages and become "a
humble, affectionate, determined reformer." He advocated a nationwide educational crusade
to teach people about the evils of alcohol. He endorsed voluntary abstinence but argued that
it would not solve the problem over the long term. The ultimate remedy would be removing
"ardent spirits from the list of lawful articles of commerce." Beecher urged all religious groups
to petition their state legislatures and the U.S. Congress "for legislative interference to protect
the health and morals of the nation."[15]

Beecher's homilies were published as *Six Sermons on the Nature, Occasions, Signs, Evils, and Remedy of Intemperance.* The book had multiple printings and was translated into several languages, extending Beecher's influence far beyond his pulpit in Connecticut. As powerful as his rhetoric was, it wasn't always effective, even in his own backyard. His famous daughter, author Harriet Beecher Stowe, once asked her publisher to send her six bottles of Catawba wine to help her meet a deadline.[16]

Dr. Benjamin Rush, a prominent Philadelphian who signed the Declaration of Independence, was the first American physician to strongly advocate temperance. His views were largely shaped by his medical experience, including his service as Surgeon-General of the Revolutionary Army. He stated that distilled spirits harmed both individuals and society because drunkenness led to illness, crime, poverty, insanity, and broken homes. He argued that beer and wine could be beneficial if used moderately, but long-term consumption of hard liquor would ruin a person's health and lead to an early death. Regular use of distilled spirits made the drinker susceptible to jaundice, diabetes, yellow fever, flatulence, epilepsy, gout, colic, apoplexy, and "dropsy of the belly."[17]

Rush viewed drunkenness as a condition or disease, which evolved over time because the habitual drunk gradually lost the ability to control his liquor intake. The doctor stated that drunkards suffered "paroxysms," or bouts of uncontrollable drunkenness. As their disease progressed, they lost "free agency" and began to drink "from necessity." His observations about habitual drinking foreshadowed modern concepts of alcoholism.

In the nineteenth century a growing number of well-educated, informed public figures viewed drunkenness as a health problem. Nathan Beman, president of Rensselaer Polytechnic Institute, declared that "drunkenness is itself a disease." He said, "When the taste is formed, and the habit established, no man is his own master." Secretary of War Lewis Cass stated that habitual drunkenness "equally debilitated" the mind and the body. "The pathology of the disease is sufficiently obvious," he said. "The difficulty consists in the entire mastery it attains." Samuel Woodward, superintendent of a mental hospital, published a series of articles based on his professional experience. He stated that drunkenness must be treated as a "physical disease." John Gough, a famous orator and reformed drunkard, called intemperance "a physical as well as moral evil."[18]

How Much Is Too Much?

As Americans became more aware of the negative impact of heavy drinking, the public discourse focused on temperance as the best way to prevent chronic drunkenness. But there was no consensus on exactly what temperance entailed. Some temperance advocates demanded total abstinence from all alcoholic beverages. Others wanted to ban hard liquor but allow the sale of beverages with low-alcohol content. A third group felt that moderation was the essential element, so a person could drink any beverage as long as he didn't get drunk.

The differing concepts of temperance may have been the origin of the term "teetotaler." According to a dry historian, the word originated in a temperance society in Hector, New York. The group asked members to sign one of two pledges. The "old pledge" called for abstinence from distilled spirits but permitted the consumption of low-alcohol beverages. Members choosing the "total pledge" refused to drink any intoxicating liquor, fermented or distilled, regardless of alcohol content. The society's secretary recorded each member's choice with OP for old pledge or T for total. Thus someone who opted for complete abstinence was a "teetotaler."[19]

Temperance societies proliferated as Americans banded together to reform the nation's drinking habits. The country's first temperance society was probably the farmers' group formed circa 1789 in Litchfield, Connecticut. Other early groups included the Total Abstinence Society in Virginia, the Sober Society in New Jersey, the Massachusetts Society for the Suppression of Intemperance, and the Union Temperance Society of Moreau and Northumberland in New York.[20]

Black men in Philadelphia founded the Free African Society in 1778. Membership was open only to sober men, but the group was not a temperance society per se. Rather, it was a benevolent society; the members pledged to "support one another in sickness" and to aid the widows and children of deceased members. The New Haven Temperance Society of the People of Color, formed in 1829, was likely the first African American group with sobriety as its primary mission.[21]

A group of ministers led by the Reverend Justin Edwards formed the American Society for the Promotion of Temperance in 1826. The society called for total alcohol abstinence and for laws banning the sale and consumption of distilled spirits. Edwards' movement grew rapidly, and in 1833 it merged with other groups to become the United States Temperance Union (later called the American Temperance Union). This new organization claimed five thousand local chapters with more than one million members.[22]

In the decades before the Civil War, the ranks of the temperance crusade swelled as new groups were born and old ones added members. The new societies included the Cadets of Temperance, the National Temple of Honor and Temperance, the Knights of Jericho, the Society of Good Samaritans, and the Independent Order of Rechabites of North America. Some dry groups adopted the trappings of fraternal orders — ritual, regalia, a secret handshake, and complicated bylaws. The officers had fancy titles, like Worthy Patriarch, Exalted Scribe, or Grand Worshipful Potentate. In general, white males ran the temperance societies and created auxiliaries for women, teens, and African Americans.

The temperance crusade was closely associated with mainstream Protestant sects, but it also attracted Catholic activists. Bishop Francis Patrick Kenrick of Philadelphia started the Pennsylvania Catholic Total Abstinence Society. In a very short time, more than 5,000 Catholics joined the Philadelphia group, pledging "to abstain from all intoxicating drinks, except used medicinally" and "to discountenance the cause and practice of intemperance." The new abstinence society set up a chapter in each of Philadelphia's Catholic parishes.[23]

Following Kenrick's lead, activists formed temperance groups for Catholics in other cities, including Boston and New York. In some parishes Catholics could choose to join the American League of the Cross, which had three divisions. Members in the first division took a total abstinence pledge. In the second division, a member could drink socially but was not allowed to buy drinks for others at a bar or accept a free drink in a saloon. Individuals in the third division drank but didn't patronize saloons.[24]

The Catholic temperance crusade received a boost when Father Theobald Mathew visited the United States in 1849–1851. Father Mathew was a charismatic Irish, Capuchin friar who had traveled widely in his homeland, persuading drinkers to choose sobriety. As he crisscrossed America, he inspired countless Catholics to take the abstinence pledge, and many parishes started a Father Mathew Society to promote temperance.[25]

Millions of Americans joined temperance societies, took the pledge, and received a certificate like this one from the 1840s (Library of Congress).

The Army of Red Noses

Dry leaders believed that the road to habitual drunkenness began in childhood, so adults must teach youngsters to hate alcohol. Childhood habits that seemed innocuous could start a youngster on the path to alcoholism. Giving children too many sweets or using alcohol as medicine had hidden dangers. "All that is necessary to make a drunkard is a good healthy boy ... and plenty of candy, pastry, pickles, and medicine," a book warned. Wise fathers pointed out drunks to their sons as repulsive specimens of decaying manhood. Smart mothers taught their young ones "to shrink at the approach of the drunkard." They warned their children that the drunkard "shall drink the wrath of God — forever — forever — forever."[26]

Grownups told youngsters scary "true" tales about the horrors of alcohol use. In the era of candlelight and fireplaces, death by burning was a common theme. An oft-told tale recounted the tragedy of an intoxicated mother who dropped her baby on the hearth and watched him burn to death. An old sot risked dying a horrific death by spontaneous combustion; his body could ignite because it was saturated with alcohol! The chronic drunkard must avoid bright sunlight because his body might heat up until it burst into flame. When a drunkard blew out a burning candle, his breath could start a fire and burn his face and hair. One children's book told the tale of a drinker so full of alcohol that he exploded when he lit his pipe![27]

Thomas Poage Hunt was a Presbyterian minister, writer, and temperance lecturer who strongly believed in the necessity of warning children about Demon Rum. Due to a childhood illness, Hunt's body was dwarfish and slightly deformed. Despite his handicap, he sought the spotlight and became an eloquent speaker who drew large crowds. In 1836 he started the Cold Water Army (CWA) to teach youngsters to spurn alcohol. CWA chapters sprang up across the nation, often affiliated with a Sunday school.

Hunt warned children that "a great army of drunkards" could harm them and their parents because a toper would do anything when he needed a drink. The liquor sellers were evil because they made money peddling poison to the "army of red noses." When a drunkard needed to satisfy his craving, he must take "his money to the poison-seller and give it to him for intoxicating liquors.... If his wife and children cry for bread, he must beat them, or turn them out of doors, or kill them. He must sing filthy, foolish songs, keep low company, curse and swear and lie, quarrel and fight, and steal. He must not be too proud to sleep with the hogs," Hunt wrote.[28]

To recruit new members, the CWA youngsters paraded through the streets wearing their uniforms and carrying colorful banners with temperance slogans. Other children would follow the procession to a CWA meeting where they could join — with their parents' permission, of course. Across America the CWA "came out in all its glory" on the Fourth of July — a holiday when dry activists merged love of country with hatred of alcohol. In a typical town, the entire juvenile population showed up, attracted by the hoopla and free food. As the local marching band played stirring music, the CWA children paraded, waving American flags and banners with anti-alcohol mottoes. When the parade ended, proud parents beamed as their offspring recited the abstinence pledge:

> We, Cold Water girls and boys,
> Freely renounce the treacherous joys

Of brandy, whiskey, rum, and gin —
The serpent's lure to death and sin.
Wine, beer, and cider we detest,
And thus we'll make our parents blest.
So here we pledge perpetual hate
To all that can intoxicate.[29]

Reforming the Reformers

Churchgoing, middle-class adults formed the backbone of the temperance movement. Firm believers in lifelong abstinence, they didn't drink socially or fraternize with drinkers. A significant number had never tasted alcohol or seen the inside of a saloon. Yet they knew that whiskey did the devil's work, and they abhorred it with a deep hatred. This earnest loathing of alcohol colored their attitude toward the drunkard, so they were more likely to feel contempt than compassion for someone with a drinking problem.

In general, dry activists didn't regard rescuing the individual drunkard as their mission. They thought it was a waste of time to try to reform the chronic inebriate because habitual drunkenness could not be cured. "Habitual drunkards, held to be irredeemable, were expected to drink themselves to death and thus spare society the trouble of dealing with them, except as temporary denizens of the almshouses and jails," a scholar wrote.[30]

The dry activists were dedicated to the monumental task of creating an ideal temperate nation where sobriety saved souls, families, and society in general. One dry leader envisioned a sober utopia where "all who are intemperate will soon be dead" and "the earth will be eased of an amazing evil." Another leader said, "We must have a nobler, higher, holier ambition than to reform one generation of drunkards after another."[31]

The Massachusetts Society for the Suppression of Intemperance (MSSI), like other temperance groups, grappled with the issue of saving drunkards. For years MSSI leaders debated the possibility of reforming chronic drunks. The majority felt that drunkards had lost "their moral sensibility" and lacked "the very foundation on which reformation should be laid." As one minister put it, "Their condition affords scarce a ray of hope." A dissenting MSSI leader argued in favor of helping drunkards, saying the sot "has yet, perhaps, intervals of thought — moments of compunction." Other members didn't agree with him. They insisted that the group's mission was "to keep sober those who are sober."[32]

The Washington Revival added a new dimension to the temperance movement by drawing drunkards into the dry crusade. In 1840 six drinking buddies were hanging out at a tavern in Baltimore, Maryland. A noted minister/orator was slated to give a temperance lecture at a nearby church that evening. The drinkers delegated two of their number to go hear him and report back. They expected to enjoy a few laughs at the minister's expense.

The two emissaries were not prepared for what happened at the church. As they listened to the minister, his message struck home. He seemed to be talking directly to them, and they felt that he understood their love-hate relationship with whiskey. His words of redemption inspired them. Both felt a sudden, intense desire to begin life anew as sober men. Bursting with fresh hope and purpose, they hurried back to the tavern to share their amazing news with their pals. Their story elicited skepticism, disbelief, and derision. But the fire of reform burned within them. They knew what they must do, and they wanted their friends

their lobbying on the state legislatures because they believed success was more likely at the state level than nationally. Although they won some battles, the results were ultimately disappointing. Lawmakers in Maine, Pennsylvania, Delaware, New Hampshire, Michigan, and the Oregon Territory enacted prohibitory statutes before 1850. None of those laws produced a lasting, satisfactory result.

The anti-alcohol forces were especially active in Maine, where Portland Mayor Neal Dow lent his political clout to the dry crusade. For years the Maine legislature grappled with the issue of prohibition, trying to pass an enforceable law that would actually dry up the state. After repeated failures, in 1851 the lawmakers enacted a strict statute, the Dow Prohibition Law, named for the mayor. When the Dow law failed to kill the liquor traffic, the statute was beefed up with harsher penalties. In 1856 the tougher law was repealed, only to be reinstated the next year.[39]

In 1858 Maine's legislature submitted the liquor question to the voters, who overwhelmingly approved prohibition. The resulting law banned the manufacture and sale of intoxicating liquors, "except for medical and mechanical uses, by agents duly appointed for that purpose." Chemists, artists, and manufacturers who used alcohol in their work could purchase it through legal channels. Church congregations could legally use wine for religious rituals. The statute sought to put the onus on the liquor trafficker rather than the drinker. An individual arrested for drunkenness or disturbing the peace would be released if he identified the person who sold or gave him the liquor. The statute specified a range of fines and jail time for manufacturing and/or selling illegal alcohol.[40]

Maine's prohibition law failed to turn the Pine Tree State into a desert. Booze flowed into the state by land and by sea. Bootleggers and illicit saloons thrived. Unlicensed stills and breweries prospered. Despite the robust illegal liquor traffic, temperance forces used Maine's law as a prototype in other places. Eleven states and two territories passed prohibitory statutes similar to the Maine law. Some states chose another option: laws that regulated liquor sales but didn't try to completely prohibit them. For example, Kansas permitted the sale of liquor except "to drunkards and also to married men against the known wishes of their wives." (This must've set off a bitter argument in more than one marriage.)

The antebellum skirmishes over state prohibition prepared the dry forces for the national battle that lay ahead. The dry leaders learned how to lobby, how to mobilize their members, and how to pressure politicians to vote for their agenda. Seeing that political activism was an effective tool, they expanded their efforts in that arena. The American Temperance Union urged its members to vote dry and to support politicians who would pass strict dry laws. The Sons of Temperance took a very bold step: advocating an amendment to the U.S. Constitution that would make prohibition the law of the land.[41]

The temperance movement gained momentum before the Civil War, but it would soon be sidetracked. With the United States divided by so many life-or-death issues, lawmakers moved the liquor issue to the back burner while they grappled with more urgent problems.

30. The Dry Women versus the Wet Workingmen

Defending the saloon is just as impossible as defending Benedict Arnold, John Wilkes Booth, Guiteau, or Mr. Luetgert of Chicago, who became annoyed one morning because his wife served cold coffee, and so he ran her through a sausage machine. — George Ade, playwright and newspaper columnist[1]

While the men went off to fight the Civil War, the women stayed behind to keep the home fires burning. By necessity, they assumed new roles. The wife-mother stepped into her absent husband's shoes to run the family business or the farm. Young ladies who had never worked at anything more strenuous than needlepoint found the strength to be nurses, caring for wounded troops in military hospitals. Women with wealth and social standing took charge of the charity work, raising money to care for disabled soldiers, war widows, and orphans. As a group, American women expanded their horizons and met the challenges that wartime forced on them. Spending more time outside the home led them to greater awareness of political issues and social problems. When peace returned, confident women stepped forward to assume leadership roles, using the skills they had honed during the war. When the temperance movement regrouped, legions of ladies were ready to do their part to make America a better, drier place.

A Woman's Prayer

After the war religious leaders and do-gooders set out to resurrect the dry crusade, but the movement had lost its momentum. Dry activism lacked vigor, cohesion, and a vision for the future. Then in 1873-74 the crusade came alive when a group of Ohio women launched an audacious campaign inspired by the true story of a drunkard's wife.

Diocletian Lewis had many interests; he was an educator, a traveling lecturer, a homeopathic doctor, and an exercise enthusiast who invented the beanbag. On lecture tours Lewis sometimes told audiences about his mother, Dilecta, and his father, a habitual drunkard who wasted many hours at the saloon. Papa Lewis abused his wife and spent his money on whiskey, impoverishing the family. Dilecta, who didn't believe in divorce, was determined to keep her family together. She found work to support her children and "bore all her sorrows with Christian fortitude."

Dilecta couldn't keep her husband from going to the bar, so she pleaded with the saloonkeeper to stop serving him. The barkeep refused because he didn't want to lose a steady customer. In desperation, Dilecta asked her female friends to go with her to the bar and pray that God would open the publican's eyes so he could see the harm he caused by selling liquor. The women's prayers touched the man's heart; he took the sobriety pledge and closed his saloon.[2]

A few days before Christmas 1873, Lewis told Dilecta's story when he gave temperance lectures in two Ohio towns, Hillsboro and Washington Courthouse. His message about the power of a woman's moral courage and prayer inspired his female listeners. Like Dilecta, they knew that heavy drinking could destroy a marriage and turn home into hell. They wanted to rescue families from the plague of drunkenness, so they formulated a plan of action. Under Ohio law liquor dealers could sell wine and beer but not distilled spirits. Unethical barkeepers routinely sold hard liquor labeled as beer or wine. Drugstores could legally dispense liquor by prescription; many also sold illegal booze by the bottle or by the drink at the soda fountain.[3]

On Christmas morning a group of dedicated, motivated dry women met at a Presbyterian church in Hillsboro. After praying and singing hymns, the ladies marched forth to stop the liquor sales at the local saloons, hotels, and drugstores. Like Dilecta, they chose prayer as their weapon, praying inside or in front of the places they wanted to close. They divided into small groups, so they could take turns praying; when one group got tired, another took over.[4]

Initially, the saloonkeepers viewed the praying women as a curiosity or a minor annoyance. The men were polite but refused to close. The ladies were also courteous. They "knelt down on the floor and offered prayers of such an earnest kind that the most obdurate old liquor dealer could not fail to be affected by them." The ladies prayed for the saloon owner, his family, and his customers. They ended their prayers by asking for the strength to continue their crusade until they triumphed.[5] In only six weeks, more than half of Hillsboro's bars closed. In addition, two druggists agreed to stop selling illegal liquor.

When the ladies confronted a doctor/druggist and accused him of illegal sales, he denied any wrongdoing. He stated that he complied with all the laws and didn't "sell to any person whose father, mother, wife, or daughter" made a written request to deny liquor to that family member. The temperance ladies weren't satisfied. They built a "tabernacle" in front of his drugstore and prayed there from early morning until late at night. He went to court, secured an injunction, and sued the ladies for illegal trespass and defamation of character. This forced them to tear down their tabernacle and stop harassing the doctor, but it didn't stop their activism. They continued to hold temperance meetings that attracted large, fervent crowds.[6]

Soon after Hillsboro's praying bands began their crusade, women in Washington Courthouse started their own campaign. As church bells tolled, they marched through the streets, stopping at the saloons. They went inside each barroom and sang a hymn; then their leader read an appeal asking the saloonkeeper to close; if he didn't agree to do so, they prayed. That first day the barkeepers were courteous but determined to stay open.

The next day a larger group of ladies sallied forth, braving the cold, inhospitable winter weather. At the first saloon, they found the doors locked, so they knelt outside in the snow to pray. For three days they prayed at the bars. On the fourth day they had their first success; a liquor dealer agreed to close his business. He poured his entire inventory down the gutter

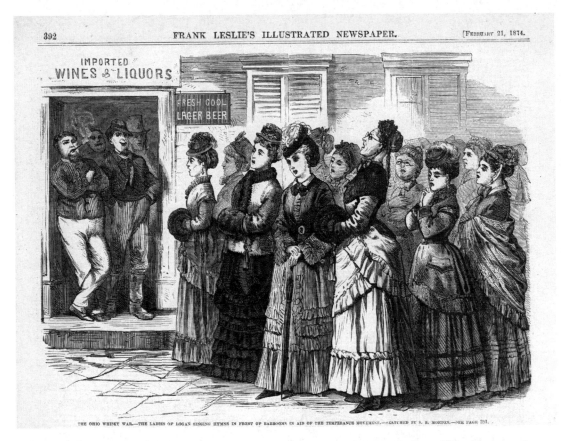

THE OHIO WHISKY WAR.—THE LADIES OF LOGAN SINGING HYMNS IN FRONT OF BARROOMS IN AID OF THE TEMPERANCE MOVEMENT.—SKETCHED BY S. B. MORTON.—SEE PAGE 391.

This 1874 magazine illustration depicts temperance women protesting outside a barroom in Logan, Ohio (Library of Congress).

while the ladies sang and the church bells pealed. This set off a domino effect; soon all of the town's saloons closed and the drugstores pledged to sell by prescription only.[7]

The Woman's Crusade spread to other Ohio towns, including Xenia, Oxford, Bellefontaine, Elysia, Bucyrus, Moscow, Greenfield, Logan, and Waynesville. In some saloons the barflies didn't approve of the ladies' activism. In Clyde, rowdy drinkers heckled the ladies and the barkeep threw cold water on their leader. In Norwalk, the women withstood a barrage of dirty water that soiled their clothes. At one saloon the bartender did a naughty, suggestive dance while the women sang a hymn. In Madisonville, bar owners flooded the sidewalk with water to prevent the ladies from kneeling in front of their saloons.[8]

Crusading women surrounded a beer wagon in Wilmington and kept the teamster from delivering his product to the saloon. "The driver escaped, after they had prayed him crazy," an observer said. The teamster headed for the nearby town of Sabina, planning to make a delivery there. A quick-thinking Wilmington woman sent a telegram to the ladies in Sabina, so they were waiting for him when he arrived. They "prayed for him till, like Saul, he gave up in despair."[9]

In Columbus, an angry publican grabbed the leader of the praying band and roughed her up. He was later arrested. A Vienna barkeeper seemed friendly; he even volunteered to lead the ladies in prayer. With proper magniloquence he prayed that the Lord would show the women how to mind their own business and leave him alone. Then he shook up a keg of beer, pulled out the plug, and sprayed foam on the ladies. They hurried out of the saloon, with wet dresses and drooping feathers on their hats. After going home to change clothes, they returned to the saloon to resume their prayers.[10]

The Cleveland Woman's Crusade started peacefully but became violent after a few days. A mob of angry, vicious men attacked the ladies, kicking, punching, and striking them with bricks. The women scrambled to take refuge inside a store, where they waited until the police dispersed the mob. The following day more women ventured forth and were attacked by a crowd of rowdy men. This finally roused Cleveland's law-abiding males to do their chivalrous duty. When the women ventured out to pray again, a thousand "manly men went out to defend" them. A mob of drinkers congregated on the street and threatened to attack the men who were protecting the ladies. Police and militia units hurried to the scene; the mob melted away.

For several months, Cleveland women went from saloon to saloon without violence, and many publicans agreed to close their shops. The ladies converted a few former pubs into Friendly Inns, where they held temperance meetings. Inspired by the women's activism, a group of wealthy temperance men hired detectives and obtained hundreds of indictments against Cleveland liquor sellers who were violating the law.[11]

In Cincinnati temperance ladies took to the city streets, praying in front of saloons. On one occasion, forty-three praying women were arrested and jailed for obstructing the sidewalk. In jail they spent their time trying to convert the other prisoners to Christianity. Not everyone applauded their religiosity. Judge Alphonso Taft showed little sympathy for the pushy praying ladies. "It is an objectionable feature of the present crusade that it intrudes religious observances on those who do not ask for them," the judge said. "Prayer with or for those who desire it is commendable; but when forced upon the unwilling it is a mockery of God."[12]

Despite critics like Judge Taft, the general public lauded the Ohio Woman's Crusade, which soon spread to neighboring states. In one Indiana town the women sat on camp stools outside the busiest saloon, praying and singing. The saloon owner politely asked them to leave, but they ignored him. Growing angry, he ordered them to leave. The women stood their ground, saying that he didn't own the sidewalk. He left briefly, then returned carrying a chamber pot. He sat on his pot on the sidewalk in front of the ladies, trying to embarrass them into leaving. They focused on singing hymns and reading Scripture, pretending they didn't see him. It was an impasse. No clear victor emerged that day.[13]

In April 1874 news reports said the woman's crusade had abolished the liquor traffic in thirty-seven towns and closed more than 1,750 saloons in Ohio, Indiana, and Illinois. During the course of the crusade, thousands of women participated in at least twelve states. In most locations, the ladies formed praying bands and used the Ohio tactics. Occasionally barkeeps or drinkers attacked them verbally or physically. Sometimes the women fought back using their parasols, hatpins, and purses as weapons. However, in general, the crusade was peaceful.[14]

Tremble, King Alcohol

Ebullient over the success of the Woman's Crusade, the temperance ladies decided to form their own national society. If small prayer groups could accomplish so much, think what a unified, nationwide organization could achieve! Less than a year after the Ohio crusade began, activists founded the Woman's Christian Temperance Union (WCTU), which would soon surpass all previous dry groups in power and influence. Women were no longer relegated to the ladies' auxiliary while the men made policy and planned the strategy. Now they controlled their own organization from top to bottom.

The WCTU quickly became the largest women's club in the United States. Its members were known as "white ribbon ladies," referring to the ribbons they wore to symbolize the purity of womankind and motherhood. As a vital part of the WCTU mission, the group owned a publishing house that churned out tons of didactic literature. In the days before electronic media, printed matter was the surest means of informing the masses, and WCTU leaders were well aware of that. The Women's Temperance Publishing Association issued approximately 25 million pages of printed matter each year. Women did all the editing, managed the finances, sat on the board of directors, and owned all the stock in the company.

The WCTU greatly expanded its mission after dynamic do-gooder Frances Willard took the helm. Willard was an educator and, for a time, served as president of Evanston College for Women. When that college became part of Northwestern University, she was appointed dean of women. During a seaside holiday in Maine, teetotaler Willard met influential temperance activists, including Neal Dow, Portland's former mayor. She found the dry activists to be kindred spirits who shared her passion for improving society and elevating mankind. Their zeal drew her into the temperance crusade. She became a temperance lecturer, aided in the creation of the WCTU, and served as president of the Chicago WCTU. In 1879 she moved up to head the national organization.[15]

For almost two decades, Willard provided vigorous leadership, vastly enlarging the WCTU's mission and power. A human whirlwind, she declared that she wanted to "do everything!" She created numerous WCTU departments to tackle such issues as woman's suffrage, child labor, domestic violence, divorce laws, prostitution, illegal narcotics, workers' rights, world peace, and the Americanization of immigrants. She demanded equal opportunity for the sexes and for all socioeconomic groups. A Christian socialist, she called socialism "the higher way" and argued that it carried "the ethics of Christ's gospel" into everyday life. "In every Christian there exists a socialist, and in every socialist a Christian," she said.[16]

WCTU leaders knew that political action was the key to passing strict liquor control laws. If the majority of the electorate voted dry, lawmakers would be forced to enact stringent statutes limiting, or even abolishing, the liquor traffic. To increase the number of dry voters, the WCTU had a two-pronged strategy: (1) passing woman's suffrage and (2) raising children to vote dry. Temperance sentiment was very strong among women, and distaff voters would constitute a formidable dry bloc if they were enfranchised. Willard and other WCTU activists joined forces with the suffragettes in an all-out effort to obtain the vote for women.

To indoctrinate children, the WCTU offered programs for different age groups. The Loyal Temperance Legion (LTL) enrolled boys and girls aged six to twelve. The LTL's motto was "Tremble, King Alcohol, We Shall Grow Up." The LTL children were taught to abstain from liquor, be kind to their pets, prevent animal cruelty, shun tobacco products, and use "clean language."

According to the WCTU handbook, "the little people ... are drilled and disciplined in the fight for a clear brain and fitted for active temperance service." The white ribbon ladies used stories, cheers, slogans, Bible readings, lessons, and group-action songs to indoctrinate the youngsters. "In the Loyal Temperance Legion the children catch the spirit that dominates the WCTU," said the superintendent of juvenile work. "Their little feet step to white ribbon songs; they learn to love our mottoes and watchwords of victory, and are systematically taught our plans of work." The women strove to make the meetings fun so the children would connect "good times with temperance."[17]

Each LTL member was called a National Prohibition Guard, and some activities had military overtones. The LTL boys were taught to march, salute, and drill with toy firearms. Despite Willard's belief in gender equality, the girls' drill teams used brooms and paper fans instead of guns. At first the drill teams were immensely popular, but some parents worried about the militarism inherent in them. After a time, the LTL replaced the quasi-military drills with less controversial activities.[18]

Like other dry groups, the LTL had a pledge:

> Desiring to obey the laws of health,
> The laws of my country, and the laws of God,
> I promise, God helping me,
> Not to buy, drink, sell or give
> Alcoholic liquors while I live;
> From all tobacco I'll abstain,
> And never take God's name in vain.

In order to reach as many youngsters as possible, WCTU leaders had a plan to teach "scientific" temperance education in all public schools. The emphasis would be on explaining the effects of alcohol on human biology and health. Initially, few school boards agreed to add temperance to the curriculum, but the ladies doggedly pursued their goal. They circulated petitions and explained their plan to parents; they lobbied educators, school board members, and legislators. Ultimately, they convinced every state in the Union to teach temperance in the public schools.

The temperance textbooks emphasized the WCTU's views on "the laws of health," based on the belief that the human body is the temple of the Holy Spirit. The children were told to avoid "alcohol and nicotine poisons" as well as "bad food, unnatural dress, bad ventilation, and ill-proportioned exercise." Students were specifically urged to shun narcotics, pork, spicy foods, stimulating beverages, and tight, restrictive clothing. In a popular, quasi-scientific classroom activity, the temperance students grew houseplants in pots. They poured water into half of the plants and whiskey into the other half. Of course, the plants dosed with whiskey withered away — just as the children would if they drank alcohol.[19]

The Workingman's Club

In the late nineteenth century, opposition to the liquor trade crystallized around one institution: the saloon. Dry leaders chose to focus on the saloon due to its monumentally bad image. It was the ugly antithesis of respectability, and a wide spectrum of Americans hated everything it stood for. Prohibitionists said the barroom's swinging doors led straight to the gates of hell. Popular culture depicted the saloon as a smoky, dimly-lit dive with smelly, battered spittoons and tobacco-stained sawdust on the floor. Sots, brawlers, fallen women, and ne'er-do-wells hung out there. The saloon nurtured vice and crime, especially prostitution and illegal gambling. It abetted corrupt political machines by trading drinks for votes. It sucked up the workingman's wages, leaving him little or no money to support his family.

To a certain extent, the dry activists were waging class warfare because the saloon was a blue-collar institution. The affluent classes drank at posh watering holes with glittery chandeliers, ornate mirrors, shiny brass rails, and well-dressed patrons. A rich man had the option of joining an exclusive private club. A middle-class man could join a fraternal order. The poor guy had only the humble saloon, the so-called "workingman's club." Prohibitionists said the workingman's club had by far the most expensive dues because the poor man paid all his hard-earned wages to join.

After a grueling workday at the foundry, on the docks, or in the stockyards a tired man needed to relax. The saloon beckoned. It was Shangri-la compared to a squalid tenement where screaming kids and a nagging wife gave a man no peace. The corner saloon offered numbing alcohol, male camaraderie, and good cheer. A man could smoke a big cigar or chew tobacco without taking any flak from a woman. He could tell a dirty joke, talk politics, or curse the boss. He could play cards or shoot dice in the backroom. He could drink until he ran out of money.

Dry leaders felt an urgent need for a coordinated, forceful campaign against the saloon. In 1893 the Reverend Howard Hyde Russell, a Congregational minister, joined with other activists to form the Anti-Saloon League (ASL) in Oberlin, Ohio. The new group worked closely with the Methodist Church and the Oberlin Temperance Alliance. Russell took the lead in mobilizing dry voters and pressuring the Ohio state legislature to pass strict anti-alcohol laws. He also worked tirelessly to raise money for the cause, and he secured substantial donations from John D. Rockefeller.

In 1895 the Ohio ASL merged with a similar group in Washington, D.C., to form the American Anti-Saloon League. Dry activists started local chapters of the ASL, which became a powerful political force in a remarkably short time. In the early 1900s the ASL had active chapters in forty-three states and territories.[20] While the WCTU worked to enact woman's suffrage, the ASL molded dry males into a voting juggernaut. The leadership formed alliances across party lines and endorsed any politician who would vote dry, even if he took a nip in private.

In keeping with the dry coalition's penchant for pledges, there was one for the anti-saloon crusade:

> I stand for prohibition,
> The utter demolition
> Of all this curse of misery and woe;
> Complete extermination,
> Entire annihilation —
> The saloon must go!

The anti-saloon forces faced a seasoned adversary with a long tradition of wielding political clout. The saloons were especially powerful in big cities, and more than one corrupt political machine owed its supremacy to the liquor trade. Saloons served as informal campaign headquarters where candidates hung out and courted the voters. Liquor interests donated huge sums of money to wet candidates who promised to block strict regulation of the industry. The saloon owners turned out the vote on Election Day, bartering booze for ballots.

The wet forces expected the liquor industry's ties to the urban political machines to protect it from the dry fanatics. But skeptics wondered if politics might be the downfall, rather than the salvation, of the liquor trade. In an editorial, *National Liquor Dealers' Journal* said the industry had formed alliances with "the most corrupt political powers" and acted in ways "that repel all conscientious citizens." The journal forecast "doom," saying "for this the liquor business is to blame."[21]

Of course, bar owners knew that the retail liquor business had a dismal image. But they attacked the problem halfheartedly. Alarmed by the anti-saloon outcry, publicans started a trade association, the Knights of the Royal Arch. They planned to upgrade their industry and change the popular perception of the liquor trade. Royal Arch chapters sprang up in many cities, but inertia blocked the push to clean up the saloons. Some barkeeps made superficial changes, but the saloon's unsavory aspects were deeply entrenched. Barkeepers couldn't, or wouldn't, take decisive action to dissociate their business from gambling, prostitution, and dirty politics. In general, the saloon owners simply didn't see any harm in wagering or paying for sex.[22]

On the production side of the liquor industry, divisions prevented the formation of a united front against the prohibitionists. Brewers considered beer to be a benign product, not at all like distilled spirits. Beer was widely held to have nutritional value, and an astounding number of people believed it was not intoxicating. In some communities, a visit to the local beer garden was wholesome family fun and even the children drank beer. Given beer's image as less harmful than distilled spirits, brewers believed that the law might someday ban hard liquor, but never beer. Therefore, they didn't throw all their forces into the anti-prohibition fight. Their profits seemed to be guaranteed whatever happened. In fact, drinkers would consume more beer if distilled spirits were outlawed.

As the ALS grew more powerful, a few savvy brewers took steps to divorce themselves from the sleazy side of the liquor trade. With twenty-twenty foresight, Adolphus Busch saw the dry movement as a threat to his business, his wealth, and his way of life. He urged his fellow brewers to contribute money to a campaign "to win the American people over to our side, to make them all lovers of beer." He envisioned spending at least a million dollars to teach Americans "to have respect for the brewing industry and the brewer."[23]

Although the brewers tried to present their product as a wholesome beverage, they were "tied" to a large portion of the country's tawdry taverns. The big breweries owned prime urban real estate that they leased to barkeepers, and they held the mortgages on many saloons. In return for an exclusive sales contract, a brewer would give free furnishings and equipment to a publican. The major breweries bought huge quantities of food cheaply and wholesaled it to saloons for the famous free lunch.

The Anheuser-Busch brewery undertook "the suppression of lawless saloons" by closing disreputable bars that it owned or controlled. But only a handful of brewers joined Anheuser-Busch in shuttering the vile, vice-ridden saloons that plagued society. Apathy seemed to pervade the brewing sector. The fatalists believed that prohibition would come no matter what they did. "We will not fight it," said brewer Leopold Schmidt. "It is a disease and must run its course."[24]

Trade groups, including the National Wholesale Liquor Dealers' Association and the Distillers' Association of America, mounted lackluster campaigns to stop the passage of new dry laws. They argued that prohibition curtailed personal freedom and harmed the economy by closing prosperous businesses. Although these issues merited discussion, dry leaders dominated the public discourse and they chose to demonize the wets rather than debate them. Zealous dry spokesmen sought the spotlight and became very visible, well-known public figures. The wet forces had no comparable cadre of spokesmen. Moreover, the dry activists were motivated by an altruistic fervor to improve society while the wets generally had selfish goals, like preserving their access to liquor and/or protecting their financial interests.

Although the drys seemed to be winning the public relations battle, the wets had a powerful, practical argument that might save the day. For much of the nation's history, liquor taxes had been a major revenue source for the government. Although the liquor trade had often protested and evaded these taxes, the wet faction argued that losing this source of revenue would adversely impact everyone — even teetotalers. Liquor taxes constituted up to forty percent of the nation's tax revenue in the early 1900s. If liquor money stopped flowing into the public coffers, the government would have to tax something else, and nobody wanted to pay a personal income tax.[25]

Temperance leaders understood that the tax argument was a powerful weapon for the liquor industry, so they set out to disarm it. Dry lobbyists played a major role in persuading Washington to diversify its revenue stream. In 1909 the U.S. Congress approved the Sixteenth Amendment to override language in the Constitution that greatly restricted the federal government's right to collect an income tax. The ratification process was completed in 1913. Several months later Congress passed an income tax law to implement the new levy. Initially, the income tax affected few people, but dry leaders knew that it had the potential to replace liquor taxes, which would make the whiskey industry entirely dispensable.

While the wet forces struggled to find a winning strategy, the cold water men ran toward the goal line. Led by the ASL, dry groups aggressively mobilized public opinion and formed political coalitions to pass strict state liquor laws. By 1906 thirty states had local option laws that permitted prohibition by townships, municipalities, and/or counties. Nationwide, dryness reigned in more than half of all counties, more than sixty percent of incorporated towns, and almost seventy percent of townships. In 1907 the residents of Oklahoma, in preparation for statehood, voted to make statewide prohibition part of their new constitution. When Oklahomans passed the measure by a substantial margin, it "electrified the moral forces of other states." By 1913 nine states had passed statewide prohibition.[26]

While the dry forces forged ahead, realists questioned the impact of prohibitory laws. *The American Magazine* published an account of one traveler's quest to buy liquor in dry towns. The man arrived in Jackson, Mississippi, on the day the legislature passed statewide prohibition. The legislators celebrated by consuming "a carload of wine and intoxicants," courtesy of the soft-drink companies that expected their sales to soar. In Shreveport, Louisiana, the traveler paid dues to join two locker clubs. At one club, he used his member's key to open a locker that held bottles of booze. He chose one and poured himself a drink. At the other club, he unlocked the door on his locker, the back side popped open, and a bartender took his order.

The traveler found it easy to buy moonshine throughout the rural South. In Asheville, North Carolina, he patronized "near-beer palaces" that served the real thing. In Oklahoma City, he bought pints of whiskey at a hotel and visited an illegal barroom where drinkers were packed in like sardines. He purchased beer and whiskey at drugstores in Redlands, California. In Topeka, Kansas, he bought booze at a hotel, a drugstore, and multiple cigar stands. His longest dry spell came in Wichita — a notoriously arid town; it took him an hour and twenty minutes to find a drink.[27]

A National Solution

Even the most nearsighted prohibitionists could see that the dry states were moist, if not sopping wet. The bootleg traffic kept intoxicants flowing from wet states to dry ones, supplying drinkers with their favorite alcoholic beverages. Dry activists proposed an obvious remedy: national Prohibition. The WCTU, the Prohibition Party, the Independent Order of Good Templars, and several other dry groups called for a Prohibition amendment to the U.S. Constitution. At first the ASL didn't jump on the band wagon because its strategists believed the states wouldn't ratify such an amendment. Delegates at the ASL's 1913 national convention debated the pros and cons of a nationwide ban on alcohol. After sober discussion, the ASL delegates "unanimously and enthusiastically" joined other drys in demanding a constitutional amendment.[28]

Wayne Wheeler, a famous attorney who ran the ASL's legal department, led the lobbying effort in Washington. Wheeler understood both pressure politics and public relations, which was in its infancy as a tactic for molding legislation. He was a master strategist who deftly manipulated press coverage in order to sway public opinion. He pioneered many tactics still used by special interest groups, and his relentless crusade made "Wheelerism" slang for high-pressure lobbying. During his regime, the ASL ranked among the most respected *and* the most hated forces on Capitol Hill. At his request, dry voters inundated lawmakers with letters and telegrams urging them to pass national Prohibition. He applied more pressure by personally confronting Congressmen. If he couldn't sweet talk them into voting his way, he didn't hesitate to bully them or threaten to block their re-election.[29]

In December 1917, the dry faction's tenacious, high-powered lobbying paid off. Both houses of Congress adopted the National Prohibition resolution, starting the process that would allow the states to ratify or reject the proposed constitutional amendment. The state legislatures were given seven years to vote for or against the amendment. If the amendment were ratified, the liquor trade would be given one year to dispose of its inventory and prepare for Prohibition.[30]

With the ratification process underway, dry leaders pursued a dual agenda: they pushed the state legislatures to vote for the Prohibition amendment and they pressured Congress to pass special wartime controls on liquor. They argued that the liquor industry was using grain, railcars, and manpower needed to fight the war. Grains going into alcoholic beverages could feed the troops. According to the drys' data, liquor manufacturers used enough grain to bake eleven million loaves of bread every day. Dry posters asked, "Shall the many have food, or the few have drink?" The cold water men argued that stopping the shipment of liquor would free up at least 100,000 railcars for the war effort. Closing the distilleries, breweries, and saloons would furlough thousands of able-bodied men, who could join the military or work in defense plants.[31]

When Congress passed the Lever Food and Fuel Control Act in 1917, it included a ban on the distillation of foodstuffs for ardent spirits, but it didn't prohibit the production of beer or wine. In 1918 President Woodrow Wilson went a step farther and approved controls to reduce the amount of grain used by breweries. The alcohol content of beer was capped at 2.75 percent, and production was limited to seventy percent of the previous year's output.[32]

The new restrictions on liquor production put the dry activists a little closer to their goal of abolishing the industry. Total victory seemed to be near at hand. In 1918 Congress passed a wartime prohibition law, a temporary measure that didn't require ratification by the states. This statute specified that the ban would last until U.S. military forces were officially demobilized by the President. Even many wets endorsed this emergency ban as a patriotic sacrifice. Dry leaders viewed it as a stopgap measure that would shut down the liquor industry until the states could ratify permanent Prohibition.[33]

World War I aided the dry lobbyists, who exploited anti–German sentiment to further their cause. Zealous nativists vilified everything German, including sauerkraut, pretzels, beer, dachshunds, and Wagnerian opera. Beer was derisively called "Kaiser brew." In Milwaukee, self-proclaimed patriots manned a machinegun in front of a theatre to scare people away from a performance of *Wilhelm Tell*. New York's Metropolitan Opera House banned Wagner's music. True-blue Americans coined new terms for things associated with Germany: sauerkraut became liberty cabbage, hamburger was liberty meat, and the German shepherd was upgraded to Alsatian shepherd. The acme of absurd name changes was liberty measles, which replaced the unpatriotic German measles.[34]

Hatemongers burned books written by German authors and/or published in the German language. They poured yellow paint on German-American churches and homes belonging to families with German ancestry. In Oklahoma two Mennonite churches were set on fire by someone identified as "a patriotic arsonist." Also in Oklahoma, "self-proclaimed defenders of the American way" marched into a Mennonite church and demanded that services be conducted in English. They posted a bizarre notice on the church door: "GOD ALMIGHTY UNDERSTANDS THE AMERICAN LANGUAGE. ADDRESS HIM ONLY IN THAT TONGUE."[35]

Dry zealots depicted the liquor industry as the enemy within, wasting resources and leading young soldiers astray. The ASL singled out liquor as "the Kaiser's mightiest ally" and popularized a new slogan: Kaiser-ism abroad and booze at home must go. A typical ASL pamphlet railed against "the un–American, pro–German, crime-producing, food-wasting, youth-corrupting, home-wrecking, treasonable liquor traffic."[36]

Nativists called people with German ancestry 3.5 percent Americans, referring to the alcohol content of beer. A Wisconsin politico said brewers Pabst, Schlitz, Blatz, and Miller were "the most treacherous, the most menacing" enemies of America. The United States had never faced "power so brutal, so domineering, so corrupt ... as the brewers of America," wrote a former Indiana governor. Congressman John Tillman (D-AR) said, "The most arrogant, the least polite, the most disdainful citizen is that haughty plutocrat, the American brewer, usually tainted with Teuton sympathies and damned by a German conscience."[37]

Right and Righteousness

The wartime ban on alcohol disappointed the dry faction because it had limited impact. Initial efforts to enforce it were restrained because legal authorities questioned the statute's constitutionality. The Department of Justice announced that it would make only a few arrests, to be used as test cases in the courts to resolve the constitutional issues. Many jurisdictions stated that they simply didn't have enough money or lawmen to enforce the ban. Sales of beer and wine "continued over thousands of bars in every state in the Union, and even ardent liquors were sold in many places."[38]

Even though the wartime ban failed, dry leaders didn't waver in their commitment to Prohibition. They felt confident that the constitutional amendment would be ratified because the wet forces were putting up little resistance. The liquor industry and a few veterans groups mounted disjointed, ineffectual campaigns. World War I soldiers argued that they had fought for freedom, risking their lives on foreign soil, and Prohibition would deny them personal freedom at home. As one wet put it, "Our army was brave enough, moral enough and dependable enough to stop the German hordes on the way to Paris, but the National Prohibitionists say they cannot be trusted to drink a glass of beer or wine!" While Americans admired the soldiers and their patriotism, their resistance was simply too little, too late.[39]

In January 1918, Mississippi claimed the honor of being the first state to ratify the proposed National Prohibition amendment. On January 16, 1919, Nevada became the thirty-sixth state to vote for ratification, thereby adding the Eighteenth Amendment to the U.S. Constitution. By the end of February 1919, forty-four states had ratified. Only New Jersey, Connecticut, and Rhode Island failed to approve the resolution before it became law. (New Jersey finally ratified the amendment in 1922; the other two states never voted for it.)[40]

In July 1919, the U.S. House of Representatives passed the Volstead Prohibition Enforcement Act, which added the meat to the Eighteenth Amendment's skeleton. Congressman Andrew Volstead (R-MN), chair of the House Judiciary Committee, was officially in charge of writing the statute. In reality, the ASL's Wayne Wheeler controlled the entire process. "Representative Volstead never in his life wrote his name at the bottom of a temperance pledge, never in his life has been a member of a teetotaler's society, nor even made a speech on Prohibition," a newsman noted.[41] Yet his name would forever be associated with national Prohibition.

In September 1919 the Senate passed an enforcement bill similar to the House's. After reconciling the two bills, the U.S. Congress sent the measure to President Woodrow Wilson, who vetoed it. (Wilson had suffered a debilitating stroke, and his wife probably made this decision based on what she knew about his views on drinking.) Congress quickly, resoundingly overrode the Presidential veto. National Prohibition would go into effect at 12:01 a.m. January 17, 1920.[42]

As America looked forward to the dawn of the new decade, happy prohibitionists foresaw a dry utopia. Law enforcement forecast a sharp drop in crime and prison populations. Whiskey widows were excited about having sober husbands who would magically morph into loving, responsible family men. Social workers predicted a decline in poverty, divorce, venereal diseases, and other societal ills. Business leaders declared America would have a sober, dependable workforce. Political reformers said politics would be cleaner without alcohol's corrupting influence. Religious leaders believed Prohibition would save millions of souls who would otherwise drink themselves into hell on earth and eternal hell after death.

U.S. Senator Morris Sheppard (D-TX) summed up the high hopes, saying Prohibition "means a rise to a higher and better plane of civilization for the United States. It means more savings, more homes, better health and better morals. It means that the American republic has achieved a distinctive triumph for right and righteousness in the long and bitter struggle between good and evil." Prohibition would "reach the uttermost limits of the earth to uplift, to encourage and to bless all the millions of mankind."[43]

What could possibly go wrong?

31. Corruption: Gangsters and Graft

"There were no civil service requirements and, as a result, the most extraordinary collection of political hacks, hangers-on, and passing highwaymen got appointed as Prohibition agents."—Elmer Irey, Special Intelligence Unit, United States Treasury[1]

The dry activists knew that some drinkers would violate the Volstead law at the dawn of the Golden Age of Sobriety, but the offenders would soon change their ways. Every American, even the old sot, would experience the wonderful benefits of sober living, so the demand for alcohol would taper off until it vanished. Without demand, there would be no incentive for anybody to sell booze, so the bootleggers would have to find honest work. As the demand for alcohol plummeted, the need for Volstead enforcement would diminish until the glorious day when it disappeared altogether.

Even the Pollyanna Prohibitionists understood that the dry law would initially require an enforcement apparatus. State and local police forces would add enforcing the dry law to their long list of duties, but they could allocate only part of their resources to Volstead. To spearhead the fight against the illegal liquor traffic, the federal government created the Prohibition Unit (later the Prohibition Bureau). Headquartered in Washington, D.C., the unit had field offices across the United States.

From the very beginning to the bitter end, funding shortfalls crippled dry law enforcement. In Volstead's first year, Congress appropriated only $6.35 million to enforce the nationwide ban on alcohol. Drys voted for the small appropriation because they believed most Americans would gladly comply with the law and recalcitrant drinkers would soon give up their wicked habit. The wet members of Congress voted against funds for enforcement because they wanted Prohibition to fail. The sooner Americans realized Volstead couldn't be enforced, the better.

The federal Prohibition commissioner, working under the Treasury secretary, made policy and directed Volstead enforcement. The commissioner's job proved to be a political hot potato, and it turned into a nightmare for more than one appointee. Ohio attorney John Kramer was the first man appointed to the post. He was a Democrat, an Evangelical Lutheran, a Sunday school teacher, and a former state legislator. As for his attitude toward Prohibition, he claimed to be "a man with strong convictions ... without being a crank." Although he had never worked in law enforcement, dry leaders believed that his education and experience qualified him to be Volstead's supreme dry spy.[2]

During Prohibition countless bottles of illegal whiskey were poured into city sewers (Library of Congress).

Kramer directed the work of nine assistant commissioners, each of whom supervised a district made up of two or more states. Within the districts, each state had a director with a staff to do the office work. The actual job of hitting the streets and arresting violators fell to the federal Prohibition agents, who were assigned based on the perceived need in each district. Over the course of Prohibition, Washington revamped the federal enforcement apparatus several times. For the most part, these shakeups shuffled personnel and resources but didn't change the basic structure.

For the first decade of Volstead, the Prohibition Unit was part of the Treasury Department, primarily because Treasury collected the taxes on alcohol. Even before Prohibition, Treasury employed revenue agents to track down moonshiners and others who evaded the liquor tax. Enforcing Volstead was a logical extension of this work. The Department of Justice (DOJ) prosecuted Volstead cases after the Prohibition Unit had collected the evidence and made arrests.

Treasury Secretary Andrew Mellon showed little enthusiasm for enforcing Volstead. According to published reports, he attended parties where whiskey was served and he broke the law by buying liquor from bootleggers. Before Prohibition he had been part owner of a distillery, which became a bonded warehouse when the dry law took effect. Governor

Gifford Pinchot (R-PA) complained that Mellon made money on the sale and withdrawal of liquor from this bonded facility. Pinchot said, "I do not know whether it is legal for a man who has been in the whiskey business for forty years to be at the head of the [dry] law enforcement, but I do know that it is wrong."[3]

Mellon's expertise lay in financial matters, and he preferred to focus on fiscal policy. Dry leaders attacked him for failing to make Volstead enforcement a top priority. Bone-dry Senator Smith Brookhart (R-IA) wanted to replace Mellon with someone "who means to enforce the law." Elizabeth Tilton of the WCTU actually accused the Treasury secretary of "indulging in the illicit liquor traffic." The Methodist Church Board of Temperance took the position that Mellon "should not have the responsibility of Prohibition enforcement. Neither by conviction nor inclination is he fitted for that responsibility." Nevertheless, he remained in charge until 1930.[4]

Even though dry leaders complained about Mellon, they repeatedly blocked efforts to transfer the Prohibition Unit from Treasury to the DOJ. This was largely due to their distrust of the men who served as attorney general. Congressional drys knew that Harry Daugherty, President Harding's attorney general, was both wet and corrupt. They viewed his successor, Harlan Fiske Stone, with suspicion, labeling him a "New York liberal." The next attorney general, John Garibaldi Sargent, made impressive speeches about Volstead enforcement, but dry leaders felt he was not suited to the job. Finally, when President Hoover chose William DeWitt Mitchell as attorney general, the dry faction was happy. Mitchell vowed to enforce Volstead with every tool at his disposal, so the DOJ took over all facets of federal enforcement, with a few very minor exceptions.[5]

Underfunded and Understaffed

During the early 1920s, Prohibition agents were hired outside the civil service system, so political patronage ran rampant. As a rule, an agent received his job as payment for services rendered to a political boss or party. Of course, this was not the best way to find qualified lawmen. In fact, many agents had no law enforcement training or experience. Assistant U.S. Attorney General Mabel Willebrandt spoke bluntly about the general incompetence of the federal dry sleuths. She said the typical Prohibition agent was the "ward-heeler type" who was "as devoid of integrity and honesty as the bootlegging fraternity." She accused the government of "committing a crime against the public when it pins a badge of police authority on, and hands a gun to, a man of uncertain character...." She said some dry agents were "no more fit to wear a badge and carry a gun than Jesse James."[6]

Background checks were haphazard at best, so a shocking number of Prohibition agents had shady pasts, including prison records. Two sensational shootings in New York City raised public awareness of this problem. Only two months after Volstead began, Prohibition agent Stewart McMullin shot and killed an unarmed bootlegger. In court, agent McMullin admitted that he was an ex-con who had been convicted of involuntary manslaughter, forgery, and highway robbery. He had served prison time in Texas, Indiana, and New York. State Senator Jimmy Walker (later the mayor of NYC) had pulled strings to get McMullin a job with the Prohis.[7]

Jeremiah Bohan, a Prohibition inspector, shot and killed a pal after a night of hard drinking in the Big Apple. Police identified Bohan's drinking buddy/victim as Monk Eastman, a notorious gang leader with a long rap sheet. The two men had quarreled over how much to tip a waiter at a café. On the sidewalk outside the café, their loud bickering continued. The quarrel escalated until inspector Bohan drew his revolver and shot Eastman at close range. While stunned onlookers watched, Bohan tossed his gun away and hitched a ride on the running board of a passing taxi. Eastman died on the sidewalk.

A week after the shooting, Bohan turned himself in to police. He confessed he had shot Eastman but claimed it was self-defense. His story had a serious flaw: the gangster wasn't carrying a gun. Newspapers revealed that inspector Bohan had a criminal past; he had been arrested multiple times and had even been indicted for murder. A glowing reference from a Brooklyn politico seemed to be his sole qualification for his Volstead job. At trial he was convicted of manslaughter in the Eastman shooting.[8]

In 1926, after it became widely known that the ranks of the dry sleuths included an alarming number of ex-cons, Washington finally took steps to improve the screening process. Volstead policy makers decided to fingerprint all Prohibition agents and applicants, in order to weed out those with criminal records.[9]

Due to chronic underfunding, personnel shortages plagued the federal Prohibition Unit. In 1921 the unit had nearly four thousand employees, but less than twenty percent of them were agents working the streets.[10] Because of the manpower shortage, the Prohis couldn't arrest all the bootleggers, so they had to choose their targets. In general, the federal agents worked in the big cities and gave top priority to the urban bootleg gangs. They made only occasional forays to small towns, focusing on the wettest ones and leaving the merely moist villages alone. Smart small-town bootleggers went fishing when the Prohis arrived. After a short stay and a few high-profile raids, the federal agents would leave town and the leggers would resume their business.

The sheer number of Volstead violators overwhelmed the federal apparatus in most districts. At the beginning of 1921 fewer than three hundred Prohibition agents and inspectors were assigned to the State of New York, which had numerous wet towns as well as the nation's most populous city. Due to a budget shortfall, in May 1921 the number of agents fell to less than fifty—a ludicrously small force for a large state riddled with speakeasies, rum rings, and gateways for foreign liquor. Nevertheless, New York's Prohibition director had to wait for additional funding before he could re-staff his force.[11]

Even thinly-populated districts could be a problem because Prohibition agents had to cover vast geographic areas. In 1926 the Pacific Northwest district had only fifty agents to cover more than 800,000 square miles in Oregon, Washington, and the Alaska territory. The federal Prohibition office in Seattle owned only one car, and the managers monopolized it. Few of the poorly-paid agents could afford a personal auto. To conduct official business, an agent had to take a taxi, borrow a car, or hitch a ride. One lucky agent had a car-owning, action-loving pal who drove him to raids and stakeouts.[12]

Initially, the entire state of California was a single enforcement district with only thirty-six Prohibition agents. Later the state was divided into two enforcement districts: northern and southern. The northern district covered sopping-wet San Francisco, Sacramento, Napa-Sonoma Wine Country, and numerous mountain towns plus all of Nevada. When Prohibition official Ned Green supervised the northern district, he called enforcement a "joke" because he had only one agent for every one hundred thousand residents.[13]

Before the Arid Era, the federal government deployed few agents along the U.S. borders because smuggling and illegal immigration were relatively minor problems. This changed during Prohibition, as an endless river of liquor flowed across the international borders. Washington responded by beefing up homeland security in the mid–Twenties. The Treasury Department expanded the mission of its special narcotics force, roughly three hundred agents, to encompass the smuggling of all illegal substances along the border. In 1924 the Customs Marine Patrol, an arm of the Customs Service, began operating on the northern waterways.[14]

The United States Immigration Border Patrol was formed primarily to prevent illegal entry into the USA. The border patrolmen, who carried firearms and had police powers, focused on stopping illegal immigrants, but they also searched for contraband goods, such as liquor. In 1925 the largest contingent of border patrolmen, nearly one hundred, worked in the sector around El Paso, Texas. Another large group operated in upstate New York, along the border from Ogdensburg to Rouses Point. Due to limited funding, the border patrol relied heavily on contraband seized from smugglers. When the lawmen went out on patrol, they used cars and boats confiscated from liquor traffickers. Public sales of smuggled goods helped to pay the patrolmen's wages.[15]

In 1926 the border patrol undertook a substantial expansion, increasing the number of patrolmen by eighty-five percent. The new manpower went primarily to Detroit and New York City, busy gateways for smuggling both liquor and illegal aliens into the USA. Despite Montana's sparse population, the state had a sizeable force of border patrolmen, deployed to stop the smuggling of cattle and wheat as well as alcohol. In 1929–1931 the government hired more than four hundred new border patrolmen to fill gaps along the international boundaries.[16]

By 1929 federal manpower for Volstead enforcement totaled roughly ten thousand persons if the count included customs, immigration, and military personnel who spent part of their time enforcing the dry law. As always, the Prohis had a shortage of agents working the streets. Assistant U.S. Attorney General Aaron Youngquist called federal dry law enforcement "pitifully inadequate." He noted that the Prohibition Bureau had roughly 1,750 agents and investigators, or one for every seventy thousand Americans. He said that enforcing Volstead with such a small force was an "utter impossibility."[17]

Greasy Mitts

Cynics predicted that corruption would accompany Prohibition, but even they were surprised by the massive scope of the graft and malfeasance. Corruption on such a grand scale was unprecedented in U.S. history. Illegal liquor traffickers paid top dollar for lawmen willing to shirk their duty. An epidemic of greed, ineptitude, and hypocrisy infected the agencies charged with enforcing Volstead. The horde of poorly trained, dishonest Prohibition agents negated the work of the honest, competent ones. The public quickly learned to distrust the federal dry sleuths, and pop culture stereotyped them as venal, double-dealing jerks. The federal Volstead agents did more to "make Prohibition detested than anyone else, even the drys," opined a newspaper editor.[18]

The poorly-paid Prohibition agents were expected to subsist on an annual income as low as $1,200 in some districts. "Anybody who believed that men employable at thirty-five or forty or fifty dollars a week ... would surely have the force of character to resist corruption by men whose pockets were bulging with money would be ready to believe in Santa Claus, perpetual motion, and pixies," wrote a historian.[19]

Despite the low pay for Prohibition agents, the job was highly sought after because a dry sleuth could pick up extra money, if his scruples didn't get in the way. A dishonest agent could take bribes or extort money from Volstead violators, such as bootleggers and speakeasy owners. He could sell the government permits required to obtain industrial alcohol, medical whiskey, or sacramental wine. He had access to liquor seized by lawmen, so he could steal confiscated booze and sell it. All these endeavors paid well and entailed little risk.

The public heard sensational get-rich-quick stories about agents on the take. The press printed articles about Prohibition agents who joined "the millionaire's club," but corrupt Prohis usually accumulated a smaller fortune. Even tens of thousands counted as big bucks in the Roaring Twenties. While an honest dry agent could barely support his family, a corrupt one could amass enough money to buy luxuries most Americans only dreamed of.

In California a woman filed for divorce from her estranged husband, a Prohibition agent who made only $35 per week. She demanded her fair share of his impressive assets: a townhouse, a country home, two cars, a speedboat, and multiple bank accounts. In a similar divorce case in New York City, the Prohibition agent's assets included two houses, two automobiles, a motorboat, and several parcels of land — all acquired while he made less than $50 per week.[20]

Across the nation, dishonest Prohibition agents exploited their position to make money. A sampling of cases illustrates the scope of the corruption. In Chicago an investigation by the district attorney's office exposed "systematic graft on a very large scale" among the Prohis. Windy City bootleggers paid dry agents $1 per gallon for permits to withdraw alcohol from bonded warehouses. Two "aces of the federal Prohibition squad in Milwaukee" were convicted of taking "shut-eye bribes." A Prohibition administrator in Wisconsin pled guilty to taking bribes from industrial alcohol wholesalers and falsifying official reports to conceal the illegal transactions.[21]

Prohibition officials helped bootleggers withdraw large quantities of whiskey from bonded warehouses in Philadelphia. Two administrators were accused of issuing permits for withdrawals amounting to more than $1 million in only one day. Five federal agents in Philadelphia were fired for forging permits used to remove liquor from warehouses. Another Philadelphia Prohibition agent was arrested and charged with "aiding in the illegal transportation" of whiskey withdrawn from a bonded facility. Although the whiskey was designated for non-beverage use, it was delivered to outlets selling alcohol for public consumption.[22]

One official called the federal Prohibition Bureau "a training school for bootleggers." While working for the bureau, agents "naturally learn all the ropes of the underworld as well as the government's methods in attempting to apprehend and convict violators," said the administrator. "Naturally, when leaving the service of the Prohibition forces, they are sought after by those engaged in the illicit business." Nobody knew precisely how many agents became bootleggers, but it happened often enough to deepen the public disdain for the Prohis.[23]

The case of "Handsome Larry" Davidson showed the public how easy it was to go from dry sleuth to liquor trafficker. Davidson was a highly regarded special Prohibition agent — until he switched sides and started his own rumrunning syndicate. He bought liquor in Ontario, ran it across Lake Erie in speedboats, and sold it in Ohio and Pennsylvania.

There was so much demand for his potent cargo that he bought Middle Island on the Canadian side of Lake Erie and used it as a liquor storage facility. In a short time Davidson amassed a personal fortune of roughly $2 million.

A disgruntled underling turned on Davidson and exposed his operations to the police. Handsome Larry was arrested in Cleveland and subsequently indicted on Volstead charges. Before the informant could testify against his former boss, he was taken for a one-way ride. Nevertheless, prosecutors had enough evidence to convict Davidson, who was sentenced to three years in federal prison.[24]

Despite the public outcry over corruption in the Prohibition Unit, Congress hesitated to change the hiring process. Politicians liked the patronage system because they used the jobs to repay favors and reap good will among their constituents. After years of debate, Congress finally made civil service exams a requirement for both new and old agents. In 1927 more than twelve thousand candidates took the test to become an agent or junior agent. Almost two-thirds failed to make a passing grade. Of the Prohibition agents already on the job, roughly sixty percent failed. Prohibition administrators, attorneys, and legal advisors didn't have to take a written test but were subjected to rigorous oral interviews.[25]

By 1929 the federal government had fired and/or prosecuted 963 Prohibition agents, according to a Treasury Department report. Hundreds more had resigned to avoid termination. When Seymour Lowman headed the Prohibition Bureau, he complained, "There are many incompetent and crooked men in the service. Bribery is rampant.... Some days my arm gets tired signing orders of dismissal." However, he assured Americans that most federal Prohibition agents were "splendid, fearless men ... who are entirely dependable. Fortunately, they greatly outnumber the crooks."[26]

Faking It

Since Prohibition agents could make easy money by threatening to arrest liquor traffickers, scam artists sometimes posed as Prohis. In Philadelphia, lawmen arrested Joseph Carson, the ringleader of a gang that impersonated Prohibition agents. In one incident, Carson went to a drug supply company, showed the proprietor what appeared to be a valid search warrant, and confiscated a truckload of alcohol. Then Carson offered to let the proprietor keep his liquor in return for $500. The proprietor paid the ransom but later told his story to officials. Philadelphia police said that Carson's gang had pulled similar scams in other Eastern cities.[27]

A gang in Chicago ran a two-part scam: some of the gangsters sold booze to saloonkeepers and the others posed as Prohibition agents. Gang members would deliver a barkeeper's order and take payment. As soon as those gangsters left, their accomplices would appear, pretending to be Prohibition agents. The fake Prohis would confiscate the liquor and offer the barkeep a choice: pay a bribe or be arrested. At least two of the gang members were former federal agents. Officials estimated that the men extorted more than $100,000 from bar owners in the Windy City.[28]

Two deputy sheriffs and an accomplice posed as federal Prohibition agents to extort money from owners of illegal saloons in San Francisco. In one case, a barkeeper paid the trio $300 for two weeks' protection. When real Prohibition agents raided his bar and arrested him, the angry barkeep realized he'd been duped. He helped law enforcement track down the phony Prohis.[29]

In New York City fake Prohibition agents mulcted money from the owners of speakeasies in danger of being padlocked. When the U.S. attorney's office filed for injunctions against speakeasies, the names of the targeted places were published on a list at the courthouse. The lag time between the application for an injunction and the actual closing ranged from several weeks to a year or longer. During this time, a fake federal agent would approach the owner of a targeted speakeasy and offer to stop the padlocking. The proprietor usually paid, figuring it was money well spent.

Thomas Harris (AKA James Marshall) extorted a small fortune from NYC speakeasies in only a few weeks. Harris would walk into a speakeasy, ask the barkeeper pointed questions, and hint that he was a Prohibition agent. Sometimes he brandished a revolver or pretended to call headquarters. If the barkeep didn't offer him a bribe, he would threaten to raid the place and make arrests. Officials learned about his scam when speakeasy owners called the Prohibition Unit to complain that they had already paid their protection money.[30]

Enough for Everybody

Local and state officials, like their federal counterparts, happily filled their wallets with the bootleggers' bucks. The public heard countless stories of misconduct by sheriffs, police officers, constables, magistrates, and others sworn to uphold the law. Volstead was "the cause of more police delinquency than all other laws put together," according to the mayor of Seattle, Washington. Seattle's police chief agreed. He said that "the dry law has created an opportunity for graft in law enforcement such as never before existed."[31]

A look at a few notable cases shows that the lure of easy money seduced local officials across the United States. A federal investigation of a rum ring smuggling Cuban liquor into New Orleans led to the indictment of the sheriff of St. Bernard Parish, two deputy sheriffs, a police sergeant, and several former policemen. Two of the accused men confessed their guilt and testified for the state at trial. Federal agents in Memphis, Tennessee, seized a "payoff book" in a raid. The ledger revealed that a bootleg gang was paying bribes to more than forty policemen, constables, and deputy sheriffs. The police department in Evansville, Indiana, bought a boat for chasing rumrunners on the Ohio River. Although the boat dashed up and down the river on dark nights, the police caught nary a rumrunner — for good reason. While the lawmen pretended to chase outlaws, they were actually hauling liquor for a local rum ring.[32]

Records kept by Chicago's notorious Genna gang showed that at least 250 policemen were on the mob's payroll. A federal investigation in Chicago Heights exposed a major rum ring and led to the arrest of dozens — including a policeman, a deputy sheriff, and two former police chiefs. In Madison County, Illinois, several constables and justices of the peace were charged with collecting illegal fines and extorting money from liquor traffickers. Some of the men confessed and cooperated with law enforcement. During a raid in Robinson, Illinois, federal lawmen nabbed a "confessed" bootlegger and the state's attorney. The legger claimed he had been paying protection money to the state's attorney.[33] (Apparently, he wasted his money.)

A jury convicted the mayor of Hamtramck, Michigan, of being a ringleader in a syndicate that sold high-octane beer. Hamtramck's former police commissioner and a police lieutenant were also found guilty. All three were sentenced to federal prison. On Michigan's

Belle Isle the harbormaster, who doubled as police chief, was arrested for rumrunning. Under his orders, employees in the harbormaster's division had convoyed boatloads of Canadian rum to Detroit. On one occasion he had ordered his underlings to guard a boatload of liquor to prevent Prohibition agents from seizing it. At trial the harbormaster pled guilty to conduct unbecoming an officer. He paid a fine, accepted a reduction in rank, and retired.[34]

After Wyoming's state law enforcement commissioner resigned in 1928, he was indicted as the central figure in a massive extortion scheme. The prosecution alleged that he had extorted protection money from bootleggers, moonshiners, and barkeepers in Cody, Thermopolis, Kirby, Basin, Greybull, Rawlins, and other towns. Before the trial started, a suspicious gas explosion killed the prosecution's star witness. Nevertheless, the state went forward with the case.[35]

At trial, the U.S. attorney called known liquor traffickers who testified about paying protection money to the commissioner's henchmen. In return, the commissioner kept local and state lawmen from arresting the traffickers and also gave them advance notice when federal Prohibition agents were coming to town. Governor Frank Emerson, who had appointed the commissioner, was subpoenaed to testify against his political ally. The governor stated that he had become suspicious of the commissioner and had started his own investigation after receiving mysterious late-night phone calls. The commissioner abruptly resigned while the investigation was underway.[36]

The jury found the former commissioner and four codefendants guilty of conspiracy to violate the Prohibition law. The court fined the commissioner and sentenced him to eighteen months in the federal prison at Leavenworth. He declined to appeal his conviction and chose to begin serving his term immediately.[37]

Money played a most unsavory role in Volstead enforcement in Ohio, where the state's unusual pay scheme almost guaranteed corruption. Ohio put twenty Prohibition inspectors and a commissioner on the state payroll. An additional 110 unpaid "card men" were also licensed to enforce the dry law. A card man didn't receive a salary but worked on commission; each time he arrested a Volstead violator he received a percentage of any fine paid by the lawbreaker. Likewise, constables and justices of the peace were paid a portion of the fines and court costs in Volstead cases. Since there were no jury trials for minor Volstead offenses, this system rewarded the judge for finding a defendant guilty and levying a large fine. A not-guilty verdict simply didn't pay.

A shocking number of Ohio's constables and card men were convicted felons and/or Ku Klux Klansmen. They were allowed to carry guns and clubs, which they used with gusto, especially when a suspect was slow to follow orders. Some card men committed crimes to fill their wallets. To ensure a guilty verdict, they planted evidence before a raid. In some instances, they stole valuables from a home or business that they raided. They took bribes and extorted money from bootleggers. They sold confiscated liquor instead of pouring it down the sewer.[38]

The abuses of Ohio's card-man system became so blatant, especially in Cleveland, that the public would no longer tolerate it. In May 1924 Governor Alvin Victor Donahey summarily dismissed all of the card men. Subsequently, thirty constables and justices in Cuyahoga County were prosecuted for official misconduct and sent to prison or the workhouse. In order to avoid a similar fate, other Cuyahoga County justices resigned or announced that they would no longer hear Volstead cases.

In 1927 the U.S. Supreme Court handed down a ruling that made it illegal for magistrates and justices of the peace to pay themselves a share of the fines and court costs in Volstead cases. Chief Justice William Howard Taft stated that no judge should rule in any case where he had a monetary interest in finding the defendant guilty but did not have an equivalent stake in acquitting him. Thereafter, the Ohio legislature passed a law that changed the rules so constables and justices of the peace were paid whether the defendant was convicted or acquitted.[39]

Drunk for Three Weeks

Corrupt police officers didn't always demand money from bootleggers or barkeepers. Sometimes they were happy to be paid with free food and drinks at a blind pig. Or a bottle of fine sipping whiskey. The following anecdote is based on the reminiscences of a bootlegger who plied his trade in Florida in the Roaring Twenties.

One day I was riding along in an old Dodge, several cases of whiskey showing plainly on the backseat, when I noticed a motorcycle policeman behind me. I kept going: what else could I do? He stayed on my tail. Finally, I stopped and he pulled alongside.

"What you got there, boy?"

"Got a load of whiskey," I said, knowing it would be useless to lie.

"Well, I figured you did, so I was following along in case you had a flat. Got a bottle of that Three-Star Hennessey?"

I handed him a bottle.

When he followed me the next day, I gave him another bottle. And another the next, for about three weeks. Then he didn't show up.

After a few more days, I asked a police officer about my motorcycle friend.

The officer shook his head sadly. "You know, we had to fire him. He stayed drunk for three weeks."[40]

32. The Enforcement Follies

Now I lay me down to sleep,
May Hoover my life safely keep.
May no lawman looking for a still
Raid my home and shoot to kill.
May no dry agent fire his gun
At my innocent young son.
May no dry spy shoot without warning
And give my family cause for mourning.
— Anonymous

Over the course of Prohibition, enforcement tactics evolved as policy makers searched for the best strategy to end the bootleg traffic. Dry sleuths raided thousands of establishments that made and/or sold illegal alcohol. In the beginning, the public generally approved of raids as an enforcement tool. As Volstead wore on, everyone saw that they had little effect. Wets became openly hostile to raids as a waste of taxpayer money, and realistic drys knew that raids would never produce an arid utopia. Padlocks, like raids, showed the public that officials were making an honest effort to enforce the Volstead law. Although padlocks shuttered illegal businesses, they had little lasting impact because the owners closed up shop and reopened elsewhere.

The dry faction argued that harsher punishment would stop the bootleg traffic. Their theory was put to the test when Congress passed the Jones Law, which increased the penalties for Volstead offenses. The stiffer punishment put many bootleggers in federal prison for lengthy terms, and it changed the liquor traffickers' cavalier attitude about arrests. When a bootlegger expected to spend little or no time in jail, he could shrug off an arrest as no big deal. When he faced the prospect of five years in prison plus a hefty fine, the stakes were high and he was likely to use a firearm to avoid capture. The casualty list grew long as bullets killed lawmen, gangsters, and even innocent citizens. The heartbreaking loss of life alarmed the public and gave citizens another reason to ask if Americans were paying too dearly for Prohibition.

Raid!

In the early days of the Great Drought, lawmen favored flashy, photo-op raids to show the public that they were doing their duty. For a really sensational raid, Prohibition officials

346

would mass a squad of dozens of lawmen. Generally, federal agents formed the nucleus of the raiding force, with state and local police assisting them. The lawmen took reporters, photographers, and newsreel crews into the fray with them. When the dry sleuths climbed onto rumrunning boats and threw booze overboard, flashbulbs popped and movie cameras rolled. Lawmen posed for photographs as they wielded axes, smashing vats in a wildcat brewery or an illegal distillery. News photographs showed federal agents using sledgehammers to demolish stills in the woods. Lawmen smiled for the cameras as they poured gallons of liquor down the sewer.

In one notable raid, the Prohibition chief for the Carolinas and Georgia assembled a force of one hundred-plus Prohibition agents, deputy U.S. marshals, and Coast Guardsmen. The drys in Charleston, South Carolina, applauded when this force staged raids in a crime-ridden area known as the Hell Hole. The raiders nabbed more than thirty men, including the area's busiest bootlegger, a state constable, a police officer, and the sheriff of Williamsburg County. Federal lawmen searched the home of a Prohibition agent and found a large quantity of moonshine along with marked money paid to him in a sting operation. The raiders destroyed seventeen stills and seized more than eight hundred gallons of moon. Local churches celebrated with prayers of thanksgiving.[1]

Of course, not everyone applauded raids. Drinkers and onlookers sometimes became unruly at a raid, especially in Volstead's latter years when disdain for the dry law reached high levels. On numerous occasions, citizens attacked the lawmen sent to confiscate illegal liquor and make arrests. In Baltimore a mob armed with rocks, sticks, bricks, and bottles fought with the Prohibition agents and policemen who seized high-voltage beer from a blind pig on Green Mount Avenue. A city police sergeant and a Prohibition agent suffered serious injuries during the brawl. Trucks stood by to haul away the confiscated brew, but rioters dragged the drivers out of the cabs and punched them. The frightened drivers broke free and ran away. The raiders called the city police for reinforcements. Officers answered the call, racing to the scene in taxis and a fire engine. Electric railway trouble trucks, hearses, and rescue squads with Pulmotor resuscitating machines also came to help. The show of force persuaded the crowd to disperse.[2]

Also in Baltimore, a large crowd gathered outside a corner saloon on Barre and Woodward Streets when Prohibition agents and "two Negro assistants" raided the place. When the Prohis tried to load the confiscated liquor onto a truck, the mob attacked them. The lawmen took shelter inside the saloon and were trapped there while the crowd rioted outside. Rowdies on the street and on rooftops hurled bricks, breaking the saloon's plate glass windows and knocking out streetlamps. The rioters threw bricks at the agents' car and also slashed the tires. City police and soldiers from Fort Holabird came to help the Prohis; it took two hours to get the mob under control.[3]

New York Prohis raided a bar in the bowling alley where the Yorkville Women's Bowling Club played. A distaff crowd was enjoying the afternoon, bowling and drinking beer. Two agents entered the bar, and two waited outside. The agents found the pipe that transported beer from the basement to the bar and went downstairs to disconnect it. When they came upstairs, the ladies ambushed them. Wielding bowling pins and balls, the women swung at the men, causing real pain when they hit their target. Outside, the two agents heard the commotion and rushed in to help. The battle raged until the men overpowered the ladies. Luckily, no one was seriously hurt. After order was restored, the agents seized a large quantity of beer. They also arrested the bowling alley manager and bartender but not the women.[4]

Prohibition agents raided a small distillery/winery in the basement under a bank on Mulberry Street in New York City. With pistols drawn, the agents broke down the door and arrested the occupants, who were tending a still. The Prohis ordered the alky cookers to move the barrels of aging wine and a vat of mash to the sidewalk. Mulberry Street was a very busy roadway with lots of foot traffic, and people gathered to watch. A dry agent told the bystanders to move on, but not everyone obeyed. Spectators attacked the agent, knocked him down, and took his pistol. When another agent ran to assist him, someone hit the lawman on the head with a club. The onlookers took sides, with some attacking the Prohis and others helping the agents fight back. An agent fired his pistol into the air, trying to disperse the crowd. This enflamed the mob, and angry rioters beat the agent, severely injuring him. The fracas continued until city police arrived to rescue the Prohis.[5]

On East 150th Street in the Bronx, Prohibition agents raided a winery, setting off a full-scale riot. A big crowd assembled on the street, jeering and yelling threats at the Prohis, who confiscated barrels of wine and set them on the sidewalk while they waited for a truck to arrive. Scores of men climbed onto roofs and threw rocks at the dry agents. While the agents dodged the flying rocks, rioters attempted to steal the barrels of vino. When the truck arrived to haul the confiscated wine away, the throng surged around it. The rowdies threw stones and other missiles, smashed the truck's windshield, and cut the magneto wires. City policemen came to save the dry sleuths. Some of the cops climbed onto the rooftops and subdued the rock throwers while others dealt with the crowd on the street.

The next day the Prohis raided another winery in the same neighborhood. This time, they wisely called the police before the raid began. The cops cordoned off the premises and kept the public away from the scene.[6]

The peaceful villagers in quiet, quaint Hastings-on-Hudson were aroused to violence when Prohibition agents raided a tavern on the Albany Post Road. When the Prohis entered the roadhouse, they ordered the patrons to leave. The villagers went only as far as the tavern's front yard, where dozens of other residents soon joined them. Angry men damaged the Prohis' squad cars and slashed the tires to shreds. Inside the tavern, the dry agents were busy arresting the owner and the manager. When they tried to take their prisoners to the squad cars, they were bombarded with a barrage of rocks. The agents saw two local policemen looking on and yelled for help, but none was forthcoming. The Prohis retreated into the roadhouse and phoned the state police headquarters at White Plains. Headquarters dispatched a squad of troopers, and the crowd wisely dispersed before the reinforcements arrived.[7]

In North Hudson, New York, state troopers stopped a bootleggers' convoy on a busy road. When one of the leggers spun his car around and tried to abscond, a trooper aimed his gun at the gas tank, shot, and scored a solid hit. While the troopers were arresting the bootleggers, a crowd of locals gathered and began stealing liquor from the vehicles in the convoy. A bystander climbed into the driver's seat of a bootlegger's truck and sped away before the cops could stop him. Local men armed with revolvers surrounded the troopers and liberated the leggers. Luckily, no one was shot, but the state police lost both their prisoners and the liquor.[8]

On Long Island, armed men in motorcars kept deputy sheriffs from raiding a barn where bootleggers were unloading a cargo of whiskey. The sheriff of Suffolk County ordered the raid because he had information that trucks were delivering liquor to a farm between Greenport and Southold. The deputies drove their squad car down a private road toward the barn. A fast touring car overtook the deputies' vehicle and swung across the road, blocking the squad car. Other autos roared down the road to confront the deputies, who "recognized some well-known citizens" of nearby towns. The "more determined" citizens brandished pistols and passed guns from one car to another. The delaying tactics worked, keeping the lawmen away from the barn long enough for the leggers to escape in their trucks.[9]

Federal Prohibition agents raided a liquor warehouse at Market and Broad streets in Trenton, New Jersey. A mob of drinkers congregated outside to prevent the Prohis from trucking away the potent potables. When a Prohibition agent fired a warning shot into the air, a local police officer rushed over to take control of the situation. He immediately arrested the federal lawmen for carrying guns without a license! The Trenton police chief advised the feds to keep their "gun-toting operatives" in Newark. "We don't want them here," he declared.[10]

Prohibition agents in Pennsylvania staged a series of raids "by automobile under secret orders" in Lehigh and Northampton Counties. Following a raid on a hotel in Rosetto, a crowd of more than 500 people hurled rocks at the Prohis. The rioters broke the windows in the agents' cars and slashed the tires. The feds took cover until state police from Reading showed up to subdue the mob. A local policeman, whose sympathy lay with the rioters, harassed one of the federal agents by arresting him for DWI.[11]

Raids weren't the only occasion when crowds assaulted Volstead enforcers. The lawmen were sometimes attacked as they went about their routine daily duties. A Prohibition agent was driving down North Pearl Street in Baltimore when he spotted a man toting a container of alcohol. The agent parked his car and followed the suspect on foot. As if on cue, scores of people surrounded the dry agent. He drew his gun and backed up against a wall. The mob rushed him, knocked him down, threw rocks at him, and kicked his teeth loose. He tried to resist but was greatly outnumbered. City police officers rescued him and took him to the stationhouse. When the agent decided to leave, he needed a police escort because the mob was waiting for him outside the station. During the commotion, someone stole twenty gallons of confiscated booze from his car.[12]

An angry mob attacked a "Negro policeman" after he arrested the bartender in an illegal saloon on Eighth Avenue in New York City. The saloon's patrons "resented the sending of a Negro officer to search the place." When the cop and his prisoner started walking to the police station, the bar patrons followed. People on the street joined the procession, and the officer felt threatened. When he paused at the door of a grocery store, several men lunged at him. He drew his blackjack, but someone snatched it and hit him on the head. Others joined in the attack, battering him from head to toe. Someone put in a riot call to the police station. The wounded officer managed to draw his revolver and shoot, but it jammed and failed to fire. Policemen arrived to corral the mob. In the chaos, the bartender escaped, but he later turned himself in at the police station.[13]

In Little Rock, Arkansas, a moonshiner was tipped off that cops were headed to his house to arrest him. He barricaded himself in the attic with his bottles of shine and waited for his visitors to arrive. When the police detectives got out of their car, he hurled the bottles at them through an attic window. The detectives called headquarters for help. When more officers arrived, the cops hammered in the man's front door. The moonshiner didn't put up a fight since he had thrown the evidence out the window and the grass was soaking it up.[14]

In Chicago's Fourth Precinct, policeman Howard Ogle was a well-known, unpopular figure because he was the officer assigned to enforce Prohibition. On one occasion Ogle ran down an alley, chasing a bootlegger. To lighten his load, the legger dropped his containers of corn liquor and sprinted away, with Ogle on his heels. Bystanders joined the chase, caught up with officer Ogle, and attacked him. One woman pummeled him while another woman struck him over the head with a bottle. Other police officers came to his rescue, subdued the women, and arrested them for assault and disorderly conduct. This melee was the fourth attack on Ogle in only two months — simply because he was trying to do his job.[15]

Padlock That Tree!

Padlocking the front door of a speakeasy or an illegal liquor plant was a favorite tactic for enforcing Volstead, especially in big cities. Sometimes zealous officials went overboard in their padlocking crusades and closed more than the garden-variety speakeasy. Princeton University, the New York Public Library, the U.S. Postal Service, and churches were among the august institutions caught up in padlock cases.

In 1927 law enforcement padlocked the ornate FitzRandolph Gate at Princeton University due to Volstead violations on campus. Before graduation, a maintenance man had to cut off the lock, so the gate could be opened for the ceremonies. Federal prosecutors named the New York Public Library as the codefendant in a padlocking case because it held the mortgage on the premises occupied by the notorious Melody Club speakeasy.[16]

In Lowell, Massachusetts, a U.S. Post Office substation was located in a building padlocked as a "liquor nuisance." The postal service defied an injunction to illegally open the substation and deliver the mail. The Pilsen postal station in suburban Chicago had a similar situation. Prohibition agents found a fully-equipped winery plus barrels of beer and wine in the basement of the post office. The Prohis were skeptical when postal workers claimed they didn't know about the winery, even though the liquor was loaded onto trucks in the mail-wagon freight yard. Since the winery operated in the basement of the post office, officials had the option of padlocking only the cellar.[17]

In Jersey City, New Jersey, the members of St. Paul Baptist Church arrived to dedicate their new sanctuary. To their utter dismay, they found Prohibition agents padlocking the front door. The agents declared that the three-story building housed a speakeasy. The church folk insisted that the speakeasy had closed, but the agents were skeptical because "the church social rooms occupied the upper floors." The pastor and the owner of the building pleaded with the Prohis to leave and take their padlock with them. The parishioners wept and prayed. A crowd gathered on the sidewalk, booing and hissing at the Prohis, who stayed focused on the task at hand. The agents finished their work and drove away, leaving the devout church folk locked out of their sanctuary.[18]

In the annals of padlocking crusades, the strangest case involved a tree in Humboldt County, California. A clever moonshiner hollowed out a cavity in a giant redwood tree, stashed a still inside, fueled it with kerosene, and made a flue for the smoke to escape. Finally, he covered the opening with canvas that looked like bark. Acting on a tip, agents found the redwood and seized the still. Then they stretched a chain around the tree trunk and padlocked it. Finally, they nailed a sign to the redwood: "Closed for One Year for Violation of the National Prohibition Act."[19]

The Five & Ten

By the late 1920s Americans generally agreed that Volstead enforcement needed an overhaul. Liquor traffickers arrogantly defied the dry law with little fear of punishment. Dry leaders complained that the penalties for Volstead offenses weren't harsh enough to be a deterrent. Many police officials agreed, so Congress passed the Jones Law to beef up the punishment. Beginning in March 1929 the new law allowed judges to fine a Volstead violator up to $10,000 and sentence him to five years in prison for his first offense. Repeat offenders were subject to longer prison terms.[20]

Representative Gale Stalker (R–NY) and Senator Wesley Jones (R–WA) coauthored the new statute, and Congress called it the Jones Law. The Washington lawmaker was known as a straight talker, a workaholic, and a dry fanatic who had no patience with his wet colleagues. In a Senate debate on Prohibition, a wet argued that Volstead infringed on personal liberty. Jones snapped, "[T]here is no such thing as personal liberty in a republic!"[21]

Although Jones was proud of his role in passing the new law, he didn't like having his name on it. He feared becoming synonymous with Prohibition, like Andrew Volstead, who was plagued with hate mail and crank phone calls. Drunks and pranksters, who seemed to have no trouble finding Volstead's home phone number, often called in the middle of the night to rant at him. He also received hate mail, including a strangely pompous letter on NYPD stationery calling him "an infinitely despicable specimen of the genus vermin." Given Volstead's plight, Jones was pleased when the press dubbed his law "the Five & Ten," referring to the sentence and fine. Nevertheless, a letter addressed to "Senator Sourpuss, Washington, D.C." reached Jones' office.[22]

Wet leaders argued that the new penalties were too severe for all but the most egregious Volstead crimes. Even a few influential drys agreed that the Five & Ten went too far. Newspaper magnate William Randolph Hearst, who favored temperance, wrote that the Jones Law was "the most menacing piece of repressive legislation ... since the Alien and Sedition laws." He said it "adds persecution to Prohibition, and ... substitutes fanaticism for freedom." He condemned the "un–American methods of spying and sneaking and snooping and keyhole peeping" used to enforce Volstead.[23]

In New York wet lawyers formed the Personal Liberty Committee to defend pro bono "worthy cases" when the defendants were unjustly punished under the Five & Ten. In Philadelphia the Voluntary Committee of Lawyers likewise agreed to represent worthy defendants but not "wealthy bootleggers" or "owners of disreputable clubs." On the other side of the issue, dry lawyers met in Washington to organize the Bar of the United States to ensure that the new statute would be used to impose severe penalties.[24]

In general, law enforcement hailed the Five & Ten as a much-needed weapon in the fight against booze. George E.Q. Johnson, U.S. attorney in Chicago, said the new statute would "make the Loop absolutely dry" and would send big bootleggers "to the penitentiary for a long time." Officials in Kansas City, Missouri, reported that fear of the Jones Law closed 257 local speakeasies in only one month. Baltimore police said that the severe penalties prompted 250 of the city's illegal liquor outlets to close. Bootleggers warned that the new statute would change their business for the worse. The fear of doing hard time would prompt the friendly neighborhood legger to find a safer line of work. He would be replaced by a hardened, ruthless mobster, and the price of liquor would rise.[25]

U.S. District Court Judge Louis Fitzhenry stated that the Five & Ten would turn millions of Americans into felons. He pointed to the misprision of felony law, which makes it a crime to conceal a felony committed by another person. (Misprision falls short of being an accessory because the individual concealing the crime has no prior agreement with, and gives no subsequent aid to, the felon.) Fitzhenry said, "Any person who buys a drink of liquor from a bootlegger and does not make a report to the authorities has committed a felony and is equally guilty as the person making the sale."[26]

Luckily for drinkers, the courts were already overloaded with Volstead cases. As a practical matter, the legal system simply couldn't prosecute millions of Americans for buying a cocktail.

They Shoot Agents, Don't They?

Volstead enforcers carried guns for good reason, but the ill-advised, and occasionally criminal, use of firearms worried the public. Of course, most lawmen used their guns only if necessary in the line of duty. Bootleggers packed heat, and Volstead enforcers needed firearms to fight on a level playing field. But citizens were rightly concerned when lawmen misused their weapons. Too often newspaper readers opened the morning paper to see a disturbing story about an innocent citizen killed by dry sleuths. In a typical case, the death resulted from a car chase. The incidents often followed the same scenario: the lawmen set up a roadblock to stop bootleggers or they spotted a suspicious vehicle on the highway. They ordered the driver to stop but he sped away or didn't appear to be stopping. In either case, they shot at him.

After the fatal shooting of Henry Virkula, the City Council of International Falls, Minnesota, telegraphed President Hoover, imploring him to end the "Prohibition reign of terror." Virkula, who owned a candy store in Big Falls, took his wife and children on a visit to International Falls. As the sun was setting, the family headed home, driving along a country road. Suddenly two men jumped in front of Virkula's car. They held up a sign: "Stop! U.S. Customs Officers." Virkula slammed on the brakes. Before the car stopped, bullets flew through the window, hitting Virkula in the back of the neck. He died instantly, and his car plunged into the ditch beside the road. Even though the car carried no liquor, the customs officers said the shooting was justified because Virkula didn't stop fast enough.[27]

After a customs officer shot an alleged bootlegger in upstate New York, the president of a Plattsburgh bank sent an angry letter to the Treasury Department. "One of your customs guards shot a Plattsburgh boy in the back in broad daylight," he wrote. "The people of this community are getting tired of such actions on the part of your employees and wonder if we are rapidly approaching conditions which exist in Russia. We presume that the usual statement, that this assassin was acting within his authority under the law, will be issued." The Treasury Department classified this shooting as an accident because the customs officer said he had stumbled, causing his gun to discharge.[28]

Law officers in Olive Hill, Kentucky, saw what appeared to be a bootlegger's car and shouted an order for the driver to stop. When the automobile kept going, they fired at it with shotguns, seriously wounding three children inside the car. The family was returning from a fishing trip and didn't hear the order to halt because the youngsters were singing. In Smithfield, North Carolina, lawmen suspected a local attorney was hauling liquor in his car. They followed him and fired shots. The gunfire killed him, but the officers found no liquor in his vehicle. His death left his wife and six children without the family breadwinner.

In Malone, New York, two Prohibition agents and a customs officer were charged with second-degree assault after they unleashed a fusillade at a car driven by a teenage girl. Bullets pierced the car and struck the girl in the hip. The lawmen said her car looked like a bootlegger's. Prohibition agents driving around town in Knoxville, Iowa, almost collided with another automobile. The agents drew their guns and fired at the car, which held two women, both nurses. One of the nurses was wounded. The Prohis claimed they were shooting at the ground beneath the car. Why they shot at anything was unclear.[29]

A federal Prohibition agent shot and killed the town marshal at a dance hall in Cromwell, Oklahoma. The agent stated that the marshal had interfered when he tried to raid the place. At trial the federal agent was acquitted of murder, but he went to jail on a weapons charge. In Falls County, Texas, the Prohis searched a farm belonging to a suspected bootlegger. When they found no liquor, one of the dry agents became infuriated and severely beat the suspect. At trial the lawman was convicted of aggravated assault and sentenced to a term in the county jail.[30]

A constable in Buchanan, Georgia, saw a car filled with young men driving down the street that passed by his house. He suspected that the men were drinking because he heard them cursing and talking loudly. As the car cruised by, he stepped into the street and shouted an order to halt, but the driver didn't stop. In fact, the car almost hit the constable. He aimed his gun at the automobile, opened fire, and shot a young man sitting in the back seat. Later, the constable claimed that he had aimed at the car tires and hit the young man by accident. He admitted that he had found no booze in the automobile. The occupants said they hadn't heard his order to stop because they were talking.[31]

The gunshot victim, who suffered a serious head injury, died at the local hospital. The deceased, a farmer who had also worked at a sawmill, left a wife and two small children. His widow said, "He had never given anybody any trouble and didn't fool in any way with whiskey, neither drinking it nor toting it around in his pockets. We had great plans for the future." She vowed to work in the fields, tending the crops and keeping their dream alive for her children.[32]

The constable was arrested and indicted for first-degree murder. "Whatever I did, I did my duty, and I am no murderer," he said.

At trial, the defense claimed the constable hadn't shot the young farmer. Rather, an unknown person had fired the fatal bullet. The evidence showed that a bullet had been found on the road near where the constable shot at the car. Defense witnesses testified that they had heard five or six shots on the night in question. Only one bullet had been found on the road, and no one knew what had happened to the others. After many hours of deliberating, the jury announced that it was deadlocked. The judge declared a mistrial, and the retrial was postponed indefinitely.[33]

The town of Lorain, Ohio, had a special squad of dry sleuths supervised by the mayor. One night the sleuths spotted a car carrying two men, three women, and a baby. They suspected that the car was a scout for a convoy of liquor trucks. They hollered at the driver, ordering him to stop. The driver applied the brakes, but his wife said that the strange men looked like robbers. The driver stepped on the accelerator and sped away. A volley of bullets hit the rear of the car, and the driver's twenty-something daughter slumped over in her seat. The driver braked to a sudden stop. The dry sleuths advised him to take the girl to the hospital but didn't offer to escort him there.

Later the sleuths claimed that that the girl's injuries were superficial. However, the doctor said he had removed a bullet from her head and her skull was fractured. A jury indicted the officer who had fired the shot that injured her. At trial, the head of the special dry squad testified that he had ordered his men not to fire at the car. The jury found the shooter guilty of assault and battery.[34]

A deputy sheriff in Newport, Arkansas, arrested an amateur prizefighter for being intoxicated and possessing liquor. Shortly after taking the young, unarmed boxer into custody, the deputy shot him twice in the back. The prizefighter was taken to a hospital, where he soon died. The deputy stated that he had drawn his gun because his prisoner tried to run away, but he hadn't intentionally shot the boxer. The weapon had discharged accidentally.

"Citizens of both Newport and Batesville were incensed over the killing," wrote a reporter. A mob formed on the outskirts of Newport and started for Batesville, where the deputy was jailed after the shooting. To protect the deputy, a police convoy rushed him from Batesville to the state prison at Little Rock. The county prosecutor filed a first-degree murder charge against the deputy. "The killing was the most brutal and uncalled for I have ever known," said the prosecutor. He declared that the deputy deserved the death penalty. "I shall do my utmost to see that he gets it," vowed the attorney. The sheriff agreed that his deputy, who had previously served a prison term for shooting a man, "was known as too quick on the trigger."[35]

When the murder case went to trial, the state called eyewitnesses who had seen the deputy shoot the boxer at close range as he tried to run away. They stated that the lawman took deliberate aim at his prisoner. On the witness stand, the deputy said he had merely fired warning shots and didn't intend to hit the boxer. Defense witnesses stated that the deputy's first bullet had hit the ground, then he stumbled, and the second shot struck the young man. The jury acquitted the deputy.[36]

Henry Joy, a dry activist and president of the Packard Motor Company, owned a waterfront estate in Grosse Pointe, Michigan. Rumrunners often landed liquor cargos on a stony point where Joy's land jutted out into Lake St. Clair. On more than one occasion dry sleuths entered Joy's property to shoot at liquor smugglers. A Prohibition agent shot and killed a boater on the water near Joy's house. The agent said the man had ignored an order to stop his boat for a search. The boater was returning from duck hunting and had dead ducks, not liquor, onboard. Joy switched from supporting Volstead to demanding repeal. He complained that citizens lived in fear of "unlawful search of their homes and their motor cars as they travel and unlawful shootings and killings by the officers of the Treasury Department."[37]

The Association against the Prohibition Amendment (AAPA) issued a pamphlet, "Reforming America with a Shotgun," to increase public awareness of the tragic shootings due to Volstead enforcement. To quell the public outcry over the use of guns, Washington released a report on deadly incidents involving federal Prohibition agents, customs officials, and/or Coast Guards between January 1928 and April 1929. During that time span, nine federal Volstead enforcers and sixteen suspects had been killed. According to the report, three-fifths of the deaths occurred because the suspects resisted arrest. A high-ranking Treasury official said that every federal officer had been "absolved from blame for a Prohibition tragedy by a coroner's jury or a grand jury" or "had been found to have acted in the performance of his duty" after being indicted and taken to trial. However, several cases were still in the court system, awaiting resolution. The report, which emphasized that Washington dealt only with federal enforcement, noted that local lawmen often fired the fatal shots in the controversial Volstead killings.

In response to the federal report, the AAPA president said, "Nobody need be surprised at all this free and easy killing. It always happens when a minority of the people try to ram an unreasonable law down the throats of the majority.... The Mexicans have nothing on us."[38]

33. Open the Spigots, Drown the Bigots: The End of the Prohibition Error

Prohibition is here to stay. You can no more repeal the Eighteenth Amendment than you can dam Niagara Falls with toothpicks. — Billy Sunday, evangelist[1]

Over the course of the Great Drought public support for Prohibition waned. Of course, the militant dry fanatics never changed their position: every American must, for his own good, be a teetotaler. If that required a draconian law, so be it. At the other end of the spectrum, stalwart wets never budged; they always believed that drinking was a personal choice and, in essence, a civil right. Between these extremes, moderates vacillated or simply ignored the liquor issue as much as possible. Many moderates initially supported Prohibition but, as they watched Volstead in action, their attitude changed. They saw the futility of trying to outlaw a popular commodity with huge consumer demand. They deplored the violence that accompanied Volstead, especially the tragic shootings that killed lawmen and innocent citizens. As Americans coped with the Great Depression, they saw the virtue of legalizing the liquor industry to siphon bootleg money out of the mob coffers into legitimate business. Legal breweries, distilleries, and bars would provide jobs and tax revenue in the hard economic times.

Over a ten-year period (1922–1932) *Literary Digest* conducted a series of public opinion polls on Prohibition. The polls asked respondents to choose from three options: retaining Volstead, repealing Volstead, or modifying Volstead to legalize light wines and beer. Over the decade, the percentage for repeal nearly doubled, while support for Prohibition showed a decisive downward trend. When respondents choosing modification were added to those wanting complete repeal, the total wet vote reached a whopping 73.5 percent in 1932.[2]

The momentum for repeal could not be denied when high-profile drys began to publicly question the wisdom of the Volstead law. Major Frederick Silloway endorsed the dry law and, as a high-ranking Prohibition official, worked to enforce it. But he spoke for many drys when he expressed his disenchantment after nine years of Volstead. "I believed in Prohibition," he said. "I still believe in Prohibition. I'd like to see real Prohibition in this country — but I don't think that I ever will. It's against all human nature. It's against all the rights guaranteed in the Constitution. It's a legal, psychological, physical impossibility."[3]

The Power of Protest

When the Golden Age of Sobriety dawned in 1920, wet activists were demoralized and poorly organized. They had lost the liquor war. They needed time to rethink their strategy and regroup their forces. Individual drinkers subverted the dry law by breaking it, but as a group the wets had no blueprint for repealing Volstead. When wet leaders organized marches or other protests, the results were disappointing. Relatively small crowds turned out for events that were supposed to be a show of strength. In 1921 the American Liberties League planned an anti–Volstead march for one hundred thousand wet activists in New York City on Independence Day. After the event, organizers claimed that at least seventy-five thousand wets had marched, but the ASL, using comptometers, counted less than fifteen thousand. A newspaper estimated that fewer than twenty thousand protestors had participated.[4]

The AAPA, which had fought against dry laws in the days before Volstead, stayed in the shadows in the early Twenties. The group didn't disband entirely, but it went into hibernation. In the mid–1920s the impetus for reviving the AAPA came from wealthy wets disgusted with Prohibition and willing to bankroll a repeal crusade. Before Volstead, wet activism had been closely associated with the liquor industry, which had narrow, selfish reasons for opposing Prohibition. The new wet activists had wider concerns; they worried that lawlessness and organized crime were destroying America. They believed that Volstead deprived Americans of individual freedom and personal choice. Moreover, rich Americans were tired of paying high taxes. Wealthy citizens had seen their tax burden rise due to the cost of Volstead enforcement and the dearth of revenue from liquor taxes. They wanted to reduce both their personal tax bite and the national debt by collecting more liquor taxes while spending less on law enforcement.

On George Washington's Birthday in 1926 the AAPA held a rally and dinner within sight of the Capitol Building. AAPA leaders touted the event as the start of a new push to topple Volstead. Roughly one thousand people attended the rally, and the crowd was almost evenly divided between the sexes. Wet politicos fired up the activists with spirited speeches. In a departure from pre–Volstead practice, the wet speakers included a woman, Representative Mary Teresa Norton (D-NJ). The first female Democrat in the House of Representatives, Norton was known as "Battling Mary." According to press reports, she once rebuffed a male colleague by saying, "I'm no lady. I'm a member of Congress, and we'll do business on that basis." She demanded repeal, declaring, "The shocking and immoral conditions which have been brought about by the Eighteenth Amendment and the Volstead Act cannot be defended."[5]

Senator Edward Edwards (D-NJ) rebuked the ASL for demonizing wets, and he defended the honor of the repeal crusaders. He railed against the ASL for accusing the wets of being unpatriotic and irreligious. He told the crowd, "If I am a traitor, if you are traitors, then Christ himself was a traitor, for He not only drank intoxicating liquor but turned water into wine for the glorification and edification of His disciples."[6]

James Empringham, national secretary of the Church Temperance Society of the Episcopal Church, made news at the rally. Empringham announced that the church was changing its official stance from supporting Prohibition to advocating revision of the Volstead law. Henceforth, the Church Temperance Society would stand "with Christ for moderation."

Empringham, who had a long history as an influential dry leader, noted that "God breaks man's Prohibition law every moment by fermentation." He said, "Laws to be effective must first be written in the hearts of the people."[7]

In 1928 the AAPA reorganized with a new board of directors to lead the wet revival. Heading the crusade were powerful business and civic leaders, including banker Charles Sabin, attorney Henry Hastings Curran, and the du Pont brothers — industrial magnates Pierre, Irénée, and Lammot II. Other high-profile men with leading roles were Marshall Field, Vincent Astor, William Wallace Atterbury, Hunter Liggett, Grayson M.P. Murphy, Ulysses S. Grant Jr., and former U.S. Senator James Wadsworth.

The AAPA's new agenda focused on documenting Volstead's harmful impact, educating the public, and taking political action to promote change. The AAPA demanded the "restoration to the several states of the right of their peoples to enact such liquor laws as they may respectively choose ... provided that such legislation shall not conflict with the duty of the federal government to protect each state against violation of its laws by citizens of the other states." The AAPA's new regime, much like the pre–Volstead system, would limit the federal government to a secondary role in regulating the liquor industry.[8]

For several years AAPA had a woman's auxiliary, the Molly Pitcher Club, named for the Revolutionary War's legendary water carrier. This distaff group undertook a few lobbying chores but never really got off the ground. It vanished before the AAPA got its second wind.[9] Yet women seemed more willing than ever before to join the wet crusade. Socialite and political activist Pauline Sabin stepped forward to rally wet women to join the repeal campaign.

Pauline Sabin, wife of banker Charles Sabin, came from a political family. Her grandfather had served as a legislator in the Nebraska Territory, as governor of Nebraska, and as U.S. Secretary of Agriculture. Although her grandfather and her husband were Democrats, Pauline voted Republican. She chaired the Women's National Republican Club and served on the GOP executive committee for the State of New York. She was the first woman chosen to join the Republican National Committee (RNC), and twice she was a delegate to the GOP's national convention.

Pauline Sabin was among the millions of women who initially supported Prohibition because she wanted her children to grow up in a sober society. "I thought a world without liquor would be a beautiful world," she said. Over time, she became disillusioned due to the crime, corruption, and hypocrisy that accompanied Volstead. Most of all, she was troubled because young people took great joy in breaking the dry law. They felt a special thrill when drinking because it was an illegal act. Defying Volstead was a game to them, and she feared it was teaching them disrespect for all laws. She worried about the excesses of youth and the rising per capita consumption of alcohol by the younger generation. Youngsters were drinking bootleg liquor that caused headaches, vomiting, and other minor maladies. Sometimes the tainted alcohol even killed a bright, talented youngster who seemed destined for a great future.[10]

During a Congressional hearing, Sabin listened as the head of the WCTU answered questions. The dry leader proclaimed, "I speak for the women of America!" Sabin's gut said, "No, you don't." At that moment, her political priorities changed. She startled her fellow Republicans by resigning from the RNC in order to devote her time to Prohibition reform. She spoke publicly about the failure of Volstead. Women bombarded her with letters and phone calls, saying they favored repeal or modification. She saw enormous potential for mobilizing women in a new group that would work alongside the revamped AAPA. She soon recruited a team of prominent, savvy socialites to be the founding members of the Women's Organization for National Prohibition Reform (WONPR).[11]

In many ways, the WONPR ladies were the opposite of the straitlaced, uptight women who lobbied for tougher Volstead enforcement. The WCTU's preachy party poopers had little time for frivolity. Their meetings tended to be staid affairs with no hint of levity. In contrast, wealthy, well-educated, urbane socialites ran WONPR. When they weren't busy with their charity work or civic projects, they played bridge, golf, or backgammon. They dressed to the nines in fashionable clothes and wore the latest hairstyles. The WONPR ladies threw lively cocktail parties and gala charity balls.

In the frumpy-versus-chic battle, dry fanatics sank to name-calling and personal attacks. They called the WONPR ladies "Sabine women" and "Bacchantian maids, parching for wine." A dry leader said the WONPR women "would take the pennies off the eyes of the dead for the sake of legalizing booze." Muckraker Ida Tarbell warned, "[T]hese insidious and sinister ladies at the bar are too sinister a fact to deny.... They are spreading a fatal poison." The rabidly-dry *American Independent* depicted the wet ladies as immoral hussies who seduced other women's husbands "at drunken and fashionable resorts." The paper didn't mince words, declaring that "most of them are no more than the scum of the earth, parading around in skirts." One maniacal dry wrote Pauline Sabin a letter, saying, "Every evening I get down on my knees and pray to God to damn your soul."[12]

Ignoring the shrill dry rhetoric, the WONPR women soldiered on. Despite their socialite image, the ladies were more than stylish airheads. They knew how to organize and mobilize. More than one million women joined the wet sisterhood in less than three years. As the WONPR grew, the WCTU's clout ebbed. The dry forces could no longer count on women to be a solid pro–Volstead voting bloc.

As the repeal crusade gained momentum, activists founded new groups. Debutantes and clubmen formed the nucleus of the Blue Cockade, which sought to restore the traditional role of moderate social drinking in American life. Members pledged to oppose any politician or political candidate who did not support repeal. The Blue Cockade sponsored anti–Volstead rallies and events to raise money for the repeal effort. The group stirred up controversy when it planned to hold a Repeal Ball, billed as a "Protest against Hypocrisy," at the Congressional Country Club in Washington, D.C. Pro-Volstead members of the club's governing board forced the Blue Cockade to find another venue because the club was officially dry.[13]

A rich oilman founded the Crusaders to involve more men in the repeal movement. The Crusaders organized the "poor man's campaign"—a disingenuous public relations ploy that belonged in the irony hall of fame. The poor man's crusade was led by super rich business tycoons, including Walter Chrysler, E.F. Hutton, Harry Sinclair, Edward Bausch, and Lammot du Pont II. The Crusaders wanted to repeal Volstead and replace it with liquor control laws that would allow drinking, yet prevent the return of the old-time saloon. On Election Day the Crusaders supported wet candidates regardless of their party label.

The Moderation League and the Voluntary Committee of Lawyers (VCL) also belonged to the informal pro-repeal coalition. The Moderation League had a small but influential membership of business and academic leaders active in the public discourse on Volstead. The group sponsored research on Prohibition and collected statistics on arrests. The VCL claimed more than four thousand members, including many of America's best-known attorneys. The VCL focused on legal issues related to Prohibition and urged the nation's bar associations to take a stand against Volstead.[14]

High-ranking legal officials endorsed repeal, citing the impossibility of enforcing the dry law. Former U.S. Attorney General A. Mitchell Palmer bemoaned "the enormous and useless expense which the government has expended in its futile efforts to enforce" Volstead. He declared, "The many and too well-known abuses brought about by the Eighteenth Amendment can only be abolished and eliminated by its repeal." As a high-ranking Prohibition official, James Shevlin had spent years fighting the illegal liquor traffic. He stated that the dry law supported "thousands of outlaws, who in turn were financing other rackets." He said, "Repeal the Volstead act and you will go far toward solving the crime problem."[15]

As the Great Depression descended on the United States, dire economic problems added weight to the arguments for repeal. Banks failed; businesses closed their doors; unemployment soared. Bootleggers wallowed in ill-gotten wealth while honest workers couldn't pay their rent. Mobsters lived like kings while blue-collar families went hungry. Wets argued that legalizing liquor would take money away from the beer barons and shrink the underground economy while stimulating lawful business. The manufacturing sector would invest money in modern plants and new equipment for making alcohol. Throngs of unemployed workers would find steady jobs at breweries and distilleries. Bars and liquor stores would hire people, too. Trucking companies and freight trains would ship legal liquor, putting the gin joggers out of business. Alcohol taxes would provide funds for running the government and paying down the war debt. Liquor revenue would pour into the IRS, so individuals and corporations would pay lower taxes.

Beer for Taxes

Wet strategists knew that voters, even those who didn't care about the liquor issue, hated to pay taxes. While freedom and personal liberty were abstract, philosophical issues, taxes were an ordinary, real world matter that everybody grappled with. The idea of taxing liquor to reduce other levies appealed to millions of Americans. To exploit this for the repeal crusade, New York's soaking-wet Mayor Jimmy Walker announced that he would lead a Beer for Taxation Parade in the Big Apple on May 14, 1932. He urged other mayors to hold beer parades in their cities on the same day.

An enormous crowd of marchers and spectators showed up for the NYC beer parade. "An almost endless line of marchers started out before noon" and late at night "they were still walking bravely along." Brass bands and bagpipers played lively tunes. Recorded music blared from amplifiers mounted on trucks. Groups of marchers sang old drinking songs as they strutted down the street. Gleeful spectators threw confetti and an occasional pretzel. They cheered as the units passed by: military veterans, firemen, Olympic athletes, prizefighters, Broadway actors, clowns, showgirls, business leaders, German-American clubs, railroad workers, "youthful salesmen," and "a Negro group from Harlem." Other marchers represented the Anti-Profanity Society, the Gold Star Mothers, Société Français, the House Wreckers' Union, the Compressed Air Workers, and the Greenwich Village Mummers. Floats carried replicas of old-time taverns and scenes depicting happy workers in post-repeal America. Airplanes and a blimp flew over the parade route. The press estimated the number of spectators at five hundred thousand to two million. Radio announcers riding in the blimp described the spectacle for listeners who didn't go to the parade.[16]

Outside New York City, efforts to stage beer parades met with mixed results. In Gotham's suburbs, the mayor of White Plains said a beer parade would be too tacky for his "high-class city." However, suburbanites paraded in nearby towns, including Croton-on-Hudson and Irvington-on-Hudson. In Mamaroneck hundreds of residents participated in the beer parade, which featured floats "representing barrooms" with happy patrons hoisting their mugs. A "noisy throng" watched a parade of fire trucks, automobiles, clowns, and drum corps in Hudson.[17]

Despite heavy rain and a hailstorm, thousands showed up for a truly wet beer parade in Syracuse, New York. Military bands played, and units of World War I veterans marched along with union members, local politicos, and neighborhood groups. The beer parade in Scranton, Pennsylvania, drew a huge crowd of spectators and an estimated five thousand marchers. In Daytona Beach, Florida, thousands of people formed a procession more than two miles long. New Orleans staged a beer parade worthy of a city famous for jazz, marching bands, and Mardi Gras. About fifteen thousand people, accompanied by a dozen bands, danced and pranced through the Big Easy.

Wets in Boston planned a two-day event: a beer rally on Saturday and a beer parade on Sunday. Thousands of motivated citizens showed up for the rally at Boston Common. They left disgruntled because the organizers had promised free near beer, but city officials stopped the suds giveaway, even though it didn't violate the Volstead law. The pouting public boycotted Sunday's beer parade. Five military bands played, but fewer than one hundred people marched.[18]

Milwaukee, famous for its breweries and beer gardens, had a mile-long parade led by American Legion bands. The city's wet, socialist mayor refused to march in the beer parade. He said legalized beer would boost the nation's economy but not enough to end the financial crisis, so he shunned the parade. In Chicago only one beer truck and no marchers showed up at the staging venue, so the parade was cancelled by the organizer (who hadn't done much organizing). In Lexington and Newport, Kentucky, the beer parades were cancelled "when discord broke out" between the sponsors, the American Legion and the Building Trades Union.[19]

At colleges and universities, students staged their own beer parades. At Amherst College the student body was divided over the issue of a beer parade. After wet students announced that they would stage a parade, they faced opposition from a dry group led by a football player and the editor of the school newspaper. The college held a referendum on the matter. Sixty percent of the students voted against the parade to "save the fair name of Amherst from the hands of sensational tabloid headline writers." The majority of Amherst men didn't want "to be classed as disciples of Jimmy Walker."[20] Nor Johnnie Walker.

Dry leaders disparaged the beer parades as raucous events drawing mobs of lower-class rabble with nothing better to do. The WCTU's Ella Boole said that New York City's beer parade was nothing more than "a slumming party." With a touch of pride, she declared, "I never go slumming!" In Los Angeles the WCTU called "an indignation meeting" after the ladies failed to convince the city government to deny the wets' request for a parade permit. Old-time beer trucks rolled along the L.A. parade route; a movie star and a municipal judge led hundreds of enthusiastic marchers.[21]

Banners with pithy slogans abounded in the beer parades. Crowd favorites included "Never Say Dry," "Down with Bootleg," "Help the Taxpayer," "Vote as You Drink," and "Bye-bye Mr. Dry, You're All Wet." A stilted attempt at a rhyming slogan said "End Business Stagnation with Beer Taxation." In keeping with the tough economic times, one group carried a banner saying "We Want Beer" followed by another declaring "We Want Work, Too." A rhyme with attitude proved to be a real crowd pleaser: "Open the Spigots, Drown the Bigots."

A Plank to Stand On

When the major political parties met at their national conventions in 1932, the power-brokers gave top priority to the failing economy, undeniably the nation's most urgent problem. Although Prohibition was a secondary issue, the repeal movement had gained so much momentum that neither party could afford to ignore it. The platform writers knew they must debate the liquor issue and craft an acceptable plank. Predictably, the Democrats and Republicans took different approaches to the liquor question.

The Republicans nominated incumbent President Herbert Hoover for re-election. The GOP was known as the anti-alcohol party, but savvy Republican politicians could see the rising tide of public sentiment against Prohibition. After stormy debate, the GOP adopted a wordy, vague platform plank that did not explicitly endorse either repeal or the status quo. The plank would allow "states to deal with the problem as their citizens may determine, but subject always to the power of the federal government to protect those states where Prohibition may exist and safeguard our citizens everywhere from the return of the saloon and attendant abuses." The plank held out the possibility of a national plebiscite on Volstead but didn't promise one. In the event of a referendum, the platform ruled out a simple up or down vote and said the electorate must have the option of modification as well as repeal or the status quo.[22]

Taking a predictably partisan stance, the chairman of the Democratic National Executive Committee accused the GOP of trying to appease both wets and drys. He called the Republican plank "a straddle" and a "weasel-worded" evasion. He said it was "susceptible of any meaning that the driest dry or the wettest wet might desire to read into it."[23]

The Democratic Party platform met the liquor issue head-on, saying, "We favor the repeal of the Eighteenth Amendment." The plank called on Congress to "immediately propose a Constitutional Amendment" and submit it to the citizenry for ratification via the state convention method. The electorate in each state would choose delegates to attend a convention to vote for or against repeal. This would avoid giving control to state legislators who might be bullied by dry lobbyists. Dry voting blocs could pressure wet legislators into upholding Prohibition, but the convention delegates would be able to vote wet without worrying about their prospects for re-election.[24]

Because the ratification process would take time, the Democrats promised "immediate modification of the Volstead Act to legalize the manufacture and sale of beer and other beverages of such alcoholic content as is permissible under the Constitution." While repeal could take up to seven years, reopening the breweries and wineries would quickly revive large segments of the liquor industry.[25]

Democratic Presidential nominee Franklin D. Roosevelt made the economy the central

Brewery workers in California loaded kegs of beer onto trucks that would deliver them to bars and hotels when the legal sale of beer resumed in April 1933 (San Francisco History Center, San Francisco Public Library).

issue in his campaign, but he enjoyed drinking and favored the repeal of Prohibition. After he won the election in November 1932, the lame-duck Seventy-second Congress met for its final session. On the session's opening day, the Speaker of the House announced that he would entertain a motion for a constitutional amendment to repeal Prohibition according to the terms in the Democratic Party platform. The motion was proposed but fell five votes short. The wets knew this was only a temporary setback because public sentiment strongly favored repeal.

On January 9, 1933, the Senate Judiciary Committee approved a repeal resolution, but it had two controversial provisions. One gave the federal government synchronous power with the states to regulate drinking establishments, which would perpetuate Volstead's failed concurrent enforcement and dilute the state government's regulatory power. The other provision specified the legislative method of ratifying the amendment, even though the Democrats' platform called for state conventions. The majority leader used his clout to remove those provisos, and the Senate passed the resolution by a wide margin. A few days later the House overwhelmingly approved it.

In April 1933, Michigan's state convention became the first to vote for the repeal amendment. Wisconsin, Rhode Island, New Jersey, Wyoming, New York, Delaware, Nevada, and Illinois soon followed suit. The dry strongholds of Iowa and Indiana seemed likely to vote against repeal, but the wets battled hard and triumphed in both states. Dry leaders confidently predicted victory in a trio of anti-alcohol Southern states: Alabama, Arkansas, and Tennessee. Although the vote was quite close in Tennessee, all three states surprised the drys by voting for repeal. After winning these arid states, the wet crusaders saw easy sailing ahead.

This Bud's for Al

After Roosevelt's election victory, the pacesetters in the beer industry made plans to reopen their breweries. Although Prohibition repeal was not guaranteed, brewers felt confident that beer would soon be legal. Roughly 160 breweries were already licensed to make near beer. Since the process entailed producing high-octane beer and then removing the alcohol, these plants would be able to deliver the real thing quickly when the law changed.

Pre-Volstead brewers Lion, Schaefer, Doelger, Piel, Loewer, and Trommers began modernizing their facilities. Brewer Jacob Ruppert announced that he could reopen his NYC plant "on a moment's notice." He approved a big-budget print ad campaign to run as soon as the law changed. Yuengling brewery applied for and received an advance permit to start bottling the real stuff in Pennsylvania. The Pabst Corporation and the Premier Malt Products Company merged to strengthen their position in the post-repeal marketplace.[26]

Missouri's premier brewers, Falstaff and Anheuser-Busch, made large investments to prepare for beer's reentry into the legal marketplace. Falstaff announced a million-dollar expansion that would include a modern bottling unit to fill 240 bottles per minute. Anheuser-Busch's near beer plants had roughly fifty thousand gallons of real beer maturing in storage vats, and the company planned to bottle the suds as soon as it could legally do so.[27]

To reintroduce the Budweiser brand to the public, Anheuser-Busch decided to use a nostalgic advertising gimmick: an ornate, old-fashioned beer wagon pulled by a team of horses. August Busch Jr. purchased sixteen handsome Clydesdale horses through the Kansas City Stockyards. The brewery removed several of its dust-covered beer wagons from storage to be refurbished by skilled artisans. Three weeks before the return of legal suds, a matched team of Clydesdales pulled an Anheuser-Busch beer wagon through downtown St. Louis, launching a million-dollar ad campaign. A pair of teamsters wearing bright green uniforms perched atop the wagon, which carried beer cases with the Budweiser label. Anheuser-Busch also shipped a wagon and a team of Clydesdales to New York City to await beer's rebirth as a legal commodity.[28]

While Americans waited for the state conventions to repeal Prohibition, President Roosevelt urged Congress to legalize beer "and other beverages of such alcoholic content as is permissible under the Constitution." The Eighteenth Amendment banned intoxicating liquors but didn't specify the alcohol content that transformed a legal beverage into an inebriant. This gave Congress leeway to decide how much alcohol produced an intoxicant. Although the Volstead law limited alcohol content to one-half of one percent, Congress had the power to revise the statute to raise that number. A popular scheme called for legalizing beer with an alcohol content of 3.2 percent, roughly the median of the major pre–Volstead brands, which had ranged from 2 percent for Pabst Blue Ribbon to 3.8 percent for Budweiser. (Under Volstead, beer drinkers generally chugged stronger brew. When specimens of illegal beer were collected from saloons in NYC, lab tests showed that 5.89 percent was the average alcohol content.)[29]

Congress responded promptly to Roosevelt's request to revise the Volstead law so drinkers could sip something stronger than soda pop. The House of Representatives passed a bill to legalize low-alcohol beer and fermented fruit juice. The Senate approved the same measure, and the President signed it into law. The statute set up a new licensing system for breweries and businesses selling beer. It also prohibited the sale of beer to persons in automobiles and/or under eighteen years of age. Nineteen states had anticipated the new federal law and changed their state statutes to allow beer sales. Other states had decided to stay dry or were still debating the issue.[30]

Beginning at 12:01 a.m. on April 7, 1933, Americans could legally produce, sell, and transport beer and wine with an alcohol content of not more than 3.2 percent. The media dubbed the date "New Beer's Eve," and it would open the floodgates to end the Great Drought.

In America's cities, drinkers turned out to celebrate on New Beer's Eve. Falstaff and Anheuser-Busch were the only St. Louis brewers licensed to make deliveries that night. Thousands of people congregated outside the two breweries, thirsting for a taste of the new legal lager. More than one hundred delivery trucks waited at the Falstaff brewery, and a line of trucks stretched for twenty-one blocks from the Anheuser-Busch plant. Sixteen railcars waited on a siding, ready to transport beer to other cities. A brass band entertained the happy, upbeat crowd at Anheuser-Busch. At the bewitching hour, whistles, horns, and sirens sounded across St. Louis. Anheuser-Busch employees gave free suds to the crowd standing outside the plant.[31]

A fleet of Anheuser-Busch trucks, with a police escort, rolled away from the brewery at midnight. Within a half-hour, St. Louis hotels and restaurants were serving legal beer that had just been delivered. Cases of Falstaff beer were loaded onto an airplane and flown to Jefferson City, Missouri's state capital. An eager state senator claimed the first bottle at the airport, and cases were rushed to thirsty officials waiting at a downtown hotel. Anheuser-Busch also hired airplanes to fly cases of beer to the state capital and to New York City.[32]

Milwaukee's Wisconsin Avenue was jammed with drinkers celebrating New Beer's Eve. A crowd congregated at City Hall, waiting for the beer that was scheduled to arrive shortly after midnight. A limousine pulled up, carrying a representative of Blatz Brewing with a carton of Old Heidelberg Beer. Close on his heels came a car delivering suds from Schlitz and then, with a police escort, the car from the Independent Milwaukee Brewery. Soon other vehicles arrived with Pabst Blue Ribbon, Cream City Pilsner, Miller High Life, and Gettelman's $1,000 Beer. All the packages of beer were crated up and driven to the Milwaukee County airport, where a plane christened "The Spirit of 3.2" was ready for takeoff. The airplane would fly the Milwaukee beer to Washington for delivery to President Roosevelt.[33]

At Milwaukee's breweries roughly fifteen million bottles of beer were loaded onto trucks and express freight trains for delivery in the city and beyond. In the run-up to New Beer's Eve, Milwaukee's city government had issued licenses to more than four thousand taverns. Pabst delivery trucks, escorted by police vehicles, arrived at bars only minutes after midnight. At the Miller Brewery workers poured free beer into empty milk bottles and other containers brought by the public.[34]

Chicago residents greeted New Beer's Eve with little fanfare. To herald the advent of legal beer, sirens, gunfire, and cowbells sounded at midnight, but few revelers turned out to celebrate. Although the watering holes had prepared for a crush of drinkers, they reported no more than an average night's business. About four hundred people, mostly German-Americans, gathered to sample the new legal beer at the Bismarck Hotel. Smaller groups drank 3.2 suds at German restaurants and beer stubes. Although the police had expected rowdy crowds, they made no arrests for drunkenness or disorderly conduct.[35]

Washington, D.C., had a reputation as a sedate town, but throngs of people gathered around the White House to celebrate New Beer's Eve. At midnight, horns, sirens, and firecrackers shattered the quietude. A delivery truck with a sign saying, "President Roosevelt, the First Beer Is for You" left the Abner Drury Brewery and headed down Pennsylvania Avenue to the White House. A second brewery truck followed, carrying beer and a Hawaiian guitar band. At the White House, a Secret Service agent, acting on behalf of the sleeping President, accepted two bottles of beer in a glass display case. The Hawaiian band played FDR's rousing theme song, "Happy Days Are Here Again." Men riding on the trucks handed out bottles of beer to the crowd.[36]

Baltimore drinkers braved a steady rain to see the hands of Big Sam, the clock on City Hall, signal the rebirth of legal beer. In preparation for New Beer's Eve, the city had issued more than seventeen hundred licenses to sell beer. At midnight a cacophony of horns, whistles, guns, and small cannon woke virtually everyone in the city. Within minutes dozens of beer trucks were clattering along Baltimore's streets, delivering suds to hotels, taprooms, rathskellers, and private clubs. Bars were jammed with people trying to buy a stein of lager, but the drinkers were orderly and the police recorded no arrests.[37]

In Louisville, Kentucky, steam whistles and "enthusiastic horn-tooting" marked the midnight hour. Authorities had issued licenses to nearly four hundred Louisville businesses, which would allow them to sell beer beginning at six a.m. The city's breweries had more than one million gallons of legal brew on hand, and 360 delivery trucks from six states were standing by to carry suds to thirsty beer lovers.[38]

On New Beer's Eve hordes of San Francisco residents flocked to the city's breweries, creating a massive traffic jam. A tangle of cars and trucks blocked the Southern Pacific railroad tracks, stopping trains until traffic cops could break the gridlock. At midnight, delivery trucks and railcars, loaded to capacity, left the breweries. Drinkers followed the delivery trucks. Whenever one stopped to make a delivery, thirsty volunteers rushed to unload the kegs and carry them into the bar, where they were immediately tapped. East Bay beer lovers didn't have suds until breakfast because the delivery trucks got caught in the traffic snarl.[39]

At 12:01 a.m. in Manhattan, Anheuser-Busch's neon clock lit up Times Square and electric chimes played "Happy Days Are Here Again." However, parched New Yorkers had to wait until morning for beer because the Brewers' Association had decreed that no suds would be sold before daybreak. Crowds hoping to buy beer assembled at the city's breweries, but only

On April 7, 1933, a well-dressed crowd celebrated the return of legal beer at a San Francisco hotel (San Francisco History Center, San Francisco Public Library).

a few small brewers defied the association and sold beer. At Hittleman Brewery in Brooklyn the impatient crowd became unruly and men tried to steal beer from a delivery truck; police rushed to the scene to restore order.

In NYC's White Light district most watering holes served bootleg liquor on New Beer's Eve, but a few speakeasies managed to import 3.2 beer from New Jersey. At midnight a funeral for near beer drew a noisy crowd on Broadway. Men dressed in tuxedos carried a keg of temperance beer from a restaurant to a waiting hearse. A band of musicians, wearing colorful Bavarian costumes, played somber funeral dirges and raucous drinking songs. As the hearse moved slowly along the street, about two thousand pedestrians joined the procession.[40]

When legal beer sales began in the morning, New Yorkers flocked to buy suds. In Manhattan, drinkers crowded around street stands to buy beer, forcing pedestrians off the sidewalks. Yorkville's large German-American community sampled the legal brew at the Hall of the Austrias, the German-American Athletic Club, and other locations. On Coney Island, Nathan's Famous hot dog stand gave unlimited free beer to its customers. Predictably, the giveaway attracted so many guzzlers that the police department had to send a squad to control the crowd.

At the Big Apple's posh hotels, the dining room clientele kept the staff busy serving beer. In the business district, everyone seemed to be taking a long lunch hour to savor a beer or two. "Shop girls and stenographers ... who would never have dared before" ordered lager for lunch. "Employees and employers alike lingered over their beer and liked it." Business boomed at "the lunch stands, the candy stores, and every other place where beer could be sold with a semblance of propriety." A chophouse on West Thirty-sixth Street offered free beer with lunch. So many thirsty diners showed up that the police were called "to preserve a faint semblance of order."[41]

While New Yorkers enjoyed beer at lunch, the Anheuser-Busch Clydesdales were preparing for their Big Apple debut. Grooms braided red and white roses into the horses' manes and wove white and green ribbons around their tails. At mid-afternoon, the eye-catching Clydesdales pulled a vintage beer wagon to the entrance of the Empire State Building. Former New York governor Al Smith emerged from the building to accept a case of Budweiser. Smiling for the news cameras, he said, "This is surely a happy day for all because it will in some measure deplete the ranks of the unemployed and promote happiness and good cheer.... My only regret is that the wagonload is not all mine." Actually, only the case given to Smith held beer; the other boxes were empty because Budweiser was in short supply in New York.[42]

Although many breweries were operating at top capacity to make legal suds, it would take time to smooth out the kinks in the pipeline. There was enormous pent-up consumer demand; licensed breweries had limited supplies of real beer on hand and proper aging was essential for a full-flavored brew. Spot shortages were inevitable until the industry found its new normal. Imported German beer quickly went on sale in some markets, but Americans wanted their own domestic beer industry to prosper and create jobs.

Old timers who remembered pre–Volstead beer said the new 3.2 beverage tasted very similar to what they had consumed before Prohibition. A bartender with decades of experience rhapsodized about the good old days when drinkers imbibed to become "pleasantly mellow," not "gloriously tight." He frowned on "hilarious drunks" who awoke after a night of heavy drinking to wonder just what they had done. "It will take considerable re-learning before the bad drinking habits developed during Prohibition can be dropped," he opined. "But if the people will stop and realize that they can get more pleasure from drinking good liquor slowly and moderately, they will enjoy themselves more."[43]

In addition to legalizing low-alcohol beer, Congress had cleared the way for vintners to produce wines with 3.2 percent alcohol content. Since the standard alcohol content for a quality wine was ten percent or higher, viticulturists generally regarded light wine as an inferior product. With deep disdain, vintners called 3.2 wine "mouthwash." Viticulturists in California, the source of most American wine, showed no enthusiasm for watering down their beloved vino.[44]

H.T. Dewey and Sons didn't share the Californians' contempt for light wine. The New York firm decided to sell low-alcohol, wine-based beverages in its store in Manhattan. Before Prohibition, the Dewey family had made wine and patent medicines. After New Beer's Eve, the Deweys began selling low-alcohol wines that mimicked claret and sparkling Burgundy. On the first day of sales, their store was jammed with customers. To satisfy as many people as possible, they imposed a limit of two bottles per customer. They weren't able to clear out the crowd and close the doors until late evening.[45]

While wets welcomed New Beer's Eve, dry leaders reiterated their opposition to all alcoholic beverages. "To sell beer is now legal in some states, but because the sale is legal does not mean the effects of alcohol are changed," said a WCTU official. "It is the same alcohol to be found in distilled liquors and is still a habit-forming narcotic drug, which taken in small quantities has the power to create the appetite for more." Diehard dry Senator Sheppard (D-TX) declared, "We must resist the return of this liquor traffic with all the fervor and power at our command."[46]

John Barleycorn Reborn

On December 5, 1933, Utah's state convention voted to ratify the Twenty-first Amendment. The Beehive State was the thirty-sixth to endorse repeal, thereby fulfilling the constitutional requirement that three-fourths of the states approve the amendment. People listening to the radio broadcast of Utah's convention heard the delegates vote, and the wire services quickly flashed the news across the country. Utah officials immediately sent telegrams verifying the vote to officials in Washington, D.C. That same afternoon the Acting Secretary of State certified the nullification of the Eighteenth Amendment and the end of Prohibition. President Roosevelt issued the formal Repeal Proclamation.[47]

Surprisingly, repeal did not set off a round of raucous celebrations. To prepare for repeal, eighteen states had already passed laws to institute new licensing systems for distilleries, but it would take time to implement them. Distillers had to obtain permits, reopen their plants, hire workers, and start the distilling process. While a substantial quantity of aged whiskey was stored in bonded warehouses, the owners must comply with the new regulations before they could sell it. Countless speakeasies were still serving illegal spirits, and many saloon owners wanted to join the legitimate business sector. The cautious speakeasy owner closed temporarily to avoid being raided while he applied for a liquor license.

In the Repeal Proclamation, President Roosevelt called upon all citizens "to cooperate with the government in its endeavor to restore greater respect for law and order." He asked "every individual and every family" to obey the new liquor laws, in order to facilitate "the breakup and eventual destruction of the notoriously evil illicit liquor traffic." He urged the state governments to prevent "the return of the saloon, either in its old form or in some modern guise." He called on Americans to "remove forever from our midst the menace of the bootlegger and such others as would profit at the expense of good government, law, and order." He endorsed voluntary temperance as the replacement for Prohibition. "I trust in the good sense of the American people that they will not bring upon themselves the curse of excessive use of intoxicating liquors to the detriment of health, morals, and social integrity."[48]

Thus ended the lofty experiment that began with the promise of utopia and expired in a morass of lawlessness.

You Can Legislate Morality

"You cannot legislate morality" became a very popular catchphrase for the opponents of Prohibition, and countless Americans accepted this simple statement as the rationale for repealing Volstead. Although the cliché may seem incontrovertible at first glance, it is nonsense at a very basic level. Every society with a criminal code legislates morality. Laws against murder, robbery, rape, and so forth are legislation clearly intended to enforce a moral code.

"You cannot legislate an end to addiction" would've been a more accurate sentiment for the wet activists. The dry faction's basic miscalculation was assuming that a law could cure a complex, chronic illness that medical science had barely begun to understand in the early twentieth century. If Prohibition proved anything, it surely proved that alcoholism and substance abuse cannot be abolished simply by passing a law. Cancer cannot be cured by legislation. Neither can addiction.

The dry activists were afflicted with a malady deeply ingrained in human nature: they wanted to take a shortcut — to find a simple, quick solution to an intractable problem. However, complex problems almost always require complex solutions. Simplistic ideas, like "Just Say No," ignore the nuanced complexity of addiction. The dry groups loved pithy mottos and temperance pledges. But catchy, clever slogans only work for individuals who are not vulnerable to addiction anyway. Medical science is still searching for the best treatments for substance abuse, and thus far there are no quick shortcuts to recovery. Outlawing liquor proved to be one of the many dead ends on the road to sobriety.

The cold water coalition had the best of intentions, and the dry activists honestly believed that Prohibition would cure virtually all societal ills. They fervently believed that their lifestyle, values, and social customs were superior to everybody else's. They did not shrink from passing laws to ensure conformity with their standards. Far from seeing the benefits of diversity, the dry activists wanted a homogeneous America where they could impose their values on everyone, regardless of race, gender, ethnicity, or religion. They were destined for ultimate failure because the individual prefers to think for himself and make his own choices.

Glossary — Volstead Vocabulary

Ack-Ack—Thompson sub-machinegun.

Airedale—A lookout, especially one who signaled rumrunners when the coast was clear.

Alky Cooker—A person who distilled liquor in his home or apartment and sold it to a mob or a bootlegger.

Alley Brewery—A small illegal brewery, often located in a cellar.

Angel Teat—Moonshine whiskey.

Auto-Truck—A car with the backseat removed to make space for a cargo of liquor.

Baby Volstead—A state law for enforcing Prohibition, enacted to supplement the federal Volstead law.

Baptized Booze—Diluted liquor.

Bargain Day—Court session dedicated to clearing minor Volstead cases off the docket. The defendant pled guilty and gave up his right to a jury trial; in return, he paid a small fine and served little or no time in jail.

Barley Broth—Beer.

Barrel House—A saloon where the bartender ejected a drunk who had run out of money by putting him in a barrel and rolling him out the door.

Barrel-House Bum—A drunkard begging for money.

Bathtub Gin—An intoxicating beverage made of ethyl alcohol, juniper oil, glycerin, and water, often concocted in small batches at home.

Beer Lugger—A small rumrunning boat.

Big Fix—A mob boss.

Black Thunder—Moonshine whiskey.

Blind Pig—An illegal saloon or bar.

Blind Pigger—A person who owned and/or operated a blind pig.

Block-and-Fall—Very strong, possibly poisonous, bootleg liquor.

Block Car—An automobile that followed a bootlegger's car or convoy to run interference if lawmen or hijackers chased the legger.

Blockade—Moonshine whiskey.

Blockader —A person delivering moonshine whiskey to the marketplace.

Blue John —Moonshine whiskey.

Blue Ruin —Distilled spirits, especially cheap gin or bourbon.

Boat —A railroad freight car carrying a load of beer.

Boiler —A still for making alcohol.

Booster —An additive, such as urea, used to speed fermentation.

Bootician —A bootlegger.

Bootleg Bonnet —A moonshiner's felt hat, sometimes used to filter raw whiskey.

Bootlegger's Den —A small illegal saloon, often located in a cellar or a back room.

Booze Foundry —A speakeasy.

Border Runner —A bootlegger who smuggled liquor across the Canada-USA border, particularly in the western states.

Bottle Man —A bootlegger or his underling who delivered bottles of booze to customers.

Bottling Works —A speakeasy.

Bruiser —A strong arm for the mob.

Bumper Joint —An illegal, big-city saloon that sold moonshine.

Bung Smeller —A lawman, especially a federal agent, who enforced Prohibition.

Bung Starter —A person selling illegal liquor.

Burlock —A bag, usually burlap, filled with liquor bottles surrounded by straw or another cushioning material to protect the booze cargo in an automobile or boat.

Bust-Head —Moonshine whiskey.

Button or **Button Man** —A low-ranking member of a mob.

Cab-Driver Gin —Inferior liquor.

Cab Joint —An illegal bar/bordello where taxi drivers took male passengers looking for a good time.

Can —A moonshine still.

Chatterbox —Thompson sub-machinegun.

Chaulk —Watery, whitish ale made with barley and hops.

Chef —A moonshiner or alky cooker.

Chicago Chopper —Thompson sub-machinegun.

Chicago Ride —A gangland murder.

Chicago Typewriter —A sub-machinegun.

Chicagorilla —A gangster, especially a hit man or a bomb thrower.

Chock Beer —Potent beer made by the Choctaw Indians using malt, molasses, hops, corn kernels, and raisins.

Coal Juice —Moonshine filtered through charcoal.

Coasties —U.S. Coast Guard personnel.

Cobweb —A backwoods moonshiner, especially in Virginia.

Coffin Still —A small, rectangular still that fits over two burners on a kitchen stove.

Coffin Varnish —Very strong or poisonous liquor.

Coke Party —A speakeasy.

Cold Bang —Positive identification of the perpetrator of a crime.

Cold-Water Brewery —A large illegal brewery, either a pre–Volstead plant operating without a permit or a new one built by mobsters.

Cold Water Coalition —The informal alliance of groups that advocated Prohibition, including the Anti-Saloon League and the Woman's Christian Temperance Union.

Cold Water Men —Dry activists who supported Prohibition.

Corked Lightning —Moonshine whiskey.

Corn Clique —Moonshiners.

Corn Mule —Moonshine whiskey.

Corner Boys —Petty criminals, especially young hoods who hung out on the streets.

Coroner's Cocktail —Poisonous bootleg liquor.

Crashing the Pavement —Strict enforcement of the Volstead law by the police in a specific neighborhood or section of town.

Crazy Apple —A mixture of brandy and grain alcohol.

Creep Joint —A sleazy illegal bar.

Cut —Dilute or water down whiskey.

Cutting House —A place where bootleggers diluted liquor and repackaged it in bottles with phony labels.

Dehorn —To clean denatured alcohol.

Democratic Headquarters —A buffet flat.

Dew Boys —Moonshiners, especially in the Deep South.

Dock Fixer —A person who arranged for illegal liquor cargoes to be unloaded at a dock without interference from law enforcement.

D.O.D —"Death on Delivery." Extremely potent or poisonous bootleg liquor.

Doggery —An illegal saloon.

Doublings —Drinkable moonshine; the second distillate in the moonshine-making process, produced by redistilling the singlings.

Drag —Clout, influence.

Drench the Gizzard —Get drunk.

Drop —A warehouse, garage, or other place used for the storage of illegal liquor.

Drugstore Whiskey —Liquor purchased at a pharmacy, usually with a prescription.

Dry Fleet or **Dry Navy** —The vessels and personnel of the U.S. Coast Guard and other government entities that enforced Prohibition on the waterways.

Dry Sleuths —Lawmen, especially federal Prohibition agents, who enforced Volstead.

Drymedary —A Prohibitionist or dry activist.

Dump —A device used by a bartender to dispose of liquor during a raid; often a large funnel with a hose leading to an ash pile in the basement.

Egyptian Cocktail —A mixture of corn liquor and port wine.

Embalmer —A bootlegger.

Embalming Fluid —Liquor, especially bootleg whiskey.

Feeler —An escort car leading a convoy of bootleggers.

Flasher —A revenuer or Prohibition agent who quickly raided a moonshine operation.

Forty Rod —Liquor, especially moonshine whiskey.

Frog Eyes —Large bubbles in moonshine, indicating a low proof.

Frontiersman —A border patrolman or other law officer who enforced Volstead along the U.S. border.

Frown —The coloring added to raw alcohol to make it look like aged whiskey.

Fruit-Jar Trade —Moonshine buyers.

Fruit Whiskey —Bootleg whiskey made by redistilling paint thinner.

Funnel —A heavy drinker.

Furniture Polish —Bootleg liquor.

Gat —A gun, especially a sub-machinegun.

Get a Load of Pig Iron —Buy liquor.

Giggle Juice or **Giggle Soup** —Liquor.

Gin Drops —Juniper extract and glycerin, used in making bathtub gin.

Gin Jogger —A bootlegger.

Good Time Flat —A buffet flat.

Goofer —A gang member or low-ranking mobster. Originally referred to members of New York City's Gopher Gang.

Government Alcohol —High-quality liquor obtained from bonded warehouses, licensed distilleries, or Prohibition agents.

Granny Fee —Bribe money paid by a moonshiner to a lawman.

Grappa —An un-aged brandy distilled from the pulpy residue created by crushing and squeezing grapes in a wine press.

Gravy —Bribe money, graft.

Grease —Bribe.

Grease Spot —Location where a moonshiner paid a bribe so he could transport his liquor without being arrested.

Greased —Slightly intoxicated.

Groundhog —A moonshine still hidden in a man-made cave or dugout on the side of a hill.

Guard or **Guardsman** —A member of the U.S. Coast Guard.

Halfway House —A speakeasy or other establishment selling liquor.

Ham —Another name for a burlock.

Hatchet Man —A law officer who smashed moonshine stills.

Heat Boys —Criminals wanted by law enforcement, especially mobsters on the Public Enemies list.

Hell Kettle —An illegal distillery, especially one in a rural area.

Hiccough Hideaway —A small speakeasy.

Hipster —A man with a flask in his hip pocket.

Homebrew —A generic term for homemade liquor, especially beer.

Homespun —Homemade beer.

Hooch Hauler —A bootlegger or rumrunner.

Hooch Hound or **Hooch Hunter** —A federal Prohibition agent or other law officer who enforced Volstead.

Hooch-Mobile —A bootlegger's car.

Horse Liniment —Bad liquor.

Hoss Eyes —Very strong moonshine.

Hush Parlor —A speakeasy.

Ice —Bribe money paid to a policeman or a Prohibition agent.

Irons —Guns.

Jackass —Moonshine whiskey.

Jackass Brandy —Illegal distilled spirit made of fruit juice, sugar, and wheat.

Jersey Lightning —Applejack.

Jimmy —A blind pig or an illegal saloon.

Joy Parlor —A speakeasy.

Judas Hole —The peephole in the front door of a speakeasy.

Jump the Line —Smuggle liquor from Canada across the border into the USA.

Jumped —Raided.

Juniper Juice —Gin.

Keg Man —A middleman who worked for a mob or a syndicate and picked up moonshine from backwoods stillers.

Keg Party —A speakeasy or illegal bar.

Kicker —An additive used to accelerate the fermentation of mash.

Knee Walker —A drinker who imbibed too much moonshine.

Knocked Off or **Knocked Over** —Arrested or caught by the police.

Laid Out —Intoxicated.

Land Runner —A bootlegger, especially in the Pacific Northwest.

Land Shark —A bootlegger who picked up liquor from boats at the dock or on the beach.

Legal Suasionists —Dry activists who believed that prohibitory statutes would produce a sober society because most citizens obey the law.

Legger —Short form of "bootlegger."

Mabel's Boys —Federal Prohibition agents. (Refers to Mabel Willebrandt, Assistant U.S. Attorney General in charge of prosecuting Volstead cases.)

Mash Hound —A drinker who imbibed directly from a moonshine still.

Meal Mammy —Fermented mash.

Militiaman —A low-ranking mobster.

Modificationist —A person who wanted to modify the Volstead law to legalize light wines and beer.

Moon —Moonshine whiskey.

Moonlight Inn —A speakeasy.

Moonlighter—A bootlegger or rumrunner.

Moonshine Belt—The states that produce most of the moonshine in the United States.

Mop Men or **Mop Squad**—Federal Prohibition agents and other lawmen who enforced the Volstead law.

Moral Suasionists—Dry activists who believed that moral arguments and Christian teachings, not laws, would create a sober society.

Mother Ship—A large watercraft holding a cargo of liquor, usually riding at anchor on Rum Row and selling booze that would be transported to shore by smaller vessels.

Mountain Dew or **Mountain Dynamite**—Moonshine whiskey.

Mountain Teapot—A small moonshine still.

Mule—Moonshine whiskey.

Muscler—A thug or low-ranking mobster.

Near Beer—Under the Volstead law, beer with an alcohol content less than one half of one percent.

Needle Beer—Near beer fortified with grain alcohol; typically, using a syringe to inject alcohol through the neck of a beer bottle.

Nip Joint—A saloon, especially an illegal one in the South.

Nosedive—A jigger of rotgut liquor submerged in a glass of ginger ale or another mixer.

Nullificationist or **Nullifier**—A person who wanted to repeal the Volstead law.

Oil—A bribe.

Oiled—Intoxicated.

Pack—Moonshine whiskey.

Painter's Piss—Cheap liquor, especially moonshine whiskey.

Parlor Social—A buffet flat.

Percentage Bull—A police officer who took bribes.

Piano—A Thompson sub-machinegun.

Pifflicated—Inebriated.

Pineapple—A hand grenade or a bomb.

Pineapple Merchant—A person who fabricated and/or sold illegal bombs.

Pink Ladies—Concoctions containing no alcohol but sold as cocktails in speakeasies.

Pint Peddler—A moonshiner.

Piss Pot—A small moonshine still.

Pocket Pistol—A liquor flask, especially one small enough to fit in a pocket in slacks or a jacket.

Polished Up—Intoxicated.

Pop-Skull—Moonshine whiskey.

Pot—A moonshine still.

Potboy—A waiter in a tavern.

Privilege Corner—The section of a speakeasy reserved for gangsters and their guests. Usually situated so the gangsters could keep an eye on the front door.

Prohibition Error—The Volstead Era (1920–1933).

Prohibition Water —Gin.

Prohis —Nickname for Prohibition agents, the Prohibition Unit, or the Prohibition Bureau.

Puke —The overflow from an overheated still pot.

Pull the Copper —To quickly disassemble a moonshine still because lawmen are in the area.

Pulled —Raided, confiscated, or destroyed.

Rat Dive —A dingy, sleazy illegal bar, often located in a cellar.

Rat House —A roadside blind tiger, especially in Appalachia.

Rat-Track Whiskey —Moonshine.

Rattler —A car or truck used by a bootlegger to transport liquor.

Red Dog —Ground rye meal used in making moonshine.

Red Eye —Moonshine colored to resemble aged whiskey.

Red Ink —Homemade red wine.

Red Onion —A speakeasy.

Red Stockings —Bootleg whiskey sold in a woman's dress shop, especially in Harlem.

Relief Column —A convoy of automobiles carrying illegal liquor.

Repealer —A person who wanted to repeal Prohibition.

Rerun —Liquor made by redistillation of denatured alcohol.

Roasting-Ear Wine —Corn whiskey.

Rooty-Toot-Toot —A machinegun.

Rub-a-Dub —Rubbing alcohol.

Ruckus Juice —Moonshine whiskey.

Rum —Generic term encompassing all types of liquor.

Rum Chaser —A federal Prohibition agent or other lawman who enforced Volstead, especially on the waterfront or the waterways.

Rummer —A shortened form of "rumrunner."

Rumrunner —A person engaged in illegal liquor trafficking, especially on the waterways.

Run Goods —A cargo of illegal liquor.

Running Wet —Hauling a cargo of moonshine in an automobile.

Sample Room —A speakeasy.

Sanglings or **Singlings** —The distillate produced by the first condensation in a moonshine still.

Schooner —A speakeasy or blind pig.

Sea Foam or **Seafood** —Beer.

Seeing Snakes —Drunk, intoxicated.

Shake Down —To extort money.

Shine —Moonshine whiskey.

Shiner —A person who makes moonshine.

Shinny Joint —An illegal saloon, especially one selling moonshine in the Deep South.

Shock House —A sleazy bar serving strong, noxious liquor.

Shoe Polish —Liquor.

Shot Beer —Near beer fortified with grain alcohol.

Show-Up —A police line-up.

Skat —Moonshine whiskey.

Skee —Liquor.

Smoke —A cloudy, inferior, sometimes deadly ardent spirit made by re-distilling denatured alcohol.

Smokehouse —An illegal saloon that served smoke.

Snakes —Delirium tremens.

Sneaky Pete —Cheap liquor, especially booze consumed by bums on Skid Row.

Society Bootlegger —A bootlegger with an exclusive clientele of wealthy consumers.

Soda-Pop Moon —A vile liquid made of "cleaned" rubbing alcohol mixed with other ingredients and packaged in soft drink bottles.

Spiffled —Inebriated.

Spiked Beer —Near beer fortified with grain alcohol.

Sponge Squad —Lawmen, especially federal Prohibition agents, who enforced Volstead.

Spot Killing —A mob hit.

Squatting and Scooting —A description of a loaded whiskey six on the highway.

Squirrel —Moonshine whiskey.

Stash House Boy —A hired hand who carried moonshine from the still to a hidden storage space.

Steam Plant —A large moonshine still.

Still Cutter —A Prohibition agent or other lawman who specialized in smashing stills.

Stiller —A person operating a moonshine still.

Stillin' or Stilling —The act or process of making whiskey in a moonshine still.

Stuccoed —Intoxicated.

Stump Juice —Moonshine whiskey.

Submarine —A moonshine still with a large, elongated wood tub wrapped in copper or galvanized sheet metal.

Sugar Head —Cheap whiskey made from mash with extremely high sugar content, a specialty of urban alky cookers.

Suitcase Brigade —Train passengers, including bootleggers and amateur smugglers, who carried bottles of illegal liquor in suitcases.

Swamp Root —Moonshine whiskey.

Tanglefoot —Illegal whiskey, especially moonshine.

Tarantula Juice —Bootleg liquor.

Tea —Whiskey.

Temperance Beer —Beer-like beverage containing little or no alcohol.

Texas Guinan Champagne —Fake champagne made by adding grain alcohol to sparkling cider. Named for speakeasy hostess Texas Guinan.

Third Rail —Strong liquor, especially moonshine.

Thumbing — The act of placing one's thumb over the neck of a bottle of near beer and shaking it to mix in grain alcohol, thereby increasing the alcohol content.

Tickler — A substance added to mash to accelerate fermentation.

Tiger Spit — Cheap whiskey or moonshine.

Toddy Wagon — A bootlegger's car.

Torpedo — Professional gunman or hit man.

Tow — An escort car leading a bootleggers' convoy.

Town — Bribes paid to city policemen or municipal officials.

Trailer — A gunman riding in a car behind a truckload of illegal liquor to protect it from hijackers.

Trap — A hidden storage space for illegal liquor, especially a space entered via a trapdoor or a secret sliding door in a house.

Trucketeer — The driver of a truck hauling bootleg liquor.

Turnip Still — A round, squat still pot.

Ukelele — The drum holding the bullets in a Thompson sub-machinegun.

Ukelele Music — The sound of a Thompson sub-machinegun when fired.

Undertaker's Delight — Strong whiskey made by a moonshiner or alky cooker.

Up-and-Down — A police investigation.

Varnish — Bootleg liquor.

Vulcanized — Intoxicated.

Walking Cellar or **Walking Speakeasy** — A bootlegger who walked along the street selling liquor out of containers hidden in his clothing.

Walking Drop — A smuggler or bootlegger with bottles or flasks of liquor concealed in special pockets in his clothes.

Wassailer — A drinker.

Wet Goods Importer — A bootleg boss or a rumrunning kingpin.

Whale — Someone who drinks a lot.

Whammy — A strip of metal with spikes, used by lawmen to puncture the tires on a bootlegger's automobile.

Whist Club — A buffet flat.

White or **White Lightning** — Moonshine.

White Stockings — Illegal gin sold in women's dress shops, especially in Harlem.

Who Shot John? Illegal liquor.

Whoopee or **Whoopee Water** — Champagne.

Wildcat Brewery — A large illegal facility producing beer; either a pre–Volstead plant operating without a permit or a new one built by a mob or rum ring.

Wildcatter — A moonshiner.

Wine Vault — A speakeasy.

Wood — A keg of beer.

Worm — Coiled copper tube at the top of a still; acts as a condenser during distillation.

Yack-Yack Bourbon — Bootleg whiskey made by flavoring grain alcohol with iodine and burnt sugar.

Chapter Notes

Chapter 1

1. Wayne B. Wheeler, "Five Years of Prohibition and Its Results," *North American Review* 222 (September 1925): 35.

2. Paul Isaac, *Prohibition and Politics*, 148; Ida B. Wells-Barnett, *The Red Record*, 83.

3. *Congressional Record* XLIV (December 17, 1917): 449.

4. "John Barleycorn Burned in Effigy Thursday Night," *Atlanta Constitution*, January 16, 1920.

5. "Jubilee Follows Funeral Cortege," *Boston Daily Globe*, January 17, 1920.

6. "J. Barleycorn Moves from Loop to Homes," *Chicago Daily Tribune*, January 17, 1920.

7. "WCTU Folk Celebrate End of Barleycorn," *San Francisco Chronicle*, January 17, 1920.

8. "Joy, Grief Will Mark End of Rum's Reign in Los Angeles Tonight," *Los Angeles Times*, January 16, 1920.

9. Charles Phillips, "January 16, 1920," *American History* 39, no. 6 (2005): 38; Virginia W. Wolcott, *Remaking Respectability*, 103; "Bryan, Daniels and Others Help to Bury Barleycorn," *Boston Daily Globe*, January 17, 1920.

10. Eric Mills, *Chesapeake Rumrunners*, 3–4; "John's Funeral," *Racine Journal News* (Racine, WI), January 17, 1920; Paul Sann, *Lawless Decade*, 21.

11. "John Barleycorn Died Peacefully at the Toll of Twelve," *New York Times,* January 17, 1920; "25,000 Sleuths Are Ready to Nab Dry Lawbreakers," *Appleton Daily Post* (Appleton, WI), January 17, 1920; "Federal Agents Ready to Uphold Prohibition Law," *Oneonta Daily Star* (Oneonta, NY), January 17, 1920.

12. "New York Stages Mock Funeral for D. Rum," *San Francisco Chronicle*, January 17, 1920; "John Barleycorn Died Peacefully at the Toll of Twelve," *New York Times,* January 17, 1920; Christine Sismondo, *America Walks into a Bar*, 211.

13. "Saturday, January 17, 1920," *Newport Mercury* (Newport, RI), January 17, 1920; "John Barleycorn Takes Final Count in Nation," *Boston Daily Globe*, January 17, 1920.

14. "Two Hundred Dry Enforcement Agents Cover Chicago," *San Francisco Chronicle*, January 16, 1920; "Tonight to See Last Rites for J. Barleycorn," *Kokomo Daily Tribune* (Kokomo, IN), January 16, 1920; "J. Barleycorn Moves from Loop to Homes," *Chicago Daily Tribune*, January 17, 1920.

15. "12:01 a.m., Jan. 17 Last Wet Minute," *San Francisco Chronicle*, January 11, 1920.

16. "Joy, Grief Will Mark End of Rum's Reign in Los Angeles Tonight," *Los Angeles Times*, January 16, 1920.

17. "Nation Goes Dry at Midnight," *Ironwood Daily Globe* (Ironwood, MI), January 16, 1920.

18. Ronald Jan Plavchan, *Anheuser-Busch*, 168, 171–172, 174–175, 178–179, 181, 190, 192.

19. "More Whiskey for Ireland," *Cumberland Evening Times* (Cumberland, MD), November 7, 1919; "Yankee Whiskey Is to Become German 'Schnapps,'" *Lima News* (Lima, OH), December 23, 1919.

20. "Distillery Machinery Will Be Sold as Junk," *Decatur Daily Review* (Decatur, IL), March 1, 1919.

21. "New York Goes on Great Final Spree," *Dallas Morning News*, January 17, 1920.

22. Vivienne Sosnowski, *Rivers Ran Red*, 55.

23. Mark A. Noon, *Yuengling*, 118; Daniel Okrent, *Last Call*, 90, 120; Sismondo, *Walks into a Bar*, 211; "Robbers Loot Cellar of Rare Liquors," *New York Times*, January 19, 1922; "Robbers Driven from Wine Cellars," *New York Times*, May 12, 1922; "$300,000 Worth of Leiter Liquors Stolen from Financier's Country Home in Virginia," *New York Times*, October 10, 1921; "Rob Leiter's Cellar of $50,000 in Liquor," *New York Times*, November 23, 1924.

Chapter 2

1. Roy A. Haynes, *Prohibition Inside Out*, 199.

2. National Prohibition Act of 1919, Public Law 66-66, *U.S. Statutes at Large 41* (1921): 305–319.

3. "Federal Stage Set for Dry Law Entry Tomorrow," *New York Times*, January 16, 1920.

4. "Wets Have Gala Day in Capitol's Shadow," *New York Times*, February 23, 1926.

5. "Negro Editor Arrested," *Washington Post*, January 17, 1920; "New Move Started to Save Dry Fund," *New York Times*, February 2, 1929.

6. "Library Puts No Ban on Books of Liquor's Secrets," *San Francisco Chronicle*, January 16, 1920.

7. Gilman M. Ostrander, *Prohibition Movement*, 178–179.

8. *Danovitz v. U.S.*, 281 U.S. 389 (1930).

9. Liquor Advertisement, *Odessa American* (Odessa, TX), May 16, 1932.

10. Haynes, *Prohibition Inside Out*, 199.

11. "Denatured Alcohol Always a Dangerous Poison," *Popular Mechanics* 37 (1922): 402.

12. Haynes, *Prohibition Inside Out*, 204.

13. Ibid., 202.

14. Ibid., 203; "Industrial Alcohol Will Repel by Odor," *New York Times*, September 26, 1926.

15. "Prohibition Now a Chemical War," *New York Times*, January 9, 1927.

16. "Prohibition: Under Way," *Time*, August 23, 1926, 8–9.

17. Frederic Damrau, "The Truth about Poison Liquor," *Popular Science Monthly* 110, no. 4 (April 1927): 18; "New Dry Formula Hits Bootleggers," *New York Times*, October 9, 1926; "Government to Double Alcohol Poison Content and also Add Benzine," *New York Times*, December 30, 1926.

18. "Poison," *Time*, January 10, 1927, 10–11.

19. "Spoiled Eggs and Garlic," *Time*, December 22, 1930, 10; "New Denaturant without Any Poison Found for Alcohol," *New York Times*, December 11, 1930; "S.O. California Finds Alcohol Denaturant," *Wall Street Journal*, December 30, 1930.

20. John Kobler, *Ardent Spirits*, 305–306, 307; "Poison Liquor Toll Rising, Says Buckner," *New York Times*, December 18, 1925.

21. Fred D. Baldwin, "Smedley D. Butler and Prohibition Enforcement in Philadelphia, 1924–25," *Pennsylvania Magazine of History and Biography* 84, no. 3 (1960): 359.

22. "Prohibition: Questions and Answers," *Time*, August 26, 1929, 13–14.

23. "1930 Alcohol Output Reduced," *Wall Street Journal*, January 4, 1930.

24. William G. Brown, "State Cooperation in Enforcement," *Annals of the American Academy of Political and Social Science* 163 (September 1932): 30, 36; "Medical Whiskey Nears Depletion," *New York Times*, November 16, 1926.

25. Brown, "State Cooperation in Enforcement," 35; "Drastic Prohibition Law Modified by Indiana House," *New York Times*, July 26, 1932; Okrent, *Last Call*, 141; Donald Barr Chidsey, *On and Off the Wagon*, 78.

26. "Set up Machinery to Enforce Dry Law," *New York Times*, November 13, 1919.

27. Chidsey, *On and Off the Wagon*, 78.

28. "Drys Bought Liquor with WCTU Funds, Pinchot Aide Admits," *New York Times*, June 29, 1926.

Chapter 3

1. "Two Million Gallons of Whiskey Ordered," *New York Times*, July 22, 1929.

2. "Liquor as Medicine," *New York Times*, February 1, 1920; "'Dry Act' Licenses Now Exceed 57,000," *New York Times*, July 4, 1920.

3. Mills, *Chesapeake Rumrunners*, 32; "Limits Whiskey Prescriptions by Doctors to One Hundred a Quarter," *New York Times*, April 23, 1920.

4. "U.S. Attorney Asks for Whiskey Stations in War on $7 a Half-pint Druggists," *New York Times*, March 3, 1920; Mills, *Chesapeake Rumrunners*, 33; "Six Hundred Percent Profit on Liquor," *New York Times*, January 21, 1927.

5. "Day's Name Forged, Rum Seizure Charge," *New York Times*, May 16, 1922.

6. "More French Champagne Here, Presumably as Medicine," *New York Times*, April 3, 1921.

7. "Puts Medicinal Whiskey Need at Ten Million Gallons Yearly," *New York Times*, January 18, 1927; "Two Million Gallons of Whiskey Ordered," *New York Times*, July 22, 1929.

8. "Medical Whiskey Nears Depletion," *New York Times*, November 16, 1926.

9. "End Plan to Make Medicinal Liquor," *New York Times*, August 10, 1927.

10. "Treasury Acts to Replenish Whiskey Stocks with 1.4 Million Gallons of Bourbon in Year," *New York Times*, October 11, 1929.

11. "Medicinal Whiskey One Pint Every Ten Days," *New York Amsterdam News*, December 15, 1926.

12. "Important to All of Us," *New York Amsterdam News*, February 21, 1923.

13. "Physicians Accused in Huge Liquor Ring, Broken up in Fourteen Raids," *New York Times*, February 26, 1931; "Twelve Doctors Accused in Liquor 'Racket,'" *New York Times*, March 19, 1931; "Three Doctors Guilty as Liquor Agents," *New York Times*, March 24, 1931.

14. "Discover 500,000 False Prescriptions," *New York Times*, April 14, 1923.

15. Sann, *Lawless*, 132; Sosnowski, *Rivers Ran Red*, 124–125.

16. "Dry Task Hopeless, General Andrews Says," *New York Times*, October 28, 1925.

17. "Trace Many Forged Rabbi Wine Permits," *New York Times*, March 30, 1921.

18. "Withdrawals of Rabbi Wine to Be Checked," *San Francisco Chronicle*, September 10, 1922; "Trace Many Forged Rabbi Wine Permits," *New York Times*, March 30, 1921.

19. "218,000 Gallons Wine Is Taken for Sacrament," *Davenport Democrat and Leader* (Davenport, IA), June 10, 1923; "Chicago Devout on Wine," *New York Times*, June 8, 1923; "Chicago Looks on Prohibition as Big Joke," *The Bee* (Danville, VA), March 7, 1923.

20. Kenneth D. Rose, "Wettest in the West: San Francisco and Prohibition in 1924," *California History* 65, no. 4 (December 1986): 288.

21. "New Rules Govern Sacramental Wine," *New York Times*, October 15, 1922; "Sacramental Wine under Sharp Watch," *New York Times*, July 30, 1923.

22. "Limit Rabbis' Sale of Religious Wine," *New York Times*, December 2, 1925.

23. "210 Wine Shops Shut In Drive To Dry City," *New York Times*, August 27, 1926; "Thirty-one Are Indicted in Liquor Inquiries," *New York Times*, February 8, 1927.

24. "Wine Restrictions Eased," *New York Times*, February 3, 1928.

25. "No Limit on Wine for His Patients," *New York Times*, February 5, 1921; 265 U.S. 545.

26. "Liniment! That's the Rub for the Thirsty," *San Francisco Chronicle*, August 13, 1920; "Ng Ka Py, Alias J. Barleycorn, Barred," *San Francisco Chronicle*, September 9, 1920; "U.S. Order Is Joyful News to Chinatown," *San Francisco Chronicle*, November 24, 1920; "U.S. Releases Chinese Wine Held in Bond," *San Francisco Chronicle*, April 16, 1921; "Ng Ka Py Held in U.S. Warehouses Ordered Released," *San Francisco Chronicle*, April 19, 1921; "Chinese Wine Released from Custom House," *San Francisco Chronicle*, May 27, 1921.

27. "$7 Million in Chinese Wine Is Doomed under New Ruling," *New York Times*, August 23, 1922; "Fifty Thousand Wine Quarts to be Buried at Sea," *New York Times*, February 7, 1923; "Dump Chinese Wine Thirty Miles Offshore," *New York Times*, February 10, 1923.

28. "New Move Started to Save Dry Fund," *New York Times*, February 2, 1929; "New Dry Rule Hits Use of Wine Tonics," *New York Times*, September 2, 1929.

29. John R. Meers, "The California Wine and Grape Industry and Prohibition," *California Historical Society Quarterly* 46, no. 1 (1967): 20, 28; "Home Winemaking Saves Grape Growers," *New York Times*, October 30, 1921.

30. "Rush for Grapes like Street Fight," *New York Times*, October 16, 1921.

31. "Wineries Spring up All over the City," *New York Times*, June 14, 1922.

32. "Volstead Held Real Cause of Car Shortage," *San Francisco Chronicle*, November 1, 1922; "Acts to Speed up Grape Shipments," *New York Times*, September 27, 1925.

33. "Raid Fifth Avenue Shop in 'Wine Brick' Test," *New York Times*, August 6, 1931.

34. Ostrander, *Prohibition Movement*, 179.

35. "Test Fight Starts on Grape Juice Sale," *New York Times*, May 9, 1931; "Hold Grape Juice Men in Kansas City Raid," *New York Times*, June 18, 1931; "Grape Concern Indicted," *New York Times*, September 24, 1931; "Concentrate Sale Held Dry Violation," *New York Times*, October 17, 1931.

36. "Drop Grape Concentrate Appeal," *New York Times*, November 20, 1931; "Fruit Industries End 'Vine-Glo' Sale," *Wall Street Journal*, November 6, 1931.

37. "Piel Brothers Lose Medicinal Beer Suit," *New York Times*, February 9, 1922.

38. "Medical Beer Ban Upheld by Court," *New York Times*, June 10, 1924; 265 U.S. 545 (1924).

39. Plavchan, *Anheuser-Busch*, 150, 158–161, 164–166.

40. Noon, *Yuengling*, 116–117.

Chapter 4

1. Barry J. Grant, *When Rum Was King*, 72.

2. "Woman Boot-legger Caught," *New York Times*, December 6, 1897.

3. "Shut off the Liquor Flood at Its Source, Says Pinchot," *New York Times*, November 4, 1923; "Clean Philadelphia, Mayor Tells Police," *New York Times*, September 4, 1928; "Boston Gold Coast Shifts Its Locality," *New York Times*, September 2, 1928; Mills, *Chesapeake Rumrunners*, 90; Charles Merz, *The Dry Decade*, 138, 139.

4. "Blind Pigs," *Keota Eagle* (Keota, IA), August 8, 1885.

5. "Bill Nye," *Boston Daily Globe*, September 6, 1885; "Blind Swine," *St. Paul Daily Globe* (St. Paul, MN), July 26, 1885.

6. "Local Correspondence," *Freeborn Standard* (Albert Lea, MN), September 16, 1885; "Minneapolis Globelets," *St. Paul Daily Globe* (St. Paul, MN), September 7, 1884; "Anoka," *St. Paul Daily Globe* (St. Paul, MN), August 11, 1884; "A Sad Sunday," *St. Paul Daily Globe* (St. Paul, MN), August 18, 1884.

7. "Extremes in Barrooms," *San Francisco Chronicle*, March 18, 1896.

8. "Gin Bottle Cats," *Sycamore True Republican* (Sycamore, IL), April 20, 1901.

9. "'Lige Simmons of Sinkum," *Sheboygan Journal* (Sheboygan, WI), April 6, 1857; "The Blind Tiger," *Athens Messenger* (Athens, OH), May 6, 1886.

10. "A Calhoun County Man," *Indiana Weekly Messenger* (Indiana, PA), March 11, 1885.

11. "Betty Smith's Blind Tiger," *Petersburg Daily Index-Appeal* (Petersburg, VA), April 20, 1885.

12. "Local Paragraphs," *Decatur Daily Review* (Decatur, IL), July 9, 1887; "Thirsty Had No Drink but Water," *San Francisco Chronicle*, April 7, 1902.

13. "High License in Pennsylvania," *Public Opinion* 3 (April–October 1887): 127; Untitled Article, *Malvern Leader* (Malvern, IA), March 27, 1890.

14. "The Illegal Speak-easies," *New York Times*, July 6, 1891.

15. Charles Vandersee, "Speakeasy," *American Speech* 59, no. 3 (Autumn 1984): 268; "The Illegal Speak-easies," *New York Times*, July 6, 1891.

16. Clifford James Walker, *One Eye Closed, the Other Red*, 438.

17. Rufus S. Lusk, "The Drinking Habit," *Annals of the American Academy of Political and Social Science* 163 (September 1932): 48.

18. "Chicago 'Beer Flat' Raids Put 250 in Police Cells," *New York Times*, May 21, 1928; "Chicago Beer Flats Hit in Raids," *San Antonio Light* (San Antonio, TX), May 21, 1928; "Beer Flat New Dry Law Evasion,"

Bakersfield Californian (Bakersfield, CA), December 14, 1928.

19. "Seventy-five Bottles Make Home a Beer Flat," *San Antonio Light* (San Antonio, TX), September 21, 1929.

20. "Buffet Flat Solves Many of High Society's Drinking Problems," *Port Arthur News* (Port Arthur, TX), January 9, 1927.

21. "Dry Law Denounced as House Body Opens Wet Bills Hearing," *New York Times*, February 13, 1930.

22. "Sixty Gallons of Beer Taken by Dry Agents," *Sheboygan Press* (Sheboygan, WI), November 13, 1926; "'Beer Farm' Raided in Milwaukee County," *Appleton Post-Crescent* (Appleton, WI), May 13, 1929; "Occupants of Beer Farm to Face Geiger," *Sheboygan Press* (Sheboygan, WI), May 13, 1925; "Thurber Murder Calls Attention to Beer Farm Gain," *Wisconsin State Journal* (Madison, WI), October 7, 1930.

23. "Girl, Thirteen, Assaulted after Beer Party," *Wisconsin State Journal* (Madison, WI), November 3, 1930.

24. Fred D. Pasley, *Al Capone*, 344–345.

Chapter 5

1. Edmund Fahey, *Rum Road to Spokane*, 47.
2. Ibid., 127.
3. Gary A. Wilson, *Honky-tonk Town*, 81.
4. Neal Thompson, *Driving with the Devil*, 51.
5. Derek Nelson, *Moonshiners, Bootleggers, and Rumrunners*, 84.
6. Scott Wheeler, *Rumrunners and Revenuers*, 117, 133.
7. Allan S. Everest, *Rum Across the Border*, 101; Wilson, *Honky-tonk Town*, 81.
8. Fahey, *Rum Road*, 14, 16, 108.
9. "Liquor Cargo Ditched," *New York Times*, March 17, 1922.
10. Fahey, *Rum Road*, 68.
11. Ibid., 16; Thompson, *Driving with the Devil*, 63.
12. Thompson, *Driving with the Devil*, 64.
13. Joseph Earl Dabney, *Mountain Spirits*, 151–152; Thompson, *Driving with the Devil*, 10, 51.
14. "Fake Customs Guards Stop Hearse, Search Inside for Liquor," *Dallas Morning News*, October 14, 1929.
15. "Romance of Nor'west Border Rum Runners," *New York Times*, November 19, 1922.
16. Walter B. Rideout, *Sherwood Anderson*, vol. 2, 236–237; Jess Carr, *The Second Oldest Profession*, 118.
17. Dabney, *Mountain Spirits*, 151.
18. "Refuses to Extradite Dry Agent," *New York Times*, December 29, 1920; "Dry Aides Slay Man," *Carbondale Daily Free Press* (Carbondale, IL), October 12, 1920.
19. "Kill Liquor Runner, Capture Caravan," *New York Times*, December 12, 1920.
20. "Rum Runner Gives Details of Ring's Business in Confession," *San Francisco Chronicle*, October 5, 1921.

21. Paul W. Glad, "When John Barleycorn Went into Hiding in Wisconsin," *The Wisconsin Magazine of History* 68, no. 2 (Winter 1984-85): 132.

22. "Scour Lake for Rum Runner," *Chicago Daily Tribune*, May 14, 1930; "Battling the Rum Runners in No Man's Land," *New York Times*, July 29, 1923; "Dry Agents Meet Glassy Fusillade," *New York Times*, July 9, 1922.

Chapter 6

1. Stephen Schneider, *Iced*, 185.
2. Greg Marquis, "'Brewers' and Distillers' Paradise': American Views of Canadian Alcohol Policies, 1919–1935," *Canadian Review of American Studies* 34, no. 2 (2004): 138, 139, 140; "Most of Canada Is Now (Theoretically) Bone Dry," *Boston Daily Globe*, September 18, 1921.
3. "Canada Swinging into Wet Column, for Present, Anyway," *Boston Daily Globe*, August 10, 1924; "Most of Canada Is Now (Theoretically) Bone Dry," *Boston Daily Globe*, September 18, 1921; Wheeler, *Rumrunners and Revenuers*, 138.
4. James H. Gray, *The Roar of the Twenties*, 133, 136.
5. Cyril D. Boyce, "Prohibition in Canada," *Annals of the American Academy of Political and Social Science* 109 (September 1923): 228.
6. Gray, *Roar*, 136; "When the Booze Trade Was Sinful," *Alberta Report Newsmagazine* 20, no. 40 (1993): 9.
7. Boyce, "Prohibition in Canada," 228; Gray, *Roar*, 136.
8. Marquis, "'Brewers and Distillers Paradise,'" 135, 150; "Ontario Opens the Beer Spigot," *New York Times*, November 17, 1925; "Ontario Goes Wet and the Border Seethes," *New York Times*, May 15, 1927.
9. Wheeler, *Rumrunners and Revenuers*, 9.
10. "Bootleggers Carry Alcohol to Canada," *New York Times*, July 12, 1925.
11. Everest, *Rum Across the Border*, 50–51.
12. Peter C. Newman, *King of the Castle, the Making of a Dynasty*, 97.
13. "Smuggling that Goes on Across American Borders," *New York Times*, March 30, 1930; Wilson, *Honky-tonk Town*, 49, 89.
14. Everest, *Rum Across the Border*, 46–47.
15. "Dry Agents Check Border Smugglers," *New York Times*, May 19, 1921.
16. "Canadian Liquor Pours over Line," *Dallas Morning News*, July 6, 1923.
17. Everest, *Rum Across the Border*, 46–47.
18. "Flood of Liquor for the Holidays Pours over Border," *New York Times*, December 13, 1923.
19. Everest, *Rum Across the Border*, 101–102.
20. Ibid., 32–33; Wheeler, *Rumrunners and Revenuers*, 46.
21. "Guardsmen Bombard Booze-filled Woods," *New York Times*, June 27, 1921.
22. "Vermont's Toughest Town Moves to Rid Itself of Gangsters," *Boston Evening Transcript*, July 29, 1931; Wheeler, *Rumrunners and Revenuers*, 24–26.

23. Grant, *Rum Was King*, 28, 85.

24. Ibid., 17–18, 19, 20.

25. Ibid., 48–49.

26. Everest, *Rum Across the Border*, 48, 49; Grant, *Rum Was King*, 76.

27. "Golf Week in White Mountains," *New York Times*, July 25, 1926; Wheeler, *Rumrunners and Revenuers*, 155; "Summer Visitors in the White Mountains," *New York Times*, July 5, 1925.

28. "Bootlegging Fleet Keeps Down Canadian Flow," *New York Times*, July 8, 1923.

29. Wheeler, *Rumrunners and Revenuers*, 138.

30. "Brookhart Tells Story in Senate of Liquor Party," *New York Times*, November 6, 1929; "Six Are Sentenced in Border Rum Ring," *New York Times*, August 2, 1931; "Trombley Is Turned over to McMartin," *Plattsburgh Sentinel* (Plattsburgh, NY) January 23, 1931.

31. Grant, *Rum Was King*, 22.

32. Wheeler, *Rumrunners and Revenuers*, 139.

33. "Montreal Is Liquor Oasis for Thirsty U.S. Traveler," *Evening Independent* (Massillon, OH), June 3, 1929.

34. Wheeler, *Rumrunners and Revenuers*, 140.

Chapter 7

1. "Bottles Bombard Police after Raid," *New York Times*, May 23, 1921.

2. Michael A. Lerner, *Dry Manhattan*, 166.

3. "M'Laughlin Closes Cabarets at 2 a.m.," *New York Times*, June 8, 1926.

4. Lerner, *Dry Manhattan*, 74; "Wet Days Recalled by Police Dinner," *New York Times*, February 23, 1921.

5. "Police Not 'Dry Sleuths,'" *New York Times*, February 3, 1920.

6. Lerner, *Dry Manhattan*, 75, 77, 79–80.

7. "Enright Sets Force to Hunting Liquor Carried on the Hip," *New York Times*, August 10, 1921; "City Is Drying Up under Police Order," *New York Times*, April 8, 1921.

8. Lerner, *Dry Manhattan*, 78, 79.

9. "$7 Million in Liquor Taken, Says Enright," *New York Times*, April 30, 1921; Lerner, *Dry Manhattan*, 79.

10. "One Thousand Three Hundred Rum Arrests Scatter Venders," *New York Times*, April 19, 1921.

11. "Police Took 10,016 in Dry Raids in 1921," *New York Times*, January 19, 1922; "Governor to Blame, Enright Tells Jury," *New York Times*, September 17, 1921.

12. *The National Prohibition Law: Hearings before the Committee of the Judiciary, United States Senate, Sixty-ninth Congress, First Session*, vol. 1, 96, 97, 99.

13. Ibid., 98, 100; "Andrews Arrives to Pick Dry Chief," *New York Times*, September 25, 1925.

14. "Clemency Pledged if 'Wets' Confess," *New York Times*, April 26, 1921.

15. "Two Women Taken in $1 Million Fraud Laid to Whiskey Ring," *New York Times*, December 31, 1920;

"New Rum Ring Here in $1 Million Fraud," *New York Times*, January 1, 1921; "$100,000,000 Fraud in Liquor Released on Forged Orders," *New York Times,* January 7, 1921; "Liquor Fraud Trial Opens," *New York Times*, February 21, 1922.

16. "Four Agents, Three Others Held in Rum Plot," *New York Times*, January 14, 1921.

17. "Testifies Donegan Banked Big Sums," *New York Times*, February 25, 1922; "Accused Dry Clerk a Federal Witness," *New York Times*, February 22, 1922; "Rum Withdrawals Easy, Trial Shows," *New York Times*, February 24, 1922; "Anderson a Zero, Says Bishop Gailor," *New York Times*, March 1, 1922.

18. "Donegan Convicted, Miss Sassone Free," *New York Times*, March 3, 1922; "Ten Years, $65,000 Fine for Donegan," *New York Times*, March 4, 1922; "Must Serve 10-year Term," *New York Times*, December 13, 1922.

19. "Binghamton Judge to Head Dry Forces," *New York Times*, March 4, 1921; "Hart to Enforce Prohibition Here," *New York Times*, May 19, 1921.

20. "Sees Official Aid to Liquor Forgers," *New York Times*, September 24, 1921; "Indict Hart and Orr in $10 Million Rum Plot with Eighteen Others," *New York Times*, January 5, 1922; "Had Rum Permits for 400,000 Cases," *New York Times*, August 26, 1921.

21. "Names Yellowley Dry Director Here," *New York Times*, October 7, 1921.

22. "Taxed $1,635,797 as a Bootlegger," *New York Times*, November 11, 1921; "Hart and his Clerk Held in $5,000 Bail," *New York Times*, January 6, 1922.

23. "Stolen Rum Orders Certified as Good," *New York Times*, March 1, 1923; "Sold $1 Million Rum on Stolen Permits," *New York Times*, March 2, 1923; "Woman Distiller Identifies Permits," *New York Times*, March 3, 1923.

24. "Hart and Orr Freed In Rum Plot Case," *New York Times*, March 21, 1923.

25. "Pick Clothing Man to Make City Dry," *New York Times*, October 26, 1921; "Shake-up Expected among Dry Agents," *New York Times*, December 1, 1921.

26. "Drops Dry Agents on Graft Evidence," *New York Times*, December 2, 1921; "R.A. Day Resigns as Dry Chief Here," *New York Times*, October 5, 1922.

27. "Dry Director Day Is Hauled into Court," *New York Times*, October 28, 1922.

28. "Grand Jury Calls Dry Enforcement Here a Disgrace," *New York Times*, November 18, 1922; "Hidden Indictment of R.A. Day Exposed," *New York Times*, May 15, 1926.

29. "Dry Director Day Is Hauled into Court," *New York Times*, October 28, 1922; "Wants Big Dry Chief before Grand Jury," *New York Times*, November 3, 1922; "Grand Jury Calls Dry Enforcement Here a Disgrace," *New York Times*, November 18, 1922.

30. "Indict Six Dry Agents with Twenty-seven in Rum Plot," *New York Times*, November 24, 1922; "Find Kessler Guilty with Ten Others of Bootleg Plot," *New York Times*, December 5, 1923.

31. "He Upholds State Rights," *New York Times*, June 2, 1923.

Chapter 8

1. Sismondo, *America Walks into a Bar*, 221.
2. "Once-fashionable Embassy Club Closed, a Victim of Competition in Repeal Era," *New York Times*, January 26, 1934; "Salon of the Great to Be Set up Here," *New York Times*, March 8, 1928; Michael Batterberry and Ariane Batterberry, *On the Town in New York from 1776 to the Present*, 205; Burton W. Peretti, *Nightclub City*, 6; "Forty-two Resorts Served with Padlock Writs in Biggest Round-up," *New York Times*, April 15, 1926; David Wallace, *Capital of the World*, 227.
3. Batterberry, *On the Town*, 207, 226; "Prohibition Agent Detailed to Feed Three Hundred Fish after Seizure of 25-foot Aquarium Bar," *New York Times*, May 6, 1932.
4. "Dry Agents Battle in Brooklyn Raids," *New York Times*, November 24, 1922.
5. "Say Woman Carried Saloon under Skirt," *New York Times*, May 28, 1921.
6. "Coast Guard Acts to Close Cabaret Fifteen Miles out at Sea," *New York Times*, August 17, 1924.
7. "Is this Really Harlem?" *New York Amsterdam News*, November 23, 1929.
8. "Enright Lectures Vice Squad; Thinks Some Are Grafting," *New York Times*, February 26, 1924.
9. *This Fabulous Century, 1920–1930*, 85.
10. "'Shorty' of Whiskey Is Peculiar to Harlem," *New York Amsterdam News*, July 3, 1927; Batterberry, *On the Town*, 213.
11. "Is this Really Harlem?" *New York Amsterdam News*, November 23, 1929; "'Shorty' of Whiskey Is Peculiar to Harlem," *New York Amsterdam News*, July 3, 1937.
12. "Vice Graft Traced in Harlem Inquiry," *New York Times*, March 23, 1931.
13. "City Vice Conditions Worst in Twenty Years, Survey Declares," *New York Times*, July 9, 1928.
14. "Federal Speakeasy Here Cost $44,886," *New York Times*, October 24, 1927; Sismondo, *America Walks into a Bar*, 228.
15. "Bielaski Explains Federal Rum Club," *New York Times*, January 27, 1927; Lerner, *Dry Manhattan*, 236.
16. "Andrews Abolishes Buckner's Dry Unit," *New York Times*, March 25, 1927.
17. Lerner, *Dry Manhattan*, 154.
18. *The National Prohibition Law: Hearings*, vol. 1, 101, 102.
19. Lerner, *Dry Manhattan*, 155.
20. "Locks Go on Six Cafes, Last of Fourteen on List," *New York Times*, May 1, 1925; "Dry Padlocks Snapped on Nine Wet Doors," *New York Times*, June 23, 1925.
21. Lerner, *Dry Manhattan*, 157.
22. "Buckner's Father Disagrees on Beer," *New York Times*, April 16, 1926.
23. "Andrews Abolishes Buckner's Dry Unit," *New York Times*, March 25, 1927.
24. "Campbell Sworn in as Dry Chief Here," *New York Times*, July 2, 1927.
25. "Campbell Puts Ban on Dry Spying Here," *New York Times*, October 5, 1927.
26. "Dry Siege Brings Thirty-six New Padlocks," *New York Times*, August 3, 1928; "Four Dry Men Spent $60,000 to Uncover Nightclub Evidence," *New York Times*, August 1, 1928.
27. "Politics Disclaimed in Big Dry Raid Here," *New York Times*, June 30, 1928; "Manhattan Coup," *Time*, July 9, 1928, 13–14.
28. "Nightclubs Attack Pre-trial Padlocks," *New York Times*, September 11, 1928; "Twenty-Six Club Padlocks Held Illegal Here," *New York Times*, September 12, 1928.
29. "Dry Men Paid Clubs Many Costly Visits," *New York Times*, August 2, 1928; "Washington Differs on Cost," *New York Times*, August 3, 1928.
30. "Nightclub Men Get Severe Jail Terms, *New York Times*, February 1, 1929; "It's 'Nightclub Day' In Federal Court," *New York Times*, April 9, 1929; "Padlocks Ordered for Four Nightclubs," *New York Times*, November 20, 1928; "Beaux Arts Club Ordered Padlocked," *New York Times*, November 21, 1928; "Two Padlocks Ordered for Clubs," *New York Times*, December 4, 1928; "Only Fines Imposed in Nightclub Cases," *New York Times*, April 16, 1929.
31. "Prohibition: Women and Wine," *Time*, August 13, 1928, 11–12.
32. "Campbell Demands State Take Burden of Speakeasy War," *New York Times*, August 26, 1929.
33. "Whalen Turns Back the Speakeasy Task to Federal Dry Chief," *New York Times*, August 29, 1929.
34. "Whalen Says Police Do Campbell's Job," *New York Times*, September 15, 1929.
35. "No Prohibition Here, Campbell Admits," *New York Times*, February 11, 1930.
36. "Whalen Says Police Do Campbell's Job," *New York Times*, September 15, 1929; "The New York Speakeasy: Who Shall Close It?" *New York Times*, September 15, 1929.
37. "Whalen Is Caustic on Campbell Plan," *New York Times*, August 27, 1929; "Banton Assails Campbell," *New York Times*, August 27, 1929.
38. "Record Here in 1929 in Curbing Alcohol," *New York Times*, January 2, 1930.

Chapter 9

1. "U.S. Exports Surplus 'Booze' to Canada, High Spots in Senate's Liquor Inquiry," *Evening Independent* (Massillon, OH), August 4, 1926.
2. "Began as Street Hoodlum," *New York Times*, November 29, 1934; Elmer Irey, *The Tax Dodgers*, 138.
3. 1901 Census of England and Wales, Yorkshire, Civil Parish of Leeds, 15; 1910 U.S. Census Series T624, Roll 1044, 280.
4. "Knife Fight Memories Cut Deep," *San Antonio Light* (San Antonio, TX), January 14, 1958.
5. "Two Are Stabbed in Gangsters' War," *Washington Herald*, June 18, 1913.

6. "Find Madden Guilty of Manslaughter," *New York Times*, June 3, 1915.

7. Graham Nown, *The English Godfather*, 29.

8. "Detectives Capture Man Wanted for Murder of Young Woman's Escort," *New York Times*, February 13, 1912.

9. "Gangster Is Shot In Dancers' Midst," *Oakland Tribune* (Oakland, CA), December 1, 1912; T.J. English, *Paddy Whacked*, 118.

10. Nown, *Godfather*, 38; "Try Gangster for Murder," *New York Times*, May 25, 1915.

11. Nown, *Godfather*, 42.

12. "Gang Slayer's Guilty Plea," *New York Times*, March 16, 1915; "Girl's Taunt Sent Gunmen for Killing," *New York Times*, May 28, 1915; "Girl Acted as Lure in a Gang Killing," *New York Times*, May 27, 1915; "Try Gangster for Murder," *New York Times*, May 25, 1915.

13. "Why She Confessed," *Washington Herald*, May 29, 1915.

14. Nown, *Godfather*, 45; "Guard District Attorney," *New York Times*, May 29, 1915.

15. "Gangster Madden Quits Stand in Rage," *New York Times*, June 2, 1915; "Owney Madden, Found Guilty in Gang Killing, Escapes Chair by Manslaughter Verdict," *New York Tribune*, June 3, 1915; Nown, *Godfather*, 46.

16. "Blackmail Plot Charged," *New York Times*, June 26, 1915; "Madden 'Framed' Gangsters Testify," *New York Times*, October 9, 1915; "Gangster Madden Stays in Sing Sing," *New York Times*, November 5, 1915; "Gangs of New York Hear Doom When Judge Halts Their Plans To Free Owney Madden, Leader," *Washington Post*, November 5, 1915.

17. "Arrest Whiskey Thieves," *Fitchburg Sentinel* (Fitchburg, MA), December 3, 1923; Nown, *Godfather*, 57.

18. "Robbers Captured after a Hold-up," *New York Times*, February 2, 1924; James Haskins, *The Cotton Club*, 35.

19. Stanley Walker, *The Night Club Era*, 115.

20. "Larry Fay Is Slain in his Nightclub; Doorman Is Hunted," *New York Times*, January 2, 1933.

21. "Link Underworld in Big Liquor Raid," *New York Times*, March 4, 1928; "'Gin Ring' Trial Is Set," *New York Times*, July 3, 1928; "Testifies 'Gin Ring' Plans to Kill Her," *New York Times*, October 3, 1928; "Eight Found Guilty in Trial of 'Gin Ring,'" *New York Times*, October 12, 1928.

22. "Big Beer Seizure Marks Mills Drive," *New York Times*, September 12, 1926.

23. "Report A Pipe Line At Near-Beer Plant," *New York Times*, July 3, 1930.

24. "Blind Stairways Throw Agents off Trail of Brewery," *Reno Evening Gazette* (Reno, NV), August 15, 1930; "Labyrinth Baffles Raiders in Brewery," *New York Times*, July 15, 1930.

25. "Beer Odor Evidence Shuts Big Brewery," *New York Times*, December 16, 1932; "Dry Agent Accuses Policemen as Beer Aides," *New York Times*, November 30, 1932.

26. "Twenty-five Dry Agents Raid $1.5 Million Brewery," *New York Times*, July 22, 1931; "Brewery Raid Voiding Upheld by Court," *New York Times*, September 17, 1931; "Phoenix Brewery Defense Upheld," *New York Times*, May 24, 1932; "Chemist Ridicules a Dry's 'Beer Nose,'" *New York Times*, October 18, 1932.

27. "Dry Agents at Odds on Odor of Real Beer," *New York Times*, October 20, 1932; "Voiding of Raid Upheld," *New York Times*, November 24, 1932; "Phoenix Brewery Wins Beer Decision," *New York Times*, May 9, 1933; "Phoenix Seeks Permit," *New York Times*, May 30, 1933; In Re Phoenix Cereal Beverage Co., Inc., Circuit Court of Appeals, Second Circuit, May 23, 1932.

28. "Hears Padlock Is Defied," *New York Times*, January 20, 1933; "Court Urged to End Brewery Padlock," *New York Times*, April 4, 1933; "Phoenix Padlock Stands," *New York Times*, April 19, 1933.

29. "Lanphier Heads Brewing Company," *New York Times*, June 16, 1933.

30. Emily Wortis Leider, *Becoming Mae West*, 146.

31. Nown, *Godfather*, 60.

32. Haskins, *Cotton Club*, 33, 57.

33. Nown, *Godfather*, 64.

34. "Dry Padlocks Snapped on Nine Wet Doors; 'Owney' Madden's Club Is One of Them," *New York Times*, June 23, 1925; Haskins, *Cotton Club*, 39.

35. "Gangsters Wreck Harlem Night Club," *New York Times*, January 17, 1930; "Nine Men Damage Cabaret $25,000 in Bold Assault," *New York Amsterdam News*, January 22, 1930; "Gangsters Wreck Plantation Club," *Chicago Defender*, January 25, 1930; "Gangdom's Threat to Cabarets Seen in Extortion Case," *New York Amsterdam News*, May 14, 1930; "Three Wrecking Racket Suspects Arrested," *Chicago Defender*, May 17, 1930.

36. "Royal Box Club Shut By Sole Holiday Raid," *New York Times*, January 1, 1932; "Federal Agents Strip Joe Zelli's, Bronx Still Raided," *New York Times*, January 23, 1932.

Chapter 10

1. Walker, *Night Club*, 105.

2. Nown, *Godfather*, 110–111, 113–114.

3. Edward Doherty, "The Twilight of the Gangster," *Liberty* 8 (October 24, 1931): 5–9.

4. "Twenty Thousand at Meeting Protest Gang Reign; Police Start Drive," *New York Times*, August 25, 1931.

5. "The Governor's Message," *New York Times*, September 2, 1931.

6. Nown, *Godfather*, 11; "Madden Gets Writ to Stay on Parole," *New York Times*, February 14, 1931.

7. Nown, *Godfather*, 116–120.

8. Ibid., 117–118.

9. Ibid., 119.

10. Ibid., 119–120.

11. Ibid., 121.

12. "Seek Data to Return Madden to Prison," *New York Times*, December 31, 1931; Nown, *Godfather*, 121.

13. "Prison For Madden Asked On Appeal," *New York Times*, June 18, 1931; "Clears Owney Madden on Parole Charge," *New York Times*, January 24, 1932.

14. Nown, *Godfather*, 123–124.

15. "Madden Gets Writ To Stay On Parole," *New York Times*, February 14, 1932.

16. "Justice Levy Frees Madden Under Bail," *New York Times*, February 16, 1932.

17. Ibid.; Nown, *Godfather*, 126.

18. "Madden Files Brief In Fight To Go Free," *New York Times*, March 2, 1932.

19. "Officials Deny Board Discharged Madden," *New York Times*, April 1, 1932.

20. "Link Parole Future To Plea On Madden," *New York Times*, April 6, 1932; "Justice Levy Frees Madden and Three Aides," *New York Times*, April 5, 1932.

21. "Link Parole Future to Plea on Madden," *New York Times*, April 6, 1932; "Governor Backs Appeal on Madden," *New York Times*, April 7, 1932; "Madden Must Go to Prison Again," *New York Times*, July 2, 1932.

22. "Ossining, N.Y.," *New York Times*, July 8, 1932.

23. Nown, *Godfather*, 136–137.

24. "Owen Madden Loses Fight for Freedom; Appeals Court Upholds the Parole Board," *New York Times*, October 26, 1932; "Madden Loses Plea for Release On Bail," *New York Times*, July 20, 1932; "Madden Sentenced as Parole Violator," *New York Times*, November 3, 1932.

25. Nown, *Godfather*, 139; "Madden Put in Sing Sing Yard Crew," *New York Times*, July 25, 1932; "Madden Tends Flowers at Prison," *New York Times*, August 12, 1932.

26. "Madden to Go Free on Parole Today," *New York Times*, July 1, 1933; "Madden's Parole Granted for July 1," *New York Times*, June 6, 1933; Nown, *Godfather*, 142.

27. "Madden to Go Free on Parole Today," *New York Times*, July 1, 1933.

28. "Madden Is Found, Denies Reno Plan," *New York Times*, July 13, 1934.

29. "Madden May Avoid Coal Investigation," *New York Times*, July 12, 1934.

30. "Madden Defended by Parole Board," *New York Times*, July 28, 1932; "Parole Officers Protect Madden," *New York Times*, July 21, 1934; "Fraud Is Charged in City Coal Supply," *New York Times*, July 3, 1934.

31. "Madden Insists His Money Is Gone," *New York Times*, July 25, 1934; "Madden's Vacation Defended by Doctor," *New York Times*, August 3, 1934.

32. "Will Divorce Madden," *Lowell Sun* (Lowell, MA), August 14, 1934.

33. Nown, *Godfather*, 152–155.

34. "Infamous 'Clay Pigeon' Succumbs to Lung Disease," *Progress-Index* (Petersburg, VA), April 25, 1965; "On Broadway," *Wisconsin State Journal* (Madi-

son, WI), January 4, 1934; "Uncertain Days for Bold Racketeers," *New York Times*, March 5, 1933.

35. "Exploded 'Big Shots,'" *New York Times*, January 4, 1942; "Madden Is Seized in Police Round-up," *New York Times*, May 4, 1940; "Madden, Four Others Freed by Court," *New York Times*, May 5, 1940.

36. "Owney Madden, 73, Ex-Gangster, Dead," *New York Times*, April 24, 1965; Nown, *Godfather*, 171.

37. "Citizenship Is Given To Owney Madden," *New York Times*, March 18, 1943.

38. Nown, *Godfather*, 197.

Chapter 11

1. Paul Sann, *Kill the Dutchman*, 121.

2. "Schultz Product of Dry Law Era," *New York Times*, January 22, 1933; "Schultz Reigned on Discreet Lines," *New York Times*, October 25, 1935; "Schultz Declares He's a Benefactor," *New York Times*, April 15, 1935; "Crime: Bronx Boy," *Time*, April 29, 1935, 11–12.

3. "Dutch Schultz Trial Caps a Vivid Career," *New York Times*, April 28, 1935.

4. Sann, *Dutchman*, 204; "Detectives Tapped Schultz's Phones," *New York Times*, April 20, 1935.

5. "Dutch Schultz's Ghost Walks the Underworld," *New York Times*, June 12, 1938.

6. "Schultz Product of Dry Law Era," *New York Times*, January 22, 1933; "Schultz Declares He's a Benefactor," *New York Times*, April 15, 1935; "Schultz Reigned on Discreet Lines," *New York Times*, October 25, 1935.

7. Robert A. Rockaway, *But He Was Good to His Mother*, 17.

8. "Gang Drive Spurred by Schultz Capture," *New York Times*, June 19, 1931.

9. "A Product of Dry Era," *New York Times*, October 24, 1935; Craig Thompson and Allen Raymond, *Gang Rule in New York*, 334.

10. "Began as Street Hoodlum," *New York Times*, November 29, 1934; Sann, *Dutchman*, 111, 245.

11. Thompson and Raymond, *Gang Rule*, 43; Jerome Charyn, *Gangsters and Gold Diggers*, 80.

12. Charyn, *Gangsters*, 81; "Death Makes Slain Gunman Appear as Choir Boy," *Rochester Evening Journal* (Rochester, NY), December 19, 1931; Walker, *Night Club*, 234.

13. "'Legs' Diamond Jury Completed Today at Troy," *New York Times*, July 14, 1931; "Diamond Acquitted of Assault Charge," *New York Times*, July 15, 1931.

14. Charyn, *Gangsters*, 78–79.

15. Gary Levine, *Anatomy of a Gangster*, 159–160.

16. "Often Cheated Bullets," *New York Times*, December 19, 1931.

17. Thompson and Raymond, *Gang Rule*, 52.

18. "Death of 'Legs' Diamond," *Logansport Press* (Logansport, IN), December 24, 1931.

19. "Schultz Beer Rule and Link to Gangs Portrayed to Jury," *New York Times*, July 25, 1935; Sann, *Dutchman*, 111–112.

20. Levine, *Anatomy*, 56; Sann, *Dutchman*, 119.

21. "Schultz Defense Wilts when Court Admits Accounts," *New York Times*, April 23, 1935.

22. Sann, *Dutchman*, 102.

23. Ibid., 109; "Held in Double Slaying," *New York Times*, March 5, 1930.

24. "Dutch Schultz Trial Caps a Vivid Career," *New York Times*, April 28, 1935; Quentin Reynolds, *Courtroom*, 178.

25. "Seized in Double Killing," *New York Times*, March 4, 1930; "Held in Double Slaying," *New York Times*, March 5, 1930; "Dance Hall Hostess and Her Escort Shot Down by Gunmen," *Lowell Sun* (Lowell, MA), February 13, 1930; "Slaying of Couple Mystifies Police," *New York Times*, February 14, 1930.

26. "Gangster Forfeits Bail," *New York Times*, July 11, 1931; "Freed in Bronx Dual Slaying," *New York Times*, March 19, 1930.

27. "Coll Seized with His Gang; Identified as Baby Killer; Six Taken in Battle Upstate," *New York Times*, October 5, 1931.

28. "Shot Three Times, Walks to Hospital," *New York Times*, May 31, 1931.

29. "Schultz Beer Sale $2,000,000 a Year, Jurors Are Told," *New York Times*, April 17, 1935; "Schultz Aide Slain; Seventh in Five Months," *New York Times*, June 22, 1931.

30. "Schultz Jolted as Account Book Appears at Trial," *New York Times*, April 21, 1935.

31. "Gang Drive Spurred by Schultz Capture," *New York Times*, June 19, 1931; "Schultz Defense Wilts when Court Admits Accounts," *New York Times*, April 23, 1935; "Bronx Acts to Oust Schultz Beer Ring," *New York Times*, June 25, 1931; "Acquit Dutch Schultz of Assault Charge," *Syracuse Herald* (Syracuse, NY) July 3, 1931.

32. "Child Slain, Four Shot as Gangsters Fire on Beer War Rival," *New York Times*, July 29, 1931.

33. "Gang War Seen in Manhattan," *Gettysburg Times* (Gettysburg, PA), June 20, 1931; "Rao Is Convicted in Police Beating," *New York Times*, January 5, 1935; Burton B. Turkus and Sid Feder, *Murder, Inc.*, 130.

34. "Three Gangsters Named as Child's Slayer," *New York Times*, August 8, 1931; "Another 'Milk' Truck Found Full of Beer," *New York Times*, August 13, 1931.

35. "Hold New Witness in Slaying of Child," *New York Times*, August 7, 1931.

36. "Three Gangsters Named as Child's Slayer," *New York Times*, August 8, 1931.

37. "Coll Is Pointed out as Slayer of Child," *New York Times*, December 23, 1931; "Hunted Gang Chief Seen in Subway Here," *New York Times*, August 10, 1931.

38. "Gang Hurls Bomb among Bronx Dry Raiders, Who Escape Blast after Seizing Schultz Beer," *New York Times*, October 3, 1931.

39. "Alert Policeman Broke Coll Case," *New York Times*, October 6, 1931.

40. "Coll and Four Indicted for Baby's Murder," *New York Times*, October 6, 1931; "Two Coll Gangsters Guilty of Murder," *New York Times*, December 1, 1931;

"Coll to Offer Alibi in Killing of Child," *New York Times*, December 17, 1931.

41. "Two Coll Aides Doomed," *New York Times*, December 4, 1931.

42. "Coll Is Pointed out as Slayer of Child," *New York Times*, December 23, 1931; Reynolds, *Courtroom*, 180, 181.

43. "Mystery Witness Points out Harlem Baby Killers," *Milwaukee Sentinel*, December 23, 1931; "Crimson-stained Baby Buggy Trial Evidence," *Sarasota Herald-Tribune* (Sarasota, FL), December 23, 1931.

44. "Coll Defense Fails to Shake Accuser," *New York Times*, December 14, 1931; Reynolds, *Courtroom*, 182.

45. "Sole Coll Accuser Admits Lie on Stand," *New York Times*, December 25, 1931; "Coll Is Acquitted; Case to Seabury," *New York Times*, December 29, 1931; Reynolds, *Courtroom*, 183.

46. "Coll Is Acquitted; Case to Seabury," *New York Times*, December 29, 1931; "Woman, Two Men Slain as Gang Raids Home in Coll Beer Feud," *New York Times*, February 2, 1932.

47. "Hunt Hired Killer in Murder of Coll," *New York Times*, February 9, 1932; "Coll Seized and Freed Second Time in Week," *New York Times*, January 14, 1932.

48. "Woman, Two Men Slain as Gang Raids Home in Coll Beer Feud," *New York Times*, February 2, 1932.

49. "Coll Is Shot Dead in a Phone Booth by Rival Gunmen," *New York Times*, February 8, 1932; "Hunt Hired Killer in Murder of Coll," *New York Times*, February 9, 1932.

50. Reynolds, *Courtroom*, 189; "Same Gang Killed Coll and His Aides," *New York Times*, February 10, 1932.

51. "Schultz Declares He's a 'Benefactor,'" *New York Times*, April 15, 1935.

Chapter 12

1. Sann, *Dutchman*, 49.

2. 256 US 450; 256 US 462; 41 SCt 551; 260 US 477, 480; 43 SCt 197.

3. 14 F2nd 564 (1926); "Seek $748,667 Tax on 'Bootleg' Income," *New York Times*, November 21, 1923.

4. "Liquor Case Mistrial," *Journal and Review* (Aiken, SC), October 10, 1923.

5. 15 F2nd 809; 247 US 259; 47 SCt 607.

6. "Bootleggers Paying Taxes," *New York Times*, January 22, 1924.

7. "U.S. Begins Tax Drive against N.Y. City Gangs," *Syracuse Herald* (Syracuse, NY), June 18, 1931.

8. "Raid Schultz Safes for Tax Evidence," *New York Times*, June 26, 1931; "Government Refuses Schultz Compromise; 'We Want this Man,' Says Morgenthau," *New York Times*, November 27, 1934; "Hunt Dutch Schultz for Tax on Millions," *New York Times*, January 22, 1933; "Schultz Is Jailed in Tax Fraud Case," *New York Times*, November 29, 1934.

9. "New Warrant out for Dutch Schultz," *New*

York Times, January 26, 1933; "Schultz Witness Lost for Third Day," *New York Times*, April 22, 1935.

10. "Schultz Declares He's a 'Benefactor,'" *New York Times*, April 15, 1935; "Detectives Tapped Schultz's Phones" *New York Times*, April 20, 1935; "Tax Consultant Fails to Find Income Amount, Schultz Defense Rests," *Kingston Daily Freeman* (Kingston, NY), July 31, 1935.

11. "Schultz Hideout near City Traced," *New York Times*, December 10, 1934; "Schultz Hunt Is Pressed," *New York Times*, November 24, 1934.

12. Sann, *Dutchman*, 201–202.

13. Ibid., 216; "Schultz in Hiding, Ran Policy Racket," *New York Times*, February 27, 1935.

14. "Schultz Is Next on Federal List," *New York Times*, December 3, 1933.

15. "Bring in Schultz, Police Are Warned," *New York Times*, January 17, 1934; "Schultz Is Jailed in Tax Fraud Case," *New York Times*, November 29, 1934.

16. Sann, *Dutchman*, 227, 231.

17. "Federal Officials Confer on Schultz," *New York Times*, December 1, 1934.

18. "Schultz Gets Bail on a New Tax Writ," *New York Times*, February 21, 1935.

19. "Schultz Beer Sale $2,000,000 a Year, Jurors Are Told," *New York Times*, April 17, 1935; "Profit of Schultz $579,613 for 1930," *New York Times*, April 24, 1935.

20. "Deadlock of Jury Ends Schultz Trial; Seven to Five at the End," *New York Times*, April 28, 1935.

21. "Schultz Concedes $1,600,000 Accounts," *New York Times*, April 18, 1935.

22. "Detectives Tapped Schultz's Phones," *New York Times*, April 20, 1935; "Schultz Jolted as Account Book Appears at Trial," *New York Times*, April 21, 1935.

23. "Girl Tells Secrets of Schultz Office," *New York Times*, April 19, 1935.

24. "Schultz Defense Wilts when Court Admits Accounts," *New York Times*, April 23, 1935.

25. "Profit of Schultz $579,613 for 1930," *New York Times*, April 24, 1935; "$236,026.96 Graft Hinted by Schultz," *New York Times*, April 25, 1935.

26. "Schultz Offered to Pay $100,000 Tax; Defense Is Closed," *New York Times*, April 26, 1935.

27. "Jury Deadlocked in Schultz Case; Shut up for Night," *New York Times*, April 27, 1935.

28. "Deadlock of Jury Ends Schultz Trial; Seven to Five at the End," *New York Times*, April 28, 1935.

29. "Washington Forbids Schultz Compromise," *New York Times*, April 30, 1935; "Schultz Reigned on Discreet Lines," *New York Times*, October 25, 1935.

30. "Seek to Link Schultz with Liquor Gangs," *New York Times*, July 23, 1935.

31. "Schultz and Gang Face Police Drive," *New York Times*, August 4, 1935.

32. "Schultz Beer Rule and Link to Gangs Portrayed to Jury," *New York Times*, July 25, 1935; "Schultz Aide Tries Defiance of Court; Promptly Jailed," *New York Times*, July 28, 1935; "Schultz Proved to Be Gangster," *Raleigh Register* (Beckley, WV), July 25, 1935.

33. "Federal Judge Orders Black Ledger Returned to the Schultz Defense," *Kingston Daily Freeman* (Kingston, NY), July 29, 1935; "Schultz Fate to Be in Hands of Malone Jury Today," *Syracuse Herald* (Syracuse, NY), July 31, 1935.

34. "Four Schultz Pals Jailed at Trial," *Syracuse Herald* (Syracuse, NY), July 25, 1935; "Two Schultz Aides Freed from Jail," *New York Times*, July 27, 1935; "Schultz Aide Tries Defiance of Court; Promptly Jailed," *New York Times*, July 28, 1935.

35. "Police Witness Tells of a Horrible Threat Made by Dutch Schultz," *Kingston Daily Freeman* (Kingston, NY), July 25, 1935.

36. "Tax Consultant Fails to Find Income Amount, Schultz Defense Rests," *Kingston Daily Freeman* (Kingston, NY), July 31, 1935; "Schultz Fate to Be in Hands of Malone Jury Today," *Syracuse Herald* (Syracuse, NY), July 31, 1935; "Dutch Schultz a Kindly Man, Says Defense," *Syracuse Herald* (Syracuse, NY), July 31, 1935.

37. "Schultz Is Freed; Judge Excoriates Jury of Farmers," *New York Times*, August 2, 1935.

38. "Jurors Defend Verdict," *New York Times*, August 3, 1935; "Jurors Reveal Schultz 'Narrowly Beat Raps,'" *Syracuse Herald* (Syracuse, NY), August 2, 1935.

Chapter 13

1. Sann, *Dutchman*, 81.

2. "Schultz Ordered to Appear in Court in State Tax Case," *New York Times*, August 6, 1935; "State Serves Schultz with $70,000 Tax Writ," *New York Times*, September 6, 1935; "Schultz and Gang Face Police Drive," *New York Times*, August 4, 1935.

3. Thomas E. Dewey, *Twenty Against the Underworld*, 273.

4. Sann, *Dutchman*, 257, 258.

5. "Schultz in Cell, Loses Bail Battle," *New York Times*, September 28, 1935; "Schultz Is Jailed; Bail Set at $75,000," *New York Times*, September 27, 1935; "Schultz Released on Reduced Bail," *New York Times*, October 1, 1935.

6. "Schultz Warrant Out," *New York Times*, October 11, 1935; "Schultz Challenges Judge as Prejudiced," *New York Times*, October 18, 1935; "Court Denies Bias in Schultz Case," *New York Times*, October 23, 1935.

7. For accounts of Schultz's plan to murder Dewey, see Turkus and Feder, *Murder*, 128–151; Sann, *Dutchman*, 272–280, 291–293; Dewey, *Twenty Against*, 274–276; Ron Ross, *Bummy Davis vs. Murder, Inc.*, 159–160, 163–171; "Seven Gangsters Seize Schultz Rackets; Fourth Aide Dies," *New York Times*, October 26, 1935.

8. Sann, *Dutchman*, 12–15, 24–29, 32–33; "Schultz Is Shot, One Aide Killed and Three Wounded," *New York Times*, October 24, 1935.

9. Sann, *Dutchman*, 28–30; 33, 35, 36–39, 49.

10. "Schultz Is Shot, One Aide Killed and Three Wounded," *New York Times*, October 24, 1935; Sann, *Dutchman*, 55–56; "Schultz Dies of Wounds without

Naming Slayers; Three Aides Dead, One Dying," *New York Times*, October 25, 1935.

11. Sann, *Dutchman*, 58, 60–65.

12. "Schultz Funeral Is Held Secretly," *New York Times*, October 29, 1935; Sann, *Dutchman*, 93–94.

13. Sann, *Dutchman*, 65.

14. "Prisoner Indicted in Schultz Murder," *Joplin Globe* (Joplin, MO), March 28, 1941.

15. "Schultz Killer Begins Life Prison Term," *Syracuse Herald Journal* (Syracuse, NY), June 11, 1941.

16. Ross, *Bummy Davis*, 164–165, 167.

17. Sann, *Dutchman*, 275, 296.

18. Turkus and Feder, *Murder*, 145.

19. Ross, *Bummy Davis*, 169–170.

20. Sann, *Dutchman*, 35.

21. "Mystery Girl Links 'Bug' in Schultz Case," *Syracuse Herald-American* (Syracuse, NY), June 8, 1941.

22. "Life for Workman as Schultz Killer," *New York Times*, June 11, 1941; "Schultz Killer Begins Life Prison Term," *Syracuse Herald Journal* (Syracuse, NY), June 11, 1941; "Schultz's Killer Freed in Trenton," *New York Times*, March 11, 1964.

Chapter 14

1. Rockaway, *Good to His Mother*, 15; "Thirteen Seized in Offices along Broadway as Bootleg Chiefs," *New York Times*, September 24, 1925.

2. Rockaway, *Good to His Mother*, 15; "Long a Racket Chief," *New York Times*, May 22, 1933; Dewey, *Twenty Against*, 126.

3. Alan Block, *East Side, West Side*, 134.

4. "Gordon Says He Got up to $300 a Week," *New York Times*, December 1, 1933; Dewey, *Twenty Against*, 129; Daniel Waugh, *Egan's Rats*, 98; "Noted Arson Trial Opens in St. Louis," *Janesville Daily Gazette* (Janesville, WI), November 23, 1915.

5. "Max Hassel and Pal, Beer Barons, Slain by Gunmen," *Chester Times* (Chester, PA), April 13, 1933; Waugh, *Egan's Rats*, 132–133.

6. Michael Alexander, *Jazz Age Jews*, 62–63; Dennis Eisenberg, *Meyer Lansky*, 81–82; Rockaway, *Good to His Mother*, 15–16; Thompson and Raymond, *Gang Rule*, 29.

7. "Gordon Says He Got up to $300 a Week," *New York Times*, December 1, 1933.

8. Rockaway, *Good to His Mother*, 120; "Gordon to Testify He Was Underling," *New York Times*, November 30, 1933; "Seek to Nullify 'Dummy' Beer Permit," *Chester Times* (Chester, PA), May 11, 1933; Noralee Frankel, *Stripping Gypsy*, 21; Thompson and Raymond, *Gang Rule*, 30.

9. Dewey, *Twenty Against*, 41; Rockaway, *Good to His Mother*, 120.

10. Marc Mappen, *Prohibition Gangsters*, 90; Dewey, *Twenty Against*, 119, 126, 130–131.

11. Thompson and Raymond, *Gang Rule*, 29; Dewey, *Twenty Against*, 41; "Prison Ends Waxey's Vast Rum Empire," *Syracuse Herald* (Syracuse, NY), December 10, 1933; "The Play," *New York Times*, March 9, 1933.

12. Frankel, *Gypsy*, 20, 22, 23; Dewey, *Twenty Against*, 121.

13. "Thirteen Seized in Offices along Broadway as Bootleg Chiefs," *New York Times*, September 24, 1925; "Rum-runner's Wife Gave Clue for Raid on Broadway Ring," *New York Times*, September 27, 1925.

14. "Biggest Bootleg Ring in the Country, Posing as Real Estate Firm, Broken up in New York," *Gastonia Daily Gazette* (Gastonia, NC), September 24, 1925; "Andrews Arrives to Pick Dry Chief," *New York Times*, September 25, 1925.

15. "Grand Jury Indicts Fifteen as 'Rum Ring,'" *New York Times*, October 31, 1925.

16. "Twenty-four Held in Rum Plot that Cost Twelve Lives," *New York Times*, February 9, 1926; "Fears Vengeance of Rumrunners," *New York Times*, October 9, 1925.

17. "Long a Racket Chief," *New York Times*, May 22, 1933; "Believed Victim of Gang Warfare," *Portsmouth Herald* (Portsmouth, NH), September 12, 1929; "LaGuardia Says Racket Controls Milk," *Syracuse Herald* (Syracuse, NY), September 13, 1929; "Machinegun Kills Jersey Beer Rider," *New York Times*, April 28, 1930; "Racketeer Slain by Auto Gunmen," *New York Times*, September 8, 1929; "Four Kill Beer Chief, Turn Machineguns on Hoboken Police," *New York Times*, March 8, 1930; "Former New Jersey Beer Chief Killed in Hoboken," *Lowell Sun* (Lowell, MA), March 8, 1930.

Chapter 15

1. Michael Pellegrino, *Jersey Brew*, 93, 94–95.

2. Ed Taggert, *Bootlegger*, 8–9.

3. Ibid., 16–17, 18.

4. Ibid., 23, 25, 26.

5. "Perjury Charged to Reading Beer Baron," *New Castle News* (New Castle, PA), September 14, 1928; Taggert, *Bootlegger*, 80.

6. Taggert, *Bootlegger*, 170; "Beer through Sewer Pipeline," *Reading Eagle* (Reading, PA), April 14, 1933.

7. "Dress a Hobby with Hassel," *Reading Eagle* (Reading, PA), April 13, 1933; Taggert, *Bootlegger*, 139.

8. "Max Hassel, Reading 'Beer Baron,' Is Murdered in New Jersey Hotel; Associate Also Killed," *Lebanon Daily News* (Lebanon, PA), April 13, 1933; "League Votes to Send Wreath for Funeral," *Reading Eagle* (Reading, PA), April 13, 1933.

9. "Sewage System Now Threatened by Beer," *Mansfield News* (Mansfield, OH), October 28, 1923.

10. "Brewery Quits Fight; Agrees to Padlocks," *New Castle News* (New Castle, PA), July 1, 1924; Taggert, *Bootlegger*, 32–33; "State Police Raid Reading Brewery," *New Castle News* (New Castle, PA), June 7, 1924.

11. "Millionaire Beer Baron Is Freed," *New Castle News* (New Castle, PA), December 16, 1927; "Fisher Brewery Seized with Three Thousand Barrels of Beer at Reading Wednesday," *Lebanon Semi-weekly News* (Lebanon, PA), April 7, 1927.

12. "Brewery Workers Empty Beer Vats as Guards

Linger," *Helena Daily Independent* (Helena, MT), September 8, 1927.

13. Taggert, *Bootlegger*, 46, 50, 51–52.

14. "Pennsy-grams," *Clearfield Progress* (Clearfield, PA), October 6, 1925; "Held Men for Court," *Lebanon Daily News* (Lebanon, PA), October 7, 1925; Taggert, *Bootlegger*, 52–53; "Hundreds Dip up Beer in Cans from Street Gutters," *Oneonta Daily Star* (Oneonta, NY), October 6, 1925.

15. "Max Hassel Exonerated by Prohibition Agents," *Lebanon Daily News* (Lebanon, PA), February 26, 1925; "Millionaire Beer Baron Is Freed," *New Castle News* (New Castle, PA), December 16, 1927; "Hassel, Marks, Chambers Freed," *Indiana Evening Gazette* (Indiana, PA), June 15, 1927.

16. Taggert, *Bootlegger*, 101–104, 109, 176.

17. Ibid., 91–93, 95.

18. "Millionaire Beer Baron Involved in Philadelphia Mess," *Lock Haven Express* (Lock Haven, PA), September 5, 1928; "Fisher and Reading Breweries 'Dead,'" *Lebanon Daily News* (Lebanon, PA), August 1, 1929.

19. "Beer Declared Piped in Sewers of Camden," *New York Times*, August 29, 1933.

20. Taggert, *Bootlegger*, 115–117, 167.

21. Ibid., 162.

22. Dewey, *Twenty Against*, 124.

23. Ibid., 124–125.

24. Taggert, *Bootlegger*, 176, 180–181; Block, *Organizing Crime*, 137; "Action Laid to Washington," *New York Times*, April 16, 1933; "Clark Asks Facts in 'Beer Murders,'" *New York Times*, April 15, 1933.

25. Taggert, *Bootlegger*, 199–201; Gerald Tomlinson, *Murdered in New Jersey*, 45–46.

26. "Max Hassel, Reading 'Beer Baron,' Is Murdered in New Jersey Hotel; Associate Also Was Killed," *Lebanon Daily News* (Lebanon, PA), April 13, 1933; "League Votes to Send Wreath for Funeral," *Reading Eagle* (Reading, PA), April 13, 1933; Taggert, *Bootlegger*, 203–204; "Elizabeth Police Seek Solution of Dual Murder," *Reading Eagle* (Reading, PA), April 14, 1933.

27. "Waxey Present at Gun Battle," *Steubenville Herald-Star* (Steubenville, OH), May 22, 1933; "Waxey Gordon Says He Paid Income Tax," *New York Times*, May 23, 1933.

28. "Slaying of Hassel before Grand Jury," *Chester Times* (Chester, PA), May 10, 1933.

29. "Arrest Two More in Duffy Slaying," *Lock Haven Express* (Lock Haven, PA), September 3, 1931.

30. Tomlinson, *Murdered*, 46; "Seized in Double Murder," *New York Times*, January 18, 1936.

31. "Link Max Hassel in Counterfeit Plot, Agent Says," *Lebanon Daily News* (Lebanon, PA), June 2, 1933; "Means Says Lindbergh Baby Was Stolen by Rumrunners," *Lowell Sun* (Lowell, MA), May 12, 1933.

32. Eisenberg, *Lansky*, 87–88.

33. Ibid., 88–89.

34. Rockaway, *Good to His Mother*, 119–120; Eisenberg, *Lansky*, 89.

35. "Jersey Beer Baron Is Indicted by U.S.," *Chester Times* (Chester, PA), April 28, 1933; "Gordon as

Golfer Insured for $30,000," *New York Times*, November 24, 1933.

36. "Nationwide Search Starts for Irving Wexler," *Dunkirk Evening Observer* (Dunkirk, NY), April 28, 1933; "Gordon Made by Dry Era," *New York Times*, December 2, 1933; Dewey, *Twenty Against*, 121; Rockaway, *Good to His Mother*, 120–121.

37. Dewey, *Twenty Against*, 78, 118.

38. "Four Gordon Accusers Murdered to Date," *New York Times*, July 4, 1933; "Waxy Gordon Has Taken Appeal to Supreme Court," *Middletown Times Herald* (Middletown, NY), December 9, 1935.

39. Dewey, *Twenty Against*, 118, 119, 122, 136.

40. Ibid., 121, 122, 125, 142–143.

41. "Gordon to Testify He Was Underling," *New York Times*, November 30, 1933.

42. "Gordon Refused $600,000 for Plant," *New York Times*, November 11, 1933.

43. Dewey, *Twenty Against*, 120, 131.

44. "Gordon Says He Got up to $300 a Week," *New York Times*, December 1, 1933.

45. Dewey, *Twenty Against*, 132.

46. "Waxey Gordon Gets Long Term," *Lowell Sun* (Lowell, MA), December 2, 1933.

47. "Son of Beer Baron Dies in Auto Crash," *San Antonio Express*, (San Antonio, TX), December 7, 1933; Arons, *Jews of Sing Sing*, 227; "Waxy Gordon Is off to Federal Jail," *Indiana Evening Gazette* (Indiana, PA), December 8, 1933.

48. "Waxey Gordon Loses Appeal from Sentence," *Salt Lake Tribune* (Salt Lake City, UT), November 5, 1935.

49. "Waxey Gordon in 'Pen,'" *Chester Times* (Chester, PA), February 10, 1934; Aron, *Jews of Sing Sing*, 228–230.

50. "It's the Straight and Narrow, Says Waxey," *Delta Democrat-Times* (Greenville, MS), December 8, 1940.

51. "$42,957,690 Taxes Held Due U.S. Here," *New York Times*, June 25, 1954.

52. "'Waxy Gordon' Held by N.Y. Police on Vagrancy Charge," *Long Beach Independent* (Long Beach, CA), November 18, 1941; "Waxey Gordon Dies in Alcatraz at Sixty-three," *New York Times*, Jun 25, 1952; "Former Beer Baron Leaves Los Angeles on Police Invitation," *San Antonio Express* (San Antonio, TX), November 10, 1941.

53. "Four Seized in Fraud on Sugar Rations," *New York Times*, May 4, 1944; "Fence Charge Laid to Waxey Gordon," *New York Times*, November 5, 1947; "Surplus Disposal by DPC Condemned," *New York Times*, March 23, 1945; "Surplus Property: A Swell Thing," *Time*, October 2, 1944, 77–78.

54. "Agents Arrest Ex-Beer Baron in Dope Sales," *Cumberland Evening Times* (Cumberland, MD), August 3, 1951; "Government Moves to Indict Nation's Top Dope King," *Atlanta Daily World*, August 4, 1951; "Narcotics Agents Nab Waxey Gordon," *New York Times*, August 3, 1951.

55. "Fourth Offense Trial for Waxey Gordon," *New York Times*, August 21, 1951; "Waxey Gordon Faces

Life Term in Prison on Narcotics Guilty Plea to Fourth Felony," *New York Times*, October 20, 1951.

56. "Hearing Granted to Waxey Gordon," *New York Times*, November 10, 1951; "Record from 1905 Given for Gordon," *New York Times*, November 28, 1951; "Gordon's 1909 Case Left up to Court," *New York Times*, November 29, 1951; "Twenty-five Years in Prison for Waxey Gordon," *New York Times*, December 14, 1951.

57. "Heroin Indictment Names Twenty-three on Coast," *New York Times*, March 8, 1952; "Detainer Set on Gordon," *New York Times*, April 11, 1952.

58. "Waxey Gordon Dies in Alcatraz at Sixty-three," *New York Times*, June 25, 1952.

Chapter 16

1. "In Philadelphia Prohibition Is Only an Opinion," *Chicago Daily Tribune*, June 11, 1928.

2. Ibid.

3. Mark Strecker, *Smedley D. Butler, USMC*, 87.

4. Charles Merz, *The Dry Decade*, 140–141.

5. Baldwin, "Smedley D. Butler," 353.

6. "Quaker Devil Dog," *Time*, March 7, 1927, 20; "Return of Butler," *Time*, June 20, 1927, 16.

7. Geoffrey Perrett, *America in the Twenties*, 172.

8. Forrest Revere Black, *Ill-starred Prohibition Cases*, 140.

9. Baldwin, "Smedley D. Butler," 355–356.

10. Joseph K. Willing, "The Profession of Bootlegging," *Annals of the American Academy of Political and Social Science* 125 (May 1926): 48.

11. Baldwin, "Smedley D. Butler," 356.

12. Ibid., 357.

13. Ibid., 360.

14. Perrett, *America*, 173; Baldwin, "Smedley D. Butler," 359–361.

15. Baldwin, "Smedley D. Butler," 361, 362, 365; Strecker, *Butler*, 90; "The Presidency: Mr. Coolidge's Week," *Time*, November 2, 1925, 5.

16. Baldwin, "Smedley D. Butler," 366.

17. "Butler's Last Shots Hit Philadelphia, Its Mayor, and 'Gang,'" *New York Times*, December 28, 1925; Baldwin, "Smedley D. Butler," 366, 367.

18. Baldwin, "Smedley D. Butler," 367; "Political Notes: In Philadelphia," *Time*, January 1, 1926, 8–9.

19. "Butler, Marine Chief, Changes His Mind on Volstead Act," *Ogden Standard-Examiner* (Ogden, UT), January 6, 1927; Robert H. Ferrell, *The Presidency of Calvin Coolidge*, 107.

20. "Fatal Shooting at Night Club," *Tyrone Daily Herald* (Tyrone, PA), February 2, 1927; "Machine Gun War Hits Philadelphia," *New York Times*, February 26, 1927.

21. "Gangsters Pay Homage to Philadelphia Chief," *New York Times*, February 28, 1927.

22. "Goldman Admits Hoff Was Buyer of Machine Guns," *Chester Times* (Chester, PA), September 7, 1928; Celeste A. Morello, *Before Bruno*, 48, 71; "Philadelphia Center of Eastern Rum Gangs," *Decatur Evening Herald* (Decatur, IL), September 4, 1928; "Gangster Is Slain in Quaker City Feud," *New York Times*, September 11, 1928; "Philadelphia Now Has Machinegun Warfare," *Oil City Derrick* (Oil City, PA), February 27, 1927.

23. "Penitentiary Is to Be New Home," *Montana Standard* (Butte, MT), October 2, 1928; "Millionaire Fight Manager Called as Witness in Probe," *New Castle News* (New Castle, PA), August 24, 1928.

24. "Philadelphia Police Scored by District Attorney Monaghan," *New Castle News* (New Castle, PA), September 1, 1928.

25. "Charges Police in Philadelphia with Corruption," *New Castle News* (New Castle, PA), August 31, 1928.

26. "Corruption: In Philadelphia," *Time*, September 17, 1928, 10–11; "Max (Boo Boo) Hoff Dies Broke at Forty-eight," *New York Times*, April 28, 1941.

27. "Rum Organization Served Wide Area," *Charleston Daily Mail* (Charleston, WV), September 7, 1928.

28. "Text of Report Shows Probers Sought in Vain to Uncover Deposits," *Philadelphia Record*, March 21, 1929; "Philadelphia Bootleggers Put $10 Million in Leading Banks of City in Past Year," *New York Times*, August 29, 1928; "Probers Uncover Two Million More Mystery Deposits," *Philadelphia Evening Bulletin*, October 24, 1928; "Philadelphia 'Ring' Generous to Police," *New York Times*, September 14, 1928; "Declares Police Aid Bootleggers in Philadelphia," *New York Times*, September 2, 1928.

29. "In Philadelphia," *Time*, September 17, 1928, 10–11; "Philadelphia Trio Held in Liquor Plot," *New York Times*, November 16, 1928; "Store Owner in Philadelphia Is Drawn into Probe," *New Castle News* (New Castle, PA), September 6, 1928; "Brought from Jail for Quiz by Jury," *Philadelphia Evening Bulletin*, November 5, 1928.

30. "Finds Bribe Record of Bootleg Leader," *New York Times*, August 31, 1928; "Declares Police Aid Bootleggers in Philadelphia," *New York Times*, September 2, 1928.

31. "Clean Philadelphia, Mayor Tells Police," *New York Times*, September 4, 1928.

32. "In Philadelphia," *Time*, September 17, 1928, 10–11.

33. "Says 'Bootleg Ring' Is Defying Inquiry," *New York Times*, September 17, 1928.

34. "'Black Book' Lists Philadelphia 'Ring,'" *New York Times*, September 10, 1928.

35. "Twenty-three Police Caught in Philadelphia Net," *New York Times*, September 26, 1928; "Beckman Denies Taking 'Ring' Bribes," *New York Times*, October 5, 1928; "Bar Police in Raid in Philadelphia," *New York Times*, October 11, 1928.

36. "Monaghan Angry; Valuable Records Reported Missing," *New Castle News* (New Castle, PA), September 10, 1928; "Twenty-three Police Caught in Philadelphia Net," *New York Times*, September 26, 1928.

37. "Rum Racket Account Book Brands Police," *Syracuse Herald* (Syracuse, NY), October 5, 1928; Mark Haller, "Philadelphia Bootlegging and the Report of

the Special August Grand Jury," *The Pennsylvania Magazine of History and Biography* 109, no. 2 (April 1985): 224.

38. "Night Session Is Held by Grand Jury Probers," *Altoona Mirror* (Altoona, PA), November 15, 1928; "Philadelphia Gangs Routed," *Los Angeles Times*, October 8, 1928.

39. "Quaker City Misses Old Holiday Cheer," *New York Times*, December 30, 1928.

40. "Grand Jury Not Able to Indict 'Boo Boo' Hoff," *Chester Times* (Chester, PA), March 29, 1929.

41. "Lifting of Lid Now Awaited by Racketeers," *Philadelphia Record*, March 31, 1929.

42. "Declares Thug Rule Ended in Philadelphia," *New York Times*, May 31, 1929.

43. Irey, *Tax Dodgers*, 39.

44. "Max (Boo Boo) Hoff Dies Broke at Forty-eight," *New York Times*, April 28, 1941.

Chapter 17

1. "Prohibition: Questions and Answers," *Time*, August 26, 1929, 13–14.

2. Ibid.

3. Ibid.; Raymond Clapper, "Happy Days," *American Mercury* 10, no. 37 (January 1927): 26; "Care of the Body," *Los Angeles Times*, February 18, 1923; Garrett Peck, *Prohibition in Washington, D.C.*, 126.

4. "Washington's Wetness Challenges Attention," *New York Times*, March 23, 1924.

5. "Washington Police Find Stills within One Block of Capitol," *New York Times*, November 8, 1924; "Illicit Stills Defy Dry Forces," *New York Times*, October 10, 1926.

6. Alice Roosevelt Longworth, *Crowded Hours*, 314–316.

7. John Kobler, *Ardent Spirits*, 248; "The Man in the Green Hat, Part 1," *Washington Post*, October 24, 1930.

8. "Liquor Clean-up on at Washington," *Dallas Morning News*, November 11, 1923.

9. "Care of the Body," *Los Angeles Times*, February 18, 1923; "Says Capital Had Two Thousand Bootleggers," *New York Times*, September 25, 1929; "Washington's 'Wetness' Excites Warm Interest," *New York Times*, September 29, 1929.

10. "Capitol Not so Bad, Grand Jury Reports," *New York Times*, January 7, 1930.

11. "Washington's Prohibition Farce," *New York Times*, January 14, 1923.

12. Unless otherwise noted, information about Cassiday comes from his published memoirs: "The Man in the Green Hat, Part 1," *Washington Post*, October 24, 1930; "The Man in the Green Hat, Part 2," *Washington Post*, October 25, 1930; "The Man in the Green Hat, Part 3," *Washington Post*, October 26, 1930; "The Man in the Green Hat, Part 4," *Washington Post*, October 27, 1930; "The Man in the Green Hat, Part 5," *Washington Post*, October 28, 1930; "The Man in the Green Hat, Part 6," *Washington Post*, October 29, 1930.

13. "Police Seize Bootlegger at Senate Offices," *Chicago Daily Tribune*, November 1, 1929; "Widespread Crime Shown in Capital," *New York Times*, December 30, 1929.

14. "Cassiday to Await Grand Jury Action," *Washington Post*, February 22, 1930; "S.O.B. Leggers," *Time*, March 3, 1930, 15–16; "Curtis, Doran Put Dry Spy in Senate Office," *Washington Post*, November 1, 1930; "Cassiday Appeals Liquor Conviction," *Washington Post*, January 20, 1931.

15. "Man in Green Hat under Indictment," *Washington Post*, March 5, 1930; "Cassiday Acquitted on One Rum Count," *Washington Post*, June 28, 1930; "Capital's 'Man in Green Hat' Convicted on Liquor Charge," *New York Times*, July 16, 1930; "Cassiday Appeals Liquor Conviction," *Washington Post*, January 20, 1931; "'Man in the Green Hat' Must Go to Jail as Capitol Bootlegger," *New York Times*, April 7, 1931; John Kelly, "Congress Winks at Prohibition in Bootlegger's Tale," *Washington Post*, April 27, 2009.

16. "Prohibition: Washington's War," *Time*, November 11, 1929, 15; "Brookhart Recalls Liquor at Dinner to Honor Senators," *New York Times*, September 25, 1929; "Prohibition: Silver Flasks," *Time*, November 18, 1929, 13–14; "Widespread Crime Shown in Capital," *New York Times*, December 30, 1929.

17. "Prohibition: Drinks for Drys," *Time*, April 8, 1929, 14.

18. "Prohibition: A Dear Friend," *Time*, May 20, 1929, 12; "Judge Tells What He Thinks of Drinker Who Votes Dry," *Sheboygan Journal* (Sheboygan, WI), October 23, 1929.

19. "Veteran Illinois Solon Is Hit by Latest Dry-Wet Break," *Vidette Messenger* (Valparaiso, IN), November 19, 1929; "Dry Congressman Indicted, Liquor Law Violation," *Olean Times* (Olean, NY), November 19, 1929; "Denison Will Seek for Early Trial," *Logansport Pharos-Tribune* (Logansport, IN), November 21, 1929.

20. "Langley Arrested on Drunk Charge; Freed on $10 Bond," *Washington Post*, December 16, 1924; "Langley in Cell Four Hours," *New York Times*, June 11, 1925.

21. "Langley Indicted with Five Others in Liquor Plot," *New York Times*, March 28, 1924.

22. "Langley Again Indicted," *New York Times*, April 8, 1924; "Says Langley Put $115,000 in Banks," *New York Times*, May 7, 1924; "Langley Is Indicted by Kentucky Jury," *Washington Post*, April 8, 1924.

23. "Says Langley Put $115,000 in Banks," *New York Times*, May 7, 1924.

24. "Langley Convicted of Deal in Whiskey," *New York Times*, May 13, 1924; "Testify to Paying Langley for Influence," *New York Times*, May 8, 1924; "Langley Convicted of Liquor Plot by Jury in U.S. Court," *Washington Post*, May 13, 1924.

25. "Langley on Stand in Own Defense," *New York Times*, May 10, 1924; "Langley Is Sentenced to Two Years in Prison for Conspiracy to Violate Prohibition Law," *New York Times*, May 14, 1924.

26. "Langley Is Sentenced to Two Years in Prison

for Conspiracy to Violate Prohibition Law," *New York Times*, May 14, 1924.

27. "Langley, Seeking 'Vindication' from Voters, Is Re-nominated in Kentucky for Congress," *New York Times*, August 4, 1924; "Langley Appeals Verdict," *New York Times*, March 1, 1925; "Representative Langley Must Serve Term, Supreme Court Refusing to Stay Judgment," *New York Times*, January 12, 1926; "Drop Second Langley Case," *New York Times*, November 29, 1925.

28. "Mrs. Langley Seeks to Succeed Husband," *New York Times*, May 18, 1926; "Mrs. Langley Declares Husband Is Vindicated," *New York Times*, August 9, 1926; "National Affairs: Spouse," *Time*, August 23 1926, 7.

29. "Langley Is Paroled after Eleven Months; Leaves Prison for Kentucky Tomorrow," *New York Times*, December 19, 1926; "Coolidge Pardons Langley in Liquor Case; Ex-Representative to Seek Re-election," *New York Times*, December 23, 1928.

30. "Langley Writes Book," *New York Times*, July 16, 1929.

31. Mark Sullivan, *Our Times*, vol. 6, 528–529.

32. Howard Zinn, *LaGuardia In Congress*, 36, 37.

33. Ibid., 182.

34. "LaGuardia Brews; Policeman Amiable," *New York Times*, July 18, 1926.

Chapter 18

1. Francis Pridemore, "What Prohibition Has Done for the Mountaineers," *Outlook* 146, no. 12 (1927): 384.

2. "Eighteen-karat Open-face Whiskey Is Order of the Day in Dixie," *New York Times*, December 24, 1922.

3. "Illicit Stills Defy Dry Forces," *New York Times*, October 10, 1926; "Moonshine Squadron Planned by Andrews," *Portsmouth Daily Times* (Portsmouth, NH), October 23, 1926.

4. "Old War on Moonshine Has Broken out Anew," *New York Times*, May 5, 1929.

5. Francis Pridemore, "How Doth the Busy Moonshiner!" *North American Review* 228, no. 1 (1929): 14–15.

6. Nelson, *Moonshiners*, 14, 24.

7. "Old War on Moonshine Has Broken out Anew," *New York Times*, May 5, 1929; Otto Ernest Rayburn, "Moonshine in Arkansas," *The Arkansas Historical Quarterly* 16, no. 2 (1957): 169; Betty Boles Ellison, *Illegal Odyssey*, 105; S.S. McClintock, "The Kentucky Mountains and Their Feuds: The People and Their Country," *The American Journal of Sociology* 7, no. 1 (July 1901): 8.

8. Rayburn, "Moonshine in Arkansas," 169–170.

9. Carr, *Second Oldest Profession*, 95, 98; Nelson, *Moonshiners*, 26.

10. Robert Carse, *Rum Row*, 220; Carr, *Second Oldest Profession*, 113; Nelson, *Moonshiners*, 27.

11. Lerner, *Dry Manhattan*, 81; Laurence Bergreen, *Capone*, 130–131; Kobler, *Ardent Spirits*, 241; Robert J. Schoenberg, *Mr. Capone*, 110.

12. "'Have One with Me!' Cries Boy Bootlegger," *New York Times*, October 31, 1922.

13. "Moonshine Master Gets a Day in Jail," *New York Times*, June 21, 1921; "Rum Director Off to Canadian Border," *New York Times*, April 2, 1922.

14. "Eight Moonshine Stills Explode in Two Fires; Five Firemen Seriously Burned; One May Die," *New York Times*, January 8, 1922.

15. David Critchley, *The Origin of Organized Crime in America*, 143.

16. "Prohibition: Committee Hearings," *Time*, April 19, 1926, 9.

17. "Peril at Every Turn Awaits Dry Agents," *New York Times*, July 20, 1923.

18. "Old War on Moonshine Has Broken out Anew," *New York Times*, May 5, 1929.

19. Walter W. Liggett, "Ohio — Lawless and Unashamed," *Plain Talk* 7, no. 1 (July 1930): 12.

20. Patrick G. O'Brien and Kenneth J. Peak, *Kansas Bootleggers*, 3, 65–66, 80, 81.

21. "Whiskey Mine in Oklahoma," *New York Times*, January 15, 1926.

22. "Peril at Every Turn Awaits Dry Agents," *New York Times*, July 20, 1923.

23. "Sutro Tunnel Yields Heavy Liquor Cargo," *San Francisco Chronicle*, January 3, 1920.

24. "Airplane Used to Find Illicit Stills," *Boston Daily Globe*, September 29, 1920; "Romance of Nor'west Border Rum Runners," *New York Times*, November 19, 1922.

25. Wilson, *Honky-tonk Town*, 51, 74; Leona Lampi, "Red Lodge: From a Frenetic Past of Crows, Coal, and Boom and Bust Emerges a Unique Festival of Diverse Nationality Groups," *Montana: The Magazine of Western History* 11, no. 3 (Summer 1961): 26.

26. Loyal Durand, Jr., "'Mountain Moonshining' in East Tennessee," *Geographical Review* 46, no. 2 (April 1956): 181; Mark Davis, "Northern Choices: Rural Forest County in the 1920s," *The Wisconsin Magazine of History* 79, no. 2 (Winter 1995-96): 109, 110; "Uncover Three Great Stills of Kentucky Moonshine in North Woods of Wisconsin," *Capital Times* (Madison, WI), October 17, 1922; "Moonshiners Follow Ku Klux Methods," *New York Times*, June 18, 1923.

27. Walker, *One Eye Closed*, 246, 411, 70, 71–72, 75.

28. "Bootlegging in Arkansas Succeeds Farm Industry," *Washington Post*, July 28, 1929.

29. Ibid.

30. Henry M. Caudill, *Night Comes to the Cumberlands*, 156, 158–159.

31. "Governor of Kentucky Asks Dry Enforcement," *New York Times*, January 25, 1921.

32. "Five Shot in Moonshine War," *Rock Valley Bee* (Rock Valley, IA), February 25, 1921; "Dry Men Lured to Death," *New York Times*, July 26, 1921; "Eight Dead in Two Days in Moonshine War," *Gettysburg Times* (Gettysburg, PA), March 31, 1923.

33. "Moonshine Causes Murder," *New York Times*, May 12, 1921.

34. "Kentucky Jail Is Stormed by Mob," *Dallas Morning News*, December 11, 1921.

35. "Three Dry Agents Slain by Moonshiners; Wounded Kentuckian Tells of Night Battle," *New York Times*, August 11, 1923; "Unhurt in Moonshine Row," *New York Times*, August 12, 1923.

36. "Moonshiners Kill Second Dry Raider, Hold off Big Posse," *New York Times*, December 11, 1922; Henry M. Caudill, *Slender Is the Thread*, 16.

37. "Moonshiners Kill Second Dry Raider, Hold off Big Posse," *New York Times*, December 11, 1922; Caudill, *Thread*, 16, 18.

38. "Moonshiners Kill Second Dry Raider, Hold off Big Posse," *New York Times*, December 11, 1922; Caudill, *Thread*, 16–17; "Moonshiners Hold out in the Kentucky Wilds," *New York Times*, December 12, 1922.

39. "Plan to Use Airplanes against Moonshiners," *New York Times*, December 13, 1922.

40. Caudill, *Thread*, 17–18; "Moonshiner Killed, Third Raider Slain," *New York Times*, December 16, 1922.

41. "Ballard Trial Opened Yesterday," *Middlesboro Daily News* (Middlesboro, KY), June 10, 1924; "Mountain Moonshine King Gives Big Banquet to Youth Freed of Killing Two Agents," *Syracuse Herald* (Syracuse, NY), September 28, 1924.

42. "Killing Dry Agent Is No Crime in Kentuck," *Sunday Morning Star* (Wilmington, DE), September 28, 1924.

Chapter 19

1. "Detroit Is the 'Wettest City' He Worked In, Dry Administrator Says in Resigning," *New York Times*, November 4, 1925.

2. Larry Englemann, *Intemperance*, 159.

3. "Battling the Rum Runners in Prohibition's No Man's Land," *New York Times*, July 29, 1923.

4. "Ontario Opens the Beer Spigot," *New York Times*, May 17, 1925.

5. "Four Hundred Boats Run Rum Across Detroit River Is Estimate," *Bridgeport Telegram* (Bridgeport, CT), July 19, 1927.

6. Kathy Covert Warnes, *Ecorse, Michigan*, 111; "Youths Captured with Load of Beer," *Ogden Standard-Examiner* (Ogden, UT), February 28, 1923.

7. Schneider, *Iced*, 188; Warnes, *Ecorse*, 113.

8. "Rum War Forces Mass on the Detroit Front," *New York Times*, June 23, 1929.

9. Warnes, *Ecorse*, 113; "Rum Smugglers Don Sheets, Drag Sleds across Ice and Snow," *Chicago Daily Tribune*, December 25, 1929.

10. "Find Horse a Bootlegger," *New York Times*, February 23, 1926.

11. "Nation's Wettest Spot near Detroit," *Iowa City Press-Citizen* (Iowa City, IA), February 8, 1923; Schneider, *Iced*, 193–194.

12. "Submarine Cable and Sled Used to Transport Liquor from Mud Island across Line into U.S.," *Dallas Morning News*, September 15, 1929; "Submarine Rumrunner Seized," *Detroit Free Press*, December 25, 1931.

13. "Report Torpedoes Used to Shoot Whiskey into Detroit," *New York Times*, May 8, 1920.

14. "Battling the Rum Runners in Prohibition's No Man's Land," *New York Times*, July 29, 1923.

15. "Our 'Rum Capital': An Amazing Picture," *New York Times*, May 27, 1928.

16. Philip P. Mason, *Rumrunning and the Roaring Twenties*, 45.

17. Schneider, *Iced*, 185; Mason, *Rumrunning*, 45; Newman, *King of the Castle*, 74.

18. "Border Battle on Rum Grows in Intensity," *New York Times*, May 22, 1927.

19. "Liquor Smuggling," *Sandusky Star Journal* (Sandusky, OH), June 20, 1929.

20. "Prohibition: Canada Clamps Down," *Time*, June 9, 1930, 14.

21. "Plan New Attack on Border Liquor," *New York Times*, September 14, 1930; Ted R. Hennigar, *The Rum Running Years*, 91–92.

22. Paul R. Kavieff, *Detroit's Infamous Purple Gang*, 9.

23. Rockaway, *Good to His Mother*, 63–64, 76–77.

24. Robert A. Rockaway, "The Notorious Purple Gang: Detroit's All-Jewish Prohibition Era Mob," *Shofar: An Interdisciplinary Journal of Jewish Studies* 20, no. 1 (Fall 2001): 113; Edward Butts, *Outlaws of the Lakes*, 231.

25. Rockaway, "Notorious Purple Gang," 113.

26. "Crime: U.S. Murder," *Time*, March 25, 1929, 13; "Tenth Victim for Gangsters," *Dallas Morning News*, July 17, 1930.

27. "Gangsters Kill Trio in Detroit," *Los Angeles Times*, September 17, 1931; Paul R. Kavieff, *The Purple Gang*, 110–114; Butts, *Outlaws*, 234–237.

28. "More 'Blind Pigs' in Detroit than Legalized Rum Stores in Montreal," *Evening Independent* (Massillon, OH), June 13, 1929; Mason, *Rumrunning*, 74.

29. Kavieff, *Detroit's Infamous*, 40.

30. Englemann, *Intemperance*, 135, 141.

31. "Raids Are Tipped Off," *Boston Daily Globe*, June 10, 1923.

32. "'Izzy' and 'Moe' Tips Start Detroit Raid," *New York Times*, June 15, 1923.

33. Ronald Allen Goldberg, *America in the Twenties*, 110; Mason, *Rumrunning*, 73; Rockaway, *Good to His Mother*, 73.

34. "Admits 'Framing' Rum Law Lifers," *New York Times*, November 22, 1929; "Upholds Life Term for Bootleggers," *New York Times*, January 8, 1929; "Liquor Law Lifer Wins Court Review," *New York Times*, March 28, 1928.

35. "Life Term for Fourth Dry Law Offense Is Pronounced on a Michigan Bootlegger," *New York Times*, November 29, 1928.

36. "Liquor Life Sentence Reversed In Michigan," *New York Times*, March 8, 1930; "Jail Terms of Michigan Wet 'Lifers' Cut; Mrs. Miller and Four Men Will Serve Six Years," *New York Times*, January 16, 1930; "Prohibition: From and After," *Time*, January 14, 1929, 12.

37. "Repeal of 'Life-for-a-Pint' Law Signed by

Michigan Governor," *New York Times*, April 3, 1929; "'Pint Lifer' Case Dropped," *New York Times*, April 9, 1930; "Liquor Life Case Quashed," *New York Times*, April 20, 1930.

38. "Eleven States Will Go to Polls This Week," *New York Times*, September 8, 1930.

Chapter 20

1. "Rum War Forces Mass on the Detroit Front," *New York Times*, June 23, 1929.

2. "Says Liquor Flood Pours from Canada," *New York Times*, May 23, 1923; "In the 'Rum Capital' of Dry America," *New York Times*, July 14, 1929.

3. "Rum Runners Are Using Machine Guns," *Marshall Evening Chronicle* (Marshall, MI), June 1, 1929.

4. "Rum Runners Are Arming and Clash on River with Coast Guard Is Expected," *Dallas Morning News*, June 15, 1929; "Border Towns Ready to Help in Booze Drive," *Chicago Daily Tribune*, June 20, 1929.

5. "Eight Captured in Liquor War," *Los Angeles Times*, June 18, 1929.

6. "Says Liquor Flood Pours from Canada," *New York Times*, May 23, 1923.

7. Ibid.

8. "Steady Flow of Beer to Detroit," *Boston Daily Globe*, June 10, 1923.

9. Warnes, *Ecorse*, 110.

10. "Our 'Rum Capital': An Amazing Picture," *New York Times*, May 27, 1928.

11. "Hogan's Alley Laughs at Dry Army," *Manitowoc Herald-News* (Manitowoc, WI), September 27, 1924.

12. Warnes, *Ecorse*, 111.

13. "Ecorse Excited at Charges Its Rum Runners Are Rich," *Evening Courier and Reporter* (Waterloo, IA), May 25, 1923.

14. "Federal Officials Seize Two Hundred Boats in Face of Angry Mob," *Owosso Argus-Press* (Owosso, MI), July 14, 1923; "Drys Seize Fleet in Detroit River," *New York Times*, July 15, 1923.

15. "Federal Officials Seize Two Hundred Boats in Face of Angry Mob," *Owosso Argus-Press* (Owosso, MI), July 14, 1923.

16. "Eight Captured in Liquor War," *Los Angeles Times*, June 18, 1929; Warnes, *Ecorse*, 115–116.

17. "Police Head Called Liquor Runners' Aid," *Washington Post*, April 12, 1929.

18. "Muster Dry Force in Detroit Area," *New York Times*, June 7, 1929.

19. "Rum War Forces Mass on the Detroit Front," *New York Times*, June 23, 1929.

20. Ibid.; "Rum Runners Shift Scene of Operations," *News-Palladium* (Benton Harbor, MI), June 14, 1929; "Liquor Runners Unite to Fight Huge Dry Navy," *Chicago Daily Tribune*, June 13, 1929; "Dry Chiefs Order Drive in Detroit," *New York Times*, June 11, 1929; "Big Force to Combat Detroit Liquor Flow," *New York Times*, June 9, 1929.

21. "Liquor Runners Unite to Fight Huge Dry Navy," *Chicago Daily Tribune*, June 13, 1929.

22. "Send Report on Battle," *New York Times*, June 21, 1929.

23. "Lake Liquor Runners Combine for New War," *New York Times*, June 13, 1929; "Rum Craft Flee Detroit," *New York Times*, June 14, 1929.

24. "Rum-runners Fire on Customs Boat," *New York Times*, June 20, 1929.

25. Ibid.; "Rum Runners, Customs Boat in Gun Fight," *Dallas Morning News*, June 20, 1929; "Rum Runners and U.S. Craft in Gun Battle," *Portsmouth Daily Times* (Portsmouth, NH), June 19, 1929.

26. "Keep Liquor in Canada Is Aim of U.S. Dry Forces in Detroit River Rum War," *Evening Independent* (Massillon, OH), June 27, 1929.

27. "Liquor Cargoes Dumped," *New York Times*, July 5, 1929.

28. "Liquor Boats Shift Route," *New York Times*, July 8, 1929; "Rum Operators Reap Harvest of Drys' Drive," *Chicago Daily Tribune*, June 17, 1929; "Send Report on Battle," *New York Times*, June 21, 1929; "Stop that Canadian Rum Flow: Uncle Sam's Dilemma," *Galveston Daily News* (Galveston, TX), July 21, 1929.

29. "Largest Liquor Seizure on Detroit River Made," *Washington Post*, July 24, 1929.

30. "A Winning Fight," *Sterling Daily Gazette* (Sterling, IL), July 18, 1929.

31. "Land Liquor Cargoes in Heart of Detroit," *New York Times*, August 15, 1929; "Detroit Docks Are Rum Base," *Bradford Era* (Bradford, PA), August 15, 1929.

32. "To Clean up Entire Patrol," *New York Times*, December 1, 1928.

33. "Five Hundred Prohibition Men Dry Canadian Border Rum Flow," *Appleton Post-Crescent* (Appleton, WI), July 4, 1929; "Rum Immigrants Return to Detroit," *Owosso Argus-Press* (Owosso, MI), December 26, 1929.

34. "Ten Held in Detroit Grafting Case," *New York Times*, November 27, 1930; "Border Patrol Graft Charged in Detroit Area," *Dallas Morning News*, November 29, 1930; "Half Border Force Accused in Detroit," *New York Times*, November 29, 1930; "Nine Ex-customs Men Guilty," *New York Times*, December 14, 1930.

Chapter 21

1. "Happy Hunting Ground for Racketeers," *New York Times*, October 3, 1930.

2. Kenneth Allsop, *The Bootleggers*, 31.

3. "Chicago Vice Profit Put at $13,500,000," *New York Times*, May 22, 1928.

4. "Chicago Police Chief," *Oshkosh Daily Northwestern* (Oshkosh, WI), November 10, 1920; "Bolehsviki and Loafers on Chicago Police Force Must Go," *Oshkosh Daily Northwestern* (Oshkosh, WI), February 12, 1921.

5. "Nearly One Thousand Arrested in Chicago," *Bradford Era* (Bradford, PA), November 22, 1920.

6. "Entire Chicago Police Force Being Used for

Stamping out 'Vice,'" *Sandusky Star Journal* (Sandusky, OH), March 6, 1923; "Judges Scored by Police Head," *Salt Lake Tribune* (Salt Lake City, UT), March 23, 1922.

7. "Chicago Police under Federal Scrutiny; Chief Says Prohibition There Is a Failure," *New York Times*, September 26, 1921.

8. Ibid.; "Prohibition Is Failure Avers Chicago Chief," *Anaconda Standard* (Anaconda, MT), September 26, 1921.

9. "'Real Prohibition' Promised Chicago," *New York Times*, December 16, 1921.

10. "Will Enforce the Dry Law in Illinois," *Davenport Democrat and Leader* (Davenport, IA), January 8, 1922.

11. "A Wet Mayor Dries Chicago," *New York Times*, November 18, 1923.

12. "Charged Chicago Police Are in League with Vice," *Mexia Daily News* (Mexia, TX), April 18, 1923.

13. "Chicago Police Have Enough to Do, Says Chief," *Sheboygan Press* (Sheboygan, WI), October 12, 1925.

14. "115,000 'Dry' Cases Tried in Four Years," *New York Times*, February 18, 1924.

15. "Trims Dry Squad for New Drive," *Wisconsin Rapids Daily Tribune* (Wisconsin Rapids, WI), September 19, 1925; "Dry Czar Yellowley Says He Is After 'Big Fellows' First in Planning Drought," *Sheboygan Press* (Sheboygan, WI), September 12, 1925.

16. "New Year Gets Its Customary Gay Greeting," *Kokomo Tribune* (Kokomo, IN), January 1, 1926; "Pro Officers Raid Chicago Dens; New Year Will Be Dry," *Morning Avalanche* (Lubbock, TX), January 1, 1926.

17. "Brewers in Three States Must Get Special Permits," *Steubenville Herald Star* (Steubenville, OH), December 9, 1925; "City Dads, Rail Men, Police in Beer Scandals," *Decatur Review* (Decatur, IL), October 27, 1925; "Yellowley Revokes More Liquor Permits," *Daily Globe* (St. Paul, MN), February 1, 1926.

18. "Judge Rebukes Dry Agents," *New York Times*, April 23, 1926.

19. Allsop, *Bootleggers*, 42–43.

20. "Judges Scored by Police Head," *Salt Lake Tribune* (Salt Lake City, UT), March 23, 1922.

21. "Chicago Vice Crusade," *Washington Post*, May 14, 1923; "Give Chicago its Due," *San Antonio Express* (San Antonio, TX), April 8, 1923; "A Wet Mayor Dries Chicago," *New York Times*, November 18, 1923.

22. "Chicago's Jail Cells," *Rock Valley Bee* (Rock Valley, IA), November 21, 1924.

23. Ibid.

24. John Landesco, "Prohibition and Crime," *Annals of the American Academy of Political and Social Science* 163 (September 1932): 122.

25. "Plot to Kill Dry Raiders Uncovered," *San Antonio Express* (San Antonio, TX), May 29, 1924.

26. Allsop, *Bootleggers*, 73–75.

27. "Take O'Bannion as He Directs Hijacker Raid," *Chicago Daily Tribune*, January 23, 1924; "O'Bannion & McCarthy Hit by U.S. Booze Indictments," *Chicago Daily Tribune*, April 26, 1924; "Names in Little Black Book Give Needed Evidence," *Sandusky Star Journal* (Sandusky, OH), May 20, 1924.

28. "Plot to Kill Dry Raiders Uncovered," *San Antonio Express* (San Antonio, TX), May 29, 1924.

29. "Names in Little Black Book Give Needed Evidence," *Sandusky Star Journal* (Sandusky, OH), May 20, 1924; "Federal Jury Indicts Thirty-eight in Brewery Case," *Chicago Daily Tribune*, May 28, 1924; "Get Million Dollars' Worth of Liquor," *Oelwein Daily Register* (Oelwein, IA), May 31, 1924.

30. "Underworld Pomp at Burial of Chief," *New York Times*, November 15, 1924; "Church Rites Denied for Chicago Gunman," *New York Times*, November 14, 1924.

31. "'Strong Arm' Squad for Chicago Thugs," *New York Times*, November 16, 1924.

32. "Shot Down as He Steps from Auto with Wife," *LaCrosse Tribune and Leader Press* (LaCrosse, WI), January 25, 1925; "Two Suspects in Chicago Slaying Held by Police," *Logansport Press* (Logansport, IN), November 19, 1924; "Guns Bang in Chi," *Kokomo Tribune* (Kokomo, IN), November 21, 1924.

33. "Chicago Seeks Help to Check Crime," *New York Times*, March 7, 1926.

34. Allsop, *Bootleggers*, 86.

35. "King Chicago Underworld Is Sent to Jail," *Manitowoc Herald News* (Manitowoc, WI), January 17, 1925.

36. "Shot Down as He Steps from Auto with Wife," *LaCrosse Tribune and Leader Press* (LaCrosse, WI), January 25, 1925; "One Shot Down in Chicago Beer War," *Charleston Daily Mail* (Charleston, WV), January 25, 1925.

37. "Mrs. Torrio and Husband Guarded," *Sandusky Star-Journal* (Sandusky, OH), January 27, 1925.

38. Ibid.; "One Assailant of Chicago Man Is Identified," *Albuquerque Journal* (Albuquerque, NM), January 27, 1925.

39. Allsop, *Bootleggers*, 50–51, 105.

40. Sann, *Lawless*, 209–210; "Gunmen in Machines," *Kokomo Tribune* (Kokomo, IN), September 21, 1926.

41. "Hawthorne Inn Is Scene of Gun Fray; Bullets Wound Two," *Daily Illini* (Champaign-Urbana, IL), September 21, 1926.

42. "Two Killed, Four Others Wounded in Gangland War," *Evening Courier* (Waterloo, IA), October 12, 1926; Allsop, *Bootleggers*, 113.

43. "Chicago Cops Plan Warfare," *Iowa City Press-Citizen* (Iowa City, IA), October 14, 1926; "Chicago Streets Are Patrolled by Police in Autos," *Simpson's Leader-Times* (Kittanning, PA), October 13, 1926.

44. "Capone, King of Beer Gangsters, Begs for Peace," *Wisconsin Rapids Daily Tribune* (Wisconsin Rapids, WI), October 13, 1926.

45. "Gangland Lays Its Guns Aside; Peace Declared," *Chicago Daily Tribune*, October 21, 1926; John Landesco, *Organized Crime in Chicago*, 103.

46. "Capone Is in Constant Fear of Assassins," *Urbana Daily Courier* (Urbana, IL), March 29, 1929.

47. Sann, *Lawless*, 210; "Chicago Vice Profit Put at $13,500,000," *New York Times*, May 22, 1928.

48. "Chicago Gangsters Seized in New War," *New York Times*, November 22, 1927.

49. Landesco, *Organized Crime*, 103–104.

50. "'Scarface' Al Guarded Constantly against Attack by Rival Gangsters," *Ames Daily Tribune and Evening Times* (Ames, IA), March 9, 1929; "Stege Orders New Invasion of Beer Belt," *Sheboygan Press* (Sheboygan, WI), October 11, 1928.

51. "Wounded Gangster Attacked in Hospital by Gunmen," *Appleton Post-Crescent* (Appleton, WI), February 25, 1930; "'Polack Joe' Saltis Has a Crimson Life," *Oelwein Daily Register* (Oelwein, IA), July 11, 1928.

52. "Gang Guns in Chicago Blaze but Miss Mark," *Evening Independent* (Massillon, OH), June 30, 1928; "Machine Guns in Four Cars Rake Garage," *Charleston Daily Mail* (Charleston, WV), October 10, 1928.

53. "Stege Orders New Invasion of Beer Belt," *Sheboygan Press* (Sheboygan, WI), October 11, 1928; "Chicago Hoodlums Handed their Hats," *Daily Inter Lake* (Kalispell, MT), May 9, 1930.

Chapter 22

1. Sann, *Lawless*, 214.

2. "Seven Chicago Gangsters Slain by Firing Squad of Rivals, Some in Police Uniforms," *New York Times*, February 15, 1929; "Slay Doctor in Massacre," *Chicago Daily Tribune*, February 15, 1929.

3. "Slay Doctor in Massacre," *Chicago Daily Tribune*, February 15, 1929; William J. Helmer and Arthur J. Bilek, *The St. Valentine's Day Massacre*, 19.

4. Helmer and Bilek, *Massacre*, 17–19.

5. "Slay Doctor in Massacre," *Chicago Daily Tribune*, February 15, 1929.

6. "Chicago Mobilizes Police for Dry War," *New York Times*, February 17, 1929.

7. "Ransack State's Attorney's Files in Gang Killing," *Evening Courier* (Waterloo, IA), February 27, 1929; Helmer and Bilek, *Massacre*, 141.

8. "Trap Second Gangster in Chicago Murders," *New York Times*, March 1, 1929.

9. Daniel Waugh, *Egan's Rats*, 243–244.

10. Dennis E. Hoffman, *Scarface Al and the Crime Crusaders*, 72–73, 76.

11. "Five Arrests Follow Finding of Gang Car in Chicago Slayings," *New York Times*, February 23, 1929.

12. Helmer and Bilek, *Massacre*, 146–147, 282; "Gang Murder Car Believed Found," *New York Times*, February 22, 1929.

13. "Ransack State's Attorney's Files in Gang Killing," *Evening Courier* (Waterloo, IA), February 27, 1929.

14. "Capone Aide Nabbed in Chicago Murders," *New York Times*, February 28, 1929; "Six Arrested in Chicago Killings," *Montana Standard* (Butte, MT), February 23, 1929; Helmer and Bilek, *Massacre*, 142–143, 161; "Two Gangsters Booked for Chicago Killings," *The Independent* (Helena, MT), March 2, 1929.

15. "Gang Romance of 'Gunner' McGurn and His 'Baby Blonde Alibi,'" *Ogden Standard-Examiner* (Ogden, UT), April 21, 1929; "M'Gurn Jailed as Member of Massacre Gang," *Lima News* (Lima, OH), February 28, 1929; "Trap Second Gangster in Chicago Murders," *New York Times*, March 1, 1929; "Gangster's Sweetheart Spoofs Reporters," *Bismarck Tribune* (Bismarck, ND), March 1, 1929; "Genna Gangster Taken in Chicago," *San Antonio Express* (San Antonio, TX), March 7, 1929; "Take Testimony in Gang Slaying," *Evening Huronite* (Huron, SD), March 9, 1929.

16. "Gangster's Sweetheart Spoofs Reporters," *Bismarck Tribune* (Bismarck, ND), March 1, 1929; "Two Are Indicted in Chicago Slayings," *New York Times*, March 16, 1929; "Two Booked on Gang Massacre Murder Charge," *Lima News* (Lima, OH), March 2, 1929.

17. "McGurn, Scalise, Fanelli, and Blonde Gun Girl Arraigned," *Evening Courier* (Waterloo, IA), March 16, 1929; "Six Arrested in Connection with Chicago Massacre," *Coshocton Tribune* (Coshocton, OH), March 8, 1929.

18. "Chicago's Criminal 'Blue Book' To Curb Racketeers," *Fresno Bee* (Fresno, CA), November 25, 1928.

19. "McGurn, Capone Aide, Gets Mann Act Trial Delayed," *Wisconsin State Journal* (Madison, WI), April 16, 1931; Jeffrey Gusfield, *Deadly Valentines*, 304.

20. "Police Disperse Overflow Mob of Dempsey Fans," *Chicago Daily Tribune*, December 7, 1923; "Tennis Body to Ignore Bill's Threat to Quit," *Chicago Daily Tribune*, December 15, 1923.

21. Fred D. Pasley, *Al Capone*, 168.

22. "Machine Gun Roars; Two Shot," *Chicago Daily Tribune*, March 8, 1928; "Three Armed Gunmen Shoot Realty Agent," *Oshkosh Daily Northwestern* (Oshkosh, WI), March 8, 1928; "Gangsters Try to Get McGurn," *Ogden Standard-Examiner* (Ogden, UT), April 18, 1928; "McGurn Again Guns' Target; Escapes Unhurt," *Chicago Daily Tribune*, April 18, 1928.

23. "Perspective: When Machine Gun Jack Put Himself in the Rough," *New York Times*, June 8, 2003; Gusfield, *Deadly Valentines*, 238–244.

24. "Capone Aide Nabbed in Chicago Murders," *New York Times*, February 28, 1929; "Gang Romance of 'Gunner' McGurn and His 'Baby Blonde Alibi,'" *Ogden Standard-Examiner* (Ogden, UT), April 21, 1929.

25. "Gangster's Sweetheart Spoofs Reporters," *Bismarck Tribune* (Bismarck, ND), March 1, 1929.

26. "Three Killed as Flareback to Gangsters," *Newark Advocate* (Newark, OH), March 8, 1929.

27. "Three Chicago Gang Members Are Massacred," *Titusville Herald* (Titusville, PA), May 9, 1929.

28. "Gangland Violates Sacred Custom by Not Bedecking Biers of Dead Men," *Bismarck Tribune* (Bismarck, ND), May 10, 1929.

29. "Three Capone Henchmen Are Shot to Death," *New York Times*, May 9, 1929.

30. "Capone Takes Cover in Jail," *Chicago Daily Tribune*, May 18, 1929; "Triple Killing Laid to Feud in Sicilian Gang," *Chicago Daily Tribune*, May 9, 1929.

31. Luciano Iorizzo, *Al Capone*, 49.

32. "Two Booked on Gang Massacre Murder Charge," *Lima News* (Lima, OH), March 2, 1929.

33. "Trial of Two for Chicago Massacre Delayed to May 6," *Mason City Globe-Gazette* (Mason City, IA), April 29, 1929; "Continue Case," *Decatur Daily Review* (Decatur, IL), October 1, 1929.

34. "Dismiss Case against Gangster," *Oelwein Daily Register* (Oelwein, IA), December 2, 1929; "Gang Murder Charge against M'Gurn Dropped," *Chicago Daily Tribune*, December 3, 1929.

35. "Former Capone Gangster Gets Comic Valentine along with Fatal Hoodlum Bullets," *Fitchburg Sentinel* (Fitchburg, MA), February 15, 1936.

36. "Gang War Feared in McGurn Killing," *New York Times*, February 16, 1936; Gusfield, *Deadly Valentines*, 259–263; "McGurn Slain in Gang Purge," *Chicago Daily Tribune*, February 16, 1936.

37. "Noted Gunman Assassinated," *Frederick News-Post* (Frederick, MD), February 17, 1936.

38. "'Machine Gun' McGurn Is Slain in Chicago; Linked to St. Valentine 'Massacre' of 1929," *New York Times*, February 15, 1936.

39. "The Capone Gunner's Last Ride Proved that Gaudy Gangster Funerals Are Passé," *Salt Lake Tribune* (Salt Lake City, UT), April 5, 1936.

40. "Slaying of Officer Leads to Bond Find," *New York Times*, December 16, 1929; Helmer and Bilek, *Massacre*, 190–191.

41. Hoffman, *Scarface Al*, 81.

42. "Guns Link Burke to Moran Killings," *New York Times*, December 24, 1929.

43. Waugh, *Egan's Rats*, 260.

44. www.foia.fbi.gov.

45. Ibid.

46. Waugh, *Egan's Rats*, 260–265.

Chapter 23

1. Irey, *Tax Dodgers*, xvi.

2. "Crime: Glum Gorilla," *Time*, December 19, 1927, 11.

3. "Capone Enters Jail to Serve One Year," *New York Times*, May 18, 1929.

4. "Rum Genii Makes Dog Catcher's Son an Aladdin," *Chicago Daily Tribune*, June 3, 1923; "Butch's Gold Knobs Let in 'Dry' Sleuths," *New York Times*, July 22, 1923; "Gold-knob Palace of Brewer Seized," *New York Times*, July 8, 1923; "Butch Crowley Talks U.S. out of $70,000 Income Tax," *Chicago Daily Tribune*, October 22, 1924.

5. "Butch Crowley," *Chicago Daily Tribune*, November 22, 1924.

6. "U.S. Checks up Modest Terry's Beer Millions," *Chicago Daily Tribune*, December 7, 1923; "Strong Men Sob as Seventy-five Thousand Gallons of Beer Hits Sewer," *Chicago Daily Tribune*, July 20, 1924.

7. "U.S. Checks up Modest Terry's Beer Millions," *Chicago Daily Tribune*, December 7, 1923; "Druggan, Lake, Nabobs of Beer, Give up Today," *Chicago Daily Tribune*, March 7, 1924; "Druggan and Lake Sentenced to Year in Jail," *Chicago Daily Tribune*, July 12, 1924.

8. "Druggan, Lake in Tangle with U.S. over Taxes," *Chicago Daily Tribune*, January 19, 1926; "Bootleggers Net $1,500,000," *New York Times*, February 5, 1926; "Druggan, Lake Sued by U.S. for $517,000 Taxes," *Chicago Daily Tribune*, September 2, 1926; "$2,069,409 Tax Lien Filed on Rum Profits," *Chicago Daily Tribune*, July 11, 1928; "$2,069,409 Tax Suit Filed in Chicago Bootlegging," *New York Times*, July 11, 1928; "Druggan Home Auctioned," *New York Times*, December 28, 1929.

9. "Druggan, Lake Indicted by U.S. as Tax Dodgers," *Chicago Daily Tribune*, March 14, 1928; "Income Tax Prosecutions Hit Hard Blows at Racketeering," *New York Times*, April 19, 1931; "Guilt Is Affirmed for Ralph Capone," *New York Times*, July 25, 1931.

10. "End Tax Sentence Fight," *New York Times*, December 20, 1931; "Druggan Gets Favors," *New York Times*, August 3, 1933; "Six Hundred Convicts Riot at Leavenworth," *New York Times*, August 19, 1933; "Frankie Lake Dead; Ex-gang Leader, Fifty-eight," *New York Times*, January 12, 1947.

11. "Grim Two-year Hunt Traced Capone Cash," *New York Times*, June 6, 1931.

12. "Gangster Capone to Prison," *Chicago Daily Tribune*, April 26, 1930; "Ralph Capone Guilty in Income Tax Fraud," *New York Times*, April 26, 1930; "Ralph Capone Banked $1,851,840 in Five Years," *New York Times*, April 19, 1930; "Ralph Capone Pays Tax," *New York Times*, February 13, 1958; "Capone Pays $2,000," *New York Times*, July 7, 1961.

13. "Guzik, Capone Chief, Guilty," *Chicago Daily Tribune*, November 20, 1930; Allsop, *Bootleggers*, 304, 317.

14. Allsop, *Bootleggers*, 64.

15. "Four-year Federal War on Chicago Gangs Told by Prosecutor," *New York Times*, April 3, 1932.

16. "Pastor Opens Drive," *Kokomo Tribune* (Kokomo, IN), May 18, 1925; "Document Prepared by Special Agent Frank J. Wilson, Intelligence Unit, Bureau of Internal Revenue, Update on Status of Capone Investigation, December 21, 1933," 12–13.

17. "Document Prepared by Special Agent Frank J. Wilson," 10–11, 12–13.

18. Ibid., 4–5; Irey, *Tax Dodgers*, 52.

19. "Document Prepared by Special Agent Frank J. Wilson," 5, 6, 7.

20. Ibid., 6.

21. Allsop, *Bootleggers*, 306.

22. "$4,000,000 Offer Made by Capone," *New York Times*, June 14, 1931; "Capone Begs a Trial as Court Bars Deal," *New York Times*, July 31, 1931.

23. "Crime: U.S. v. Gangs," *Time*, June 29, 1931, 9–10.

24. "Capone Begs a Trial as Court Bars Deal," *New York Times*, July 31, 1931.

25. "Document Prepared by Special Agent Frank J. Wilson," 55.

26. "Judge to Rule on Al's Change of Plea Today," *Daily Illini* (Champaign-Urbana, IL), July 31, 1931; "Capone Begs a Trial as Court Bars Deal," *New York Times*, July 31, 1931.

27. "Court Lets Capone Revoke Liquor Plea," *New York Times*, September 9, 1931.

28. "Parson Depicts Tilt with Capone in Raid," *New York Times*, October 8, 1931; "Document Prepared by Special Agent Frank J. Wilson," 9, 33.

29. "Document Prepared by Special Agent Frank J. Wilson," 17; Mappen, *Prohibition Gangsters*, 136.

30. "Document Prepared by Special Agent Frank J. Wilson," 20, 23, 24.

31. Ibid., 38, 39, 40, 42, 43, 44, 46–48.

32. "Capone Loses Fight to Bar 'Confession,'" *New York Times*, October 9, 1931; "Document Prepared by Special Agent Frank J. Wilson," 25.

33. "Al Capone Now Emerges in a New Personality," *New York Times*, October 18, 1931; Iorizzo, *Al Capone*, xix.

34. "Will Rogers Pays Visit to Capone," *Urbana Daily Courier* (Urbana, IL), February 26, 1932; "Capone's Sentence Affirmed on Appeal," *New York Times*, February 28, 1932; "Capone Plea Denied by Supreme Court," *New York Times*, May 3, 1932.

35. "Al Capone Bound for Atlanta Prison," *New York Times*, May 4, 1932.

36. "Capone Making Overalls," *New York Times*, July 13, 1932; "Al Capone Model Prisoner," *New York Times*, July 10, 1932; "What! Al Capone a Sissy? 'Some of the Boys' in Atlanta Are Beginning to Believe So!" *Daily Illini* (Champaign-Urbana, IL), November 19, 1932.

37. "Lone Island Picked to Imprison Worst of Our Criminals," *New York Times*, October 13, 1933.

38. "Capone in a Cell on Alcatraz Isle," *New York Times*, August 23, 1934.

39. "Alcatraz Prison Also a Fortress," *New York Times*, September 2, 1934; "Felon Tells of Life in Grim Alcatraz," *New York Times*, August 14, 1935.

40. Mark Douglas Brown, *Capone*, 17, 43, 44, 58.

41. "Capone Improves; Mind Clear," *Daily Illini* (Champaign-Urbana, IL), February 17, 1938; Brown, *Alcatraz*, 47, 52.

42. "Capone Pays $37,692 to Federal Court to Assure His Release from Alcatraz," *New York Times*, January 5, 1939; Brown, *Alcatraz*, 52.

43. "Al Capone Pays up; Quits Prison Soon," *New York Times*, November 4, 1939.

44. "Al Capone Is Freed from Prison; Guarded in Baltimore Hospital," *New York Times*, November 17, 1939; "Capone Freed," *New York Times*, November 19, 1939.

45. "Capone Must Stay Year in Seclusion," *New York Times*, January 9, 1940; "Says Capone Is at Miami," *New York Times*, March 21, 1940; "Capone in Public Again," *New York Times*, August 1, 1940.

46. "Big Al," *Time*, February 3, 1947, 23.

47. Ibid.; "Capone Buried in Chicago," *New York Times*, February 5, 1947.

Chapter 24

1. Fahey, *Rum Road*, 85.

2. Ibid., 2, 91.

3. Newman, *King of the Castle*, 91.

4. "Bringing Rum from Canada," *Reno Evening Gazette* (Reno, NV), August 24, 1920.

5. "Rum Runners Race to Beat Chief Winter," *Morning Republican* (Xenia, OH), November 18, 1920; "Machine Guns Used to Halt Liquor Autos," *Bismarck Tribune* (Bismarck, ND), November 2, 1920.

6. Fahey, *Rum Road*, 7.

7. Ibid., 48–49.

8. Ibid., 51.

9. Ibid., 72, 74.

10. Ibid., 94, 95.

11. Wilson, *Honky-tonk Town*, 48–49.

12. Wallace Stegner, *Wolf Willow*, 97.

13. Wilson, *Honky-tonk Town*, 77.

14. Newman, *King of the Castle*, 88.

15. Gray, *Roar*, 149.

16. "Machine Guns for Border: Saskatchewan Police in Autos to Patrol for Rum Runners," *New York Times*, October 6, 1922.

17. Gray, *Roar*, 150; Wilson, *Honky-tonk Town*, 64–65.

18. Wilson, *Honky-tonk Town*, 3, 49, 51, 52.

19. Ibid., 52, 76.

20. Ibid., 52, 81.

21. Ibid., 54–55, 88–89.

22. Ibid., 79, 87–88.

23. Ibid., 52, 54–55, 79, 96.

24. Ibid., 73, 74.

25. Ibid., 56, 58, 61.

26. Ibid., 80.

27. Ibid., 89–90, 95.

28. Ibid., 90, 91, 93, 95.

Chapter 25

1. Richard F. Hamm, *Olmstead v. United States*, 3.

2. Philip Metcalfe, *Whispering Wires*, 4, 5; Norman H. Clark, *The Dry Years*, 162.

3. "Six Autos and Nine Men Held in Roundup," *Seattle Times*, March 22, 1920; Clark, *Dry Years*, 163.

4. Metcalfe, *Wires*, 8.

5. *Olmstead v. U.S.*, 277 U.S. 438 (1928).

6. Metcalfe, *Wires*, 15, 16.

7. Ibid., 30–31.

8. Ibid., 38–39, 50, 114–115.

9. Ibid., 51, 52.

10. "Bedtime Story Cut Short by Interference of Dry Agent," *Bakersfield Californian* (Bakersfield, CA), December 1, 1924; Metcalfe, *Wires*, 70; "Seattle Rum King to Have Rehearing," *New York Times*, April 1, 1928.

11. "Hubbard Coil Runs Boat on Portage Bay Ten Knots an Hour; Auto Test Next," *Seattle Post-Intelligencer*, July 29, 1920; "Hubbard Believes Mystery Motor Based on His Own Invention," *Seattle Post Intelligencer*, February 26, 1928.

12. Metcalfe, *Wires*, 100, 102, 103; "The Inside of Prohibition," *New York Times*, August 19, 1929.

13. Metcalfe, *Wires*, 105–108.

14. Ibid., 110, 118, 128.

15. Ibid., 149, 150.

16. Ibid., 148, 150, 151, 152, 154, 155, 157.

17. Ibid., 167–168.

18. Ibid., 173, 178, 179, 192, 201; Hamm, *Olmstead*, 6, 7.

19. Metcalfe, *Wires*, 181, 186, 191–192; Hamm, *Olmstead*, 7.

20. Metcalfe, *Wires*, 205, 206, 209, 211.

21. Hamm, *Olmstead*, 8; Metcalfe, *Wires*, 215–216, 217, 218.

22. Metcalfe, *Wires*, 219, 220, 221.

23. Ibid., 272, 274.

24. Ibid., 269, 272, 273.

25. Ibid., 162–163, 274, 275.

26. Ibid., 275–276.

27. 277 U.S. 438 (1928).

28. "Wiretapping as Rule Barred by Mitchell," *Chicago Daily Tribune*, February 20, 1931; Hamm, *Olmstead*, 10, 11; Clark, *Dry Years*, 178.

29. Metcalfe, *Wires*, 277, 322, 337, 339–340.

30. Ibid., 340; "Olmstead Given Pardon by FDR," *Lewiston Morning Tribune* (Lewiston, ID), December 25, 1935.

31. Metcalfe, *Wires*, 342, 343; "King of Bootleggers Served God before Death," *Fairbanks Daily News-Miner* (Fairbanks, AK), May 6, 1966.

32. Presidential Pardon #2676, December 24, 1945; "President Issues Blanket Pardon," *Montana Standard* (Butte, MT), December 25, 1945.

33. "Federal Bureau of Investigation, Freedom of Information/Privacy Acts Release, Subject: Michael M. Hubbard."

34. Martin A. Lee and Bruce Shlain, *Acid Dreams, The Complete Social History of LSD*, 49.

35. Metcalfe, *Wires*, 342.

Chapter 26

1. "Women Dry Violators May Expect No Leniency," *Sausalito News* (Sausalito, CA), April 2, 1921.

2. "Women Bootleggers Difficult Problem, Says Haynes," *Washington Post*, May 13, 1923.

3. "Women Federal Prisoners to Be Segregated," *New York Amsterdam News*, September 1, 1926.

4. "Women Dominate Arkansas Bootlegging, Say Dry Agents, Arresting Fourteen in Raids," *New York Times*, July 19, 1929; "Warns Women Bootleggers against Sick Husband Plea," *New York Times*, February 11, 1926; "Dry Heads on Trail of Mail Order Ring," *New York Times*, November 16, 1926.

5. "Warns Women Bootleggers," *Los Angeles Times*, July 18, 1924.

6. "Bootlegging in Arkansas Succeeds Farm Industry," *Washington Post*, July 28, 1929; "Jail Yawns for Woman Bootlegger," *Los Angeles Times*, September 5, 1925.

7. "War on Women Bootleggers Just Begun, Dry Agent Says," *Dallas Morning News*, July 19, 1929; "Dry Officials Jail Women Violators," *Washington Post*, December 8, 1929.

8. "Woman Bootlegger Has her Fine Paid by Sunday School," *St. Petersburg Times* (St. Petersburg, FL), April 30, 1925.

9. Tanya Marie Sanchez, "The Feminine Side of Bootlegging," *Louisiana History: The Journal of the Louisiana Historical Association* 41, no. 4 (Autumn 2000): 409.

10. "Couple Deal in Beverage, Fined $251," *Oakland Tribune* (Oakland, CA), January 24, 1920.

11. "Co-ed Pleads for Mother Sentenced as a Bootlegger," *San Antonio Light* (San Antonio, TX), August 9, 1925.

12. "Profits in Brew Disclosed in Case," *Oshkosh Daily Northwestern* (Oshkosh, WI), January 26, 1929.

13. Dabney, *Mountain Spirits*, 135.

14. "'Did It for Children' Successful Appeal of Woman Bootlegger, *Atlanta Constitution*, December 4, 1929; "Mob Fights Police in Raid on Saloon," *New York Times*, May 22, 1921.

15. Sanchez, "Feminine Side," 406–407, 408, 419, 420.

16. Wheeler, *Rumrunners and Revenuers*, 84–85.

17. Mary Murphy, "Bootlegging Mothers and Drinking Daughters: Gender and Prohibition in Butte, Montana," *American Quarterly* 46, no. 2 (June 1994): 174, 185.

18. Nelson, *Moonshiners*, 42–43.

19. "Seize Wine Found in Counterfeit Raid," *New York Times*, February 24, 1923; "Girl Bootlegger Free, Fine Paid," *New York Times*, October 4, 1927.

20. "Girl a Moonshiner at Sixteen," *New York Times*, May 28, 1922.

21. "Ruse Entraps Girl Believed Bootleg Queen," *Los Angeles Times*, November 3, 1922; "Women Bootleggers Difficult Problem, Says Haynes," *Washington Post*, May 13, 1923.

22. Wheeler, *Rumrunners and Revenuers*, 151–155.

23. "Sheriff May Seize Farm of Pretty 'Bootleg Queen,'" *Reading Eagle* (Reading, PA), August 18, 1930; "Violet Smiles as She Is Freed on Rum Charge," *Reading Eagle* (Reading, PA), September 18, 1930; "Youth Admits Liquor Charge," *Reading Eagle* (Reading, PA), September 19, 1930.

24. Sanchez, "Feminine Side," 407, 412–415.

25. John J. Guthrie Jr., "Hard Times, Hard Liquor, and Hard Luck: Selective Enforcement of Prohibition in North Florida, 1928–1933," *Florida Historical Quarterly* 72, no. 4 (April 1994): 445.

26. "Woman, 80, Blind Pigger," *Sausalito News* (Sausalito, CA), November 12, 1921; "U.S. Constitution Violators — News of the Blind Pig World," *Mountain Democrat* (Placerville, CA), November 12, 1921.

27. Ellison, *Odyssey*, 92–93; "Queen of the Mountain Bootleggers Dies at Age 101," *Lexington Herald-Leader*, December 6, 2005.

28. Sanchez, "Feminine Side," 417.

29. Ibid., 418.

30. "Mob Fights Police in Raid on Saloon," *New York Times*, May 22, 1921.

31. "Woman Acquitted of Violating Dry Laws," *Marshall Evening Chronicle* (Marshall, MI), June 1, 1929.

32. Sanchez, "Feminine Side," 407–408, 411, 421.

33. "Policeman Chases Woman Bootlegger and Grabs Whiskey," *Dallas Morning News*, December 25, 1931.

34. "Tony Cornero Knows," *Los Angeles Times*, September 7, 1926.

35. "Women Bootleggers Difficult Problem, Says Haynes," *Washington Post*, May 13, 1923.

36. "Police Trace Leak of Embassy Liquor," *New York Times*, January 8, 1923.

37. "Dixie Highway Now Called 'the Alcohol Trail,'" *Atlanta Constitution*, February 13, 1921.

38. "Police Accuse Denver Priest," *Salt Lake Tribune* (Salt Lake City, UT), March 23, 1923; "Try Denver Priest on Dry Law Charge," *New York Times*, July 25, 1923; "Denver Society Woman Fined in Liquor Case," *New York Times*, August 2, 1923.

39. "Women Bootleggers Difficult Problem, Says Haynes," *Washington Post*, May 13, 1923; "Berkeley Woman Bootlegger Who Sold to U.C. Boys Given Jail Term," *San Francisco Chronicle*, October 5, 1922.

40. Sanchez, "Feminine Side," 426–427.

41. "Liberty Bell Rings for Belle of Bush," *Capital Times* (Madison, WI), January 17, 1928; "Arrest Jennie Justo in Booze Raid," *Capital Times* (Madison, WI), June 5, 1931; "See Bootlegger War Here as Jennie Justo Is Seized," *Capital Times* (Madison, WI), June 5, 1931.

42. "Bootleg Queen Is Sentenced," *Sheboygan Press* (Sheboygan, WI), January 16, 1932; "Jennie Justo to Serve Year, Geiger Order," *Wisconsin State Journal* (Madison, WI), May 7, 1933; "Obituary," *Wisconsin State Journal* (Madison, WI), November 28, 1991.

43. Wheeler, *Rumrunners and Revenuers*, 103.

44. "Hold Queen of the Bootleggers," *Star and Sentinel* (Gettysburg, PA), December 23, 1922; "Hold Woman in Distillery Raid," *Reading Eagle* (Reading, PA), December 15, 1922; "Fifty Men Rob Distillery," *New York Times,* July 16, 1922; "Distillery Case Opens Thursday, Ten under Arrest," *Frederick Post* (Frederick, MD), December 14, 1921; "Distillery Case Falls Through; Woman Cleared," *Frederick Post* (Frederick, MD), December 20, 1921; "Big Distillery Robbed Again," *Gettysburg Times* (Gettysburg, PA), March 8, 1922.

45. "'Queen of the Bootleggers' Is Found Guilty," *Beatrice Daily Sun* (Beatrice, NE), December 3, 1921; "Revelations of Bootleg Queen Land Gary Officials in Dry Net," *Sandusky Star Journal* (Sandusky, OH), January 25, 1923; "Mayor, Sheriff, City Judge, and Prosecuting Attorney All Given Jail Sentences in Amazing Rum Scandal," *Boston Daily Globe*, April 15, 1923; "Fifty-five out of Sixty-two Guilty in Gary Rum Plot," *New York Times,* April 1, 1923.

46. "Japanese and Sake Are Held," *Los Angeles Times*, March 30, 1922.

47. "Alcohol Company and Twenty-seven Indicted," *New York Times*, January 16, 1926; "$500,000 in Liquor and Thirteen Men Seized," *New York Times*, December 30, 1925.

48. "May Press Liquor Case," *New York Times*, June 14, 1925.

49. "Woman Bootlegger Slain," *New York Times*, January 23, 1928.

50. "Murder Attributed to a Bootleg Feud," *New York Times*, July 15, 1922.

51. "Gun Spitting Fire, Woman Bootlegger Is Killed by Police," *Atlanta Constitution*, November 25, 1921.

52. "Sheriff Who Slew Woman Rum Runner Freed by Verdict of Lawful Shooting to Defend Life," *Atlanta Constitution*, November 17, 1929; "Jury Absolves Woman-Killer," *Los Angeles Times*, November 18, 1929.

53. "Wetness Poor Politics, Declared Taggart," *New York Times*, July 19, 1924.

54. "Woman Prohibition Sleuth Is Wounded in Gun Fight," *Nevada State Journal* (Reno, NV), October 13, 1923; "Daisy Simpson Did Work for Drys in State of Montana," *Helena Daily Independent* (Helena, MT), March 25, 1926.

55. "Daisy Simpson Fights for Life," *Boston Daily Globe*, March 23, 1926; "Girl Detective's Ire Is Aroused," *Reno Evening Gazette* (Reno, NV), May 24, 1924.

56. "Stage Lost a Great Actress in Daisy Simpson, Sleuth," *Milwaukee Journal*, July 4, 1926; "Daisy Simpson Fights for Life," *Boston Daily Globe*, March 23, 1926.

57. "Woman Sleuth Makes Raid on Booze Party," *Oakland Tribune* (Oakland, CA), September 13, 1921.

58. "Epicurean Joys of Dry Sleuths Bared in Court," *Oakland Tribune* (Oakland, CA), October 31, 1921; "Techau Tavern Manager Found Guilty by Jury," *San Francisco Chronicle*, November 1, 1921; "Techau Tavern Men Sentenced to Jail Terms," *San Francisco Chronicle*, November 5, 1921.

59. "Fair Sleuth Nears," *Ukiah Republican Press* (Ukiah, CA), July 16, 1924; "Woman Dry Sleuth Working in Sonoma," *Ukiah Republican Press* (Ukiah, CA), November 29, 1922.

60. "Judge Dismisses Woman Dry Spy's 'Hell Diver' Case," *Oakland Tribune* (Oakland, CA), February 18, 1925; "Inducing Dry Law Violation Angers Court," *San Francisco Chronicle*, March 22, 1922.

61. "Petticoat Rum Raider Quits Task," *Los Angeles Times*, November 5, 1925; "Daisy Simpson Fights for Life," *Boston Daily Globe*, March 23, 1926; "Suicide Attempt Made by Former Prohi Enforcer," *Kingsport Times* (Kingsport, TN), March 22, 1926.

62. "Daisy Simpson, Former Sleuth, Is out on Bond," *Las Vegas Optic* (Las Vegas, NV), April 22, 1926; "Texas Indicts Daisy Simpson," *Oakland Tribune* (Oakland, CA), May 13, 1926; "Daisy Simpson Enters Plea," *Dallas Morning News*, September 18, 1926.

Chapter 27

1. "Rum-runners of the Air," *New York Times*, January 20, 1924.

2. "Trap-bottom Rum Planes," *New York Times,* October 5, 1922; "Seaplanes to Raid Bootleg Air Fleet," *New York Times,* August 27, 1922.

3. "Blinds Pilot with Gas and Seizes Rum Plane," *New York Times,* September 3, 1931.

4. Frederic F. Van de Water, *The Real McCoy,* 134, 137.

5. "Rum-runners of the Air," *New York Times,* January 20, 1924.

6. Newman, *King of the Castle,* 97; "Fourteen Held in Detroit Rum Plane Rings; Twelve of Smugglers' Thirty Machines Seized," *New York Times,* November 19, 1930; "Reports Liquor Made within Leavenworth," *New York Times,* December 30, 1931.

7. "Uncover Rum Ring Using Air Transport," *New York Times,* March 1, 1930.

8. "Liquor Plane Seized after Pilot's Error," *New York Times,* September 1, 1929; "Dry Officers Nab Pilot of Rum Laden Plane at Detroit," *Burlington Hawkeye* (Burlington, IA), November 27, 1929.

9. "Rum Row Seaplane Seized under Treaty," *New York Times,* March 31, 1925; "Canadian Raids," *Times Recorder* (Zanesville, OH), November 27, 1929.

10. "Huge Fortune Amassed by Flying Bootlegger," *Los Angeles Times,* October 30, 1926.

11. "Fly $1,000,000 Rum to City," *Chicago Daily Tribune,* May 9, 1930.

12. John H. Lyle, *The Dry and Lawless Years,* 52, 179; "Inquest Fails to Solve Death of Rum Flyer," *Chicago Daily Tribune,* August 30, 1925.

13. "'Flying Bootlegger' Slain in Chicago," *New York Times,* August 29, 1925; Lyle, *Dry and Lawless,* 179.

14. "Inquest Fails to Solve Death of Rum Flyer," *Chicago Daily Tribune,* August 30, 1925; "Flying Bootlegger and Comrade Slain in Feud, Police Say," *Washington Post,* August 30, 1925.

15. James A. Carter III, "Florida and Rumrunning during National Prohibition," *The Florida Historical Quarterly* 48, no.1 (July 1969): 48; Sally J. Ling, *Run the Rum In,* 107.

16. "The Story from the Other Side," *Update* 2, no. 3 (February 1975): 4.

17. "Oregon Toddy Is Brought in through Air," *San Francisco Chronicle,* February 7, 1920; "Airplanes Used in Smuggling Liquor, Canada to U.S.," *San Francisco Chronicle,* January 14, 1921.

18. Clark, *Dry Years,* 156.

19. Brian Shute, "Rum Running during the Prohibition Era," *Nostalgia Magazine* 13, no. 1 (January-February 2011): 38.

20. "Rum-runners of the Air," *New York Times,* January 20, 1924.

21. Ibid.

22. Walker, *One Eye Closed,* 75.

23. Nelson, *Moonshiners,* 74.

24. "Move Disabled Rum Plane," *New York Times,* May 21, 1922.

25. "Rum-runners of the Air," *New York Times,* January 20, 1924.

26. "Seaplane Had Whiskey Load," *New York Times,* July 4, 1922; "First Telepix Picture Shows Bootleg Airplane Captured in New York Harbor," *Atlanta Constitution,* April 1, 1925; "Rum Row Flier Freed," *New York Times,* April 2, 1925.

27. "Airplanes Capture Rum-running Ship," *New York Times,* February 21, 1922; "Seaplanes to Raid Bootleg Air Fleet," *New York Times,* August 27, 1922.

28. "First Air Attack on Liquor Ship," *New York Times,* July 1, 1922; "Rum-runners of the Air," *New York Times,* January 20, 1924.

29. Nelson, *Moonshiners,* 115.

30. Ibid.; Harold Waters, *Smugglers of Spirits,* 169, 200.

31. "Air Fleet Planned in Whiskey Battle," *Dallas Morning News,* September 4, 1929; "Third Rum Plane Seized in Detroit," *New York Times,* September 8, 1929; "Airplane Will Aid Detroit Rum Chases," *Detroit Free Press,* March 8, 1930.

Chapter 28

1. David O. Stewart, *The Summer of 1787,* 248, 249, 250.

2. Edward Arber, ed., *Travels and Works of Captain John Smith,* vol. 1, 57; Edward R. Emerson, *Beverages, Past and Present,* vol. 2, 458–459.

3. Richard Hayes Barry and Richard Barry, *Mr. Rutledge of South Carolina,* 74.

4. Clayton Colman Hall, *Narratives of Early Maryland, 1633–1684,* 292.

5. Mills, *Chesapeake Rumrunners,* 5–6; Ian Lendler, *Alcoholica Esoterica,* 109; Emerson, *Beverages,* vol. 2, 462; C.C. Pearson and James Edwin Hendricks, *Liquor & Anti-liquor in Virginia, 1619–1919,* 38, 43–44.

6. George Francis Dow, *Every Day Life in the Massachusetts Bay Colony,* 117–118.

7. Stuart C. Henry, *Unvanquished Puritan,* 95.

8. Ibid., 92–93; John Allen Krout, *The Origins of Prohibition,* 84.

9. Ernest H. Cherrington, *The Evolution of Prohibition in the United States of America,* 29–30, 33, 34; Mills, *Chesapeake Rumrunners,* 10.

10. Gregory A. Austin, *Alcohol in Western Society from Antiquity to 1800,* 256.

11. John W. Frick, *Theatre, Culture, and Temperance Reform in Nineteenth-Century America,* 21.

12. Harry G. Levine, "The Discovery of Addiction: Changing Conceptions of Habitual Drunkenness in America," *Journal of Studies on Alcohol* 39, no. 1 (1978): 146, 149–150.

13. Thomas Jefferson and Henry Augustine Washington, *The Writings of Thomas Jefferson: Correspondence,* 515; James Ford Rhodes, *History of the United States from the Compromise of 1850 to the Final Restoration of Home Rule at the South in 1877,* vol. 3, 96.

14. Cherrington, *Evolution of Prohibition,* 17; Fairfax Downey, *Our Lusty Forefathers,* 6; George F. Weston, Jr., *Boston Ways,* 214.

15. Pearson and Hendricks, *Liquor and Anti-liquor,* 305; Downey, *Forefathers,* 6.

16. Cherrington, *Evolution of Prohibition*, 24.

17. Ibid., 18, 22, 26; Krout, *Origins*, 17.

18. W.H. Daniels, *The Temperance Reform and Its Great Reformers*, 6, 9; Esther Kellner, *Moonshine*, 22.

19. "Sketches of Early Life in Boston, Part II: How They Tried to Regulate Life and Manners in Boston," *Appleton's Journal* 1, no. 3 (April 17, 1869): 86.

20. Ibid.; Edmund S. Morgan, *The Puritan Family*, 141.

21. Morgan, *Puritan Family*, 148–149; Cherrington, *Evolution of Prohibition*, 17.

22. Austin, *Alcohol*, 313, 320.

Chapter 29

1. John Norris, *Profitable Advice for Rich and Poor, in a Dialogue or Discourse between James Freeman, a Carolina Planter, and Simon Question, a West-country Farmer, Containing a Description or True Relation of South Carolina, an English Plantation or Colony in America*, no page number.

2. Berton Roueché, *The Neutral Spirit*, 36–37, 178; William B. Weeden, *Economic and Social History of New England, 1620–1789*, vol. 2, 501, 641, 756.

3. Mills, *Chesapeake Rumrunners*, 8.

4. Mark Edward Lender and James Kirby Martin, *Drinking in America*, 31.

5. Rick Beyer, *The Greatest Presidential Stories Never Told*, 16–17; Mills, *Chesapeake Rumrunners*, 5.

6. Kellner, *Moonshine*, 61.

7. Lender and Martin, *Drinking*, 16.

8. Krout, *Origins*, 53; Austin, *Alcohol*, 291–292.

9. Austin, *Alcohol*, 296.

10. Mason I. Lowance, Jr., *Increase Mather*, 122.

11. Herbert Asbury, "The Father of Prohibition," *American Mercury* 9, no. 35 (November 1926): 344–348.

12. Krout, *Origins*, 55, 81, 112; Cherrington, *Evolution of Prohibition*, 51–52.

13. Cherrington, *Evolution of Prohibition*, 72, 80; Krout, *Origins*, 112–113.

14. Krout, *Origins*, 68, 81; Cherrington, *Evolution of Prohibition*, 89; Vincent Harding, *A Certain Magnificence*, 204.

15. Krout, *Origins*, 87; Lyman Beecher, *Six Sermons on the Nature, Occasions, Signs, Evils, and Remedy of Intemperance*, 6, 7, 8, 9, 11, 62, 64, 90, 95–96, 107.

16. Henry, *Puritan*, 94.

17. Levine, "Discovery of Addiction," 151, 152; J.C. Furnas, *The Life and Times of the Late Demon Rum*, 40.

18. Levine, "Discovery of Addiction," 151–152, 156.

19. Cherrington, *Evolution of Prohibition*, 82–83.

20. Ibid., 59, 61, 79, 90.

21. Ibid., 48–49; Frick, *Theatre, Culture and Temperance*, 37.

22. Furnas, *Demon Rum*, 53, 55; Cherrington, *Evolution of Prohibition*, 93, 95.

23. Edith Jeffrey, "Reform, Renewal, and Vindication: Irish Immigrants and the Catholic Total Abstinence Movement in Antebellum Philadelphia," *The Pennsylvania Magazine of History & Biography* 112, no. 3 (July 1988): 407–408; John F. Quinn, "Father Mathew's Disciples: American Catholic Support for Temperance 1840–1920," *Church History* 65, no. 4 (Dec 1996): 625.

24. Noon, *Yuengling*, 108.

25. Quinn, "Father Mathew's Disciples," 625.

26. Mary Cable, *American Manners and Morals*, 255; Pearson and Hendricks, *Liquor and Anti-liquor*, 66.

27. Cable, *Manners*, 299; Ruth M. Elson, *Guardians of the Tradition*, 319.

28. Furnas, *Demon Rum*, 22, 122, 133–34; Thomas P. Hunt, *The Cold Water Army*, 8.

29. Mary A. Livermore, *The Story of My Life*, 377–378.

30. John William Crowley, ed., *Drunkard's Progress*, 7.

31. Ibid., 7; Cherrington, *Evolution of Prohibition*, 133.

32. Robert L. Hampel, *Temperance and Prohibition in Massachusetts, 1813–1852*, 18–19; Krout, *Origins*, 92–93.

33. Hampel, *Temperance*, 103–104.

34. Ibid., 104; Crowley, *Drunkard's Progress*, 8.

35. Krout, *Origins*, 185–186.

36. Hampel, *Temperance*, 104.

37. *Centennial Temperance Volume: A Memorial of the International Temperance Conference Held in Philadelphia, June, 1876*, 462; Hampel, *Temperance*, 104–105, 109, 121.

38. Hampel, *Temperance*, 124; Cherrington, *Evolution of Prohibition*, 94, 95; Levine, "Discovery of Addiction," 160.

39. Cherrington, *Evolution of Prohibition*, 135–139.

40. Henry Stephen Clubb, *The Maine Liquor Law*, 331, 341–342, 345.

41. Cherrington, *Evolution of Prohibition*, 141–142, 151, 153.

Chapter 30

1. George Ade, *Old-time Saloon*, 90.

2. J.E. Stebbins and T.A.H. Brown, *Fifty Years History of the Temperance Cause*, 308, 311; T.S. Arthur, *Grappling with the Monster*, 211–213.

3. *Centennial Temperance*, 715.

4. Ibid., 706–707.

5. "The Whiskey War," *New York Times*, February 14, 1874.

6. Ibid.; *Centennial Temperance*, 707–708; "Prayer vs. Whiskey," *New Philadelphia Ohio Democrat* (New Philadelphia, OH), February 13, 1874.

7. *Centennial Temperance*, 708–709.

8. Ibid., 710–712.

9. "The Whiskey War," *Eau Claire Daily Free Press* (Eau Claire, WI), February 9, 1874.

10. Ibid.

11. *Centennial Temperance*, 712–715.

12. Ibid., 710–712; Cable, *Manners*, 299.

13. Kellner, *Moonshine*, 76–77.

14. "The Temperance Cause," *New York Times*, April 7, 1874; *Centennial Temperance*, 719–720.

15. Arthur Strawn, "Saint Frances of Evanston," *American Mercury* 14, no. 54 (June 1928): 236.

16. H. Mark Roelofs, "Socialism and Christianity," *The Review of Politics* 51, no. 4 (Autumn 1989): 638.

17. Frances Elizabeth Willard, *Do Everything*, 54, 59, 60.

18. Jack S. Blocker, David M. Fahey, and Ian R. Tyrell, *Alcohol and Temperance in Modern History*, vol. 1, 387.

19. Norman H. Clark, *Deliver Us from Evil*, 86; Willard, *Do Everything*, 46.

20. Thomas R. Pegram, *Battling Demon Rum*, 114.

21. Lerner, *Dry Manhattan*, 27.

22. Clark, *Deliver Us from Evil*, 116.

23. Maureen Ogle, *Ambitious Brew*, 152.

24. Ogle, *Brew*, 155–156; Clark, *Dry Years*, 145.

25. Ogle, *Brew*, 151.

26. Cherrington, *Evolution of Prohibition*, 254–255, 281, 284.

27. "Drinking in Dry Places," *The American Magazine* 71 (November 1910–April 1911), 371–373.

28. Cherrington, *Evolution of Prohibition*, 317–321.

29. Lender and Martin, *Drinking*, 128.

30. Cherrington, *Evolution of Prohibition*, 326.

31. Plavchan, *Anheuser-Busch*, 143.

32. Clark, *Dry Years*, 128–129.

33. Plavchan, *Anheuser-Busch*, 148.

34. Ogle, *Brew*, 172; Noon, *Yuengling*, 111.

35. Davis D. Joyce, *Oklahoma I Had Never Seen Before*, 82–84.

36. Lerner, *Dry Manhattan*, 31.

37. Ogle, *Brew*, 172–173; *Congressional Record* 56, pt. 1 (1918): 442–451.

38. W.C. King, *King's Complete History of the World War*, 613.

39. Lerner, *Dry Manhattan*, 37.

40. Cherrington, *Evolution of Prohibition*, 329–330.

41. "Volstead Who Dug and Kramer Who Guards the Grave of John Barleycorn," *Current Opinion* 69 (July–December 1920): 50.

42. Cherrington, *Evolution of Prohibition*, 381–382.

43. "Prohibition Will Bring Higher Plane of Life," *Evening Gazette* (Cedar Rapids, IA), January 16, 1920.

Chapter 31

1. Irey, *Tax Dodgers*, 5.

2. "Volstead Who Dug and Kramer Who Guards the Grave," 51.

3. "Says Mellon Owned Whiskey Last March," *New York Times*, May 12, 1924.

4. "Prohibition: Silver Flask," *Time*, November 18, 1929, 13–14.

5. "The Cabinet: Enforcer-in-chief," *Time*, January 27, 1930, 11–12.

6. "Prohibition: Questions and Answers," *Time*, August 26, 1929, 13–14; Thomas Repetto, *American Mafia*, 94.

7. "Dry Agent Held on Murder Charge," *New York Times*, March 13, 1920; "Dry Agent's Picture Resembles Convict," *New York Times*, March 15, 1920; "McMullin Indicted for Murder; in Cell," *New York Times*, March 16, 1920; "Girl Says Dry Agent Killed Needlessly," *New York Times*, October 12, 1920; "Dry Agent Admits Killing," *New York Times*, October 16, 1920.

8. Lerner, *Dry Manhattan*, 61–62; "Dry Agent Admits Killing Eastman," *New York Times*, January 4, 1921; "Eastman's Slayer Freed," *New York Times*, June 24, 1923.

9. "Will Fingerprint Prohibition Agents," *New York Times*, February 3, 1926.

10. Haynes, *Prohibition Inside Out*, 275.

11. "Bottles Bombard Police after Raid," *New York Times*, May 23, 1921.

12. "Vast Northern Area Wet," *New York Times*, March 22, 1926; Metcalfe, *Wires*, 156.

13. Ostrander, *Prohibition Movement*, 162, 163.

14. "Patrol on Border to Reach to Pacific," *New York Times*, August 9, 1925.

15. "New U.S. Police Force Now Combats Smugglers," *New York Times*, May 10, 1925; "Seized Liquor Autos to Hunt Rum Runners," *New York Times*, May 22, 1925; "Dry Unit Adds 235 Men to Border Patrol to Crush out Rum-running from Canada," *New York Times*, July 22, 1926.

16. "Is Named Head of Border Patrol," *Dallas Morning News*, March 25, 1926; "Muster Dry Force in Detroit Area," *New York Times*, June 7, 1929; "Twelve Men to Be Added to U.S. Border Patrol," *Dallas Morning News*, June 11, 1931.

17. "Youngquist Holds Force Inadequate to Dam Liquor Flow," *New York Times*, August 29, 1930.

18. Lerner, *Dry Manhattan*, 71.

19. Frederick Lewis Allen, *Only Yesterday*, 216.

20. Walker, *One Eye Closed*, 4; "Agents Out of the Service," *New York Times*, January 18, 1930.

21. "Say Dry Agents Got $100,000 in Graft," *New York Times*, June 23, 1928; "Federal Prohibition Raider Surrenders on Bribe Charge," *Stevens Point Daily Journal* (Stevens Point, WI), March 5, 1929; "O'Neill Pleads Guilty to Dry Law Violation," *Eau Claire Leader* (Eau Claire, WI), January 31, 1922.

22. "Ex-Agents Called in Bootleg Case," *New York Times*, October 20, 1921; "Ousted Dry Agent Is Held," *New York Times*, July 15, 1920.

23. Joe Alex Morris, *What a Year!*, 42–43.

24. Liggett, "Ohio — Lawless and Unashamed," 12.

25. Metcalfe, *Wires*, 290–291.

26. Sann, *Lawless*, 203; "Prohibition: New Sponge," *Time*, September 19, 1927, 8–9.

27. "Charge Liquor Blackmail," *New York Times*, February 2, 1921.

28. "Chicago Dry Officer Arrested for Graft," *San Francisco Chronicle*, August 30, 1921.

29. "Three Charged with Posing as Revenue Men," *San Francisco Chronicle*, April 25, 1920.

30. "DeGroot Warns of Fake Agents," *New York Times*, February 5, 1928.

31. Clark, *Dry Years*, 158, 159–160.

32. "Colossal Scandal over Rum Running," *Sheboygan Press* (Sheboygan, WI), August 28, 1925; "Negro Customs Collector Freed," *Port Arthur News* (Port Arthur, TX), December 20, 1925; "Forty-one Memphis Policemen Accused of Graft Revealed by Alleged 'Pay-off' Book, *New York Times*, September 23, 1927; "Federal Agents on Trail of Indiana 'Whiskey Ring,'" *Des Moines News* (Des Moines, IA), May 1, 1920.

33. "Genna Gang's Book Lists 250 Chicago Police as Sharing $6,926 Monthly Bootleg Graft," *New York Times*, November 5, 1925; "Ninety-six Indicted in Day for Chicago Plots," *New York Times*, May 4, 1929; "Indictments Are Returned by Wholesale," *Urbana Daily Courier* (Urbana, IL), October 25, 1927; "Arrest Robinson State's Attorney," *Decatur Sunday Review* (Decatur, IL), December 9, 1923.

34. "Michigan Mayor Gets Two Years under Dry Act," *New York Times*, July 13, 1924; "Police Captain Ousted," *New York Times*, June 23, 1929.

35. "Federal Petit Jury for Wyoming Faces Hard Task," *Billings Gazette* (Billings, MT), January 4, 1930; "One Dollar a Gallon Levied on Stills by Wyoming Enforcement Officer, Prosecutor Tells Jurors at Trial," *San Antonio Express* (San Antonio, TX), January 28, 1930; "Charge Officer with Conspiracy," *Oelwein Daily Register* (Oelwein, IA), January 27, 1930.

36. "Case Outlined against Wyoming Former Dry Chief," *Billings Gazette* (Billings, MT), January 28, 1930; "Wyoming Governor Testifies," *Montana Standard* (Butte, MT), January 29, 1930.

37. "Five Wyoming Wets Convicted by Jurors," *Helena Independent* (Helena, MT), February 2, 1930; "Wyoming Booze Law Violators Are Sentenced," *Billings Gazette* (Billings, MT), February 4, 1930; "Irving Starts Trip to Cell," *Billings Gazette* (Billings, MT), February 6, 1930.

38. Liggett, "Ohio — Lawless and Unashamed," 7.

39. Ibid., 8, 9.

40. Jerry Pardue, "The Story from the Other Side," *Update* 2, no. 3 (February 1975), 4.

Chapter 32

1. "One Hundred Prohibition Agents Arrest Thirty-three in Raid in South Carolina," *Atlanta Constitution*, September 6, 1926.

2. "Dry Raiders Are Mobbed," *New York Times*, May 18, 1922; "U.S. Dry Raid Leads to Baltimore Riot," *Oakland Tribune* (Oakland, CA), May 18, 1922.

3. "Mob of Thousands Holds Dry Raiders," *San Francisco Chronicle*, October 7, 1922.

4. "Women Bowlers Fight to Save Beer," *New York Times*, January 6, 1923.

5. "East Side Dry Raid Winds Up in a Riot," *New York Times*, December 10, 1920.

6. "Dry Raiders Stoned from Bronx Roofs," *New York Times*, October 26, 1922; "Call Police First, Raid Second Winery," *New York Times*, October 27, 1922.

7. "Stoned by Citizens, Dry Raiders Report," *New York Times*, March 3, 1927.

8. Philip G. Terrie, *Contested Terrain*, 154.

9. "Forty Armed Autoists Block Dry Raiders," *New York Times*, June 20, 1923.

10. Pellegrino, *Jersey Brew*, 80.

11. "Pennsylvania Mob Attacks Dry Raiders," *New York Times*, April 8, 1929.

12. Mills, *Chesapeake Rumrunners*, 89.

13. "Two Thousand in Bushwick Hold a 'Wet' Parade Reviewed by Hylan," *New York Times*, May 15, 1921.

14. "Hooch Used to Hold Coppers at Bay," *Chicago Defender*, November 13, 1920.

15. "Policeman Saved from Crowd for Fourth Time," *Chicago Defender*, November 8, 1924.

16. "Padlocked," *Time*, June 20, 1927, 18; "Prohibition: Co-defendant," *Time*, June 17, 1929, 13.

17. "Post Office Is Padlocked," *New York Times*, July 28, 1929; "Uncle Sam Gone Wrong," *Logansport Pharos-Tribune* (Logansport, IN), June 10, 1926; "Wine Is Found in Post Office," *Sioux City Journal* (Sioux City, IA), June 8, 1926.

18. "Dry Padlock Shuts New Negro Church," *New York Times*, July 13, 1930.

19. "Redwood Tree Padlocked by Officers," *Havre Daily News-Promoter* (Havre, MT), April 8, 1926.

20. "Prohibition: The Five and Ten," *Time*, March 25, 1929, 14.

21. "The Five and Ten," *Time*, April 1, 1929, 11–12.

22. Lerner, *Dry Manhattan*, 73; Clark, *Dry Years*, 207.

23. Clark, *Deliver Us from Evil*, 196–197.

24. "Lawyers Volunteer to Fight Jones Law," *New York Times*, March 15, 1929.

25. "Will Start Drive under Jones Law," *New York Times*, March 13, 1929; "Jones Law Feared by Prohibition Men," *New York Times*, March 31, 1929; "Jones Law Hits Kansas City," *New York Times*, March 31, 1929.

26. "Prohibition: Millions of Felons," *Time*, December 2, 1929, 15.

27. "Minnesota Council Pleads," *New York Times*, June 18, 1929; Elizabeth Johanneck, *Twin Cities Prohibition*, 41.

28. "'Deplores' Killing of any Person," *Sandusky Star-Journal* (Sandusky, OH), June 18, 1929.

29. "Arrest 'Dry' Agents in Shooting of Girl," *New York Times*, July 6, 1923; "Suspends Dry Agents Who Shot Iowa Nurse," *New York Times*, February 16, 1930.

30. "Dry Agent Faces Trial for Tilghman's Death," *Dallas Morning News*, May 22, 1925; "One Year in Jail for Pro Agent Upheld," *Dallas Morning News*, February 14, 1924.

31. "Constable Is Indicted in Death of Motorist," *Joplin Globe* (Joplin, MO), July 17, 1929; "Ballenger Takes Stand," *Thomasville Times-Enterprise* (Thomasville, GA), July 25, 1929.

32. "Widow of Slain Man Will Work Her Crops," *Burlington Daily Times* (Burlington, NC), June 18, 1929.

33. "Constable is Awaiting Trial," *Newark Advocate* (Newark, OH), July 17, 1929; "Georgia Officer Offers

Alibi," *Burlington Daily News* (Burlington, NC), June 18, 1929; "Seek to Show that Ballenger Did Not Fire Fatal Shot," *Thomasville Times-Enterprise* (Thomasville, GA), July 24, 1929; "Ballenger Takes Stand," *Thomasville Times-Enterprise* (Thomasville, GA), July 25, 1929; "Jury Deadlocked in Ballenger Case after 24 Hours," *Thomasville Times-Enterprise* (Thomasville, GA), July 26, 1929.

34. "Dry Squad Held Shooting Girl," *Oelwein Daily Register* (Oelwein, IA), September 27, 1928; "Dry Raider Convicted in Wounding of Girl," *New York Times*, October 30, 1928; "Dry Raider Recites How Girl Was Shot," *New York Times*, October 25, 1928.

35. "Taken to Pen," *Sandusky Star Journal* (Sandusky, OH), June 18, 1929; "Mob Organizes after Shooting of Prizefighter," *Olean Times* (Olean, NY), June 18, 1929; "Death Penalty Will Be asked for Official," *Montana Standard* (Butte, MT), June 19, 1929.

36. "State Ends Case against Newport Deputy Sheriff," *Fayetteville Democrat* (Fayetteville, AR), December 6, 1929; "Newport Deputy Freed of Murder," *Fayetteville Democrat* (Fayetteville, AR), December 7, 1929.

37. Pegram, *Battling Demon Rum*, 175.

38. "One Hundred Ninety Deaths in Raids under Prohibition; Search Curb Issued," *New York Times*, April 6, 1929.

Chapter 33

1. "Billy Sunday Again Hits the Train Here," *New York Times*, April 16, 1925.

2. John C. Gebhart, "Movement against Prohibition," *Annals of the American Association of Political and Social Science* 163 (September 1932): 173.

3. "Prohibition's Failure Explained by Silloway," *Sheboygan Press* (Sheboygan, WI), March 14, 1929.

4. "Fewer than Twenty Thousand in Anti-dry Parade; Slogans from Bible," *New York Times*, July 5, 1921.

5. "Wets Have Gala Day in Capitol's Shadow," *New York Times*, February 23, 1926.

6. Ibid.

7. Ibid.

8. Gebhart, "Movement against Prohibition," 176.

9. David E. Kyvig, "Women against Prohibition," *American Quarterly* 28, no. 4 (August 1976): 466–467.

10. David Kyvig, *Repealing National Prohibition*, 119.

11. Gebhart, "Movement against Prohibition," 177; Kobler, *Ardent Spirits*, 342.

12. "Says Wet Women Only Wish to Drink," *New York Times*, May 23, 1932; Kobler, *Ardent Spirits*, 343; Kyvig, *Repealing*, 126.

13. "Blue Cockade Expands," *New York Times*, May 6, 1932; "Congress Dry and so Are Wets Who Planned Ball," *Wisconsin State Journal* (Madison, WI), July 28, 1932.

14. Gebhart, "Movement against Prohibition," 177.

15. "'People' Repeal, Palmer Insists," *New York Times*, January 2, 1933; "Ex-Dry Chief Now a Wet," *New York Times*, August 23, 1930.

16. "Ask 'Tax for Prosperity,'" *New York Times*, May 15, 1932; "Beer Parade Broadcast to Nation," *New York Times*, May 15, 1932; "New York, Los Angeles Parade for Dry Repeal," *Nevada State Journal* (Reno, NV), May 15, 1932; "Marched to Tune of Sweet Adeline," *Daily Capital News* (Jefferson City, MO), May 15, 1932.

17. "White Plains Mayor Bars Parade," *New York Times*, April 21, 1932; "Mamaroneck Parade Gay," *New York Times*, May 15, 1932; "Noisy Throng at Hudson," *New York Times*, May 15, 1932.

18. "'Keg of Beer' and Marchers Are Lacking in Boston Parade," *New York Times*, May 16, 1932.

19. "Milwaukee Has Mile-long Parade," *Wisconsin State Journal*, May 15, 1932; "Crowds Cheer Beer Parade," *San Antonio Light* (San Antonio, TX), May 15, 1932.

20. "Students at Amherst Rescind Decision to Hold Beer Parade," *New York Times*, May 6, 1932.

21. "100,000 March in New York's 'Beer Parade,'" *Lima News* (Lima, OH), May 15, 1932; "New York, Los Angeles Parade for Dry Repeal," *Nevada State Journal* (Reno, NV), May 15, 1932.

22. Gebhart, "Movement against Prohibition," 179; "GOP Liquor Plank Blamed on Dry South," *Salt Lake Tribune* (Salt Lake City, UT), June 17, 1932.

23. "Shouse Jeers at Republican Liquor Plank," *Salt Lake Tribune* (Salt Lake City, UT), June 17, 1932.

24. Gebhart, "Movement against Prohibition," 179; "AAPA, Its Work Well Done, Passes out of Existence," *New York Times*, December 31, 1933.

25. Gebhart, "Movement against Prohibition," 179.

26. "Prohibition: Beer for Revenue?" *Time*, November 28, 1932, 13; Noon, *Yuengling*, 129; Thomas C. Cochran, *The Pabst Brewing Company*, 352, 354.

27. "Say Falstaff," *Burlington Hawkeye* (Burlington, IA), May 21, 1933; "Sixteen States Will Have Beer if U.S. Says So," *Charleston Gazette* (Charleston, WV), March 16, 1933.

28. Plavchan, *Anheuser-Busch*, 217, 218, 221; "Paint Beer Wagons," *Jefferson City Post-Tribune* (Jefferson City, MO), March 21, 1933; "Anheuser-Busch Launches Ad Drive to Spend Million," *Syracuse Herald* (Syracuse, NY), March 19, 1933.

29. "Present Day Beer in New York 5.89 Per Cent Alcohol," *Waterloo Daily Courier* (Waterloo, IA), March 21, 1933.

30. "Big Cities Prepare for Beer Zero Hour," *New York Times*, April 6, 1933.

31. "Cheering Crowds at Brew Centers," *Monitor-Index and Evening Democrat* (Moberley, MO), April 7, 1933; "Thirsty Celebrate as Beer Returns Today," *Carroll Daily Herald* (Carroll, IA), April 7, 1933.

32. Playchan, *Anheuser-Busch*, 219, 220; "Cheering Crowds at Brew Centers," *Monitor-Index and Democrat*, April 7, 1933; "Jefferson City's Thirsty Gulp Down All Available Beer and Go Back to Retailers for More," *Jefferson City Post-Tribune* (Jefferson City, MO), April 7, 1933.

33. Ogle, *Brew*, 200–201; "Roosevelt Gets First Cases of Capital's 3.2 Beer," *New York Times*, April 7, 1933.

34. "Teutonic Flavor in Milwaukee," *New York Times*, April 7, 1933; "Prohibition: Prosit," *Time*, April 17, 1933, 13–14.

35. "Decorous Welcome in Chicago," *New York Times*, April 7, 1933.

36. "Roosevelt Sleeps as Beer Returns," *Moberley Monitor-Index and Evening Democrat* (Moberley, MO), April 7, 1933; "Two Cases Sent to Roosevelt," *Oakland Tribune* (Oakland, CA), April 7, 1933.

37. "Many Cities Celebrate," *New York Times*, April 7, 1933; "Holiday Air in Baltimore," *New York Times*, April 7, 1933.

38. "One Million Gallons at Louisville," *New York Times*, April 7, 1933.

39. "Beer's Flow Greeted in Cities of Bay Region by Rush for Legal Beverage," *Oakland Tribune* (Oakland, CA), April 7, 1933.

40. "Broadway Disappointed," *New York Times*, April 7, 1933.

41. "Thirsty Throngs Jam City Streets," *New York Times*, April 8, 1933.

42. "Six Big Horses Bring Smith a Case of Beer," *New York Times*, April 7, 1933.

43. "Drink to be Mellow, Not to be Tight," *Southtown Economist* (Chicago, IL), April 7, 1933.

44. Sosnowski, *Rivers Ran Red*, 182; "Vineyardists of State Unhappy," *Bakersfield Californian* (Bakersfield, CA), April 7, 1933.

45. Sosnowski, *Rivers Ran Red*, 185.

46. "Temperance Forces Plan War on Beer," *Oakland Tribune* (Oakland, CA), April 7, 1933; "They Say," *Olean Time-Herald* (Olean, NY), April 19, 1933.

47. "Utah Vote Ends Prohibition Era," *Salt Lake Tribune* (Salt Lake City, UT), December 6, 1933.

48. "Text of Roosevelt's Repeal Proclamation," *Salt Lake Tribune* (Salt Lake City, UT), December 6, 1933.

Bibliography

Ade, George. *Old-time Saloon: Not Wet—Not Dry, Just History*. New York: Long and Smith, 1931.

Alexander, Michael. *Jazz Age Jews*. Princeton: Princeton University Press, 2001.

Allen, Frederick Lewis. *Only Yesterday: An Informal History of the 1920's*. New York: Perennial Classics, 2000.

Allsop, Kenneth. *The Bootleggers: Story of Chicago's Prohibition Era*. New Rochelle, NY: Arlington House, 1968.

Arons, Ron. *The Jews of Sing Sing*. Fort Lee, NJ: Barricade Books, 2008.

Arthur, T.S. *Grappling with the Monster: Or, the Curse and the Cure of Strong Drink*. New York: John W. Lovell Company, 1877.

Asbury, Herbert. "The Father of Prohibition." *American Mercury* 9, no. 35 (November 1926): 344–348.

Austin, Gregory A. *Alcohol in Western Society from Antiquity to 1800: A Chronological History*. Santa Barbara: ABC-CLIO, 1985.

Baldwin, Fred D. "Smedley D. Butler and Prohibition Enforcement in Philadelphia, 1924-25." *Pennsylvania Magazine of History and Biography* 84, no. 3 (July 1960): 352–368.

Barry, Richard Hayes, and Richard Barry. *Mr. Rutledge of South Carolina*. New York: Duell, Sloan and Pierce, 1942.

Batterberry, Michael, and Ariane Batterberry. *On the Town in New York from 1776 to the Present*. New York: Charles Scribner's Sons, 1973.

Beecher, Lyman. *Six Sermons on the Nature, Occasions, Signs, Evils, and Remedy of Intemperance*. Boston: T.R. Marvin, 1828.

Bergreen, Laurence. *Capone: The Man and the Era*. New York: Simon & Schuster, 1996.

Beyer, Rick. *The Greatest Presidential Stories Never Told*. New York: HarperCollins, 2007.

Black, Forrest Revere. *Ill-starred Prohibition Cases: A Study in Judicial Pathology*. Boston: R.G. Badger, 1931.

Block, Alan. *East Side, West Side: Organizing Crime in New York, 1930-1950*. Cardiff: University College Cardiff Press, 1980.

Blocker, Jack S., David M. Fahey, and Ian R. Tyrell. *Alcohol and Temperance in Modern History: An International Encyclopedia*, vol. 1. Santa Barbara: ABC-CLIO, 2003.

Boyce, Cyril D. "Prohibition in Canada." *Annals of the American Academy of Political and Social Science* 109 (September 1923): 225–229.

Brown, Mark Douglas. *Capone: Life behind Bars at Alcatraz*. San Francisco: Golden Gate National Parks Conservancy, 2004.

Brown, William G. "State Cooperation in Enforcement." *Annals of the American Academy of Political and Social Science* 163 (September 1932): 30–38.

Butts, Edward. *Outlaws of the Lakes: Bootlegging and Smuggling from Colonial Times to Prohibition*. Toronto: Lynx Images, 2004.

Cable, Mary. *American Manners and Morals: A Picture History of How We Behaved and Misbehaved*. New York: American Heritage Publishing Company, 1969.

Carr, Jess. *The Second Oldest Profession: An Informal History of Moonshining in America*. Radford, VA: Commonwealth Press, 1972.

Carse, Robert. *Rum Row*. New York: Rinehart and Company, 1959.

Carter III, James A. "Florida and Rumrunning during National Prohibition." *The Florida Historical Quarterly* 48, no.1 (July 1969): 47–56.

Caudill, Henry M. *Night Comes to the Cumberlands: A Biography of a Depressed Area*. Ashland, KY: Jesse Stuart Foundation, 2001.

_____. *Slender Is the Thread: Tales from a Country Law Office*. Lexington: University Press of Kentucky, 1992.

Centennial Temperance Volume: A Memorial of the International Temperance Conference Held in Philadelphia, June, 1876. New York: National Temperance Society and Publication House, 1877.

Charyn, Jerome. *Gangsters and Gold Diggers: Old New York, the Jazz Age, and the Birth of Broadway*. New York: Thunder's Mouth Press, 2003.

Cherrington, Ernest H. *The Evolution of Prohibition in the United States of America: A Chronological History*. Montclair, NJ: Patterson Smith, 1920.

Chidsey, Donald Barr. *On and Off the Wagon.* New York: Cowles Book Company, 1969.

Clapper, Raymond. "Happy Days." *American Mercury* 10, no. 37 (January 1927): 25–29.

Clark, Norman H. *Deliver Us from Evil: An Interpretation of American Prohibition.* New York: W.W. Norton, 1976.

_____. *The Dry Years: Prohibition and Social Change in Washington.* Seattle: University of Washington Press, 1965.

Clubb, Henry Stephen. *The Maine Liquor Law: Its Origin, History, and Results, Including a Life of Honorable Neal Dow.* New York: Fowler and Wells, 1856.

Cochran, Thomas C. *The Pabst Brewing Company: The History of an American Business.* Westport, CT: Greenwood Press, 1975.

Critchley, David. *The Origin of Organized Crime in America: The New York City Mafia, 1891–1931.* New York: Routledge 2009.

Dabney, Joseph Earl. *Mountain Spirits: A Chronicle of Corn Whiskey from King James' Ulster Plantation to America's Appalachians and the Moonshine Life.* New York: Charles Scribner's Sons, 1974.

Damrau, Frederic. "The Truth about Poison Liquor." *Popular Science Monthly* 110, no. 4 (April 1927): 18.

Daniels, W.H. *The Temperance Reform and Its Great Reformers.* New York: Nelson and Phillips, 1877.

Davis, Mark. "Northern Choices: Rural Forest County in the 1920s." *The Wisconsin Magazine of History* 79, no. 2 (Winter 1995-96): 109–138.

"Denatured Alcohol Always a Dangerous Poison." *Popular Mechanics* 37 (1922): 402.

Dewey, Thomas E. *Twenty against the Underworld.* Garden City, NY: Doubleday, 1974.

Dow, George Francis. *Every Day Life in the Massachusetts Bay Colony.* New York: Benjamin Blom, 1935.

Downey, Fairfax. *Our Lusty Forefathers: Being Diverse Chronicles of the Fervors, Frolic, Fights, Festivities, and Failings of Our American Ancestors.* New York: Charles Scribner's Sons, 1947.

"Drinking in Dry Places." *American Magazine* 71 (November 1910–April 1911): 371–377.

Drunkard's Progress: Narratives of Addiction, Despair, and Recovery. Edited by John William Crowley. Baltimore: Johns Hopkins University Press, 1999.

Durand, Jr., Loyal. "'Mountain Moonshining' in East Tennessee." *Geographical Review* 46, no. 2 (April 1956): 168–181.

Eisenberg, Dennis. *Meyer Lansky: Mogul of the Mob.* New York: Paddington Press, 1979.

Ellison, Betty Boles. *Illegal Odyssey: Two Hundred Years of Kentucky Moonshine.* N.P.: First Book Library, 2003.

Elson, Ruth M. *Guardians of the Tradition: American Schoolbooks of the Nineteenth Century.* Lincoln: University of Nebraska Press, 1964.

Emerson, Edward R. *Beverages, Past and Present,* vol. 2. New York: G.P. Putnam's Sons, 1908.

Englemann, Larry. *Intemperance: The Lost War against Liquor.* New York: Free Press, 1979.

English, T.J. *Paddy Whacked: The Untold Story of the Irish American Gangster.* New York: HarperCollins, 2009.

Everest, Allan S. *Rum Across the Border: The Prohibition Era in Northern New York.* Syracuse: Syracuse University Press, 1991.

Fahey, Edmund. *Rum Road to Spokane: A History of Prohibition.* Missoula: University of Montana, 1972.

Ferrell, Robert H. *The Presidency of Calvin Coolidge.* Lawrence: University Press of Kansas, 1998.

Frankel, Noralee. *Stripping Gypsy: The Life of Gypsy Rose Lee.* New York: Oxford University Press, 2009.

Frick, John W. *Theatre, Culture, and Temperance Reform in Nineteenth-Century America.* Cambridge, UK: Cambridge University Press, 2003.

Furnas, J.C. *The Life and Times of the Late Demon Rum.* New York: G.P. Putnam's Sons, 1965.

Gebhart, John C. "Movement against Prohibition." *Annals of the American Academy of Political and Social Science* 163 (September 1932): 172–180.

Glad, Paul W. "When John Barleycorn Went into Hiding in Wisconsin." *Wisconsin Magazine of History* 68, no. 2 (Winter 1984-85): 119–136.

Goldberg, Ronald Allen. *America in the Twenties.* Syracuse: Syracuse University Press, 2003.

Grant, Barry J. *When Rum Was King: The Story of the Prohibition Era in New Brunswick.* Frederickton, NB, Canada: Fiddlehead Poetry Books, 1984.

Gray, James H. *The Roar of the Twenties.* Calgary, AL, Canada: Fifth House, 2007.

Gusfield, Jeffrey. *Deadly Valentines: The Story of Capone's Henchman "Machine Gun" Jack McGurn and Louise Rolfe, His Blond Alibi.* Chicago: Chicago Review Press, 2012.

Guthrie, Jr., John J. "Hard Times, Hard Liquor, and Hard Luck: Selective Enforcement of Prohibition in North Florida, 1928–1933." *Florida Historical Quarterly* 42, no. 4 (April 1994): 435–452.

Hall, Clayton Colman. *Narratives of Early Maryland, 1633–1684.* New York: Charles Scribner's Sons, 1910.

Haller, Mark. "Philadelphia Bootlegging and the Report of the Special August Grand Jury." *The Pennsylvania Magazine of History and Biography* 109, no. 2 (April 1985): 215–233.

Hamm, Richard F. *Olmstead v. United States: The Constitutional Challenges of Prohibition Enforcement.* Washington, D.C.: Federal Judicial Center, Federal Judicial History Office, 2010.

Hampel, Robert L. *Temperance & Prohibition in Massachusetts, 1813–1852.* Ann Arbor: UMI Research Press, 1982.

Harding, Vincent. *A Certain Magnificence: Lyman Beecher and the Transformation of American Protestantism, 1775–1863.* Brooklyn: Carlson Publishing, 1991.

Haskins, James. *The Cotton Club.* New York: Hippocrene Books, 1994.

Haynes, Roy A. *Prohibition Inside Out.* Garden City, NY: Doubleday, Page, 1923.

Helmer, William J., and Arthur J. Bilek, *The St. Valentine's Day Massacre: The Untold Story of the Gangland*

Bloodbath that Brought Down Al Capone. Nashville: Cumberland House, 2004.

Hennigar, Ted R. *The Rum Running Years.* Hantsport, NS, Canada: Lancelot Press, 1981.

Henry, Stuart C. *Unvanquished Puritan: A Portrait of Lyman Beecher.* Grand Rapids: William B. Eerdmans, 1973.

"High License in Pennsylvania." *Public Opinion* 3 (April–October 1887): 127.

Hoffman, Dennis E. *Scarface Al and the Crime Crusaders: Chicago's Private War Against Capone.* Carbondale: Southern Illinois University Press, 1993.

Hunt, Thomas P. *The Cold Water Army.* Boston: Whipple & Damrell, 1841.

Iorizzo, Luciano. *Al Capone: A Biography.* Westport, CT: Greenwood Press, 2003.

Irey, Elmer. *The Tax Dodgers: The Inside Story of the T-Men's War with America's Political and Underworld Hoodlums, as Told to William J. Slocum.* New York: Greenberg, 1948.

Isaac, Paul. *Prohibition and Politics: Turbulent Decades in Tennessee.* Knoxville: University of Tennessee Press, 1965.

Jefferson, Thomas, and Henry Augustine Washington, *The Writings of Thomas Jefferson: Correspondence.* New York: Derby and Jackson, 1859.

Jeffrey, Edith. "Reform, Renewal, and Vindication: Irish Immigrants and the Catholic Total Abstinence Movement in Antebellum Philadelphia." *The Pennsylvania Magazine of History and Biography* 112, no. 3 (July 1988): 407–431.

Johanneck, Elizabeth. *Twin Cities Prohibition: Minnesota's Blind Pigs and Bootleggers.* Charleston, SC: The History Press, 2011.

Joyce, Davis D. *Oklahoma I Had Never Seen Before: Alternative Views of Oklahoma History.* Norman: University of Oklahoma Press, 1994.

Kavieff, Paul R. *Detroit's Infamous Purple Gang.* Charleston, SC: Arcadia, 2008.

_____. *The Purple Gang: Organized Crime in Detroit, 1910–1945.* Ft. Lee, NJ: Barricade Books, 2005.

Kellner, Esther. *Moonshine: Its History and Folklore.* Indianapolis: Bobbs-Merrill, 1971.

King, W.C. *King's Complete History of the World War.* Springfield, MA: History Associates, 1922.

Kobler, John. *Ardent Spirits: The Rise and Fall of Prohibition.* Cambridge, MA: Da Capo Press, 1993.

Krout, John Allen. *The Origins of Prohibition.* New York: Russell & Russell, 1967.

Kyvig, David. *Repealing National Prohibition.* Kent, OH: Kent State University Press, 2000.

_____. "Women against Prohibition." *American Quarterly* 28, no. 4 (August 1976): 465–482.

Lampi, Leona. "Red Lodge: From a Frenetic Past of Crows, Coal, and Boom and Bust Emerges a Unique Festival of Diverse Nationality Groups." *Montana: The Magazine of Western History* 11, no. 3 (Summer 1961): 20–31.

Landesco, John. *Organized Crime in Chicago: Part III of the Illinois Crime Survey 1929.* Chicago: University of Chicago Press, 1968.

_____. "Prohibition and Crime." *Annals of the American Association of Political and Social Science* 163 (September 1932): 120–129.

Lee, Martin A., and Bruce Shlain. *Acid Dreams, The Complete Social History of LSD: The CIA, the Sixties, and Beyond.* New York: Grove Weidenfeld, 1985.

Leider, Emily Wortis. *Becoming Mae West.* New York: Reed Business Information, 1997.

Lender, Mark Edward, and James Kirby Martin. *Drinking in America: A History.* New York: The Free Press, 1982.

Lendler, Ian. *Alcoholica Esoterica.* New York: Penguin, 2005.

Lerner, Michael A. *Dry Manhattan: Prohibition in New York City.* Cambridge: Harvard University Press, 2007.

Levine, Gary. *Anatomy of a Gangster: Jack "Legs" Diamond.* New York: A.S. Barnes, 1979.

Levine, Harry G. "The Discovery of Addiction: Changing Conceptions of Habitual Drunkenness in America." *Journal of Studies on Alcohol* 39, no. 1 (1978): 143–174.

Liggett, Walter W. "Ohio — Lawless and Unashamed." *Plain Talk* 7, no. 1 (July 1930): 1–22.

Ling, Sally J. *Run the Rum In: South Florida During Prohibition.* Charleston, SC: The History Press, 2007.

Livermore, Mary S. *The Story of My Life: Or the Sunshine and Shadow of Seventy Years.* Hartford, CT: A.D. Worthington & Company, 1897.

Longworth, Alice Roosevelt. *Crowded Hours: Reminiscences.* New York: Charles Scribner's Sons, 1933.

Lowance, Jr., Mason I. *Increase Mather.* New York: Twayne, 1974.

Lusk, Rufus S. "The Drinking Habit." *Annals of the American Academy of Political and Social Science* 163 (September 1932): 46–52.

Lyle, John H. *The Dry and Lawless Years.* Englewood Cliffs, NJ: Prentice-Hall, 1960.

Marquis, Greg. "'Brewers' and Distillers' Paradise': American Views of Canadian Alcohol Policies, 1919–1935." *Canadian Review of American Studies* 34, no. 2 (2004): 135–166.

Mason, Philip P. *Rumrunning and the Roaring Twenties: Prohibition on the Michigan-Ontario Waterway.* Detroit: Wayne State University, 1995.

Mappen, Marc. *Prohibition Gangsters: The Rise and Fall of a Bad Generation.* New Brunswick, NJ: Rutgers University Press, 2013.

McClintock, S.S. "The Kentucky Mountains and Their Feuds: The People and Their Country." *The American Journal of Sociology* 7, no. 1 (July 1901): 1–28.

Meers, John R. "The California Wine and Grape Industry and Prohibition." *California Historical Society Quarterly* 46, no. 1 (March 1967): 19–32.

Merz, Charles. *The Dry Decade.* Seattle: University of Washington Press, 1969.

Metcalfe, Philip. *Whispering Wires: The Tragic Tale of an American Bootlegger.* Portland, OR: Ink Water Press, 2007.

Mills, Eric. *Chesapeake Rumrunners of the Roaring*

Twenties. Centreville, MD: Tidewater Publishers, 2000.

Morello, Celeste A. *Before Bruno: The History of the Philadelphia Mafia, Book One, 1880–1931.* Philadelphia: Celeste A. Morello, 1999.

Morgan, Edmund S. *The Puritan Family: Religion and Domestic Relations in Seventeenth-century New England.* New York: Harper & Row, 1966.

Morris, Joe Alex. *What a Year!* New York: Harper, 1956.

Murphy, Mary. "Bootlegging Mothers and Drinking Daughters: Gender and Prohibition in Butte, Montana." *American Quarterly* 46, no. 2 (June 1994): 174–194.

The National Prohibition Law: Hearings before the Committee of the Judiciary, United States Senate, Sixty-ninth Congress, First Session. Vol. 1. Washington, D.C.: Government Printing Office, 1926.

Nelson, Derek. *Moonshiners, Bootleggers, and Rumrunners.* Osceola, WI: Motorbooks International, 1995.

Newman, Peter C. *King of the Castle, the Making of a Dynasty: Seagram's and the Bronfman Empire.* New York: Atheneum, 1979.

Noon, Mark A. *Yuengling: A History of America's Oldest Brewery.* Jefferson, NC: McFarland, 2007.

Norris, John. *Profitable Advice for Rich and Poor, in a Dialogue or Discourse between James Freeman, a Carolina Planter, and Simon Question, a West-country Farmer, Containing a Description or True Relation of South Carolina, an English Plantation or Colony in America.* London: J. Howe, 1712.

Nown, Graham. *The English Godfather.* London: War Lock, 1987.

O'Brien, Patrick G., and Kenneth J. Peak. *Kansas Bootleggers.* Manhattan, KS: Sunflower University Press, 1991.

Ogle, Maureen. *Ambitious Brew: The Story of American Beer.* New York: Harcourt, 2006.

Okrent, Daniel. *Last Call: The Rise and Fall of Prohibition.* New York: Scribner, 2010.

Ostrander, Gilman M. *The Prohibition Movement in California, 1848–1933.* Berkeley: University of California Press, 1957.

Pardue, Jerry. "The Story from the Other Side." *Update* 2, no. 3 (February 1975): 4.

Pasley, Fred D. *Al Capone: The Biography of a Self-made Man.* Garden City, NY: Garden City Publishing Company, 1930.

Pearson, C.C., and James Edwin Hendricks. *Liquor & Anti-liquor in Virginia, 1619–1919.* Durham: Duke University, 1967.

Peck, Garrett. *Prohibition in Washington, D.C.: How Dry We Weren't.* Charleston, SC: The History Press, 2011.

Pegram, Thomas R. *Battling Demon Rum: The Struggle for a Dry America, 1800–1933.* Chicago: Ivan R. Dee, 1998.

Pellegrino, Michael. *Jersey Brew: The Story of Beer in New Jersey.* N.p.: Lake Neepaulin Publishing, 2009.

Perrett, Geoffrey. *America in the Twenties: A History.* New York: Simon & Schuster, 1983.

Peretti, Burton W. *Nightclub City: Politics & Amusement in Manhattan.* Philadelphia: University of Pennsylvania Press, 2007.

Phillips, Carter. "January 16, 1920." *American History* 39, no. 6 (2005): 38.

Plavchan, Ronald Jan. *A History of Anheuser-Busch, 1852–1933.* North Stratford, NH: Ayer Company Publishing, 1975.

Pridemore, Francis. "How Doth the Busy Moonshiner!" *North American Review* 228, no. 1 (July 1929): 13–16.

_____. "What Prohibition Has Done for the Mountaineers," *The Outlook* 146, no. 12 (1927): 384–385.

Quinn, John F. "Father Mathew's Disciples: American Catholic Support for Temperance 1840–1920." *Church History* 65, no. 4 (Dec 1996): 624–640.

Rayburn, Otto Ernest. "Moonshine in Arkansas." *The Arkansas Historical Quarterly* 16, no. 2 (Summer 1957): 169–173.

Repetto, Thomas. *American Mafia: A History of Its Rise to Power.* New York: Macmillan, 2005.

Reynolds, Quentin. *Courtroom: In the Criminal Courtroom with Samuel S. Leibowitz, Lawyer and Judge.* New York: Farrar, Strauss, 1950.

Rhodes, James Ford. *History of the United States from the Compromise of 1850 to the Final Restoration of Home Rule at the South in 1877*, vol. 3. New York: Macmillan, 1906.

Rideout, Walter B. *Sherwood Anderson: A Writer in America*, vol. 2. Madison: University of Wisconsin Press, 2007.

Rockaway, Robert A. *But He Was Good to His Mother: The Lives and Crimes of Jewish Gangsters.* Lynbrook, NY: Gefen Books, 2000.

_____. "The Notorious Purple Gang: Detroit's All-Jewish Prohibition Era Mob." *Shofar: An Interdisciplinary Journal of Jewish Studies* 20, no. 1 (Fall 2001): 113–131.

Roelofs, H. Mark. "Socialism and Christianity." *The Review of Politics* 51, no. 4 (Autumn 1989): 638–640.

Rose, Kenneth D. "Wettest in the West: San Francisco and Prohibition in 1924." *California History* 65, no. 4 (December 1986): 288–295.

Ross, Ron. *Bummy Davis vs. Murder, Inc.: The Rise and Fall of the Jewish Mafia and an Ill-fated Prizefighter.* New York: St. Martin's Griffin, 2003.

Roueché, Berton. *The Neutral Spirit: A Portrait of Alcohol.* Boston: Little, Brown, 1960.

Sanchez, Tanya Marie. "The Feminine Side of Bootlegging." *Louisiana History* 41, no. 4 (Autumn 2000): 403–433.

Sann, Paul. *Kill the Dutchman: The Story of Dutch Schultz.* New Rochelle, NY: Arlington House, 1971.

_____. *The Lawless Decade.* New York: Bonanza Books, 1957.

Schneider, Stephen. *Iced: The Story of Organized Crime in Canada.* Mississauga, ON, Canada: John Wiley and Sons, 2009.

Schoenberg, Robert J. *Mr. Capone: The Real & Complete Story of Al Capone.* New York: Perennial, 2001.

Shute, Brian. "Rum Running during the Prohibition Era." *Nostalgia Magazine* 13, no. 1 (January–February 2011): 34–40.

Sismondo, Christine. *America Walks into a Bar: A Spirited History of Taverns and Saloons, Speakeasies and Grog Shops.* New York: Oxford University Press, 2011.

"Sketches of Early Life in Boston, Part II: How They Tried to Regulate Life and Manners in Boston." *Appleton's Journal* 1, no. 3 (April 17, 1869): 85–87.

Smith, John. *Travels and Works of Captain John Smith,* vol. 1. Edited by Edward Arber. Edinburgh: John Grant, 1910.

Sosnowski, Vivienne. *When the Rivers Ran Red: An Amazing Story of Courage and Triumph in America's Wine Country.* New York: Palgrave Macmillan, 2009.

Stebbins, J.E., and T.A.H. Brown, *Fifty Years History of the Temperance Cause: Intemperance, the Great National Curse.* Hartford, CT: L. Stebbins, 1874.

Stegner, Wallace. *Wolf Willow: A History, a Story, and a Memory of the Last Plains Frontier.* New York: Penguin Press, 2000.

Stewart, David O. *The Summer of 1787: The Men Who Invented the Constitution.* New York: Simon & Schuster, 2007.

Strawn, Arthur. "Saint Frances of Evanston." *American Mercury* 14, no. 54 (June 1928): 230–239.

Strecker, Max. *Smedley D. Butler, USMC: A Biography.* Jefferson, NC: McFarland, 2011.

Sullivan, Mark. *Our Times: The United States, 1900–1925,* vol. 6. New York: Charles Scribner's Sons, 1935.

Taggert, Ed. *Bootlegger: Max Hassel, the Millionaire Newsboy.* New York: Writer's Showcase, 2003.

Terrie, Philip G. *Contested Terrain: A New History of Nature and People in the Adirondacks.* Syracuse: Adirondack Museum and Syracuse University Press, 1997.

Thompson, Craig, and Allen Raymond. *Gang Rule in New York: The Story of a Lawless Era.* New York: Dial Press, 1940.

Thompson, Neal. *Driving with the Devil: Southern Moonshine, Detroit Wheels, and the Birth of NASCAR.* New York: Crown, 2006.

Tomlinson, Gerald. *Murdered in New Jersey.* New Brunswick, NJ: Rutgers University Press, 1997.

Turkus, Burton B., and Sid Feder. *Murder, Inc.: The Story of the Syndicate.* Cambridge, MA: Da Capo Press, 1992

Vandersee, Charles. "Speakeasy," *American Speech* 59, no. 3 (Autumn 1984): 268–269.

Van de Water, Frederick F. *The Real McCoy.* New York: Doubleday, Doran, 1931.

"Volstead Who Dug and Kramer Who Guards the Grave of John Barleycorn." *Current Opinion* 69 (July–December 1920): 49–51.

Walker, Clifford James. *One Eye Closed, the Other Red: The California Bootlegging Years.* Barstow, CA: Back Door Publishing, 1999.

Walker, Stanley. *The Night Club Era.* Baltimore: Johns Hopkins University Press, 1999.

Wallace, David. *Capital of the World: A Portrait of New York City in the Roaring Twenties.* Guilford, CT: Lyons Press, 2011.

Warnes, Kathy Covert. *Ecorse, Michigan: A Brief History.* Charleston, SC: The History Press, 2009.

Waters, Harold. *Smugglers of Spirits: Prohibition and the Coast Guard Patrol.* New York: Hastings House Publishers, 1971.

Waugh, Daniel. *Egan's Rats: The Untold Story of the Prohibition-Era Gang that Ruled St. Louis.* Nashville: Cumberland House, 2007.

Weeden, William B. *Economic and Social History of New England, 1620–1789,* vol. 2. New York: Hillary House Publishers, 1963.

Wells-Barnett, Ida B. *The Red Record: Tabulated Statistics and Alleged Causes of Lynching in the United States.* Salem, NH: Ayer Company Publishing, 1987.

Weston, Jr., George F. *Boston Ways.* Boston: Beacon Press, 1957.

Wheeler, Scott. *Rumrunners and Revenuers: Prohibition in Vermont.* Shelburne, VT: The New England Press, 2002.

"When the Booze Trade Was Sinful." *Alberta Report Newsmagazine* 20, no. 40 (1993): 9.

Willard, Frances Elizabeth. *Do Everything: A Handbook for the World's White Ribboners.* Chicago: The Woman's Temperance Publishing Association 1895.

Willing, Joseph K. "The Profession of Bootlegging." *Annals of the American Association of Political and Social Science* 125 (May 1926): 40–48.

Wilson, Gary A. *Honky-tonk Town: Havre's Bootlegging Days.* Havre, MT: High Line Books, 1985.

Wolcott, Virginia W. *Remaking Respectability: African American Women in Interwar Detroit.* Chapel Hill: University of North Carolina Press, 2000.

Zinn, Howard. *LaGuardia In Congress.* Ithaca, NY: Fall Creek Books, 2010.

Index